Armageddon Deception
The Eschatology of Islam & Zionism

A Biblical Response

Michael Sullivan

Armageddon Deception

The Eschatology of Islam & Zionism

A Biblical Response

Michael Sullivan

Revised 2023

Copyright © 2021 by Michael Sullivan

ISBN 978-1-61529-204-2

For information on reordering, please contact:

Vision Publishing
P.O. Box 1680
Ramona, CA 92065
(760) 789-4700
www.booksbyvision.org

All rights in this book are reserved worldwide. No part of the book may be reproduced in any manner whatsoever without written permission of the author except in brief quotations embodied in critical articles or reviews.

About the Cover

Imagine the World Economic Forum (WEF) leaders, Klaus Schwab and Yuval Noah Harari, sitting around a table at Davos with the corrupt and unelected elite—the Rothschilds, the IMF, and the Bilderberg Group—hashing out plans to impose on the world. Front and center on the agenda of these puppet masters is ushering in their centuries long plan of WWIII—a holy war between Israel (the State of Rothschild) and the Muslim world. The purpose? To create global chaos and instability through "plandemics," lockdowns, the climate cult, economic collapse, starvation, reverse migration, and nuclear genocide. This will guarantee a smooth rollout of their intended one world CBDC digital currency, which will enslave the masses and create a modern-day feudal system.

Their goal is a "Great Reset," to "Build Back Better" out of the ash heap of a once great Western Civilization built upon Christianity and freedom. The eschatological endgame of this elite group is to bring about their Fourth Industrial Revolution guided by the religious philosophy of Nihilism, Technocracy, and Transhumanism. Believing the world should be governed by a class of scientists, engineers, and bankers (not by "We the People"), they play God by planning a 95% reduction in world population and merging themselves with computers/droids/robots to download their souls and "live forever." Israeli Professor Yuval Noah Harari, who functions as the high priest and top advisor of Klaus Schwab's death cult, is crucial to ushering in this Fourth Industrial Revolution of Transhumanism. The following boastful statements by Harari, taken from his lectures, public interviews, and World Economic Forum events, reveal the depth of this evil agenda:

- "Humans are now hackable animals. The whole idea that humans have this 'soul' or 'spirit,' and nobody knows what's happening inside them, and they have free will—that's over!"
- "I strongly believe that given the technologies we are now developing, within a century or two at most, our species will disappear. I don't think that in the end of the 22nd century, the earth will still be dominated by homo sapiens."
- "What you tried to do a thousand years ago with the priest preaching from the pulpit you will be able to do in a far more invasive way in ten or fifteen years with all kinds of brain-computer interfaces and direct biological interventions."
- "Data might allow elites to do something more radical than just build digital dictatorships. By hacking organisms, elites may gain the power to reengineer life itself. Once you hack something, you can usually reengineer it."
- "Now in the past many tyrants and governments wanted to do it, but nobody understood biology well enough, and nobody had enough computing power and data to hack millions of people. Neither the Gestapo or the KGB could do it. But soon, at least some corporations and governments will be able to systematically hack all the people."

- "And if indeed we succeed in hacking and engineering life, this will be not just the greatest revolution in the history of humanity, this will be the greatest revolution in biology since the very beginning of life four billion years ago."
- "Science is replacing evolution by natural selection with evolution by intelligent design. Not by intelligent design of some God above the clouds, but our intelligent design and the intelligent design in our clouds—the IBM cloud, the Microsoft cloud—these are the new driving forces of evolution."
- "Today we have the technology to hack human beings on a massive scale. In this time of crisis, you have to follow the science. It's been often said, 'You should never allow a crisis to go to waste.' People could look back a hundred years from now and define the Corona epidemic as the moment when a new regime of surveillance took over, especially surveillance under the skin."
- "My brain, my body, my life—does it belong to me, or to some corporation or government, or perhaps to the human collective?"

The United Nations and World Economic Forum are run by the children and grandchildren of the WWII Nazi regime cult and their "scientists" – some of whom the U.S. government protected and took in to perform deadly research and experiments. The above quotes accurately portray where Klaus Schwab and the global elite want to take humanity. Through their Fourth Industrial Revolution of Transhumanism, their One World Government system will finally be able to control the population. This group wants to play God by hacking the human body and taking away human rights and foundational freedoms.

At present (2023), this group is fomenting more and more hatred and division with their race wars, class wars, ethnic wars, and gender wars. Using the politically ill-informed "useful idiots" to further their goals, they also make a "Trojan Horse" of the "Christian" or Evangelical Zionist movement, Talmudic Zionist movement, and Islamic Sharia law to embed themselves in governments around the world—especially the U.S. government. It is quite revealing that the majority of U.S. senators and congressmen must sign an agreement with the Jewish lobby, AIPAC, pledging their unwavering support for Israel both financially and in Middle East conflicts. There is also the problem of many of our politicians having dual citizenship with Israel. This allegiance to Israel trumps any interests of their constituents, state, or country. A governing body whose alliance is to a foreign state undermines the national security of the country and the people they are supposed to represent.

The purpose of this book is to educate and give the reader a true understanding of "end times" according to scripture. Knowing the eschatological beliefs of the main religions of the world is key to understanding global politics. An educated public will be able to see through the fog and confusion perpetrated on them by a small group in power, a group who uses insidious and subtle tactics of entire governments to manipulate populations into accepting—and even welcoming—their own demise.

Cover artist: Michael J. Sullivan and Robert E Cruickshank Jr.

In Gratitude

I wish to express my everlasting gratitude to my beloved wife, Denise, whose patience and longsuffering toward me and loving support in writing this volume has meant the world to me.

This book would have never come to fruition without Pastor David Curtis of Berean Bible Church inviting me to speak at one of our annual conferences where I lectured on the contents of this book. I had so many people over the years tell me that those lectures and subsequent articles needed to be turned into a book, so here it is.

Special thanks to Jeff McCormack in his labors on the cover design work and to Adam Maarschalk for his meticulous editing. It's a blessing to have Full Preterist Christians gifted in these areas.

Table of Contents

Preface 13

Prologue 15

Chapter One: *Islam, an Eschatology of Violence: Holy Land and a "Very Soon" Second Coming of Jesus and Holy War to Destroy the Infidels (Jews, Christians, etc.)* 21

Chapter Two: *Talmudic or Messianic Zionism: Holy Land and an Imminent Messianic Deliverer and Holy War to Enslave or Destroy the Gentiles (Islam, Christians, etc.)* 37

Chapter Three: *Evangelical Zionism: Holy Land and a "Very Soon" Second Coming of Jesus to "Rapture" the Church and Start a Holy War to Destroy the Sinners (Islam, Jews, etc.)* 61

Chapter Four: *The Christian Full Preterist Solution: Believers in Messiah/Jesus Are God's New Covenant Sacred Space – the Kingdom is Now "Within" and "in Christ," Not "in the Land"* 71

Chapter Five: *The Christian Full Preterist Solution: The "Big Three" (Mt. 10:22-23; Mt. 16:27-28 & Mt. 24:34) – Jesus Promised His Second Coming and End of the Old Covenant Age/World Would Occur in the Lifetime and Generation of the First Century Church—Promised Fulfilled by AD 70* 105

Chapter Six: *The Christian Full Preterist Solution: The End of the Old Covenant Age Battle of Armageddon / Gog and Magog Fulfilled AD 67 – AD 70* 221

Chapter Seven: *How was the Resurrection Fulfilled by AD 70?* 245

Chapter Eight: *How was the "Rapture" Fulfilled by AD 70?* 319

Chapter Nine: *How did Jesus Come "In Like Manner" in AD 70?* 337

Chapter Ten: *How was the Millennium Fulfilled Between AD 27 – AD 67?* 345

Chapter Eleven: *How is the Promise of No More Death, Tears and Pain Fulfilled Today?* 353

Chapter Twelve: *How to Evangelize Muslims, Zionists and Reach Evangelical Zionists* 357

Chapter Thirteen: *Pentecostal or Charismatic Zionists Giving Conflicting or Manipulative False Prophecies* 413

Chapter Fourteen: *Refutation of Pacifism What Just War Theory in the Middle East is and isn't* 433

Conclusion: *Identifying the enemies and putting together a Christian Bible-centered Republic foreign policy* 443

Appendix A: *The Roman Catholic Church and Sacred Space and Holy War* 461

Appendix B: *Two Movie Proposals Designed to be Biblical Information Warfare* 467

What others are saying about *Armageddon Deception*...

Don K. Preston, D. Div., author of multiple books and President of Preterist Research Institute www.donkpreston.com, calls it a powerful, fully documented book:

> "Far too many people are unaware that the Palestinians and the Jews lived in peaceful co-existence in the land called Israel/Palestine, until British and American foreign policy intervened and decided, based on a false view of eschatology, that they would support Israel in claiming that the land belonged exclusively to the Jews. With the Balfour Declaration and ensuing actions on the part of Britain and the US, the Middle East has been a cauldron of violence and bloodshed. Palestinians, thousands of them Christians - were violently forced from their generational homes.
>
> All the while, American Dispensational Zionists, such as John Hagee, Jerry Falwell, Pat Robinson all sat by silently, refusing to condemn the violence against their Christian brethren! Why? Because of their false eschatology that insisted (insists still!!) that modern day Israel remains as God's chosen, covenant people and that the land belongs to them by divine right.
>
> Do you catch the power of the fact that people are dying because of a false view of the end times? For generations now, even American young people have died supporting Israel's "divine right" to own the land. America's support of that false doctrine and the ensuring violence against Arabs and Palestinians has resulted in turning the Islamic world into a growing threat against America.
>
> In this powerful, fully documented book, *Armageddon Deception*, Mike Sullivan pulls back the veil on the shocking, troubling and dangerous doctrine of Zionism in all of its forms, whether political or religious. Citing a host of recognized sources, Sullivan powerfully shows that it is far past time that America - and the world - wakes up to the danger posed by the virulent Zionist movement as well as the radical Islamic ideology. In sum, bad theology is killing thousands of young people! This should concern everyone who claims to believe in Christ!
>
> This book may well shatter any naive worldview that you have of politics, of Israel and of Islam. Sullivan has done the world and Christianity a massive favor by bringing this work to the public and it deserves widespread circulation. What he has produced will not be welcomed with open arms by many. But for those who are looking for the Truth, and some solid suggestions for future peace, this book should be read and seriously considered by everyone - including the world leaders!"

Pastor David Curtis, www.bereanbiblechurch.org, explains why reading this book matters:

> "This is a thought-provoking book by my good friend Mike Sullivan. This book will help you understand why eschatology matters. Mike demonstrates how a faulty eschatology is driving American politics. He pulls back the curtain to expose what is behind Zionism and the players involved. This book exposes the evil behind Zionism in a clear and concise way. You are guaranteed to learn some things about eschatology as Mike exegetes many biblical texts. Give it a read, you won't regret it."

Pat Miletich, former UFC Champ, Trainer of Champions, UFC Hall of Fame member, Biological Soil to human health advocate, says the book provokes important questions:

> "Armageddon Deception will bring the reader to a point, if they are self-searching and honest, to ask themselves what their beliefs truly are and are they concrete. This book will expose questions never before thought of, let alone asked of themselves. Are we really in the end times? How many generations have asked the same question?"

TJ Smith, author of *The Last Semite*, has high praises for the book:

> "Armageddon Deception is an all-in-one, top-to-bottom, front to back compendium on the evil creation of Zionism. Sullivan leaves no stone unturned as he deep dives into the Scriptural, and historical evidence that should dissuade all well-meaning Christians from following this ill-guided Rothschild-created political demonasty. Mike Sullivan has long been known as a biblical theologian who takes the study of Scripture to new levels. Mike covers all tentacles of Zionism, from Islam, Israeli, and Evangelical. Keep an open mind and prepare to ingest numerous "red pills of truth." Monumental work, Mike!"

Karen Rogers, author of *Racing With My Shadow*, gives it two thumbs up:

> "Spot on. This book is a must read, especially in today's climate. To expose the lies, one must know the truth. 'Then you will know the truth, and the truth will set you free.' –John 8:32. Thank you, Mike, for writing this book. Two thumbs up!"

Pastor Zach Davis of First Baptist Church Marked Tree in Arkansas calls it a must read:

> "Bad theology has consequences. In this well written book, Mike Sullivan obliterates the irrational view of Zionism and exposes its faults to the core. Though secondary sources are included, you will find Mike's exegetical work useful for your worldview and theology, especially his work in the Olivet Discourse. This is a must read for the serious student of Bible prophecy, and a piece that every political leader in America should have their hands on."

Bible teacher Travis Drum calls *Amageddon Deception* a thought-provoking, exegetical masterpiece:

> "Whenever I think of *Armageddon Deception*, the first word the comes to my mind is this—treasure. Mike has gifted the church a truly invaluable gem with this work, covering a vast array of subjects under the blanket of eschatology. In typical Mike Sullivan fashion, *Armageddon Deception* is a thought provoking, exegetical masterpiece that is sure to challenge your beliefs about Zionism, the last days, the second coming, and so much more. For any serious student of God's Word, this is one that you can't afford to miss."

Actor and Producer Brett Prieto says this book should be in everyone's library:

> "In the age where leading pastors – even political leaders – Shout, "we are living in "The End Times," or decry "time is short for this planet," author, speaker and apologist Michael Sullivan puts that rhetoric to rest with his masterful work, which is aptly titled, "Armageddon Deception." In this Clarion Call to the evangelicals who are held captive to the concept(s) of faulty [political] paradigms and bad eschatology, Sullivan peels the mask off to reveal the puppet Master's behind it all. He successfully documents his work and expounds upon it not only with history, but with biblical truth, which he skillfully exegetes from the Bible.
>
> *Armageddon Deception* is a must have in your library. It will shatter worldviews only to help rebuild a biblical one. The results of this book will pull any honest Bible believing Christian [who is held captive to concepts], from their holy huddle, to only take action for Christ's Kingdom! The days of waiting to be whisked away in a "Rapture" are done! The guess work of who are Gog and Magog is finished. If one is triggered from the aforementioned statements, let me offer this trigger for those who subscribe to Darbyism (i.e. Premillennial Dispensationalism): Sullivan's treatise will challenge your current position on eschatology, your stance on geopolitical Israel, and whether Jesus is a true or a false prophet in your model of End Times Bible prophecy. Run to gauntlet, and get and read this book!"

Authors of *The Return of Christ: Why are we still waiting?*, Pete and Rachael Wrue, call it a well researched resource:

> "This book is a great resource and very well researched. We find ourselves referencing it time and time again. Mike has done an excellent job covering the many facets of Eschatology. Everything is thoroughly explained and includes several parallel charts comparing Scripture with Scripture. He also shows the other side of the story regarding Zionism and Israel, making this book very relevant to the current controversy in the Middle East. He does a great job explaining the imminecy passages in both the Old and New Testaments, as well as expounding the Olivet Discourse. We highly recommend this book to anyone interested in learning more abou wha the Bible REALLY has to say about the end times!"

Author and Bible teacher Robert Cruickshank highly recommends this timely book and gives the reasons why:

> "This book reminded me of the question asked in the classic song: "War, what is it good for?" For many today, war is good for bringing about God's plan and purpose in our own day and age. But as Michael Sullivan demonstrates in this much needed work, the wars and rumors of wars, of which Jesus spoke, are in our distant past, not our future. Armageddon is behind us; the Battle of Gog and Magog is over. These, along with the rest of the "end times" prophecies of the New Testament, find their fulfillment in the first century AD.
>
> While eschatology is not essential to one's salvation, the implications of eschatology are nevertheless no trival matter. As Sullivan points out, misinterpreting fulfilled prophecy as unfulfilled is more than just an academic or intellectual mistake. Eschatology matters, and ideas have consequences. Serious cconsequences. In this case, such misinterpretation can be (and often is) used to justify militant movements, horrific violence and even all-out war.
>
> Sullivan's contribution to this debate demonstrates that war is not the answer to the problems facing our world. The answer is peace—peace that comes through the Prince of Peace. It is only as people embrace Jesus and enter into the everlasting kingdom that He established, that God's place and purpose can truly be realized in our own day and age and in our lives. I highly recommend this timely book!"

Preface

As this second printing of *Armageddon Deception* is released, the events foretold within this book are starting to unfold. The first printing of *Armageddon Deception* (2021) predicted how the religions of Islam, Talmudic Zionism, and Evangelical Zionism desired to self-fulfill an end time holy war and that the global "elite" would help to facilitate it. This global cabal (New World Order/World Economic Forum/U.N./Rothschild Zionism and International Banksters) could start WWIII between Israel and the Muslim world. This would usher in their "Great Reset," "Build Back Better," or "2030 Agenda" one world global government goals. The Rothschild dynasty has been involved in starting and profiting from previous World Wars, Revolutions, Civil Wars, etc., and it is no secret that they have been working on their global one world Central Bank Digital Currency (CBDC), which is about to be rolled out. Like CV-19, the lockdowns, and the climate hoax/cult, all that is needed now is a string of global "crises" designed to weaken the financial institutions of the world to enable them to step in as the saviors. While Islam, Talmudic Zionism, and Evangelical Zionism are trying to *fulfill their end time "holy war" or "prophecies,"* one must also focus on the globalists who know how to bring that war about and profit from it (both financially and through control) when the dust settles.

Albert Pike (or whoever penned the famous letter ascribed to him detailing how three world wars would be rolled out) made it clear that one of the goals in starting WWIII between Israel and the Muslim world was to create a religious vacuum which this global cabal intended to fill. When the Muslim version of the Second Coming of Jesus doesn't happen, Israel's Jewish militaristic Messiah doesn't show up to usher in their version of a paradise on earth, and the "rapture" doesn't take place for the Evangelical Zionists, one of two things will happen: there will be a religious vacuum that will be filled by this cabal of Technocrats/Transhumanists, or there will be a reformation in the area of eschatology whereby Preterism will greatly increase in popularity. With the pressing realization that this inevitable clash could take place within the next ten to thirty years, I decided to write this book. In the wake of these events, a truly Biblical Christianity, one which is not interested in supporting or starting "holy wars," will be there to pick up the pieces and offer healing to the nations through the message of fulfillment and the gospel (cf. Rev. 22:2-17).

Unfortunately, since 1830 the Church has been infected with the Dispensational Zionism lie which teaches things are destined, and in fact, "prophesied" to get worse and worse in the world— and that the "end" or "rapture" is always "near" to bail out Christians right before things get really bad. While some within this group do study the evil facing our world through the likes of Klaus Schwab/W.E.F./ U.N./ Rothschilds/Global Fascism, etc…, *they do it in such a way as to make these people and organizations the imminent fulfillment of Matthew 24 or the book of Revelation and use this as alleged "proof" that they are going to be "raptured."* Of course, this is exactly what the New World Order group *wants* them to think. This is why these deceivers do things like use "666" for the "vaccine" passport patent number. To Christians, "666" telegraphs that "the end and the rapture is near," and so their mantra continues "why polish brass on a sinking ship," a mentality that offers no long-term strategy to fight against this group who seeks to control and destroy them.

But what if Jesus was telling the truth—that the prophetic events of Matthew 24-25 were "near," that the fulfillment of these things would happen in "this generation," meaning the generation of his first century audience? What if the prophetic book of Revelation really was to be fulfilled "shortly," with the "Beast" and "666" being Rome and Nero Caesar, and the war of Armageddon and Gog and Magog fulfilled during an imminent "3 ½ years" time frame between the Romans and Jews (AD 67 – AD 70)? Not only would this have profound theological implications proving Christ's deity and accuracy as a prophet, but the negative implications for the New World Order and Rothschild Zionist dynasty would be devastating! This would mean that the "sleeping giant" (the Church) would finally awaken from her lazy slumber to confront her enemies head-on and develop a Biblical long-term cultural worldview. The book you now hold in your hands is that wake-up call and serves as the real information warfare and message of our day! Get this book into the hands of your Pastor and your local and national politicians so that they can be guided by Christ and the Kingdom of Heaven! It is high time for truth to prevail and for just laws and wise foreign policy to be implemented.

Prologue

"The war of ideas" = "The war of theology or eschatology"

Everyone looking at the conflict in the Middle East realizes that while engaging militarily at times is necessary, the ultimate solution will have to come from another area. Therefore, many see the various conflicting religious theologies or forms of eschatology (study of prophecy) fueling these areas as being solved ultimately through a "war of ideas." What they mean by this is really a "war of theology/eschatology" that needs to change the hearts and minds within these areas before *lasting peace* can emerge.

The problem summarized

Unfortunately, these three futurist eschatological systems of Islam, Israeli or Talmudic Zionism and Evangelical Zionism all share common errors that perpetuate conflict in the Middle East and the U.S. such as:

- God allegedly has predicted for our generation to see end time "signs" that are allegedly being fulfilled right before our eyes today such as natural disasters, wars, and an imminent arrival of an evil ruler or "Antichrist", "man of lawlessness," etc. As we will see, many read their Quran, Talmud/Torah and NT through the lens of current events and news headlines.

- God allegedly will cause the evil ruler's religious system to overcome others or inherit certain local "holy land" areas and ultimately the earth, while the other groups are exterminated or end up serving their god or even them in some way.

- There is an alleged future but imminent "end time" great war (e.g. the battle of Gog and Magog or Armageddon) for us to experience in which their religion will win over the other wicked ones.

- God allegedly will send Jesus or Messiah to save Israel (or to condemn Israel, according to the Islamic view), bringing global peace, defeating the antichrist and infidels, and thus ushering in some kind of paradise or kingdom on earth.

But what if it can be proven that these Biblical "end time" signs and "holy war" scenarios have already been fulfilled and that the OT and NT predicted a "new" and spiritual kingdom to be established within the hearts of His people rather than the establishment of a physical earthly paradise on earth?

What if it can be proven according to Allah's "revelations" that Muhammad was a false prophet, and thus the Quran is not a revelation from God? What if it can be proven from their own Islamic sources that the Old and New Testaments could not be corrupted and that they do contradict the Quran? Where does this leave and lead the Muslim when he or she is commanded to go to the "people of the book" (Christians) to test and judge if the Quran is accurate and/or consistent with the Bible?

And for the Zionist, what if all of the land promises were actually fulfilled in the OT and therefore the modern state of Israel is a non-starter? What if the OT prophetic material concerning Israel being saved or gathered "in the land" was also typological, pointing to a greater and spiritual fulfillment in the prophesied coming new covenant that would be realized "in Christ"?

Therefore, does the God of the Bible really support or recognize modern day Israel as "God's people"? Is modern day Israel and the events of 1948 or 1967 a "super sign" of fulfilled Bible prophecy, or was it simply formed and funded by the Rothschild dynasty and Khazarian mafia which seeks to globally enslave the Gentiles through monetary means using modern Israel as one of many places to conduct some of its affairs?

How many passages in the OT and NT have they and Evangelical Zionists claimed were fulfilled in 1948 or 1967 that are grossly taken out of context in order to back and support their false and manipulative religious/political systems?

Are Christians in the U.S. supposed to support modern day Israel in their theft and violence because God will allegedly "bless" us if we do? Are some Evangelical Zionists such as C.I. Scofield and John Hagee correct to condemn Christians as being in "sin" if we don't support the modern Israeli agenda?

Is it just possible that modern day Israel is simply another unbelieving nation, among many others, that needs the gospel and to be held accountable for their land agreements with the Palestinians?

What if it can be proven from Jewish sources prior to Jesus and after AD 70 that Messiah would be divine and had to have arrived even upon the clouds of heaven before the second Temple fell in AD 70? What if I can show Jews that their own sources of authority teach that a spiritual resurrection and spiritual fulfillment of the Temple promises were to be fulfilled by AD 70?

And what if I can prove to the Evangelical Zionist that both the OT and NT teach that a Messianic kingdom and temple would be fulfilled spiritually and "within" the believer, and that they don't teach that a physical or earthly kingdom or temple will be set up in modern Jerusalem? And what if I can prove these to be true not only from the Scriptures, but from the teachings of the orthodox Christian Church?

What if I can prove to the Evangelical Zionist that the "rapture" of 1 Thessalonians 4:15-17 is not a promise made to them whereby they are going to disappear from planet earth just before things get really bad here on earth? If I can prove this passage was fulfilled by AD 70 and the Christian Church will never be raptured off the planet, would this affect the way the Church lives, should be involved in politics, and ought to develop long-term strategies to take back our country and fight against wicked globalism? If I can do this, perhaps we can awaken the Evangelical sleeping giant from the mentality that says, "You don't polish brass on a sinking ship."

What are we to make of the Charismatic Evangelical Zionist movement that brings false prophecies in the name of God concerning the Second Coming and the activities of our politicians and even our Presidents? Did the gift of prophet and prophecy in the OT and NT contain error or was the prophet to be 100% accurate? Did the office of prophet and the miraculous gifts of prophecy, tongues and knowledge stop or cease in AD 70? If so, what are we to make of all the false, failed and often times conflicting "prophecies" arising from the Charismatic Zionist churches?

The solution summarized

These are all very important questions when analyzing these three "end time" religious systems and trying to find an effective "war of ideas" that can bring as much peace as is possible among them. Therefore, let me answer some of these questions and give the reader my propositions and solutions from the outset. The rest of this volume is designed to prove my propositions:

- **Imminent Time of Fulfillment:** Jesus predicted that His Second Coming, the end of the (old covenant) age, and all of the signs described in Matthew 24-25 would be fulfilled (and were "near") within His contemporary "this generation" and He kept that promise (Matthew 24:34; see also Matthew 10:22-23 and Matthew 16:27-28). Therefore, the NT inspired authors who were "reminded" and "led into truth concerning things to come" like their Master also taught (as their generation was ending) that Christ's Second Coming was "at hand", "near", "soon," and was "about to be" fulfilled "in a very little while and will not delay" (ex. Rms. 13:11-12; Jms. 5:7-9; 1 Pet. 4:5-7; Heb. 10:37; Rev. 1:1—22:7, 10, 20).

  Jesus and the NT authors are consistent with OT prophets who used common apocalyptic language filled with metaphors and symbolism. When God came on the clouds in the OT and there was de-creation language, He came through an invading army and caused the nations being judged to have their civil and religious worlds come to an end. In the Olivet Discourse Jesus prophesied that the age or world (heaven and earth) of the old covenant system would end in His generation. Neither Jesus nor any NT author predicted that the end of world history was "near" or "soon" to take place.

- **Sacred Space:** Under the Old Covenant there was a literal "in the land" militaristic kingdom or theology, but this served as prophetic types and shadows of Jesus' spiritual kingdom or being "in Christ" under the new covenant which now advances through the sword of the Spirit or the everlasting gospel. However, this does not lead to pacifism, as I will discuss in a later chapter.

  The events of 1948 have nothing to do with the fulfillment of Bible prophecy, contrary to the empty claims of Zionism in its various forms. Neither modern-day Judaism nor Islam has any religious right to "holy land" in the Middle East or the planet today.

The Bible does not support a Messianic Kingdom or paradise on earth. Jesus taught that when He would be revealed from heaven like the sun shining from the east to the west, His Kingdom would not be seen with one's eyes, but rather would be realized "within the heart of a person" (Lk. 17:20-37). It is more than ironic that people refer to Islam, Talmudic Zionism, and Evangelical Zionism as the "three Abrahamic faiths." This is odd since Hebrews makes it abundantly clear that Abraham's faith was not in an earthly country or city but a spiritual or heavenly one, "For we have not here an abiding city [a city named Jerusalem on earth], but we are seeking the one [city / New Jerusalem] *about to ['mello' in Greek] come*" (Heb. 11:10-16; 13:14). This is consistent with the "Jerusalem from above" being the new covenant (Gal. 4:26) which Revelation teaches is the New Jerusalem which was in the process of coming down and did "shortly" arrive in AD 70 when the earthly Jerusalem/Babylon was destroyed (Rev. 1:1; 3:12; 22:7, 10, 20 NIV).

- **The End of the Age War:** The battle of "Gog and Magog," or "Armageddon" was prophesied to be fulfilled within a 3 ½ year period, and "shortly" or "soon," and this took place during the Roman-Jewish War of AD 67 – AD 70, resulting in the temple being destroyed. This was also the time "when the power of the holy people would be completely destroyed," thus marking the end of the old covenant age (Lk. 21:20-32; Rev. 11; Dan. 12:4-7).

- **The Office of Prophet & Prophecy:** I will prove from the OT and NT that the office of prophet and the miraculous gift of prophecy "stopped" or "ceased" when the Temple was destroyed in AD 70 at the "soon" Second Coming of Christ (Dan. 9:24-27; 1 Cor. 13:8-12; Rev. 22:4-7, 10, 20). This obviously is relevant in our discussion with Islam since because Muhammad couldn't be "God's prophet" when that office and revelation ceased in AD 70. It is also relevant since many Charismatic Zionists surround President Trump and give false and failed "prophecies" on almost a daily basis, which creates much concern. If a President has a "prophet" or "prophetess" as his council and wants WWIII to take place so they can be "raptured," – "Houston we have a problem."

Outline and Approach to the Solution

My approach is twofold: First, I will develop what each of these three systems teach concerning sacred space and an imminent Second Coming of Jesus the Messiah to usher in an end-time holy war. Secondly, I will demonstrate how these overlapping prophetic concepts have either been proven to be false and failed predictions, or are in conflict with what the Bible actually teaches.

I should also note that since Islam says that Jesus never claimed to be God and rejects the Deity of Christ, and since modern Jews claim that a divine Messiah is nowhere taught in the Torah or in their rabbinic traditions, I will deal with this subject in much detail as well. It is not sufficient to tear down a false religion, but one must do so while pointing the person to the truth and when possible do it even through their own sources of authority.

I will now begin to make my case proving that all of my propositions above are in fact true, and therefore make a truly Biblical and common-sense case which will achieve more peace in the Middle East than is present today.

I dedicate this book to President Trump who did not listen to many who wanted to lure us into the "endless wars" in the Middle East. In fact, not only did he not listen to the enticements of Islam, Israel and Evangelicals to engage in war in the Middle East, but he made peace deals. My work is simply a theological treatise which can be used for Christian politicians and presidents to take peace in the Middle East to the next level and provide a platform for "Christian Patriots" to take back this great country!

Chapter One:

Islam, an Eschatology of Violence: Holy Land and a "Very Soon" Second Coming of Jesus and Holy War to Destroy the Infidels (Jews, Christians, etc.)

The Violence of Islamic Theology / Eschatology

Before we begin, we should note that there are two religious sources within Islam which teach the "time of the end" eschatology. The first is the Quran, which is viewed as inspired and infallible, allegedly describing God giving the prophet Muhammad revelation from the angel Gabriel and compiling the doctrine which resulted from those revelations. Not much eschatology is found in the Quran except affirmations of a future coming "hour" in which Allah will resurrect men and judge the world. The second source is the Hadith, which is not considered as infallible as the Quran because it contains teachings and stories about Muhammad's life that were not considered direct revelation from Allah. These teachings were compiled some 200 years after Muhammad's death. As we will readily see, Muhammad and Islam seek to steal OT and NT Scriptures and join them and their concepts with other "revelations" from "angels" or "prophets," giving them the alleged "true" meaning (similar to what the Jehovah's Witnesses, Mormons etc. do).

The main points to cover in outlining Islamic Eschatology, which are relevant to our discussion in solving the circular religious violence in the Middle East and elsewhere, are the following:

1). **Islam and Holy War**

2). **Islam and Sacred Space – the Caliphate Conquest**

3). **Islam and a "Very Soon" Second Coming of Jesus and End Time Battle of Gog and Magog**

Islam and Holy War

I will briefly examine the evidence which demonstrates why Islam and its eschatology is inherently violent and cannot be "reformed" into a peaceful religion. The core of Islamic eschatology and theology is fulfilled through war as can be seen in studying its teachings in the following areas:

- *The doctrine of Sunnah and following Muhammad's life example and revelations in Mecca v. Medina*

- *The doctrine of abrogation*
- *The life of Muhammad and his revelations in both Mecca and then in Medina form the two divisions of the Quran*
- *The Quran is violent and perverse*
- *The three kinds and/or stages of Jihad*
- *Unity on the meaning of Sharia Law and Jihad*

The doctrine of Sunnah and following Muhammad's life and revelations in Mecca v. Medina

"Say [to people], 'If you love God, then follow me [Muhammad]; God will [then] love you and forgive your sins'" (Quran, 3:31).

"Ye have indeed in the Messenger of Allah a beautiful pattern (of conduct) for any one whose hope is in Allah and the Final Day, and who engages much in the Praise of Allah" (Quran 33:21).

"By explaining the Qur'an through his words and actions, the *Prophet through his Sunnah, gives us the best example of how this book is to be understood and practiced*" (taken from a Muslim web site).

This is somewhat similar, and a rip-off of what Jesus teaches His followers:

"Then he called the crowd to him along with his disciples and said: "Whoever wants to be my disciple must deny themselves and take up their cross and follow me" (Mark. 8:34).

As we will see, the difference of course is that following Jesus as the "way" entails humbling ourselves, denying our pride and lusts, being peacemakers, loving our enemies, etc. On the other hand, following the "conduct" and "example" of Muhammad's life and revelations feeds pride, lust and violence.

Muhammad in Mecca

Muhammad for the first 12 years preached to his home tribes a relatively peaceful message of tolerance and cooperation with the "people of the book" (Jews and Christians). It is during this period that we hear Muhammad teaching things like, "Leave unbelievers alone in their errors and bear with them for a little while" or there is "no compulsion in religion" (cf. Quran 109:1-6; 2:256; 73:10-11). He declares he is getting revelations from Allah (a monotheistic god) through his angel Gabriel. This results in very few followers and much ridicule from his polytheistic tribe and family members. Additionally, Jews and Christians did not find his "revelations" in their Scriptures, and they believed him to be gullible and uneducated to think that his revelations were consistent with theirs.

However, while preaching peace during this period, behind closed doors Muhammad was telling the leaders of his home tribes that if only they would acknowledge Allah as the only God and himself as His Apostle, Allah would give them victory (through war) over their rival Arabs and the Jews and Christians. This exposes that he had violent intentions of gaining an army and that of military conquest even at this early stage.

This message of peace (while concealing the true intent of violence through Jihad) will later be developed and known as the doctrine or practice of *taqiyya*. This doctrine allows Islam to be advanced by lying and deception when Muslims are in the minority (cf. Quran 3:26; 3:54; 9:3; 16:106; 40:28).

Muhammad's public message of peace turning more violent can be seen when he gets a bit bolder in denouncing his tribe's polytheistic gods in a harsh manner. As a result, they end up denouncing Muhammad and Islam. While Muhammad secretly desires to conquer various Arab tribes, Jews and Christians, he allows these groups at various times to help him and his small group of so-called "persecuted" followers.

Muslims claim Muhammad was being "persecuted" during this time period for preaching the truth (thus playing the victim card). Yet, it is Muhammad who denounced and mocked their gods, and this is what triggered his "persecution."

During this period "revelations" are given that Muslims may fight to defend themselves when persecuted (Quran 22:39-40). Being outnumbered and realizing that his new religion is not going anywhere, he flees to Medina.

Muhammad in Medina

While in Medina, Muhammad finds a more receptive audience. Here the Arab tribes are in civil war, fighting against each other while at the same time trying to fight Jewish tribes.

Now Muhammad's so-called "revelations" become violent, teaching that Muslims can kill unbelievers, steal their wealth, and rape and take their women as sex slaves or wives. And if they die in battle, they will inherit wealth and sex in "Paradise."

This message of greed and lust appeals to the occupants of Medina. Muhammad hopes the appeal to the carnal mind will at least unite them in forming a new religion that can be a foundation and philosophy that can be used against a common enemy – the Jews and Christians. Now the true Islam begins to emerge.

Instead of living peacefully in Medina, he returns to Mecca launching seven attacks on their caravans. Muslims attack during the sacred month of Rajab (when fighting was forbidden) and kill their first victim. Afterward, convenient "revelations" are given that this deception and killing was justified – because persecuting and criticizing Islam is worse than Muslims killing unbelievers. For Muslims, "persecution" comes in the form of disagreeing with the "revelations" of Muhammad and they are now justified in killing the unbeliever. This is somehow self-defense and a righteous form of Jihad.

The pagans realize Muslims will not stop attacking them, so they form a large army to protect and defend themselves. Muhammad continues attacking and, even with a smaller army, succeeds. This was known as The Battle of Badr. All the Quraysh were captured or killed, through beheading and other means.

Thus, within Islam one is to "strive" to wage war/Jihad against unbelievers and behead them along with apostates and hypocrites among Islam (cf. Quran 9:73; 47:4; 9:29; 9:123). This is allegedly a fight involving the followers of Allah and those of the friends of Satan (cf. Quran 4:76).

Engaging in Jihad (killing unbelievers and apostates) is the "highest rank" or calling in Islam, which produces salvation and guarantees that those who "slay and are slain" will inherit paradise (Quran 9:19; 9:111).

There is no spiritualizing away or "reforming" these passages, because their historical context of what Muhammad was doing, and how he was living out or practicing the revelations of the Quran, confirms they are meant to produce literal warfare and violence. This is the example and revelation that Muslims are to follow. There is no getting around this.

The doctrine of abrogation

"Whatever a Verse (revelation) do We {Allah} abrogate or cause to be forgotten, We bring a better one or similar to it. Know you not that Allah is able to do all things?" (Quran 2:106).

"When We substitute one revelation for another—and God knows best what He reveals (in stages)—they say, "Thou art but a forger": but most of them understand not" (Quran 16:101).

If there is a contradiction or apparent contradiction, Muslims are to follow the revelation that was the most recent, which will then serve to abrogate earlier ones. Therefore, Muslims teach and are called to follow or favor the violent passages in the Quran that come later, rather than the more peaceful ones that were given by Muhammad when he didn't have an army.

A similar concept can be seen in the Christian Scriptures in that when Jesus and the Church fulfills the old covenant promises, that covenant "soon vanished" (Heb. 8:13) and became obsolete in AD 70 and replaced with the new covenant. We understand that we don't need to be circumcised, perform animal sacrifices, and take up the literal sword taking dominion over peoples of a particular land in order to fulfill prophecy. The new covenant abrogates these covenant types and shadows, and we are now following Jesus' final marching orders in the new covenant age – that of loving our neighbor and advancing the kingdom through the Word of God (the sword of the Spirit – the gospel).

In Islam, it is the complete opposite. Their OT, so to speak, is Muhammad's life in Mecca, the portion of their holy book which contains relatively peaceful teachings. However, their final marching orders in their NT, so to speak, come from Muhammad's life in Medina where he gets an army and begins having so-called "revelations" of violence, perversions and jihad.

The teachings of the Quran

Putting this all together so far, in the Quran we see direct and explicit teachings of murder, violence, deception, and perversion as the *sunnah* or "perfect way of conduct" is carried out by Muhammad when he emulates or lives out his so-called "revelations." We also find his followers faithfully emulating them.

We further learn from the Quran and the life of Muhammad the following violent and depraved teachings:

You can rape, marry and divorce pre-pubescent girls (Quran 65:4).
You can enslave women for sex and work and form prostitution (Quran 4:3; 4:24; 5:89; 33:50; 58:3; 70:30).
You can beat sex slaves, work slaves, and wives (cf. Quran 4:34).
You can kill Jews and Christians if they do not convert or pay taxes (cf. Quran 9:29).
You can crucify and amputate non-Muslims (cf. Quran 8:12; 47:4).
You can kill non-Muslims to receive 72 virgins in heaven (cf. Quran 9:111).
You can kill anyone who leaves Islam (cf. Quran 2:217; 4:89).
You can behead non-Muslims (cf. Quran 8:12; 47:4).
You should kill and be killed for Allah (cf. verse of the sword - Quran 9:5).
You can commit acts of terror against non-Muslims (cf. Quran 8:12; 8:60).
You can steal from non-Muslims (cf. Quran chapter 8 - booty/spoils of war).
You can lie to strengthen Islam (cf. Quran 3:26; 3:54; 9:3; 16:106; 40:28).

Three kinds and stages of Jihad

There are three kinds of Jihad, developed in three stages. The three forms of Jihad are:

1). "Jihad of the heart" – fighting evil within

2). "Jihad of the mind and tongue" – agreeing with the right behavior of others while confronting those who have not fully submitted to Allah and have gone astray from his teachings

3). "Jihad of the sword" – enslaving or killing unbelievers. Many Western Muslims either try to deny or lie about the Quran teaching this third violent form of Jihad, or they seek to muddy the waters by defining Jihad within the limited categories of the first two. This is very much a part of their doctrine or practice of *taqiyya* (advancing Islam through lying and deception when Muslims are in the minority – cf. Quran 3:26; 3:54; 9:3; 16:106; 40:28).

David Wood correctly summarizes the three stages of Jihad within Islam to be the following:

"STAGE ONE OF JIHAD

When Muslims are completely outnumbered and can't possibly win a physical confrontation with unbelievers, they are to live in peace with non-Muslims and preach a message of tolerance. We see an example of this stage when Muhammad and his followers were a persecuted minority in Mecca. Since the Muslims were entirely outnumbered, the revelations Muhammad received during this stage (e.g. "You shall have your religion and I shall have my religion") called for religious tolerance and proclaimed a future punishment (rather than a worldly punishment from the sword of Islam) for unbelievers.

STAGE TWO OF JIHAD

When there are enough Muslims and resources to defend the Islamic community, Muslims are called to engage in defensive Jihad. Thus, when Muhammad had formed alliances with various groups outside Mecca and the Muslim community had become large enough to begin fighting, Muhammad received Qur'an 22:39-40:

> "Permission (to fight) is given to those upon whom war is made because they are oppressed, and most surely Allah is well able to assist them; Those who have been expelled from their homes without a just cause except that they say: our Lord is Allah..."

Although Muslims in the West often pretend that Islam only allows defensive fighting, later revelations show otherwise.

STAGE THREE OF JIHAD

When Muslims establish a majority and achieve political power in an area, they are commanded to engage in offensive Jihad. Hence, once Mecca and Arabia were under Muhammad's control, he received the call the fight all unbelievers. In Surah 9:29, we read:

> "Fight those who believe not in Allah nor the Last Day, nor hold that forbidden which hath been forbidden by Allah and His Messenger, nor acknowledge the Religion of Truth, from among the People of the Book, until they pay the Jizyah with willing submission, and feel themselves subdued."

Notice that this verse doesn't order Muslims to fight oppressors, but to fight those who don't believe in Islam (including the "People of the Book"—Jews and Christians).[1]

Unity on the meaning of Sharia Law and Jihad

Gregory M. Davis correctly points out that Sharia Law is not optional for the Muslim to follow, and yet Sharia Law necessitates a nationalistic hostile form of totalitarianism against other countries, their unbelief, and the other religions they may embrace:

Unlike many religions, Islam includes a mandatory and highly specific legal and political plan for society called Sharia, which translates approximately as "way" or "path." The precepts of Sharia are derived from the commandments of the Quran and the Sunnah (the teachings and precedents of Muhammad as found in the reliable Hadiths and the Sira). Together, the Quran and the Sunnah establish the dictates of Sharia, which is the blueprint for the good Islamic society. Because Sharia originates

---

[1] David Wood, *Jihad*, http://www.answeringmuslims.com/p/jihad.html

with the Quran and the Sunnah, it is not optional. Sharia is the legal code ordained by Allah for all mankind. To violate Sharia or not to accept its authority is to commit rebellion against Allah, which Allah's faithful are required to combat.

There is no separation between the religious and the political in Islam; rather Islam and Sharia constitute a comprehensive means of ordering society at every level. While it is in theory possible for an Islamic society to have different outward forms — an elective system of government, a hereditary monarchy, etc. — whatever the outward structure of the government, Sharia is the prescribed content. It is this fact that puts Sharia into conflict with forms of government based on anything other than the Quran and the Sunnah.

The precepts of Sharia may be divided into two parts:

[1] Acts of worship (al-ibadat), which include: ritual purification (Wudu), prayers (Salah), fasts (Sawm and Ramadan), charity (Zakat), pilgrimage to Mecca (Hajj)

[2] Human interaction (al-muamalat), which includes: financial transactions, endowments, laws of inheritance, marriage, divorce and child care, food and drink (including ritual slaughtering and hunting), penal punishments, war and peace, and judicial matters (including witnesses and forms of evidence).

As one may see, there are few aspects of life that Sharia does not specifically govern. Everything, from washing one's hands to child-rearing to taxation to military policy, falls under its dictates. Because Sharia is derived from the Quran and the Sunnah, it affords some room for interpretation. But upon examination of the Islamic sources (see above), it is apparent that any meaningful application of Sharia is going to look very different from anything resembling a free or open society in the Western sense. The stoning of adulterers, execution of apostates and blasphemers, repression of other religions, and a mandatory hostility toward non-Islamic nations, punctuated by regular warfare, will be the norm. It seems fair then to classify Islam and its Sharia code as a form of totalitarianism."[2]

Again, to believe in and implement Sharia law means to wage holy war against unbelievers (non-Muslims). Gregory Davis also exposes the violence of Islam when he writes on the unity of understanding the meaning of Jihad within Sharia Law within its various sects.

> "One of the common elements to all Islamic schools of thought is jihad, understood as the obligation of the Ummah to conquer and subdue the world in the name of Allah and rule it under Sharia law. The four [main Sunni]…schools — all agree that there is a collective obligation on Muslims to make war on the rest of the world. Furthermore, even the schools of thought outside Sunni orthodoxy, including the [Shia school Jafari], agree on the necessity of jihad."[3]

---

[2] Gregory M. Davis, *Islam 101*, http://www.jihadwatch.org/islam-10
[3] Ibid.

One of the ways to bring out the true motivation of Muslims is to poll the various sects to see how much they want the nations to which they have migrated to embrace and conform to Sharia Law:

51% of Muslims in the U.S. back some form of Sharia.
77% of Muslims in S. Asia support Sharia.
74% of Muslims in S.E. Asia support Sharia.
64% of Muslims in various areas of Africa support Sharia.
99% of Afghanistan Muslims want Sharia law (the U.S. allowed 11,000 to have green cards from Afghanistan from 2009-2013).
91% in Iraq want Sharia law (we allowed 83,000 Iraqis – during the same time period – to have green cards).
84% in Pakistan want Sharia law (we allowed 83,000 Pakistanis to have green cards – again during the same time period).

Next ask how Muhammad (as the perfect messenger of Allah) sought to bring about Sharia upon the nations and how the Quran commands them to live it out, emulating the ways of Muhammad. Again, you may get various versions and answers of what Jihad is, but this is to be properly interpreted as to how well this Muslim actually understands and follows the Quran, or if they are willfully deceiving you.

Islamic Eschatology has a sacred land / world Caliphate mandate

Islam divides the nations of the world into two houses or spheres. First, there is The House of Islam (dar al-Islam), which consists of those nations and lands that have already been conquered and submitted to Allah and Sharia Law. The second is The House of War (dar al-harb), which consists of those nations and lands that have yet to be conquered and submit to Allah and Sharia Law. Islam is called to conquer all the religions of the world (cf. Quran 61:9, 48:28, 9:3).

In Islam, land that was once conquered under Islam will always belong to Islam. For example, since Muhammad conquered Jerusalem and allegedly ascended from the site of Solomon's Temple, Islam will NEVER concede that Jerusalem belongs to any other than that of Islam and its caliphate ambitions. Even the alleged "moderate" and "peaceful reformer," Zuhdi Jasser (who appears on FOX News from time to time), made a slip of the tongue in the last five minutes of an interview challenging his "reformed" views. In that interview, he referred to Israel as "occupied territory."[4]

So, no matter how you slice it, even Jasser, who is trying to practically form his own Islam, subscribes to some form of religious divine right to "holy land," throwing more fuel on an existing fire. He is not bringing any kind of "peaceful" solution, which is what he claims to be doing and what he claims is his mission.

---

[4] Pamela Geller, *Jasser's Jihad*, http://pamelageller.com/2009/05/jassers-jihad.html/

Muhammad and the Caliphate Mandate

Muhammad sought to make his bloody conquests beyond Arabia, contacting rulers (e.g. the k ing of Persia, the emperor of Rome, and others) and inviting them to believe in Allah. "Embrace Islam and you will be safe." Obviously, he implied that if they didn't embrace Islam, they would suffer the same fate as others.[5]

Muhammad also promised that the first of his armies to invade Constantinople "will be forgiven their sins." An interesting side note here is that later the Catholic Pope and various monks would use this same manipulative technique to motivate the crusaders, granting them forgiveness of sins if they partook in this "the end is near" holy war battle against the Muslims, whom they identified as the beast of Daniel and Revelation (see Appendix section).

The Muslim Caliphate dwarfs anything the Roman Empire produced, and Muslims had a Caliphate up until WWI in Turkey. Some view Iran as an Islamic Caliphate of sorts, and of course ISIS resurrected the "end is near" and "Jesus is coming soon" Islamic Caliphate expectation before President Trump and the U.S. decimated and exposed that false and failed prophetic expectation!

Islamic Eschatology – teaches a "soon" Second Coming of Jesus and end-time battle of Gog and Magog

Islam is willing to forget its rich history of alleged "inspired" and yet *failed eschatological predictions*. There isn't enough space to address all of them, but here are a few that are relevant for our subject matter:

1) Muhammad predicted the "Last Hour" would come within the lifetime and generation of his contemporaries:

   "Anas reported: A young boy of Mughira b. Shu'ba happened to pass by (the Holy Prophet) and he was of my age. Thereupon Allah's Apostle (may peace be upon him) said: If he lives long **he would not grow very old till the Last Hour would come (to the old People of this generation).**"[6]

2) Muhammad predicted that everyone would die on the earth within a hundred years (thus predicting the end time/last hour events of the judgment and resurrection):

   "Once the Prophet led us in the 'Isha' prayer during the last days of his life and after finishing it (the prayer) (with Taslim) he said: 'Do you realize (the importance of) this night? Nobody present **on the surface of the earth tonight will be living after the completion of one hundred years from this night.**"[7]

---

[5] See *Muslim, book 19, no. 4382; Bukhari, vol. 4, book 56, no. 2941*
[6] Sahih Muslim, Book 41, Number 7053
[7] Sahih al-Bukhari, Vol. 1 Book 3, Number 116

3) Muhammad predicted the great war, the coming of the Antichrist and thus the end of the world would take place after the conquests of Jerusalem (636 AD) and Constantinople (1453 AD):

> "The Prophet (peace be upon him) said: The flourishing state of Jerusalem will be when Yathrib is in ruins, the ruined state of Yathrib will be when **the great war comes, the outbreak of the great war will be at the conquest of Constantinople and the conquest of Constantinople when the Dajjal (Antichrist) comes forth**. He (the Prophet) struck his thigh or his shoulder with his hand and said: This is as true as you are here or as you are sitting (meaning Mu'adh ibn Jabal)."[8]

Other, but more complex, views would be Muhammad's belief that the world was roughly 6,500 years old during his lifetime and that all of the prophecies would be fulfilled no later than when the earth reached her 7,000th year (by the way, many Jews and even Christians have tried this approach as well in predicting the end of the world, always ending in failure as well).

Obviously, the "last hour" (a world-wide literal resurrection and judgment of the dead and literal transformation of the planet earth, etc.) did not happen 500 years from Muhammad's death.

Since Islam teaches that Allah inspired the OT, then according to Allah, the "prophet" Muhammad was a false prophet and should have been stoned to death (Deut. 18:20-22).

Islam keeps the failed prophetic ministry and manipulation of Muhammad alive and well today. We shall look at ISIS as just one example. The title of ISIS's magazine *DABIQ* helps us understand Islamic eschatology and worldview. The Syrian town of Dabiq is where the Prophet Muhammed is supposed to have predicted that the armies of Islam and "Rome" (or the Christian West) would meet for the final battle that will precede the end of time and the triumph of true Islam. In the 15th issue of ISIS's *DABIQ* magazine is an article entitled *Break the Cross*, where they seek to persuade all gullible young men to join the final end-time holy war or Jihad. Why? Well, you guessed it. It's because their version of Jesus' Second Coming is going to take place "very soon," i.e. will be fulfilled in our lifetime (pp. 48-49), and therefore everyone needs to get on the side of Islam and accept their perverted version of Jesus' Second Coming or face imminent judgment from the Islamic Jesus.

ISIS writes, "As the world progresses towards **'the Great Battle'** to be held at Dabiq, the option to stand on the sidelines as a mere observer is being lost."

The propaganda goes something like this: "The FINAL Jihad has begun. We have captured the land, where the last holy war is now being fought. This is your 'final opportunity' because there will be no other wars in which you may martyr yourselves for Allah and secure your place in paradise." When American aid worker, Peter Kassig,

---

[8] Sunan Abu Dawud, Book 37, Number 4281

was murdered by ISIS, many ISIS videos said of Kassig: "We bury the first crusader in Dabiq, eagerly waiting for the rest of your armies to arrive."

In other words, ISIS is trying to self-fulfill their prophecies by provoking the West into invading Syria and into a ground war, which they believe will cause their version of the Second Coming of Jesus to take place, at which time He will call out to Allah in order to finish killing off the infidels.

Dr. Sebastian Gorka of FOX News writes in his book, *Defeating Jihad*:

> "Like Judaism, Christianity, or any other major religion, Islam has a well-developed eschatology. Christian eschatology, based in part on the Book of Revelation, [where there are] a series of battles before Judgment Day between the forces of an Anti-Christ and the last Christians on earth, culminates on the plains of Megiddo in northern Israel."[9]

He goes on to demonstrate that in a distinct parallel to what a lot of Christian Zionists believe, Islamic eschatology also teaches about "a diabolic figure who will lead the forces of the infidels into a series of great battles…"[10]

So, the Islamic Megiddo for Muslims is actually the territory of Syria and Iraq. ISIS in their publications claim that Jesus' Second Coming is going to take place "very soon" in our lifetime because of wars they are initiating.

The truth is that EVERY sect within Islam (not just ISIS) sees their current wars in the Middle East (even Muslims on both sides of the civil war in Syria, for example) as fulfilling their end-time prophecies and creating an atmosphere to where they all believe Jesus' Second Coming is "near."[11] Islam has their own versions of manipulative "the end is near" (again and again and again), false teacher provocateurs like Hal Lindsey and John Hagee.

In regard to how some Muslims view the end time battle of Gog and Magog, one can watch videos online where they see the immigration of modern "Jews" coming from the ancient Khazarian Empire (close to where ancient Magog was located). Since modern Israel comes from "Magog," and some within Israel believe they must wage war against the Muslim world in order to rebuild the temple and bring about their messiah, Muslims see the "end being near" and Israel (and her allies) as the great enemy in the end time battle.

---

[9] Dr. Sebastian Gorka, DEFEATING JIHAD THE WINNABLE WAR, (Washington, DC: Regnery Publishing, 2016), 116

[10] Ibid.

[11] Mariam Karounv, Apocalyptic prophecies drive both sides to Syrian battle for end of time, Reuters, April 1, 2014; Leo Hohmann, Popular Muslim Personality: Jesus Christ is Among us, http://www.wnd.com/2014/10/popular-muslim-personality-jesus-christ-is-among-us/#omxjVrhqwfLylqlS.99

Futurist Christians and Muslims Debate Who is a True Prophet -- the NT Jesus or the Quran's Muhammad

So how do Futurist Christian Apologists and Muslim Apologists deal with the fact that both Jesus and Muhammad taught the consummation would be fulfilled within the lifetimes of those standing next to them? Jesus clearly taught that He would return in the lifetime and generation of those he spoke to (ex. Mt. 10:22-23; Mt. 16:27-28; Mt. 24:3-34), and Muhammad taught that Jesus' Second Coming and the "last hour" judgment would be fulfilled in the lifetime and generation that he spoke to (or within 500 years after his death). So who's right, or were they both wrong?

It becomes very interesting, to say the least, when Futurist Christians debate Muslims on issues related to the reliability of the Bible, the reliability of the Quran, or the validity of Jesus or Muhammad as a faithful and accurate prophet when these subjects come up.

Let me give you a brief summary of how the James White (a Reformed Futurist Christian Apologist) and Shabir Alley (Islamic Apologist) series of debates went when this subject came up:

Shabir Alley – argued that since Jesus and the NT teaches the Second Coming of Jesus was supposed to occur in the lifetime and generation of the first century church, then this proves the Christian Jesus is a false prophet and that the NT has been corrupted and added to. Therefore, Allah gave Muhammad the most accurate revelations about Jesus as revealed in the Quran and Haddiths.

James White – surprisingly totally ignored Shabir's argument and his appeals to NT imminence. He referred the audience to listen to his teaching on Matthew 24 where he tells his church that he "dreads" teaching on this subject. In the debate with Alley he pointed out that the Temple was destroyed in AD 70 in Jesus' generation. Alley countered by pointing out that his argument was that Jesus promised that His Second Coming would also take place in that first century generation. White was silent from then on, because in his teaching on Matthew 24 he believes that the coming of Christ there is not a coming that was fulfilled spiritually in AD 70, but that it's a Second Coming which is future to us.[12]

So what is the REAL Christian response to the Muslim argument here of Jesus' teaching on imminence (Mt. 10:22-23; Mt. 16:27-28; Mt. 24:3-34)?

Michael Sullivan (Christian Full Preterism) – Jesus was a faithful prophet when He came upon the clouds "shortly and "soon" in the lifetime and generation of the first century church as the Ancient of Days, the Alpha and Omega, The Word of God, and the King of Kings bringing an end to the old covenant age (not to end world history and establish a paradise on earth) in AD 70.

---

[12] Interesting sidenote - passages White claims are referring to the ONE NT Parousia or Second Coming event (Mt. 24:27-30), his co-elder, Jeff Durbin, affirms were fulfilled spiritually in AD 70--thus forming my position that the ONE NT Second Coming event was fulfilled spiritually and imminently in AD 70. I have challenged both men to a public debate, but they will not respond to the challenge.

And since Jesus *did* come when He promised, this is only further evidence which proves that Muhammad is a false prophet.

As far as the Muslim argument that the Christian Bible has been corrupted or added to, we would respond, as White has responded, that this is not the position of the Quran and the early sources within Islam. Alley's "corruption of the text" argument wasn't invented until 1064 which is when Islam realized that Muhammad's teachings were not in fact compatible with the Jewish or Christian Scriptures.

These are arguments which only a Full Preterist can make when it comes to countering the Muslim argument on NT imminence, while at the same time addressing the failed imminence within their own sources. After reading my articles and response to both he and White, this is why Shabir Alley said he would only debate me on the subject of the deity of Christ and not the imminence of Jesus' eschatology or that of Muhammad's. *Telling indeed.* I countered that we could work that subject in with the issue of NT imminence and the failed prophecies of Muhammad, but Shabir would have none of it.

We should close this section on Islam by pointing out how drastically different Muhammad's depraved and non-miraculous predictions are compared to the NT Jesus and His teachings:

- Jesus was born of a virgin (having divine origins). Muhammad was born naturally, but conceded that Jesus was born miraculously of a virgin. This begs the question as to why Muslims don't embrace the OT and NT teaching of Him being God (which we will get into in chapter 12).

- Jesus claimed and proved Himself to be God. Muhammad is admittedly a mere man. A part of Jesus proving to be God and divine was by being tested of Satan (without sin), driving out demons, and ultimately "crushing" Satan "shortly" through the cross and His Second Coming between AD 30 - AD 70 (Col. 2:15; Rms. 16:20). Muhammad thought on several occasions that he himself was demon-possessed.

- Jesus taught that all of His words were those of the Father, and that those who would accept them would receive eternal life (male and female). Muhammad had to retract the "satanic verses" from his teachings, and he held that eternal life is only for men and not women in Islam.

- There are no contradictions within Jesus' teachings. There are plenty of contradictions within Muhammad's teachings, and again some of them were attributed to Satan.

- Jesus performed miracles, proving that He was a prophet. According to the Quran, Muhammad performed no miracles. Realizing this was a problem when trying to sell Muhammad's teachings and Islam to Christians, they later began attributing miracles to Muhammad hundreds of years later in the Hadiths, etc. But the Quran itself teaches that the only alleged miracle Muhammad performed was to produce the confusing and contradictory Quran (cf. Quran 29:51).

- Jesus was the Great High Priest (and Lamb of God), being the only mediator between God and man, restoring God's presence with man. Muhammad served no such role, except to deny that Jesus ever died on the cross and rose from the dead.

- Jesus is a risen and eternal King ruling from heaven, and His kingdom continues to increase. His kingdom is not of this world and His servants have never had to fight with a sword to produce converts to it. The "sword of the Spirit" (the Word of God) and the miraculous, effectual call of the Holy Spirit produce repentance, faith, and followers of Christ. Muhammad attempted to be some kind of a king (after the way of others through violence). If he ever even did exist, he is dead and long gone. His religion is spread through violence and coercion along with appealing to the depraved nature of man.

- Jesus lived a sinless life. Muhammad again thought he was demon possessed on several occasions, and lived a life of stealing, raping, and killing, leaving this as an "example" for his followers to emulate.

- Jesus rose from the dead (with up to 500 witnessing this event), proving He is God. He and the Father have made their home within believers. Muhammad, if he even existed, is long dead and gone.

- Jesus came to serve, demonstrating true humility and leadership. He was God and had nothing to prove by "lording it over" others as was, and continues to be, the corrupt way of unregenerate rulers and leaders. Muhammad came to be served and subject Jews and Christians to violence – "the way of the [unbelieving] Gentiles" (as Jesus described).

- Jesus came to fulfill the law and the prophets, and this is what He did. We have prophetic material predicting His birth thousands of years ahead of time, what He would do in His life and ministry, death, resurrection, ascension, and coming upon the clouds as the eternal Ancient of Days. Muhammad gave NEW so-called "revelations," which served only to give the Arabs a religious, political, and military movement to unite them. There were no miraculous predictions of Muhammad's life. Muhammad even conceded that Jesus was the Messiah of the Jews, thus fulfilling their prophecies concerning Him.

- Jesus is worshiped because He proved Himself to be God. Muhammad proved to be a thief, liar, pervert (having sex with a nine year old girl), killer, and founder of a false religion.

- There is historical evidence that Jesus existed and performed miracles (even from non-Christian sources) during the life of Christ and shortly after. One might be surprised to learn that there is no real historical evidence that Muhammad even existed (see Robert Spencer's books and Reformed theologian Robert Morey on this point) – during his life or shortly after. Because of this, many historians and theologians believe he was created to unite the Arabs, giving them a political/military/religious cause. Instead of converting to Christianity, they created their own version based off of bits and pieces they knew of Jewish and Christian beliefs.

- Jesus said "Blessed are the peace makers," while Islam teaches that those who perform Jihad and kill the infidels perform the highest services for god. Jesus taught that the greatest commandment is to love God and your neighbor as yourself. Islam teaches that the greatest commandment is to love Allah and wage Jihad.

- Jesus condemned anyone trying to protect him with a sword. Muhammad demanded and needed bodyguards in his presence.

- Christ was crucified for His Church, knowing all of their names from eternity past. Islam promotes the crucifying of others.

- Christ put in the hearts of the early Church to sell their possessions and give to the poor. Muhammad's followers lived off of stealing from others.

- Christ makes His people cheerful givers to encourage ministry to the poor and for the preaching of the gospel. Islamic mosques need to tax or force non-Muslims to pay for the spread of their religion.

- OT or old covenant war, prescribed to inherit "in the land" promises, pointed typologically to NT or new covenant promises to be fulfilled spiritually and peacefully "In Christ" (the ultimate fulfillment). Chronology from the Quran is from deceptive peace to violence (with later writings being most important and taking precedence over earlier ones).

- Apostates in Christianity are simply said to be professors of Christ (not true Christians) who have gone out from us, for if they were of us they would have continued with us. Apostates in Islam are a great threat to them, so they are to be killed. Professing believers in Christ that become Muslim are not killed by other Christians. Muslims who leave the empty and hateful religion of Islam for Christianity are beheaded by Muslims.

- Christ commands Christians to love their enemies. Islam teaches that one is not to befriend non-Muslims but rather to enslave them, tax them, and ultimately kill them if they do not convert to Islam.

- Christ commands husbands to love their wives as Christ loves the Church. And again, Christ gives eternal life to women. The Quran teaches men that they can beat their wives and that women cannot inherit eternal life; only men can.

- Christ (and also Christianity) doesn't need suicide bombings from His followers to survive and thrive. Islam commends and encourages suicide bombings from its followers and its children in order to thrive and survive.

- And to the subject of this book, Jesus predicted and promised that His Second Coming / Parousia would take place within the lifetime of some of those He spoke to, and in their AD 30 – AD 70 ("this generation") He promised to bring an end to the old covenant age while establishing and maturing the new covenant age. In AD 70 He did just that -coming upon the clouds of heaven "as the Ancient of Days" to be "worshiped" (cf. Dan. 7:13-14 (OG) LXX/NIV/Matt. 26:62-64/Rev. 1:7, 13-18). Muhammad taught that the "last hour" would take place within a hundred years of those he spoke to and demonstrated once again that he was a false prophet.

Conclusion - The Eschatological Goals of Islam

Clearly the eschatology of Islam calls for the military conquest of all the nations of the earth, subjecting them to Sharia Law or to be enslaved and even perish by the sword. Its violence is due to the doctrine of Sunnah (the example and pattern of Muhammad), the doctrine of abrogation (latter violent passages are the final marching orders for Islam), and what is taught in the Quran itself to militarily conquer all the religions and nations of the earth.

After studying Islam and its eschatology, there are only two kinds of Muslims claiming Islam is peaceful: 1) those ignorant or professing Muslims who haven't truly studied the life of Muhammad or the Quran, or 2) those practicing stages 1-2 of Jihad where they are called to lie and deceive in order to preserve and spread Islam in countries where they are outnumbered.

In predicting that the last hour judgment and Second Coming of Christ would occur within 100 years of the children standing next to him, or that the great end-time battle would occur no later than 500 years after his death, Muhammad has been proven to be a false prophet. But this doesn't stop virtually all sects of Islam from thinking that their civil wars, wars with the West, famines, plagues, etc. are all signs pointing to their version of the "soon" Second Coming of Jesus and end-time war.

Islam and its various groups, such as ISIS, have killed so many and have deceived millions of their young men to die early and senselessly. The final marching orders of the Quran end with chapter 9's violent Great Commission. The NT ends its revelation of Christ having come "soon" in AD 70, and then having the charge for the Church to bring healing to the nations through wielding the sword of the Spirit or preaching the everlasting Gospel (Rev. 22:6-20). Christianity has grown over the years because it miraculously confronts and heals man's depravity, while Islam has grown because it has appealed to man's depravity (greed and lust). There is simply no comparison!

Chapter Two:

Talmudic or Messianic Zionism: Holy Land and an Imminent Messianic Deliverer and Holy War to Enslave or Destroy the Gentiles (Islam, Christians, etc.)

The Violence of Israeli Talmudic Zionism

Introduction

While there are various strains and forms of Zionism, my focus will be on religious/Talmudic Zionism or Messianic Zionism. We will address Torah Judaism in a latter chapter. Talmudic Zionism is where Zionists try and equate modern Christian Arabs or Muslim Arabs living in Palestine with the ancient Amalekites under the old covenant, therefore justifying and giving them an alleged divine right and calling to perform ethnic cleansing of these groups. After all, they believe they are "God's people," that they have a "divine right to the land," and that the "Gentile was created to serve the Jew." They also believe that it is through these modern wars, theft, and ethnic cleansing that they will usher in the Messiah's coming and world "redemption."

Before we dive into the three areas of Talmudic or Messianic Zionist eschatology, it is very important to address fundamental questions such as:

1). What is the religious source of authority for this group which forms its eschatology?

2). Do modern Jews in the modern state of Israel have a racial right as "God's people" to the ancient boundaries described to Israel in the Old Testament?

3). If it can be proven that modern Jews do not have a pure racial right to the land of Palestine, then where did they come from and what are their theological or eschatological goals?

4). Do they likewise have a constantly failing imminent expectation of the coming of Messiah in the same way Muslims and Futurist Evangelical Christians do?

After the destruction of the temple during the Babylonian captivity beginning in 586 BC, the need arose for the Jews to interpret the law in Babylon without the temple. The offices of the Scribes and Pharisees would eventually be created to fill this function. These men claimed God gave the 70 elders at Mount Saini more profound revelations and traditions than that which Moses was given when he received the Torah.

Many Christians think that the modern religious Jew finds the OT Scriptures as his main and only source of authority when in fact, for many, the Talmud is his main source of religious authority in forming doctrine and how to live out his understanding of kingdom living.

So, what exactly were some of the "traditions of men" and the "hypocrisy" of the Pharisees, by which they were seeking to make "null and void the commandments of God" in the Torah, that Jesus rebuked them for in such passages as Mark 7:13 and Matthew 23? Why were they so arrogant, exclusive and violent then and now? Other than the depravity of man, the other explanation is what they had orally memorized from the Talmud, which would officially be canonized in 426 BC and believed to this day.

The authority of the Talmud

The modern religious "Jew" reaches the following conclusions about the importance and authority of the Talmud:

- The Talmud is more important than the law of Moses and it is more wicked to question a Rabbi than to question the law of Moses.

- The decisions of the Talmud are words of the living God. Jehovah Himself asks the opinions of earthly rabbis when there are difficult affairs in heaven.

- Jehovah Himself in heaven studies the Talmud, standing, since he has such respect for that book.

Wow. Since the Talmud has so much authority, what exactly is the Zionist "Jew" to submit and commit himself to believing and living out?[13]

There is a reason why the Talmud was kept unknown or secret to non-Jews for so long. It was not until 1934-1948 that it was even translated into English. As we will see, there is a reason why non-Jews exiled these modern Khazarian Jews from their countries and burned the Talmud when they found out what the Talmud taught.

The view of Gentiles in the Talmud

- Jews have souls and are humans, but Gentiles do not have souls. Gentiles are mere animals created in human form, created for the purpose of serving the Jews.[14]

- "When the Messiah comes every Jew will have 2800 slaves."[15]

---

[13] The following are the references for the above three bullet points: *Mischna Sanhedryn 11:3; Rabbi Issael, Rabbi Chasbar, et. al.; Rabbi Menachen, Comments for the Fifth Book; Tractate Mechilla/Me'ilah*).

[14] -*Saba Mecia 114, 6; Midrasch Talpioth, p. 225-L; -Simeon Haddarsen, fol. 56-D*

[15] *Simeon Haddarsen, fol. 56-D:, (Erubin 43b).*[15]

- Jews are to "make ('continuous') war with Gentiles by deceit and trickery" in order to "free themselves from them and rule over them."[16]
- "All property of other nations belongs to the Jewish nation, which, consequently, is entitled to seize upon it without any scruples." Stealing from and "cheating of a non-Jew at any time pleases the Lord."[17]
- "A Jew may do to a non-Jew female whatever he can do. He may treat her as he treats a piece of meat."[18]

Summary: A Jew could rape, steal from, deceive, and kill a Gentile at any time (if they could get away with it), because Gentiles have no souls and were only created for the purpose of being slaves to the Jews. And you thought this section was going to be less racist or violent than the Islam and Quran section? Sorry, it gets darker…

The Talmud's views on Jesus and Christians

Views on Jesus Christ

- It is taught that Jesus's mother played the whore with many carpenters. Therefore, Jesus was a bastard child. Jesus seduced and destroyed Israel by performing magic and teaching heresy and apostasy. Therefore, He is currently being punished by being boiled in His own urine and excrement never to enter the world to come.[19]

Views on Christians

- A JEW WHO KILLS A CHRISTIAN COMMITS NO SIN, BUT OFFERS AN ACCEPTABLE SACRIFICE TO GOD AND SHALL HAVE A HIGH PLACE IN HEAVEN.[20]
- Christians are idolaters; Jews must not associate with them.[21]
- It's suggested or implied that Christians are so depraved that they have sexual relations with animals.[22]
- Marriages between Christians and Jews must be made null and void.[23]

---

[16] *Talmud: Zohar, I. 160a.*

[17] *Talmud: Zohar, I. 160a.*

[18] *-Hadarine, 20, B; Schulchan Qruch, Choszen Hamiszpat 348; Moses Maimonides ("The RaMBaM"), Jak. Chasaka 2:2.*

[19] *Sanhedrin, 107b; Mishna Yebamoth 4,13; Sanhedrin 106a; Tosephta Sanhedrin X, 11: Jerusalem Sanhedrin 25c,d; Sanhedrin 107b; Taanit 65a; Gittin 56b, 57a; Mishna Sanhedrin X, 2.*

[20] *Sepher Or Israel (177b); Ialkut Simoni (245c. n. 772); In Zohar (III,227b); Zohar (I,38b, and 39a).*

[21] *Hilkhoth Maakhaloth.*

[22] *Abhodah Zarah (15b, 22a).*

[23] *Eben Haezar (44,8)*

- The Christian birth rate must be diminished to slow its spread.[24]
- Christian churches are places of idolatry.[25]
- Avoid eating with Christians because that breeds familiarity.[26]
- It is permitted to deceive Christians.[27]
- High usury or tax may be practiced and placed upon Christians (e.g. the Zionist Federal Reserve).[28]
- A Jew may lie and perjure to condemn a Christian.[29]
- Kill those who give Israelite money to Christians.[30] But they love taking money from Dispensational Zionists and of course Dispensational Zionist Pastors such as John Hagee are stupid enough to give it to them!
- Make no agreements and show no mercy to Christians.[31]

Views On Rabbis Teaching the Talmud

- Ironically, while the Talmud teaches that the greatest Rabbi ever (Jesus), who came to fulfill Torah, is being boiled in the afterlife, a Rabbi teaching the Talmud can never go to hell.[32]
- Knowledge of the Talmud for a Gentile is strictly forbidden: "Every non-Jew who studies the Talmud, and every Jew who helps him in it, ought to die." A Jew is to lie and make false vows to Gentiles if they ask what is taught in the Talmud, because if the Gentiles find out what is taught about them, they may desire to persecute or kill the Jews.[33] Now you know why some countries burned their Talmud and kicked them out of their countries!

What happens when Gentiles do find out what is in the Talmud and how these "Jews" are living it out?

Once Gentiles have found out what these so-called Jews have been teaching in their Talmud about them and what they have been up to, we find the Jews being thrown out

---

[24] *Zohar (II, 64b)*

[25] *Abhodah Zarah (78).*

[26] *Iore Dea (112, 1).*

[27] *Babha Kama (113b).*

[28] *Abhodah Zarah (54a).*

[29] *Babha Kama (113a-b).*

[30] *Choschen Ham (388,15).*

[31] *Hilkhoth Akum (X,1).*

[32] *(Hagigah 27a).*

[33] *Sanhedryn, 59a, Aboda Zora 8-6, Szagiga 13; Libbre David 37; Szaaloth-Utszabot, The Book of Jore 17*

of 47 countries in the last 1,000 years. These so-called "Jews" claim they are being persecuted for their righteousness and have been the victims of "Anti-Semitism." Yet from the perspective of these countries the reasons include:

1). their starting of revolutions and persecuting and killing Christians (e.g. the Bolshevik revolution where 66 million Christians died). While we agree that Hitler killing 1 – 6 million Jews (depending on your source) was wrong, we cannot ignore what Communist Jews did in Russia in butchering 66 million Christians.

2). their predator-lending practices and manipulation of currency (e.g. the Rothschild dynasty)

3). their arrogance and attitude toward the Gentile nations that have often times initially and graciously hosted and protected them.

4). profiting from both sides of war (e.g. the Rothschild Dynasty) and then creating a globalist banking system to enslave Gentiles.

5). The modern state of Israel and its consistent land grab in Palestine is a consistent expression of the Talmud. It is nothing but stealing land and committing racial genocide (murder) of "non-Jews" – all in the name of "God."

6). Most don't know that the modern state of Israel has committed more war crimes and violations (per the UN) than any nation in the world.

Evidence of the internal racism, hate and violence of the modern state of Israel would include:

1). According to the 1964 Jewish-American press, about half of the Jews at that time in Israel were black or dark-skinned Orientals. There is a constant charge and history of "discrimination" raised by the Oriental black Jews against the Western Jews. Israel's Interior Minister, Eli Yishai, has said of refugees coming into Israel that they "think the country doesn't belong to us, the white man."

2). Israel overwhelmingly segregates its schools, apartments, neighborhoods, whole cities and towns, and even the settlements they stole from the Palestinians. Israel even segregates public transport and has "Jews only" roads in the occupied territories.

3). In Israel it is illegal for a Jew to marry a non-Jew.

4). A Christian must renounce his faith before becoming a citizen in Israel.

5). In Israel Jews constantly hit and spit upon Christians in public and urinate on their churches.

But now that the racism and violence of the Talmud has become more public, some, such as Benjamin Netanyahu and other religious Zionist fanatics, want to make it the law of the land:

"Prime Minister Binyamin Netanyahu reportedly revealed at a Likud conference on Wednesday some remarkable facets of the Basic Law he submitted last Thursday, which would enshrine Israel's status as the nation-state of the Jewish people.

Netanyahu told the head of Likud's hareidi division Yaakov Vider at the conference that he intends to make the Hebrew calendar, which is based on Jewish law, the official calendar of Israel, reports *Kikar Hashabat*.

The new law also would establish the Talmud, the core work of Jewish law, as an official basis for Israeli state law.

"I'm going to personally be involved in the law defining the state of Israel as the nation-state of the Jewish people," Netanyahu reportedly told Vider. "It's a very important law that will influence how Israel will look in the future."

"I want to anchor in this law, that it will be a Basic Law that the state of Israel arose and exists on the basis of the Torah and the Jewish tradition," Netanyahu explained, promising to define the Hebrew calendar as the official state calendar.

Netanyahu also promised that "we will define in the law the Gemara as a basis for the Israeli legal system," referencing the Jewish legal text analyzing the Mishnah, a legal work of the Jewish sages, which together form the Talmud.

Discussing the new Basic Law on Sunday in a cabinet meeting, Netanyahu stated, "The existence of the State of Israel as a Jewish state does not actualize itself enough in our Basic Laws, which is what the proposed law aims to fix."[34]

Critics point out that this is an Israeli version of Islamic "Sharia Law":

"Netanyahu's proposed bill would make the Jewish calendar the only officially recognized calendar in the country and would move Israel's legal system ***one giant step closer to a Jewish version of Sharia law***."[35]

Another criticism sees the subtle bait and switch of the Rothchild / Khazarian / Zionist mafia-run creation and state promised to begin with Western Common Law to now be switched to the Talmud:

"…now Benjamin Netanyahu wants to have Israel declare that its legal system **is based on the Babylonian Talmud** *rather than on the secular western common law it was founded on*."[36]

And since Netanyahu also wants the law of the land to reflect the Talmudic Jewish calendar, many see him as a possible candidate for the runner-up to the Messiah or, in some circles, to be the Messiah:

---

[34] *FailedMessiah.com*, https://failedmessiah.typepad.com/failed_messiahcom/2014/05/prime-minister-benjamin-netanyahu-wants-to-move-israel-toward-jewish-sharia-law-567.html

[35] Ibid.

[36] Victoria Radin, *Who is Benjamin (Bibi) Netanyahu?*, http://www.haderekministries.com/index.php/articles/52-current-events/169-who-is-benjamin-bibi-netanyahu

> "It would seem that these proposals as well as other 'signs' have led some in the Orthodox community to believe that Bibi Netanyahu is Masiach ben Yosef (Messiah, son of Joseph)[2] the military leader that will precede the coming of the Messiah. [He will die in battle, but will make the way for the Messiah to come.] They claim that Netanyahu will be the last leader of Israel until the Messiah comes. Because Netanyahu has a military background and the fact that [they believe] he has taken on the spiritual mantle of Mordechai as is demonstrated in his speech to the U.S. Congress noted above, they are calling him Mashiach ben Yosef. Their website enumerates the many ways Bibi fulfills the requirements of this forerunner."[37]

Bibi's desire to change the law of Israel is a classic "bait and switch." The Khazarian Rothchild "Jews" deceptively convinced the Gentile nations that they would agree to a two-state Palestinian occupation of the land in 1947 and build their laws on Western Common Law values, but once in they begin driving the Palestinian Christians and Arabs out and sought to establish Talmudic law. Since the Talmud is considered more inspired than the Torah itself, if the Talmud is adopted as the law of the land, how can anyone avoid the theological racism and violence that is interwoven throughout it, which justifies and paves the way for Israel's coming Messiah?!?

Why is it that when Islam practices Sharia law in Muslim countries, conservative commentators such as Sean Hannity condemn them as not being consistent with Western or Christian values, but when Israel lives out the violent and racist ambitions and worldview contained in the Talmud (with some even wanting to make it the law of the land), not only is it not condemned, but we are actually called on by Hannity and others to continue giving Israel $10 – 15 billion a year to keep doing it?!? Why did Glen Beck and Sean Hannity obsess over trying to warn us about those Obama surrounded himself with (which would indicate his Communist destructive worldview), but not do the same with Benjamin Netanyahu who surrounds himself with violent racists and Talmudic zealots?!? I agreed with Hannity and Beck when they tried to shed light on Obama or criticize the violence and hypocrisy of Islam, but why the lack of consistency with Benjamin Netanyahu and Khazarian Talmudic Zionism? Is it because they practically own the news networks?

It seems more than hypocritical to engage in Islamic "extreme vetting" (which I agree should continue), but then allow Mossad operatives, organizations/cells and dual citizens to thrive (and even serve in high levels of our government) here in the U.S.! As I write, imposter Joe Biden is trying to fill his cabinet with them! Here are some helpful quotes from President George Washington and Benjamin Franklin that are worth meditating upon:

> "They (the Jews) work more effectively against us, than the enemy's armies. They are a hundred times more dangerous to our liberties and the great cause we are engaged in… It is much to be lamented that each state, long ago, has not

---

[37] Ibid.

hunted them down as pest to society and the greatest enemies we have to the happiness of America" (George Washington)."

"Jews, gentlemen, are Asiatics, let them be born where they will nor how many generations they are away from Asia, they will never be otherwise. Their ideas do not conform to an American's, and will not even thou they live among us ten generations. A leopard cannot change its spots. Jews are Asiatics, are a menace to this country if permitted entrance, and should be excluded by this Constitutional Convention" (Benjamin Franklin).

Sean Hannity and many on FOX News are only following Ronald Reagan's false prophetic view of modern Israel and it was public knowledge that Reagan was following the Charismatic Zionist writings of Hal Lindsey. Lindsey, of course, knows nothing about Biblical eschatology and has been proven to be a fraud, as we will see when we address Evangelical or Dispensational Zionism.

Are modern "Jews" the racial Jews of the OT and NT having a right to the land Palestine?

I would hope the encyclopedias below (especially the *Encyclopedia Judaica Jerusalem*) will not be deemed as "anti-Semitic," but one never knows today. It is usually the card the "Jew" plays when the facts are stacking against him. Consider the following quotes:

The American Peoples Encyclopedia (1954) -- "In the year 740 A.D. the Khazars were officially converted to Judaism. A century later they were crushed by the incoming Slavic-speaking people and were scattered over central Europe where they were known as Jews." *(at 15-292)*

The Encyclopedia Brittanica (1973) -- "The findings of physical anthropology show that, contrary to the popular view, there is no Jewish race... The only race to which the Jews have not achieved assimilation is the Nordic" (cf. *Vol. 12, p. 1054).*

Encyclopedia Judaica Jerusalem (1971) – "It is a common assumption, and one that sometimes seems ineradicable even in the face of evidence to the contrary, that the Jews of today constitute a race, a homogeneous entity easily recognizable. From the preceding discussion of the origin and early history of the Jews, it should be clear that in the course of their formation as a people and a nation they had already assimilated a variety of racial strains from people moving into the general area they occupied. This had taken place by interbreeding and then by conversion to Judaism of a considerable number of communities. . ."

"Thus, the diversity of the racial and genetic attributes of various Jewish colonies of today renders any unified racial classification of them a contradiction in terms. Despite this, many people readily accept the notion that they are a distinct race. This is probably reinforced by the fact that some Jews are recognizably different in appearance from the surrounding population. That many cannot be easily identified is overlooked and the stereotype for some is extended to all – a not uncommon phenomenon" *(cf. Vol. 3, p. 50; see also **The New Jewish Encylopedia (1962)**, pp. 190, 251, 265-266, 381, 411).*

Encyclopedia Americana (1986) – "Some theorists have considered the Jews a distinct race, although this has no factual basis. In every country in which the Jews lived for a considerable time, their physical traits came to approximate those of the indigenous people. Hence the Jews belong to several distinct racial types, ranging, for example, from fair to dark. Among the reasons for this phenomenon are voluntary or involuntary miscegenation and the conversion of Gentiles to Judaism" *(cf. Vol. 16, p. 71).*

Collier's Encyclopedia (1977) – "A common error and persistent modern myth is the designation of the Jews as a race! This is scientifically fallacious, from the standpoint of both physical and historical tradition. Investigations by anthropologists have shown that Jews are by no means uniform in physical character and that they nearly always reflect the physical and mental characteristics of the people among whom they live" *(cf. Vol. 13, p. 573).*

Dr. Benjamin H. Freedman correctly wrote in a letter written to New York's *National Economic Council's Newsletter* in 1947, testifying to the theft of Palestine by these Khazarian "Jews,"

"Popular ignorance of the real basis of political Zionism is beyond calculation. Vaguely most Christian Americans have the idea that the Jews claim Palestine because it was the "promised land" in which they lived for a period of a few centuries that ended 2000 years ago. And the thought of a people returning to its "homeland" seems emotionally satisfying and good.

But here are facts most Americans do not know:

Political Zionism is almost exclusively a movement by the Jews of Europe. But these Eastern European Jews have neither a racial nor a historic connection with Palestine. Their ancestors were not inhabitants of the "Promised Land." They are the direct descendants of the people of the Khazar Kingdom, which existed until the 12th century....

About the 7th century A.D., the King of the Khazars adopted Judaism as the state religion, and the majority of inhabitants joined him in the new allegiance. Before that date there was no such thing as a Khazar who was a Jew [Israelite]. Neither then nor since was there such a thing as a Khazar whose ancestors had come from the Holy Land. The Semitic people who established Judaism in Palestine many centuries before the Khazars became converts to the Hebrew faith [actually to the wicked Babylonian Talmudic faith MJS], did mostly emigrate from Palestine. But none of them [Semitic Judahites] emigrated to the Khazar Kingdom far to the North.

In view of this fact, what becomes of the cry for "repatriation" to the "homeland"? These Eastern European, Yiddish-speaking Jews have no historic or racial connection with Palestine....

...if the claim of Palestinian-descended Jews is so dubious, what of the claim of Khazar-descended Jews? Would a single Christian support their trek back to the "homeland" or want to oblige them by expelling the Arabs, if it were known that these Eastern European, Yiddish-speaking Jews who form the Zionist group practically in toto, have neither a geographic, historic nor ethnic connection with either the Jews [Judahite Israelites] of the Old Testament or the land known today as Palestine?"

Some seeing the problem here claim a "Jew" is simply a person who has converted to the religion of Judaism. But as we will see later, the covenant that undergirds "Judaism" or the "Hebrew faith" ended when the "scepter departed from Judah" (Gen. 49:10) in AD 70. Also, since the birth and genealogical records were burned when Christ came upon the clouds through the Roman armies in AD 67 - AD 70, there are no provable "racial Jews" let alone "Levites" to even get "Judaism" off the ground, even if they had a re-built Temple!

DNA Studies & the Irony of Jewish Racial Claims

History, archeology and now DNA-testing confirms that some 80% - 90% of Zionist "Jews" in the modern state of Israel today (and some 97% of the 17 million Jews in the world) have roots in the ancient and ruthless Turkish Khazarian Empire and are not Semites related to Abraham or the promised land of ancient Israel.[38] This is pathetic in that most of the Palestinians (Christian or Muslim) have more DNA relationship to Abraham and the ancient Hebrew people than these phony Zionist Khazarian "Jews" do! If you think Warren's "Pocahontas" scam was big, wait until I develop and expose the greatest racial religious scam in all of history!

It is amazing how these so-called racial "Jews" have tried to convince the world that they and they alone have the exclusive racial rights to the old covenant ancient land and boundaries of Israel. This truly is the biggest scam of ALL TIME!

The other irony here is that when you present these historical and genetic issues to the public, this powerful group seeks to silence you by calling you "anti-Semitic" when they aren't even some kind of pure, provable Jewish race! How can you be "racist" against a "Jew" who can't even tell you, let alone prove, what tribe he is from? I usually

---

[38] In 2001 Dr. Arilla Oppenheim who is a biologist at Hebrew University was the first to publish an exhaustive DNA study of the origins of the Jews. She concluded that just about all Jews came from the Khazar bloodline: see her article in American Journal of Human Genetics entitled, *The Y Chromosome Pool of Jews as Part of the Genetic Landscape of the Middle East*. Also see Dr. Eran Elhaik article, *The Missing Link of Jewish European Ancestry: Contrasting the Rhineland and the Khazarian Hypotheses*, published in Oxford Journal on behalf of the Society for Molecular Biology and Evolution. Also see: Ranajit Das, Paul Wexler, Mehdi Pirooznia and Eran Elhaik, *The Origins of Ashkenaz, Ahkenazic Jews, and Yiddish*, 2017.

know I've won a debate with a Muslim and Zionist "Jew" when they resort to calling me "Islamophobic" or I'm allegedly "anti-Semitic."

History of the Khazarian Empire

The Khazar kingdom was a large Turkish people that at one time stopped the expansion of the Islamic caliphate empire. They became wealthy through trade and placing an overbearing tax upon those they conquered. They also specialized in being a mercenary army – renting out their army of 40 – 50 thousand men to the highest bidders. After a battle took place, they were known to rape and pillage. Some report that they offered up children to Moloch, even stealing some of the children from neighboring countries. Not surprisingly, the people in the area didn't care for them much and ended up driving them out of Turkey in around 500 AD to what would be considered today as southern Russia or Georgia. From here their kingdom thrived from 660 – 1016 AD. It wasn't long before they began enslaving those in that area as well.

Russia began giving them ultimatums to convert their kingdom to a more peaceful religion or else. Eventually they were put in another dilemma. Coming down from the North was Byzantine Christianity and coming from the South was Islam. They knew that to choose either of these sides would put them in conflict with the other and this would affect their prosperous trading with both sides. So, they did the politically expedient thing and decided to make their empire convert to Judaism. They quickly saw that the wickedness, racial supremacy, and violence found in the Talmud would fit in well with their violent and immoral worldview that built their empire in the first place. It was a perfect fit!

In 965 AD they were weakened by the Vikings. In 1140 AD they were overrun by the Mongols and driven west and settled in parts of Europe. Over time they convinced themselves that they were ethnically and racially "Jewish" – even changing and adopting Jewish names, etc.

History of Rothschild Khazarian Dynasty

One of the Khazarian Talmudic "Jews" who settled in Europe was Mayer Amschel Bauer — who changed his last name to Rothschild. Rothschild means "red shield." Thus, he hung a sign of a red, six-pointed, shielded star as his logo for his money merchant shop. It is through his religious views on the Talmud, and money that he and his five sons attained, that the stage was set for financing the events of 1948 to become a reality.

Mayer Rothschild eventually befriended William the 9th who was a Hession warrior and leader of a mercenary army. For $12,000 you could hire William and his army to do anything. England hired them to keep the U.S. colonists in check. At this time William was one of the richest people in the world (worth $200 million) and the Rothschilds made a great deal overseeing his estate and making financial decisions for him. William stole millions owed to his army, and then when Napoleon came after him he entrusted $3 million to the Rothschilds, who in return ended up stealing it from him. The Rothschilds used this un-kosher and unclean money to begin their international banking venture/enslavement of the Gentile. The five Rothschild brothers obeyed their father's command and branched out into the various countries in Europe. From here, they ended up financing not just various wars, but in some instances both sides of the same war!

The Balfour Declaration in 1917 was created when the British Foreign Secretary, Arthur Balfour, declared in a letter to the Rothschilds that his government would support a Jewish homeland in Palestine. It is important to note that, before this declaration was given, it was agreed upon that if the Rothschilds could get the U.S. into WWI to help defeat the Germans, then Britain in return would give the land of Palestine to the Rothschilds and Zionists.

The Rothschilds funded the early Khazarian settlers from Europe to relocate in Palestine. In 1948 they also funded and armed terrorist groups, which bombed and terrorized 800,000 Palestinians to leave the land of their birth. *Modern Israel is simply the State of Rothschild.* This is even evident with them paying for the construction of the Israeli parliament building, the Knesset, and the Israel Supreme Court. The Israeli flag symbolizes both its territorial ambitions and that it is owned by the Rothschilds. Modern Israel uses the same six-pointed star on its flag that the Rothschilds used as their family symbol (just changing its color from red to blue). The two blue lines above and beneath the star symbolize the ancient borders / rivers given to ancient Israel under the old covenant, and thus gaining all of that land is the ultimate goal (even if modern countries surrounding them stand in the way, which by the way includes Egypt and Jordan, two of our allies)!

The Influence of the Talmud on the Rothschilds

Mayer's father's wish for his son was that he would one day become a Rabbi strictly teaching and following the Talmud. Although he didn't become a Rabbi, Biographer Frederic Morton, in *The Rothschilds*, points out how important the Talmud was in guiding the Rothschild dynasty in their unquenchable drive for money and power. He writes,

> "On Saturday evenings, when prayer was done at the synagogue, Mayer would invite the rabbi into his house. They would bend towards one another on the green upholstery, sipping slowly at a glass of wine and argue about first and last things deep into the night. Even on workdays…Mayer…was apt to tear down the big book of the Talmud and recite from it…while the entire family must sit stock still and listen."[39]

He goes on to tell us that Mayer Amschel Rothschild and his five sons were "wizards" of finance, and "fiendish calculators" who were motivated by a "demonic drive" to succeed in their secret undertakings. And Morton adds that it is difficult for the average person to "comprehend Rothschild nor even the reason why he having so much, wanted

---

[39] Frederic Morton, *The Rothschilds* (New York: Scribners, 1988), 33

to conquer more." All five brothers shared their father's spirit of Talmudic cunning and conquest.

The Influence of the Rothschild Dynasty

> "The Rothschilds are the wonders of modern banking… We see the descendants of Judah, after a persecution of two thousand years, peering above kings, rising higher than emperors, and holding a whole continent in the hollow of their hands. The Rothschilds govern a Christian world. Not a cabinet moves without their advice. They stretch their hand, with equal ease, from Petersburg to Vienna, from Vienna to Paris, from Paris to London, from London to Washington. Baron Rothschild, the head of the house, is the true king of Judah, the prince of the captivity, the Messiah so long looked for by this extraordinary people. He holds the keys of peace or war, blessing or cursing… They are the brokers and counselors of the kings of Europe and of the republican chiefs of America. What more can they desire?"[40]

President Andrew Jackson, the only one of our presidents whose administration totally abolished the National Debt, condemned the Rothschilds and international bankers as a "den of vipers" which he was determined to "rout out" of the fabric of American life. Jackson claimed that if only the American people understood how these vipers operated on the American scene "there would be a revolution before morning."

In 1911, John F. Hylan, mayor of New York, said that "the real menace of our republic is the invisible government which, like a giant octopus, sprawls its slimy length over our city, state and nation. At the head is a small group of banking houses, generally referred to as 'international bankers.'"

"The house of Rothschild has arisen from the quarrels between states, has become great and mighty from wars. The misfortune of states and peoples has been its fortune" (Friedrich Edlen von Scherb).

Having provided the reader with the proper education on the modern "Jew" and or the modern state of Israel, which he or she was never provided by the media or Hollywood, let alone Bible College or Seminary, we shall now press forward in examining the Zionist eschatology as it pertains to 1) violent "holy war" ambitions 2) sacred space / "holy land" or world domination expectations, and 3) an imminent expectation of a military Messiah to usher in the end-time war of Gog and Magog.

---

[40] Niles *Weekly Register*, 1835-1836

Religious or Messianic Zionist Eschatology is Fulfilled through Violent Holy War

There is a Messianic view within religious Zionism which is very similar to what we see in Islamic eschatology. It sees war and the suppression of the Gentiles or unbelievers and their nations taking place prior to and actually paving the way for the Messiah, who will then come to completely destroy the Gentiles and give each Jew 2,800 Gentile slaves in a "kingdom on earth" or "paradise."

Mai-mon-ides (a famous medieval Rabbi) ruled on Sanhedrin 98b., giving the following as the definitive criteria for identifying the messiah:

> "If we see a Jewish leader who…wages the "battles of God"—such a person is the "presumed messiah." If the person succeeded in all these endeavors and then rebuilds the Holy Temple in Jerusalem and facilitates the in-gathering of the Jews to the Land of Israel—then we are certain that he is the 'actual messiah.'"

Going as far back as the Jewish Zealots of AD 67 - AD 70 and up until today, there have always been those claiming to be "Jews" and "God's chosen people," who think that killing and making war will usher in the "redemption of the world" and/or the coming of Messiah and his kingdom on earth.

In the twelfth century one of those Khazarian "Jews" I addressed earlier believed he could bring Messiah's coming by conquering the land of Palestine (through war). He and his followers claimed that "…the time had come in which god would gather Israel, His people from all lands to Jerusalem, the holy city."[41]

Gershon Salomon boldly proclaims;

> "The mission of the present generation is to liberate the Temple Mount and remove the defiling abomination (the Dome of the Rock)… The Israeli Government must do it. **We must have a war…The Messiah will not come by himself; we should bring Him by fighting**."[42]

Max Mandelstam, at the July 1898 World Zionist Congress, stated:

"The Jews energetically reject the idea of fusion with the other nationalities and cling to their historical hope of world empire."

Morris A. Levy Secretary, at the 1946 World League of Liberal Jews, stated,

> "The only true path to follow to gain real peace and honest government is through Judaism. And the Jewish people can and will lead the people to lasting peace. The promise of Jehovah for the Jewish people to rule the world and for the Jews to hold high places in world government has arrived."

---

[41] cf. John L. Bray, *Israel in Bible Prophecy*, (John L. Bray Ministries, INC., P.O. Box 90129, Lakeland, FL. 33804), 42-43

[42] Sam Kiley, *'The righteous will survive and the rest will perish'* The Times, (December 13,1999), 39

So, what is the purpose of the Gentile in Jewish eschatology? Texe Marrs writes,

> "Another authoritative Jewish religious leader, the late Sepharidic Rabbi Ovadia Yosef, Chief Rabbi in Israel, further elaborated on this topic [of the Gentile's purpose] in a series of radio sermons he gave in 2010. Yosef, spiritual leader of the ultra-conservative Shas political party, a faction which helped Prime Minister Benjamin Netanyahu's rise to power, said that in the coming world, Gentiles may be likened to "donkeys and beasts of burden." The main reason for the very existence of Gentiles, the Rabbi explained is that they are to serve as slaves for the Jews. That, he said, is their "sole purpose."
>
> Quoted in *The Jerusalem Post*, Rabbi Yosef went on to say that, "without this purpose, the non-Jew, the *goy*, has no place in the world. That is why they were created."[43]

This racist and violent eschatology is consistent with the Talmud and even the teachings of some of the premier religious colleges in Israel.

Here is an article by Mr. Feldman, entitled, *Violence in the Name of the Messiah,* showing the development of a violent Zionist messianic eschatology within modern Israel:

> "…reflecting the mystical-messianic aspect of the act. *The killing was supposed to function cosmically, further awakening the messianic sparks to help bring about a new Jewish kingdom on earth.* So, who is the king messiah, and what does he want?

The kings of Israel were anointed with oil, and the word "messiah" means "the anointed one." But the ancient Israelites didn't speak of the "king messiah." It was the early Jewish community, which produced Jesus and the Christian faith, that came to understand the possibility of a messianic king whose reign would be spiritual and actual.

With a few exceptions over the centuries, the Christian associations with a king messiah have mostly stopped Jews from using the phrase to designate a living person. It re-entered contemporary Jewish religious thought roughly 30 years ago, in the lifetime of Rabbi Menachem Mendel Schneerson, the seventh grand rabbi of the Chabad-Lubavitch movement.

Schneerson, known widely as "the Rebbe," believed fervently in the ***imminent advent of the messianic age***. He taught and preached about the subject, urging followers to spread religious practices among Jews to hasten the messianic moment.

---

[43] Texe Marrs, *BLOOD COVENANT WITH DESTINY*, (Spicewood, TX: RiverCrest Publishing, 2018) pp. 93-94. The problem with men like Texe Marrs and Pastor Steve Anderson in his video "Marching to Zion," is that they think modern Israel being gathered in the land in 1948 was the work of Satan and modern Israel is necessary to fulfill the coming of the "anti-Christ" – which is also an unbiblical view of modern Israel and the Jew.

In the years before the Rebbe's death in 1994, some of his followers began to declare that he was the messiah and to implore him to reveal himself. In his presence and at his home in Crown Heights, Brooklyn, entranced followers sang songs and posted banners declaring, "Long live our master, teacher and rabbi, the king messiah." Schneerson, who had been slowed by a stroke, may not have fully understood the implications — but, in any case, he did little to dampen the hopes of his followers. After his death, the belief in his messianic status didn't abate.

What does this have to do with the settler movement?

The religious nationalists of the hilltop settlements generally aren't followers of the Rebbe. Although many believe they are *living in the beginnings of a messianic age, their messiah is more typically associated with the state of Israel* and its sovereignty, not with Schneerson.

Enter Rabbi Yitzchak Ginsburgh, the man who more than any other has fused Chabad messianism with national-religious messianism, and has emerged as a messianic candidate in his own right. Ginsburgh, who was born in 1944 in St. Louis, embraced orthodoxy as a young man. After studying philosophy and mathematics at the University of Chicago, and getting a master's degree in math from Yeshiva University, he moved to Israel in 1965, engaging there with the theology of Chabad-Lubavitch and gradually becoming a full-time teacher and writer. In 1982, he founded a school that opened at the traditional site of Joseph's tomb, in the heart of Nablus, and named it Od Yosef Chai, "Joseph Still Lives."

In the early 2000s, the school, or yeshiva, moved to the hilltop settlement of Yitzhar. There, Ginsburgh further developed his distinctive combination of Chabad Hasidism and national-religious-settler theology. His best-known writing is a short book called "Barukh ha-Gever," meaning "Blessed is the Man." That's a play on the name of Baruch Goldstein, the American-born settler who killed 29 Palestinian men and boys in prayer and injured 125 more at the mosque above the tomb of the patriarchs in Hebron in 1994. *The book is an extended justification of Goldstein's actions. It identifies the Palestinian people with the biblical Amalekites, whom God orders the children of Israel to extirpate.*

Ginsburgh's fusion of Chabad messianism and settler messianism is potent because it allows the identification of a specific figure as the messiah, or at least as the living person most qualified to become the messiah should the world merit his revelation. According to the Rutgers anthropologist, Harel, who has spent time at the yeshiva, Ginsburgh identifies Schneerson as a "messianic model."

Ginsburgh heads a quasi-political movement called Derech Chaim, "The Way of Life," which aspires to make Israel into a Jewish monarchy with Ginsburgh presented as the candidate for king. This, combined with his position on the Rebbe, effectively invites followers to identity Ginsburgh as the current messiah. To Ginsburgh's followers, the practical application of his messiahship is clear: *They must commit themselves to act on behalf of the "wholeness of the land of Israel" and awaken mystical-messianic sparks by their actions. Those actions must include violence against the Amalekite enemy.*

In other words, the **deaths of Saad Dawabsheh and his wife and son were almost certainly understood by the killers as a redemptive messianic act. This is Jewish terrorism that goes beyond even Goldstein's conflation of Palestinians and Amalekites: It conceives what the terrorists called "revenge" as a means to making the king messiah live and hastening the coming of his kingdom.**

Yet according to Jewish tradition, God's law continues to apply in the messianic age. How then could the terrorists intentionally firebomb a home that they knew might well have children inside?

As with much of Jewish law, the answer lies in a book. It's not just any book, but it's probably the most notorious work of Jewish legal and religious thought published in the last decade, "Torat ha-Melekh," which means "The Law of the King." The work exists only in Hebrew, and the translations provided here are my own. Its subtitle is, roughly, "Laws of Life and Death between Israel and the Nations." (The Hebrew phrase used, "dine nefashot," ordinarily refers to Talmudic criminal law.)

It was published in 2009 under the imprint of the Od Yosef Chai yeshiva. Its authors are two rabbis, Yitzhak Shapira and Yosef Elitzur, who are followers of Ginsburgh.

"The Law of the King" is really two books in one. The first is a legal treatise offering **new interpretations and applications of traditional Jewish legal sources regarding rules of engagement and the use of force against civilians. The second, interspersed in six "appendixes" throughout the book, is a work of mystical philosophy devoted to explaining the differences between Jewish and non-Jewish souls.** Its views are mostly drawn, the writers say, from the teachings of Ginsburgh.

Both parts of the book reach horrifying conclusions. The most well-known, and the one with chilling connections to Duma, concerns the killing of children: **"There is an argument for killing them because of the future danger that will be caused if they grow up to be evil like their parents."**

In a more expanded discussion of "revenge" — one of the words written in graffiti at the site of the Duma attack — the writers explain that **"according to this calculus, children aren't killed because of their evil, but rather because there is a general need for revenge against evildoers, and the children are those whose death will satisfy that need."**

The metaphysical dimension is equally shocking. The authors write: "In a perfected situation, there would be no prohibition on the killing of a non-Jew, because the existence of a non-Jew who does not fulfill the basic commandments is not legitimate." Behind this position lies a mystical view that the soul of the non-Jew has less value than the Jewish soul. Indeed, the authors opine that a Jew may kill an innocent non-Jew to preserve his own life, although he may not kill an innocent Jew for the same purpose.

Many conclusions of the book would be disputed by most Orthodox rabbis. But the sources cited and discussed are all perfectly ordinary Biblical and rabbinic materials. The religious tradition offers sufficient material to justify the intentional killing of innocents, provided the sources are interpreted the way the terrorists want. In short, "The Law of the King" provides a legal and theological blueprint for revenge killings of the kind undertaken by the new Jewish terrorists. As far as the terrorists are concerned, their actions are not merely permitted by Jewish law, but required.

When "The Law of the King" first appeared, more moderate religious Zionists filed a petition with Israel's High Court of Justice seeking to have it banned and its authors arrested for incitement to racism and violence. The authors were brought in for questioning. No one was prosecuted. The book went through three printings and garnered significant international attention, in part because of the efforts made to suppress it.

"The Law of the King" functions much like fatwas or other legal opinions by Muslim jihadi writers that justify the use of weapons of mass destruction against civilians. Its reasoning matters less than its existence and form, which is more or less that of a legal or theological text.

Books by themselves are rarely sufficient to cause terrorism. But in book-oriented cultures like the yeshiva or the madrasa, works written to encourage and justify the killing of innocents play a significant role in legitimizing the unthinkable. ***Muslim terrorists can't claim to be Islamic without invoking some Islamic authority to condone their actions. The same is true for Jewish terrorists. "The Law of the King's justification for revenge killings against children foretold the killing of an 18-month-old child in Duma — and foretells more attacks to come.***"[44]

This is a Zionist group that believes a violent Jewish state should govern the biblical land from the Mediterranean to the Jordan, and possibly beyond.

And of course, we can't ignore the communist "Jews" who see themselves as a corporate Messiah conquering the world with violence and bringing about Talmudic "redemption":

> "*The Jewish people as a whole will become its own Messiah. It will attain world domination by the dissolution of other races, by the abolition of frontiers, the annihilation of monarchy and by the establishment of a world republic* in which the Jews will everywhere exercise the privilege of citizenship. Thus, will the promise of the **_Talmud_** **_will be fulfilled_**, in which it is said that when the Messianic time is come, the Jews will **_have all the property of the whole world in their hands_** [this is the Khazarian mafia Zionist cabal – pushing the WHO for globalism and a one-world currency, etc.].[45]

---

[44] Noah, Feldman, *Violence in the Name of the Messiah*, https://www.bloomberg.com/view/articles/2015-11-01/violence-in-the-name-of-the-messiah), bold emphasis MJS

[45] Baruch Levy, *Letter to Karl Marx, printed in La Revue de Paris*, p. 574, June 1, 1928

In *A Program for the Jews and Humanity*, Rabbi Harry Waton, we read the following (pages 143, 148, and 206):

> "**It is not an accident that Judaism gave birth to Marxism**, and it is not an accident that the Jews readily took up Marxism; all this was in perfect accord with **the progress of Judaism and the Jews**. The Jews should realize that Jehovah no longer dwells in heaven, but he dwells in us right here on earth; we must no longer look up to Jehovah as above us and outside of us, but we must see him right within us" (p. 148). ". . . **the communist soul is the soul of Judaism . . . in the Russian revolution the triumph of communism was the triumph of Judaism . . .**" (p. 143).

> "The poor working class is the lowest and most backward class in society. It is therefore the supreme duty of the Jews to identify themselves with them. All other classes will disappear, but the working class will endure forever, for all of mankind will become workers. For identifying themselves with the working class **the Jews will incur the displeasure and hatred of the ruling classes, but the Jews must not fear the ruling classes: their rule will be only for a while.**"

> ". . . the aim of Judaism is to realize the destiny of mankind. This aim cannot and will not be changed, for the destiny of mankind was predetermined by God from eternity unto eternity. And no matter what may come to pass, races, nations, states and empires may come and go, the predetermined destiny of mankind will inevitably be realized. *What is the predetermined destiny of mankind? This is the kingdom of God on earth. What is this kingdom of God on earth? It is a human society resting on universal communism*" (p. 206).

Rabbi Harry Waton writes,

> "We can say with Nietsche that the Jews are the highest aristocrats in the world.... The **Talmud** tells us that the whole world was created only for the sake of the Jew; the *Jew is the spiritual aristocrat, the excellent man*. The Jews differ from all other races and peoples **because of Judaism**; Judaism differs from all other religions because of Jehovah; and Jehovah differs from all other gods. All other gods dwell in heaven. But Jehovah comes down from heaven to dwell on this earth and to embody himself in mankind. Judaism concerns itself only about this earth and promises all reward right here on this earth. *Judaism is communism*, internationalism, the universal brotherhood of man, the emancipation of the working class and the human society. It is with these spiritual weapons that **the Jews will conquer the world and the human race**. *The races and the nations will cheerfully submit to the spiritual power of Judaism, and all will become Jews....*"

It is this writer's conviction that the modern state of Israel poses a greater threat to the U.S. than even Islam. We are waking up to Islam, but I think we are still very much asleep when it comes to the cabal and enslaving eschatological goals of the Khazarian "Jews."

Sacred Space or Holy Land Eschatology

Because our three themes are so inseparably connected with each other, I think it is safe to say we have covered the modern Zionist's view of sacred space within Talmudic theology and eschatology. They believe they are "Jews" and "God's people" (truly human with souls) and are called to rule over and enslave the Gentile nations or non-Jews (who are more akin to animals which have no souls or a lesser degree of souls than they) **from the eternal city and land of Jerusalem / Israel**. It is from this sacred space that they will rule the world.

"It is all a matter of sovereignty. He who controls the Temple Mount, controls Jerusalem. And he who controls Jerusalem, controls the land of Israel" (*Rabbi Yisrael Meida*).

> "The Jews might have had Uganda, Madagascar and other places for the establishment of a Jewish fatherland, but they want absolutely nothing but Palestine. Because ***Palestine constitutes the veritable center of world political power, the strategic military center for world control***" (*Dr. Nahum Goldmann, President of the World Zionist Congress, 1960*).

> "Jerusalem is not the capital of Israel and world Jewry; it aspires to become the spiritual center of the world...'[46] In LOOK Magazine (1962) he wrote, 'All continents will become unified in a world alliance, at whose disposal will be an international police force. All armies will be abolished and there will be no more war. In Jerusalem the united nations (a truly united nations) will build a shrine of the prophets to serve the federated union of all the continents; this will be the seat of the supreme court of mankind, to settle all controversies among the federated continents, as prophesied by Isaiah.' The irony here is that according to the Talmud Gentiles have no 'legal rights'" (*David Ben Gurion Israel's first President*).

Let's get back to **Prime Minister Benjamin Netanyahu**. Speaking on the 65th anniversary of the liberation of the Nazi concentration camp at Auschwitz in Poland, he declared that Israel becoming a state in 1948 was the fulfillment of Ezekiel 37:

> "The Jewish people rose from ashes and destruction, from a terrible pain that can never be healed... Armed with the Jewish spirit, the justice of man, and the vision of the prophets, we sprouted new branches and grew deep roots. Dry bones became covered with flesh, a spirit filled them, and they lived and stood on their own feet, as Ezekiel prophesized: '*Then He said to me, 'Son of man, these bones are the whole house of Israel. They indeed say, 'Our bones are dry, our hope is lost, and we ourselves are cut off!' Therefore, prophesy and say to them, thus says the Lord God, 'Behold, O My people, I will open your graves and cause you to come up from your graves and bring you into the land of*

---

[46] *Jewish Chronicles*, London, Dec. 16, 1949

Israel. Then you shall know that I am the Lord, when I have opened your graves, O My people, and brought you up from your graves.'"[47]

The Prime Minister is very tight with the American Dispensational Zionist movement (often speaking with them when arriving in the U.S. before our Presidents) and shares their erroneous view that 1948 was a fulfillment of Ezekiel 37. This is important since our next section discusses what Zionists believe about the next chapters of Ezekiel 38-39 concerning the last days, end-time war of Gog and Magog. As we saw earlier, Bibi is looked at as some kind of military warrior to pave the imminent coming of Messiah, or Messiah Himself who will be engaged in the end-time war. This gives an entirely new meaning to the phrase of having a "Messiah complex."

Before leaving the topic of the Prime Minister, it should be noteworthy that he and his political heroes drove Palestinians out of their land, a people who have more in common with racial and ancient Israelites than himself (being a descendant of European Jews).

In Zionist eschatology, the Messiah will gather the people back in the land (which necessitates war, violence and theft) and/or will be the one who will regain the territory of Muslims (Dome of the Rock) in order to re-build the temple (again requiring war). It is taught that the one paving the way for Messiah, or the coming of Messiah Himself, will help wage this war to regain all of the land of Israel. The Jews themselves are called to wage holy war from their land to usher in the coming Messiah. No matter how you slice it up, Talmudic or Messianic Zionism is racist and either justifies and promotes violence or looks to a future end-time bloody war. And to this theme we turn next.

A Talmudic Zionist understanding of the end-time battle of Gog and Magog

Rabbi Dr. Louis Jacobs (1920-2006) was a Masorti rabbi, the first leader of Masorti Judaism (also known as Conservative Judaism) in the United Kingdom, and a leading writer and thinker on Judaism. He wrote the following concerning the end-time battle of Gog and Magog within Judaism:

> "**Gog and Magog are the peoples who will wage war against the Jews before the advent of the Messiah**. These two names appear in the vision of the prophet Ezekiel (Ezekiel 38, 39) where Gog is the ruler of the country of Magog. Gog will lead his people in war against the land of Israel but will be defeated and God alone will reign supreme. Since Ezekiel prophesied in exile about the return of the Jewish people to its land, ***it is possible that he was thinking of contemporary events***. Attempts have been made to identify Gog and Magog with nations whom the prophet may have thought to pose a threat in the immediate future to the Jews who were to return to the land."

---

[47] See his speech here: *http://www.youtube.com/watch?v=BAuZA17genk&feature=related*

On the other hand, as a number of biblical scholars understand it, the prophet himself may have had in mind events in the remote future as part of his apocalyptic vision. In subsequent Jewish eschatology, both Gog and Magog are understood to be persons and the "wars of Gog and Magog" become part of the whole eschatological scheme.

As with regard to Jewish eschatology as a whole, there is a considerable degree of uncertainty about what is said to happen at the "end of days." The picture is really an amalgam of various folk-beliefs, some of them contradictory.

In the eschatological account given by Saadiah Gaon (*Belief and Opinions*, viii. 6), an attempt is made to accommodate the wars of Gog and Magog into the scheme. Interestingly enough, however, in Maimonides' scheme at the end of his great code, the *Mishneh Torah*, in which messianism is interpreted in largely rationalistic terms, there is no reference to the wars of Gog and Magog, only to the Messiah fighting "the battles of the Lord" in order to reconquer the land of Israel, rebuild the Temple, and establish God's reign on earth. Even in Orthodox Judaism, the details of these terrible events are vague, and wars of Gog and Magog do not feature at all prominently in Orthodox theology.

Yet, at the time, World Wars I and II did tend to be seen as the wars of Gog and Magog, as the essential prelude to the coming of the Messiah. Some of the Hasidic masters saw the **struggle between Napoleon and Russia as the wars of Gog and Magog**.

This of course begs the question that if Jews (and Christians) could view the "current events" at the time of Napoleon and World War I and II as the fulfillment of Bible prophecy and the end-time battle of Gog and Magog, **then they will just re-work the failed system to suit OUR current events** and seek to self-fulfill them! And as we have seen, they are working hard to fit and pressure Bibi to usher in the "imminent" war and coming of their version of Messiah!

Modern Jewish Rabbis' failed Messianic prophecies and date-setting - who really teaches a Messianic failure?

Just as there are crazy sensational and charismatic date-setting figures in the Middle East within Islam predicting their version of a "very soon" Second Coming of Jesus and end-time war, and Evangelical Hal Lindsey and John Hagee types within Evangelical Zionism predicting the end is near (again), so it is true among famous and popular Rabbis in Israel. I will cite for you a fairly recent article on this subject which, after citing all of the failed predictions among his rabbis, concludes:

> "Let us be clear that these high-ranking Rabbis, learned as they may be, have no special revelation from God - despite what they might believe. It appears that through their vigorous study of the scriptures (Torah + Tanakh), plus a few "prophetic dreams and visions" (which I suggest did *NOT* come from God), they have come to the same conclusion that watching Christian believers have - *the state of the world today is strongly indicative of the imminent coming of*

the Messiah. Have no doubt, satan is also WELL aware that the ***Messiah is near***."[48]

So, instead of concluding that the bizarre study methods, let alone "revelations/dreams," of date-setting Rabbis and Christians are way off, the author continues to look to current events as the guiding light instead of the Scriptures.

Like Islamic Apologists, Jewish Apologists also claim that the Christian New Testament Jesus was just a heretical man and the NT is likewise guilty of producing false prophecy since Jesus didn't come upon the clouds to usher in a physical, militaristic kingdom on earth in His generation. They claim all one needs to do is look out their window and they can clearly see that Messiah and his kingdom have not been established or set up upon the earth.

What they don't tell you is that within their own sources, it is taught that Messiah needed to come before the destruction of the temple in AD 70. Not only this, but Messiah would be the divine cloud rider of Daniel 7:13. As I will document later, many Jews didn't understand according to Daniel 9:24-27 why Messiah didn't come before the destruction of the second temple in AD 70. Some thought he may never come if he didn't come then. Others said he was alive on earth during that time but because Israel wasn't ready for him, God took him to heaven only to reveal him at another time. Others just concluded that Daniel's prophetic calculation was wrong!

Jesus claimed to be the Messianic divine cloud rider of Daniel 7:13-14 worthy of worship, and He connected this coming with the destruction of the second temple in AD 70. I will prove in a later chapter that, according to their own sources, ONLY Jesus is qualified to be the Messiah. Yet isn't it more than telling that Judaism stopped teaching Messiah was a divine being around 100 AD, because Jesus claimed to be Him and Christians were preaching this message from the rooftops and winning debates with them?

Not only do the Dead Sea Scrolls posit Messiah arriving around AD 17 – AD 28 based on Daniel 9:24-27 and other texts, but they also support that the imminent, end-of-the-age war would be between the Romans and apostate Jerusalem in the events of AD 67 – AD 70! More on these issues and details that modern Jews don't want to discuss in chapter 12. We will address these issues further when we present the case for the truth of Christian Full Preterism and learning how to go to the Quran and Jewish sources of authority to not only refute their system, but to lead them to Christ.

Concluding Israeli Talmudic or Messianic Zionism

Due to the events of 9/11 and the actions of ISIS, many now know of the violent beliefs of Islam and the Quran and their desire to manipulate their followers to self-fulfill their prophecies. Unfortunately, however, not many have been educated on the racism and violence contained in the Talmud and how this too perpetuates war in the Middle East.

---

[48] Stephanie Dawn, *Jewish Rabbis: "Messiah is Coming This Year – We Need To Prepare"* https://www.unsealed.org/2019/03/jewish-rabbis-messiah-is-coming-this.html

Just as ISIS seeks to manipulate Muslims into Jihad in order to usher in their version of a "very soon" Second Coming of Jesus and end-time battle of Gog and Magog, we can see how Talmudic Messianic Zionists are doing the very same thing – waging war with Islam to pave the way for the coming of their Messiah. Both false religious systems and eschatologies see themselves as righteous, persecuted victims, and both systems believe that their imminent coming Messianic figure will deliver them and punish the others, ending in a violent global war. Until the real "war of ideas" emerges – that is, until a real biblical education emerges (Christian Full Preterism) – both of these violent religious systems will create unrest for the rest of the world.

Unfortunately, the WOKE popular face of Christianity today is a 150 year old heretical system called Premillennial Dispensational Zionism. As we are about to see, this system is not much farther adrift than Islam and Talmudic Zionism when it comes to wanting and thinking that current events will once again prove an imminent "holy war" or "soon" Second Coming of Jesus (or Messiah) is right around the corner.

Chapter Three:

Evangelical Zionism: Holy Land and a "Very Soon" Second Coming of Jesus to "Rapture" the Church and Start a Holy War to Destroy the Sinners (Islam, Jews, etc.)

Christian Premillennial or Dispensational Zionism

Introduction

The Premillennial Dispensational Christian eschatological view of Bible prophecy has only been around for about 150 years. Premillennialism itself was condemned as heresy in early creeds and confessions (by those who adhered to Amillennialism) because its hyper-literal hermeneutic of a Messianic Kingdom on earth was based upon the beliefs of the unbelieving Jews of Jesus' day and not the teachings of Christ and the NT. Dispensationalism was founded and systematized by the teachings of John Nelson Darby, and then picked up and popularized through Cyrus Scofield (*The Scofield Reference Bible*), D.L. Moody and Donald Barnhouse. Its largest boost has come through the radio and television airwaves.

Popular, so-called "prophecy expert" authors that litter the contemporary Christian store shelves include Charles Ryrie (*The Ryrie Study Bible*), John Walvoord, Tim LaHaye, Thomas Ice, Grant Jeffrey, John Hagee, Chuck Smith and Hal Lindsey. Religious institutions peddling this false view of Bible prophecy include the Moody Bible Institute, Dallas Theological Seminary, Assembly of God Bible Colleges, Calvary Chapel Bible College, The Master's Bible College and Seminary, etc.

U.S. presidents who have embraced this system have included Jimmie Carter and unfortunately even Ronald Reagan. As an example, Reagan told Tom Dine, AIPAC's executive director, "I turn back to your ancient prophets in the Old Testament and the signs foretelling Armageddon, and I find myself wondering if we're the generation that is going to see that come about."

This remark was published by the Jerusalem Post and widely distributed by the Associated Press. This raised red flags not just among the liberal left, but among conservative Christians who understood their Bibles better than Reagan and the "prophecy experts" he and his mother had been influenced by.

The ICEJ (The International Christian Embassy, Jerusalem) was founded in 1980 with the goal to "comfort" Israel by educating Jews on their national heritage and convince them to leave other countries and come back into the land of Israel. I write "comfort" in quotations because it is the ICEJ's agenda to usher in the "rapture" of the church, which would involve, in their theology, the deaths of 2/3 of the Jewish population during the Great Tribulation. This is ironic since they claim that Preterists, or those who don't support their cause, are anti-Semitic, and yet their theology is the most insulting and dangerous view toward the modern "Jew" today! This organization has joined up with the already entrenched and powerful Jewish lobbyists to support the Israeli land and policy agendas of the U.S. and other foreign nations.

The Violent History of Premillennial Dispensational Christian Zionism

This eschatological system is violent in that its theology forces its followers to financially fund and prayerfully support the Talmudic Zionist terrorism of modern Israel in its land stealing through murderous aggression. If there is no modern Israel in the land and no rebuilt temple, its "Christian" eschatology is destroyed. They claim that the modern "Jew" and "Israel" are "Gods people" and that if we "bless them" in their theft and aggression, "God will bless us" back. If the Church doesn't support modern Israel, then we are in "sin."

John Nelson Darby was the founder of Dispensationalism (late 1800's - 1900's). He taught that Christ would rapture up the elect (the spiritual bride), and after they disappeared from the face of the earth God would then deal with the Jews (his alleged earthly bride) by causing them to return to Palestine and exterminate all the Muslims, inheriting the Holy Land. **Therefore, per Darby, AFTER Christ returned, the "Jews" would inherit Palestine by exterminating Muslims**.

William Blackstone (1800's - 1900's) took some of Darby's concepts and meshed them with the Zionist false teachings and philosophies of his day (e.g. Theodor Herzl / Rothschild). **He pushed for an early inheritance of Palestine (prior to the second coming and millennial period). He was looking for a pre-second coming and millennial inheritance of, and extermination of Muslims from, Palestine.**

Blackstone published his first eschatological book on this subject in 1878 entitled *Jesus Is Coming*. As most Dispensationalists constantly teach no matter what period of time they are in, he claimed there were various "signs" in his day which he thought conclusively demonstrated that the end was near – one of which was the emergence of political Zionism among Jews in Europe.

Around 1917 many Evangelical leaders voiced their support for the Jewish people to conquer Palestine and exterminate all Muslims because, they maintained that (yes, you guessed it) the Jews are God's "Chosen People." They made comparisons between early Americans taking the land from Indians (American Manifest Destiny) and "Gods people" liberating the land of Palestine, which included unbelieving Muslims but ironically also included Christian Palestinians. American Christian Zionists and these so-called "Jews" were seen as forming a holy alliance as God's people to expand the Judeo-Christian ethic or civilization as far as they could.

By far the most influential Christian Zionist was Scofield. The Oxford University Press (Zionist funded) owned *The Scofield Reference Bible* from the beginning, and Scofield was housed and funded to write his "notes" while also receiving handsome royalties from Oxford. Oxford and the Zionists successfully marketed Scofield's bible, with its "Christian" Zionist footnotes, making it a standard for interpreting scripture in "Judeo-Christian" churches, seminaries, and Bible study groups. **The Bible notes heretically teach that if a Christian or the U.S. doesn't support the modern Zionist state of Israel, we are in "sin" and will be judged. No manipulation there – nothing to see; keep walking.**

Modern Evangelical Dispensational Zionists are on par with "the end is very soon" eschatology of Islam and, as we saw earlier, even some sects of Israeli Zionism. John Hagee (known as "Dr. Armageddon") is very excited to fly "Jews" into Israel so that some can be slaughtered in a "Tribulation" period so as to hasten the "rapture" of the Church. Hagee is known as "Dr. Armageddon" because many of his critics not only have discerned that he wants Armageddon to take place in his lifetime, but he is willing to be a very active participant in order to bring it about. At a July 19, 2006 CUFI event in Washington D.C., Hagee gave his prophetic scenario for Israel and the U.S.:

> "The United States must join Israel in a pre-emptive military strike against Iran to fulfill God's plan for both Israel and the West … a biblically prophesied end time confrontation with Iran, which will lead to the Rapture, Tribulation … and [the] Second Coming."

John Hagee has built a foreign policy advocacy organization called Christians United for Israel (CUFI), centered around this false doctrine and false interpretation of Scripture. He is pushing for a pre-emptive war with Iran to quicken the "rapture." In 2006 while lobbying in Washington Hagee was clear in his agenda: "The United States must join Israel in a pre-emptive military strike against Iran to fulfill God's plan for both Israel and the West," he said. This was supposed to be a step in the right direction as allegedly mapped out in the Bible, "a biblically prophesied End Time confrontation…which will lead to the Rapture, Tribulation…and the Second Coming of Christ."

Hagee not only uses guilt manipulation techniques on the members of his church and T.V. audiences to tithe to his "ministries" through his false prosperity gospel, but also uses guilt manipulation to push his false Dispensational Zionism doctrine. Hagee clearly insists that if you are not on board with him and his alleged Holy Spirit-led agenda of believing Jews coming back in the land in 1948 was a fulfillment of prophecy, and that God has a literal real estate "forever" in the literal city of Jerusalem today, any other view for a Christian to embrace is "sin."[49]

It is sad that this false doctrinal system / "gospel" of Hagee is tolerated among Evangelicals and it gets even more scary when he is allowed to lecture and manipulate

---

[49] See his speech here: *http://www.youtube.com/watch?v=BAuZA17genk&feature=related*

our politicians and give them "altar calls" while pushing this agenda as part of his "gospel" of redemption, etc. I would love to debate this clown.

Dispensational Zionist "In the (Holy) Land" Theology

The date of 1948, and the "Jews" inheriting their land and becoming a nation again, is **essential** to Dispensational Zionism. For without an Israel, there can be no Jerusalem. Without a Jerusalem and the Torah being active today, there can be no rebuilt temple. And without these, there can be no "Anti-Christ" to defile the temple and a Great Tribulation for two-thirds of the "Jews" to die in. And without the Anti-Christ to lead the charge, there can't be the battle of Gog and Magog or Armageddon to fight against Israel. All of these are necessary elements to be in place before the "soon" "rapture" of the Church or the "soon" Second Coming of Jesus can be fulfilled for OUR generation.

The *Scofield Reference Bible* writes of Deuteronomy 30:5, "It is important to see that the nation has never as yet taken the land under the unconditional Abrahamic covenant **nor has it ever possessed the whole land**."

Arnold Fruchtenbaum writes, "**At no point in Jewish history have the Jews ever possessed all the land from the Euphrates in the north to the River of Egypt in the south.**"[50]

Greg Laurie of Calvary Chapel appeals to Ezekiel 37-39 and Mark 13:28-29:

"On more than one occasion in Scripture, Israel is compared to a fig tree (see Judg. 9:11; Hos. 9:10; Joel 1:7-8). I believe that Mark 13:28-29, along with many other Scripture passages, **such as Ezekiel 37-39, speak of the rebirth of Israel—the re-gathering of God's people**. When the nation of Israel comes back into existence, Jesus was stating prophetically, it is a **super-sign** that His coming **is near**."[51]

But pay attention to what the borders are to the "land" these Dispensational Zionists want us to support Israel in taking. The borders of this land include parts of modern-day Egypt, Lebanon, Syria, Jordan, Palestine, Iraq, Kuwait, and parts of Saudi Arabia. Some of these countries are our allies in the region, so their greedy land grab and unbiblical agenda will inevitably put us into military conflict with even our allies!

Dispensational Zionists take OT and NT passages out of context to make the claim that Jews coming back into the land in 1948 was a fulfillment of Bible prophecy and was the "super-sign" of Jesus' "soon" Second Coming to take place in our generation. We will look at those alleged "proof texts" in a bit. I should briefly point out that even some Torah Jews and even Dispensational Zionists according to Deuteronomy 4:25-39; Deuteronomy 28-29 and Leviticus 26 don't see a gathering of Israel in unbelief as

---

[50] Arnold Fruchtenbaum, *The Land is Mine* Issues, 2.4 July 1982

[51] Greg Laurie, *ARE THESE THE LAST DAYS? HOW TO LIVE EXPECTANTLY IN A WORLD OF UNCERTAINTY,* (Ventura, CA: Regal Books From Gospel Light, 2005), 20

a fulfillment of 1948. That's how desperate the 1948 "prophetic gathering" position is – even some of their best theologians have to part ways with it.

Premillennial Zionism and the Battle of Armageddon or Gog and Magog

Like Talmudic Zionism and Bibi, Dispensational Zionism appeals to Ezekiel 37-39 to prove that not only was Bible prophecy fulfilled in 1948 when modern Israel became a nation again (allegedly Ezekiel 37 teaches this), but also an end-of-time war of "Gog and Magog" (allegedly taught for our time in Ezekiel 38-39) is truly imminent for our generation.

In 1864 John Cumming was the first to propose that the battle of Gog and Magog supposedly involves modern day Russia. Another cult picked this up in 1940, the British Israel movement. This group believes the tribes of Ephraim and Manasseh lived on in the Anglo-Saxon races, and one of their leading teachers, A.J. Ferris, wrote a book entitled, *Armageddon Is at the Doors,* in which he proposed that Ezekiel 38-39 teaches that Russia would soon attack British Israel. But Hal Lindsey in the 70's popularized this "Gogology" theology. During the Cold War, Dispensational "newspaper eschatology" began telling everyone that Russia would play a role in this end-time battle and attack Israel in our generation. Why? Because the "prince of Meshek" – *rosh meshek* in Hebrew – **sounded a lot like** Russia and Moscow. Wow, serious scholarship there!

But as the newspapers and current events change, so too does Zionist eschatology in its various forms, be it Israeli Zionism or Dispensational Zionism:

1970 – Lindsey claimed **Russia** was the threat and focus of the Gog and Magog Battle.

1994 – Lindsey changed it to **"Islamic fundamentalism."**

1997 – Then he changed it again to "the **Russia-Muslim force**."

1999 – And then again to the "**Muslim-Russian alliance**."

In 2000 Lindsey was the first to have a Charismatic revelation that America was also found in the book of Revelation. Why? Well, because our flag has an eagle on it, so the wings of an eagle in Revelation 12:14-17 that carry the woman to safety must be a description of a U.S. airlift rescue mission of the Jews. So, I guess when your hermeneutics and exposition are so bad, you just claim the Holy Spirit is guiding you in your teaching. I see the U.S. prophesied in Revelation 12 about as much as I see Muhammad prophesied to come in Deuteronomy 18 or John 14-16. After all, who can challenge the Holy Spirit teaching of Lindsey or "revelations" of Muhammad? Ugh. Well, WE can, and we are called to do so in Scripture. Don't fall prey to this manipulative BS.

Dispensationalism's View of NT Imminence or Jesus Coming "Soon"

The Dispensational Zionist position on NT imminence is about as clear as mud. On one hand we are told when we read a NT author teaching that Christ's Second Coming was "near", "at hand", "soon", "about to be" fulfilled, will be "in a very little while and will not delay," etc., that this means:

1. For the last 2,000 years, the "rapture" (which most see as taking place seven years before the Second Coming) was truly imminent and could have happened at any time – even for the first century church.

Yet on the other hand we are told:

2. God never wanted the first century church or us to interpret these statements as literally near because God is outside of time.

But if that isn't confusing enough, the plot thickens because what was kind of, sort of literally "near" for the first century church (the "rapture") is only really "near" for us today. Why? Because allegedly our contemporary generation is the terminal "this generation" (of Matthew 24:34) that will see the rapture and Second Coming. Why? Because our generation is the only generation that has seen the "super-sign" of Israel coming back into the land in 1948.

The obvious question arises -- how could the coming of Christ have been literally "near" for the first century church when the 1948—1988 (and counting) "this generation" was thousands of years away?!? In other words, we have a "carrot and stick" alleged real "nearness" for 2,000 years which only becomes truly or really "near" for OUR generation.

"Our generation will be the generation that sees the Lord's return"

Hal Lindsey popularized the idea that Christ had promised to return in our generation in his book, *The Late Great Planet Earth*:

> "The most important sign in Matthew has to be the restoration of the Jews to the land in the rebirth of Israel. Even the figure of speech 'fig tree' has been a historic symbol of national Israel. When the Jewish people, after nearly 2,000 years of exile, under relentless persecution, became a nation again on 14 May 1948 the 'fig tree' put forth its first leaves. Jesus said that this would indicate that He was 'at the door,' ready to return. Then He said, 'Truly I say to you, *this generation* will not pass away until all these things take place' (Matthew 24:34, NASB). What generation? ***Obviously, in context, the generation that would see the signs—chief among them the rebirth of Israel. A generation in the Bible is something like forty years. If this is a correct deduction, then within forty years or so of 1948, all these things could take place. Many***

> *scholars who have studied Bible prophecy all their lives believe that this is so.*"[52]

Of course the truth is the "obvious" meaning of "this generation," when you look at how the phrase is used in the NT and look up *genea* in the dictionaries, is referring to Jesus' contemporary generation. And Luke's account adds that it isn't just the one fig tree but "all the trees," so what happened to all the "nations/trees" in 1948? The "obvious" meaning is that the budding of the fig tree and all the trees is a parable of seeing all the signs fulfilled in Jesus' contemporary generation, and the arrival of "summer" is the fulfillment of Christ's coming and inheriting the Kingdom in the same time frame.

One of my former pastors when I was a new believer (Chuck Smith of the Calvary Chapel movement) followed Lindsey's sensationalistic prophetic calculations and thus gained a large following for himself, preaching and writing things like:

> "If I understand Scripture correctly, Jesus taught us that the generation which sees the 'budding of the fig tree,' the birth of the nation of Israel, will be the generation that sees the Lord's return. I believe that the generation of 1948 is the last generation. Since a generation of judgment is forty years and the Tribulation period lasts seven years, I believe the Lord could come back for His Church any time before the Tribulation starts, which would mean any time before 1981 (1948 + 40 − 7 = 1981)."[53]

Smith joined Hal Lindsey in making a career and gaining a large following from this kind of sensationalistic manipulation. Gary DeMar would agree with me in addressing Smith's fundamental flaw:

> "In Chuck Smith's Revelation Commentary, *Dateline Earth* he informed his readers in 1989 that "the rapture is at hand." Before this he wrote, "Very soon there are going to be some strange and terrible things happening on this planet of ours." These "very soon" happenings are based on his reading of Revelation. He reinforces this claim when he argues emphatically, *"Jesus is coming back, and He's coming back soon."* In his book *The Final Curtain*, he writes, "It is later than you think. It is time to wake up from your lethargy and realize that the coming of the Lord is at hand!" Notice the use of "soon" and "at hand," a phrase that is most often translated as "near" (Matt. 24:32–33; 26:18; James 5:8; 1 Pet. 4:7; Rev. 1:3; 22:10).
>
> As a reader, what do you think Smith wants to convey when he uses "soon" and "at hand"? He sees them as time indicators. By his use of them, Smith is conveying his belief that the prophetic events he has been describing in all his prophecy books since 1976 is that the "rapture" is on the horizon not thousands of years in the future. So why is it when the Bible uses "at hand" (lit., "near")

---

[52] Hal Lindsey, *The Late Great Planet Earth* (Grand Rapids, MI: Zondervan, 1970), 53–54
[53] Chuck Smith, *End Times, (Costa Mesa, CA:* The Word for Today, 1978) 35.

that it does not mean soon to take place? Skirting the implications of the time references in the Bible is a major problem with dispensationalism."[54]

For "prophecy experts" or "teachers" like Chuck Smith and Hal Lindsey, the rapture or Second Coming is only really imminent for people in our generation who allegedly witnessed the "super-sign" of the Jews returning to their land in 1948 as allegedly being the fulfillment of Old Testament prophecy. When Smith says Jesus is coming "soon" he means it literally, but somehow when the New Testament authors claim this, we apparently shouldn't interpret their *inspired* comments so literally!

In 1997, Lindsey wanted to keep a good thing going for his book sales, so once again he started claiming that through his prayers the Holy Spirit was giving him special insights into the Book of Revelation in order "to crack the Apocalypse Code." Apparently, these were insights only recently given to the Church, through him of course. Lindsey claims God had not given previous generations the insights he had been given related to the issue of imminence because the time of fulfillment was ***only now drawing near for us***.[55]

Jon Courson is another very influential pastor within the Calvary Chapel movement who, instead of exposing Lindsey's and Smith's false predictions, decided he wanted to get into the prophetic game too and see if he could salvage the system. He admits:

> "1981 came. So did 1982, '83, '84, '85, and '86. And then something began to happen. A whole bunch of radical Christians began to ***cool off***, saying, 'Maybe we're here for a while after all. Maybe we shouldn't be so committed to this kingdom thing.' Oh, they didn't say it in those exact words, but that's what they were thinking. And ***a dulling*** of expectancy swept over our generation."[56]

Courson, instead of saying these men were not interpreting the Bible correctly, decided Jesus' "this generation" prediction was not really a 40 year time period, but was actually a period of 51 years. So 1999 became the new target date: "…Thus, scripturally, there is validity for a Biblical generation to be 51.4 years."[57]

"God's week of human history is rapidly coming to completion"

Various Jews and Muhammad tried this theory, so why not Zionist Charismatics, right? This false view teaches that a day is equal to a literal 1,000 years and thus the following prophetic equation emerges: 4,000 years (the earth's alleged age) + 2,000 years (since the time of Christ) = the earth's age nearing 6,000. Therefore, many so-called "prophecy experts" speculated and continue to speculate that sometime around AD 2000 Christ would, or still will, return and propel the earth into a literal Sabbath rest.

---

[54] Gary DeMar, *Chuck Smith's Prophetic Confusion* http://www.americanvision.org/article archive2007/11-20-07.asp www.americanvision.org/

[55] See Hal Lindsey, *Apocalypse Code* (1997), back cover and p. 38

[56] Jon Courson, *Jon Courson's Application Commentary* (Nashville, TN: Thomas Nelson, 2003) 179, emphasis MJS

[57] Ibid., 179.

This rest is allegedly accomplished with Christ's return and He establishes his reign in literal Jerusalem for another literal 1,000 years (Rev. 20).

Grant Jeffrey, another lovely and annoying self-acclaimed "prophecy expert," writes, "We could look for the beginning of the seventh day (the Millennium—a thousand years of peace, Revelation 20:2-6) to commence in the fall of the year 2000 on the fifteenth of Tishri, the first day of the Feast of Tabernacles—exactly two thousand years from Christ's birth."[58]

Courson, trying to find further support that our generation is the one that will see Jesus return, also jumped on this train:

> "When is the seven thousandth year? When will Christ return? Thus, the calculation is complete:
>
> Day 1 Adam is created - 4000 B.C.
> Day 4 The coming of Jesus Christ A.D. 1
> Days 5–6 Israel goes through hard times A.D. 1–2000
> Day 7 Israel revived during millennium A.D. 2000
>
> I am not alone in this interpretation. **God's week of human history is rapidly coming to completion.** *The return of Christ is nigh*. **I believe you who are in your teens and early twenties are very possibly the last generation**. Set your heart on things above. Live for heaven. Seek first the kingdom, and you will be happy presently, rewarded eternally, and grateful constantly. You who are older, continue setting an example for us who are younger. Continue to make the Lord top priority in your life. We're looking to you in a very real sense. Please keep the fire hot. **Fellow baby boomers, we need to realize that *Jesus Christ is coming soon*.** We don't have time to play around. We don't have time to chase worldly pursuits any longer. We need to return to ministry and service, worship and prayer, Bible study and street witnessing. **Whatever it was you used to do when you were fired up about Jesus in the 70's, *do it again*.** Maranatha!"[59]

Jon Courson was right about a couple of things. He's right that he's not "alone" in this bizarre view – there is a long list of prophetic failures and heretics who have embraced it! And he is also correct that Christians do go away in total disillusionment and their faith "dulled" and hearts turned cold as ice due to his false teaching and that of his spiritual fathers – Lindsey and Smith. Instead of repenting, these "prophecy experts" just reformulate their prophetic calculations and continue to stretch out the meaning of "this generation" just like the last days cults of Mormonism and the Jehovah's Witnesses have had to do.

---

[58] Francis X. Gumerlock, *The Day and the Hour Christianity's Perennial Fascination with Predicting the End of the World*, (Powder Springs, GA: American Vision Pub., 2000), 319-322.

[59] Jon Courson, Ibid., 179

It also reminds me of the "global warming" or "climate change" folks who constantly tell us the world is going to end every 12 years, and when it doesn't they just rework the system to tell us it will end in another 12 years – and on and on it goes. It's sad that this "the terminal generation is our generation", "Jesus is coming soon for us" carrot-and-stick eschatology is the main "distinctive" of the "growth" and "success" of these cults, and it is the same and main "distinctive" to the "growth" of even my former church - the Calvary Chapel movement – and the Dispensational Zionist movement as a whole.

As we will see in the next chapter, the truth is that Jesus' "this generation" (Mt. 24:34) was His contemporary generation (AD 30 – AD 70) and that is why as that generation was ending the NT authors (under divine inspiration) said His Second Coming was truly "near." I will demonstrate that this inspired promise was fulfilled in the events of AD 67 – AD 70. It's always nice when you vote for a president and he faithfully keeps his promises. But it's an entirely different thing when God incarnate keeps His promises to support one of His titles, "the Faithful and True Witness."

Concluding Islamic, Talmudic and Christian Zionist Eschatology

As we have seen, both Islam and Zionism believe the Quran and the Talmud call them to help usher in their version of the Second Coming of Jesus, or a Messianic deliverer through waging literal war in order to pave the way for the imminent end-time war of Gog and Magog. This is necessary for them in order to take control of sacred space and land as a platform to eventually rule the world and enslave others.

Since Dispensational Zionism shares the same faulty hyper-literal hermeneutic of the so-called "Jewish" Zionists, they too encourage Christians to give money to the Zionist cause. This cause includes the theft of property and killing of Palestinians (even Christian Palestinians). Like the others, this group exhibits a morbid desire to see war in the Middle East, and in some cases is willing to pressure our politicians to involve ourselves in wars so as to usher in the battle of Armageddon or Gog and Magog to make the Second Coming take place "soon." This group would also have Christians believe bizarre teachings such as the idea that the many OT prophecies made to Israel cannot be fulfilled in the church – not even the New Covenant itself! If that wasn't heretical enough, we are actually supposed to tithe our money to rebuild a temple to help Israel reinstitute a sacrificial system. And, lastly, if we don't support Israel, then we are allegedly in sin, guilty of anti-Semitism, and God's wrath is resting upon us.

But the truth of the matter is that all three of these religious systems have blood on their hands and their concept of Messiah's kingdom couldn't be further from the truth.

Chapter Four:

The Christian Full Preterist Solution: Believers in Messiah/Jesus Are God's New Covenant Sacred Space – the Kingdom is Now "Within" and "in Christ," Not "in the Land"

The Peaceful Christian Full Preterist Solution
Sacred Space - Israel's Kingdom Promises Fulfilled "in the land" or "in Christ"?
Introduction – The Constituent Elements of Israel's Old Covenant World / Heavens and Earth

In this chapter we will look at the physical typological constituent elements that formed Israel's old covenant world or "heavens and earth," and how they pointed to the spiritual new covenant anti-types or true realities "in Christ."

When God delivered the Hebrews out from the bondage of the Egyptians and established His covenant with them, He "established the heavens" and "laid the foundations of the earth" (Isa. 51:15-16). Of Isaiah 51:15-16, *The New Treasury of Scripture Knowledge* accurately states:

> "…'Heaven' and 'earth' are here put by **symbolic language for a political universe**. That is, that I might make those who were but scattered persons and slaves in Egypt before, a kingdom and polity, to be governed by their own laws and magistrates."[60]

And probably the greatest Reformed and Puritan theologian of all time likewise agrees that the creation of the heavens and earth of Isaiah 51:15-16 is Israel's old covenant world:

> "Then we must consider in what sense men living in the world are said to be the 'world,' and the 'heavens and earth' of it. I shall only insist on one instance to this purpose, among the many that may be produced, Isa. 51. 15, 16. The time when the work here mentioned, of planting the heavens, and laying the foundation of the earth, was performed by God, was when he 'divided the sea,' verse 15, and gave the law, verse 16, and said to Zion, 'Thou art my people,'" – that is, when he took the children of Israel out of Egypt, and formed them in the wilderness into a church and state. Then he planted the heavens, and laid the

---

[60] Jerome Smith, *The New Treasury of Scripture Knowledge Revised and Expanded* (Nashville, TN: Thomas Nelson Publishers,1992), 802

foundation of the earth, – made the new world; that is, brought forth order, and government, and beauty, from the confusion wherein before they were. This is the planting of the heavens, and laying the foundation of the earth in the world."[61]

God's covenant community became His special creation, world or heavens and earth. But what constituent elements made up this world? What did citizenship look like in her old covenant kingdom which was a type of the Messianic prophesied new covenant kingdom to come?

To be a part of Israel's world or heavens and earth, one was born a physical descendant of father Abraham (Gen. 12:3; 17: 6; 21:12; 26:3-4; 28:14-15). After eight days an infant boy needed to undergo physical circumcision and a baptism/washing for purification (Gen. 17:10; Lev. 12:3).

As one grew up being a citizen of the old covenant kingdom creation, his or her faith and worship were inseparably connected to residing in a physical promised land (Gen. 15:18-21).

In the promised land, citizens of Israel's kingdom were required to offer up physical sacrifices (Lev. 4:35, 5:10). These sacrifices required a physical priesthood from the sons of Aaron and the tribe of Levi who were sanctified or set apart for this purpose through the sprinkling of blood and washing/baptism (Ex. 6:18, 20; 28:1; 29:4, 20-21; Lev. 8:6, 22-29). They were to offer up sacrifices for their sin and that of the people (Lev. 4:3-35).

This physical sacrificial system and priesthood was to be conducted within the physical structure of a tabernacle or temple (Ex. 25-40; 1 Kings 6-8). Although God wanted to be Israel's King over His Kingdom, He allowed her to have a physical king to sit on a literal throne in Jerusalem (1 Sam. 8). Ultimately, the Messiah would come as King and sit on the Davidic throne and rule from heaven (cf. 2 Sam. 7:10-13; 1 Chron. 17:11-14; 2 Chron. 6:16; Jer. 23:5; 30:9; Isa. 9:7; 11:1; Acts 2:33-36).

I cannot stress enough the importance of the Jew understanding his covenant with God in connection with the temple, and the city of Jerusalem being a cosmos or "heavens and earth." Amillennialist scholar, G.K. Beale, correctly points this out, saying "…that **'heaven and earth'** in the Old Testament may **sometimes be a way of referring to Jerusalem or its temple, for which 'Jerusalem' is a metonymy**."[62]

The Jew understood his covenant, city, temple and land to be a heavens and earth filled with the light of Torah while the Gentile nations were outside the covenant relationship lost in outer darkness, needing to come in the gates of the city for conversion. If a Gentile wanted to renounce his gods and follow Yahweh and become a citizen of old

---

[61] John Owen, *The Works of John Owen*, Vol. 9 (Edinburg: Banner of Truth pub., 1850), 132-135, 138-139, emphasis added MJS

[62] G.K. Beale, *The Temple and the Church's Mission A biblical theology of the dwelling place of God*, (Downers Grove, Illinois: Inter Varsity Press, 2004), 25

covenant Israel, he likewise would undergo a physical circumcision, baptism/washing and offer up sacrifices - after which time the Rabbis would pronounce him a "new creation" and he would then be a part of the "heavens and earth" of Israel.

According to the OT prophets, Israel in her last days would reject her Messiah/Groom and God would cause the old covenant heavens and earth kingdom or people to pass away and He would establish a new covenant heavens and earth or people. Under the new covenant, man was about to be transformed.

The Spiritual New Covenant Birth

Jesus chided Nicodemus for not knowing His Scriptures when He said that in order for one to be a part of His Kingdom he or she needed to be "born again", "born from above" or "born of water even the Spirit" (John 3:2-10). According to the OT and NT, did Jesus ever undergo a "firstborn" or type of born-again experience, and to what OT Scriptures could He have been exhorting Nicodemus on?

Paul in Acts 13 references Psalm 2:7 and establishes that Christ's resurrection was when the Father says to the Son, "You are My Son, today I have begotten you" (cf. Acts 13:26, 30-32; Ps. 2:7).

Christ's resurrection is described as Him being the "firstborn" or "first fruits" from among the dead ones. That is, while Christ was physically raised (as a "sign"), He was not the first to rise from physical death, but He was the first to overcome the spiritual death that came from Adam and the death the old covenant system could only magnify but not overcome.

Our Lord was "…put to death in the flesh but made alive in the Spirit" (1 Pet. 3:18). That is, Christ was put to death under the weak old covenant system of flesh but was the first to be raised in the glorious new covenant system of the Spirit of which He is the Head and Trailblazer for His posterity.

In Acts 3 we learn that Israel had entered into her "last days" of Joel 1-3 in which the Spirit would be poured out. In Ezekiel 36-37 we learn that at this time God would establish His new covenant with Israel by sprinkling clean water on her and giving her citizens a new heart. That is, Israel would undergo an individual and corporate-body new birth or resurrection. When Jesus says to Nicodemus that he should have understood what He meant by him needing a new covenant birth by "water even the Spirit," He is referring to the promise of Ezekiel 36-37.

The Spiritual New Covenant Circumcision and Baptism

Paul, both in Galatians and Colossians, is battling the Judaizers and their Gentile proselytes who were seeking to influence the Church. He is concerned over the Christian Jews and particularly Gentiles who put their faith in Christ, and does not want them to go back under the "bondage of the elements" of the old covenant world (Gal. 4:3, 9; Col. 2:8, 20). The first Christian Gentiles were probably Gentile proselytes Paul had preached to in the synagogues. They had been circumcised and were under the elements of the old covenant world as were the Jews.

Paul taught that their "citizenship" was in heaven and that they were not to place their minds and hopes upon the things of the earth or, better translated, "land" (Col. 3:1-2, Greek *ge*) – as in the old covenant land of Palestine – as the Judaizers and their Gentile proselytes were doing.

Paul informs them that not only was their new covenant citizenship spiritual, but so was their circumcision and baptism that was necessary to become a citizen:

> "**In him** (not "in the land" of the OC world) you were also circumcised. It was **not a circumcision performed by human hands**. But it was a removal of the corrupt nature in the circumcision **performed by Christ**. *This happened when you were placed in the tomb **with Christ** through **baptism/union/induction**. In baptism you were also brought back to life with Christ through faith in the power of God, who brought him back to life*" (Col. 2:11-13 GWT).

Paul is consistent – new covenant salvation "in Christ" involves a SPIRITUAL "putting on of Christ" (Gal. 3:27), undergoing a SPIRITUAL circumcision (Cols. 2:11), and a SPIRITUAL baptism (Gal. 3:27/Col. 2:12/Eph. 4:5), which are necessary to place us into the SPIRITUAL corporate "ONE Body" or SPIRITUAL "Jerusalem from above" (1 Cor. 12:13; Gal. 4).

No doubt Jesus and Paul have Ezekiel 36-37 and Isaiah 52:1-2, 15 in view here when it comes to entering into Israel's spiritual new covenant salvation: 1) being spiritually circumcised 2) being spiritually sprinkled / washed / baptized in order to enter 3) the spiritual New Jerusalem.

John the Baptist knew his OT Scriptures when he proclaimed that, while he baptized with water in the Jordan, Messiah would baptize with the Spirit in the living waters/river of eternal life that would flow through His people (Mt. 3:11; Ezek. 36:25/Isa. 52:15; Ezek. 47/John 7:37-39/Rev. 22:17).

The Spiritual New Covenant Land

After the prideful rebellion at the Tower of Babel (man seeking to force God to come down on *his terms and fill his temple – perhaps the 300 foot high ziggurat temple of Marduk at Babylon*), the nations were judged and divided into 70 (cf. Genesis 10-11). God, in effect, disinherited them and would eventually start over by making one nation as His inheritance and heritage. It would be through Abraham's seed (and the formation of a covenant made with national Israel) that Messiah and salvation would come – in order to reconcile the nations to Himself once again. As briefly as possible, we will demonstrate how the OT and NT see this process being played out through physical old covenant Israel being blessed "in the land," designed to point her to her Messianic new covenant, spiritual NT fulfillment realized "in Christ."

Since Talmudic Zionism, Islam and Premillennial Zionism are termed the "three great Abrahamic faiths" of the world, it is probably best to begin with the Abrahamic covenant. In Genesis and Exodus, God promises Abraham that through his descendants 1) He would form a great nation 2) He would give them a land, and 3) the nations would be blessed.

Promise #1: A Great Nation

God promised Abraham that through him he would form **a great nation** – to be as numerous as the stars in the sky, the dust of the earth, and as numerous as sand on the seashore.

    a) *Genesis 46:3* - God tells Jacob or Israel to "not be afraid to go down to Egypt," because He was going to "make him a **great nation there**."

Fulfillment:

    a) *Deuteronomy 10:22* – Here we read of the fulfillment. "Your fathers went down to Egypt seventy persons in all, and now the Lord has made you **as numerous as the stars of heaven**."

The NT confirms this:

    b). *Acts 7:17* - "But as the time of the promise was approaching which God had assured to Abraham, the people **increased and multiplied in Egypt**."

    c). *Hebrews 11:11-12* - "even Sarah received ability to conceive…since she considered Him faithful who had promised; therefore, also, there was born of one man, and him as good as dead at that, **as many descendants as the stars of heaven in number, and innumerable as the sand which is by the seashore**."

While this promise was physically fulfilled under the Mosaic old covenant, the NT writers inform us that it would be fully fulfilled in Christ forming the Church as His new "nation." In AD 70 He "took" the kingdom from physical Israel and "gave it" to "another nation" – which is the spiritual new covenant "elect nation" or "Israel of God" (cf. Mt. 21:43-45; 1 Pet. 2:9; Gal. 6:16). It is through this "nation" or "New Jerusalem" "from above" that the gospel of Christ is preached and flows - healing and reconciling the rest of the nations of the world back to Himself (cf. Gal. 4:21-31; Heb. 11—13:14YLT; Rev. 21-22:17).

Promise #2: A Land

God promised Abraham that through his descendants he would inherit **a land**.

    a) *Genesis 15:18* – Here we learn what the boundaries of the land promise entailed. "On that day the Lord made a covenant with Abram and said, 'To your descendants I give **this land, from the river of Egypt to the great river, the Euphrates**.'"

Talmudic Zionists and Evangelical Zionists argue:

Since Israel never inherited all the land God promised to Abraham and his descendants, we need to financially and politically support modern Israel in taking as much of it back (even if this means military action and killing Christian Arabs). Wow.

Scriptural response:

a). *Joshua 21:43-45* - "So the LORD gave Israel **all the land he had sworn to give their ancestors**, and they took possession of it and settled there. The LORD gave them rest on every side, just as he had sworn to their ancestors. Not one of their enemies withstood them; the LORD gave all their enemies into their hands. **Not one of all the LORD's good promises to Israel failed; every one was fulfilled**."

b). *2 Samuel 8:3-4* - We learn that King David "went to restore his control along the Euphrates River," which means the kingdom had extended this far north.

c). *1 Kings 4:20-21* - "The people of Judah and Israel were **as numerous as the sand on the seashore (this means he understood this to be a fulfillment of the Abrahamic promise)**; they ate, they drank and they were happy. And Solomon ruled over all the kingdoms from **the Euphrates River** to the land of the Philistines, **as far as the border of Egypt**. These countries brought tribute and were Solomon's subjects all his life."

d). *1 Kings 8:56* - "Praise be to the LORD, who has given rest to his people Israel just as he promised. **Not one word has failed of all the good promises he gave through his servant Moses**."

e). *Nehemiah 9:7-8, 24* - "You are the LORD God, who chose Abram and brought him out of Ur of the Chaldeans and named him Abraham. You found his heart faithful to you, and you made a covenant with him to give to his descendants the land of the Canaanites, Hittites, Amorites, Perizzites, Jebusites and Girgashites. **You have kept your promise because you are righteous**… Their children went in and took possession of the land. You subdued before them the Canaanites, who lived in the land; you gave the Canaanites into their hands, along with their kings and the peoples of the land, to deal with them as they pleased."

Again, the physical old covenant blessing of being "in the land" of Israel was typological, pointing to the ultimate blessing of being spiritually "in Christ" in the new covenant Israel of God (the Church). Fighting wars over sacred space, such as modern "Israel" or "Jerusalem," is completely unbiblical.

Not only is financially supporting modern Israel in their killing and theft of land unbiblical, but it also creates problems for us with other allies in the region. If we support and give Israel all of her land ambitions, this would consume Saudi Arabia, Egypt, etc.

Promise #3: The Seed Promise

The inspired NT authors make the case that the seed promise made to Abraham is fulfilled "in Christ" and the Church:

- a). *Acts 3:25-26* - "It is you who are the sons of the prophets, and of the covenant which God made with your fathers, saying to Abraham, `And in your seed all the families of the earth shall be blessed. For you first, God raised up His Servant, and sent **Him** to bless you by turning every one {of you} from your wicked ways."

- b). *Acts 13:32-33,38* - "We preach to you the good news of the promise made to the fathers, that God has **fulfilled this promise** to our children in that He raised up **Jesus…that through Him** forgiveness of sins is proclaimed to you."

- c). *Galatians 3:8-9* - "And the Scripture, foreseeing that God would justify the Gentiles by faith, preached the gospel beforehand to Abraham, saying, 'All the nations shall be blessed in you.' So, then **those who are of faith are blessed with Abraham, the believer**."

- d). *Galatians 3:16* – "Now the promises were made to Abraham and to his offspring. It does not say, 'And to offsprings,' referring to many, but referring **to one, 'And to your offspring,' who is Christ**."

- e). *Galatians 3:18* - "For if the inheritance is based on law, it is no longer based on a promise; **but God has granted it to Abraham by means of a promise**."

  That land "inheritance" "promise" comes through having faith in the seed of Messiah:

- f). *Galatians 3:29* - "**if you belong to Christ, then you are Abraham's offspring, heirs according to promise**."

Scripture could not be clearer. The author of Hebrews says Abraham longed for a "heavenly country/land" and "city" that was **"about to come"** in their day (Heb. 11:10-16/13:14 - Worrell NT, Weymouth NT, Smith's Literal Translation). Paul affirms that all of the OT promises of God are "yes and amen" **"in Christ,"** and thus he indirectly teaches that they would no longer be realized "in the land" (2 Cor. 1:20).

God placed old covenant Israel at the center of the Gentile nations as a light to those outside the covenant with Abraham. But even in the OT, Gentiles were allowed to partake in covenant with God – being circumcised, worshipping Yahweh through the sacrificial system, and even living and inheriting land that God promised to Israel.

The Exodus was not just to deliver Israel from the bondage of Egypt, but to demonstrate God's power and glory to all nations and have His name "proclaimed in all the earth" (Exodus 9:14, 16). In chapter twelve we learn that some Egyptians did see God's power and believed in Yahweh, forming the "mixed multitude [that] went up with" the children of Israel (Ex. 12:38).

Therefore, believing Egyptians and other Gentile servants, along with Israel, experienced deliverance from Pharaoh at the Red Sea. They were present at the giving of the law when God shook Mount Sinai. They were with the Hebrews when together they were "baptized into Moses in the cloud and in the sea," eating from the same manna and drinking from the same water which flowed from the rock (both of which pointed to Messiah/Christ - John 6; 1 Cor. 10:1-4, 11). They, along with the Hebrews, came "out of the iron furnace, out of Egypt" and became for the LORD "…**a people of inheritance**" (cf. Deut. 4:20; 1 Kings 8:51; Jer. 11:4).

It was a common practice in Israel that an **adopted heir** could inherit the land:

"A wise servant shall have rule over a son that causeth shame, **and shall have part of the inheritance among the brethren**" (Proverbs 17:2).

Even a famous Rabbi, Rashi, comments on this verse:

> "A righteous **proselyte** is better than a wicked person who was home born, and in the future, he will share the spoils and the inheritance among the children of Israel, as it is said (Ezek. 47:23): "And it shall be, in whatever tribe the stranger will live, etc,…"

I agree with biblical scholars who see Ezekiel 47:21-23 referring first to the scattered remnant of the 12 tribes of Israel and believing Gentiles inheriting the land under Ezra and Nehemiah after a second exodus from the 70 years of Babylonian captivity. Gentiles inheriting the land was a feature of the law of Moses:

> "When an alien **lives with you in your land**, do not mistreat him. The alien living with you **must be treated as one of your native-born**. Love him as yourself, for you were aliens in Egypt. I am the LORD your God" (Lev. 19:33-34).

Therefore, even early on God sees believing Gentiles as "a people of inheritance" partaking in Israel's deliverance, redemption, and salvation promises, which helps create a covenant people in the land "**as numerous as the sand on the seashore**" (participating in the fulfillment of the Abrahamic covenant). Both believing Jews and Gentiles were involved in helping to rebuild Jerusalem's walls and to build up the temple during the restoration led by Ezra and Nehemiah.

This all served as typological fulfillments of what God was going to do spiritually in gathering believing Jews and Gentiles "in Christ" under Messiah and building up His spiritual Temple, the Israel of God, New Jerusalem, etc. in the coming new covenant age.

The "Everlasting" Nature of the Land and Circumcision Promises

Israeli and Dispensational Zionists love to discuss that the Abrahamic and Israel's land promises were "everlasting." Yet they don't do a very good job of demonstrating how the "everlasting" circumcision promise (Gen. 17:13-14), required to not be "cut off" from being in the land, has been working out or will work out in the future.

Like the issue of animal sacrifices, Dispensationalist Zionists also struggle over this issue. Some claim that, "yes," circumcision is required by all Jews in the land "forever" and through the future millennial period. Circumcision would also be required by the believing Gentiles who will allegedly come to worship in a fourth physical temple (Ezek. 40 – 46). Other Zionists see this as more symbolic language and spiritually fulfilled today in the new covenant. However, even though there is nothing mentioned in the OT about a transference from physical circumcision and physical sacrifices to spiritual circumcision and spiritual sacrifices, that is exactly how the inspired NT authors see them being fulfilled.

So, if animal sacrifices and "everlasting" circumcision are not physically everlasting and can be fulfilled today spiritually in the new covenant, then this type versus anti-type fulfillment can and has been fulfilled for ALL of Israel's promises. As we will see in Hebrews and Colossians, Gentile Christians were commanded to not set their eschatological hopes on the old covenant types and shadows of the old covenant age which were "about to" come to an end because they only pointed to the new covenant realities "in Christ" that were likewise "about to come" and did come in AD 70. The Judaizers would have loved the eschatology of Dispensational Zionism while Paul would condemn it as the heresy it is!

The Spiritual Sacrifices of the New Covenant

Israel's atoning sacrifice system began in Egypt when the firstborn of the Egyptians and a lamb were substitutes for appeasing God's wrath. Jesus is both the "firstborn" and the "lamb" slain to take away the sin of His Church – the new covenant Israel of God.

Christ's blood in the new covenant is spiritually sprinkled and applied to the hearts and consciences of His people and accomplishes what the old covenant sacrificial system could not (Heb. 10:22). Through Adam came spiritual sin, spiritual death, and condemnation, and thus "the sin," "the death" and "the law" (Mosaic Law) reigned until Christ. But through Christ's High Priestly atonement process in His passion at the cross, resurrection and then appearing a Second time out of the temple at His "in a very little while and will not delay" Second Coming event at the end of the old covenant age, He has brought spiritual eternal life, righteousness and pardon and has thus overcome the condemnation of sin, death and the law (Rom. 5-8; 11:26-27; 13:11-12; 1 Cor. 15; Heb. 9:26-28—10:37).

The Apostle Peter tells us that we "offer up *spiritual* sacrifices" (1 Pet. 2:5). The author of Hebrews informs us that these consist of "offering up a sacrifice of praise to God", "acknowledging His name" and "doing good" to others (Heb. 13:15-16). We are called to "present" ourselves to God with "spiritual worship" (Rom. 12:1). The Apostle Paul was a priest "offering the Gentiles" through the gospel which sanctifies through the Holy Spirit (Rom. 15:16).

One of the most deplorable aspects of Premillennial Zionism is interpreting the sacrifices of Ezekiel's temple literally. While C.I. Scofield had no doubt that these sacrifices were to be interpreted literally and Christ would smell the stench of them while on a literal throne in Jerusalem someday, the newer editors of his "Study Bible" were not so sure and suggested,

> "The references to sacrifices is **not to be taken literally**, in view of the putting away of such offerings, but is rather to be regarded as a presentation of the worship of redeemed Israel, in her own land and in the millennial temple, **using the terms with which the Jews were familiar in Ezekiel's day**."

But obviously if the sacrifices need not to be interpreted literally then neither does the temple in which they are performed in. And if the sacrifices and temple need not be interpreted with a hyper-literalism, then neither does the city and land in which they/it reside and are performed in. This of course is the inspired hermeneutic of Christ and the NT authors which the Zionists reject. The OT was filled with prophetic material "…using terms with which the Jews were familiar in Ezekiel's day" that included concepts of not just sacrifices, but land, temple and priesthood promises.

The Spiritual Priesthood of the New Covenant

The Apostle Peter tells us that we are "a royal priesthood" (1 Pet. 2:5, 9). John confirms this in the book of Revelation when he writes that Christ through His blood has "made us priests to God" (Rev. 1:6; 5:10; 20:6).

In order to be a priest, one had to be from the right family - Aaron or the tribe of Levi. We have been "born again" and thus placed into Christ's family or priesthood (1 Pet. 1:22; Heb. 7:11-12).

Aaron and the Levites were sanctified and separated by the sprinkling of blood and the washing / baptism of water and oil. As members of the new covenant Israel of God we are all priests set apart by the sprinkling and washing of Christ's blood upon our hearts (cf. Heb. 10:19-22), which "purifies our souls" (1 Pet. 1:22).

Priests could not have any physical defects (cf. Lev. 21:17-23), being typological of Christ's perfect righteousness as our High Priest and Him imputing that righteousness to our account (cf. Heb. 4:15; Rom. 5:15-21; 2 Cor. 5:21).

The priests, such as Aaron and his sons, partook of a meal of which they were permitted to eat the remainder of the flesh of the ram of consecration (cf. Exod. 29:31-34; Lev. 8:31-32). We spiritually eat and partake of the flesh of Christ daily to sustain us (Jn. 6:50-54).

The Spiritual New Covenant Temple

Jesus said that the living water of eternal life through His Spirit would flow out from within believers "as the [OT] Scripture has said" (Jn. 7:37-39). In Ezekiel 37:26 and chapters 40-48 we get the prediction of the new covenant temple, and through it flows the river of eternal life (cf. Ezek. 47).

In John 14 Jesus taught that in His Father's "house" (or temple) are many "rooms" (side rooms to this temple), and that He was preparing them so that at His return He and His Father would dine within believers.

In Revelation the New Jerusalem is a perfect cube and thus becomes the Most Holy Place structure of the tabernacle/temple system that was in the process of "coming down" to earth and "shortly" would arrive in AD 70 for God to dwell within (Rev. 1:1; 3:12 NIV; 21:16ff). John describes the living and healing water flowing from the temple of Ezekiel 47 being the New Jerusalem with her gates being open for the nations to drink from as the source for their healing (Rev. 22:1-17).

James was given the miraculous gift of knowledge to understand the OT Scriptures and to discern that the Gentiles being saved and given the Holy Spirit was the fulfillment of Amos 9:11-12, and thus David's tent / tabernacle / dynasty was in the process of being rebuilt (cf. Acts 15:6-21).

Peter and Paul instruct us that Christ is the "Cornerstone" of this spiritual new covenant temple, the 12 apostles and prophets are the "foundation," and the Church is the "living stones" (1 Pet. 2:5; Eph. 2:19-22).

The typology of Hebrews 9 depicts the "first" compartment of the Holy Place being symbolic or typological of the "present" old covenant age in which the writer and his audience were living. The "second" section of the Most Holy Place represented the new covenant economy and worshippers of God. The old covenant Law was still "imposed" until the first would be removed—this being in the time of reformation. Between AD 30 – AD 70 the two covenants overlapped, with the first being "ready to vanish" (Heb. 8:13) at the "in a very little while" and "would not be delayed" Second Coming of Christ (Heb. 10:37). This is why the new covenant Jerusalem is the shape of a perfect cube (cf. Rev. 21:16) of the Most Holy Place of God and no other section (e.g. the Holy Place – a long rectangle) of the temple remains after the "soon" and "at hand" Second Coming of Jesus was fulfilled in AD 70 (Rev. 22:6-7, 20).

The Spiritual New Covenant Kingdom

It is regularly taught by Dispensational or Premillennial Zionists that Christ offered and predicted a physical earthly kingdom. However, all one needs to do is read the gospels to see this is false. Jesus says His words and teachings are "spirit" and "life" (John 6:63). Jesus offers a spiritual kingdom where His citizens are sovereignly and spiritually born from above (Jn. 3), eat and drink spiritual water and bread (Jn. 6), receive spiritual eternal life and thus never die (Jn. 8 & 11). The Jews did not understand their OT scriptures and expected the Messiah to bring a carnal earthly kingdom, which Jesus clearly rejects (Jn. 6). If all of this is not clear enough, He clearly says His "Kingdom is not of this world" and at His return in their generation they would not be able to say, "see here or see there, for the kingdom of God is within" the heart of a person (Jn. 18:36; Lk. 17:20-37; Lk. 21:27-32).

Both King David and King Solomon reigned for 40 years. David was a mighty warrior putting his enemies under his feet and Solomon built the Temple up and established peace in the kingdom for 40 years. Both were typological of Christ ascending to a spiritual throne in AD 30 and placing His enemies under His feet and then returning imminently in AD 70 to burn those first century enemies (cf. Heb. 10:13-37). We are placed in the kingdom or New Jerusalem of the "Prince of Peace" and He has overcome "the sin", "the death," and "the law."

The Spiritual New Covenant Heavens and Earth

Isaiah foretold a time when God would perform a "new thing" and the "former things" would no longer be remembered (Isa. 42-43). This is the promise of the passing of the old covenant heavens and earth and people of God, and the arrival of the new covenant heavens and earth and New Jerusalem "seed" or people of God taking their place (Isa. 65-66). This new "seed" (new covenant people) consists as a spiritual "nation" (Isa. 65:1, 66:7-9), which Paul interprets as the Jew / Gentile Church (Rom. 10:19-21). The Apostle Paul also identifies believers as the spiritual "new creation" or heavens and earth of Isaiah 65:17 (cf. 2 Cor. 5:17). The promise and arrival of the new covenant creation and New Jerusalem are synonymous both in Isaiah 65-66 and in Revelation 21-22.

As we noted earlier, the Jew understood the old covenant, his land and temple to be God's creation of "heaven and earth" (Isa. 51:15-16). At Christ's "soon" Second Coming in AD 70, God caused His physical old covenant kingdom heavens and earth to be replaced by the followers of Messiah/Jesus -- depicted as the arrival of the new covenant kingdom or heavens and earth. It should be abundantly clear that this is not referring to a physical, global removal / renewal, since in both Isaiah 65-66 and in Revelation 21-22 sinners remain in the new creation and are evangelized.

Revelation 21-22 ends with the familiar world view of the Jew. Remember, the Jew understood his covenant, land and temple to be a heavens and earth in which the light of Torah shone, and the Gentiles were outside in darkness needing to come through the gates of Jerusalem to become converted to Yahweh and become citizens of Israel. Well, Revelation ends with the New Jerusalem being the new temple and new creation with sinners in darkness needing to come through the gates of the city to be healed and converted to the light of the gospel. This is not as complicated as so many have made it.

Literal land or global real-estate inheritance concepts coming from, say, Christian Premillennialism and or even Postmillennialist systems were deemed to be "heretical" by the early church and even some today who were and are primarily Amillennialists. They correctly saw/see these views to be on par with unbelieving "Jewish dreams and myths" originating in a hyper-literal, non-apostolic hermeneutic that connected God's kingdom to earthly real-estate, and we too reject them as such.

Refuting the Zionist "Prooftexts" for 1948

Let's briefly address some of the passages which Dispensational Zionists and even Israeli Zionists use as their "prooftexts" to prove that "Jews" coming back into the land in 1948 and forming "Israel" was somehow a fulfillment of prophecy.

Ezekiel 20:33-38

The context of this passage is dealing with the Babylonian captivity and has nothing to do with Israel being re-gathered back into the land in 1948! The context is that Israel was being unfaithful to God and wanted to be like the heathen nations around them. Therefore, God would take Israel out of her land in the wilderness (symbolic of the Babylonian captivity) and "purge" the wicked there so that the unbelievers would perish as God had purged the unbelieving generation under Moses in the wilderness. So this text actually teaches the opposite of what Dispensationalists say, because it would be the unbelievers who would be purged and die outside the land and not enter it. How is this passage teaching us that unbelievers would be re-gathered in the land of Israel in 1948 "in unbelief"? This teaching is baffling, to say the least!

Paul combines and applies both Isaiah 52:11 and Ezekiel 20:34 to the Church age in II Corinthians 6:17, which Dispensationalists claim cannot be done in any way.

Ezekiel 22:18-22

Again, the context is the "near" (vss. 3-4) judgment of Israel by means of the Babylonians in BC 586 for their sins of spilling innocent blood and idolatry. The unbelievers are "dross" and would "melt." This prophecy has nothing to do with God gathering Israel in the land in 1948 as a covenant gathering blessing, and it definitely does not teach a gathering of Israel in unbelief in 1948 either!

Ezekiel 36:22-24

The immediate context of this chapter is describing Israel's sins of idolatry and her sins of blood guilt. For these reasons she was scattered into the Gentile nations and made slaves. As slaves they remained unfaithful to God and were thus a poor witness of Jehovah to the nations in which they were scattered. But God, for His own great name's sake, would cleanse them from their sins and call them back into their land to rebuild the waste places. In type form, this prophecy (and chapter 37) was fulfilled under the restoration of Nehemiah and Ezra when the people came back into the land in repentance and began re-building the waste places of Jerusalem. There is NO contextual evidence whatsoever that there was a "re-gathering" of Israel in "unbelief," let alone any suggestion whatsoever that 1948 is the focus of this prophecy!

Ezekiel 37:40-48

Everyone agrees that the resurrection depicted in Ezekiel 37 is a "national" resurrection. In other words, Israel experienced national and covenantal "death" when she was scattered from her land and experienced a "resurrection" when she was restored back into the land. Again, like chapter 36, this prophecy was partially fulfilled through typology when the two houses of Israel came back into the land under the restoration and leadership of Ezra and Nehemiah. However, both chapters contain elements of Messiah's work of salvation (the anti-type) with the coming Messianic new covenant.

The New Covenant promises

Since the gathering back into the land and the new covenant prophecies of Jeremiah 30-31parallel much of the same historical re-gathering and new covenant material found in Ezekiel 36-37, we should probably examine the blatantly unbiblical comments of Dispensationalists who claim that the new covenant promises made to Israel are not being fulfilled nor can they be fulfilled in the Church today. Dwight Pentecost writes,

> "The Church cannot be presently fulfilling the New Covenant."[63]

John Walvoord agrees, saying,

> "The New Covenant is with Israel and awaits the second coming of Christ for its fulfillment."[64]

Pentecost concedes that if the Church has been redeemed with the blood of Christ under the new covenant, then the other covenants must also be applied to the Church and that would mean the Bible does not teach an earthly millennium:

> "The whole covenant takes on importance, in addition, for amillennialism attempts to show that the church is fulfilling Israel's covenants because the church today is redeemed by the blood. If the church fulfills this covenant, she may also fulfill the other covenants made with Israel and there is no need for an earthly millennium."[65]

We would agree with Charles Ryrie when he claims that the Bible condemns Dispensationalism if the new covenant is being fulfilled in and through the Church:

> "If the church is fulfilling Israel's promises as contained in the new covenant or anywhere in the Scriptures, then [dispensational] premillennialism is condemned."[66]

These are obviously startling statements, to say the very least. How can any Christian claim that he or she has not been redeemed by Christ's blood under the new covenant when the Scriptures are so clear that we are? The answer is that these men have become so engrossed in defending their eschatological system that this has forced them into rejecting foundational elements to the gospel and indeed the Christian faith.

Per Jeremiah 31:31-34 and how the authors of the NT develop this text, new covenant promises made to Israel through Jeremiah apply and are fulfilled in the Church (cf. Lk. 22:20; Heb. 7-12 - especially see 8:6-13; 2 Cor. 3:6). I have already demonstrated how Jesus and Paul identified the new covenant temple promises of Ezekiel 37 and Ezekiel 47 to the Christian and Church today (cf. Jn. 7:37-39 = Ezek. 47 and 2 Cor. 6:16 =

---

[63] Keith Mathison, *DISPENSATIONALISM Rightly Dividing the People of God?*, (Phillipsburg, NJ: P&R Publishing, 1995), 28

[64] Ibid.

[65] Ibid.

[66] Charles Ryrie, *THE RELATIONSHIP OF THE NEW COVENANT TO PREMILLENNIALISM* (unpublished Master's Thesis, Dallas Theological Seminary 1947), 31

Ezek. 37:27). Thus we are destroying the foundational pillars on which the corrupt Evangelical Zionist movement rests.

Ezekiel 38-39

There is nothing in these two chapters that even remotely suggests that Israel was "re-gathered in unbelief" in 1948 to fulfill this prophecy. It is said that God's judgment of the wicked will be a witness of Himself to the nations. He also states that He will make Himself holy in the ones He calls back into the land (39:27-29) – functioning as a witness to the nations. Again repentance, faith, cleansing, and restoration in the hearts of Israel are necessary requirements to be gathered from among the nations back into the land. We can understand from the text how FIRST the wicked being judged are a witness to the nations of God's holy character, but how was 1948's alleged re-gathering in unbelief a witness of God's holiness and faithful covenant dealings with Israel? The answer is that it isn't, and that what took place in 1948 simply does not meet the covenantal requirements as laid out in Torah.

We will come back to the last days' war of Gog and Magog in Ezekiel 38-39 in our next chapter.

Isaiah 11:1-12 - 1948's "Second Exodus" Leading to a Millennial Period for Modern Israel?

Dispensational Zionists understand this section of Isaiah 11 to be teaching a literal future thousand year millennial period, and/or some cite it as some kind of proof text for a gathering of Israel in unbelief in 1948, marking the beginning of the second exodus running into Israel's millennial period in our imminent future.

But again, the text only supports a gathering of the remnant of Israel and the Gentiles into the kingdom **in belief,** not unbelief (vv. 11-12)!

Virtually everyone agrees that Isaiah 11 is Messianic. After the Assyrian desolation and then the Babylonian captivity in 586 BC, Judah was desolate like a stump. But within the Davidic dynasty and promises would eventually arise the Messianic King like a branch emerging from the stump. Assyria functioned as God's rod (10:5, 24) desolating the land, and in Israel's last days God would use the Roman armies to desolate the land of Israel.

Isaiah 11 is addressing the coming of Messiah as the "branch" (Isa. 11:1) to fulfill the "in that day" second exodus gathering (Isa. 11:10-11). The promises of peace that the Messiah would bring, described as the "wolf laying with the lamb" and "the earth being full of the knowledge of the LORD," would be fulfilled "in that day" (Isa. 11:10-11).

The Apostle Paul in Romans states that the "in that day" Messianic period had arrived. Quoting Isaiah 11:10, Paul writes,

> "And again, Isaiah says, 'The Root of Jesse will spring up, one who will arise to rule over the nations; the Gentiles will hope in him'" (Rom. 15:12).

G.K. Beale and D.A. Carson correctly note,

"...for Paul, that time [of salvation] has arrived (see Isa. 11:1-9)."[67]

"Paul, too, understands the text to speak of the Messiah, the new David, who has arisen to rule over the Gentiles. Yet Jesus rules not by the sword, but rather by his resurrection from the dead (see 1:1–7). The nations enter into the salvation that he brings as they place their hope in him. It is in this way that they submit to him. Paul's mission of effecting the "obedience of faith" (1:5; 15:18; 16:26) is embedded within this citation. His apostolic "priestly service" (*hierourgeō* [15:16–18; cf. 1:9]), by which the Gentiles are reclaimed, is thus an echo of the Messiah's "service" (*diakonos* [15:8])."[68]

The wolf lying with the lamb (Isa. 11:6-8)

Paul applies this passage to himself as being the Apostle to the Gentiles and fulfilling the Jew / Gentile "mystery" and fulfilling Isaiah 66:20 with him being a priest offering up the Gentiles as a sweet sacrifice to God (Rom. 15:16). Paul is taking the poetic language of Isaiah 11—the "in that day", "wolf laying with the lamb" – as the Gentile / Jew union *presently being fulfilled spiritually* in the Messianic Kingdom rule of God.

"They will neither harm nor destroy on all my holy mountain" (Isa. 11:9)

The old covenant kingdom did advance through the literal sword, with Jews being commanded to subdue and have dominion over the Gentiles, but the new covenant kingdom of Jesus advances through the sword of the Spirit – or the Word of God/the everlasting gospel which brings unity to the ONE Jew / Gentile "nation" whereby the rest of the "nations" receive "healing" and peace (Mt. 21:43-45/1 Pet. 2:9/Isa. 66/Rev. 21–22:17).

Knowledge of the LORD covering the earth (Isa. 11:9)

Virtually everyone agrees that the promise of the knowledge of the Lord covering the earth is the fulfillment of the Great Commission taught by Christ and the Apostle Paul. Therefore, it is critical to see when they see it fulfilled:

- **(1) Prophecy**: "And this gospel of the kingdom shall be preached in all the world [Greek *oikumene*] for a witness unto all nations; and then shall the end come" (Matt. 24:14).

- **(1) Fulfillment**: "But I say, have they not heard? Yes indeed: 'Their sound has gone out to all the earth, and their words to the ends of the world'" [Greek *oikumene*] (Rom. 10:18).

- **(2) Prophecy**: "And the gospel must first be published among all nations." [Greek *ethnos*] "And Jesus came and spoke to them, saying, 'All authority

---

[67] G.K. Beale, D.A. Carson, COMMENTARY on the NEW TESTAMENT Use of the OLD TESTAMENT, (Grand Rapids, MI: Baker Academic, 2017), 690-691

[68] Ibid.

has been given to Me in heaven and on earth. Go therefore and make disciples of all the nations'" [Greek *ethnos*] (Mark 13:10).

(2) **Fulfillment**: "...My gospel... has been made manifest, and by the prophetic Scriptures has been made known to all nations..." [Greek *ethnos*] (Rom. 16:25-26).

(3) **Prophecy**: "And He said to them, 'Go into all the world [Greek *kosmos*] and preach the gospel to every creature" (Mark 16:15).

(3) **Fulfillment**: "...of the gospel, which has come to you, as it has also in all the world [Greek *kosmos*], and is bringing forth fruit..." (Col. 1:5-6).

(4) **Prophecy**: "And he said unto them 'Go into all the world and preach the gospel to every creature'" [Greek *kitisis*] (Mark 16:15).

(4) **Fulfillment**: " . . . from the gospel which you heard, which was preached to every creature [Greek *kitisis*] under heaven, of which I, Paul, became a minister" (Col. 1:23).

(5) **Prophecy**: "But you shall receive power when the Holy Spirit has come upon you; and you shall be witnesses to Me in Jerusalem, and in all Judea and Samaria, and to the end of the earth/land" [Greek *ge*] (Acts 1:8).

(5) **Fulfillment**: "But I say, have they not heard? Yes indeed: 'Their sound has gone out to all the earth/land [Greek *ge*], and their words to the ends of the world'" (Rom. 10:18).

The Holy Spirit had the Apostle Paul use every Greek word which Jesus used to describe the Great Commission, to make it CLEAR that it was fulfilled in Paul's day! The "knowledge of the Lord" (the gospel through Messiah) had covered the then known world. This is also parallel to the knowledge of Messiah increasing at that time (Dan. 12:4). This knowledge has nothing to do with the TV or our technology in any way, per some Evangelical Zionist speculations.

The second exodus gathering (Isa. 11:10-11)

The Jews prior to Christ and during his day, based upon Psalm 90:15 and other OT passages, believed that **"the days of Messiah" would be a transition period between the old covenant "this age" and the Messianic new covenant "age to come" and that this would be another 40 year-long second exodus period:**

> "How long will the days of Messiah last? R. Akiba said, **Forty years**, as long as the Israelites were in the wilderness."[69]

The NT follows this first century Jewish teaching and eschatological expectation that their "this age" was the old covenant age (not the new covenant Christian age), that the "age about to come" was the Messianic new covenant age (not the end of world

---

[69] Dr. BOAZ COHEN, *NEW AMERICAN EDITION Everyman's TALMUD*, (New York: E.P. Dutton & CO., 1949), 356

history), and that there was a 40 year-long "this generation" second exodus between them. There was a first exodus from physical slavery to sabbath rest in inheriting and being "in the land," and there was a predicted second exodus from the slavery of sin to sabbath rest of inheriting and being "in Christ."

This is seen in the following parallels:

1). Moses threatened at birth (Ex. 1:22). Jesus threatened at birth (Mt. 2:16).

2). Moses fled to Midian until the wrath of the king passed (Ex. 2:15). Joseph and Mary fled with Jesus to Egypt until the wrath of the king passed (Mt. 2:14).

3). God called Moses back to his country to be his people's deliverer (Ex. 3:10). Jesus was called back to His country to be their deliverer (Mt. 2:20).

4). Moses fasted 40 days and nights in the wilderness before he was given the law on a mountain (Deut. 9:11; Ex. 19). Jesus was taken into the wilderness where He fasted for 40 days and nights before going on a mount to give the proper interpretation of the law and new covenant kingdom principles of living it out (Mt. 4:1- chapter 5).

5). Moses' face shone with God's glory on a mountain (Ex. 34:29). In a vision given to Peter, James, and John, they saw Christ's face shine like the sun (Mt. 17:2).

6). While being tested by Satan for 40 days, Jesus quotes three scriptures found in the Exodus wilderness testing (Mt. 4:4/Deut. 8:3; Mt. 4:7/Deut. 6:16; Mt. 4:10/Deut. 6:13 & Deut. 10:20).

7). God through Moses appointed 70 elders to exercise authority with Moses to judge the people (Num. 11:16). Jesus appointed 70 disciples to exercise authority with Him (Luke 10:1-17).

8). Old covenant Israel consisted of 12 tribes (Gen. 32:28; 49:1-28). Jesus begins restoring and forming the new covenant Israel with an inner core of 12 disciples or apostles being the foundation (Mt. 10:1-4; Eph. 2:20; Rev. 21:14).

9). God's old covenant people were delivered from His judgment upon Egypt by the first Passover which was substitutional (death of the Egyptian firstborn and by the blood of a lamb). God's new covenant people were delivered from the wrath (Jesus being the "firstborn" and "Lamb" of God).

10). There was a miraculous outpouring of the Spirit's work in building the old covenant tabernacle (Ex. 31:1-11) before God's presence would move in. The AD 30 – 70 generation also saw the miraculous work of God in the "last days" in which the building and erecting of the spiritual new covenant tabernacle/temple of God was taking place. The first was a physical building with the hands and the latter was a spiritual temple built up by the preaching of the Word and by the *laying on of hands* of the apostles. Micah 7:15 predicted miracles would occur in this new exodus under Messiah. The NT confirms miracles lasted until He would return "soon" to bring an "end" to the old covenant age, at which time the sign and revelatory gifts would "cease" and the office of prophet would be "stopped" (cf. Mk. 16:15-18/Mt. 28:18-20; Mt. 24:3-34/Lk. 21:22-32; Dan. 9:24-27/1 Cor. 13:8-12/Rev. 22:4-7).

11). 3,000 die at the giving of the law and 3,000 are saved at the giving of the Spirit (cf. Ex. 32:28; Acts 2:41).

12). God was grieved with the unbelieving old covenant generation and did not allow them to enter the promised land and Sabbath rest (cf. Heb. 3-4). God was grieved with the adulterous and wicked generation of His day and did not allow them to inherit His heavenly rest in His kingdom – "in Christ" (cf. Mark 8:31-9:1, Matthew 23:34-46, Hebrews 3-4, 10). The wilderness wandering generation was baptized into Moses (by believing in his doctrine and the revelation given to him), passing through the Red Sea whereby they would receive a physical salvation from their persecutors – with the water not touching them but destroying their enemies (cf. I Cor. 10:1-2). This was a "type" for Paul's contemporary generation that would see "the end" of the old covenant age (1 Cor. 10:11 DBT/BLB). There likewise was a baptism of fire and persecution which the first century Church underwent that was separating the gold (true believers) from the wood (professing believers) and would eventually burn up the persecutors in God's wrath, to which the believers were not appointed (Mt. 3:11; Lk. 8:13-14; 1 Cor. 3:13; 1 Pet. 4:12; 1 Thess. 5:9; 2 Thess. 1:4-12).

The children or remnant (Joshua & Caleb) of Moses generation that went through the Red Sea would enter into the rest and salvation of the Promised Land. The remnant of spiritual Israel would inherit and enter the Heavenly Country Sabbath Rest (the "another day" that was "at hand") "in Christ" (cf. Heb. 3-4, 10:25, 37), with Peter describing the spiritual new covenant salvation and entrance into the kingdom as the "salvation of the soul…ready to be revealed" and thus "near" to arrive in AD 70 (1 Pet. 1:4-7; 4:5-7).

As we saw Paul interpret Ezekiel 37:27 in 2 Corinthians 6:16 (the so-called future physical millennial temple of Premillennial Zionist theology) as the Church in his day, Paul once again dismisses the Dispensational Zionist theory that Isaiah 11 is dealing with a future millennial period when he quotes Isaiah 11 in Romans 15:8-12 as being fulfilled in his day. *Here Paul makes it crystal clear that God was in the process of fulfilling His covenant promises to Israel because this fulfillment was resulting in the salvation of the Gentiles in the Church. Clearly if the "gathering" of Israel is the "in that day" millennial period which results in the salvation of the Gentiles, then Paul is emphatically teaching that this prophecy was being fulfilled and that the Church was already in the millennial period.*

How the NT authors understand and interpret Isaiah 11 destroys virtually every pillar of Premillennial Zionism!

Isaiah 35:10

John Hagee appears to believe that Isaiah 35, 43, 44 and 6 are dealing with literal "agricultural accomplishments" fulfilled in 1948 and today:

> "If Israel as a nation had not been reborn, if the Jews had not returned to the land, if the cities of Israel had not been rebuilt, if the Judea and Samaria (the West Bank) had not been occupied, if the trees that the Turks cut down had not been replanted, if the agricultural accomplishments of Israel had not been miraculous, there would be a valid reason for every person to doubt that the Word of God is true. But listen to the prophets of God declare his intention for the Jews of the world to reinhabit Israel."[70]

It is indeed true that, under the blessings and curses of the old covenant Mosaic Law, God would withhold rain (harden the land) or give rain (cause fruitful produce) for Israel in order to picture the state of their hearts. The desert beginning to blossom and bloom is really dealing with the hearts of God's people turning to Him in faith and repentance under Ezra and Nehemiah, but is ultimately fulfilled in the outpouring of the Holy Spirit upon Jew and Gentile (the Church) in the NT.

Verse 3ff. is quoted in Hebrews 12:12. Within the immediate context, this passage is designed to comfort the fearful among Israel in the face of the invading Gentile lords. Eventually God would come and deliver them and bring them back into their land through Cyrus, Nehemiah, and Ezra – all types of Christ. Therefore, in type form, this historical coming of the Lord in judgment and salvation would picture the imminent "in a very little while and will not delay" return of Jesus in the events of AD 67 – AD 70 (Heb. 10:37). In Hebrews 12:11-13, the writer interprets the agriculture, the way/path, and healing of Isaiah 35 as a "harvest of righteousness" and "peace" to be realized in the salvation of Jesus. Unfortunately for Hagee and Dispensational theology in general, the writer to the Hebrews in chapter 12 does not teach that Israel's kingdom promises of salvation and a new covenant were "postponed" until 1948 (and counting into the "literal" 1,000 years millennial period), but rather that they were being fulfilled and received in the first century by the Church!

Jesus performed literal miracles of deliverance in the gospels for the "unclean" from their blindness, deafness, not being able to speak, leprosy and being lame (vv. 5-6), because these infirmities pictured the bondage of sin in the heart of man. Jesus would bring the ultimate healing (the forgiveness of sins) through the cross, outpouring of the Holy Spirit and at His Parousia in AD 70.

---

[70] John Hagee, *IN DEFENSE OF ISRAEL, THE BIBLE'S MANDATE FOR SUPPORTING THE JEWISH STATE*, (Lake Mary, FL: FrontLine Publishing, 2007), 150-151

Isaiah's promises to Israel of a "highway of holiness" and "way" that the "redeemed" travel on (vv. 8-10), have not been postponed for thousands of years, but are being fulfilled today in the Church age through faith in Christ (cf. John 14:6).

Isaiah 43:5-6

Clearly God did bring His scattered children back into the land from the south, north, east and west from the Assyrian and Babylonian (cf. v.14) captivities through the deliverance of Cyrus and the restoration period of Ezra and Nehemiah's day. As in Isaiah 11, the "second" or "new" exodus under Messiah is the contextual setting here and was ultimately fulfilled in Christ's blood and Parousia.

God gathered His children from the east, west, north, and south into His kingdom through the preaching of the gospel and at His return in AD 70 (Isa. 27:13/Mt. 24:14-30-31; Lk. 21:22-32). These children included not just the remnant of Israel, but also the Gentiles, and they were gathered into the kingdom when the old covenant kingdom was judged and taken from the Jews and given to the Church in AD 70 (Mt. 21:33-43; Lk. 13:28-30).

Again, Christ and His New Covenant salvation is the "way" and "new thing" (cf. Jer. 31:21-22, 31) in the desert which causes men's hearts to blossom as the very garden of God (43:19-21).

Isaiah 44:24, 26

Here it becomes abundantly clear that the prophet Isaiah identifies the miraculous "agricultural accomplishments," which Hagee literalizes, as the water and outpouring of the Holy Spirit into the hearts of His people. The water is the Holy Spirit, and the grass, meadow and poplar trees are God's people (vv. 1-4).

The time of deliverance here is clearly typified during the time of Cyrus who functioned as God's shepherd and would, "…accomplish all that I please; he will say of Jerusalem, 'Let it be rebuilt,' and of the temple, 'Let its foundations be laid'" (v. 28).

Perhaps there is some application for false prophets such as Hal Lindsey, Chuck Smith, Jon Courson and John Hagee in verse 25. God clearly has made "foolish" their "Holy Spirit led" false predictions of the 1948 "this generation" scenario – "overthrowing" them, and making them "nonsense" and "fools" in His sight!

Isaiah 61:4 and Daniel 9:24-27

Premillennial Christian Zionists assume the rebuilding and agricultural accomplishments in Isaiah 61 refer to modern day Israel[71] as they likewise assume there is a 2,000 plus year gap between the 69th seven and the 70th seven in Daniel's seventy sevens prophecy found in Daniel 9:24-27. When Israel became a nation in 1948, we are told by these self-proclaimed "prophecy experts" that "Israel's prophetic time clock of Daniel 9:24-27 began running again."

---

[71] Hagee, Ibid.

Since both Isaiah 61:1-11 and Daniel 9:24-27 deal with the coming Messianic soteriological and eschatological Jubilee salvation, I will address them together here.

The miraculous "agricultural accomplishments" or the "planting of the Lord," according to Isaiah, has to do with His people being "oaks" and displaying the sprouting of His righteousness and praise before the nations (vv. 3, 11).

Examining the Context of Isaiah 61 in the NT - Luke 4 / Luke 21

Old Testament scholar Margaret Barker points out that the Jews in Jesus' day were looking for Messiah to arrive in the 10th Jubilee prophesied in Isaiah 61 and Daniel 9:

> "The first miracle was an exorcism (Mark 1.21-26), setting one of his own people free from the power of Belial. He spoke of a woman bound by Satan and released her (Luke 13.16), of slaves to sin whom the Son could release (John 9.31-38). He forgave sins and illustrated his teaching with a parable of two debtors whose debts were cancelled (Luke 7.41-48). The healing miracles restored to the community people who would have been excluded as ritually unfit: the disabled, the lepers, a woman who was bleeding. This was the great ingathering of the Jubilee. Jesus spoke of those who would inherit the earth (Mat. 5.5) and at the Last Supper, he spoke of the New Covenant and of his blood poured out for the remission of sins (aphesis, the Jubilee word, Mat. 26.28).

> The Jubilee also brought the Day of Judgement, vividly described in 11QMelch. Melchizedek would take his place in the heavenly assembly and, as described in Psalm 82.1, begin to judge the `elohim, the heavenly beings. This was to be the year of Melchizedek's favour, a very significant alteration to Isaiah 61.2, which proclaims the Jubilee as the year of the LORD's favour. Similarly, with Psalm 82.1; it is Melchizedek who takes his place in the heavenly assembly, whereas in the original Psalm it is God. The only possible conclusion is that Melchizedek, the heavenly high priest, was the LORD, the God of Israel. In 11 QMelch he has armies and brings the vengeance of divine judgement, and these were expected to appear in the tenth Jubilee. 11 QMelch explains why Jesus is depicted as judge and warrior in the Book of Revelation and why the Book of Revelation is described as 'The revelation of Jesus Christ which God gave him to show to his servants what must soon take place' (Rev.1.1). These were the teachings of Melchizedek, revealing in the tenth Jubilee the ends times of the world. When the Lamb takes his place in the heavenly assembly (Rev. 5.6-14 fulfilling Ps. 82.1) the judgement begins. The Word of God rides out from heaven, wearing a white robe sprinkled with blood; he is the high priest who has taken the atonement blood into the holy of holies. He rides out with his army (Rev.19.11-16) and the judgement follows."

> "There is insufficient evidence to say with confidence how closely the Parousia expectations of the early church were bound up with the Jewish nationalism of the first century CE. They had Jubilee expectations in common, but the present form of the gospels invites us to believe that Jesus spiritualized the Jubilee,

interpreting release from debt and slavery as forgiveness of sins and release from the power of Satan. This, however, is exactly the interpretation in 11QMelch, which was quite clear about the events of the tenth Jubilee. A spiritual interpretation of Jubilee does not necessarily indicate a separate agenda from the nationalists. Jesus did warn that the blood of the prophets would be required of his generation (Luke 11.50), in other words, that the Day of Judgement would occur within the lifetime of his hearers. This explains the urgency of his words: 'The time is fulfilled and the kingdom of God is at hand. Repent and believe in the good news.'"[72]

Jesus begins His ministry by quoting Isaiah 61:1-2a. The Jews of Yeshua's day understood Isaiah 61 and Daniel 9:24-27 to be Messianic and that He would come to usher in the soteriological and eschatological Jubilee (Daniel 9:17-27 based off of Lev. 25-26). They understood from Daniel 9 that He would arrive on the 10th cycle of the Jubilee (49 x 10 = 490). In their calendar the first temple's destruction was around 424/422 BC, and therefore they were expecting Messiah right around AD 17 – AD 28 to reveal Himself and begin to establish the Messianic Kingdom.

Again, in the Jewish mind,

> "422 BC is associated with when the first temple burned 70 Sabbaticals (490 years) before the second temple burned in 70 AD."[73]

And,

> "The 2nd century CE rabbinic work of Seder Olam Rabbah, which formed the basis of the era counting of the Hebrew calendar, interpreted the prophecy of seventy weeks in Daniel 9:24-27 as referring to a period of 490 years, with a "week" being interpreted as a period of seven years, which would pass between the destruction of the First and Second Temple. This is used to date the destruction of the First Temple to 423 BCE (3338 AM) – about 165 years after the current scholarly dating of the event. The discrepancy between these two dates is referred to as "missing years."[74]

To further support Barker's research of the first century Jewish understanding Isaiah 61 in an eschatological and Messianic way, M.P. Miller adds:

---

[72] Margaret Barker,*THE TIME IS FULFILLED JESUS AND THE JUBILEE*, 1999, http://www.margaret barker.com/Papers/JesusAndTheJubilee.pdf).

[73] *A Treatise on the Sabbatical Cycle and the Jubilee*, 1866, by Dr. B. Zuchermann, Professor at the Jewish Theological Seminary

[74] *Missing Years*, https://en.wikipedia.org/wiki/Missing_years_%28Jewish_calendar%29).

"In 11Q13 phrases from **Isa. 61:1–2** are linked with Lev. 25:13; Deut. 15:2; Ps. 7:8–9; 82:1–2; Isa. 52:7 to portray the expectation of the eschatological Jubilee."[75]

Based upon these historical facts of what the Jews were expecting in the first century, below are the various ways in which they were calculating Messiah's coming based upon a 49 year or 50 year cycle for the Jubilee, or from the 424 or 422 BC starting date. At best they could calculate the end of the 10th Jubilee to be within 1-2 years, but definitely not know the "day and hour" (Mt. 24:36) of Israel's end. I have calculated the Jubilee periods off of the 50 years model (the two on the left) which puts the beginning of the 10th Jubilee at the beginning of Christ's earthly ministry. His Second Coming, or day of vengeance, is still within the 10th Jubilee period (AD 67 – AD 70). On the right of the chart is Margaret Barker's calculations based upon the 49 year period of the Jubilee. She has the 10th Jubilee beginning around AD 17/19 and AD 70, still falling within the last Jubilee period:

Michael Sullivan calculating a Jubilee using the 50 yrs. Jewish tradition of counting & starting at 424 BC	Michael Sullivan calculating a Jubilee using the 50 yrs. Jewish tradition of counting & starting at 422 BC	Margaret Barker calculating a Jubilee using the 49 yrs. Jewish tradition of counting & starting at 424 BC	Margaret Barker calculating a Jubilee using the 49 yrs. Jewish tradition of counting & starting at 422 BC
1st Jubilee 424 BC	1st Jubilee 422 BC	1st Jubilee 424 BC	1st Jubilee 422 BC
2nd Jubilee 374 BC	2nd Jubilee 372 BC	2nd Jubilee 375 BC	2nd Jubilee 373 BC
3rd Jubilee 324 BC	3rd Jubilee 322 BC	3rd Jubilee 326 BC	3rd Jubilee 324 BC
4th Jubilee 274 BC	4th Jubilee 272 BC	4th Jubilee 277 BC	4th Jubilee 275 BC
5th Jubilee 224 BC	5th Jubilee 222 BC	5th Jubilee 228 BC	5th Jubilee 226 BC
6th Jubilee 174 BC	6th Jubilee 172 BC	6th Jubilee 179 BC	6th Jubilee 177 BC
7th Jubilee 124 BC	7th Jubilee 122 BC	7th Jubilee 130 BC	7th Jubilee 128 BC
8th Jubilee 74 BC	8th Jubilee 72 BC	8th Jubilee 81 BC	8th Jubilee 79 BC

---

[75] M. P. Miller 1969; J. A. Sanders 1975: 85). (Pao, D. W., & Schnabel, E. J. (2007). Luke. In Commentary on the New Testament use of the Old Testament (p. 288). Grand Rapids, MI; Nottingham, UK: Baker Academic; Apollos).

9ᵗʰ Jubilee 24 BC	9ᵗʰ Jubilee 22 BC	9ᵗʰ Jubilee 32 BC	9ᵗʰ Jubilee 30 BC
10ᵗʰ Jubilee begins in AD 26 during Jesus' earthly ministry and includes the time of His Second Coming AD 66/67 – AD 70.	10ᵗʰ Jubilee begins in AD 28 during Jesus' earthly ministry and includes the time of His Second Coming AD 66/67 – AD 70.	10ᵗʰ Jubilee begins in AD 17 which is NOT during Jesus' earthly ministry and only extends to the beginning of AD 66.	10ᵗʰ Jubilee begins in AD 19 which is NOT during Jesus' earthly ministry and only extends to the beginning of AD 68.

Also, based upon Josephus, one can calculate a seventh year Sabbath around AD 27. Based on this information and my math, the 10th Jubilee cycle begins around AD 26/28 and this is when Jesus declared in the synagogue that He is the fulfillment of the Jubilee of Isaiah 61:1-11 in Luke 4:16-21. This would give a Jubilee Sabbatical or seventh year Sabbatical in the following years (all falling within the last 10th Jubilee cycle of the 490 years):

> 1). *AD 26/28 — Jesus begins fulfilling the soteriological and eschatological 10th cycle of the Jubilee — ministry — "cut off" — inaugurates NC age — First half of Daniel's last "7."*
>
> 2). AD 33/35 – Seventh year Sabbath
>
> 3). AD 40/42 – Seventh year Sabbath
>
> 4). AD 47/49 – Seventh year Sabbath
>
> 5). AD 54/56 – Seventh year Sabbath
>
> 6). AD 61/63 – Seventh year Sabbath
>
> 7). *AD 67/69 — Jesus fulfilling "Days of vengeance" — end of OC age — maturity of NC age — last half [3 ½ yrs.] of Daniel's last "7"*

AD 67 falls within the Second Coming of Christ event — that is the "day of vengeance" of Isa. 61:2, which was fulfilled within Jesus' contemporary "this generation" and described by Him as "the days of vengeance in fulfillment of all that has been written" and Israel's "redemption" (Lk. 21:20-22; 27-32 = Dan. 9:24-27/Isa. 61:1-11). Josephus also records that the temple was destroyed on the 10th of Ab, the same date on which the first temple was destroyed.[76]

Amos 9:11-15 is a parallel prophecy to Isaiah 61:4 and the rebuilding and restoration here is clearly identified as the salvation of the remnant of Jews and Gentiles in Acts 15:16-17. This rebuilding of the ancient ruins was fulfilled in type form during

---

[76] Josephus, *Wars*, 6:4:5

Nehemiah's ministry and fulfilled in anti-type form through the building up of Christ (the "Chief Cornerstone") and His master builders, the NT apostles and prophets as the "foundation" to the Jew / Gentile Church ("living stones").

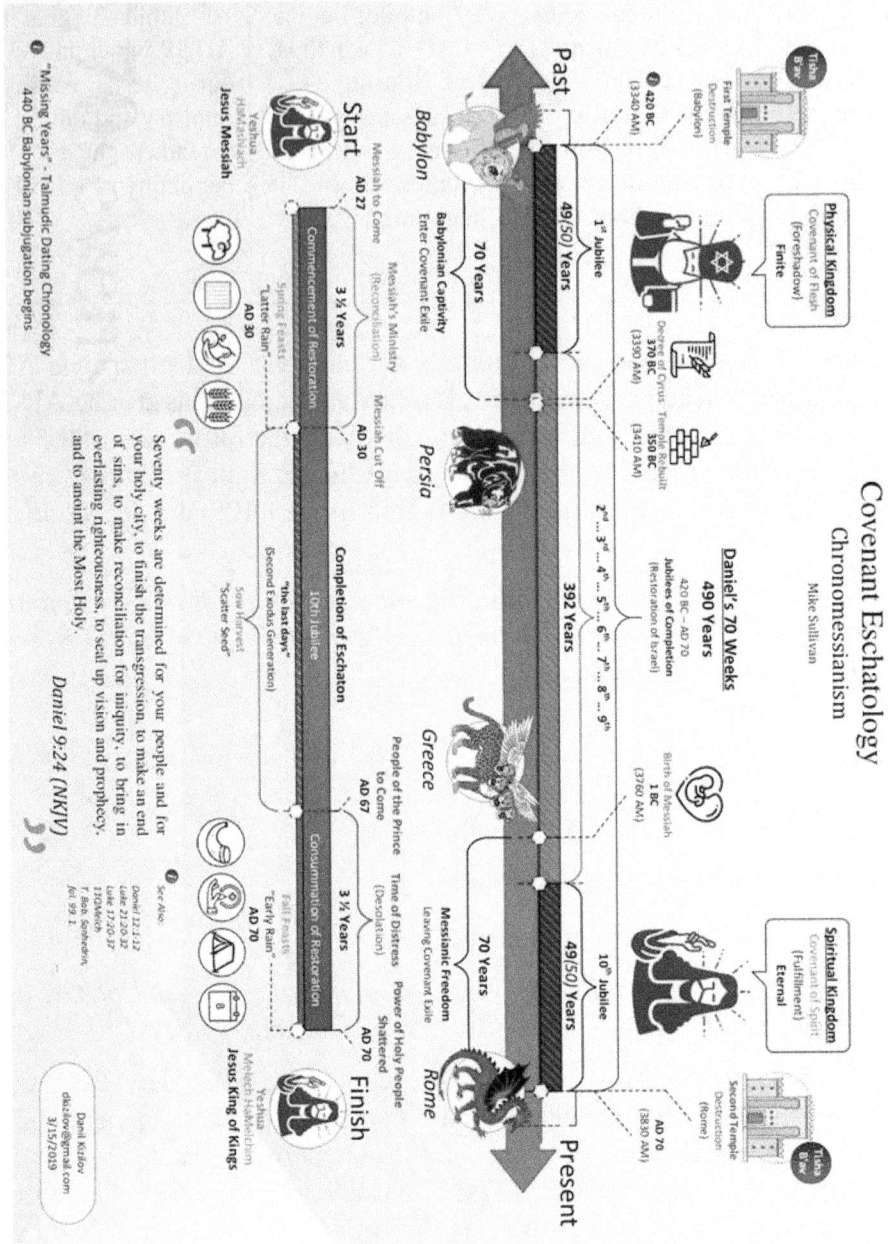

Theology of the Jubilee Sabbath – "Edenic Reset"

During the Jubilee (cf. Lev. 25-26) every 49th-50th year, the land would not be worked for two years and experienced a Sabbath rest. Jews who were poor and had to lease their land and work for other wealthier Jews as servants were "set free" from their debts and allowed to once again live in their rightfully inherited family and tribal-allotted land.

The idea is that the land and people would experience an "Edenic reset" of sorts. The unclean sins of the people and land would be cleansed and restored. They would not have to work the land, because God Himself would cause the land to provide in abundance what they would need (as in Eden). This picture, with the Day of Atonement taking place in this Sabbath year, foreshadowed Messiah coming to cleanse us of our sin and restore us to our inheritance in Him – the Tree of Life.

The NT also develops the imminent AD 70 judgment of the fallen Watchers and Satan (Gen. 3-6), thus restoring and making right what took place in Eden.

This Edenic reset would include God inheriting the nations once again and restoring what was lost in Genesis 10-11 (cf. Acts 1:8/Acts 2 = Rom. 10:18; 16:25-26; Col. 1:5-6, 23; Rev. 22:17).

It should not surprise us that Jesus begins His ministry in Luke 4:18 giving a "proclamation of liberty" (cf. Deut. 15:12-18) in fulfillment of this long expected soteriological and eschatological 10th Jubilee Sabbath period or cycle (Dan. 9:24-27). In 11 QMelch we learn that a Messianic figure would fulfill Isaiah 61:1-11 and Daniel 9:24-27, with the "last days" of Israel being grounded in their understanding of Leviticus 25 and Deuteronomy 15.

The Six Events of Daniel 9:24 Fulfilled by AD 70

1). Finish transgression

Jerusalem "filled up" or "finished transgressions" against God and His Messiah within Jesus' "this generation" (Mt. 23:31-38; Dan. 9:24a). Premillennial "Jewish" Zionist Dr. Michael Brown cites James E. Smith as understanding this verse,

> *"To fill up* [or restrain] *the transgression.* Within the 490 years period the people of Israel would commit their final transgression against God. Jesus indicated that the leaders of his generation were about to fill up the measure of the sin of their forefathers (Matt. 23:32)…"[77]

And Dr. Brown himself takes this interpretation when he writes,

> "…take seriously Yeshua's words spoken in Matthew 23:32, when he sarcastically exhorted the hostile Jewish leaders of his day, "Fill up the measure of the sin of your forefathers!" Thus, **the generation that rejected the Messiah** would suffer the **culmination of the sins of all the previous generations**: "Upon you will come all the righteous blood that has been shed on earth…I tell the truth, all this will come upon **this generation**" (Matt. 23:35a, 37)."[78]

---

[77] Michael Brown, *AJOJ, Vol. 3*, (Grand Rapids, MI: Baker Books, 2003), 93

[78] Ibid., p. 96, bold emphasis MJS

Unfortunately, Brown's commitment to Premillennial Zionism causes him to **not** "take seriously Yeshua's words spoken in Matthew 23...," because this is the consummative judgment of the living (the Pharisees) and the dead (martyrs) going all the way back to Genesis.

As that contemporary generation was ending, the book of Revelation confirms the same first century time frame of fulfillment in that the vindication of the martyrs' blood at the hands of the great harlot city Babylon (which is OC Jerusalem where the Lord was crucified – Rev. 11:8) would be fulfilled in a "very little while" at the "soon" Second Coming of Christ to vindicate them (Rev. 6:10-11; 17–22:6-7, 10-12, 20). The judgment (vindication) and resurrection of the dead is once again connected with the fall of Jerusalem in Daniel 12:1-7 – during a "3 ½ years" period (AD 67 – AD 70) "when the power of the holy people would be shattered" (Dan. 12:7).

Peter also affirms that the judgment of the living (e.g. the Pharisees) and the dead (e.g. the martyrs) was "at hand" (1 Pet. 4:5-7).

2). Put an end to sin

As we have seen in our brief discussion of entering into the Sabbath rest in the book of Hebrews, Christ put an "end to sin" at His imminent, "in a very little while," Second Appearing as the Great Anointed High Priest fulfilling the new covenant promises made to Israel and to close the "last days" of the old covenant age in AD 70 (Heb. 9:26-28/10:37; Rom. 11:26-27/13:11-12; Dan. 9:24b.).

3). To atone for wickedness or the covering over of iniquity

See references in #2. In the new covenant creation, our sins are remembered no more and covered in the depths of the sea (Isa. 65-66; Micah 7:19).

4). To bring in everlasting righteousness

Per Peter, at the Day of the Lord in AD 70, He brought in "everlasting righteousness" or a **"world of righteousness" which was to arrive in an AD 70 "at hand" time frame – "the end of all things is <u>at hand</u>"** – in Peter's day (1 Pet. 4:5-7; 2 Pet. 3). This was the "inheritance" and "salvation of the soul" that was "**<u>ready to be revealed</u>**" to Peter and his contemporaries (1 Pet. 1:4-12; Acts 2:20-40).

Paul likewise preached that this righteousness was about to be given to the early Church:

> "But also, on ours, to whom it **[righteousness] <u>is about to be reckoned</u>** — to us believing on Him who did raise up Jesus our Lord out of the dead" (Romans 4:24).

> "For through the Spirit we <u>eagerly await</u> by faith the righteousness for which we hope" (Galatians 5:5).

5). To seal up vision and prophet

Many commentators agree that Daniel 9:24-27 is a tiny snapshot of fulfilling the first and second redemptive comings of Jesus. Yet at the same time, commentators struggle with the fact that the prophecy ends with the destruction of Jerusalem in AD 70 per Jesus (Lk. 21:20-22ff). Jesus' teaching is clear that all of Israel's OT promises and prophetic material concerning His redemptive work (including His Second Coming) would be accomplished within the AD 30 – AD 70 "this generation" (Luke 21:22-32).

OT scholars Keil and Delitzsch correctly give the meaning of "seal up vision and prophet" to be:

> "Prophecies and prophets are sealed, when by the full realization of all prophecies prophecy ceases, no more prophets any more appear."[79]

I like this definition because it addresses the office of prophet ceasing at the same time the seventy sevens prophecy is fulfilled. The Hebrew *nabiy'* is used 316 times in the OT and is translated as "prophet" 312 times, and only once is it translated 'prophecy,' which is here in Daniel 9:24. I used this argument in my public debate over prophecy, tongues and knowledge ceasing in AD 70 (per 1 Cor. 13:8-12) with Charismatic Zionist Dr. Michael Brown and he had no counter argument.

Charles John Ellicott echoes similar thoughts, correctly connecting the ceasing of the miraculous sign and revelatory gifts of 1 Corinthians 13:8-12 when Daniel 9:24-27 is fulfilled:

> "The impression of translators being that all visions and prophecies were to receive completed fulfillment in the course of these seventy weeks. It appears…, to be more agreeable to the context to suppose that the prophet is speaking of the absolute cessation of all prophecy" (I Cor. 13:8).[80]

Premillennial Zionist James Leon Wood agrees:

> "The words taken together refer to the final fulfillment of revelation and prophecy, i.e., when their functions are shown to be finished."[81]

6). To anoint the most holy place

Christ anointed and consummated the new covenant Church as His Most Holy Place and Bride in AD 70 (Ex. 20, 29-31, 40; cf. Hebrews 9:6-10; Revelation 11:18-19, 19–21:16). As David Green writes,

> "Finally, it was through the anointing of the Holy Spirit that the whole city of Jerusalem was made new and became "the Tabernacle of God," when the worldly Holy Place fell in 70 (Heb. 9:1, 8). Under the old covenant, every article of God's tabernacle was consecrated by the anointing of oil (Ex. 30:25-30; 40:9; Lev. 8:10, 12). In the same way, in the Last Days, God taught His elect ones the truth of His gospel through the anointing of the Holy Spirit (2 Cor. 1:21,22; I Jn. 2:20,27), until all of them had come to know Him (Jn. 6:39). Then came

---

[79] Keil and Delitzsch, *Commentary on the Old Testament, Vol. 9*, (Grand Rapids; Eerdmans, 1975), 344

[80] Charles John Ellicott, *Commentary on the Whole Bible*, (Cassell and Co; London, 1884), 387

[81] James Leon Wood, *A Commentary on Daniel*, (Grand Rapids; Zondervan, 1973), 250

"the end" (Dan. 9:26), when the Body of Christ, all His holy ones, the living and the dead, were raised up to become His anointed (God-taught) "Most Holy Place" in the new covenant world (Jn. 6:44-45; Eph. 2:21-22; Heb. 8:11-13; Rev. 21:3)."[82]

As we have seen, there is no 2,000 year plus gap between the 69th and 70th seven of Daniel 9:24-27 with the "prophetic clock starting up again with the events of 1948." The prophecy, and how the NT develops it, clearly places all of the soteriological and eschatological events to be fulfilled when the temple is destroyed in AD 70 and the people judged or rewarded.

Zephaniah 2:1-2

This is but yet another prophetic passage that has to do with the Babylonian captivity, which was "near" and would hasten "quickly" during the time the prophecy was written (Zeph. 1:7, 14). The context is dealing with a casting out of Judah from the land in judgment because of sin and not a "re-gathering" back into the land in unbelief in 1948! God was calling Judah to gather together in repentance or face her imminent judgment. They refused this exhortation (3:6-8).

This is another passage where "near" or "quickly" is language to be taken literally and fulfilled within the lifetime of the prophet's contemporary audience – just as Jesus and the NT authors use these terms.

Matthew 24 / Luke 21

I will give an in-depth exegesis of the Olivet Discourse later. But for this section we must note the Premillennial Dispensational Zionist appeal to Jesus connecting His return and wrath upon the "land" of "Jerusalem" / "this people" (Jews) and her "temple" - connected with a flight from "Judea" – as somehow necessitating the event of 1948.[83]

Of course, the painful and contextual truth is that Jesus and the disciples were discussing the destruction of the temple they were actually looking at. This would be connected with His wrath upon the "land" they were currently standing on. The armies that would surround the "Jerusalem" in view would be the Roman armies, and "Jerusalem" was the city they were actually in. And they and other first century Christian Jews would "flee Judea" (not the modern "West Bank") to Pella right before the wrath and events of AD 67 – AD 70 had begun.

Zionists have no problem discarding sound hermeneutics and failing to honor context when reading into Matthew 24 and Luke 21. Instead they point to the events of 1948 with a modern "Jerusalem", "Judea," and "land," anticipating a rebuilding and destruction of a "temple" that is nowhere found in the actual passage. I guess reading these things into the passage and discussing the imminent end of the world is more exciting to pawn off, and it sells more books.

---

[82] David Green, *From Babylon to Babylon,* preteristcosmos.com

[83] Hagee, *In Defense of Israel*, Ibid., 155-157

Romans 11 and the Salvation of All Israel

Similar to the butchering of Matthew 24 and Luke 21, Premillennial Zionists assume that, just because Paul is addressing "Jews" and the "salvation of all Israel" in the book of Romans, this must mean Paul has the salvation of "all Israel" (modern Jews) and 1948 and beyond in his mind.

Even though God's old covenant people in their last generation were being hardened and excluded from the coming inheritance, this did not mean that God had rejected old covenant Israel (Rom. 11:1–2). Although it may have looked like Israel was being utterly cut off in her last generation, the truth was that old covenant Israel was being saved in her last days. God was actually saving "*all Israel*"—fulfilling His promises to "*the fathers*"—partly by means of the hardening of its last generation. Here's how:

- By means of old covenant Israel's transgression/failure and rejection in her last days, riches and reconciliation (through the gospel) were coming to the Gentiles (Acts 13:46; 18:6; 28:18). As Paul said, "*They are enemies for your sakes*" (Rom. 11:28).

- The salvation of the Gentiles was making last days Israel "*jealous*" so that a remnant was becoming zealous for righteousness and being saved. (Rom. 11:2-11,13-14)

- The hardening, or reprobation, of old covenant Israel in her last generation was to continue until the fullness of the Gentiles came in, i.e., *came into Israel* (Rom. 11:25).

- In this manner, or by this process, all of the saints of historic, old covenant Israel were going to be saved (resurrected) along with the last days remnant, and with the believing Gentiles who had been grafted into historic Israel. The consummation of this process took place in the Parousia of Christ in AD 70, according to the promises made to the fathers (Rom. 11:26). That is when Israel died, and was raised up a new, transformed Israel. That is when all of the elect (the Old Testament saints, the last days Jewish remnant, and the believing Gentiles) were consummately *united* in Christ and became the fulfilled "*Israel of God.*" It was thus that all Israel was saved.

Concluding the Zionist "Prooftexts" for 1948

Ripping these OT passages out of their historical contexts, or from how the NT writers teach they are spiritually fulfilled in Christ and through the Church, is an interpretive scam of great proportions!

Concluding the Sacred Space and Typological World of Old Covenant Israel

In typological form, Israel's land promises were fulfilled during the reign of Solomon. God's promise to make Abraham a great nation and make his descendants as numerous as "the dust of the earth" and as the stars of the heavens was fulfilled in the OT (Gen.

12:2; 13:16 = 2 Chron. 1:9; 1 Chron. 27:23; 1 Kings 4:11). Even Israel's land promises "from the river of Egypt as far as the great river, the river Euphrates" were fulfilled (Gen. 12:7; 22:17 = 1 Kings 4:20; Josh. 11:23; 21:41-45; Neh. 9:21-25).

Once we reach the NT, we learn that Israel's promises have their ultimate fulfillment not in the literal land or literal real-estate, but rather in the new covenant or being "in Christ." Christ Himself and those united to Him through faith are blessed with Abraham and fulfill the seed promise (Gal. 3:9, 16, 18, 28-29). We also learn that Abraham's faith in the promise was rooted in a spiritual fulfillment of a heavenly land and city that were "about to" be received at Christ's "in a very little while" Second Coming to close the old covenant age (cf. Heb. 9:26-28—10:37—11:10-16—13:14).

Or in the context of the book of Revelation we can say that the heavenly land and city (New Jerusalem) that Abraham looked for was in the process of coming down in John's day, and "shortly" did arrive at Christ's "soon" Second Coming in AD 70 (cf. Rev. 1:1, 3:12, 21:1–22:20). The New Jerusalem / New Creation is not a literal cubed city that will someday float down to earth, but rather is the perfecting of the new covenant people of God within the new covenant (the "Jerusalem from above" – Gal. 4).

The coming tabernacle/temple of Ezekiel 37: 40-48 is referring to the body – the Church (Ezek. 37:27=2 Cor. 6:16). The new creation is not physical real-estate, but rather new covenant believers (Isa. 65:17=2 Cor. 5:17) and God tabernacling within them. Even Paul's statement that believers would inherit "the world" (Rom. 4:13) is understood in context to mean believers (Jew and Gentile) in all nations (Rom. 4:11-12, 16-17).

The hearts, minds and souls of God's people (not a sacred land or globe) are His sacred space today in the new covenant age post AD 70.

Premillennial Zionist "proof-texts" in the OT and NT that allegedly prove a 1948 re-gathering, second exodus leading to modern Israel being "saved" and entering into a future, literal, thousand years millennial period has been debunked for the hoax it is!

This position plays loose with the Scriptures. OT passages that refer to Jews being regathered in the land (with repentance and faith) through the restoration and re-building efforts under Nehemiah and Ezra are somehow turned into God regathering modern "Jews" to become "Israel" in 1948 through unbelief! They claim OT passages given to Jews (including new covenant promises) cannot be fulfilled today in and through the Gentile Church – which of course is how virtually ALL of the NT authors clearly apply them!

Here is a helpful chart that summarizes what old covenant, "in the land" Israel's function was in pointing to the spiritual "in Christ" coming Messianic new covenant age and kingdom:

Old Covenant (OC) Physical "In the Land"	New Covenant (NC) Spiritual "In Christ"
Physical OC Heavens and Earth or "World passing away" (Isa. 51:15-16; Mt. 5:17-18; 24:35; 1 Jn. 2:17-18; Rev. 21:1ff.; 1 Cor. 7:31)	Spiritual NC New Heavens and Earth "soon" to come or World/Age "about to Come" (Isa. 65-66; Rev. 21-22; Heb. 2:5 – Greek *mello* "about to")
Physical OC Seed/Birth (Gen. 12:1-3; Jn. 8:33-39)	Spiritual NC Seed/Birth (Jn. 1:12-13; 3:3ff.; Gal. 3:16-29/Gen. 12:1-3)
Physical OC Circumcision / Baptism(s) (Gen. 17:10 / Ex. 24:8; Heb. 6:2)	"ONE" Spiritual NC Circumcision / Baptism (Isa. 52:1, 15; Ezek. 36:25-27; Rom. 2:25-29; Col. 2:11 / Heb. 10:22; Mt. 3:11; Acts 1:5; 1 Cor. 12:12-13; Eph. 4:5; Col. 2:12; Rom. 6:3-5; Gal. 3:27)
Physical OC Tabernacle / Temple (Amos 9:11-12; Ezek. 37:26, 27 / 2 Sam. 7:4, 5; 2 Chron. 22:6-10; Heb. 7-9)	Spiritual NC Tabernacle / Temple (Acts 15:6-21; Heb. 8:1-3; 9:23-24/ 2 Cor. 6:16; Eph. 2:19-22; 1 Pet. 2:5; Rev. 3:12NIV; 21:16)
Physical OC Priesthood (Heb. 9:6-8; 7:11-12)	Spiritual NC Priesthood (1 Pet. 2:5-9; Heb. 7:11-12; Rms. 15:16; Rev. 1:6; 5:10; 20:6)
Physical OC Sacrifices (Heb. 10:1-6; 9:9-10)	Spiritual NC Sacrifices (1 Pet. 2:5; Heb. 13:15-16; Rms. 12:1; 15:16)
Physical OC Mountain / Sinai (Heb. 12:18; Gal. 4:25)	Spiritual NC Mountain/ Zion (Heb. 12:22; Rms. 11:26)
Physical OC Land (Gen. 13:14-15; 15:18)	Spiritual NC Land (Mt. 5:5; Heb. 12:22-28)
Physical OC Resurrection from the Graves and Slavery of Babylon – Back "in the Land" (Ezek. 37:12). Through Elijah, the Father (the great "I Am") in the OC raised a dead boy and spiritually raised corporate and covenantal Israel "in the land" (Jn. 5:21)	Spiritual NC Resurrection from the Graves and Slavery of Sin & Death Are Realized "In Christ" the "I AM" and "Better Resurrection" (Jn. 5:22-29; 11:25-26; 1 Cor. 15:44-49; 2 Cor. 1:20; 5:1-5; Heb. 10:37—11:35)
Physical OC Jerusalem / Israel (Gal. 4:25 / Rom. 9:6-8)	Spiritual NC Jerusalem / Israel / "City About to Come" (Heb. 12:22; 13:14YLT; Gal. 4:26; 6:16-29; Rev. 3:12NIV; 21:2ff.; Rms. 9:6-8)
Physical OC Throne / Kingdom (1 Kings 2:12; Ezek. 21:27 / Mt. 21:43-45)	Spiritual NC Throne / Kingdom (Heb. 1:1-3; Acts 2:25-36; 7:49-50 / Heb. 12:28; Mt. 21:43-45; Lk. 17:20-37; Lk. 21:30-32; Rev. 1:6; 5:10; 11:15)
Physical OC "This Age"/ "This Present Evil Age"/ Christ Appeared at the End of the [OC] Age(s) (Mt. 13:39-43; 24:3; Gal. 1:4; Heb. 9:26-28)	Spiritual NC "Age About to Come" & "Without End" (Mt. 12:32 – Greek *mello* "about to"; Eph. 3:20-21; Heb. 6:5 – Greek *mello* "about to come" WUESTNT)

Physical OC Kingly Rule – Davidic Covenant "Anointed One" / "Messiah" & 40 year reigns of David and Solomon as Types: (cf. 1 Sam. 16:1, 12-13; 2 Sam. 7; 23:5; Isa. 7:14-16; 9:1-7; 11:1-16; 1 Kings 2:11; 11:42). OC Israel ruled with the literal sword.	Spiritual NC Kingly Rule – Ascended ruling from throne in spiritual realm (Acts 2:34-35); built a spiritual "house / tabernacle / temple" forever (Acts 15:6-21). **Reigned over fleshly Israel for 40 years putting them "under His feet" and judging them with fire at His "in a little while" Second Appearing** (Heb. 10:13-37). We rule w/ Christ in the NC age through the gospel/sword of the Spirit.

Chapter Five:

The Christian Full Preterist Solution: The "Big Three" (Mt. 10:22-23; Mt. 16:27-28 & Mt. 24:34) – Jesus Promised His Second Coming and End of the Old Covenant Age/World Would Occur in the Lifetime and Generation of the First Century Church—Promised Fulfilled by AD 70

The third area we are critiquing Islam, Israeli Zionism and Premillennial Zionism on is their understanding of an imminent Second Coming of Jesus (Islam & Premillennial Zionism) or an imminent arrival of a Messianic deliverer (Israeli Zionism).

In previous chapters we noted how Islam and Muhammad predicted an imminent Second Coming of Jesus and last hour of judgment to occur within his generation or within a hundred years of him passing. This alone disqualifies Islam. But ironically, modern Islamic apologists seek to disqualify the Christian NT Jesus, since He clearly predicted that His Second Coming and the end of the world would occur within His generation. Since the end of world history did not occur in His generation, they reason he is a false prophet, and we need to trust the Quran's teaching on Jesus. But as pointed out, Muhammad's Jesus failed to come when he said He would too.

Modern apologists of Judaism use the same "argument" as to why Jesus could never be the Messiah – He failed to come when He said He would – "Just look around. Obviously the glorious Messianic earthly kingdom has not arrived," they reason.

And as we noted earlier, Premillennial Zionists simply stick their heads in the sand and pretend that Jesus and the NT authors never really predicted a first century Second Coming of Jesus. They also have the same carnal misunderstanding of the Messianic Kingdom being a physical, glorious kingdom on earth. They likewise reason that "since the planet earth didn't dissolve in AD 70 and Jesus didn't float down on a literal cloud in AD 70 to rule and reign on earth from Jerusalem, then Christ's kingdom must be "postponed" until He comes in our near future to set up an earthly Kingdom.

All three of these religious systems fail to understand and embrace either the imminent time or apocalyptic nature of the Second Coming as taught by Christ and the authors of the NT. And to this subject we turn our attention.

The Big Three

Here I will exegete correctly what Islamic and Jewish apologists (along with other Bible critics) appeal to as "the big three" texts where Jesus allegedly is found to be a false prophet. They also point out that these three passages were understood by the writers of the NT to buttress their doctrine of a first century Second Coming and end of world history event, which they say failed to happen. They reason that this failure proves the NT is not an inspired book as it claims to be.

While I agree with my critics that Jesus and the NT authors claimed both divine inspiration and the fulfillment of a first century Second Coming event, their failure is in not understanding the familiar OT apocalyptic (symbolic & metaphorical) language of Christ coming upon the clouds, stars falling, etc., and that neither Jesus nor any other NT writers ever predicted the end of world history, but rather they predicted the end of the old covenant world/age.

If I can prove the above premise, then I will have proven the following:

1). Jesus is both Messiah and God (as He claimed).

2). The NT is an inspired document whereby we learn to live out our lives with grace and peace.

3). Islam, Israeli Zionists and Premillennial Zionists need to come to the Jesus of the Scriptures and not the one they have imagined and fashioned to fit their carnal political and religious agendas.

#1 Matthew 10:17-23

- *"Behold, I send you out as sheep in the midst of wolves. Therefore, be wise as serpents and harmless as doves. But beware of men, for they will deliver you up to councils and scourge you in their synagogues. You will be brought before governors and kings for My sake, as a testimony to them and to the Gentiles. But when they deliver you up, do not worry about how or what you should speak. For it will be given to you in that hour what you should speak; for it is not you who speak, but the Spirit of your Father who speaks in you. "Now brother will deliver up brother to death, and a father his child; and children will rise up against parents and cause them to be put to death. And you will be hated by all for My name's sake.* **But he who endures to the end will be saved. When they persecute you in this city, flee to another. For assuredly, I say to you, you will not have gone through the cities of Israel before the Son of Man comes"** *(Mt. 10:17-23)*

The first century disciples were clearly told that **they** (not us) would not run out of cities within Israel to flee to (for protection – cities of refuge) **before** the Son of man came upon the clouds to judge Jerusalem in AD 70. As D.A. Carson correctly points out,

> "vv. 17–22, pictures the suffering witness of the church in the **post-Pentecost period** during a time **when many of Jesus' disciples are still bound up with the synagogue.** vv. 23 The **"coming of the Son of Man" here refers to his**

coming in judgment against the Jews, culminating in the sack of Jerusalem and the destruction of the temple."[84]

Unfortunately, not many Reformed Christians or Evangelicals are as honest as Carson is on our first text. Most can't comprehend how Christ could "come" in judgment upon Jerusalem in AD 70, so they simply make up the idea that somehow His "coming" was fulfilled in the events of the cross, resurrection or Pentecost. There are two main problems with this theory.

First, Jesus is very specific that there were some events that would transpire before His "coming" "salvation" and "end" would arrive:

1). Some would be scourged in synagogues.

2). Some would be brought before governors and kings.

3). The Holy Spirit would be given as a miraculous defense.

4). Some would be put to death during a period of severe persecution.

NONE of these events took place before the crucifixion, but ALL of these are laid out for us in the book of Acts and took place before Christ came in the judgment upon Jerusalem in AD 70.

Secondly, Jesus' teaching here in Matthew 10:17-23 is a snapshot and introduction of the same event described more in-depth in Matthew 24. The **persecution**, the **power** of the Holy Spirit for a defense, the **preaching** (GC – still local – known Roman world), and **Parousia** (or Second Coming of the Son of Man) are **all said to be fulfilled in the same first century time period** (i.e. **their "this generation"** in vs. 34).

Matthew 10:17-23 and the Olivet Discourse – the Analogy of Faith (Jesus interprets Jesus)

Matthew 10:17-23	Olivet Discourse
1). Delivered up to **local councils** and **synagogues** (Mt. 10:17)	1). Delivered up to **local councils** and **synagogues** (Mrk. 13:9)
2). Brought before **governors and kings** to be witnesses to the Gentiles (Mt. 10:18)	2). Brought before **governors and kings** to be witnesses to the Gentiles (Mrk. 13:9)
3). **Holy Spirit** would speak through them (Mt. 10:19-20)	3). **Holy Spirit** would speak through them (Mrk. 13:11)

---

[84] Carson, D. A., *The Expositor's Bible Commentary: Matthew, Mark, Luke*, Vol. 8, (Grand Rapids, MI: Zondervan Academic, 2017), 252, bold emphasis MJS

4). **Family members would betray and kill each other**; all men would hate the disciples, but he who would stand firm to **"the end"** would be **"saved"** (Mt. 10:22)	4). **Family members would betray and kill each other**; all men would hate the disciples, but he who would stand firm to "the end" would be **"saved"** (Mrk. 13:12-13)
5). The disciples would not have run out of cities of refuge to flee to as they were being persecuted in **preaching the gospel to the cities of Israel** before the "end" and the **Son of Man would come** (Mt. 10:23)	5). The disciples & Paul were to **preach the gospel to the then known "world" and "nations"** at that time before "the end" (of the OC age) and coming of the **Son of Man would take place** (Mt. 24:14/Mrk. 13:10)

Jesus is **not** saying in this text that the first century disciples would not be able to finish evangelizing all the towns of Israel before His Second Coming would be fulfilled. Rather, He is comforting and instructing them that while completing their mission to Israel (roughly between AD 26 - AD 66) they would not have run out of cities to flee to for safety before He returned. Some, like B.M. Metzger, have understood the Greek here to refer to the disciples not being able to exhaust cities of refuge to flee to before Christ would come:

> "...the Committee preferred to regard the words as a natural continuation, inserted in order to explain the following statement, οὐ μὴ τελέσητε τὰς πόλεις τοῦ Ἰσραὴλ ἕως [ἂν] ἔλθῃ ὁ υἱὸς τοῦ ἀνθρώπου (which was taken to mean, *"You will not exhaust the cities of Israel [as cities of refuge], before the Son of Man comes"*)."[85]

Right up to the end, He would provide them with a city of refuge, somewhere in Israel. After all, Paul confirms that all nations throughout the then known Roman world had heard the gospel in his day (cf. Rom. 10:18; 16:25-26; Col. 1:5-6, 23).

#2 Matthew 16:27-28 / Mark 8:38—9:1

- *"For the Son of Man will (or is "about to..." YLT) come in the glory of His Father with His angels, and then He will reward each according to his works. Assuredly, I say to you, there are some standing here who shall not taste death till they see the Son of Man coming in His kingdom"* (Mt. 16:27-28).

- *"For whoever is ashamed of me and of my words in this adulterous and sinful generation, of him will the Son of Man also be ashamed when he comes in the glory of his Father with the holy angels."* And he said to them, *"Truly, I say to you, there are some standing here who will not taste death until they see the*

---

[85] B.M. Metzger, *A textual commentary on the Greek New Testament, second edition a companion volume to the United Bible Societies' Greek New Testament* (4th rev. ed.), (London; New York: United Bible Societies, 1994),

*kingdom of God after it has ["**already**" Rotherham Translation] come with power" (Mrk. 8:38—9:1).*

Before I begin my exegesis of this key text, it is important for others to see that conservative Christians have correctly pointed out that our passage is both referring to Jerusalem being destroyed in AD 70 and that it also functions as a guide to understanding Christ's coming as apocalyptic language with NT imminence to be interpreted literally.

Matthew Henry correctly points out that **the coming of the Son of Man in judgment** here is referring to:

> "…**the destruction of Jerusalem,** and the taking away of the place and nation of the Jews, who were the most bitter enemies to Christianity. **Many then present lived to see it, particularly John, who lived till after the destruction of Jerusalem, and saw Christianity planted in the world. "Behold, the Lord is at hand. The Judge standeth before the door**; be patient, therefore, brethren." (Jms. 5:7-9)."[86]

Reformed theologian and Westminster "divine" John Lightfoot also agrees,

> "[The kingdom of God coming in power.] In Matthew, it is the Son of man coming in his kingdom. The coming of Christ in his vengeance and power to destroy the unbelieving and most wicked nation of the Jews is expressed under these forms of speech. Hence the day of judgment and vengeance: I. It is called "the great and terrible day of the Lord," Acts 2:20; 2 Thess. 2:2,3. II. It is described as "the end of the world," Jeremiah 4:27; Matthew 24:29, &c. III. In that phrase, "in the last times," Isaiah 2:2; Acts 2:17; 1 Tim 4:1; 2 Peter 3:3; that is, in the last times of that city and dispensation. IV. Thence, the beginning of the "new world," Isaiah 65:17; 2 Peter 3:13. V. The vengeance of Christ upon that nation is described as his "coming," John 21:22; Hebrews 10:37: his "coming in the clouds," Revelation 1:7: "in glory with the angels," Matthew 24:30, &c. VI. It is described as the 'enthroning of Christ, and his twelve apostles judging the twelve tribes of Israel,' Matthew 19:28; Luke 22:30. Hence this is the sense of the present place: Our Saviour had said in the last verse of the former chapter, "Whosoever shall be ashamed of me and of my words in this adulterous and sinful generation; of him also shall the Son of man be ashamed, when he cometh in the glory of his Father with the holy angels," to take punishment of that adulterous and sinful generation. And he suggests, with good reason, that his coming in glory should be in the lifetime of some that stood there."[87]

---

[86] Matthew Henry, *Matthew Henry's Commentary on the Whole* (Peabody: Hendrickson, 1995), 1699, bold emphasis MJS

[87] John Lightfoot, *COMMENTARY ON THE NEW TESTAMENT FROM THE TALMUD AND HEBRAICA*, Vol. 2, (Hendrickson pub. 1979), 422 emphasis MJS

*1). "For the Son of Man is **about to** come..." (Mt. 16:27YLT)*

The YLT, DARBY, WUESTNT, and WEY translations correctly translate Jesus' return here as "about to come" or "soon to come." These translations are accurate since this is the consistent usage of the Greek word *mello* in Matthew's gospel, let alone its predominated usage in the rest of the New Testament. Let's briefly see how *mello* is used in Mathew's gospel:

- A). In Matthew 2:13 WEY, Herod is "about to" seek to kill Jesus, and therefore Joseph and Mary need to "escape." *Mello* here is communicating a near imminent danger, not just a certain or general danger to be aware of.

- B). In Matthew 3:7 GNT, John was preaching to the Pharisees concerning a "wrath about to come." The GNT of *mello* here as "about to" is supported by the immediate context in that John was preaching a kingdom that was "at hand" (Mt. 3:2), in which both the wrath and kingdom would be manifested imminently because God already had His ax at the root of the trees (Mt. 3:10) and His harvesting winnowing fork was already in His hand (Mt. 3:12). This "winnowing fork" was the tool used at the end of the harvest period to separate the wheat from the chaff. Jesus likewise teaches that the "end of the [Old Covenant] age" resurrection harvest gathering would be fulfilled in His contemporary generation (cf. Mt. 13:39-43/Mt. 24:3, 31-34).

- C). In Mathew 17:10-13, *mello* is used twice. The first occurrence refers to the Jews expecting Elijah "about to" come to prepare the way for Messiah. In other words, Elijah was the one the entire nation understood to be "about to come" in their day, and the text tells us that he had already come in the person of John the Baptist.

  Many Premillennial Zionists reject Jesus' direct teaching here that John is the fulfillment of the one who would prepare the way for Christ's "about to come", "great and dreadful day" of Malachi 4:5-6. They instead ***speculate*** that he will again appear in the future as one of the witnesses in Revelation 11!

  The second occurrence of *mello* in this passage is not referring to the general fact that Jesus was going to suffer, but that He was "about to" suffer and be mistreated as John the Baptist was.

- D). In Matthew 24:6 WEY, "before long" the disciples would begin hearing of a general sign of "wars and rumors of wars," but Jesus said the "end" (of the old covenant age) was not yet. Jesus gave general signs that they would begin hearing about in their near future, while the two specific ones (the Great Commission - Mt. 24:14) and the "armies surrounding Jerusalem" (Lk. 21:20) would mark that Christ's Second Coming was indeed "near."

To conclude this point, Christ's "about to" coming (Mt. 16:27) is consistent with Christ's coming in the lifetime of "some" of the crowd listening to him in the next verse

– 28! After thousands of years of the world and Israel awaiting the Seed of the woman, or the coming of the Messiah and His kingdom, the span of some of the crowd's lifetime was a short time for them to wait and thus it was "about to" be fulfilled.

2). *"**Verily I say unto you**..."* (Mt. 16:28)

Jesus' phrases "verily", "truly," or "most assuredly I say unto you" are used some 99 times in the gospels and give the meaning of "absolutely", "really", and "may it be fulfilled." They are used as a phrase of emphasis to drive home a point that has gone before it. It is **never** used to introduce a new subject. Yet in spite of this fact, Thomas Ice, who is a Dispensational Premillennial Zionist, has sought to refute our exegesis of this text by claiming:

> "...verse twenty-seven looks at the establishment of the kingdom in the future, while a promise of seeing the Messiah in His glory is the thought of verse twenty-eight. They are two separate predictions separated by the words 'truly I say to you.'"[88]

But Mr. Ice does not produce one passage where Jesus' phrase "Truly I say unto you" is ever used to separate the subject matter previously discussed and to introduce a new subject! Since he cannot produce any evidence for his statement, his point at the very least is unscholarly, and at worst irresponsible and deceptive.

I remember attending the Evangelical Theological Society one time where a Premillennial Zionist was speaking on the subject of Preterism. When he approached Matthew 16:27-28, he regurgitated Thomas Ice's point that "verily I say unto you" can be used to introduce a new subject. In the Q&A session I publicly asked, "Can you give me just ONE instance in the teachings of Jesus where the phrase 'verily I say unto you' is used to introduce a new subject?" He stalled for a long time and said, "No." I then responded, "Please do not parrot the so-called 'scholarship' of other Zionists who likewise have not done the homework you clearly haven't done either. I have looked up the phrase everywhere it is used and haven't found one place where it introduces a new subject. Just the opposite in fact is the truth. It is always used to link the previous subject matter with what follows and that is how it is used here in Matthew 16:27-28. The fact that Christ was 'about to come' was exciting and startling to the crowd listening and Jesus wanted to ram home the point by pointing out it was so near in fact that 'some of you standing here shall not die until" you see it fulfilled.'" The man had nothing to say. It was a mic drop moment and I enjoyed it.

3). *"**Some standing here shall not taste of death**" and "the **kingdom** of God"* (Mt. 16:28)

As we study Christ's teachings elsewhere in the Gospels and other related passages in the Old and New Testaments concerning 1) the physical death of some of the 12 and their first century contemporaries along with 2) the Son of Man coming and the arrival

---

[88] Tim LaHaye, Thomas Ice, *END TIMES CONTROVERSY THE SECOND COMING UNDER ATTACK*, (Eugene, OR: Harvest House Publishers, 2003), 87, emphasis MJS

of the kingdom of God in power, we discover Christ is addressing a very specific and prophetic persecution coming in the apostolic generation and not just alluding to some of them dying off because of mere old age. The only event in the teachings of Jesus that associates the death of some of the apostles or saints with the kingdom of God is the persecution preceding his Second Coming event (cf. Mt. 10:16-23; Lk. 21:16-32; Mt. 23:31-36; Jn. 21:19-22; Rev. 6:10-11, 17; 16:6, 15; 18:5, 20). The only exception to this is the death of Judas.

Daniel's prophecy confirms Jesus' teaching. In Daniel 2, 7, 9, and 12 we learn the following:

A) The kingdom would come and be established during the time of the Roman Empire

(cf. Dan. 2 & 7).

B) There would be a time of persecution and death for believers before the Son of Man would come upon the clouds in judgment and the kingdom would be inherited (Dan. 7:13-22).

Some of our opponents have made some real crucial mistakes in trying to refute us. Again, Thomas Ice, a prominent Premillennial Zionist, makes another blunder in trying to refute us on this critical passage:

> "A further problem with the preterist view is that our Lord said 'some of those standing here…' It is clear that the term 'some' would have to include at least two or more individuals… Peter notes that 'John only survived among the 12 disciples till the destruction of Jerusalem.'"[89]

In other words, Ice is claiming that the 12 apparently were the only ones Jesus was addressing in this text, and therefore if only John was alive till the destruction of Jerusalem then that does not meet the definition of "some" because "some" necessitates more than one. However, Mark's account clearly states, "Then he called **the crowd** to him along with his disciples and said…" (Mk. 8:34 – 9:1).

This is but yet another embarrassing printed "argument" that is blatantly false. The first was that "verily I say unto you" (Mt. 16:28) was allegedly used to introduce a new subject (the transfiguration), when the truth is it is never used to introduce a new subject but rather to connect what went before with what follows. Now we have a second embarrassing "argument" which exposes the fact that this Premillennial "prophecy expert" and "debater" doesn't even take the time to read Mark's account to see that Jesus was speaking to an entire "crowd" and not just the 12! Amazing!

4). *"…in **this adulterous** and **sinful generation**, the Son of man also shall be **ashamed** of him, **when he cometh**…" (Mk. 8:38).*

This passage is not dealing with Jesus' listeners sleeping with women other than their wives. It is referring to Israel being known as committing spiritual and covenantal adultery by

---

[89] Ice, Ibid., 88

rejecting the Messiah / Groom standing right in front of them. While Christ does not specifically mention Jerusalem's divorce and remarriage directly in our text, it is implied in Him being "ashamed" of His contemporary "*adulterous* generation" at His Second Coming event, which necessitates both of these eschatological motifs. , and one of Jesus' OT sources here, addresses Him coming with His "reward" and the eschatological wedding motif (cf. Isa. 62:4-5, 11).

Under the old covenant, God was married to Israel (cf. Israel Ex. 19-24). This marriage was both pictured as a monogamous marriage (God married to a Mother/Israel) and then, after the splitting of the northern kingdom and the southern kingdoms, a polygamous marriage. The picture then becomes God taking two daughters (or sisters) as His wives: 1) Israel (Aholah / Samaria capital of Israel) and 2) Judah (Aholibah / Jerusalem capital of Judah; cf. Jer. 31:31-32; Ezek. 1:1-4; 1 Kings 11:9-13). These two sisters were notorious for their adultery and playing the prostitute (cf. Ezek. 23:3;Jer. 3).

Although God divorced Israel through the Assyrian captivity, He remained married to His other harlot wife, Judah, from which line Jesus would come. Judah/Jerusalem was judged by the Babylonian captivity but never divorced (Ezek. 23:22-45).

The book of Hosea describes God divorcing Israel through the Assyrian captivity. He divorced her and put her to death by burying her like a seed in the land of the Gentiles. Hosea also predicts Judah's harvest divorcement / judgment in her last days. But there is hope in that Hosea also predicts a time when God will betroth her in the desert and thus re-marry Israel in those same last days.

Under the old covenant, a wife caught in adultery would be stoned and the wife of a priest would be burned. As we looked at in Revelation 19 the harlot wife of Old Covenant Jerusalem was both stoned and/or burned!

Therefore, Jesus in Matthew 16:27/Mark 8:38 was describing the judgment of the "adulterous generation/wife" in an "about to be" AD 70 time frame. Concerning the phrase "be ashamed of," the adulterous old covenant wife would be left without a wedding garment, stripped naked and left ashamed (Rev. 17:6), while His new covenant wife would be clothed in Christ's righteousness as His New Jerusalem or "house from above" - unashamed and "further clothed" with costly gold, gems, etc… (cf. Mt. 22:1-14; Rev. 3:18; 19:8/2 Cor. 5:1-21; Rev. 21:11ff.).

We will pick up the divorce and re-marriage motif in connection with Christ's first century Second Coming again in Matthew 25:1-12 and in Revelation 17-21 (where it is more directly mentioned).

*5). "…There are certain of those here standing, who shall in nowise taste of death, until they see the kingdom of God, **already come** in power" (Mrk. 9:1 Rotherham Translation).*

In Mark's parallel account, we learn that some within the crowd Jesus is addressing would live to see His return and His kingdom coming in power. Mark uses the perfect participle while Matthew uses the future tense. In other words, Mark is saying that some of the disciples would *live to be able to look back on this event knowing that the* *coming of the Lord and His kingdom had **already come in power**.* Kenneth Gentry concedes this point, citing J.A Alexander:

> "Here "come" is "not, as the English words may seem to mean, in the act of coming (till they see it come), but actually or already come, the only sense that can be put upon the perfect participle here employed."[12] Thus, His disciples were to expect its exhibition in power. It was not powerfully to evidence itself immediately, for many of His disciples would die before it acted in power. Yet it was to be within the lifetimes of others, for "some" standing there would witness it. This seems clearly to refer to the A.D. 70 destruction of the temple and removal of the Old Testament means of worship (cf. Heb. 12:25-28; Rev.1:1, 3, 9). This occurred as a direct result of Jesus' prophecies (John 4:21-23; Mt. 21:33ff.; 23:31-34:34)."[90]

Jesus tells the disciples that some of them would live to "see" His coming and that the kingdom would have "already come" in power to bear witness of His return. The Greek word here for "see" is *eido*. Strong's Concordance defines *eido* as to "know how" and "perceive" as well as physical sight.

Through observing with the physical senses Christ coming through the power of the Romans to desolate the outer shell of the old covenant kingdom, temple and city in AD 70, "some" of Jesus' contemporary audience would be able to "perceive" and "know how" Christ's spiritual kingdom had "already come" "within" them (cf. Mrk. 8:38-9:1; Lk.17:20-37; Col.1:27; Jn. 14:2-3, 23). By connecting Mark 8:38--9:1 with Luke 17:20-37, Christians today can also experientially know and can see from reading our Lord's words (the testimony of the Scriptures) that Christ's Second Coming and His kingdom have "already come" and that His kingdom has been established "within" us.

Just as a sidenote, this text is one of many that refutes a literal, so-called "rapture" off the earth for the living and remaining at Christ's return! The fact that they would remain on the earth and "know" that He had "already come" coincides with what the prophet says in Isaiah, when we learn there are "survivors" of the "Day of the Lord" who continue preaching the gospel to "sinners" in the new creation (cf. Isa. 65-66).

6). Matthew 16:27-28 and the Olivet Discourse – the Analogy of Faith (Jesus interprets Jesus)

Earlier we saw that the content of the coming of the Son of Man as developed in Matthew 10:17-23 was a snapshot of what Jesus would develop more fully in the Olivet Discourse. The same can be said of Matthew 16:27-28 being an abbreviated form of Jesus' teaching in the Olivet Discourse concerning the same events and same first century time of fulfillment.

---

[90] Kenneth L. Gentry Jr., *HE SHALL HAVE DOMINION A POSTMILLENNIAL ESCHATOLOGY*, (Draper, VA: Apologetics Group Media, third edition 2009), 219-220, emphasis MJS

Matthew 16:27-28 & Parallels	The Olivet Discourse
1). Christ comes in **glory** (Lk. 9:26)	1). Christ comes in **glory** (Mt. 24:30)
2). Christ comes **with angels** (Mt. 16:27)	2). Christ comes **with angels** (Mt. 24:31)
3). Christ comes in **judgment** (Mt. 16:27)	3). Christ comes in **judgment** (Mt. 24:28-31; 25:31-34)
4). Christ and the **kingdom come in power** (Mrk. 8:38)	4). Christ and the **kingdom come in power** (Lk. 21:27-32)
5). Some of the disciples **would live** (Mt. 16:28)	5). Some of the disciples **would live** (Lk. 21:16-18)
6). Some of the disciples **would die** (Mt. 16:28)	6). Some of the disciples **would die** (Lk. 21:16)
7). Christ would be ashamed of some in His **"this adulterous generation"** (Mrk. 8:38)	7). All of this would occur in His contemporary **"this generation"** (Mt. 24:34)

7). How the NT authors develop Matthew 16:27-28 confirms our exegesis/ interpretation

If the Preterist exegesis of Matthew 16:27-28 is correct in that Jesus' "about to be" Second Coming event (vs. 27) was so imminent, that it would be witnessed in the lifetimes of some of those listening to Him (vs. 28), and thus He would be ashamed of their contemporary "this adulterous generation" at His coming (Mrk. 8:38--9:1), then as that first century audience and generation was closing the same events of Matthew 16:27-28 listed would be connected to a "soon" Second Coming event. And that is exactly what we see:

Matthew 16:27-28 / Mark 8:38—9:1	Revelation 22:12 / Revelation 17:16
1). "The Son of Man is about to come in the glory of His Father with His angels,…"	1). "Behold I am coming soon;…"
2). "then he shall reward every man according to his works."	2). "…bringing my reward with me, to give every man according as his work shall be."
3). "For whoever is ashamed of me and my words in this adulterous and sinful generation, of him will the Son of Man also be ashamed when he comes in the glory of his Father with the holy angels."	3). "They will make her (the adulterous prostitute – old covenant Jerusalem) desolate and naked…". *Adulterous women in the ancient world were put to shame and stripped naked (cf. Isa. 47:2-3; Jer. 13:26; Lam. 1:8-9; Ezek. 16:37, 39; 23:29; Hos. 2:10; Nah. 3:5).

The Apostle Paul taught that some of his contemporaries would live to witness Christ's Second Coming event – *"we shall not all die… we who are alive…"* (1 Cor. 15:51; 1 Thess. 4:15).

8). Matthew 16:27-28 and the Transfiguration event

Premillennial Zionists such as Thomas Ice, who seek to disprove that some of the first century disciples Jesus addressed in Matthew 16:28 would live to witness the Second Coming event in verse 27, try to argue that since the transfiguration event is followed by Jesus' teaching here in all three synoptic gospels, then this must be the event Jesus was referring to.[91]

Remember that Dr. Ice claimed "verily I say unto you" can be used to introduce a new subject – when in fact it is never used to do such. So Mr. Ice is attempting to pawn off the theory that the event that some of the first century disciples would live to witness is the transfiguration event in the following chapter. And while "verily I say unto you" is never used to transition to a new subject matter (rather it is used to link the subject which has gone before with what follows), the Greek word *kai* (meaning "and") is used often as a change of subject and Jesus uses it here - "and after six days Jesus..." (Mt. 17:1).

Since the transfiguration event does follow Jesus' teaching in Matthew 16:27-28, is there a relationship? We believe there is. In the vision, when Peter wants Moses and Elijah to remain and abide with the other disciples and Jesus, God causes the glory of Moses and Elijah to disappear. The theology of the vision is directed at the appearing and disappearing of the old covenant order pictured in the glory of Moses and Elijah (the law and the prophets), with an emphasis on the eternal abiding glory of the new covenant words of Christ – "hear Him" (Mt. 17:5-8; cf. Mt.24:35). Seeking the abiding glory and nature of the old covenant (Moses and Elijah) along with the new (the glory of Christ) was the theological error that the Judaizers and mockers of Peter's day were making! With this in mind we can now understand Peter's appeal to the vision as an apologetic against the mockers and false teachers of his day.

The 1 Peter 1:16-19 passage is now very easy to understand. Peter is under attack by the Judaizers who are claiming that he and the other disciples have been teaching Christians "cleverly devised stories" about the Second Coming (2 Pet. 1:16a). Peter's apologetic against this charge is that he has two other apostolic witnesses that will bear witness that they got their teaching of the Second Coming as direct revelation from the Father and the Son on the Mount of Transfiguration–verses 16b-18. Although Peter does not use the Greek word *metamorphoo*, he describes the Church going through a similar process in verse 19a when he says it is "…a light shining in a dark place, until the Day dawns and the Morning Star rises in your hearts." The "day" (singular) is none other than the "last day" of John's gospel and the "in that day" or last day (singular) of (Lk. 17/Mt. 24-25).

There are only two other places in the New Testament where this Greek word "transfigured" or "transformed is used": Romans 12:2 & 2 Corinthians 3:18. Paul's "therefore" of Romans 12:1 is linking it with his teaching on the unsearchable riches of the new covenant "mystery" (Jew/Gentile) or salvation that he has been developing throughout, which reaches its peak here in Romans 11:15, 25-36. In Romans 7-8, the

---

[91] Ice, Ibid., 88

issue with the old covenant law of sin and death and the new covenant law of the Spirit is realized within the "mind" and walking in this newness. In chapters 12 and on are the practical applications of living out this new covenant salvation and life which was imminently coming at Christ's return, described as the "night" (of the old covenant age) fading away or being "far gone" and the "day" (of the new covenant age) being "at hand" (cf. Rom. 13:11-12.)

The only other New Testament passage in which *metamorphoo* is used is 2 Corinthians 3:18. This text is even a clearer covenantal contrasting section within Paul's writings. The Church was in the process of "being transformed" into the likeness of Christ which was connected with the old covenant veil being lifted from the eyes of their minds and hearts. This was obviously not a literal or biological transformation process, but rather a spiritual and covenantal one! The old covenant glory was "passing away" (2 Cor. 3:7-11) just as the glory of Moses and Elijah had disappeared in the vision given on the mount! The old covenant glory was like Moses seeing God's face and then that glory fading away, while the new covenant glory of the gospel is like the creation of the light of day manifested in our hearts – resulting in seeing Christ's face which does not fade away (2 Cor. 4:6/Rev. 22:4-7ff.).

Since we agree with most who understand the transfiguration event to be a foreshadowing or pre-figuring of the Parousia or Second Coming event, we need to ask where in the vision are the following:

A) the passing and burning of the planet earth?

B) Christ floating down on a literal cloud someday?

C) corpses flying out of their caskets at the end of time to be united with their spirits?

The vision of the Parousia in the transfiguration event gives us a theological picture/description of what the Parousia was going to be all about – the passing and fulfilling of the old covenant promises contained in the law (Moses) and prophets (Elijah) and the bringing in and establishing of the abiding new covenant by AD 70.

The first two (of "the big three") coming of the Son of Man passages in Matthew 10:17-23 and Matthew 16:27-28/Mark 8:38—9:1 are small snapshots and actually form the main content of Christ's teaching of His Second Coming in the Olivet Discourse:

Matthew 10:17-23/16:27-28 & Parallels	The Olivet Discourse
1). Delivered up to **councils** and **synagogues** (Mt. 10:17)	1). Delivered up to **local councils** and **synagogues** (Mrk. 13:9)
2). Brought before **governors and kings** to be **witnesses to the Gentiles** (Mt. 10:18)	2). Brought before **governors and kings** to be **witnesses to the Gentiles** (Mrk. 13:9)
3). **Holy Spirit** would speak through them (Mt. 10:19-20)	3). **Holy Spirit** would speak through them (Mrk. 13:11)
4). Family members would **betray and kill each other**, all men would hate the	4). Family members would **betray and kill each other**, all men would hate the disciples,

disciples, but he that would stand firm to **"the end"** would be **"saved"** (Mt. 10:22)	but he that would stand firm to **"the end"** would be **"saved"** (Mrk. 13:12-13)
5). The disciples would not have run out of cities of refuge to flee to as they were being persecuted preaching the gospel **to the cities of Israel before the Son of Man would come** (Mt. 10:23)	5). The disciples (and later Paul) were to preach the gospel to the **then known "world" and "nations"** at that time **before "the end" (of the OC age) and the coming of the Son of Man would take place** (Mt. 24:14/Mrk. 13:10)
6). Christ comes **in glory** (Lk. 9:26)	6). Christ comes **in glory** (Mt. 24:30)
7). Christ comes **with angels** (Mt. 16:27)	7). Christ comes **with angels** (Mt. 24:31)
8). Christ comes **in judgment** (Mt. 16:27)	8). Christ comes **in judgment** (Mt. 24:28-31;25:31-34)
9). Christ and the kingdom come **in power** (Mrk. 8:38)	9). Christ and the kingdom come **in power** (Lk. 21:27-32)
10). Some in the **crowd would live** to witness the Second Coming (Mt. 16:28)	10). Some in the **crowd would live to** witness the Second Coming (Lk. 21:16-18)
11). Some in the **crowd would die** before the Second Coming (Mt. 16:28)	11). Some in the **crowd would die** before the Second Coming (Lk. 21:16)
12). Christ was **"about to come"** and would be ashamed of some in His contemporary **"this generation"** (Mt. 16:27YLT/Mrk. 8:38)	12). All of this would occur and be **"near" and "at the door"** in His contemporary **"this generation"** (Mt. 24:33-34/Lk. 21:27-32)

#3 The Olivet Discourse Matthew 24-25 / Mark 13 / Luke 21

- *"Truly, I say to you, **this generation** will not pass away until all these things [Temple's destruction, signs, end of the Old Covenant age and coming of the Son of Man] take place" (Mt. 24:34)*

- *"So also, when you see these things taking place [signs, coming of the Son of Man, armies surrounding Jerusalem, etc.], you **know that the kingdom of God is near**. Truly, I say to you, **this generation** will not pass away until all has taken place" (Lk. 21:31-32).*

Before giving a rigorous exegesis of the Olivet Discourse, it may be good to see how it ties into the previous context of Matthew 23. Some commentators connect Matthew 23-25 with a chiasm which begins with the Pharisees hypocritically judging the people *from Moses' seat* and ends with the Son of Man *sitting upon His throne* righteously judging those same hypocrites. The issues in the middle are found primarily in Matthew 23-24 with the promise of Christ's coming to judge the living and the dead and destroy the temple within Jesus' contemporary generation. While I won't develop a chiasm here, we should point out some comparisons, contrasts and issues that link them inseparably together.

The context and connections between Matthew 23-24

Matthew 23	Matthew 24-25
1). The Pharisees sit in Moses' seat and hypocritically judge the people and therefore will not inherit the Kingdom and are sentenced to hell (Mt. 23:2ff.).	1). Jesus would sit on His glorious throne and judge those very hypocrites and they would not inherit the Kingdom (Mt. 25:31, 41-45).
2). The "blind" Pharisees and Scribes' evangelism produced "sons of hell" (Mt. 23:15).	2). The evangelism of Jesus' disciples would produce the end of the age and "look[ing] up" to [metaphorically] see the "near" "redemption" or inheritance of the Kingdom (Mt. 24:14/Lk. 21:28-32).
3). They swore by the gold and beauty of the temple, but Jesus prophesied the destruction of their temple (Mt. 23:16-36).	3). Jesus prophesied the destruction of their temple and cursed them to eternal punishment (Mt. 24:1-2).
4). The Pharisees would "fill up" the sin of Israel's blood guilt and it would be completed after they persecuted and killed some of those Jesus would send to them (Mt. 23:31-36).	4). The Pharisees would experience "wrath" and the "days of vengeance" for beating [in their councils and synagogues] and killing those whom Jesus sent to evangelize Israel and nations (Mrk. 13:9-13; cf. Mt. 10:17-23).
5). This would be the time for the judgment of the living (the Pharisees) and the dead (vindication of the martyrs) (Mt. 23:31-36).	5). This would be the time for the judgment of the living ("wrath against this people", "fall by the sword", "be led captive") and the dead (Lk. 21:20-24; Mt. 25:31-46).
6). The Pharisees had seven woes pronounced upon them and they would be judged when Christ came "again" to desolate their temple (Mt. 23:13ff.)	6). The "stars [Israel's religious and civil rulers] would fall from heaven to earth when Jesus came upon the clouds to judge them and desolate their temple (Mt. 24:3,29-30).
7). In their contemporary "this generation," they would see Him come "again" to judge them and "desolate" their temple (Mt. 23:31-39).	7). The contemporary "this generation" of the disciples and Pharisees would witness Christ come in judgment and "desolate" their Temple (Mt. 24:1-2—34, cf. Mt. 26:62-64).

If we allow for some connections between Matthew 23 and Luke 17 (the same Second Coming event, even with Christ coming as the great light of the sun shining from east to west), the Pharisees would be judged for what was **"within"** their unclean hearts, and when Christ and His kingdom came in AD 70 it would be realized "**within** the hearts of a person [i.e. a believer] (Mt. 23:27). Let's now turn our attention to how the Second Coming of Christ is described in Matthew 23:

> "For I tell you, you will not see me **again** until you say, 'Blessed is he who comes in the name of the Lord." (Matt. 23:39 / Psalm 118:26).

The Song of Ascent of Psalm 118:26 (and taken from other Psalms) was supposed to be a song of joy and salvation that the Jews would sing on the walls of Jerusalem, welcoming the pilgrims to their feast days, but God turned it into a "stage work" for their judgment (not the judgment of their enemies, the Romans). The Jews were bottled up in Jerusalem (in AD 67 - AD 70), deceiving themselves into thinking God was going to save them from the Romans and usher in a carnal earthly kingdom in fulfillment of OT prophecies (the very mentality that Jesus warned about concerning the coming false prophets in Matthew 24). In essence, God was forcing them to welcome their own judgment (in song form). Instead of being met and welcoming pilgrims for the feasts (seeking peace and salvation), they were met with and forced to welcome God coming in judgment through the Roman armies (as God had "come" in the OT through the Assyrians, Babylonians, etc...).[92] After all it was prophesied that Messiah would spread a "trap" and "snare" for them when they came to feast at their "table" (Ps. 69:22). Josephus confirms for us the Roman Jewish war began when the Jews were trapped in the city while celebrating the Feast of Passover.

That the Jews would not "discern what their end would be" was predicted in yet another song - the Song of Moses (Deut. 32:29). God/Messiah as their "Rock" is also a common theme in Deuteronomy 32. Because they forsook God as their "Rock" (Jesus the coming "Corner Stone" of Psalm 118) and trusted in others, He brought upon them certain "disaster" in a particular "perverse generation" which the NT declares was the AD 30 - AD 70 one (cf. Deut. 32:5, 20/Acts 2:40). The OT prophets would go on to describe this coming judgment as God's "strange work" (judging them at a time when they expected God to judge their enemies).

The exegete also needs to pay attention to how Jesus uses Psalm 118 elsewhere. Psalm 118:22 sheds light on how Jesus is using verse Psalm 118:26 in Matt. 23:39. If Jesus uses Psalm 118:22 as being fulfilled in the AD 70 judgment (cf. Matt. 21:42-45), then the burden of proof is upon the Zionist to demonstrate that He is using Psalm 118 in a completely different way, ie. referring to a 2,000+ year distant future context for Israel's alleged salvation.

Three simple points on Matthew 23:39:

> 1). Since Jesus used Psalm 118 elsewhere in Matthew to refer to the judgment coming in AD 70, this directs us to see that He is using Psalm 118 in Matt. 23:39 to refer to the same event.
>
> 2). The immediate context of Matthew 23-24 points to AD 70. It is this discussion of Christ "coming" in their (AD 30 - AD 70) "this generation" to destroy their "house" or "temple" which spurs on a continued discussion regarding the SAME "coming," the SAME time frame ("this generation"), and the destruction of the SAME "temple." It is commonplace for commentators to acknowledge that the disciples understood the temple's destruction to take place at Christ's coming at the end of the age. However, these same commentators,

---

[92] Special thanks to my friend Don K. Preston for pointing this interpretation out to me.

based upon a Futurist bias, claim that the disciples were "mistaken" to connect these events. The disciples "understood" Jesus' teaching on the "end of the age" (Matt. 13:39-51), and when we identify the "end of the age" to be the end of the old covenant age instead of the end of world history, all three (temple's destruction, coming of Christ, and end of the age) fall naturally within the "this generation" time frame.

3). Their "stumbling" over Christ produced a "strange work" (Isa. 28:21, etc. - God would come to judge them, not deliver them) and thus there was irony in Jesus using a song of salvation for their judgment!

Matthew 23 *ends* with Christ coming again to judge the Pharisee and desolate their temple in Jesus' contemporary "this generation." There is a subtle "sign" in that Jesus hints that this will be during one of their feasts when they sing the song of ascent from Psalm 118 upon their walls ("blessed is he who comes in the name of the Lord").

Matthew 24 *begins or picks up* where Matthew 23 left off. The temple's destruction, Jesus' coming, and the signs are now developed in more detail, but again with the alarming declaration that all of this will be fulfilled in their "this generation."

The importance of the Olivet Discourse – the Rosetta Stone of all Bible prophecy

We definitely agree with our Premillennial Zionist opponents on the importance of correctly interpreting the Olivet Discourse, because how one understands it will dictate how one understands Bible prophecy throughout the Bible:

> "A proper understanding of the Olivet Discourse is absolutely essential for anyone who wants to gain a clear picture of God's plan for the ages. This discourse is so significant that **the way a person interprets it will impact his understanding of the rest of the prophecy in the Bible**."[93]

Thomas Ice writes the following on the alleged differences between Jesus' use of "this generation" in Matthew 23 and 24:

> "In fact, when one compares the use of "this generation" at the beginning of the Olivet Discourse in Matthew 23:36 (which is an undisputed reference to AD 70) with the prophetic use in the Matthew 24:34, a contrast becomes obvious. Jesus in contrasting the *deliverance* for Israel in Matthew 24:34 with the predicted *judgment* stated in Matthew 23:36."[94]

In both Matthew 23-24 there are themes of deliverance and judgment. In Matthew 23 there is the theme of *vindication / deliverance* for the martyrs and *judgment* upon those who have persecuted them, resulting in Christ coming and destroying the temple, with both to take place in their contemporary "this generation." In Matthew 24, there are likewise the same themes of *vindication / deliverance* for the persecuted in the city with

---

[93] Ibid., 151
[94] Ibid., 93

their flight from Judea and then that of *judgment* upon those who persecuted them, resulting in Christ coming and destroying the temple, with both to take place in their contemporary "this generation."

While Zionists like Ice admit that "this generation" in Matthew 23 is "an undisputed reference to AD 70," meaning the contemporary generation of Jesus, they give "this generation" in Matthew 24 an entirely different meaning in order to defend their false Futuristic Zionist theology. We are told that their re-definition of "this generation" in Matthew 24 is justified because "…it is obvious that these things did not occur…in AD 70."[95]

When we allow the Bible to interpret itself, it becomes very easy to see how "all these things" in Matthew 24:3-34 were fulfilled in Jesus' contemporary "this generation." So, let's turn our attention to proving just that!

- *The end of what age? (Mt. 24:3)*

- *"As he sat on the Mount of Olives, the disciples came to him privately, saying, "Tell us, when will these things be, and what will be the sign of your coming **and of the end of the age** (Mt. 24:3)"?*

- *"And they asked him, "Teacher, when will these things be, and what will be the sign when these things are about to take place" (Lk. 21:7)?*

The first thing we notice between Matthew's account placed alongside Mark's and Luke's is that after Jesus predicts the destruction of the temple, Mark and Luke do not include the "and end of the age" (Greek *suntéleia ó ho aiṓn*) in the disciple's question(s). The fact that this phrase is only used in Matthew's gospel three times (cf. Mt. 13:39-43; 24:3 and 28:18-20) and in the book of Hebrews (cf. Heb. 9:26-28) communicates its Jewishness.

Since the "end of the age" is referring to the end of the old covenant age when the temple would be destroyed, there is no conflict between the accounts. If so, are we to expect that Mark and Luke were so careless as to not introduce the subject of the alleged end of world history into the most important account of Jesus' teaching on Bible prophecy? For Mark and Luke, when the Son of Man comes upon the clouds in judgment, this is when the temple would be destroyed (which for Matthew is when the old covenant age would end as well).

We should briefly examine Matthew 13:39-43 where Jesus has used "end of the age" (Greek *suntéleia ó ho aiṓn*) before. Partial Preterist Joel McDurmon, commenting on the end of the age in Matthew 13:39-43, concedes it is the end of the old covenant age:

> "It is clear that Jesus did not have in mind the end of the world, nor did He mean the final judgment. Rather, Matthew 13:2430, 36-43 describe the judgment that would come upon unbelieving Jerusalem. During this time, the angels would "gather out of his kingdom all things that offend, and them which do iniquity"

---

[95] Ibid.

(13:41) and these would be judged with fire. Many of them literally were burned in fire during the destruction of Jerusalem. During this same time, however, the elect of Christ— "the children of the kingdom" (v. 38)—will be harvested. While the explanation of the parable does not tell us their final end, the parable itself has the householder instructing the harvesters to "gather the wheat into my barn." In other words, they are protected and saved by God.

This, of course, is exactly what happened to the Christians. Not only were they saved in soul, but they mostly fled Jerusalem before the Roman siege. This was consequent to Jesus' advice to flee and not look back once the signs arose (Matt. 24:16-22); indeed, this would correspond with the angels' work of harvesting the elect (24:30)."[96]

McDurmon even develops Jesus' two age model ("this age" = old covenant age) and "age to come" or "age about to come" (the new covenant age) in Pauline eschatology to be one and the same. After making his case in Ephesians 1:21; 2:1-7; 3:8-11; Colossians 1:26; 1 Corinthians 10:11; Hebrews 9:26, he concludes:

"So, from the teaching of Jesus, Paul and the author of Hebrews, we get a very clear picture of the two primary ages: one that endured up until the time of Christ, and another that began around that same period. I believe these two periods, being hinged upon the coming and work of Christ, pertain obviously to the Old and New Covenant administrations."[97]

Getting back to the disciple's question in Matthew 24:3, DeMar correctly writes:

"The disciples question involves three interrelated, contemporary events: (1) the time of the temple's destruction; (2) the sign that will signal Jesus' coming related to the destruction of the temple; and (3) the sign they should look for telling them that "the end of the age" has come. These questions are related to the destruction of the temple and the end of the Old Covenant redemptive system and nothing else."[98]

In the 1994 version of DeMar's *Last Days Madness,* he connects Matthew 23 with 24 and adds that the maturity or "consummation" of the new covenant arrived in AD 70 as well:

"The "woes" of Matthew 23 and the destruction of the temple and the city of Jerusalem were a result of all that John the Baptist and Jesus had been warning the scribes, Pharisees, and chief priests regarding the judgment that would come upon them if they did not repent. "All these things," Jesus cautioned, "shall come upon this generation" (23:36). It is after hearing about the desolation of

---

[96] Joel McDurmon, *Jesus v. Jerusalem: A Commentary on Luke 9:51 – 20:26, Jesus' Lawsuit Against Israel* (Powder Springs, GA: The American Vision, Inc., 2011), 48-49; see entire section 43-51.

[97] Ibid., 46-47.

[98] Gary DeMar, *Last Days MADNESS Obsession of the Modern Church*, (Powder Springs, GA: Fourth revised edition, 1999), 68.

> their "house" – the temple – that the disciples ask about the "temple buildings" (24:1). ***Jesus answered the disciples' questions relating to the time and signs of Jerusalem's destruction, always with the background of Matthew 23 in view, since His comments in that chapter had precipitated the questions (24:3). The Old Covenant order would end with the destruction of Jerusalem. This would be the "sign" of the "end of the age," the end of the Old Covenant, and the consummation [MJS - bringing to maturity] of the New Covenant.***"[99]

DeMar explains his position on the "end of the age" and then uses a quote from George Hill to support its historical relevance:

> "Notice that the disciples did not ask about the end of the "world" (kosmos), as some Bible versions translate the Greek word *aion*. In context, with the temple and city as their primary focus, they asked about the end of the "age." They were asking when time would run out for the temple, the city of Jerusalem, and the covenant promises that were related to the Mosaic system of animal sacrifices, ceremonial washings, and the priesthood.
>
> Time was divided by the Jews into two great periods, **the age of the law and the age of the Messiah**. The conclusion of the one was the beginning of the other, the opening of that kingdom which the Jews believed the Messiah was to establish, which was to put an end to their sufferings, and to render them the greatest people upon the earth. The apostles full of this hope, said to our Lord, immediately before his ascension, "Lord, wilt thou at this time restore the kingdom to Israel? [Acts 1:6]. Our Lord uses the phrase of his coming to denote his taking vengeance upon the Jews by destroying their city and sanctuary. **The "end of the age" refers to the end of the Old Covenant redemptive system with its attendant sacrifices and rituals**."[100]

"End of the age" – were the disciples confused?

All Dispensational Zionists begin with the disciples' question in Matthew 24:3 and simply *assume what they need to prove* when they assume that the disciples were "confused" in associating Jesus' coming and the end of the age with the destruction of the temple. Since Zionist theology separates these events by thousands of years and the disciples linked them to be fulfilled altogether, they merely assume the disciples were mistaken and not themselves, or they assume their Zionist Futurist system. Here are some key hermeneutical steps the Zionists willfully skip:

> 1). The Jews of Jesus' day understood and connected the phrase "this age" to the old covenant age of Moses and the prophets, with the desolation of Jerusalem and the temple, as predicted in Daniel. They understood the "age to come" as the new covenant or Messianic age. The context supports the

---

[99] Gary DeMar, *Last Days Madness Obsession of the Modern Church*, (Powder Springs, GA: American Vision, 1994), 41, bold and underline emphasis MJS

[100] Ibid., 68

destruction of the temple the disciples and Jesus were actually looking at. This would mark the "end of the age" that they were currently living in, the old covenant age, not the end of world history.

Daniel in chapters 7, 9 and 12 was told that the eschatological "time of the end" events such as the desolation of the temple, the resurrection, the tribulation, the coming of the Son of Man and the arrival of the kingdom were "all" to take place together when the city and temple would be destroyed or "when the power of the holy people would be completely shattered" (cf. see the consummation and recapitulation scenes in Dan. 7:13-22; 9:24-27, climaxing in Dan. 12:1-7).

2). Isaiah, in his "little apocalypse" (cf. Isiah 24-27), posits all of the eschatological events (judgment, de-creation, avenging the sin of blood guilt, the blowing of the trumpet / eschatological gathering / resurrection, etc.) to be fulfilled when Israel violated the old covenant, and thus would take place together when the temple would be destroyed or "when he makes all the altar stones to be like chalk stones crushed to pieces" (Isaiah 27:9). Again, the judgment and destruction of the city and temple were inseparably connected together just as in Daniel. Why are they "confused" to link them together when the OT prophets connected them together?!?

3). In Matthew 13:39-43, 51 Jesus taught the judgment and resurrection ("the time of the end" of the eschatological events in Daniel 12:2-3) would "all" take place at the end of their old covenant "this age." Jesus specifically asks them if they understood His teaching on the time of this harvest at the end of their "this age" and they emphatically responded **"Yes"** (vs. 51). We have direct evidence that they DID understand Jesus' teaching on the "end of the age," contrary to the false assumptions pawned off by Zionists.

4). As we have seen and proven thus far, Jesus had previously taught the disciples that He would return in some of their lifetimes and be ashamed of some within their contemporary "this generation" (Matthew 10:22-23; 16:27-28/Mark 8:38-9:1).

So, before we even get to Matthew 24, the disciples could have discerned from such prophets as Daniel and Isaiah that all of the eschatological events would be fulfilled together when Jerusalem was judged and her temple destroyed. And before we get to Matthew 24, Jesus had already clearly stated that He would return in some of their lifetimes and connected this coming with the desolation of their "house" / temple (Mt. 10:22-23; 16:27-28; 23:36-39). If this isn't clear enough, the record clearly confirms the disciples understood Jesus' teaching on the end of their "this age" with a resounding "yes" (Mt. 13:39-51)! We do not seek to divide what God has joined together or go beyond what Scripture teaches – while the Premillennial Zionist does.

Since there is no direct evidence here in Matthew 24 that the disciples were "confused," Zionists and other Futurist systems appeal to the fact that the Gospels often point out that the disciples were confused over various issues. But this proves nothing here in Matthew 24, or it is a classic example of "proving too much." Here is how. In each case, Jesus (or Matthew as a responsible narrator of his gospel) explicitly points out when the disciples are confused or ask a question that needs correction (cf. Mt. 16:6-12, 21-23; 17:4-5; 19:13-15; 20:20-25). Therefore, since we don't find Jesus or Matthew claiming the disciples were "confused" in asking the question they did, the burden of proof is now thrown in the lap of Futurist Premillennial Zionists to prove the disciples are confused in Matthew 24.

Milton Terry was spot on when he wrote of Jesus' teaching on the "end of the age" in the Olivet Discourse and elsewhere in the NT (such as Hebrews 9:26-28) as the end of the old covenant age and not the end of world history:

> "The 'end of the age' means the close of the epoch or age—that is, the Jewish age or dispensation which was drawing nigh, as our Lord frequently intimated. All those passages that speak of 'the end,' 'the end of the age,' or 'the ends of the ages,' refer to the same consummation, and always as nigh at hand." "...the writer regarded the incarnation of Christ as taking place near the end of the aeon, or dispensational period. To suppose that he meant that it was close upon the end of the world, or the destruction of the material globe, would be to make him write false history as well as bad grammar. It would not be true in fact; for the world has already lasted longer since the incarnation than the whole duration of the Mosaic economy, from the exodus to the destruction of the temple. It is futile, therefore, to say that the 'end of the age' may mean a lengthened period, extending from the incarnation to our times, and even far beyond them. That would be an aeon, and not the close of an aeon. The aeon of which our Lord was speaking was about to close in a great catastrophe; and a catastrophe is not a protracted process, but a definitive and culminating act."[101]

After all, the Second Appearing or coming of Christ to close the old covenant age is further described as Christ's coming "...in a very little while" which "would not tarry" (Hebrews 10:37). Again, the inspired NT authors both understood **what** "age" would end and **when** Christ would come to bring its end!

If Jesus' coming in AD 70 ended and changed the old covenant age, then there is really no justification for reading into the text (eisegesis) that the disciples were "confused" or that the Olivet Discourse has anything to do with the end of world history.

How were all the signs fulfilled prior to AD 70?

While it is easy to show how all of the signs Jesus gave to mark His coming and end of the old covenant age would be "near" and thus fulfilled by AD 70, it is important to point out that there are two groups of signs Jesus discusses. The first set would be general signs of the times that would "not" mark the near end of the age and His coming, while there would be two that would. The two that would mark the "near" end of the age and His coming were the fulfillment of the Great Commission and the Roman

---

[101] Milton S. Terry, *Biblical HERMENEUTICS A Treatise on the Interpretation of the Old and New Testaments,* (Rand Rapids, MI: Zondervan Publishing House, 1986), 441-442.

armies surrounding Jerusalem. Let's first address the general signs that were fulfilled within Jesus' contemporary generation.

- *"False Messiahs and Prophets" (Mt. 24:5)*

    Jesus predicted that false messiahs would come in the generation of the first century disciples and they did - Theudas (Acts 5:36; 13:6), Judas of Galilee (Acts 5:37), and Simon (Acts 8:9-11), to name a few. In the epistles of John, John writes (as that generation was ending) that they knew it was "the last hour" because the antichrists had arrived (1 John 2:17-18).

    The Jewish historian, Josephus, writes of a false prophet during the destruction of Jerusalem who deceived the Jews to stay and fight the Romans:

    "Of so great a multitude, not one escaped. Their destruction was caused by a false prophet, who had on that day proclaimed to those remaining in the city, that "God commanded them to go up to the temple, there to receive the signs of their deliverance." There were at this time many prophets suborned by the tyrants to delude the people, by bidding them wait for help from God, in order that there might be less desertion, and that those who were above fear and control might be encouraged by hope. Under calamities man readily yields to persuasion but when the deceiver pictures to him deliverance from pressing evils, then the sufferer is wholly influenced by hope. Thus, it was that the impostors and pretended messengers of heaven at that time beguiled the wretched people." (Josephus, Wars, 6.3.6.).

- *"Wars and Rumors of Wars" (Mt. 24:6-8, 23-26)*

    "In AD 40 there was a disturbance at Mesopotamia which (Josephus says) caused the deaths of more than 50,000 people. In AD 49, a tumult at Jerusalem at the time of the Passover resulted in 10,000 to 20,000 deaths. At Caesarea, contentions between Jewish people and other inhabitants resulted in over 20,000 Jews being killed. As Jews moved elsewhere, over 20,000 were destroyed by Syrians. At Scythopolis, over 13,000 Jews were killed. Thousands were killed in other places, and at Alexandria 50,000 were killed. At Damascus, 10,000 were killed in an hour's time."[102]

    "The Annals of Tacitus, covering the period from AD 14 to the death of Nero in AD 68, describes the tumult of the period with phrases such as "disturbances in Germany", "commotions in Africa", commotions in Thrace", "insurrections in Gaul", "intrigues among the Parthians", "the war in Britain", and "the war in Armenia". Wars were fought from one end of the empire to the other. With this description we can see further fulfillment: "For nation will rise against nation, and kingdom against kingdom." (Matthew 24:7)[103]

---

[102] John L. Bray, MATTHEW 24 FULFILLED, Fifth Edition (Powder Springs, GA: 1996), 28

[103] Gary DeMar, Ibid., 1994 edition, 62

When Jesus was addressing wars and rumors of wars, He was not referring to what is going on in modern day Russia, China, Israel, Iraq, the United States, or Europe today. To reach into Matthew 24 and back into the OT and twist these passages and prophecies by asserting that they are referring to these modern-day countries is irresponsible exegesis at best, or willful deception at the worst.

- *"Famines & Pestilence" (Lk. 21:11)*

Again, the Bible and history record famine and pestilences during "the last days" (AD 30 – AD 70) of the Mosaic old covenant age and generation (cf. Acts 11:27-29; 1 Cor. 16:1-5; Rom. 15:25-28).

In AD 40 and AD 60 there were pestilences in Babylon and Rome where Jews and Gentiles alike suffered. Tacitus, Suetonius and Orosius all record a famine in the Autumn of AD 65 that killed more than 30,000 throughout the Roman Empire. Sorry, but natural corona viruses or government-engineered, manipulated ones are NOT the subject of the Olivet Discourse.

- *"Earthquakes" (Lk. 21:11)*

The book of Acts records for us an earthquake occurring in the apostolic generation (cf. Acts 16:26). "…just previous to 70 AD there were earthquakes in Crete, Smyrna, Miletus, Chios, Samos, Laodicea, Hierapolis, Colosse, Campania, Rome, and Judea."[104]

- *"Put to Death" (Mt. 24:9)*

As we discussed in our treatment of Matthew 10:17-23, first century Christians were expected to be brought before Gentile kings and rulers, and also imprisoned and beaten for the sake of Jesus. Please read Acts 4:3,17; Acts 5:40; Acts 7:54-60; Acts 8:1; Acts 9:1; Acts 12:1-3; and Acts 14:19 to see the fulfillment of Jesus' prophecy here in Luke 21:12 and Matthew 10:17-23.

In fulfillment of our Lord's words, Paul and Silas were beaten (Acts 26:23) and Paul was brought before rulers and kings – Gallio (Acts 28:12), Felix (Acts 24), Festus and Agrippa (Acts 25). Peter and Paul were put to death in the persecution of Nero.

- *"And this gospel of the kingdom will be preached in the whole world as a testimony to all nations, and then the end will come." (Matthew 24:14)*

The reader at this point says, "I got you. How are you going to be able to prove the gospel was preached throughout the entire globe before AD 70?!?" Allowing Scripture to interpret Scripture, this is not difficult to prove at all:

---

[104] DeMar, ibid., 64

Prophecy	Fulfillment
1). "And this gospel of the kingdom shall be preached in all the <u>world</u> [Greek oikumene] for a witness unto all nations; and then shall the end come." (Matt. 24:14)	1). "But I say, have they not heard? Yes indeed: 'Their sound has gone out to all the earth, and their words to the ends of the <u>world</u>.'" [Greek oikumene] (Rom. 10:18)
*One definition of oikumene – "The Roman Empire (Acts 17:6); the Jews in the world (Acts 24:5). Of Palestine and the adjacent countries (Luke 2:1; Acts 11:28)."	
2). "And the gospel must first be published among <u>all nations</u>." [Greek ethnos] "And Jesus came and spoke to them, saying, 'All authority has been given to Me in heaven and on earth. Go therefore and make disciples of <u>all the nations</u>.'" [Greek ethnos] "'... I have commanded you; and lo, I am with you always, even to the end of the age.' Amen." (Mark 13:10; Matt. 28:19-20)	2). "...My gospel... has been made manifest, and by the prophetic Scriptures has been made known to <u>all nations</u>. . . ." [Greek ethnos] (Rom. 16:25-26)
*These are "all the nations [Greek ethnos] under heaven" that were gathered in (Acts 2:4-5) and they returned to those "nations" to preach the gospel and would be followed up by Paul preaching to those same nations prior to AD 70.	
3). "And He said to them, 'Go into <u>all the world</u> [Greek kosmos] and preach the gospel to every creature"	3). "...of the gospel, which has come to you, as it has also in <u>all the world</u> [Greek kosmos], as is bringing forth fruit..." (Col. 1:5-6)
*One definition of kosmos - "The then–known world and particularly the people who lived in it..."	
4). "And he said unto them 'Go into all the world and preach the gospel to <u>every creature</u>.'" [Greek kitisis] (Mark 16:15)	4). "...from the gospel which you heard, which was preached to <u>every creature</u> [Greek kitisis] under heaven, of which I, Paul became a minister." (Col. 1:23)
*The creation [kitisis] of men – "in rabbinical usage (by which a man converted from idolatry to Judaism was called)." The creation of men is preached to.	
5). "But you shall receive power when the Holy Spirit has come upon you; and you shall be witnesses to Me in Jerusalem, and in all Judea and Samaria, and to the end of the <u>earth/land</u>." [Greek ge] (Acts 1:8)	5). "But I say, have they not heard? Yes indeed: 'Their sound has gone out to all the <u>earth/land</u> [Greek ge], and their words to the ends of the world
*One definition of ge – "The *then known* lands, regions, territories, countries, etc..."	

It's no accident that the Holy Spirit led the Apostle Paul to use ALL of the very same Greek words Jesus used to describe the extent of the Great Commission — to proclaim this "end" time sign had already been fulfilled and therefore teach an "at hand" and "about to be" Second Coming and resurrection event (Phil. 3-4:5; Acts 24:15YLT; Rom. 13:11-12). I'm not sure how else Paul could have communicated that Jesus' "end" of the age sign had been fulfilled exactly when Jesus said it would be, within Paul's contemporary "this generation."

Let's spend a little time in Acts 2 and the Great Commission developed there. I believe that Jonah was not just a type of Christ, but that perhaps he was a type for Peter and Paul as well, being that they were instruments of crossing the Jew/Gentile barrier in fulfilling the Great Commission to the nations of the then known world. This is the same area into which the nations in Genesis 10-11 were dispersed, and Acts 2 is reversing the curse.

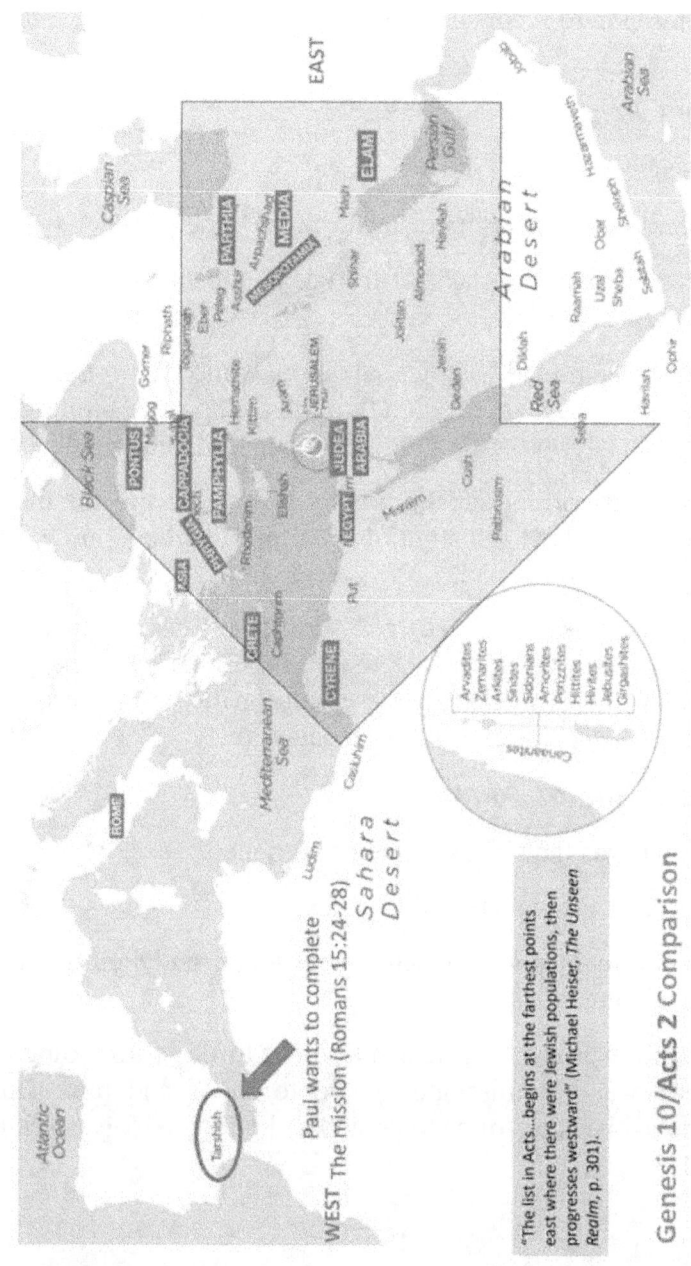

Genesis 10/Acts 2 Comparison

I will address more of how Acts 2 reverses the curses laid upon the nations in Genesis 10-11 when I address the question, "What about Acts 1:9-11?" For now, here are just some brief typological thoughts. We know how Jonah was a type of Christ, but I want to explore how the life of Jonah shares some characteristics with "Peter son of Jonah" and Paul in their mission to reconcile the nations to Christ. First the familiar typology of Christ:

Jonah a type of Christ

- Both preached a message of repentance.
- Both appeared alive after three days or from "Sheol."
- Jonah gave Nineveh 40 days of testing to repent. Jesus gave Israel and the nations 40 years.
- Jonah's mission granted Gentiles salvation, while later bringing judgment upon unrepentant Israel. Jesus' mission through the apostles brought salvation to the Gentiles while later bringing judgment upon unrepentant OC Israel in AD 70.
- Jonah offered a willing substitutionary death (his life for the sailors), while Jesus offered a willing substitutionary death for the Church, those whom He calls in faith to follow Him.

In Acts 2, Peter preached to Jews gathered "from every nation under heaven." After 3,000 were converted, they returned back to those "nations" with the gospel and shared it with others. Paul then traveled to these same nations and further preached and *established* the gospel and churches in those nations.

*Jonah and "Peter **son of Jonah**"*

- The Bible records the sin and pride of both men.
- Jonah and Peter faced a crisis during a storm.
- And, for our main purpose here, both Jonah and Peter were first to cross Jew/Gentile boundaries.
- Jonah fled from Joppa to Tarshish in order to flee from going to the Gentiles, while Peter was commissioned to go to Joppa and raise Dorcas and then commissioned back to Joppa to preach and give the Holy Spirit to Cornelius in Acts 9-11.

Jonah and Paul:

- Both were heading to Spain. Jonah fled to Tarshish (in Spain), which was the end of the world in the ancient world (Jonah 1:3) and Paul wanted to go to Spain/Tarshish, with tradition teaching that he did (cf. Rom 15:24, 28).
- Both sailed on the Mediterranean. Jonah boarded a ship on the Mediterranean to get away from the Lord's calling (cf. Jonah 1:3) and Paul was led by the Spirit to sail on the Mediterranean to fulfill his calling (cf. Acts 27:1).

- Both experienced a great storm on the sea (cf. John 1:4; Acts 27:13-14).
- Both crews threw cargo overboard to lighten the ship (cf. Jonah 1:4; Acts 27:18).
- There was a presence or absence of seeking the Lord's guidance. Jonah was exhorted by a pagan to pray, while Paul through answer to prayer assured the captain and crew (cf. Jonah 1:6; Acts 27:24).
- The miraculous sign of the great fish caused the Ninevites to be amazed and played a part in their repentance while the miraculous sign of Paul being bitten by a poisonous snake played a role in the conversion of crew members and foreigners on an island.

The Church's Great Commission today in the new covenant age, post AD 70, is found in Revelation 22:17 where the "Spirit and the Bride" invite sinners from the darkness outside the New Jerusalem to come through her gates through faith and drink the waters of eternal life.

- *"Abomination that causes desolation" or "When you see Jerusalem surrounded by armies its desolation has come near" (Mt. 24:15 / Lk. 21:20).*

Let's compare and look at how Matthew and Luke's parallel accounts fulfill "the end" of the old covenant age "war" and "desolation" of Daniel 9:26-27:

- "And after threescore and two weeks shall Messiah be cut off, but not for himself: and the people of the prince that shall come shall destroy the city and the sanctuary; and **the end** thereof shall be with a flood, and unto the end of **the war** desolations are determined." And he shall confirm the covenant with many for one week: and in the midst of the week he shall cause the sacrifice and the oblation to cease, and for the overspreading of **abominations he shall make it desolate**, even until the consummation [the end], and that determined shall be poured upon the desolate" (Dan. 9:26-27).
- "So, when you see the **abomination of desolation spoken of by the prophet Daniel, standing in the holy place** (let the reader understand), then let those who are in Judea flee to the mountains" (Mt. 24:15-16).
- "But when **you see Jerusalem surrounded by armies, then know that its desolation has come near**. Then let those who are in Judea flee to the mountains, and let those who are inside the city depart, and let not those who are out in the country enter it, for these are days of vengeance, to fulfill all that is written" (Lk. 21:20-22).

Luke's account of Daniel's "desolation" differs slightly from Matthew's. Matthew adds *"abomination"* with "desolation" and "when you see the abomination of desolation spoken of by the prophet Daniel, *standing in the holy place…*," whereas Luke's account only mentions "desolation" and replaces "standing in the holy place" with "seeing Jerusalem surrounded by armies." When we first read "holy place" we are tempted to think this is taking place in the temple itself. But as John L. Bray points out,

> "…in the Apocrypha (inter-biblical writings) "the holy place" meant the whole area of the "holy land." In 2 Maccabees 2 it said, "As he promised in the law, will shortly have mercy upon us, and gather us together out of every land under heaven into the holy place." This included the city and the temple, all of which were looked on as "holy." The land was called "holy" (2 Maccabees 1:7), and the city was called holy (2 Maccabees 3:1).
>
> Meyer's Commentary on the New Testament, on Matthew 24:15 says, "Others, and among them de Wette and Baumgarten-Crusius (comp. Weiss on Mark), understand the words as referring to Palestine, especially to the neighborhood of Jerusalem (Schott, Wiesler), or to the Mount of Olives (Bengel), because it is supposed that it would have been too late to seek escape after the temple had been captured, and so the flight of the Christians to Pella took place as soon as the war began" (Meyer, vol. 1, 414-415).
>
> By standing in the holy place, or where it ought not, needs not to be understood the temple only, but Jerusalem also, and, any part of the land of Israel (Lardner, 49)."[105]

Godet agrees but adds the observation that the slight difference is for Luke's primarily Gentile audience:

> "The sign indicated by Luke is the investment of Jerusalem by a hostile army. We see nothing to hinder us from regarding this sign as identical in sense with that announced by Matthew and Mark in Daniel's words (in the LXX.): *the abomination of desolation standing in the holy place*. Why not understand thereby the Gentile standards planted on the sacred soil which surrounds the holy city? Luke has substituted for the obscure prophetic expression a term more intelligible to Gentiles."[106]

Now it is much easier to harmonize Matthew and Luke's account of Daniel's abomination that causes or brings about desolation which is connected to the end time war with armies surrounding Jerusalem. Let me harmonize and summarize:

> "when you [the disciples and first century Christians] see the abomination of [the Gentile Roman] armies surrounding and standing in/on the holy place of the land of Jerusalem, then know it's desolation has drawn near. Then let those who are in Judea flee to the mountains, and let those who are inside the city depart…"

- *"Great Tribulation" = "Great Distress" (Mt. 24:21 / Lk. 21:23)*

---

[105] Bray, Ibid., 58

[106] Godet, F. L. (1881). *A Commentary on the Gospel of St. Luke*, <u>A commentary on the gospel of St. Luke</u>. (E. W. Shalders & M. D. Cusin, Trans.) (Vol. 2, p. 266). New York: I. K. Funk & co.

Luke's parallel account differs slightly on the great tribulation period as it does on the "abomination that causes desolation," so let's compare both and then look at the language of contemporary authors such as Josephus and the Dead Sea Scrolls:

- "For then there will be ***great tribulation***, such as has not been *from the beginning of **the world** until now, no, and never will be*" (Mt. 24:21).

- "For there will be ***great distress*** upon the earth and wrath against this people. They ***will fall by the edge of the sword and be led captive*** among all nations, and Jerusalem will be trampled underfoot by the Gentiles, until the times of the Gentiles are fulfilled" (Lk. 21:23-24).

- "Now this vast multitude is indeed collected out of remote places, but the entire nation was now shut up by fate as in prison, and the Roman army encompassed the city when it was crowded with inhabitants. Accordingly, *the multitude of those that therein perished **exceeded all the destructions that either men or God ever brought upon the world***; for, to speak only of what was publicly known, **the Romans slew some of them, some they carried captives**,…[107]

- And it shall be a ***time of distress***…their afflictions there will have been ***nothing to equal it from its beginning until its end***…"[108]

Matthew writes "great tribulation [Greek *thlipsis*]" while Luke writes "great distress [Greek *ananke*]." This is easy to harmonize since The Abbott-Smith Lexicon lists the two as *synonyms*.

Both Matthew and Luke's accounts begin with "For…" which inseparably connects the tribulation/distress with their versions of the "desolation" of Jerusalem and her temple, along with the same exhortation to flee from Judea to the mountains (Mt. 24:16-21; Lk. 21:21-24). This is the same historical flight the Christians obeyed when they saw the Roman armies surrounding Jerusalem and fled to Pella to escape God's covenantal wrath upon Jerusalem. History records the Romans under Cestius Gallus initially surrounding Jerusalem and then mysteriously retreating only to come back later under Vespasian and Titus. In between these two periods the Christians escaped Jerusalem to Pella.

Josephus records that "many of the most eminent of the Jews swam away from the city."[109] Similarly, the ecclesiastical historian Eusebius writes,

> "The whole body, however, of the Church at Jerusalem, having been commanded by a divine revelation, given to men of approved piety there before the war, removed from the city, and dwelt at a certain town beyond the Jordan,

---

[107] *Josephus The Complete Works*, Chapter 9:4, https://ccel.org/ccel/josephus/complete/complete.iii.vii.ix.html

[108] *1QM 1:11-12*

[109] *Jewish War* 2, 20, 1

called Pella. Here those that believed in Christ, having removed from Jerusalem, as if holy men had entirely abandoned the royal city itself, and the whole land of Judea; the divine justice, for their crimes against Christ and his Apostles finally overtook them, totally destroying the whole generation of these evildoers form the earth."[110]

Luke also adds that the desolation and tribulation period would be God's "wrath" upon "this people" (Jews) in their local "land" (not the globe!). This is the same "wrath" that John the Baptist told the Pharisees was "about to" be unleashed upon them in their lifetimes (Mt. 3:7, 10-12 GNT).

Matthew, addressing a Jewish audience, adds some commonly known Hebraic hyperbole: "…such as has not been *from the beginning of the world until now, no, and never will be*" (Mt. 24:21).

Compare this language with:

- "Behold, I now do according to your word. Behold, I give you a wise and discerning mind, so that *none like you [Solomon] has been before you and none like you shall arise after you."* (1 Kings 3:12)

- He [Hezekiah] trusted in the LORD, the God of Israel, so that *there was none like him among all the kings of Judah after him, nor among those who were before him* (2 Kings 18:5).

- "Before him [Josiah] there was *no king like him*, who turned to the LORD with all his heart and with all his soul and with all his might, according to all the Law of Moses, *nor did any like him arise after him*" (2 Kings 23:25).

Is there a contradiction in the Bible as to which king was the greatest in Israel and or had the most loyal heart for God – Solomon, Hezekiah or Josiah? Or is this common Hebraic hyperbole to stress that these three kings were great within the history of Israel and loyal to God? The latter is obviously the case.

And even more applicable is the common Hebraic hyperbole connected with historical judgments upon Jerusalem such as:

"And because of all your abominations I will do with you what *I have never yet done, and the like of which I will never do again*" (Ezek. 5:9).

This was referring to the "Day of the Lord" that was "near" in Ezekiel's day when God came through Nebuchadnezzar's armies (cf. 2 Kings 25; Ezek. 7:7; 33:21) to judge Jerusalem around 586 BC. This historical judgment by the Babylonians can help us understand the Olivet Discourse:

1). The "Day of the Lord" judgment was manifested through an invading Gentile army (Babylonians).

---

[110] Eusebius, *History of the Church 3, 5*

2). These historical judgments were described as God figuratively coming on the clouds (cf. Ezek. 30-32).

3). There was the darkening of the heavens, sun, moon and stars or de-creation type language (Ezek. 32:7-8).

4). The language of imminence concerning this judgment being "near" and "without delay" is interpreted literally in relationship to the lifetime of the prophet and his contemporaries (Ezek. 7:7ff. 12:25; 30:3).

5). *The prophet uses common Hebraic hyperbole; this judgment was the worst in relation to Israel's past and future (Ezek. 5:9).*

This fits perfectly with Jesus' teaching in the Olivet Discourse:

1). The judgment "Day" of the Lord would be manifested through an invading Gentile army (Romans).

2). This historical judgment was described as Christ figuratively coming upon the clouds.

3). The sun and moon would not give their light (de-creation language).

4). The language of imminence, such as "near" and "this generation," is to be interpreted literally and referring to the fulfillment being within the lifetimes of the prophet's contemporary audience.

5). *The prophet uses common Hebraic hyperbole (this judgment was the worst in relation to Israel's past and future).*

- *"They will fall by the edge of the sword and be led captive among all nations" (Lk. 21:24)*

Luke's description also depicts the Jews falling by the sword of the Romans and being led captive. Adam Clarke gives a good description of this fulfillment as documented by John Bray,

> "The number of those who fell by the sword was very great. Eleven hundred thousand perished during the siege. Many were slain at other places, and other times... Besides those many of every age, sex, and condition were slain in the war, who are not reckoned, but, of those who are reckoned, the number would have appeared incredible, if their own historian had not so particularly enumerated them. See Josephus, WAR, book li. C. 18,20; book iii. c. 2,7,8,9; book iv. c. 1,2,7,8,9; book vii. c. 6,9,11; and Bp. Newton, Vol. li. P. 288-290.
>
> Many were also led away captives into all nations. There were taken at Jotapa, 1,200. At Tarichea, 6,000 chosen young men, who were sent to Nero; others sold to the number of 39,400, besides those who were given to Agrippa. Of the Gadarenes were taken 2,200. In Idumea above 1,000. Many besides these were taken in Jerusalem; so that, as Josephus says, the number of the captives taken in the whole war amounted to 97,000. Those above seventeen years of age were sent to the works in Egypt, but most were distributed through the Roman

provinces, to be destroyed in their theatres by the sword, and by the wide beasts; and those under seventeen years of age were sold for slaves."[111]

- *"...and **Jerusalem will be trampled underfoot by the Gentiles**, until the times of the Gentiles are fulfilled." (Lk. 21:24)*

Pat Robertson interprets the "times of the Gentiles" as a sign that took place in 1967, marking out 40 years until the rapture must take place, i.e. 2007. Oops!

> "The year 586 B.C. was the time that Nebuchadnezzar took over Jerusalem, and that condition lasted…until the Six Day War that took place not too long ago. When did it happen? 1967. …The Jews took over Jerusalem for the first time since Nebuchadnezzar took it. What is the significance of all this? …At this point of time, a clock began to tick. A generation is 40 years, and a clock began to tick that said there's 40 years from 1967."[112]

Here are some passages that will help us understand what Jesus means by the "times of the Gentiles" and "treading underfoot Jerusalem":

- "The Lord has rejected all my strong men in my midst; He has called an **appointed time** against me to crush my young men; the Lord has **trodden as in a wine press the virgin daughter [Jerusalem] of Judah**" (Lam. 1:15). [The Jewish Targum adds, 'established a time to shatter…defile the virgins of the House of Judah until their blood…was caused to flow like wine from a wine press when a man is treading grapes and grape-wine flows.']

- "But do not measure the court outside the temple; leave that out, for it is given over to the nations (Gentiles), and they will **trample** the **holy city** (Jerusalem) **for forty-two months** (3 ½ yrs.)" (Rev. 11:2).

- "…the one who had the sharp sickle said, 'Put in your sickle and gather the clusters from the vine of the earth, for its grapes are ripe.' So the angel swung his sickle across the earth and gathered the grape harvest of the earth and threw it into the great winepress of the wrath of God. And the winepress was trodden outside the city, and blood flowed from the winepress, as high as a horse's bridle, for 1,600 stadia" (Rev. 14:18-20).

Lamentations 1:15 [and the Targum referred to] is looking back at a past event [Babylon's military desolation of Jerusalem in 586/587BC] as an "appointed time" when the Lord had "trodden" down Jerusalem like grapes crushed in a winepress in which her blood flowed and she was "shattered." This is talking about a very specific and limited time of military treading down of the city, not a protracted period of hundreds of years. Babylon surrounded Jerusalem and the military campaign of treading her down lasted roughly 2-3 years (from 589 BC to 586/587BC).

---

[111] Bray, Ibid., 91-92

[112] Don K. Preston, *The Times of the Gentiles? Past-Present-Or What?* https://donkpreston.com/the-times-of-the-gentiles-past-present-or-what/

Revelation 11 and Daniel 12 describe the trampling of Jerusalem by Rome (the 4th Gentile Empire in Dan. 2 and 7) as a period of 3 ½ years which would be a "*complete shattering* of the holy people." Therefore, when we compare Scripture with Scripture and honor this event to take place when Jerusalem would be "surrounded by armies" in Jesus' contemporary generation, the 3 ½ year war (Dan. 9:26-27/12:7) between AD 67 – AD 70 is what Jesus prophesied about – nothing else, not 1967 nor any other event!

Revelation 14:18-20 confirms the treading down of Israel's land in a winepress with her blood flowing throughout the exact dimensions of the land of Israel. As John Gill points out these would be the known dimensions of the land of Palestine:

> "…the measure of the land of Israel, and the common notion of it among the Jews, who make it to be the square of four hundred parsoe: hence they often speak of the land of Israel shaking and moving four hundred "parsoe", upon some extraordinary occasions; and a "parsa" contained four miles, so that four hundred "parsoe" made a thousand and six hundred miles; and if miles and furlongs are the same, in which sense only the land of Israel could be so large, here is the exact space; for Jerom, who was an inhabitant of it, says, it was scarce ***160 miles in length, to which agrees R. Menachem; and it may be observed, that the Arabic version renders the words, "by the space of a thousand and six hundred miles."***[113]

- *"These are the days of vengeance to **fulfill all that is written**" (Lk. 21:22)*

Some of our Partial Preterist Reformed opponents have attempted to argue that Jesus is only referring to "all" OT prophecies concerning the fall of Jerusalem and not His Second Coming, end of the age, resurrection, etc…. They appeal to Luke 18:31, where Jesus says that when He and His disciples go up to Jerusalem (in about AD 30), "*all things that are written by the prophets concerning the Son of Man will be accomplished.*" They argue that since the Second Coming did not occur at that time, it follows that when Jesus says in Luke 21:22 that "*all things written*" will be fulfilled when Jerusalem is destroyed in AD 70, He is referring only to prophetic predictions that concerned the destruction of Jerusalem and not to all eschatological prophecy in general.

Of course, no one disagrees with the observation that the context of Luke 18:31 limits "all things written" to prophetic material pertaining to Jesus' passion. But Partial Preterists assume what they need to prove when they assume that Christ's coming in Luke 21:27-28 was only "a" coming and was not the "actual Second Coming" which fulfills all prophecy in general. Reformed Partial Preterists, such as Keith A. Mathison and Gary DeMar, are having a hard time convincing anyone that Christ's coming in the Olivet Discourse is not His Second Coming event.

---

[113] John Gill, *John Gill's Exposition of the Whole Bible*, Ibid., free online at biblehub.com

Luke here also varies from Matthew's account in that he adds that the events of AD 67 – AD 70 would be the fulfillment of "all that is written" in the OT, while Matthew teaches the abomination of desolation is the fulfillment of Daniel 9:24-27 and Daniel 12:1-7. These are easily harmonized since these two sections of Daniel encapsulate in a nutshell pretty much all of the end of the age eschatological events predicted in the rest of the OT:

Daniel 9:24-27	Daniel 12:1-12	Matthew 24/Luke 21
1). Abomination that causes desolation (9:27).	1). Great Tribulation & Abomination of Desolation (12:1,2).	1). Great Tribulation & Abomination of Desolation (Mt. 24:15, 21/Lk. 21:20-23)
2). Judgment upon the Jews and city & atonement made (9:24, 26-27)	2). Judgment & Deliverance (12:1).	2). Judgment & Deliverance (Mt. 24:13/Lk. 21:18-22, 28).
3). Bring in everlasting righteousness & fulfill all OT vision and prophecy (9:24 - i.e. Isa. 25:6-9; Hos. 13).	3). Resurrection & Evangelism (12:2-3).	3). Resurrection, Evangelism & fulfill "all" OT prophecy (Mt. 13:39-43; Mt. 24:30-31; Lk. 21:22-32).
4). "**The end** will come like a flood" (9:26, 27).	4). "**The end**" or end of the old covenant age (Dan. 12:4, 6, 8-9, 13).	4). **The end or end of the old covenant age** (Mt. 24:3, 14).
5). **When Fulfilled?** a. Using the Jewish (not Gentile) calendar, within a period of **490 years** (10 Jubilees - 49/50 year periods of time - 10 x 49 or 70 x 7 = 490) from the "word" of Jeremiah and the destruction of the first temple to the second (**420 BC – AD 70 = 490**). b. The prophecy of the 70 7's ends with the abomination of desolation, which is the main sign Jesus gives (Lk. 21:20-24/Mt. 24:15ff.).	5). **When Fulfilled?** "**All these things**" (vss. 1-7) will be fulfilled: a. **"Far off"** from Daniel b. **In a "3.5 year" time frame.** c. **"When the power (the old covenant) of the holy people (1st century Jews) is completely shattered."**	5). **When Fulfilled?** "**All these things**" (Mt. 24:34/Lk. 21:32) would be fulfilled: a. **"Near"** in the **AD 30 – AD 70 "this generation."** b. "when you see **Jerusalem surrounded by armies,**" its **"desolation" will be near** & will be the **"times of the Gentiles"** (or 3.5 yrs. – AD 67 – AD 70) when **"Jerusalem is trampled" under their feet** (cf. Lk. 21:20, 24/Rev. 11:1-2, 8ff.).

Since it is agreed upon that the book of Revelation is John's version of the Olivet Discourse and that it has more references to OT prophecies than any other NT document, is it in line with Jesus' teaching that "all that is written" in the OT would be fulfilled by AD 70?

In the book of Revelation, it is said from the beginning to the end (Rev. 1:1; 22:6–7, 10–12, 20) that the prophecy of this book (not prophecies of books) would be fulfilled "shortly." Those soon-to-be-fulfilled prophecies included the Second Coming, the resurrection of the living and the dead, the judgment, the passing of the first heavens and earth and the arrival of the new heavens and the new earth—in other words, literally "all things written."

In Revelation 10:6-7 we learn that there would be "no more delay" to the blowing of the seventh trumpet (the last trumpet) ushering in the maturing and fulfilling of the mystery of God as predicted by "His servants and the prophets." Paul identifies this "mystery" as the Jew/Gentile, one new covenant body (cf. Eph. 3), of which he proclaimed was predicted in the "prophetic writings" (or OT Scriptures). Therefore, Revelation is consistent with Jesus in Luke 21:22 in that "all" that had been written in the OT prophetic Scriptures would be imminently fulfilled by AD 70.

Paul in 1 Corinthians 10:11 is also in line with Jesus' teaching. Here he tells his first-century audience, "Now all these things happened to them as examples [types], and they were written for our admonition, upon whom the ends of the ages have come." As stated earlier, Jesus' and Paul's audience understood the phrase "this age" to be a reference to the old covenant age, and the "age to come" as a reference to the Messianic or new covenant age. They also understood that under the umbrella of the old covenant "age" (singular) there were various "ages" (plural), or covenants. The covenant that God made with David is an example of this and yet being within the promises of the old covenant age. Thus, when the old covenant age was consummated, it was then that all of Israel's "ages," as contained in "the Law and the Prophets" ("all things written"), were consummated.

Peter's eschatology is in line with that of Jesus, John, and Paul. Per Peter, his contemporaries were living in Israel's "last days", "crooked and perverse generation" that Moses said would witness the "near" end of Israel, and that is why Peter said, "the end of all things is near" (Deut. 32=Acts 2:40=1 Pet. 4:5-7; 2 Pet. 3). Peter is very clear in telling his contemporaries that all the OT prophets spoke of a fulfillment and eschatological "inheritance" which was "ready to be revealed" for them at an "at hand" resurrection and judgment event (1 Peter 1:4-12; 4:5-7, 17).

What about a Double Fulfillment of the Olivet Discourse?

I think everyone agrees that many prophecies in the Old Testament were typologically fulfilled and awaited full realization in the New Testament. This phenomenon reflected the contrast between Old Testament types and shadows, and the New Testament anti-type or body, i.e., Christ (Col. 2:17).

But this principle in no way implies or leads to the notion that New Testament prophecies, which are fulfilled in Christ, will be fulfilled multiple times over potentially millions of years of time. The fact that the Old Testament was "typical" and "shadowy" in no way suggests that the New Testament is of the same pre-Messianic character. The cross of Christ will not be fulfilled multiple times until the end of human history, and neither will Christ's Second Coming (Heb. 9:26–28).

Ken Gentry, who is a Partial Preterist, teaches that the time texts of the New Testament "demand" a fulfillment in AD 70, and that the theory of "double fulfilling" the book of

Revelation, for example, is "pure theological assertion" that has "no exegetical warrant."[114]

Another Partial Preterist, Gary DeMar, also rejects the double fulfillment theory here in the Olivet Discourse:

> "Either the Olivet Discourse applies to a generation located in the distant future from the time the gospel writers composed the Olivet Discourse or to the generation to whom Jesus was speaking; it can't be a little bit of both. As we will see, **the interpretation of the Olivet Discourse in any of the synoptic gospels does not allow for a mixed approach, a double fulfillment, or even a future completion. Matthew 24:34 won't allow for it**."[115]

The fulfillment that has been wrought in Christ is no piecemeal fulfillment that has remained a "yes and no" fulfillment/non-fulfillment for 2,000 years, as futurists such as Mathison imagine. The Law of Moses does not remain "imposed" as it did between the Cross and the Parousia (Heb. 9:10, NASB). Rather, Christ returned, and the old covenant vanished in His presence 40 years after His cross (Heb. 8:13). If He did not return, and if the dead were not raised in Him, then the old covenant never vanished and we are still in our sins. This is the inevitable implication of denying that literally "all things written" are fulfilled in Christ today.

While I agree with the Partial Preterist comments on the Olivet Discourse and the book of Revelation not being "double fulfilled," I disagree with these men that the coming of Christ in Revelation and Matthew 24:27-31 "is not the actual Second Coming event."

NT eschatology is not new; it is the fulfillment of all that is written in the OT, and Jesus places that fulfillment to be imminently fulfilled in His contemporary generation, as do all of the other NT writers.

The OT did not prophesy that when Messiah showed up there would be two end of the age(s) connected with two cloud comings of Messiah, two last days, two judgments and resurrections of the living and dead, two de-creations / new creations, etc.

- *Apocalyptic language - "The stars shall fall from heaven" and "the Son of Man coming on the clouds" (Mt. 24:29-30)*

The first thing that we need to take note of is that the de-creation language of Matthew 24:29 is associated with the same time frame and events of the tribulation, distress, abomination, desolation, the Roman armies surrounding Jerusalem, wrath upon the Jews and the flight of the Christians from Judea to Pella – in that it says, "immediately after those days…" And the coming of the Son of Man in verse 30 begins with "then," also connecting all of these events together in the unfolding events of AD 67 – AD 70.

---

[114] Kenneth Gentry, *Four Views on the Book of Revelation*, ed. C. Marvin Pate (Grand Rapids, MI: Zondervan, 1998), 43–44.

[115] Gary DeMar, *The Olivet Discourse: The Test of Truth*, http://www.americanvision.org/blog/?p=190).

There is no gap of thousands of years between these events if we want to be honest with the language and interpret holy Scripture with integrity.

God's coming on the clouds and stars falling from heaven (de-creation language), as used elsewhere in the Bible, are metaphors or symbolic language referring to in-time historical judgments of nations, obviously not the destruction of the physical planet. This can be seen in such OT passages referring to:

1). the fall of Babylon (cf. Isa. 13:6) and Egypt (cf. Ezek. 30:2-3).

2). judgments upon Idumea, Bozrah and all the local nations of that time (cf. Isa. 34).

3). a shaking of the then known nations through Darius, king of Persia (cf. Hag. 2:6).

4). historical judgments upon Judah and Israel (cf. Isa. 13:9-10; 19:1; 34:4-5; Ezek. 32:7-8; Amos 5:21-22; Zeph. 1:7, 14; Zech. 14:1; Psalm 18; Psalm 104; Hab. 1:2ff.).

Did God come on a literal cloud when He judged Egypt by means of the Assyrians in 670 BC?

- "Behold, the **LORD rideth upon a swift cloud**, and shall come into Egypt" (Isa. 19:1).

Was the literal heaven "dissolved" and rolled back like a scroll and did literal stars fall down from heaven to earth when national Idumea (or Edom) was judged by God in the OT?

- "And **all the host of heaven shall be dissolved, and the heavens shall be rolled together as a scroll: and all their host shall fall down**, as the leaf falleth off from the vine, and as a falling *fig* from the fig tree. For my sword shall be bathed in heaven: behold, it shall come down upon Idumea, and upon the people of my curse, to judgment" (Isa. 34:4-5).

Another striking passage is found in Jeremiah 4 concerning the judgment of Jerusalem in 586 BC:

- "I looked at the **earth/land, and it was formless and empty; and at the heavens, and their light was gone**. I looked at the **mountains, and they were quaking**; all the hills were swaying. I looked, and there were no people; every bird in the sky had flown away. I looked, and the **fruitful land was a desert**; all its towns lay in ruins before the LORD, before his fierce anger. This is what the LORD says: **"The whole land will be ruined, though I will not destroy it completely**. Therefore, the **earth will mourn** and the **heavens above grow dark**, because I have spoken and will not relent, I have decided and will not turn back." At the sound of horsemen and archers every town takes to flight. Some go into the thickets; some climb up among the rocks. All the towns are deserted; no one lives in them. What are you doing, O devastated one? Why

> dress yourself in scarlet and put on jewels of gold? Why shade your eyes with paint? You adorn yourself in vain. Your lovers despise you; they seek your life. I hear a cry as of a woman in labor, a groan as of one bearing her first child— the cry of **the Daughter of Zion gasping for breath, stretching out her hands and saying, "Alas! I am fainting; my life is given over to murderers"** (Jer. 4:23-31).

Jeremiah is reaching back into Genesis 1-2 and applying that language to the de-creation of Jerusalem (as John will do in Rev. 21-22). As we pointed out before, old covenant Israel understood her land and covenant to be a "heaven" and "earth," and here they are being desolated through an in-time local judgment that sounds as if it is the destruction of the globe and/or the end of world history.

Most Evangelical Zionists are clueless that for centuries older and modern commentaries described the de-creation language and coming of Christ in Matthew 24/Luke 21/Mark 13 as common apocalyptic language that was fulfilled in the events of AD 67 – AD 70. John Bray's book, *Matthew 24 Fulfilled,* offers the most documentation of Christian commentators (past and present) that I know of. I will offer just a few examples. Bray quotes N. Nisbett on the de-creation language of Matthew 24:29:

> "[T]his language was borrowed from the ancient hieroglyphics: for as in hieroglyphic writing, the sun, moon, and stars were used to represent states and empires, kings, queens, and nobility; their eclipse and extinction, temporary disasters or overthrow, & so in like manner, the holy prophets call kings and empires by names of the heavenly luminaries; their misfortunes and overthrow are represented by eclipses and extinction; stars falling from the firmament are employed to denote the destruction of the nobility, & (Warburton's Divine Legation, vol. 2, book 4, section 4, quoted by N. Nisbett, Our Lord's Prophecies of the Destruction of Jerusalem, 22-23)."[116]

Adam Clarke, after addressing the historical judgments and apocalyptic language of Isaiah 13:9-10; Ezek. 32:7-8, goes on to address:

> "The destruction of the Jews by Antiochus Epiphanes is represented by casting down some of the host of heaven, and the stars to the ground. See Dan. Viii. 10. And this very destruction of Jerusalem is represented by the Prophet Joel, chap ii. 30, 31 by showing wonders in heaven and in earth—darkening the sun, and turning the moon into blood. This general mode of describing these judgments leaves no room to doubt the propriety of its application in the present case (Adam Clarke, commentary on Matthew 24:29)."[117]

As we have seen, the context in Matthew 23-24 is the fall of Jerusalem and the destruction of the temple. The sun, moon, and stars represented the universe of Israel

---

[116] Bray, Ibid., 136

[117] Ibid. 137

and her rulers which would fall from her covenantal significance by AD 70 for rejecting Christ and His apostles and prophets (cf. Matthew 23:31-36).

Reformed and Puritan theologian John Owen had this to say of the de-creation language in Matthew 24:29:

> "And hence it is, that when mention is made of the destruction of a state and government, it is in that language that seems to set forth the end of the world. So, Isa. 34:4; which is yet but the destruction of the state of Edom. And our Saviour Christ's prediction of the destruction of Jerusalem, Matthew 24, he sets it out by expressions of the same importance. It is evident then, that, in the prophetical idiom and manner of speech, by 'heavens' and 'earth', the civil and religious state and combination of men in the world, and the men of them, are often understood."[118]

John L. Bray correctly writes of the stars falling from the heavens in Matthew 24:29:

> "Jewish writers understood the light to mean the law; the moon, the Sanhedrin; and the stars, the Rabbis."[119]

- *"Heaven and earth will pass away"* (Mt. 24:35)

So far, we have found contextual and grammatical reasons to interpret the "end of the age" as the old covenant age (v. 3), the stars falling from the heavens in vs. 29 to be the religious and civil rulers falling from the places of power (within that old covenant age) when Jerusalem and her temple was destroyed in AD 70, but what of verse 35 which addresses the "heaven and earth" passing away? Surely that is referring to the end of planet earth, right? Once again, we must follow a contextual, grammatical and historical hermeneutic that is within the Christian church to help understand that this kind of language can also be referring to the old covenant heavens and earth and its temple.

While not a Preterist, G.K. Beale's research indicates "…that **'heaven and earth'** in the Old Testament may sometimes be a way of **referring to Jerusalem or its temple, for which 'Jerusalem' is a metonymy**."[120]

Reformed theologian John Brown, in identifying the passing of "heaven and earth" in Matthew 5:18, writes:

> "But a person at all familiar with the phraseology of the Old Testament Scriptures, knows that **the dissolution of the Mosaic economy, and the**

---

[118] Owen, Ibid., 134

[119] Bray, Ibid., 125

[120] G.K. Beale, *The Temple and the Church's Mission A biblical theology of the dwelling place of God*, (Downers Grove, Illinois: Inter Varsity Press, 2004), 25

> **establishment of the Christian, is often spoken of as the removing of the old earth and heavens, and the creation of a new earth and new heavens.**"[121]

Commentators are correct to identify the "heaven and earth" (of Matthew 5:18) as the "heaven and earth" (of Matthew 24:35), but the context of both point us to the old covenant system passing away and not the planet earth. According to Jesus' teaching in Matthew 5:17-18, if heaven and earth (and all OT prophecy) have not passed away (or been fulfilled), then we are currently under all of the "jots and tittles" of the old covenant Law of Moses.

And now, specifically of the passing of heaven and earth here in our text, Evangelical Crispin H.T. Fletcher-Louis makes the following comments on Mark 13:31/Matthew 24:35:

> "The temple was far more than the point at which heaven and earth met. Rather, it was thought to correspond to, represent, or, in some sense, to be 'heaven and earth' in its totality." ". . . [T]he principal reference of "heaven and earth" is the temple centered cosmology of second-temple Judaism which included the belief that the temple is heaven and earth in microcosm. **Mark 13[:31] and Matthew 5:18 refer then to the destruction of the temple as a passing away of an old cosmology.**"[122]

Indeed, the temple was set forth as a creation of heaven and earth:

Day	Creation	Tabernacle
Day 1	Heavens are stretched out like a curtain (Ps. 104:2)	Tent (Exod.26:7)
Day 2	Firmament (Gen. 1:2)	Temple veil (Exod.26:33)
Day 3	Waters below firmament	Laver or bronze sea (Exod. 30:18)
Day 4	Lights (Gen.1:14)	Light stand (Exod. 25:31)
Day 5	Birds (Gen. 1:20)	Winged cherubim (Exod. 25:20)
Day 6	Man (Gen. 1:27)	Aaron the high priest (Exod. 28:1)
Day 7	Cessation (Gen. 2:1) Blessing (Gen. 2:3) Completion (Gen.2:2)	Cessation (Exod. 39:32) Mosaic blessing (Exod. 39:43) Completion (Exod. 39:43)[123]

---

[121] John Brown, *Discourses and Sayings of Our Lord* (Edinburg: The Banner of Truth Trust, 1990 [1852]), 1:170

[122] Crispin H.T. Fletcher-Louis a contributing author in, *ESCHATOLOGY in Bible & Theology Evangelical Essays at the Dawn of a New Millennium*, (Downers Grove, Illinois: Inter Varsity Press, 1997), 157

[123] See also, J.V. Fesko, *Last things first Unlocking Genesis 1-3 with the Christ of Eschatology*, (Scotland, UK, 2007), 70.

Neither Jesus nor any NT writer ever predicted the end of the planet earth or world history as is simply assumed by so many here in Matthew 24:3, 29, 35 and elsewhere in the NT.

When we take a combined look at some of the best theologians within the Reformed and Evangelical communities, we find a Full Preterist interpretation of virtually every eschatological de-creation prophecy in the Bible. Combined, John Owen, John Locke, John Lightfoot, John Brown, R.C. Sproul, Gary DeMar, Kenneth Gentry, James Jordan, Peter Leithart, Keith Mathison, Crispin H.T. Fletcher-Louis, Hank Hanegraaff, and N.T. Wright (to name just a few) teach that the passing away of heaven and earth (cf. Matt. 5:17–18; 24:3, 29, 35; 1 Cor. 7:31; II Peter 3; I Jn. 2:17–18; Rev. 21:1) refers to the destruction of the temple or to the civil and religious worlds of men—either Jews or Gentiles; and that the rulers of the old covenant system or world, along with the temple, were the "sun, moon, and stars," which made up the "heaven and earth" of the world that perished in AD 70. See the following works:

> John Owen, *The Works of John Owen*, 16 vols. (London: The Banner of Truth Trust, 1965–68), 9:134–135. John Lightfoot, *Commentary on the New Testament from the Talmud and Hebraica: Matthew – 1 Corinthians, 4 vols.* (Peabody, MA: Hendrickson Publishers, [1859], 1989), 3:452, 454. John Brown, *Discourses and Sayings of our Lord, 3 vols.* (Edinburgh: The Banner of Truth Trust, [1852] 1990), 1:170. John Locke, *The Clarendon Edition of the Works of John Locke: A Paraphrase and Notes on the Epistles of St Paul Volume 2*, (NY: Oxford University Press, 1987), 617–618. R.C. Sproul, *The Last Days According to Jesus* (Grand Rapids, MI: Baker Books, 1998). Kenneth Gentry, *He Shall Have Dominion* (Tyler TX: Institute for Christian Economics, 1992), 363–365. Kenneth Gentry (contributing author), *Four Views on the Book of Revelation* (Grand Rapids, Michigan: Zondervan, 1998), 89. Gary DeMar, *Last Days Madness: Obsession of the Modern Church* (Powder Springs: GA, 1999), 68–74, 141–154, 191–192. James B. Jordan, *Through New Eyes Developing a Biblical View of the World* (Brentwood, TN: Wolgemuth & Hyatt, Publishers, 1998), 269–279. Crispin H.T. Fletcher-Louis (contributing author) *Eschatology in Bible & Theology* (Downers Grove, Illinois: Inter Varsity Press, 1997), 145–169. Peter J. Leithart, *The Promise of His Appearing: An Exposition of Second Peter* (Moscow, ID: Canon Press, 2004). Keith A. Mathison, *Postmillennialism: An Eschatology of Hope* (Phillipsburg, NJ: P&R Publishing, 1999), 114, 157–158. N.T. Wright, *Jesus and the Victory of God* (Minneapolis, MN: Fortress Press, 1996), 345–346. N.T. Wright, *The Resurrection of the Son of God* (Minneapolis, MN: Fortress Press, 2003), 645, n.42. Hank Hanegraaff, *The Apocalypse Code* (Nashville, TN: Thomas Nelson Publishers, 2007), 84–86.

These interpretations are, individually considered, "orthodox." Yet when Full Preterists consolidate the most defensible elements of Reformed and Evangelical eschatology, anti-Preterists unite in opposition to even some of their own stated views. The Full Preterist combines the two competing "orthodox" views on the coming of the Lord and de-creation of Jesus' teaching in Matthew 24-25 to form a consistently exegetical and historical position:

> **Major Premise – Classic Amillennial:** The coming of the Son of Man in Matthew 24-25 is the ONE second coming event and the de-creation spoken of here is the consummative end of the age event.
>
> **Minor Premise – Partial Preterist View:** But the coming of the Son of Man happened spiritually and the end of age, de-creation of verses 3, 29 and 35 are descriptive of the passing of the old covenant creation/age and the establishment the new covenant age by AD 70.
>
> **Conclusion – Full Preterist View:** Therefore, the coming of the Son of Man is the ONE Second Coming event fulfilled spiritually, with the end of the age and de-creation language spoken of in verses 3, 29, 35 being the consummative event and referring to the old covenant creation/age passing away in the events of AD 67 – AD 70, while establishing and maturing the new (Synthesis of above views – "Reformed and always reforming").

Having given an exegetical analysis and orthodox/historical evidence that the Olivet Discourse predicts the end of the old covenant age/heavens and earth, and that Christ's coming upon the clouds is common apocalyptic language of God coming through an invading army (the Romans) in the events of AD 67 – AD 70, let's dig a little deeper into the coming of Christ texts mentioned in Matthew 24:27 and verses 30-31.

- *"For as the **sunshine** comes out from the **east** and is seen even in the **west**, thus will be the coming of the Son of man" (Matthew 24:27 Aramaic English New Testament)*

Matthew 24:27 is usually interpreted by Futurists, Partial Preterists and many Full Preterists to mean Christ's coming here is as "lightning." Preterists who see Christ coming as "lighting" here describe Him coming through the means of the Roman armies to be sudden and quick like lightning, which very well may be true.[124] But there are other Partial Preterists and Full Preterists like myself who believe Jesus' Second Coming (Greek *parousia*) here is being described as the sun with its great light shining or flashing from east to west. For this reason, I have chosen the Aramaic English New Testament translation of Matthew 24:27 for its accuracy here.

I agree with Partial Preterist author Steve Gregg who points out that translators have done us a disservice on this text:

> "The word "lightning" is the Greek *astrape*. This word is in fact, the correct term for lightning, but this is not always its meaning. When defined in the lexicons, *astrape* is said to mean either "lightning" or, more generally, "bright shining." It is in this latter sense that the word is used in Luke 11:36—"If then

---

[124] Bray, Ibid., pp. 120-128

> your whole body is full of light, having no part dark, the whole body will be full of light, as when the bright shining [*astrape*] of a lamp gives you light.
>
> Interestingly, the same translators who rendered *astrape* as "lightning," in Matthew 24:27, quite reasonably chose to translate the same word as "bright shining," in Luke 11:36, where it refers to the brightness radiating from a light source. But what prevented them from translating the word this way in Matthew 24:27? Would it not present a very different image if Jesus were to have said, "For as the bright shining comes from the east and flashes to the west, so also will the coming of the Son of Man be"? Instead of a lightning bolt, this would clearly be comparing His coming to a glorious sunrise!"
>
> If one should arise before the dawn and watch the eastern horizon, the sky will be observed to change from nearly black to a lighter blue. On the edge of the horizon a ribbon of red-orange will gradually appear, and the whole sky will become progressively lighter and lighter, nearly like daytime even before the upper rim of the sun is visible. Within seconds, the sun will fully present itself, and the dawning of the day is complete."[125]
>
> "...the Kingdom's glory will increase more and more until the moment Jesus appears..."[126]

Christ's *Parousia* (presence) here and the Greek word associated with it, *astrape*, is making reference to Christ's presence and kingdom being manifested "within the hearts" of His people in AD 70 using the illustration of the sun's rays shining "from east and flashing to the west" (see my exegesis of Luke 17:20-37 later on).

And it seems to me that there may be a *contrast* being made between the false prophets and Messiah's hiding in a **dark secretive** "inner room" of the temple in the previous verse, with Christ being **revealed openly and dramatically as the sun and daylight itself is**.

Christ's salvation manifested in both His first and Second Coming events are referred to as Him coming as the "sun," associated with the "day" bringing "healing," or as the "morning star dawning" as His Word and presence within the hearts of His people:

- "But for you who fear my name, the **Sun of righteousness shall rise** with healing in its wings" (Mal. 4:2).

- And you, child, will be called the prophet of the Most High; or you will go before the Lord to prepare his ways, to give knowledge of salvation to his people in the forgiveness of their sins, because of the tender mercy of our God, whereby **the sunrise shall visit us from on high to give light to those who sit**

---

[125] Steve Gregg, *EMPIRE of the RISEN SON A TREATISE ON THE KINGDOM OF GOD—WHAT IT IS AND WHY IT MATTERS BOOK ONE: THERE IS ANOTHER KING*, Maitland, FL: 2020), 388-389
[126] Ibid., 389

in darkness and in the shadow of death, to guide our feet into the way of peace" (Lk. 1:78-79).

- "Besides this you know the time, that the hour has come for you to wake from sleep. For salvation is nearer to us now than when we first believed. The **night is far gone; the day is at hand**" (Rms. 13:11-12).

- "…as a **light that shines** in a dark place, until the **day dawns** and the *morning star rises* **in your hearts**" (2 Pet. 1:19).

- "…I will give Him **the morning star**" (Rev. 2:28).

- "**I am the bright and morning star**" (Rev. 22:16).

Malachi 3:1—4:1-6:

- "Behold, I send my messenger (John as Elijah), and he will prepare the way before me (Christ). And the Lord whom you seek **will suddenly come to his temple** (in judgment – at Christ's Second Coming); and the messenger of the [New] covenant (Christ) in whom you delight, behold, **he is coming**, says the Lord of hosts. But **who can endure the day of his coming**, and who can stand when he appears? For he is like a **refiner's fire**…"

- "For behold, **the day is coming, burning like an oven**, when all the arrogant and all evildoers will be stubble. The day that is coming shall **set them ablaze**, says the Lord of hosts, so that it will leave them neither root nor branch. But for you who fear my name, **the SUN of Righteous-ness shall rise with healing in its rays/wings**. You shall go out … leaping like calves from the stall… Behold, I will send you Elijah (John) the prophet before **the great and awesome day of the Lord comes**. And he will turn the hearts of fathers to their children and the hearts of children to their fathers, lest I come and strike the land with a decree of utter destruction."

Malachi 3-4 predicts TWO messengers: 1) John being the eschatological Elijah preparing the way for 2) the Second Coming of Jesus as the Messiah fulfilling and bringing to maturity the new covenant promises.

"The day" that is "coming" is the Second Coming which is described here not only as "the great and awesome day of the Lord," but also as the "Sun of Righteousness" "rising" or manifesting Himself with healing rays for the righteous and yet burning the unrepentant.

Ellicott's has some helpful comments:

"The fathers and early commentators have understood Christ by the Sun of Righteousness, and they are so far right that it is the period of His advent that is referred to… As the rising sun diffuses light and heat, so that all that is healthy in nature revives and lifts up its head, while plants that have no depth of root are scorched up and wither away, so the advent of the reign of righteousness, which will reward the good and the wicked, each according to his deserts..."[127]

John Gill writes,

"...Christ: and thus it is interpreted of him by the **ancient Jews**, in one of their Midrashes or expositions (a); they say... until **the Messiah comes**, as it is said, "unto you that fear my name shall the sun of righteousness arise," and **Philo the Jew (b) not only observes, that God, figuratively speaking, is the sun; but the divine "Logos" or Word of God, the image of the heavenly Being, is called the sun**; who, coming to our earthly system, helps the kindred and followers of virtue, and affords ample refuge and salvation to them; referring, as it seems; to this passage: indeed, they generally interpret it of the sun, literally taken, which they suppose, at the end of the world, will have different effects on good and bad men; they say (c), "in the world to come, God will bring the sun out of its sheath, and burn the wicked; they will be judged by it, and the righteous will be healed by it:"[128]

John Lightfoot sees the connection with John as the fulfillment of Elijah and the "wrath" of God coming in Matthew 3:7ff. and Malachi 4 as Christ coming spiritually in the destruction of Jerusalem in AD 70:

"...To fly from the wrath to come.] These words respect the very last words of the Old Testament, "lest I smite the earth with a curse," Mal. 4:[6]; and denote the most miserable destruction of the nation, and now almost ready to fall upon them."[129]

Adam Clarke is most helpful and the clearest that Malachi 4:2 is Christ's spiritual coming in the events of AD 67 – AD 70:

"Malachi 4:1: Behold, the day cometh, that shall burn as an oven – **The destruction of Jerusalem by the Romans**. And all the proud – This is in reference to Mal 3:15 of the preceding chapter. The day that cometh shall burn them up – Either by famine, by sword, or by captivity. All those rebels shall be destroyed. It shall leave them neither root nor branch – A proverbial expression for total destruction. Neither man nor child shall escape.

Malachi 4:2: You that fear my name – The persons mentioned in the sixteenth verse of the preceding chapter, ye that look for redemption through the Messiah. **The Sun of righteousness – The Lord Jesus, the promised Messiah; the Hope of Israel. With healing in his wings – As the sun, by the rays of light and heat, revives, cheers, and fructifies the whole creation, giving, through**

---

[127] *Ellicott's Commentary for English Readers*, https://www.studylight.org/commentaries/ebc/malachi-4.html

[128] *John Gill's Exposition*, https://biblehub.com/commentaries/gill/malachi/4.htm

[129] Lightfoot, J. (2010). *A Commentary on the New Testament from the Talmud and Hebraica, Matthew-1 Corinthians, Matthew-Mark* (Vol. 2, p. 78). Bellingham, WA: Logos Bible Software.

> **God, light and life everywhere; so Jesus Christ, by the influences of his grace and Spirit, shall quicken, awaken, enlighten, warm, invigorate heal, purify, and refine every soul that believes in him, and, by his wings or rays, diffuse these blessings from one end of heaven to another; everywhere invigorating the seeds of righteousness, and withering and drying up the seeds of sin. The rays of this Sun are the truths of his Gospel, and the influences of his Spirit. And at present these are universally diffused.**
>
> And ye shall go forth – **Ye who believe on his name shall go forth out of Jerusalem when the Romans shall come up against it. After Cestius Gallus had blockaded the city for some days, he suddenly raised the siege. The Christians who were then in it, knowing, by seeing Jerusalem encompassed with armies, that the day of its destruction was come, when their Lord commanded them to flee into the mountains, took this opportunity to escape from Jerusalem, and go to Pella, in Coelesyria; so that no Christian life fell in the siege and destruction of this city."**[130]

So, we learn from the ancient Jewish commentators and Christian commentators that Christ coming as the "Sun of Righteousness" in Malachi 4:2 is:

1). understood to be *Messianic*

2). the *Second Coming event*

3). *Christ coming spiritually in salvation for the Christians (an inner spiritual infusion of imputed righteousness) while at the same time a physical salvation or flight to Pella - while being a judgment of fire burning up the wicked and their temple in the events of AD 67 – AD 70.*

All three of these the author defends to be true and supporting the premise of this work.

The other references to Christ being the Morning Star at His Second Coming event, manifesting His inner salvation within the hearts of His people as an "inheritance ready to be revealed," or to receive His "soon" reward/presence in the New Creation at His "soon" spiritual Second Coming in AD 70, the author also fully agrees with (Rev. 2:16, 28; Rev. 22:7-16). Again, commentators are divided as to whether the coming of Christ and inheritance of Christ being the "Morning Star" was received at His spiritual "soon" coming in AD 70 or will be fulfilled at a future Second Coming event. This, of course, is not an "either or" but a "both and" Futurist dilemma which Full Preterism solves.

And, of course, the "Sun of RIGHTEOUSNESS" (Mal. 4:2) caused us to "inherit" the new covenant "world of RIGHTEOUSNESS" when He fully arose in the hearts of His people – described as the "salvation of the soul" (1 Pet. 1:4-12/4:5-7; 2 Pet. 1:19/2 Pet. 3).

Paul likewise taught that Christ's Second Coming being "at hand" was the "Day" light and life for Christians in the new covenant age looking to AD 70, while the "night" of

---

[130] Adam Clark, *Commentary on the Bible* [1831], free online at: biblehub.com

the old covenant age was passing away had to do with the "salvation" of inner forgiveness and not the transformation of physical bodies at the end of world history (Rom. 11:26-27/13:11-12).

Here in our text (Mt. 24:27), the *Enhanced Strong's Lexicon* gives *astrape* the meaning of a "bright light," so the question arises as to what great light Jesus is referring to – lightning or the sun? The Greek word for "shine" is *phaino,* which according to the *Greek English Online Bible Greek Lexicon* can mean "of growing vegetation, to come to light." Well, is there a "bright light" that causes "vegetation to grow" that shines "from east to west"? To me the great light being the sun, and shining from the east to the west giving light and life to the Church as His garden in salvation, makes more sense than Him coming as lightning, which is, generally speaking, more north to south.

Jesus would not be revealing Himself in some **dark** inner secret room of the temple as the false Messiahs and prophets would shamefully be doing, for they were of the darkness, but on that **day** "*they may know **from the rising of the sun and from the west, that there is none beside me. I am the LORD, and there is none else***" (Isa. 45:6; 19-25; cf. Mal.1:1, 4:1-2, 5-6).

Perhaps a type of eternal life can be found in Joshuah10:12-14 when God listened to Joshua and the sun stood still. Every day in the new creation is a day without darkness or bearing the reproach of our sins (Isa. 60:19-20; Rev. 21:23-26). In Joshua's day this miracle was a sign to all that Jehovah was fighting for Israel. When those who are in darkness outside the gates of the city look at your life and see the joy, light, and warmth of God's presence radiating from your inner being, God uses this to cause His elect to crave this enduring light and righteousness that can only come from your Lord. This also serves to harden the reprobate, as the sun melts the wax and hardens the clay.

In Joshua's day this was a sign that the Lord was fighting for Israel, and today Christ's presence and eternal Day within His Church demonstrates that nothing will ever be able to withstand her.

As plants receive life from the sun's light and energy through photosynthesis, so the Church receives eternal life from Christ alone. In union with Christ, the Church becomes the leaves on the Tree of Life and the Light of the New Jerusalem/Creation brings healing to the nations of the world. It is the light and living waters of the gospel preached to sinners that serve as "special revelation" to a thirsty sinner's soul. No luminary lights of the physical creation can fully demonstrate the righteous ways of God! Only Christ and His Church serving as a heavenly kingdom can bring the revelation needed for sinners to be saved. Without the "Sun of Righteousness," the light and glory of God's imputed righteousness beaming in upon the heart and mind of man, all is lost. The world truly does revolve around the "Sun/Son of Righteousness."

- *"Then the sign of the Son of Man will appear in heaven, and then all the tribes of the earth will mourn, and they will see the Son of Man coming on the clouds of heaven with power and great glory. And He will send His angels with a great*

> *sound of a trumpet, and they will gather together His elect from the four winds, from one end of heaven to the other." (Mt. 24:30-31)*

Before beginning an exegesis of our text, let's first point out a similar passage where Jesus again promises that His contemporaries (the religious rulers) could live to witness Him coming upon the clouds in judgment:

> "And the high priest stood up and said, "Have you no answer to make? What is it that these men testify against you?" But Jesus remained silent. And the high priest said to him, "I adjure you by the living God, tell us if you are the Christ, the Son of God." Jesus said to him, "You have said so. But I tell you, **from now on you will see the Son of Man seated at the right hand of Power and coming on the clouds of heaven.**" Then the high priest tore his robes and said, "He has uttered blasphemy. What further witnesses do we need? You have now heard his blasphemy. *"Then, the sign, of the Son of Man in heaven"* (Mt. 26:62-64).

The above passage also supports the deity of Christ. The Jew knew that only God comes upon the clouds in judgment, and therefore Jesus was equating Himself with God. As I will demonstrate later in chapter 12, it was a Jewish view that the Son of Man coming upon the clouds in Daniel 7:13 meant He was understood to be not only the Messiah but divine. The Old Greek LXX makes the union stronger when it translates the Son of Man coming *"**as** the Ancient of Days."* So, this view of Daniel 7:13 was very present in Jesus day and the high priest was aware of it. We don't know how hostile or open he was to this interpretation, or if his main blasphemous charge came from the fact that Jesus was the one claiming to be the one mentioned in Daniel 7:13. After all, if it were true, the high priest would have to acknowledge that Messiah and possibly the divine "second power of heaven" was right all along and that his entire system was the offspring of Satan himself. Therefore, it was more convenient to go the route of charging Jesus with "blasphemy" than to be open to the view of Daniel 7:13 being a divine power of heaven.

Getting back to our text, the first thing we need to point out is that the de-creation of the preceding verse 29 begins with ***"immediately after those days*** (the distress/tribulation and wrath upon the land and their flight from Judea)..." Then verse 30 begins with ***"then"*** *– **demonstrating that all these events transpire together and there is no gap of thousands of years between them**.*

Some commentators, such as Hofman and Meyer, thought the sign here was possibly when Josephus discusses how the Jews during the AD 67 – AD 70 time-frame saw an apparition of a glorious man in the clouds above the temple while Jerusalem was under siege:

> "R. Hofman thinks that the reference is to that **apparition in the form of a man** which is alleged to have stood over the holy of holies for a whole night while

the destruction of the capital was going on (Meyer's Commentary on the New Testament, vol. 1, 423)."[131]

Sepher Yosippon (with Steven B. Bowman translating the Hebrew) writes of this event,

> "…Now it happened after this that there was seen from above the over the Holy of Holies for the whole night the **outline of a man's face, the like of whose beauty had never been seen in all the land, and his appearance was quite awesome**. Moreover, in those days were seen chariots of fire and horsemen, a great force flying across the sky near to the ground coming against Jerusalem and all Judah, all of them horses of fire and riders of fire."[132]

> "When the holiday of Shavu'oth came in those days, during the night the priests heard within the Temple something like the sound of men going and the sound of men marching in a multitude going into the Temple, and a terrible and mighty voice was heard speaking: 'Let's go and leave this House."[133]

Here is another description of the same event from another source,

> "Also, after many days a **certain figure appeared of tremendous size**, which many saw, just as the books of the Jews [Yosippon?] have disclosed, and before the setting of the sun there were suddenly seen in the clouds chariots and armed battle arrays, by which the cities of all Judaea and its territories were invaded."[134]

Others point out that the Greek of the text is not referring to a sign in the sky, but rather the destruction of the desolation of Jerusalem and the temple by the invading Roman armies is the actual sign pointing to the unseen reality of the Son of Man sitting at the right hand of the Father ruling in heaven. Keith Mathison writes,

> "The Greek text of this verse does not state that the Son of the Man will appear in the heavens. Rather, what appears is the sign of the Son of Man in heaven. In other words, the destruction of the Jerusalem will be the sign that the Son of Man, who prophesied the destruction of Jerusalem, is in heaven."[135]

Marcellus Kik similarly writes,

---

[131] Bray, Ibid., 161

[132] Sepher Yosippon, *A Mediaval History of Ancient Israel*, translated from the Hebrew by Steven B. Bowman

[133] Ibid.

[134] Pseudo-Hegesippus, online text, public domain, translated from the Latin into English by Wade Blocker, made available online by Roger Pearse in 2005. This taken from chapter 44, corresponding to pp. 391-394 in Latin critical text edited by Vincente Ussani entitled, Hegesippi qui dicitur historiae libri V, found in the Corpus Scriptorum Ecclesiasticorum Latinorum series, volume 66, Vienna: Holder-Pichler-Tempsky (1932). Special thanks to Ed Stevens for sending me these sources.

[135] Keith A. Mathison, *Postmillennialism An Eschatology of Hope*, (Phillipsburg, NJ: P&R Publishing, 1999), 114

"One must note that the verse speaks of a "sign" and not of the personal appearance of Christ Himself. If Christ had referred to his visible coming in the heavens, he would have said, "And then shall appear the Son of man in heaven." But he prophesied the appearance of a sign of the Son of Man who dwells in heaven.

To what sign did Christ have reference? This had been the question of the disciples: "Tell us, when shall these things be? And what shall be the sign of they coming, and of the end of the age?" Christ had informed them of the destruction of Jerusalem and its Temple, and when they asked, "when shall these things be?" he indicated to them the sign of his coming and the end of the pre-Messianic age. The sign of the passing away of the pre-Messianic age and the beginning of the Messianic reign was the destruction of Jerusalem and its Temple. As the old dispensation passed away, the sign would introduce the new dispensation."[136]

- *"...and then all the **tribes** of the earth/**land** will mourn,..."*

Many assume that the entire "tribe" of the globe of mankind and/or all nations of the globe therein is supposed to physically see Jesus return someday because many translations translate the Greek word *ge* as "tribes of the *earth*" instead of correctly translating it, "tribes of the *land*," as the International Standard Version and Darby Bible Translation correctly have. And *ge* can be seen as the local land of Palestine in the following texts: Matthew 2:6, 20; 27:45; Mark 15:33; Luke 4:25; 21:23; John 3:22; Acts 7:3.

The Greek word here for "tribes" is *phule* and is another clear link to the tribes of Israel in the local "land" of Palestine, which is the subject of the coming of the Son of Man in judgment - not a global event. Jesus' OT reference here is to Zechariah 12:10-12, and in that context the mourning involves the "tribe of David", "tribe of Nathan", "tribe of Levi", and "tribes of Shimeites" and are connected to a "mourning in Jerusalem." Again, the subject matter concerns the tribes of Israel not the globe.

I would agree with James Stuart Russell who pointed out when *ge* (land) and *phule* (tribes) are used together as they are here, "...its limitation to the land of Israel is obvious...restricted," and "undisputed."[137]

D.A. Carson, connecting Matthew 24:30 with Revelation 1:7, 6:15-17, points out that "most scholars" agree that the "mourning" involved here is that of "despair, not repentance."[138]

---

[136] J. Marcellus Kik, *An Eschatology of Victory* (Phillipsburg, NJ: P&R Publishing, 1971), 137-138

[137] James Stuart Russell, *The Parousia A Study of the New Testament Doctrine of Our Lord's Second Coming*, (Grand Rapids, MI: Baker Book House, third printing 1990), 77

[138] D.A. Carson, F. E. Gaebelein (Ed.), *The Expositor's Bible Commentary: Matthew, Mark, Luke, Vol. 8*, (Grand Rapids, MI: Zondervan Publishing House, 1984), 505

Since both Matthew 24:30 and Revelation 1:7 draw from and are the fulfillment of Zachariah 12:10, and both are seen to be the same eschatological event, we should give it a brief exegesis at this point.

- *"Lo, he doth come with the clouds, and see him shall every eye, **even those who did pierce him**, and wail because of him shall all the **tribes of the land**. Yes! Amen!" (Rev. 1:7 YLT DARBY).*

The immediate context tells us that the content of Revelation (thus Rev. 1:7) would be fulfilled "shortly" and within John's contemporary audience (the seven churches in Asia – Rev. 1:1).

Contextually, "every eye" that sees Him are "*even* those who did pierce him" – that is, "all the tribes of the land." So, those who "see" Him coming upon the clouds are first century Jews who by their own hands crucified Christ (Acts 2:23).

The Greek word for "see" is *horao* and has the meaning "of mental and spiritual perception *perceive, take note, recognize, find out* (AC 8.23);[139] to see with the mind, to perceive, know. **3** to see, i.e. become acquainted with by experience, to experience."[140]

We use this same sense or definition of see as to perceive or understand today. For example, "do you *see* (understand) what I'm saying?"

These first century Jews would understand and perceive that Christ was coming upon them in judgment, just as He said He would and as God had come upon the clouds judging their nation in the past (e.g. through the Babylonians, Assyrians, etc.).

Josephus records the Jews saying, "The Son cometh," as the Romans hurled 100 pound boulders over the walls to crush them.[141]

These apostate Jews knew of Christ pronouncing that they would see Him coming upon the clouds of heaven to judge them through the Roman armies and had heard the NT authors proclaim the same message. Even before they killed James in around AD 63 James once again uttered,

> "And he answered with a loud voice, Why, do ye ask me concerning Jesus, the Son of Man? He himself sitteth in heaven at the right hand of the great Power, and *is about to come upon the clouds of heaven*."[142]

The Church understood that Christ and the kingdom had "already come" in power (Mrk. 8:38—9:1) when looking back upon their deliverance from the destruction of

---

[139] Friberg, Timothy ; Friberg, Barbara ; Miller, Neva F.: *Analytical Lexicon of the Greek New Testament*. Grand Rapids, Mich. : Baker Books, 2000 (Baker's Greek New Testament Library 4), S. 284

[140] Strong, James: *The Exhaustive Concordance of the Bible : Showing Every Word of the Text of the Common English Version of the Canonical Books, and Every Occurrence of Each Word in Regular Order*. electronic ed. Ontario : Woodside Bible Fellowship., 1996, S. G3708

[141] Josephus, *The Jewish Wars*, v.vi.3

[142] Eusebius' *Ecclesiastical History*, Vol. II, ch. 23:13

Jerusalem, and the apostate Jews "saw" and understood this event to be their doom (mockery or not). In spite of knowing His predictions, they believed the false prophets' predictions until the end - that God would deliver them from the Romans and establish their earthly, carnal kingdom. They would not have Christ rule over them, so they were "slain before Him" (Lk. 19:14-27).

Jesus' OT sources for Matthew 24:30

As we have previously seen in Luke 21:22-32, Jesus states very clearly that all OT scripture would be fulfilled and brought to maturity in His contemporary "this generation." Therefore, we should look at two of those OT passages Jesus is drawing upon here in Matthew 24:30: 1) Zechariah 12 – 14 and 2) Daniel 7:13.

Zechariah 12 – 14

Note the parallel subject matter between Zechariah 12-14 and Jesus' teaching in the Olivet Discourse:

1). A gathering and siege of Jerusalem by the surrounding nations takes place (Zech. 12:2-3 = Lk. 21:20-22).

2). Judgment of the nations takes place while Jerusalem (the remnant or New Jerusalem) is saved (Zech. 12:7-9 = Lk. 21:27-28; Mt. 25:31-46).

3). They look upon Jesus whom the Jews had pierced and mourn (Zech. 12:11-12 = Mt. 24:30). The false prophets and demons are cleansed and judged from the land (Zech. 12:2-3 = Mt. 23—25:31-46).

4). In that day the Lord would prepare a way of escape for the righteous remnant (Zech. 14:4 = Lk. 21:20-22).

5). This day is only known by the LORD (Zech. 14:6 = Mt. 24:36).

6). There is always light (Zech. 14:7=Mt. 24:27/Lk. 21:30-32/Rev. 21:25; 22:5-7) —Christ comes as the Sun/Son and His light shines from east to west and is the light of the New Jerusalem that never ceases in the kingdom.

7). Living waters of salvation or redemption flow from the New Jerusalem when the King and the kingdom arrive (Zech. 14:8-9=Lk. 21:27-32/Rev. 11; 21-22:7-17).[143]

The last three eschatological fall feasts of Zechariah 12-14 (Trumpets / Ingathering / Day of Atonement) were fulfilled by AD 70. I agree with Premillennial Zionist Dr. Michael Brown that we can see the last three eschatological feasts of Israel being fulfilled between Zechariah 12-14.[144] But since these feasts are a part of the Mosaic Law (cf. Lev. 23/Cols. 2), they had to have been fulfilled by AD 70 or the Church

---

[143] For a great exegesis of Zech. 14 read David A. Green, pretcosmos.com Q&A #80
[144] Brown, *Ibid., Vol. 1*, 83-84

remains under "all" of the Mosaic Law (cf. Mt. 5:17-18) in observing its feasts, sacrifices and sabbaths – all of which formed it.

Pastor David Curtis explains these three feasts – 1) Trumpets 2) Ingathering and 3) Tabernacles:

> "There were "ten days of awe and repentance" between the Feast of Trumpets and the Day of Atonement (Israel's redemption) – which was to be in preparation for the time of judgment. During the 10 days they would prepare their hearts for the judgment when the "books were opened." But they didn't know when it would take place (the "day and hour") because the "new moon" had to be visible before the trumpet would sound and the feast to take place. The High Priest would send three witnesses on three different mountains to look for the moon to be visible emerging from the clouds so that the trumpet and atonement process could be finished for the year. **It was the ONLY feast of which it was said, "But of that day and hour knows no man**…".[145]

The Day of Atonement looks back at the sacrifice of Christ in His first coming (the first four spring feasts) but also anticipated Christ as the Church's High Priest returning a "second time" out of the temple to apply His blood and salvation to the eagerly awaiting congregation. This "Second Appearing" is described in Hebrews to take place in the last days of Israel's old covenant age, and thus "in a very little while" it would "not tarry," and thus by AD 70 (Heb. 9:26-28; 10:37).

Curtis continues explaining the Feast of Tabernacles,

> "The Feast of Tabernacles (Sukkot) is not just a harvest celebration, but the time when Solomon completed and dedicated the Temple in Jerusalem (2 Chron. 5:1-3). It took Solomon 20 years to complete the Temple (1 Kings 9:10) and when it was finished and dedicated to God, the shekinah glory filled God's House so strong that the priests could not stand to minister (2 Chron. 5:13-14).

> During Sukkot 70 bulls were sacrificed daily according to the pattern designed by King David and carried out by his son Solomon. The nations of the world are connected to the Feast of Tabernacles through Solomon's dedication of God's Temple during Sukkot with his sacrificing of 70 bulls. God had originally disinherited the seventy nations of the world in Genesis 10-11, but through Israel being a light to the Nations, they once again would be united to Messiah and He would bring them to the New Jerusalem for healing. Add to this that Zechariah 14:16-17 speaks of a time when the nations, which came against Jerusalem, go up year to year to worship the King of Kings and Lord of Hosts during the Feast of Tabernacles, else they won't receive a physical and spiritual refreshing of rain."[146]

---

[145] See David Curtis' 8-part series on the Feasts of Israel fulfilled by AD 70 https://www.bereanbible church.org/studies/series.php I highly recommend this series.

[146] Curtis, Ibid.

Some have given good evidence that Jesus was born on the first day of the Feast of Tabernacles (Jn. 1:14) and circumcised on the eighth day of Sukkot. If so, perhaps John is using the Feast of Tabernacles to be two theological bookends in describing Christ's First and Second Comings. He came from heaven to earth and "pitched his booth/tent" among us, and in AD 70 He brought His heavenly presence (kingdom of heaven) to be "within" us as His Most Holy Place / temple / city at His *Parousia* – again, during the Feast of Tabernacles when He destroyed the old covenant temple and established the new covenant in September of AD 70 (Lk. 17:20-37/Jn. 14:2-3, 23, 29; Rev. 21:16 - 22:17).

In Isaiah 2-3 and in Israel's "last days" and at the "day of the Lord," there would be a godly remnant of survivors, and the nations would begin to flow to Zion or the New Jerusalem to receive healing through the gospel. This is exactly what Zechariah 12-14, the Olivet Discourse and Revelation 21-22 teach us. In AD 70 at the trumpet call, God gathered all of His Elect Jews/Gentiles into His Kingdom and then post AD 70 the nations continue to be gathered within the New Jerusalem **to drink of the living waters** which flow from her.

If the eschatological gathering at the sound of *a trumpet* in Matthew 24:30-31, 1 Corinthians 15:52, and 1 Thessalonians 4:16-17 has not been fulfilled, then this means that the last three feasts of Israel's ceremonial laws have not been fulfilled. And if those ceremonial laws have not been fulfilled, then the Church is under "every jot and tittle" of the Mosaic Law (cf. Mt. 5:17-19). According to Colossians 2-3 and Hebrews 9-10, the ceremonial laws with their types and shadows were "about to be" fulfilled at Christ's "in a very little while and will not delay", "Second Appearing" as the High Priest finishing the atonement process and thus finishing fulfilling the last three typological feast days.

Daniel 7:13

The other OT fulfillment or echo Jesus is appealing to in His coming upon the clouds in Matthew 24:30 is Daniel 7:13. Many assume that Daniel 7:13 is the ascension event and somehow Jesus is applying it to both His ascension and His coming in AD 70. I personally believe Christ and the NT authors are following the (OG) LXX where Christ is coming "as" the Ancient of Days and not "up to" the Ancient of Days. However, for the sake of argument, let's look at other concepts that could be seen as Christ coming "up" to the Ancient of Days, not at His ascension, but connected with His *Parousia* in AD 70. Then I will present my view.

The presentation of the Son of Man to the Ancient of Days in Daniel 7:13 is perhaps a reference to Christ in His *Parousia* delivering up the kingdom ("*the saints*") to the Father ("*the Ancient of Days*") in AD 70.

"Then cometh the end, when he shall have delivered up the kingdom to God, even the Father; when he shall have put down all rule and all authority and power" (1 Cor. 15:24).

Or perhaps *"the Son of Man"* in Daniel 7:13 signifies the body of Christ (the saints, *"the fullness of Christ"*) in His Parousia (Eph. 4:13). In this view, the universal church (*"the New Man"*, *"the Son of Man"*) was presented to Christ (*"the Ancient of Days"*) and united with Him at the end of the age in His Parousia in AD 70 (2 Cor. 4:14; 11:2; Eph. 5:27; Col. 1:22, 28; Jude 1:24).

However, my preferred interpretation is similar to that of F.F. Bruce. According to the Old Greek Septuagint translation of Daniel 7:13, the Son of Man came *"as* the Ancient of Days" on the clouds of heaven, not *"to* the Ancient of Days." This translation is in harmony with verse 22, which says that it was the Ancient of Days Himself who came in judgment and gave the saints the kingdom. Also, the New Testament does not give the slightest hint that "the coming of the Son of Man" on the clouds of heaven would be fulfilled in the ascension. As Keil and Delitzsch point out, Daniel 7:13-14 is addressing Christ coming *down in the Second Coming event*:

> "…it is manifest that he could only come from heaven to earth. If the reverse is to be understood, then it ought to have been so expressed, since the coming with the clouds of heaven in opposition to the rising up of the beasts out of the sea very distinctly indicates **a coming down from heaven**. The clouds are the veil or the "chariot" on which God comes from heaven to execute judgment against His enemies; cf. Ps. 18:10f., 97:2–4; 104:3, Isa. 19:1, Nah. 1:3. **This passage forms the foundation for the declaration of Christ regarding His future coming**, which is described after Dan. 7:13 as a coming of the Son of man with, in, on the clouds of heaven; Matt. 24:30; 26:64; Mark 18:26; Rev. 1:7; 14:14."[147]

It is also important to point out that John in the book of Revelation alludes to Daniel 7:9, 13 in his description of Christ as both the Son of Man who comes on the clouds to judge those who had pierced Him (first century Jews) and as the eternal Ancient of Days in Revelation 1:7, 13-16. Again, the context concerns Christ's "soon" (Rev. 1:1) Second Coming, not His Ascension.

- *"And He will send His angels with a great sound of a **trumpet**, and they will **gather** together His elect from the four winds, from one end of heaven to the other" (Mt. 24:31).*

The Futurist system is conflicted over this passage. Some teach that the coming of Christ here was fulfilled spiritually in AD 70, while others say this could be a "thorny problem" for their creedal system in that the analogy of faith teaches us this coming of Christ is the same as that of 1 Corinthians 15 and 1 Thessalonians 4.

In the *Reformed Study Bible* edited by Postmillennial Partial Preterists R.C. Sproul and Keith Mathison, we learn this of Matt. 24:30-31:

> "But the language of Matt. 24:31 is **parallel** to passages like **13:41**; **16:27**; and **25:31 [passages which Postmillennialists such as Mathison and DeMar**

---

[147] Keil, C. F., & Delitzsch, F., *Commentary on the Old Testament.* (Peabody, MA: Hendrickson, 2002), (Daniel 7:13-14), bold emphasis MJS.

say were fulfilled in AD 70], as well as to passages such as **1 Cor. 15:52** and **1 Thess. 4:14-17**. *The passage most naturally refers to the Second Coming."*

This is more than a bit odd since R.C. Sproul and Keith Mathison believe and teach that the coming of Christ in Matthew 24:27-30 (and Mathison 25:31) was spiritually fulfilled in AD 70, and yet we learn in their own Study Bible that these passages "most naturally refer to the Second Coming"!

John Murray, appealing to the **"analogy of faith"** principle of interpretation in examining this passage, also correctly observes,

> "There is ample allusion to the sound of the trumpet and to the ministry of angels elsewhere in the New Testament in connection with Christ's advent (**1 Cor. 15:52; 1 Thess. 4:16**). Hence verse 31 can **most readily** be taken to refer to the gathering of the elect **at the resurrection**."[148]

Some Partial Preterists, while admitting that the coming of Christ in Matthew 24:30 was fulfilled spiritually in AD 70, have thought the gathering of the elect here refers to a post AD 70 evangelism, when in fact the analogy of faith principle of interpretation teaches us that this is the resurrection event to take place at the end of the old covenant age. Let's pay attention to another passage where Jesus mentions that the eschatological "gathering" and judgment which was to take place at the "end of the age" is the fulfillment of the resurrection of Daniel 12:2-3:

> "The enemy who sowed them is the devil, the harvest is the end of the age, and the reapers are the angels. Therefore, as the tares are gathered and burned in the fire, so it will be at the **end of this age**. The Son of Man will send out **His angels**, and they will **gather** out of His kingdom all things that offend, and those who practice lawlessness, and will cast them into the furnace of fire. There will be wailing and gnashing of teeth. Then the **righteous will shine forth as the sun in the kingdom** of their Father. He who has ears to hear, let him hear" (Mt. 13:39-43).

The parallels between Matthew 13 and Matthew 24, forming the fulfillment of the resurrection of Daniel 12, cannot be denied by any honest exegete of holy Scripture:

Since A (Daniel 12) is = to B (Matthew 13):		
Tribulation on national Israel as never before	12:1	13:40-42
Time of the end / end of "this" OC age separation	12:1, 4, 9, 13	13:39-41
Saints rise and shine in the eternal kingdom	12:2-3	13:43
Wicked rise to shame in eternal condemnation	12:2	13:39-42
And if B (Matthew 13) is = to C (Matthew 24-25):		
Pre-kingdom evangelism by Jesus' evangelism	13:37-38	24:14

---

[148] John Murray, *COLLECTED WRITINGS OF JOHN MURRAY 2 Systematic Theology*, (Carlisle, PA: THE BANNER OF TRUTH TRUST, 1977), 391

Tribulation on national Israel as never before	13:40-42	24:21-22
End of "this" age / end of the age separation	13:39-41	24:30-31; 25:31-41
Sons of the day / hour shine with the Son	13:43	24:27, 30-31, 36
Inheritance of and entrance into the kingdom	13:43	25:34/Luke 21:30-32
Then A (Daniel 12) is = to C (Matthew 24-25)		
Tribulation and sanctification / Great Tribulation	12:1, 10	24:21-22
Hour / day / time of the judgment (aka separation)	12:1-2, 4 (OG) LXX	24:36; 25:31-33
Fulfillment at the time of the end / end of the age / the shattering of Israel's world / power or her "heaven and earth" (the temple, etc…)	12:4, 7, 9, 13	24:3, 13-14, 28-29, 34-35
Inheritance of and entrance into the kingdom	12:2-3, 13	25:34/Luke 21:30-32
The sons of the day / hour shine with the Son of life	12:3	24:27, 30-31, 36
Kingdom age evangelism via God's shining ones	12:3	24:14, 25:29
Two or more things that are equal to another thing are also equal to each other		
Kingdom age evangelism	Dan. 12 = Mt. 13 = Mt. 24-25	
Tribulation like never before	Dan. 12 = Mt. 13 = Mt. 24-25	
Time of the end (shattering of Israel's power) / end of the old covenant age (destruction of OC Israel's temple)	Dan. 12 = Mt. 13 = Mt. 24-25	
Chosen ones raised and shine to eternal life and wicked raised to eternal condemnation / the righteous raised to shine and tares burn / sheep inherit eternal life / goats to eternal punishment	Dan. 12 = Mt. 13 = Mt. 24-25	

Premillennial Zionists claim there are two future physical resurrections, one before the thousand year millennial period and another after that period. However, Daniel and Jesus teach that there is only one judgment / resurrection / separation for both believers and unbelievers at the end of the old covenant age – in Daniel 12, Matthew 13, Matthew 24, and John 5.

Unfortunately, Pre-tribulation Zionists also believe there are two different comings or two phases of one coming separated by seven years. They give two main arguments for this.

The first "argument" is that Christ must come in a secret rapture "for" Christians separated by seven years. After this, the Second Coming is fulfilled when Christ comes "with" the Church. The "rapture" coming is for the Church while the Second Coming is for Israel to fulfill and bring God's kingdom and millennial promises for her to earth.

The second "argument" is that the Second Coming is a "sign-less" coming while the "rapture" could happen at any time. Mark Hitchcock presents this "argument":

> "The rapture is an imminent, signless event, which, from the human perspective, could occur at any moment. But in contrast, the Second Coming will be preceded by many signs (see Matthew 24:1-29). The same event cannot logically be both signless and yet portended by numerous signs. This is flatly contradictory."[149]

And, looking for support, he appeals to John MacArthur:

> "Scripture suggests that the Second Coming occurs in two stages—first the Rapture, when He comes *for* His saints and they are caught up to meet Him in the air (1 Thessalonians 4:14-17), and second, His return to earth, when He comes *with* His saints (Jude 14) to execute judgment on His enemies. Daniel's seventieth week must fall between those two events. That is the only scenario that reconciles the immanency of Christ's coming *for* His saints with the yet unfulfilled signs that signal His final glorious return *with* the saints."[150]

Early founders of Dispensational Zionist eschatology, such as John Nelson Darby and William E. Blackstone, back as early as 1925 cited Matthew 24:36-42 as arguing for the rapture, so we will add it here for their two-coming theory:

Signs mentioned, so this is the Second Coming event	No signs mentioned, so this must be the Secret "Rapture" coming of Jesus
Matthew 24:27-31	Matthew 24:36-42
Luke 17:20-37 / Luke 21:25-28	1 Thessalonians 4:13-18

It should be clear enough that the Apostle Paul is following Jesus' teaching in the Olivet Discourse, virtually almost in the same order. There is no exegetical evidence that Jesus or Paul are teaching or expecting two comings or two eschatological hopes, one for the Church and another for Israel:

If A (Matthew 24) is = B (1 Thessalonians 4-5)		
Christ returns from heaven	24:30	4:16
With voice of Arch Angel	24:31	4:16
With trumpet of God	24:31	4:16
Caught/gathered together with/to Christ	24:31	4:17
"Meet" the Lord in the clouds	24:30 & 25:6	4:17
Exact time unknown	24:36	5:1-2
Christ comes as a thief	24:43	5:2
Unbelievers caught off guard	24:37-39	5:3
Time of birth pangs	24:8	5:3

---

[149] Mark Hitchcock, *COULD THE RAPTURE HAPPEN TODAY?*, (Sisters, OR: Multnomah Publishers, 2005) 80-81

[150] Ibid., 81

Believers not deceived	24:43	5:4-5
Believers to be watchful	24:42	5:6
Exhorted to sobriety	24:49	5:7
Son/sunlight shinning from e. to w. / Sons of the Day	24:27, 36, & 38	5:4-8
And if B (1 Thessalonians 4) is = to C (1 Corinthians 15)		
The sleeping to be raised	4:13-14	15:12-18
The living to be caught/changed	4:15-17	15:51-52
Christ's coming (Greek: *Parousia*)	4:15	15:23
At the sound of the trumpet	4:16	15:52
Encouraged to stand firm	4:18	15:58
Same contemporary "we"	4:15-17	15:51-52
Then A (Matthew 24 & Parallels) is = to C (1 Corinthians 15)		
Christ to come (Greek: *parousia*)	24:27	15:23
His people to be gathered/changed	24:31	15:52
To come with the sound of a trumpet	24:31	15:52
To be "the end" (Greek *telos*, the goal)	24:3, 14	15:24
Kingdom consummation (goal reached)	Luke 21:30-32	15:24
All prophecy fulfilled at this point	Luke 21:22	15:54-55
Victory over the Mosaic Law/temple	Mt. 24:1	15:55-56
Same contemporary "you" or "we"	Mt. 24:2ff	15:51-52
Two or More Things that are Equal to Another Thing are Also Equal to Each Other		
Matthew 24	**1 Thessalonians 4**	**1 Corinthians 15**
At His coming (24:27-31)	At His coming (4:16)	At His coming (15:23)
At the trumpet (24:31)	At the trumpet (4:16)	At the trumpet (15:52)
Dead raised, all gathered (24:31)	Dead raised (4:16)	Dead raised (15:35-44)
All living gathered (24:31)	Living caught together to Him (4:17)	Status of living changed (15:51)

First, let me address the treatment of NT "imminency" given by my former pastor and college president, John MacArthur. Sadly, MacArthur's attempt at explaining NT imminence was not only an embarrassment to the Church on an exegetical level, but it was also an embarrassment in response to liberal skeptics, Muslims and Jewish Zionists.[151]

MacArthur provided no Greek word study on the various words the NT uses for Christ's imminent "rapture" or Second Coming. He admits that Paul taught under the inspiration of the Holy Spirit that Christ could have come at any time for Paul and his contemporaries, and this is indeed what Paul was expecting for his contemporaries and thus those living in his generation.[152] Apparently it hasn't dawned on MacArthur that if Paul was inspired and believed and taught that Christ's coming would take place

---

[151] John MacArthur, THE SECOND COMING, pp. 51-68

[152] Ibid., 52

within the lifetime of some of his contemporaries, then Paul was a false prophet! Paul does not give us his *opinion* on when he thought Christ would return. He *gives us divine revelation* that Christ would come within some of the lifetimes of his contemporaries – as Jesus did (as we have seen in Mt. 10:22-23; 16:27-28; Mt. 26:62-64).

MacArthur, like many Dispensational Zionists, believes the return of Christ was just as imminent in the first century as it is today, and oddly concludes his section on an "imminence" in the NT (that isn't really imminent at all) by writing, "I suppose it is also possible that Christ could delay His coming another 2,000 years or longer."[153]

Something cannot be truly imminent and "delayed" at the same time. This of course is the *exact opposite* of the Greek and English languages and position of the Biblical testimony of Christ coming in "a very little while" and that He "would **not delay**" (Heb. 10:37).

Premillennial Zionists have a very hard time explaining how the "rapture" or the Second Coming events were truly imminent for the first century Christians since the temple had not been destroyed in AD 70 when Paul was writing, let alone another alleged "re-built" one. But perhaps we should back up even further. How could they have expected a truly imminent coming of Christ if, in the Zionist view, the gospel had not been preached throughout the entire globe? Or when Paul was writing, the Jews being scattered throughout the world, let alone being re-gathered in unbelief in 1948, hadn't even taken place or wasn't even close to being fulfilled.

Since all of these events are necessary to take place before the "rapture" or Second Coming could be fulfilled, how can MacArthur even pretend to say that the "rapture" was "imminent" and therefore Paul and his contemporaries expected it to happen? Perhaps MacArthur's explanation of NT imminence should be equivalent to what he has to say about Charismatics speaking in "tongues" today — just plain, unbiblical "gibberish." Selah.

Now let's address the two arguments concerning signs and no signs and Christ coming for the saints versus His coming with the saints.

First, there is no "contradiction" in Christ coming "with" the dead saints that He just raised out of Hades (and coming with the angels) "for" the living, whereby they would both reside in the kingdom and God's presence. The view that there is a seven-year gap between these two comings of Christ is no less heretical and unbiblical than the Partial Preterist view which sees thousands of years between two comings of Christ (one in AD 70 and another at the end of world history), or that of the Jehovah Witnesses for that matter! The idea that Jesus in the Olivet Discourse, or Paul in 1 and 2 Thessalonians (or the NT in general), teaches two different comings of Christ separated by seven or seven thousand years is nothing but pure eisegesis and created out of thin air to uphold their eschatological system.

---

[153] Ibid, 57

Secondly, both Dispensational Zionists and Partial Preterists make a distinction in Matthew 24 and Thessalonians that is not present when it comes to a "coming of Christ preceded by signs" versus another one "without signs." And to that subject we turn our attention.

Division Theories to justify two comings of Christ refuted - Signs vs. no signs & Luke 17:20-37

- *For as were the days of Noah, so will be the coming of the Son of Man. For as in those days before the flood they were eating and drinking, marrying and giving in marriage, until the day when Noah entered the ark, and they were unaware until the flood came and swept them all away, so will be the coming of the Son of Man. Then two men will be in the field; one will be taken and one left. Two women will be grinding at the mill; one will be taken and one left. Therefore, stay awake, for you do not know on what day your Lord is coming. But know this, that if the master of the house had known in what part of the night the thief was coming, he would have stayed awake and would not have let his house be broken into. Therefore, you also must be ready, for the Son of Man is coming at an hour you do not expect. "Who then is the faithful and wise servant, whom his master has set over his household, to give them their food at the proper time? Blessed is that servant whom his master will find so doing when he comes. Truly, I say to you, he will set him over all his possessions. But if that wicked servant says to himself, 'My master is delayed,' and begins to beat his fellow servants and eats and drinks with drunkards, the master of that servant will come on a day when he does not expect him and at an hour he does not know and will cut him in pieces and put him with the hypocrites. In that place there will be weeping and gnashing of teeth" (Matthew 24:37-51).*

Let's review the Zionist Pre-tribulationalist and Partial Preterist "arguments" that this section allegedly proves two different comings of Christ.

A Dispensational Zionist view:

Signs mentioned, so this is the Second Coming Event	No signs mentioned, so this must be the Secret "Rapture" coming of Jesus
Matthew 24:27-31	Matthew 24:36-42
Luke 17:20-37 / Luke 21:25-28	1 Thessalonians 4:13-18

A Partial Preterist view:

Signs mentioned, so this must be Christ's spiritual coming in AD 70	No signs mentioned, so this must be the future physical Second Coming
Matthew 24:3-34	Matthew 24:36ff.
Luke 17:20-37	Luke 17:20-37

It is always humorous to watch these two views attack and debate each other over the Olivet Discourse and Luke 17, and try to explain which verses are referring to AD 70, which verses are Second Coming verses, and which ones could or shouldn't be "rapture" verses distinct from Second Coming verses. What a mess! Some Dispensationalists think Matthew 24:36-42 is the Second Coming while others think it's the secret rapture. Some Partial Preterists think Luke 17:20-37 is referring to Christ coming spiritually in AD 70 while others think it's a future Second Coming event. It's like the blind leading the blind. There is no consistency and thus no real answer to the Bible skeptic, Talmudic skeptic or Muslim. But that's all changing!

Recapitulation in Matthew 24-25 Disproves the two-coming theory

Jesus is using common Hebraic or prophetic recapitulation in Matthew 24-25 concerning just ONE coming. This is even more obvious when the parallels in Luke 21 and Mark 13 are reviewed, and they are only addressing ONE coming of Christ. Are we really to believe Mark and Luke forgot to mention that Christ taught TWO different comings spanning seven years, or thousands of years per Dispensational or Partial Preterist interpretations?

Matthew's account is simply emphasizing recapitulation and adding more parables, due to his Jewish audience, when addressing the same coming of Christ and same judgment. Matthew 24 is addressing only one coming of Christ, and it was either fulfilled by AD 70 or it is a future-to-us event. While not a Preterist, John Murray correctly points out that Matthew 24 is "recapitulatory" in its structure concerning one coming and one judgment:

> "The [Olivet Discourse here in Mt. 24], **as to structure, is *recapitulatory*…**"
> "It is not, therefore, continuously progressive. We are repeatedly brought to the advent and informed of its various features, [i.e. contemporary, concurrent or interrelated events], and consequences (vss. **14, 29-31, 37-41; 25:31–46**."[154]

And is it even true that Jesus is not addressing signs in Matthew 24:36-42ff.? The truth of the matter is that when Jesus exhorts the disciples to "watch and pray" or to "be ready," this is contextually tied to His discussion of the signs the disciples asked about and of which He just covered in Matthew 24:3-30.

And if Jesus was trying to use Noah as an example of a "sign-less", "secret rapture" (per Dispensationalism) or a future Second Coming event (per Partial Preterism), wouldn't building an ark for a very long time be a sign to Noah's contemporaries?!?

There simply is no exegetical evidence that there are two different comings of Christ (a sign coming and a non-sign coming of Christ) taught by Jesus in Matthew 24-25.

---

[154] John Murray, Ibid., 398

The parallels between Matthew 24-25 and Luke 17 disprove the two comings theory

When we compare Jesus' teaching of His coming in Matthew 24 and Luke 17, it becomes even more obvious that He is not addressing two different comings, or Matthew has "two sections" to his account.

Gary DeMar is a Partial Preterist who, like me, disagrees with other Partial Preterists and Dispensational Zionists who try to make this two comings of Christ distinction of signs v. no signs argument. We disagree with Kenneth Gentry and other Partial Preterists who argue that Christ's coming in Matthew 24:27-30 is His coming in AD 70 because Jesus gives "signs," and Christ's coming in Matthew 24:36—chapter 25 is allegedly His future coming because no signs are allegedly mentioned. We also disagree with Dispensational Zionists who claim that the coming of Christ in Matthew 24:27-30 is the Second Coming event because signs are discussed while Matthew 24:36-42 is a different rapture coming due to no mention of signs. Gary writes,

> "Many futurists claim that the phrase "took them all away" (Matt. 24:39) refers to a rapture that is still in our future. On the contrary. "In the context of 24:37–39, 'taken' presumably means 'taken to judgment' (cf. Jer. 6:11 NASB, NRSV)" (Craig S. Keener, *The IVP Bible Background Commentary: New Testament* (Downers Grove, IL: InterVarsity Press, 1993), 115.) The phrase ties the judgment of the world in Noah's day with the judgment of the Jews' world in Israel's day that took place with the destruction of the city of Jerusalem and the temple.
>
> Who was taken away in the judgment of the flood? Not Noah and his family. They were "left behind" to carry on God's work. John Gill writes in his commentary on this passage: "the whole world of the ungodly, every man, woman, and child, except eight persons only; Noah and his wife, and his three sons and their wives. . . ." were taken away in judgment. And what does Gill say about those in the field? They shall be taken away "by the eagles, the Roman army, and either killed or carried captive by them." The Bible gives its own commentary on the meaning of "took them all away" in Luke 17:27, 29: "Destroyed them all" is equivalent to "took them all away."

A number of commentators (e.g., J. Marcellus Kik and Kenneth Gentry) argue that Matthew 24:35 is a "transition text." It's at this point, they argue, that Jesus is referring to a time period that is still in our future. Luke 17:22–37 describes five Olivet Discourse prophetic events that are identical to those found in Matthew 24. The difference between Matthew 24 and Luke 17 is in the order of the events, a characteristic of the passages that few commentators can explain. Ray Summers writes:

> This is a most difficult passage. The overall reference appears to be to the coming of the Son of Man—Christ—in judgment at the end of the age. Some small parts of it, however, are repeated in Luke 21 in reference to the destruction of Jerusalem (A.D. 70), and larger parts of it are in Matthew 24,

also in reference to the destruction of Jerusalem. The entire complex cautions one against dogmatism in interpreting. (Ray Summers, *Commentary on Luke: Jesus, the Universal Savior* (Waco, TX: Word Books, 1972), 202.)

Taking Matthew 24 as the standard, Luke places the Noah's ark analogy (Matt. 24:37–39) before the events of Matthew 24:17–18 ("let him who is on the housetop not go down"), verse 27 ("for just as the lightning comes from the east…"), and verse 28 ("wherever the corpse is, there the vultures will gather"). If the five prophetic events of Matthew 24 that are found in Luke 17:22–37 are numbered 1–2–3–4–5, Luke's numbering of the same events would be 2–4–1–5–3. While this is not positive proof of an A.D. 70 fulfillment for chapters 24 and 25, it certainly adds credibility to the position.

MATTHEW 24:1-41

1
"Whoever is on the housetop must not go down to get the things out that are in his house. Whoever is in the field must not turn back to get his cloak" (24:17-18).

2
"So if they say to you, 'Behold, He is in the wilderness,' do not go out, or, 'Behold, He is in the inner rooms,' do not believe them. For just as the lightning comes from the east and flashes even to the west, so will the coming of the Son of Man be" (24:26-27).

3
"Wherever the corpse is, there the vultures will gather" (24:28).

"Heaven and earth will pass away, but My words will not pass away. But of that day and hour no one knows, not even the angels of heaven, nor the Son, but the Father alone" (Matt. 24:35-36).

4
"For the coming of the Son of Man will be just like the days of Noah. For as in those days before the flood they were eating and drinking, marrying and giving in marriage, until the day that Noah entered the ark, and they did not understand until the flood came and took them all away; so will the coming of the Son of Man be" (24:37-39).

5
"Then there will be two men in the field; one will be taken and one will be left. Two women will be grinding at the mill; one will be taken and one will be left" (24:40-41).

LUKE 17:20-37

2
"They will say to you, 'Look there! Look here!' Do not go away, and do not run after them. For just like the lightning, when it flashes out of one part of the sky, shines to the other part of the sky, so will the Son of Man be in His day" (17:23-24).

4
"And just as it happened in the days of Noah, so it will be also in the days of the Son of Man: they were eating, they were drinking, they were marrying, they were being given in marriage, until the day that Noah entered the ark, and the flood came and destroyed them all" (17:26-27).

1
"On that day, the one who is on the housetop and whose goods are in the house must not go down to take them out; and likewise the one who is in the field must not turn back." (17:31)

5
"There will be two women grinding at the same place; one will be taken and the other will be left. Two men will be in the field; one will be taken and the other will be left" (17:35-36).

3
"And answering they said to Him, 'Where, Lord?' And He said to them, 'Where the body is, there also the vultures will be gathered'" (17:37).

Another line of evidence, offered by those who believe that the events following Matthew 24:34 refer to a yet future personal and physical return of Jesus, is the meaning given to "after a long time" (24:48; 25:19) and the "delay" by the bridegroom (25:5). On the surface these examples seem to indicate that two different events are in view, one near (the destruction of Jerusalem) and one distant (the Second Coming of Christ). This is the view of Stephen F. Hayhow:

> Both parables, the parables of the virgins (vv. 1–13), and the parable of the talents (vv. 14–30), speak of the absence of the bridegroom/master, who is said to be "a long time in coming" (v. 5) and "After a long time the master of the servants returned" (v. 19). This suggests, not the events of A.D. 70 which were to occur in the near future, in fact within the space of a generation, but a distant event, the return of Christ. (Stephen F. Hayhow, "Matthew 24, Luke 17 and the Destruction of Jerusalem," *Christianity and Society* 4:2 (April 1994), 4.)

Notice that the evil slave says, "My master is not coming for a long time" (Matt. 24:48). The evil slave then proceeds to "beat his fellow-slaves and eat and drink with drunkards" (24:49). But to the surprise of the "evil slave," the master returned when he least expected him (24:50). The master did not return to cut the evil slave's distant relatives in pieces (24:51); he cut *him* in pieces. The evil slave was alive when the master left, and he was alive when the master returned. In this context, a "long time" must be measured against a person's lifetime. In context, two years could be a long time if the master usually returned within six months.

The same idea is expressed in the Parable of the Talents. A man entrusts his slaves with his possessions (25:14). The master then goes on a journey (25:15). While the master is gone, the slaves make investment decisions (25:16–18). We are then told that "after a long time the master of *those slaves* came and settled accounts *with them*" (25:19). In this context "a long time" is no longer than an average lifetime. The settlement is made with the same slaves who received the talents. In every other New Testament context, "a long time" means nothing more than an extended period of time (Luke 8:27; 23:8; John 5:6; Acts 8:11; 14:3, 28; 26:5, 29; 27:21; 28:6). Nowhere does it mean centuries or multiple generations. The delay of the bridegroom is no different from the "long time" of the two previous parables. The bridegroom returns to the same two groups of virgins (25:1–13). The duration of the delay must be measured by the audience.

This brief analysis helps us understand the "mockers" who ask, "Where is the promise of His coming?" (2 Peter 3:3–4). Peter was aware that Jesus' coming was an event that would take place before the last apostle died (Matt. 16:27–28; John 21:22–23). The doctrine of the soon return of Christ was common knowledge (Matt. 24:34; 26:64; Phil. 4:5; Heb. 10:25; 1 John 2:18; Rev. 1:1, 3). It is not hard to imagine that the passage of several decades would lead some to doubt the reliability of the prophecy, especially as the promised generation was coming to a close. The horrendous events of A.D. 70 silenced the mockers."[155]

---

[155] Gary DeMar, *Is the Rapture Found in Matthew 24?* https://christianfamilystudycentre.home.blog/2020/12/07/is-the-rapture-found-in-matthew-24/

Luke 17:20-37

Just as Matthew 23-25 is written with a common chiastic structure connecting these chapters, Luke 17:20-37 is also structured with a chiasm. Some may be asking, "What in the world is a chiasm?" So let me briefly point out its basic structure. Here is a classic example.

(A) No one can serve two masters,

    (B) for either he will hate the one

        (C) and love the other,

        (C) or he will be devoted to the one

    (B) and despise the other.

(A) You cannot serve God and money.

Usually in a chiasm, the beginning and end correspond with each other and ram home the point. The middle parts also correspond with each other, and the beginning and end, and can serve as the main point or the meat in the middle. In ancient Hebrew and Biblical times, this form of teaching was popular because the parallel structure made it easy to memorize the teaching.

Now notice that the chiasm structure in Luke 17:20-37 begins and ends with two questions, and the point Jesus is addressing is when and how His kingdom will be manifested. It's at His Second Coming:

(A) The question by the Pharisees - When will the kingdom come or be realized (17:20-21)? It will come "within the heart of a person."

    (B) When the coming of the Son of Man is revealed as the sun (17:22-25)

        (C) This will be like in the days of Noah (17:26-27)

        (C) This will be like in the days of Lot (17:28-29)

    (B) When the Son of Man is revealed (17:30)

(A) The question by the disciples – Where, Lord? "Where the dead body is."

Luke 17:20-37 is a chiasm centered around two questions (asked by the Pharisees and then the disciples) addressing the eschatological point as to when, how and where the kingdom will come and be realized. The answer for the Pharisees is that when the kingdom comes, it will be unseen and realized "within" the hearts of their enemies - when the Son of Man is revealed from heaven (which will be like the days of Noah or Lot). The answer to the disciple's question, as to when, how or "where" the kingdom comes, is connected to when their enemies would be "gathered" together in order to be slain like a dead body that the birds of the air would pick apart. This too would be realized when Christ would be revealed from heaven (which would be like the days of Noah or Lot). Remember, Jesus taught elsewhere that the kingdom would be "taken" from the Pharisees and "given" to the Church or "nation" bearing the fruits thereof (Mt.

21:43-45). Our text here in Luke 17 DESCRIBES HOW, WHEN and WHERE that transfer would be accomplished in the events of AD 67 – AD 70.

"Within you"

Some modern translators translate *entos* as "among you" or "in your midst" without any linguistic justification. They appear to do this for two reasons. First, they can't have Jesus' spiritual "within" kingdom associated with the eschatological "not yet" or with Christ's Parousia, so translating it as "among you" or currently "in your midst" places the phrase comfortably in the here and now of the "already." And, secondly, they think that if you translate the passage as "within you," this would have Jesus saying that the unbelieving Pharisees had the kingdom within them.

Therefore, let's consider the linguistic evidence for "within you" or "within your heart," and also to whom Jesus is referring when He says within "you."

Strong's Concordance pretty much nails the definition of *entosas* as "within you":

> "1787. ἐντός entós; adv. from en(1722), in. Within. Used also as a prep. with the gen. (Luke 17:21, "the kingdom of God is within you," meaning it is located in your heart and affections, not external). With the neut. def. art., tó entós, the inside (Matt. 23:26; Sept.: Ps. 39:4; 109:22). Zodhiates, S. (2000)."

Consider the following arguments which prove with 100% certainty that *entos* should be translated as "within you" or, even better, "within the heart of a person":

1). The context of Luke 17:21 is giving a contrast between something that is outward and physically seen – "lo here or lo there" – as opposed to something that is spiritual and therefore is unseen and "within."

2). *Entos* is only used one other time in the NT and it is located in Matthew 23:26, where again there is a contrast being made between what the hypocritical Pharisees did outwardly – sitting in Moses' seat and doing their deeds to be "SEEN by men," dressing to be SEEN by men, and loving the best seats so as to be SEEN by men. But Jesus drives the point home when He teaches that they were overly concerned about outward washings and cleanliness, not realizing that they were unclean and spiritually dead from the *"inside" (entos)* – (23:25-28).

3). Strong's also appeals to the LXX which universally translates the OT Hebrew being "within" a building such as the temple, or something taking place "within" a person's "inward parts" or within the spiritual nature of man as contrasted with the outward. See also the LXX in Psalm 103:1; Psalm 109:22; Isaiah 16:11.

4). Outside the NT, *entos* never means "among."

5). In order to express "among, amidst," or "in the middle of," the New Testament always uses *mesos* already employed in the Old Testament 307 times, and in the New Testament there are 27 occurrences with Luke, who uses *mesos* much more than any of the other gospel writers. This clearly implies that Luke would certainly have used *mesos* in 17:21 if the meaning were "among you."

6). Therefore, it shouldn't surprise us that Liddell-Scott (p. 577) gives Luke 17:21 the translation of *entosas,* to be *"in your hearts."*

7. All the early church fathers who were closer to koine Greek than we are, universally understood *entosas* to be "within you."

8). It has only been in recent times that some translations have rendered *entos* as "among you" in the fear that Jesus is teaching the kingdom of God would be "within" the unbelieving Pharisees. But as William Hendriksen points out, "The pronoun you (whether singular or plural) have more than one meaning such as 'a person' or 'one.'"[156] Therefore, Jesus is teaching that when the kingdom of God comes (at His Second Coming) you will not be able to physically see it, because it will be realized and fulfilled "within the heart of a person."

Here's one last point on Luke 17:20-37. Luke's account of Jesus' teachings often closes a discourse with a parable (6:20-49; 10:1-37; 11:14-36; 11:37-12:21; 12:22-48; 16:9-31; 17:20-18:8). Thus the "day(s) of the Son of Man" will include inheritance of the kingdom & Parousia, but also severe persecution requiring vindication, to which Jesus now turns His attention. While the disciples may be tempted to want the kind of kingdom the Pharisees wanted (a violent vindication from their Roman enemies), due to the coming persecutions, Jesus does assure them that His Parousia would include an aspect of physical deliverance and vindication of their enemies. This would occur "quickly" (Lk. 18:8) at His Second Coming and not thousands of years in the future.

Concluding the parallels of Matthew 24:37-51 and Luke 17:20-37

There is no exegetical evidence to support the idea that Matthew 24-25 is addressing two comings of Christ, as some Dispensational Zionists have taught (e.g. Darby) and as some Partial Preterists (e.g. Gentry) teach.

Was Luke so confused and forgetful, that when Christ taught on His Second Coming in Luke 17 and Luke 21, Luke only addressed ONE coming while Matthew pointed out that there are really TWO comings? If Luke understood Christ teaching two comings in the Olivet Discourse, then why does he mix up the order of those events in Luke 17 to be one and the same event?

When we compare Jesus' teaching on His Second Coming and the arrival of His kingdom in Luke 17:20-37 with Luke 21:27-32 we realize that both His kingdom and Second Coming would be fulfilled within Jesus' contemporary "this generation" and His kingdom and Parousia presence would not be physically seen, because it would be revealed "within the hearts" of His people. He would come as "The Sun of

---

[156] William Hendriksen, *Gospel of Luke*, (Grand Rapids, MI: 1978), 805

Righteousness...shining from the east to the west," "healing" and bring resurrection life "within the hearts" of His people, while the old covenant kingdom would be desolated and never remembered.

- *"From the **fig tree learn its lesson**: as soon as its branch becomes tender and puts out its leaves, you know that summer is near. ³³ So also, when you see all these things, you know that **He is near, at the very gates/door**"* (Matthew 24:32-33) / *"Look at the **fig tree**, and **all the trees**. As soon as they come out in leaf, you see for yourselves and know that the summer is already near. So also, when you see these things taking place, you know that the **kingdom of God is near**"* (Lk. 21:30-32)

Premillennial Zionist "prophecy experts" claim that this text is a "super sign" teaching us that when Israel (the fig tree) became a nation in 1948, Christ's coming and the arrival of His Kingdom became "near" for our contemporary "this generation." In a similar way, some like Pat Roberts reasoned the "times of the Gentiles" was somehow fulfilled in 1967, so we are the "this generation" that will experience the secret "rapture." So the embarrassing theory goes.

But the clear contextual meaning is that the fig tree *and all the trees* beginning to put forth their leaves is equal to the signs being fulfilled (specifically the sign(s) of the great commission and the Roman armies surrounding Jerusalem). This would indicate that the arrival of "summer" being "near" is equal to the desolation of Jerusalem being near or the kingdom and Second Coming being "near."

*"Look at the **fig tree**, and **all the trees**. As soon as they come out in leaf,...*	When the disciples would see the **sign** of "Jerusalem being surrounded by [Roman] armies [& or the GC of Mt. 24:14]...
*...you see for yourselves and know that **summer is already near**. So also, when you see these things taking place, you know that the **kingdom of God is near**"* (Lk. 21:30-32)	*...know that its desolation **is near*** (Lk. 21:20). Or, they would know that the **coming of the Son of Man and His Kingdom** would be "near" or "at the door" in their "this generation" (cf. Lk. 21:27-32).

In Matthew and Luke's accounts, there is a slight difference. In Matthew's account of the parable, the disciples are exhorted to just look at the fig tree (one tree), while Luke adds *"and all the trees."* So, if modern Israel becoming a nation in 1948 is the "fig tree" beginning to bring forth her leaves, then they need to explain what "and all the trees" sprouting forth their leaves means in Luke's account, which of course they never attempt to do. If the fig tree is Israel, then "all the trees" would be the other nations, right? If so, what happened to all of the modern nations of the globe in 1948 per this bizarre twisting of God's Word?

It is true that in the OT and even the NT the fig tree can represent Israel. But Jesus on a previous occasion cursed the fig tree (Israel after the flesh) so that it would never bear forth fruit again (Mt. 21:18-19). Not only this, but the kingdom would be "taken" from the Pharisees and Jews and "given" to "another nation" [the Church] that would bear fruit after Israel was judged in AD 70 to never bear fruit again (Mt. 21:43-45/1 Pet. 2:15).

The other slight difference between Matthew's account and Luke's is that Luke includes the "kingdom" being near at this point while Matthew does not mention the kingdom being near but rather Christ Himself. As we saw in our study of Luke 17:20-37, the coming of Christ and the kingdom are once again linked together.

The best evidence that our exegesis is accurate is if the inspired NT writers taught that the Second Coming was "at the very gates/door" (Mt. 24:33). And of course, that is exactly what we find James writing:

> "…the ***coming of the Lord is at hand***. Do not grumble against one another, brothers, so that you may not be judged; behold, ***the Judge is standing <u>at the door</u>***" (Jms. 5:8-9).

- *"Verily I say unto you, '**This generation** shall not pass, till **all these things be fulfilled**'"* (Mt. 24:34 KJV).

Other relevant translations which understand that this is referring to Jesus' contemporary generation include these:

> "Remember that all these things will happen ***before the people now living have all died***" (Mt. 24:34 GNT).

> "I tell you the truth, all these things will happen while the people of this time are still living" (Mt. 24:34 NCV)

There are three texts which answer the disciples' question as to ***when*** the Temple would be destroyed and the signs, coming of the Son of Man and the end of the age would be fulfilled. They are:

1). After the gospel had been preached throughout the then know "whole world" or Roman Empire "***then*** the **end** [of the old covenant age asked about in v. 3] will come" (Mt. 24:14).

2). "***When*** you see ***Jerusalem surrounded by armies*** then know that its desolation ***has come near***" (Lk. 21:20).

3). And the third is here when Jesus sums up that everything the disciples asked about, and which He just finished answering, would ***"all"*** be fulfilled in their contemporary ***"this generation"*** (Mt. 24:34/Lk. 21:31-32).

In the immediate context here in Matthew 24:1-34 and Luke 21:5-32 there is no confusion on what the "all these things" are. They are the following:

1). All of the general signs that would "not" mark the near coming of the Lord and end of the old covenant age.

2). The two specific signs of the gospel being preached throughout the then known world (or "nations") within the Roman Empire and the armies surrounding Jerusalem would mark the "near" end.

3). The Great Tribulation.

4). All OT prophecy would be fulfilled.

5). The casting down of Israel's "stars" or religious rulers.

6). The flight of Christians from "Judea" to escape the "wrath coming upon this people" (Jews), which would be "the days of vengeance" when those Jews would "fall by the end of the sword" or "Jerusalem would be trodden down" during the "times of the Gentiles."

7). The "gathering of the elect" or "redemption" (resurrection) that would occur at the coming of the Son of Man upon the clouds or when the "kingdom" would arrive.

When we understand that Matthew 24-25 is written in the common prophetic and Jewish genre of recapitulation, then we understand that the "day and hour", "passing of heaven and earth," and the time of the parables [including Israel's wedding] describing His coming to judge the nations, the Devil and his angels also all fall under the umbrella of being fulfilled within Jesus' contemporary "this generation."

The *Thayer Greek-English Lexicon* and *Vine's Expository Dictionary of Old and New Testament Words* defines "generation" (Greek *genea*) here in Matthew 24:34 as Jesus addressing His contemporary generation (AD 30 - 70) and no other generation:

> "**the whole multitude of men living at the same time: Mt.xxiv. 34; Mk. xiii. 30**; Lk. i. 48; xxi. 32; **Phil. ii. 15**; used esp. of the Jewish race living at one and the same period: Mt. xi. 16; xii. 39, 41 sq. 45; xvi. 4; xxiii.36; Mk. Viii. 12, 38; Lk. Xi. 29 sq. 32, 50 sq.; xvii. 36; Heb. iii. 10…" "…who can describe the wickedness of the present generation, Acts viii. 33 (fr. Is. Liii. 8 Sept.)."[157]

> "…of the whole multitude of men living at the same time, Matt. 24:34; Mark 13:30; Luke 1:48; 21:32; Phil. 2:15…**a period ordinarily occupied by each successive generation, say, of thirty or forty years**, Acts 14:16; 15:21; Eph. 3:5; Col. 1:26; see also, e.g., Gen. 15:16."[158]

Although somewhat inconsistent, the most impressive Greek work on *genea* comes from Collin Brown:

> "In Matt. it has the sense of *this generation*, and according to the first evangelist, *Jesus expected the end of this age (Time, art. aion) to occur in

---

[157] Joseph Henry Thayer, D.D., *A GREEK-ENGLISH LEXICON OF THE NEW TESTAMENT*, (Grand Rapids, MI: Baker Book House, 1977), 112, bold emphasis MJS

[158] W.E. Vine (edited by F.F. Bruce), *VINE'S Expository Dictionary of Old and New Testament Words* (Iowa Falls, Iowa: World Bible Publishers, 1981), 42, bold emphasis MJS

> *connection with the judgment on Jerusalem at the end of that first generation* (see Mk. 9:1 and Matt. 16:28)."[159]

And again,

> "But if these events were expected within the first generation of Christians (and 'generation' is the most probable translation of *genea*), either Jesus or the evangelists were mistaken…or…*there is an alternative interpretation of the passage which points out that insufficient attention has been paid to the prophetic language of the passage as a whole.*
>
> The imagery of cosmic phenomena is used in the OT to describe this-worldly events and, in particular, historical acts of judgment. The following passages are significant, not least because of their affinities with the present context: Isa. 13:10 (predicting doom on Babylon); Isa. 34:4 (referring to "all the nations", but especially to Edom); Ezek. 32:7 (concerning Egypt); Amos 8:9 (the Northern Kingdom of Israel); Joel 2:10 (Judah). The cosmic imagery draws attention to the divine dimension of the event in which the judgment of God is enacted. The use of Joel 2:28-32 in Acts 2:15-21 provides an instance of the way in which such prophetic cosmic imagery is applied to historical events in the present (cf. also Lk. 10:18; 1 Jn. 12:31; **1 Thess. 4:16; 2 Pet. 3:10ff**; Rev. 6:12-17; 18:1). Other OT passages relevant to the interpretation of the present context are Isa. 19:1; 27:13; Deut. 30:4; Zech. 2:6; 12:10-14; Mal. 3:1. In view of this, Mk. 13:24-30 may be interpreted as a Son of man will be vindicated. Such prophecy of judgment on Israel in which a judgment took place with the destruction of Jerusalem, the desecration of the Temple and the scattering of Israel – all of which happened within the lifetime of "this generation." "…Such an interpretation fits the preceding discourse and the introductory remarks of the disciples (Mk. 13:1ff. par)."[160]

Brown is at least attempting to allow the Bible to interpret itself, unlike Dispensational Zionists. And, if I'm not mistaken, he seems to be consenting that the "rapture" or resurrection passage of 1 Thessalonians 4:16 and de-creation of 2 Peter 3 were fulfilled by the "historical event" of AD 70 just as the apocalyptic language of Matthew 24 can and should be interpreted.

False interpretations of "this generation"

There have been many false interpretations of "this generation" given by Dispensational Zionists and even other Futurist Christian systems. These include the following:

---

[159] Colin Brown, *The New International Dictionary of New Testament Theology Vol. 2*, (Grand Rapids MI: Zondervan Publishing House, 1986), 37-38, bold emphasis MJS

[160] Ibid., 38-39

1). Popularized by the Zionist funded and friendly *Scofield Study Bible*, this view teaches that Jesus meant the entire *Jewish race* would not pass away until all things were fulfilled.

Response - If this was Jesus' meaning, He would have used the Greek word *genos* which means "1) kindred 1a) offspring 1b) family 1c) stock, tribe, **nation** 1c1) i.e. nationality or descent from a particular people 1d) the aggregate of many individuals of the same nature, kind, sort."[161] But clearly Jesus did not use *genos*. He used *genea*.

2). *Our contemporary generation* which saw Israel (the "fig tree") become a nation in 1948, and the "times of the Gentiles" ended in 1967. This is the end-time generation. Hal Lindsey, an alleged "prophecy expert" who, based on current events and not the Bible, claimed:

> "WE are the generation that will see the end times… and return of Christ." And "unmistakably… this generation is the one that will see the end of the present world and the return of Christ."[162]

And then this view was fueled from the pulpit by mega church pastors, such as one of my former pastors, Chuck Smith, of the Calvary Chapel movement:

> "…that the generation of 1948 is the last generation. Since a generation of judgment is forty years and the Tribulation period lasts seven years, I believe the Lord could come back for His Church any time before the Tribulation starts, which would mean any time before 1981 (1948 + 40 – 7 = 1981)."[163]

That 1981 was the alleged date was further solidified in his book *Future Survival* (1978) where he writes:

> "From my understanding of biblical prophecies [and *genea*], I'm convinced that the Lord is coming for His Church before the end of 1981."[164]

Response – As we have seen in our exegesis of these passages, the parable of the "fig tree…and all the trees" is referring to the disciples seeing the signs being fulfilled in their generation. These signs being fulfilled would mark the "near", "at the door" arrival of "summer," which is the arrival of the Son of Man upon the clouds and inheritance of the kingdom event.

---

[161] *Greek English Online Bible Greek Lexicon, Online Bible Software*, Ibid, emphasis MJS

[162] Hal Lindsey, The 1980's: Countdown to Armageddon, (New York: Bantam, 1980), see back-cover, and p.144

[163] Chuck Smith, *End Times,* (Costa Mesa, CA: The Word for Today, 1978), 35.

[164] Francis X. Gumerlock, *The Day and the Hour Christianity's Perennial Fascination with Predicting the End of the World*, (Atlanta, GA: American Vision, 2000), 290.

The "times of the Gentiles" is when the Gentiles would tread down Jerusalem. And according to Luke 21, Rev. 11 and Daniel 12, this would be the period of 3 ½ years or from AD 67 – AD 70. The dates of 1948 and 1967 are simply read into these texts by the Evangelical Zionists.

3). Jesus uses the phrase "this generation" to refer to a future generation that is alive to witness these signs whenever they begin to be fulfilled.

Response – Jesus does **not** say "that [as in a future] generation." He says "*this* [His contemporary] generation." And we have seen *how* all of the signs and Christ's kingdom were fulfilled when Jesus said they would be.

4). Jesus is simply describing an evil generation of people that is descriptive of the last days generation, whoever that may be.

Response – Just because Jesus adds adjectives of "evil", "sinful," or "adulterous" before "this generation" does not justify changing the meaning of *genea* to be spanning thousands of years as an "evil people." The commonsense understanding is that Jesus was describing His contemporary generation as being evil, sinful and adulterous, because they had rejected Him and would crucify Him. Because of that, they (the tribes of the land of Israel) would mourn and see Him coming in judgment using the Roman armies. This is not difficult.

Uses of "generation(s)" or "this generation"

We will start with how "generation(s)" or "this generation" is used within the gospel of Matthew itself.

1). "So, all the ***generations*** from Abraham to David were ***fourteen generations***, and from David to the deportation to Babylon ***fourteen generations***, and from the deportation to Babylon to the Christ ***fourteen generations***" (Mt. 1:17).

Obviously 42 "races" which came from Abraham does not work here. Clearly, genea means "the whole multitude of men living at the same time, a period ordinarily occupied by each successive generation, say, of thirty or forty years."

2). "But to what shall I compare ***this generation***? It is like children sitting in the marketplaces and calling to their playmates" (Mt. 11:16).

In context, "this generation" is the contemporary generation Jesus is speaking to who falsely accused John the Baptist of "having a demon" (v. 18) and Himself of being "a glutton and drunkard, a friend of tax collectors and sinners" (v. 19). It is the same generation that was expecting the "about to coming" of Elijah, which Jesus said was John, and thus were also expecting the about-to-be coming of the great day of the Lord to be imminent after Elijah/John appeared (cf. vss. 8-15).

3). But he answered them, "An evil and ***adulterous generation*** seeks for a sign, but no sign will be given to it except the sign of the prophet Jonah. For just as Jonah was three days and three nights in the belly of the great fish, so will the Son of Man be three days and three nights in the heart of the earth. The men of Nineveh will rise up at the judgment with ***this generation*** and condemn it, for they repented at the preaching of Jonah, and behold, something greater than Jonah is here. The queen of the South will rise up at the judgment with this generation and condemn it, for she came from the ends of the earth to hear the wisdom of Solomon, and behold, something greater than Solomon is here. "When the unclean spirit has gone out of a person, it passes through waterless places seeking rest, but finds none. Then it says, 'I will return to my house from which I came.' And when it comes, it finds the house empty, swept, and put in order. Then it goes and brings with it seven other spirits more evil than itself, and they enter and dwell there, and the last state of that person is worse than the first. So also, will it be with ***this evil generation***" (Mt. 12:39-45).

Jesus' contemporary generation was "evil" and "adulterous," always seeking a sign. But just as Jonah being raised out of the great fish after three days was a sign to Nineveh that they needed to repent, Jesus' contemporary generation would experience the "sign" of Him being raised after three days and nights, demanding repentance and faith or be judged.

Jesus' contemporary "this generation" was so "evil" that it was like a demon who possessed a man, who after having the demon driven from him was not thankful or repentant (did not get his house/heart in order with such graces), and thus the later state (the demon got seven others to enter the man) was worse than before. Israel's history was that of persecuting the prophets, but her judgment coming in AD 70 would be a sevenfold severe one because, in killing Christ and the NT messengers that He sent to her, she would "fill up the measure" [store up severe wrath] of her sins throughout her history.

4). "And Jesus answered, "O ***faithless and crooked generation***, how long am I to be with you? How long am I to bear with you? Bring him here to me." And Jesus rebuked the demon, and it came out of him, and the boy was healed instantly. Then the disciples came to Jesus privately and said, "Why could we not cast it out?" He said to them, "Because of your little faith. For truly, I say to you, if you have faith like a grain of mustard seed, you will say to this mountain, 'Move from here to there,' and it will move, and nothing will be impossible for you" (Mt. 17:17-20).

Here Jesus is echoing the language and prophecy of Deuteronomy 32:5, 20 which would be Israel's terminal generation. The disciples' contemporary generation was characterized as not having faith in its Messiah and even the disciples needed to increase their faith in order to engage in imprecatory prayers to uproot and move the apostate mountain(s) of Israel, to cast it/them into the sea in the imminent judgment of fire that would come upon that generation (cf. Mt. 21:18-21/Rev. 8:3-8/Deut. 32:5, 20, 22[165]).

---

[165] I would agree with Lightfoot who takes Deuteronomy 32:22 as the judgment of Jerusalem in AD 70. And other commentators who see the "mountains" (plural) to be referring to the seven hills/mountains that represented and were present within Israel. Israel was also known as a "mountain" (singular) or "Mount Zion." The Church had become the new covenant Mount Zion, and old covenant Israel had become apostate and rejected her Messiah.

5). "Truly, I say to you, all these things will come upon *this generation*" (Mt. 23:36).

The context is clear that the contemporary generation of the Pharisees, of whom Jesus is speaking, would "fill up the measure" of the sin of blood guilt and it would be manifested in the destruction of "their house" or the temple in AD 70.

Now we will move beyond Matthew's gospel and see if the meaning is the same throughout the NT.

6). *"*And his mercy is for those who fear him from *generation to generation*" (Luke 1:50).

The same understanding and interpretation of *genea* as in Matthew 1:17 is to be understood. Or as Ecclesiastes 1:4 teaches, "A generation goes, and a generation comes, but the earth remains forever." These are "successive generations," or periods of 35-40 years of people living at the same time.

7). "But first he must suffer many things and be **rejected by *this generation***. Just as it was in the days of Noah, so will it be in the days of the Son of Man. They were eating and drinking and marrying and being given in marriage, until the day when Noah entered the ark, and the flood came and destroyed them all. Likewise, just as it was in the days of Lot—they were eating and drinking, buying and selling, planting and building, but on the day when Lot went out from Sodom, fire and sulfur rained from heaven and destroyed them all— so will it be on the day when the Son of Man is revealed" (Lk. 17:25-30).

It should go without saying that it was the first century contemporary "this generation" of Jesus that would cause her Messiah to "suffer" and be crucified. And as we have pointed already, the context before this verse, and after, is referring to the coming of the Son of Man in the judgment of AD 70. I think it is safe to say that the references of that generation crucifying Christ and experiencing judgment in AD 70 are two themes brought together well in Revelation (cf. 1:7; 11:8ff.; chapters 17-19; and also see Matthew 21:33-45; 22:1-14; 23:1-36).

8). "And with many other words he bore witness and continued to exhort them, saying, **"Save yourselves from *this crooked generation*"** (Acts 2:40).

This passage falls within Peter's sermon in which his contemporary generation was living in the "last days" of the old covenant Mosaic age, having with their own hands crucified the Lord of Glory (Acts 2:14-23). Therefore, they needed to "call upon the name of the Lord" in repentance and thus be "saved" from the "great day" of the Lord's coming in their "crooked generation" (v. 20-40).

Peter, like the Lord, appeals to the terminal "last days", "crooked generation" of Deuteronomy 31-32 that would see her "end." Peter clearly understood that his contemporary generation would experience the final end of Israel when he taught that "the end of all things is near" (cf. 1 Pet. 4:5-7, 17).

9). "that **you** may be blameless and innocent, children of God without blemish in the midst of a ***crooked and twisted generation***, among whom you shine as lights in the world, holding fast to the word of life, so that **in the day of Christ** I may be proud that I did not run in vain or labor in vain" (Phil. 2:15-16).

Being consistent with Jesus and Peter, Paul will likewise teach that his contemporary generation is Israel's last days was the "crooked generation" (Deut. 32:5, 20) that would experience "the day of Christ," which he says in chapter 4:5 was "at hand" and thus to be fulfilled in AD 70.

One last example will do.

10). "Therefore, I was provoked with ***that generation***, and said, 'They always go astray in their heart; they have not known my ways'" (Heb. 3:10).

The first thing we notice is that if an NT author wants to communicate a past or different generation than the one He is addressing, "**that** generation" is referred to. So again, if Jesus meant that a future generation would witness "all these things" listed in the Olivet Discourse, He would have naturally said *"that* generation." Hebrews 3:10 uses the Greek word ***ekeinos,*** *which is primarily translated by the KJV and Strong's (1565) as "that" in the NT -* ***that (99x)****,* those (40x), the same (20x), they (14x), misc. (38x). In Matthew 24:34 Jesus uses the Greek word ***houtos,*** *which is primarily translated by the KJV and Strong's (3778) as "this" in the NT -* ***this (157x),*** these (59x), he (31x), the same (28x), this man (25x), she (12x), they (10x) and misc. (34x).

The context of Hebrews 3-4 and 10 is that the forty years wilderness wandering "generation" was a type of "another day" of receiving Sabbath rest in Christ. The author in chapter 10 says this "another day" he spoke of in the earlier chapters "was drawing near" when Christ would come in judgment and salvation "in a very little while and would not delay" (Heb. 10:25-37).

When we piece together the evidence of "this generation," it's pretty clear that the 40 years wilderness wandering generation was typological of the imminent judgment and salvation that would be realized in Christ's contemporary and terminal generation.

I was very disappointed in my former pastor and college president John MacArthur's attempted refutation of my/our position here of "this generation" (Mt. 24:34). He claims that Preterists use a "wooden literalness"[166] *when interpreting it. If my former pastor means I/we allow the rest of Scripture to give us the literal meaning of Jesus' words, then I guess I'm gladly guilty. It's odd that a "wooden literal" Dispensational Zionist is accusing us of giving "this generation" its "literal" normal meaning. Go figure.*

Having already addressed and connected the "heaven and earth" passing away with the end of the old covenant "age" passing away, along with the de-creation of Matthew 24:29 being the civil and religious rulers falling from their place of authority in AD 70, we shall now turn to the "day and hour" of Matthew 24:36.

---

[166] MacArthur, Ibid., 80

- *"But concerning that day and hour no one knows, not even the angels of heaven, nor the Son, but the Father only" (Mt. 24:36).*

While Jesus predicted that His Second Coming event would occur "near" and within His contemporary "this generation," He said that no one would know the exact "day and hour" of it. Here are other commentators who correctly understand/see the "day and hour" of His coming being fulfilled by AD 70.

Adam Clarke writes:

> "Verse 36. But of that day and hour—…here, is translated season by many eminent critics, and is used in this sense by both sacred and profane authors. As the day was not known, in which Jerusalem should be invested by the Romans, therefore our Lord advised his disciples to pray that it might not be on a Sabbath; and as the season was not known, therefore they were to pray that it might not be in the winter; Matthew 24:20.[167]

Even Premillennialist John Gill correctly noted that Matthew 24:36 is referring to AD 70:

> "Ver. 36. But of that day and hour knoweth no man, &c.]… …the coming of the son of man, to take vengeance on the Jews, and of their destruction; for the words manifestly regard the date of the several things going before, which only can be applied to that catastrophe, and dreadful desolation: now, though the destruction itself was spoken of by Moses and the prophets, was foretold by Christ, and the believing Jews had some discerning of its near approach; see #Heb 10:25 yet the exact and precise time was not known: it might have been: calculated to a year by Daniel's weeks, but not to the day and hour; and therefore our Lord does not say of the year, but of the day and hour no man knows; though the one week, or seven years, being separated from the rest, throws that account into some perplexity; and which perhaps is on purpose done, to conceal the precise time of Jerusalem's destruction: nor need it be wondered at, notwithstanding all the hints given, that the fatal day should not be exactly known beforehand; when those who have lived since, and were eyewitnesses of it, are not agreed on what day of the month it was; for, as Dr. Lightfoot {i} observes, Josephus {k} says,

> "that the temple perished the "tenth" day of "Lous", a day fatal to the temple, as having been on that day consumed in flames, by the king of Babylon."

> And yet Rabbi Jochanan ben Zaccai, who was also at the destruction of it, as well as Josephus, with all the Jewish writers, say it was on the "ninth of Ab"; for of this day they {l} say, five things happened upon it:

---

[167] See Clarke's comments on Mark 13:32, *Adam Clarke's Commentary* – available online https://www.studylight.org/commentary/matthew/24-36.html

"On the "ninth of Ab" it was decreed concerning our fathers, that they should not enter into the land (of Canaan), the first and second temple were destroyed, Bither was taken, and the city ploughed up."

Though the words of R. Jochanan, cited by the doctor, refer to the first, and not to the second temple, and should have been rendered thus:

"If I had been in the generation (which fixed the fast for the destruction of the first temple), I would not have fixed it but on the tenth (of Ab); for, adds he, the greatest part of the temple was burnt on that day; but the Rabbis rather regarded the beginning of the punishment {m}."

And so, the fasting of Rabbi, and R. Joshua ben Levi, on the "ninth" and "tenth" days, were on account of the first temple; for they were under the same difficulty about the one, as the other:

no, not the angels of heaven; who dwell there, always behold the face of God, stand in his presence ready to do his will, and are made acquainted with many of his designs, and are employed in the executing of them, and yet know not the time of God's vengeance on the Jews; to this agrees the sense that is given of the day of vengeance in # Isa 63:4 it is asked {n},

"what is the meaning of these words, "the day of vengeance is in my heart?" Says R. Jochanan, to my heart I have revealed it, to the members I have not revealed it: says R. Simeon ben Lakish, to my heart I have revealed it, ytylg al trfh ykalml, "to the ministering angels I have not revealed it.""

The Ethiopic version adds here, "nor the son", and so the Cambridge copy of Beza's; which seems to be transcribed from #Mr 13:32 where that phrase stands; and must be understood of Christ as the son of man, and not as the Son of God; for as such, he lay in the bosom of the Father, and knew all his purposes and designs; for these were purposed in him: he knew from the beginning who would betray him, and who would believe in him; he knew what would befall the rejecters of him, and when that would come to pass; as he must know also the day of the last judgment, since it is appointed by God, and he is ordained to execute it: but the sense is, that as he, as man and mediator, came not to destroy, but to save; so it was not any part of his work, as such, to know, nor had he it in commission to make known the time of Jerusalem's ruin: but my Father only; to the exclusion of all creatures, angels and men; but not to the exclusion of Christ as God, who, as such, is omniscient; nor of the Holy Spirit, who is acquainted with the deep things of God, the secrets of his heart, and this among others."[168]

---

[168] See John Gill's Commentary on Matthew 24:36 – free online https://www.studylight.org/commentary/matthew/24-36.html

Clearly, Matthew 24:36 is not evidence of another coming of Christ at the end of world history. Partial Preterists like Kenneth Gentry simply abuse its context in hopes of tolling the creedal line in order of keeping their creedal "orthodox" jobs.

The eschatological marriage

- *"As the bridegroom was delayed, they all became drowsy and slept. But at midnight there was a cry, 'Here is the bridegroom!* **Come out to meet him**.*' Then all those virgins rose and trimmed their lamps. And the foolish said to the wise, 'Give us some of your oil, for our lamps are going out.' But the wise answered, saying, 'Since there will not be enough for us and for you, go rather to the dealers and buy for yourselves.' And while they were going to buy, the bridegroom came, and those who were ready went in with him to the marriage feast, and the door was shut. Afterward the other virgins came also, saying, 'Lord, lord, open to us.' But he answered, 'Truly, I say to you, I do not know you.'* [13] *Watch therefore, for you know neither the day nor the hour" (Matthew 25:5-12).*

Classic Premillennial Dispensational Zionism teaches that there are two kingdoms, two elect predestined peoples of God (earthly Israel and the heavenly Church), two plans of salvation, two gospels, two hopes, and two Second Comings all mysteriously and mystically coexisting in the Scriptures. So it should not surprise us that they teach two eschatological weddings, one for the Church (His heavenly people/bride) and another for Israel (His earthly people). Of course, there is no hint of this two-coming or two-wedding eschatology anywhere in the OT or NT. So it shouldn't surprise us that there is no hint of it here in our Lord's teaching on the eschatological wedding.

I think Reformed eschatology also has a problem with a two-coming or two eschatological wedding and wedding feast doctrine. Partial Preterists teach that the eschatological wedding and/or wedding feast in the following passages indicate that Christ consummated His marriage to His new covenant wife/Jerusalem in AD 70 when He divorced and judged His old covenant wife/Jerusalem in the following texts: Matthew 8:11-12; 22:1-14; 25:1-13; Revelation 19-21.

Classic Amillennialist authors point out that this eschatological wedding and wedding feast motif found in these Scriptures is the fulfillment of the resurrection "in that day" of Isaiah 25:6-9 and therefore must be fulfilled in the future. Since Partial Preterism has evolved into also teaching two resurrections (a spiritual one in AD 70 and a so-called physical one at the end of world history), it too must necessitate a two eschatological wedding and wedding feast motif to match. I'm wondering which Partial Preterist will be the first to try and develop that.

Matthew 8:10-12:

"When Jesus heard this [expression of the Gentile's faith], he marveled and said to those who followed him, "Truly, I tell you, with no one in Israel have I found such faith. I tell you, many will come from east and west [Gentiles] and recline at the table [wedding feast of Isa. 25:6-9] with Abraham, Isaac, and Jacob in the kingdom of

heaven [in the resurrection], while the sons of the kingdom [Pharisees and unbelieving Jews] will be cast out into the outer darkness. In that place there will be weeping and gnashing of teeth" (Mt. 8:10-12).

Kenneth Gentry writes:

> "In Matthew 8:11-12 we read of the faithful gentile who exercises more faith than anyone in Israel. We hear once again of the people from the east. This time they sit with Abraham, Isaac, and Jacob (the rightful place of the Jews). While the Jews themselves are "cast out" into "outer darkness" (He Shall Have Dominion, p. 175). And, "God is preparing to punish his people Israel, remove the temple system, and re-orient redemptive history from one people and land to all peoples throughout the earth… This dramatic redemptive-historical event…ends the old covenant era…"[169]

Strengths:

The "casting out" of the "subjects of the kingdom" is a reference to OC Israel being judged in AD 70, at which time the believing Jewish/Gentile Church takes her place at the end of the OC era (but notice he is afraid of using the term "age").

The "casting out into darkness" where there is "weeping and gnashing of teeth," he says, refers to AD 70.

Weaknesses:

There is no mention of Isaiah 25:6-9 as Jesus' source and this is odd both because Jesus says He came to fulfill all of the Law and Prophets (cf. Mt. 5:17-18) and because He said this would be fulfilled in His generation (Luke 21:20-32).

There is no inconsistency in Jesus' use of the phrases "cast out into darkness" and "weeping and gnashing of teeth" in Matthew 24:51 and 25:30. There is simply nothing throughout Matthew's gospel which indicates there are TWO (casting out into outer darkness / weeping and gnashing of teeth) judgments in Jesus' teaching.

Unanswered questions – Since, according to Gentry and James Jordan, Daniel 12:2-3 teaches that there was a spiritual resurrection which was fulfilled in AD 70, why isn't this the fulfillment of that resurrection?

Commentators who are not Postmillennial Partial Preterists have no problem pointing out the OT passages Jesus is referring to when He addresses the eschatological wedding feast.

D.A. Carson writes:

> "The picture is that of the "messianic banquet," derived from such OT passages as Isaiah 25:6–9 (cf. 65:13–14)…" "…the presence of Gentiles at the banquet, symbolized the consummation of the messianic kingdom (cf. Mt 22:1–14;

---

[169] Gentry, *Dominion*, Ibid., 342

25:10; 26:29). "Son of" or "sons of" can mean "sons of the bridal chamber" [9:15; NIV, "guests of the bridegroom."[170]

Bloomberg writes:

> "Jesus characterizes that bliss as taking "their places at the feast," the messianic banquet image depicting the intimate fellowship among God's people in the age to come (cf. Isa 25:6–9; 65:13–14)."[171]

Leon Morris connects this "feast" with "the coming bliss of the messianic banquet," to be fulfilled "in the world (or age) to come."[172]

R.C. Sproul's *Reformation Study Bible* admits that the table and feast of Matthew 8:11 is "a reference to the messianic banquet theme of Is. 25:6-9. Gentiles now appear in place of the natural sons" (p. 1684).

Strengths:

Jesus is teaching on the fulfillment of the Messianic wedding banquet and resurrection of Isaiah 25:6-9 and inheriting the new creation of Isaiah 65:12-14 at the end of the then current age, and in the age to come.

They connect the judgment of being "cast out into darkness" where there is "weeping and gnashing of teeth" here with Matthew 24:51 and 25:30 as ONE separating judgment throughout Matthew's gospel.

Weaknesses:

They ignore the time texts and clear references to the ONE AD 70 judgment throughout Matthew's gospel and the time texts of the wedding and resurrection in Matthew 24-25 and Revelation – "this generation", "soon," etc…

The hermeneutical steps are incomplete in that no work is done on the context of Isaiah 24-25 or Isaiah 65 which demonstrate an "in time" and local judgment and not an end-of-time, global transformation event.

Matthew 22:1-14:

And again, Jesus spoke to them in parables, saying, "The kingdom of heaven may be compared to a king who gave a wedding feast for his son, and sent his servants to call those who were invited to the wedding feast, but they would not come. Again he sent other servants, saying, 'Tell those who are invited, "See, I have prepared my dinner, my oxen and my fat calves have been slaughtered, and everything is ready. Come to the wedding feast."' But they paid no attention and went off, one to his farm, another to his business, while the rest seized his servants, treated them shamefully, and killed them. The king was angry, and he sent his troops and destroyed those murderers and

---

[170] Carson, *The Expositor's Bible Commentary: Matthew, Mark, Luke*, Ibid., 202–203

[171] (Blomberg, C. (1992). *Matthew* (Vol. 22, p. 142). Nashville: Broadman & Holman Publishers).

[172] (Morris, L. (1992). *The Gospel according to Matthew* (p. 195). Grand Rapids, MI; Leicester, England: W.B. Eerdmans; Inter-Varsity Press).

burned their city. Then he said to his servants, 'The wedding feast is ready, but those invited were not worthy. Go therefore to the main roads and invite to the wedding feast as many as you find.' And those servants went out into the roads and gathered all whom they found, both bad and good. So, the wedding hall was filled with guests. "*But when the king came in to look at the guests, he saw there a man who had no wedding garment. And he said to him, 'Friend, how did you get in here without a wedding garment?' And he was speechless. Then the king said to the attendants, 'Bind him hand and foot and cast him into the outer darkness. In that place there will be weeping and gnashing of teeth.' For many are called, but few are chosen*" (Mt. 22:1-14).

Joel McDurmon writes of verses 2-7:

> "Here the first servant-messengers (another reference to the prophets, no doubt) were simply ignored. Another wave of servant-messengers (more prophets) are treated as such a nuisance that while some still ignored them, "the rest seized his servants, treated them shamefully, and killed them" (v. 6). Jesus is certainly adding [the murdering of the servants or prophets] here as part of the same indictment of Jerusalem He would give again in (Matt. 23:34-36)."

> "The murderers were the entire generation of Israelites… the armies would set the murderers' city on fire (again exactly what happened in AD 70)."

And of verses 8-14, "…yet, after this destruction… during this post-destruction wedding feast, some would sneak in who did not belong… Whether [the man w/out the wedding garment] should be interpreted as the Judaizers who would cause so much dissention in the NT Church, or whether these should just be understood as general heretics in the Church, is not clear."[173]

Strengths:

The Great Commission invitation to the feast is between AD 30 – AD 70 in verses 1-7.

The sending out, rejection and killing of the servants is equated to Matthew 23 and the AD 70 judgment.

The judgment and burning of the city closes the old covenant era/age in AD 70.

The AD 70 judgment is once again characterized as being "cast out into outer darkness where there is weeping and gnashing of teeth."

Weaknesses:

Again, there is no mention that Jesus came to fulfill Isaiah 25:6-9 or 65:12-14 because they would have to address the timing and nature of the resurrection.

Postmillennialists miss that Matthew 22:1-14 is structured with recapitulation:

---

[173] McDurmon, Ibid., 157-158, emphasis MJS

a). (vss. 1-7): 1. There is an invitation to the wedding feast. 2. It is rejected, and 3. this rejection leads to the judgment of Jerusalem in AD 70 – burning their city.

b). (vss. 8-13): 1. There is an invitation, 2. BUT there is NEW information given to us about the same time period that vss. 1-7 didn't tell us about. This rejection results in the invitation to the undesirables – the 10 northern tribes/Samaritans and Gentiles (as laid out in Acts 1:8) and describes the success of the Great Commission between AD 30 – AD 70. And then finally 3. there is a judgment for their rejection (except this time it's described differently – with a Jew or Judaizer trying to achieve salvation by works of the law and not through belief in the Son and His grace – who is then "CAST" out into outer darkness where there is weeping and gnashing of teeth. This is the same language used for the AD 70 judgment Postmillennialists assign to Matthew 8:11-12. So there is no exegetical evidence that vss. 8-13 are a post-AD 70 Great Commission resulting in a different judgment at the end of time.

As far as commentators who are not Postmillennial or Partial Preterist, they again have no problem connecting our Lord's teaching here with the eschatological wedding feast consummation and resurrection of Isaiah 25:6-9. And most give lip service to God sending His armies to burn the city as the AD 70 judgment (some such as Kistemaker try to downplay it). However, these men refuse to interpret the rest of the parable as referring to AD 70, let alone connecting Isaiah 25:6-9 with that judgment since it would destroy their Futurism.

And once again our passage: Matthew 25:1-13

As I pointed out earlier, the reference to "day and hour" not being known by the Son but only by the Father (24:36) is echoing the OT betrothal/marriage/resurrection motifs coming in Israel's last days terminal generation (AD 30 – AD 70), motifs that Jesus came to fulfill (Lk. 21:22; Mt. 5:17-18).

Others such as Kenneth Gentry see the coming of the Lord and "day and hour" in 24:36 – 25:46 as THE Second Coming consummative event with apparently another eschatological wedding and wedding feast to follow!

Again, Postmillennialists are faced with TWO consummative eschatological marriages, feasts and resurrections when the NT only knows of ONE.

So let's do what the Postmillennialists won't do (they won't even MENTION Jesus fulfilling Isa. 25:6-9) and what the other Futurists also won't do (they mention Jesus fulfilling Isa. 25:6-9 or Isa. 65:12-14, but then won't develop those OT contexts).

Context of Isaiah 25:6-9

"On this mountain the LORD Almighty will prepare a feast of rich food for all peoples, a banquet of aged wine- the best of meats and the finest of wines. On this mountain he will destroy the shroud that enfolds all peoples, the sheet that covers all nations; he will swallow up death forever. The Sovereign LORD will wipe away the tears from all faces; he will remove his people's disgrace from all the earth. The LORD has spoken.

In that day they will say, "Surely this is our God; we trusted in him, and he saved us. This is the LORD, we trusted in him; let us rejoice and be glad in his salvation" (Isa. 25:6-9).

In context, the Messianic wedding banquet comes as a result of judgment upon old covenant Israel for her breaking Torah (cf. Isa. 24:5). This makes no sense in the Futurist paradigm because all of the Mosaic Law was supposed to have been fulfilled and passed away at the cross or no later than AD 70.

The Messianic wedding banquet comes when old covenant Jerusalem is judged with her city becoming a "heap of rubble" (cf. Isa. 25:2). Again, this points to an "in time" and local event, and not an end-of-time or global destruction and renewal.

Therefore, Jesus is using Isaiah 24-25 consistently and accurately to demonstrate that the Messianic wedding banquet and resurrection would be fulfilled in AD 70 when old covenant Israel would break Torah, be judged, and her city and temple would be left in a heap of rubble.

I would further add that one of the OT references for the "trumpet" call and "gathering of the elect" (Mt. 24:30-31) is the fulfillment of the resurrection of Isaiah 26:12-21 and 27:12-13. This would also be the time of punishing "Leviathan" and the "dragon" (Isa. 27:1). According to Isaiah 27, this would be "when He makes all the stones of the altars like chalkstones crushed to pieces" and when the "fortified city [Jerusalem]" would be "forsaken" and made "like a wilderness" and He would "not have compassion on them" and "He who formed them will show no favor" (Isa. 27:9-11). Here in Matthew 24-25 the desolation of Jerusalem and her temple would be the time of Christ's trumpet gathering and the punishment of Satan and his angels.

Context of Isaiah 65:12-14

"I will destine you for the sword, and all of you will fall in the slaughter; for I called but you did not answer, I spoke but you did not listen. You did evil in my sight and chose what displeases me." Therefore, this is what the Sovereign LORD says: "My servants will eat, but you will go hungry; my servants will drink, but you will go thirsty; my servants will rejoice, but you will be put to shame. My servants will sing out of the joy of their hearts, but you will cry out from anguish of heart and wail in brokenness of spirit" (Isa. 65:12-14).

Here we are told that God was going to judge old covenant Israel "by the sword" and their fathers "in full" measure. Yet at the same time, He would save a remnant along with the Gentiles (cf. Rms. 10:20—chapter 11).

In that day of judgment, the remnant of believing Jews and Gentiles would feast at the wedding supper and be called by a new name (an everlasting new covenant name – the New Jerusalem) while old covenant Israel would not feast, but would rather starve and be remembered no more. This is in line with the "soon" AD 70 coming of the Lord throughout the book of Revelation. In Revelation 19-21, while the Church (the transformed Israel of God) feasts at the wedding feast, old covenant Israel not only starves, but is actually feasted upon by the birds of the air.

Putting it All Together "Bridging the Gap"

The Analogy of Faith or Analogy of Scripture Hermeneutic teaches us that Scripture interprets Scripture, and Scripture cannot contradict Scripture.

In mathematics and logic we learn that if A bears some relation to B and B bears the same relation to C, then A also bears relation to C. If A = B and B = C, then A = C. Therefore, things which are equal to the same thing are also equal to one another. If equals be added to equals, the wholes are equal (A=B=C).

A (Mt. 8; 22; 25) = Wedding or wedding feast, end of the age, and Parousia fulfilled by AD 70.

B (Isa. 25:6-9) = The wedding feast & resurrection are fulfilled together "in that day."

C (1 Cor. 15) = The resurrection and end of the age are fulfilled at the Parousia.

> *If A bears some relation to B* - Jesus in A (Mt. 8; 22; 25) uses B (Isa. 25:6-9) to teach that His eschatological wedding feast would be fulfilled at His Parousia to close the end of the old covenant age in AD 70
>
> *...and B bears the same relation to C* - Paul uses B (Isa. 25:6-9) in C (1 Cor. 15) to teach that the resurrection would take place at Christ's Parousia and at "the end [of the age]"
>
> *...then A bears it to C* - both Jesus in A (Mt. 8; 22; 25) and Paul in C (1 Cor. 15) use a common source B (Isa. 25:6-9) to teach that the resurrection would be fulfilled "at the end [of the OC age]" Parousia event.

Therefore, things which are equal to the same thing are also equal to one another. If equals be added to equals, the wholes are equal. The ONE Parousia/Second Coming, Eschatological Wedding, end of the age and resurrection event of A (Mt. 8; 22; 25), B (Isa. 25:6-9) and C (1 Cor. 15) was fulfilled in AD 70.

When we harmonize what Partial Preterist Postmillennialists are teaching when it comes to the eschatological wedding and wedding feast with a spiritual resurrection taking place in AD 70 at Christ's Parousia with what other Futurists are teaching on this, being THE ONE consummative event for the Second Coming, resurrection and wedding to occur at the end of the age, we get Full Preterism.

The coming of the Son of Man and the judgment of the nations

- *"When the Son of Man comes in his glory, and all the angels with him, then he will sit on his glorious throne. Before him will be gathered all the nations, and he will separate people one from another as a shepherd separates the sheep from the goats. And he will place the sheep on his right, but the goats on the left. Then the King will say to those on his right, 'Come, you who are blessed by my Father, inherit the kingdom prepared for you from the foundation of the world. For I was hungry and you gave me food, I was thirsty and you gave me drink, I was a stranger and you welcomed me, I was naked and you clothed me, I was sick and you visited me, I was in prison and you came to me.' Then the*

> *righteous will answer him, saying, 'Lord, when did we see you hungry and feed you, or thirsty and give you drink? And when did we see you a stranger and welcome you, or naked and clothe you? And when did we see you sick or in prison and visit you?' And the King will answer them, 'Truly, I say to you, as you did it to one of the least of these my brothers, you did it to me.' "Then he will say to those on his left, 'Depart from me, you cursed, into the eternal fire prepared for the devil and his angels. For I was hungry and you gave me no food, I was thirsty and you gave me no drink, I was a stranger and you did not welcome me, naked and you did not clothe me, sick and in prison and you did not visit me.' Then they also will answer, saying, 'Lord, when did we see you hungry or thirsty or a stranger or naked or sick or in prison, and did not minister to you?' Then he will answer them, saying, 'Truly, I say to you, as you did not do it to one of the least of these, you did not do it to me.' And these will go away into eternal punishment, but the righteous into eternal life" (Matthew 25:31-46).*

The coming of the Son of Man here in glory with His angels is the same coming of Christ as mentioned previously in Matthew 24:30 (and Mt. 16:27-28) to be fulfilled in Jesus' contemporary generation. Again, this is common Hebraic or prophetic recapitulation Matthew is developing while Mark and Luke do not. There is no evidence that this is a different, or future to us, coming of Christ.

The judgment separation of the sheep from the goats is the same event mentioned by Jesus in the separation of the wheat and tares in Matthew 13:39-43, or the "wrath about to come" separation in the "harvest" John the Baptist was teaching about in Matthew 3:7-12 GNT.

There are differing views as to who the "nations" are that Jesus is referring to. Are they strictly the nations of the Jews or do they include the nations of the Gentiles within the Roman Empire and previous evil kings and nations in Hades?

J. Stuart Russell makes the connection between Christ coming in judgment upon the mourning tribes of the land of Palestine in Matthew 24:30 and the Jewish "nations" here:

> "In our Lord's time it was usual to speak of the inhabitants of Palestine as consisting of several nations. Josephus speaks of 'the nation of the Samaritans,' 'the nation of the Batanaeans,' 'the nation of the Galileans,'—using the very word which we find in the passage before us. Judea was a distinct nation, often with a king of its own; so also was Samaria; and so with Idumea, Galilee, Perea, Batanea, Trachonitis, Ituraea, Abilene--all of which had at different times princes with the title of Ethnarch, a name which signifies the ruler of a nation. It is doing no violence then, to the language to understand… [this judgment to

be upon]…as referring to 'all the nations' of Palestine, or 'all the tribes of the land.'"[174]

While Russell offers a compelling argument here, I should point out that the Great Commission of Matthew 24:14 was not limited to the "nations" of Palestine, but rather the "whole world" and the "nations" that made up the Roman Empire. Paul's mission was to the Jews and Gentiles of this world and these nations. Paul would preach to the Jew first and then to the Gentile.

It was his custom to begin in the synagogues where there were Jewish members, who had been scattered throughout the Roman Empire, and their Gentile proselyte converts. Some within these synagogues were converted to Christianity and thus a Church plant had begun. Those who were not converted to Christ began to persecute the Jews and Gentiles in these early churches.

Most likely Nero being married to a Jewess who had friends in high places, such as the Pharisees who had an ax to grind with the Christians, came up with a scheme to blame the Christians for the fires Nero had started. So these synagogues for a season were somewhat protected from the wrath of Nero.

When the feasts of Israel began in and around AD 67, Jews and Gentiles (Judaizers or Christians) from the synagogues within the Roman Empire would have traveled to Jerusalem. Those who had not converted to Christ would have been deceived by the false messiahs and prophets to stay within the walls of Jerusalem and not leave (just as those Jews and their Gentile converts who lived in Jerusalem would have done), and thus Christ's wrath fell upon them and He gave them the same kind of "trouble" they had given the Jewish and Gentile Christians (cf. 2 Thess. 1:5-10) through the hands of the Romans.

When Roman / Jewish tensions began to heat up during the beginning of the war, Jews throughout the Roman Empire also revolted, and Rome was no longer favorable to them, and thus wrath fell upon them and many perished from both groups. However, the Jewish and Gentile converts would have fled to Pella and would have been safe. In this way the Great Commission and God's wrath and judgment extended to the "nations" of the Roman world as well.

The gospel itself, preached throughout the nations of Rome and the nations of Palestine, served as judgment being an "aroma of life" to those God sovereignly called and an "aroma of death" to those who rejected it (cf. 2 Cor. 2:16).

I think Russell also misses that this was likewise a judgment that took place in the spiritual realm for "the Devil and his angels" with Hades being emptied and all those in it being judged at Christ's coming. Jesus connects the vindication of the dead going as far back as Genesis in Matthew 23, so this was not just a local judgment upon Palestine. Therefore, it would have included all of the wicked Jewish and Gentile kings

---

[174] Russell, Ibid., 105.

and those "nations" of the OT who had died and were awaiting judgment at Christ's coming in AD 70 (cf. Revelation 20:5-15 and Revelation 22).

Jesus Himself identified "the day of judgment" and His coming at the end of the old covenant age as not just involving unbelievers within the disciples' local Jewish towns and nations of Israel, but also involving "Sodom and Gomorrah" (cf. Mt. 10:15, 17-23).

The author of Hebrews mentions that it is appointed to die once and then experience judgment (Heb. 9:26-28). This would apply to those who died prior to AD 70 awaiting the judgment, and to those who die post AD 70 and either continue in God's presence or are immediately cast into the lake of fire only to continue having no rest day and night, being eternally separated and tormented.

Jesus said that if anyone did not believe that He was the great "I Am," then he would "die in his sins" (Jn. 8:24). The same principle applies today as we continue to preach the everlasting gospel to the "nations" in the new covenant age (cf. Rev. 22:2, 17). In fact, the prophecy of the destruction of Jerusalem and the wrath involved is a testimony not only of the Deity of Christ, but also of one's eternal destiny in responding to His gospel. For if God took the sin of rejecting His Son so seriously that He came upon the clouds to judge His own covenant nation, how much more will He pour out His wrath upon those today who refuse to hear the message of the "Spirit and the Bride" concerning the "Faithful and True Witness" in fulfilling His prophecies of His passion and Parousia in the historical events of AD 30 – AD 70?!? Selah.

If our exegesis of the Olivet Discourse has been accurate, we should continue to let the Bible interpret itself for further support. Therefore, we will briefly examine how the language of OT imminence was interpreted in connection with metaphoric and symbolic apocalyptic language.

Harmonizing OT and NT apocalyptic language and imminence

I recently debated Charismatic Zionist Dr. Michael Brown on the subject of "that which is perfect" (1 Cor. 13:8-12), proving that the sign and revelatory miraculous gifts of prophecy, tongues and knowledge "ceased" in AD 70 at the "soon" Second Coming, and we are spiritually seeing His face today in the new covenant age (cf. Rev. 22:4-7).[175]

In that debate, knowing Dr. Brown is also an OT scholar, I challenged him with the fact that in the OT de-creation language was not only figurative and metaphorical, but these imminent judgments were fulfilled within the lifetimes of the prophets and their

---

[175] *Review of My Debate with Dr. Brown Over 1 Corinthians 13:8-12*, https://fullpreterism.com/reviewing-and-critiquing-my-debate-with-charismatic-dr-michael-brown-over-1-corinthians-138-12-and-introducing-a-full-preterist-chronomessianic-interpretation-argument-on-daniel-924-27-that-went-un/ The debate on my YouTube channel includes charts and a Power Point: https://www.youtube.com/watch?v=I5DZRv56eQg&t=185s

contemporaries. I will summarize his answer and then critique it, since it is applicable in harmonizing Jesus' teaching in the Olivet Discourse with the OT prophets.

Dr. Michael Brown's answer summarized: "OT imminence may be understood in a few ways. First, the 'Day of the Lord' being 'near' (ex. Isa. 13) may be referring to a truly imminent coming of the Lord in the lifetime and generation of those to whom the prophecy was given. Secondly, it may be referring to a coming of the Lord being 'near' to the immediate audience while at the same time being typological of the Second Coming to be fulfilled at the end of the age or to end world history. And, lastly, it may be referring to projected imminence, that is, when the prophecy would be fulfilled, or begin to unfold, it would be 'soon' at that point. I could provide you with a list if you'd like. NT imminence follows this OT pattern, and I could believe that the coming of the Lord in Matthew 24:27, for example, was imminently fulfilled in AD 70, and this wouldn't affect my position at all. And yet when I read that the coming of the Lord is 'near' in the NT, I believe God is using a different calendar (2 Pet. 3:8) or standard (than that of OT imminence?) and this is simply God wanting every generation to think that His coming is 'near' for them."

The Q&A session was very short, so we could not get into all of these OT prophecies and examine them. I did ask for a "list" of OT time texts that were not fulfilled within the lifetime of the prophet or his contemporaries so we could examine them, but he did not provide his proof texts. So, let's go to a Zionist book that Dr. Brown has endorsed hoping to refute Full Preterism, *Debunking Preterism,* for that list and see if it supports the Full Preterist exegesis or the Premillennial Zionist position. Brock Hollett writes:

- "…the historical manner of interpreting the time statements finds its origins in the Old Testament Prophets. The prophets warned of an impending judgment upon the wicked at the day of the Lord:

- "Wail, for the day of the LORD is near; as destruction from the Almighty it will come!" (Isaiah 13:6)

- "…its time is close at hand and its days will not be prolonged" (Isaiah 13:22)

- "For the day is near, the day of the LORD is near" (Ezekiel 30:3)

- "Alas for the day! For the day of the LORD is near" (Joel 1:15)

- "the day of the LORD is coming; it is near" (Joel 2:1; cf. Isaiah 9:9; Malachi 4:1)

- "For the day of the LORD is near upon all nations. As you have done, it shall be done to you" (Obadiah 1:15)

- "For the day of the LORD is near (Zephaniah 1:7)

- "…in a little while" (Haggai 2:6)"[176]

My response - There are really three issues here which we must address and unpack: 1). The OT imminence of the day of the Lord being near is a pattern which corresponds to the NT imminence of the day of the Lord being near. 2). There are OT types and NT anti-types, or double fulfillments of the day of the Lord. 3). Did or does Psalm 90:4 or 2 Peter 3:8 change the meaning of any OT or NT imminent prophetic material to mean thousands of years? We have already dealt with double fulfillments, so let's address 1 and 3.

1). OT Imminence – the day of the LORD is near

In our debate I appealed to such passages as Ezekiel 7 and 12 along with Isaiah 13:6, and asked if the day of the Lord judgments in these texts were truly "near" and "without delay" and thus fulfilled within the time of the prophet's audience. Dr. Brown affirmed that they were – kind of, sort of. I emphasized that in Ezekiel 7 and 12, where we learn that "the day of the Lord is NEAR" and would be "WITHOUT DELAY" (12:23-25; 7:7), it was the FALSE prophets who sought to change the meaning of God's revelation from "near" and "without delay" to "The vision he [Ezekiel] sees is for MANY years from now, and he prophesies about the DISTANT future" (12:27).

This misapplication and twisting of God's truly prophetic imminent coming in judgment caused God's anger to burn against those false prophets and therefore He affirmed once again, "None of my words will be delayed any longer; whatever I say will be fulfilled, declares the Sovereign LORD" (12:28). What a stinging rebuke for the Futurist (Evangelical or Reformed) and Charismatic Zionist Futurists of our day, such as Dr. Brown, who seek to change the Second Coming and Day of the Lord from being "near" / "in a very little while / would NOT be DELAYED" (ex. Heb. 10:37) / in AD 70 to be, well, in reality fulfilled in the "distant future" from the first century Church. As you can clearly see, Mr. Brock Hollett did not include a discussion of Ezekiel 7 and 12 in addressing OT imminence. How revealing indeed.

Let's go ahead and address the "list" Brown and Hollett have come up with:

A). "Wail, for the day of the LORD is near; as destruction from the Almighty it will come!" (Isaiah 13:6) and "…its time is close at hand and its days will not be prolonged" (Isaiah 13:22).

Response: Unfortunately, many think this prediction is referring to the fall of Babylon at the hands of the Medes years beyond Isaiah's contemporaries. But the truth is that this is referring to the judgment upon Babylon at the hands of Assyria some 15 years from Isaiah's prophetic word. Thus, the prophecy was literally "near" as even a Dispensationalist Zionist commentary points out:

---

[176] Brock Hollett, *DEBUNKING PRETERISM How Over-Realized Eschatology Misses the "Not Yet" of Bible Prophecy*, (Kearney, NE: Morris Publishing, 2018), 21

"After Sargon II died in 705 there was much rebellion in the Assyrian Empire. The Elamites put Mushezib-Marduk over Babylon (692–689); he made an alliance with several nations including the Medes. To subdue the rebellion in Babylon, **Sennacherib marched there in 689 and destroyed it**."[177]

"Isaiah 13:14–18 (BKC): The statement I will stir up against them the Medes (v. 17) has caused much discussion among Bible students. Many interpreters, because of the mention of the fall of Babylon (v. 19), assume that Isaiah was (in vv. 17–18) prophesying Babylon's fall in 539 (cf. Dan. 5:30–31) to the Medes and Persians. However, that view has some difficulties. In the Medo-Persian takeover in 539 there was very little change in the city; it was not destroyed so it continued on much as it had been. But Isaiah 13:19–22 speaks of the destruction of Babylon. Also the word "them," against whom the Medes were stirred up (v. 17), were the Assyrians (referred to in vv. 14–16), not the Babylonians. It seems better, then, to understand this section as dealing with events pertaining to the Assyrians' sack of Babylon in December 689 b.c. As Seth Erlandsson has noted, "The histories of the Medes, Elamites, and Babylonians converge around the year 700 in the struggle against the Assyrian world power and … Babylon assumes a particularly central position in that great historical drama from the latter years of the 8th century down to the fall of Babylon in 689."[178]

"Babylon was besieged no fewer than three times – in the lifetime of Isaiah, viz., in 710 by Sargon, and in 703 and 691 by Sennacherib." Babylon's fall in 689 is, however, "die einzige wirkliche Zerstorung von Babylon, die uberhaupt stattgefunden hat."

"With regard to Babylon's role in the history, her position mainly in the 6th century has been delineated when dealing with Old Testament texts. The main reason for this was that Babylon's history during the Assyrian period was less familiar, while, on the other hand, the historical events involving Babylon in the 6th century were well known. *It is therefore significant that when the new Akkadian text-finds from Mesopotamia began to be published towards the end of the 19th century, they gave rise to a reconsideration of the current interpretations of various passages…*".

"…we have arrived at the culmination of the many bloody struggles, namely the fall of Babylon. When the king of Elam was smitten by a stroke of apoplexy in April 689, Sennacherib took advantage of the occasion and marched against Babylon to take there his revenge against Elam and put an end to Babylon's power once and for all. In December 689 the city was captured and Mushezib-Mushezib-Arduk taken prisoner. That which no one previously had dared and

---

[177] (Martin, J. A. (1985). Isaiah. In J. F. Walvoord & R. B. Zuck (Eds.), *The Bible Knowledge Commentary: An Exposition of the Scriptures* (Vol. 1, p. 1061). Wheaton, IL: Victor Books.)
[178] Ibid., 91–2

which was considered to be out of the question, Sennacherib now accomplished. Marduk's famed and holy city had laid in ruins. "like the on-coming of a storm I broke loose, and overwhelmed it like a hurricane" (cf. Isa. 21:1). "I completely invested that city...whether small or great, I left none. With their corpses I filled the city squares (wide places)...The gods dwelling therein, –the hands of my people took them, and they smashed (*usabbiru*) them" (cf. Isa. 21:9). "The city and (its) house, from its foundation to its top, I destroyed, I devastated, I burned with fire. The wall and outer wall, temples and gods, temple towers of brick and earth, as many as there were, I razed and dumped them into the Arahtu Canal." His final gesture was to have huge volumes of water released over the ruins in order to obliterate every trace of that city which had constantly been in revolt. "I made its destruction more complete than that by a flood. That in days to come the site of that city, and (its) temples and gods, might not be remembered, I completely blotted it out with (floods of) water and made it like a meadow." That event must have had to the effect of a bomb on the contemporary world and it is significant that Sennacherib's successor, as his first measure, sets himself to the reconstruction of the "holy" city. He laid stress on Babylon's cosmopolitan character and its destiny as an open city and gathering place of the peoples. What had befallen Babylon as a result of Sennacherib's fury should never happen again. **When the Neo-Babylonian kingdom had come to an end 539 and was succeeded by the Persian, no one did violence to Babylon**.

This historical excursus has thus shown that the histories of the Medes, Elamites and Babylonians converge around the year 700 in the struggle against the Assyrian world-power and that Babylon assumes a particularly central position in that great historical drama from the latter years of the 8th century down **to the fall of Babylon in 689**.[179]

Dr. Brown, while agreeing that imminence was literal in Isaiah 13:6, 22, mentioned that Isaiah 13 was going on to deal with the destruction of the planet. Yet again the hyper-literal Zionist *Bible Knowledge Commentary* admits:

"The statements in 13:10 about the heavenly bodies (**stars.... sun ... moon**) no longer functioning may figuratively describe the total turnaround of the political structure of the Near East. The same would be true of **the heavens** trembling **and the earth** shaking (v. 13), figures of speech suggesting all-encompassing destruction" (ibid., p. 1059).

There is nothing in the passage which tells us that this is a type of a literal "day of the LORD" resulting in the end of world history and the destruction of the planet that Jesus allegedly picks up on Matthew 24:3, 29, 35 and applies to our future. This is simply assumed here in Isaiah and in Matthew 24. The truth is that both Isaiah 13 and Matthew

---

[179] Seth Erlandsson, *The Burden of Babylon A Study of Isaiah 13:2—14:23*, (Berlingska, Boktryckeriet Lund, 1970), 91-92

24 are referring to two contemporary and imminent judgments using common, non-literal apocalyptic language.

B). "For the day is near, the day of the LORD is near" (Ezekiel 30:3). "When I blot you out, I will cover the heavens and make their stars dark; I will cover the sun with a cloud, and the moon shall not give its light. All the bright lights of heaven will I make dark over you, and put darkness on your land, declares the Lord God" (Ezek. 32:7-8).

Response - This is addressing a historical judgment upon Egypt around 587 BC by the Assyrians and was literally fulfilled in a "near" time frame using symbolic, apocalyptic language. Again, there's nothing in this passage telling us this is a type of a physical cloud coming of God in the future to destroy the planet.

C). Obadiah 1:15 – The "day of the LORD is NEAR."

Response - The quote below is part of what John Gill had to say of this passage, which was true, but later he begins dropping the ball and compromising with an end-of-time judgment for Edom and Rome connected to "antichrists." However, this is the accurate statement:

> "Edom and the other surrounding nations/heathen to Jerusalem rejoiced to see God's people punished by Him through the Babylonians (somewhere between 605 – 586 BC or in the Jewish calendar 439 – 420 BC), and so God would come in a 'near' time frame upon them (within five years) after His judgment of Jerusalem. The 'nations' here are local nations: the Edomites, Egyptians, Philistines, Tyrians, Ammonites, Moabites and others…"[180]

God was able to deceive Edom and other nations – giving them over to their pride. He allowed even their "friends" to deceive them (v. 7). God likewise laid a trap for old covenant Jerusalem in AD 70, giving them over to their pride and false prophets – in thinking and calculating Daniel's seventy weeks so as to think it was the time in which God was going to deliver them from the Romans, when in fact the opposite was the case. They would be food for the vultures of Rome for rejecting their Messiah/Jesus.

We have learned from the Dead Sea Scrolls that even the Essenes were caught up in their self-righteousness, thinking God was going to deliver them (the true children of light) from the Romans and Apostate Jerusalem.

However, as the Apostate religious rulers of Jerusalem learned along with those Monkish Essenes who isolated themselves, all who rejected Jesus would perish at the hands of their own brethren, friends and Rome in the events of AD 67 - 70.

D). "Alas for the day! For the day of the LORD is near" (Joel 1:15); "the day of the LORD is coming; it is near" (Joel 2:1; cf. Isaiah 9:9; Malachi 4:1).

Response - Joel 1-3 is addressing two Days of the Lord – one that was literally "near" for Joel's immediate audience and one that would be near in the last days. The second is consistent with, say, Deuteronomy 31-32, which taught that Israel's "end" would be

---

[180] John Gill, Ibid.,

"near" in her "latter days" when a specific "perverse and crooked generation" arrived, which Peter tells us predicted his contemporary generation and therefore the time when the "end of all things is NEAR" (Acts 2:40/1 Pet. 1:10-12, 4:5-7).

Don Preston points out the following:

> "So, the language of the Day of the Lord is used in the Old Testament. When the Old Testament prophets said the Day was near, they were not referring to the end of the age, consummative Day of the Lord. When they referred to a Day of the Lord that was near, it was an event that was to occur in their lifetime (See Ezekiel 12.21f again). However, when they were speaking of the last days, when the kingdom would be established, the resurrection, etc., they were told that it was not near (cf. Isaiah 2.2-21f).
>
> This is clearly illustrated in Joel. In the first two chapters, the prophet declared "the Day of the Lord is near" (Joel 1.15; 2.1, 10). He repeatedly describes events that took place historically, in an in-time Day of the Lord, as we have documented above.
>
> However, in verse 28 the prophet said: "It shall come to pass afterward." What does "afterward" mean? It means after the events he had been describing, at another time known as the last days, the events that he then describes would be near. Notice that in 3:1, he then says "In those days (the last days, DKP) and at that time..."
>
> Joel is a case of projected imminence. That is my term to describe what happens in the O.T. when a prophet speaks of events that were not for his day, but he describes events in the distant future. As he describes those events, he says that in the days under consideration, other events would be near. Moses did this in Deuteronomy 4.25f, when he spoke of Israel's coming future. He said that after they had dwelt long in the land, and then became corrupt, that then, a long time off from his perspective, when they became corrupt, "you will soon utterly perish from the land." Moses was not saying that they were, when he wrote, about to utterly perish. He was projecting himself and his audience to a distant time, and saying that when certain things happened, their apostasy, that then their destruction would be near.
>
> This is what happens in Joel. The writer speaks of events that were for his day. They were truly near. Then, however, he turns to the distant future, and says that when those distant days came, then, and not until then, another Day of the Lord would be near (Joel 3.14). Joel was not affirming that the last days Day of the Lord was near, or else Peter was wrong in 1 Peter 1.10!"[181]

Malachi 4:1: Dr. Brown, writing of Malachi 3:1-5, says:

---

[181] Don K. Preston, *Can God Tell Time*, (JaDon publishers), 29-30

> "...God would visit the Second Temple, purifying some of his people [bringing salvation] and bringing judgment on others. There would be a **divine visitation of great import that would occur in the days of the Second Temple**... I ask you, **did this happen? If it did, then the Messiah must have come before the Temple was destroyed in 70 C.E.; <u>if not, God's Word has failed</u>.**"[182]

The context of Malachi 3:1-5 / 4:1-6 and how it is applied to John the Baptist (as Elijah) is very clearly referring to the Second Coming of Jesus in AD 70.

Brown arbitrarily divides the "divine visitation of God" in a judgment of fire, whereby He saves and purifies some and brings wrath on others, here in Mal. 3:1-5 as AD 70, from the SAME coming day of the Lord and judgment of fire in Mal. 4:1-6. Let's once again take a look at the context and description of this ONE coming of the Lord in AD 70 and John the Baptist's imminent "already" and imminent "not yet" eschatology in developing these OT passages.

1). Luke 1:77-79; 7:27: "...for you [John] will go before the LORD to prepare his ways... whereby **the sunrise [inclusive of the imminent, 'not yet' Second Coming - Mal. 4:2]** shall visit us from on high... This is the one about whom it is written: 'I will send my messenger ahead of you, who will prepare your way before you.'"

2). Malachi 3:1-5/4:1-6: "Behold, I send my messenger [John as Elijah], and he will prepare the way before me [Jesus]. And the Lord [Jesus] whom you seek **will suddenly come <u>to his temple [Second Coming]</u>**; and the messenger of the [new] covenant [Jesus] in whom you delight, behold, **he is coming [Second Coming]**, says the Lord of hosts. **But who can endure <u>the day of his coming [Second Coming]</u>, and who can stand <u>when he appears [Second Coming]? For he is like a refiner's fire</u>...** For behold, <u>**the day is coming, burning** like an oven</u>, when all the arrogant and all evildoers will be stubble. **<u>The day that is coming</u>** shall **set them ablaze**, says the Lord of hosts, so that **it will leave them neither root nor branch**. But for you who fear my name, **<u>the SUN of Righteousness [Second Coming]</u>** shall rise with healing in its rays/wings. You shall go out ... leaping like calves from the stall... **<u>Behold, I will send you Elijah [John] the prophet before the great and awesome day of the Lord comes [Second Coming]</u>**. And he will turn the hearts of fathers to their children and the hearts of children to their fathers, lest I come and **strike the land with a decree of utter destruction**."

3). Matthew 3:2: "In those days John the Baptist came preaching in the wilderness of Judea, and saying, 'Repent, for **the <u>kingdom</u> of heaven is <u>at hand</u>**!'"

The context will develop that the Kingdom being "at hand" is not just the arrival of the imminent eschatological "already" of the kingdom, but the imminent judgment or "not yet" of the kingdom as well.

---

[182] Brown, Ibid. *AJOJ, Vol. 1*, 77-78

4). Matthew 3:3: "For this is he who was spoken of by the prophet Isaiah, saying: 'The voice of one **crying** in the wilderness: "**Prepare the way** of the Lord; Make His paths straight."'"

And yet the context of what John is "crying" and the way he is preparing is one of not just salvation, but also judgment:

*5). Isaiah 40:5-10: "A voice cries... the **glory of the LORD** shall be revealed [seen], and all flesh shall see it together... All flesh is grass, And all its loveliness is like the flower of the field. The grass withers, the flower fades, Because the breath of the Lord blows upon it; Surely the people are grass. The grass withers, the flower fades, But the word of our God stands forever... Say to the cities of Judah, 'Behold your God!' Behold, the Lord God shall come with a strong hand, And His arm shall rule for Him; Behold, His reward is with Him [cf. Mt. 16:27-28], And His work before Him."*

6). Matthew 3:7: "Many Pharisees and Sadducees came to be baptized by John. He said to them, 'You children of snakes! Who warned you to escape from the angry **judgment that is [Greek *mello*] coming soon**?' (Mt. 3:7 CEB). ...the **punishment** [or wrath] God is **about to send** (WUESTNT; GNT)?"

7). Matthew 3:10-12: "And **even now the ax is laid to the root of the trees**. Therefore, every tree which does not bear good fruit is cut down and thrown into the fire. I indeed baptize you with water unto repentance, but He who is coming after me is mightier than I, whose sandals I am not worthy to carry. **He will baptize you with the Holy Spirit and fire**. **His winnowing fan *is* in His hand**, and He will thoroughly clean out His threshing floor, and gather His **wheat into the barn**; but He will burn up the **chaff with unquenchable fire**" (Matt. 3:10-12).

We prefer the Reformed Historic Premillennialist view of this passage over Dr. Brown's Dispensational or Zionist friendly one:

"...**the awful judgment of God, which Christ was ready to execute**, and in a **short time** would execute on the unbelieving and impenitent Jews: hence it is said to be '**in his hand.**' ...By '**his floor is meant the land of Israel**, where he was born, brought up, and lived; of which the Lord says, 'O my threshing, and the corn of my floor!' #Isa 21:10."[183]

Concluding Malachi 3-4 and John the Baptist's imminent "not yet" eschatology, the truth is that the Church has identified the coming of the Lord here as both His imminent coming in judgment in AD 70 and as the Second Coming event. As Full Preterists, we acknowledge both positions are true.

E). "For the day of the LORD is near upon all nations. As you have done, it shall be done to you" (Obadiah 1:15).

---

[183] John Gill's Commentary, Ibid. free online

My Response - Matthew Poole points out there was truly an imminent judgment of Edom and the surrounding nations here:

> **"For the day of the Lord,** of just revenge from the Lord upon this cruelty of **Edom**, the time which the Lord hath appointed for **the punishing of this and other nations, is near upon all the heathen; which God had given to Nebuchadnezzar**, and which by this man's arms God would punish, as **Jeremiah 27:2-7**; and that day may **justly be accounted near, which shall come within the compass of one man's life**, and that well advanced in years, as Nebuchadnezzar now was.
>
> **As thou hast done,** perfidiously, cruelly, and ravenously against Jacob, with a hostile, revengeful mind, it shall be done by thine enemies **to thee,** as **Obadiah 1:7**; and this came to pass **on Edom within five years after Jerusalem was sacked and ruined**; within which space of time Obadiah prophesied, reproving Edom, and threatening him for what he had done against Jerusalem and its inhabitants."[184]

Again, there is no exegetical evidence within Obadiah that this is a truly imminent judgment upon Edom and the surrounding nations that is typological of another NT "day of the Lord," of which "near" then means 2,000 plus years and counting. Brown's "argument" is "bizarre" and "fascinating," to use Dr. Brown's phrases in our debate.

F). "For the day of the LORD is near (Zephaniah 1:7).

Response - This is descriptive of an imminent judgment upon the Jews at the hands of the Babylonians. John Gill writes of this passage and the genuine nearness of the event:

> "For the day of the Lord is at hand; the time of his vengeance on the Jewish nation for their sins, which he had fixed in his mind, and had given notice of by his prophets: this began to take place at Josiah's death, after which the Jews enjoyed little peace and prosperity; and his successor reigned but three months, was deposed by the king of Egypt, and carried thither captive, and there died; and Jehoiakim, that succeeded him, in the fourth year of his reign was carried captive into Babylon, or died by the way thither; **so that this day might well be said to be at hand**:"[185]

Again, there is no exegetical evidence here of a truly imminent day of the LORD that is typological of a NT day of the Lord that is said to be "near," but really isn't!

G). "…in a little while" (Haggai 2:6).

Response - Here is a section taken from our book on this passage concerning its truly imminent fulfillment in Haggai's day and then the truly imminent anti-type in the

---

[184] *Matthew Poole's Commentary*, also free and available online, Biblehum.com
[185] *John Gill's Exposition of the Bible*, Ibid.

fulfillment of the book of Hebrews, which was fulfilled in that first century generation in AD 70:

> "The prophecy of Haggai 2:6–9, 21–23 was fulfilled, in a "typical" sense, in the lifetime of Zerubbabel. In about *four years* ("*in a little while*") after the prophecy was given, God overthrew all the nations, (He "*shook the heavens, the earth, the sea and the dry land*") and the desire or wealth of all nations came, and the temple was filled with glory (with gold and silver). (Compare Haggai 1:15; 2:10 and Ezra 6:15.)

This all took place when Darius King of Persia overturned Israel's enemies, who for years had been preventing the rebuilding of God's house. Darius decreed, "*May God... overthrow any king or people who lifts a hand to change this decree or to destroy this temple in Jerusalem*" (Ezra 6:11–12). Darius forced Israel's enemies themselves to pay the full cost of the rebuilding, as well as the full cost of all the daily, priestly services (Ezra 6:8–10).

The military and political power of Israel's enemies was overthrown. They had tried to turn the king against Israel (Ezra 5), but God turned their own stratagems against them. He made them subservient to His people, taking their own wealth for the building of His glorious, earthly house. God had thus "moved heaven and earth" to keep the covenant that He had made with His people through Moses (Ezra 6:18; Hag. 2:5).

The prophecy of Haggai 2:6–9; 21–23 also foreshadowed the fulfillment of the better promise (Heb. 8:6) that was fulfilled in Christ's generation. Israel's building of the greater, earthly house in Zerubbabel's generation was an example of the building of the true, heavenly "*House*" in Christ.

Within perhaps only *four years* ("*in a little while*") after Hebrews 12:26 was written, God overthrew all the nations. He "*shook the heavens, the earth, the sea and the dry land.*" The desire of all nations came, and God's Temple was filled with Glory.

This happened when God overturned His kingdom-enemies who, in their persecution of the church, had furiously resisted the construction of His new covenant temple (Eph. 2:21–22; I Peter 2:5). Despite the rage of the enemies, God enlisted countless multitudes of them to build His new House (Rom. 5:10; Col. 1:21; Rev. 5:9); and the enemies who resisted to the end were crushed, and were cast out of the kingdom in AD 70 (Matt. 8:12; 21:43; Lk. 13:28; Acts 4:25–28; Gal. 4:30; Rev. 3:9).

God "*moved heaven and earth*" to keep the covenant that He made with His elect through the blood of Christ. Now the Father, the Son, and the Holy Spirit dwell eternally in the universal church, which is the new covenant House of promise (Jn. 14:23; Gal. 4:19; Eph. 2:21–22; 3:17; Col. 1:27; II Peter 1:19; Rev. 3:20; 21:2–3). Through the power of the eternal gospel, the desire of the nations flows into *"the more perfect tabernacle"* today and forever (Heb. 9:11; Rev. 21:26–27), and God Himself is its unfading Glory (Rev. 21:23). Amen."[186]

2). *Does 2 Peter 3:8 change the meaning of NT imminence?*

"But do not overlook this one fact, beloved, that **with the Lord one day is as a thousand years, and a thousand years as one day**. The Lord **is not slow to fulfill his promise as some count slowness**, but is patient toward you, not wishing that any should perish, but that all should reach repentance" (2 Pet. 3:8-9).

Response - Peter is quoting from Psalm 90:4, which in context reads,

> "Before the mountains were brought forth, or ever you had formed the earth and the world, from everlasting to everlasting you are God. **You return man to dust and say, "Return, O children of man!" For a thousand years in your sight are but as yesterday when it is past, or as a watch in the night. You sweep them away as with a flood**; they are like a dream, like grass that is renewed in the morning: in the morning it flourishes and is renewed; in the evening it fades and withers. For we are brought to an end by your anger; by your wrath we are dismayed. You have set our iniquities before you, our secret sins in the light of your presence. For all our days pass away under your wrath; we bring our years to an end like a sigh. The years of our life are seventy, or even by reason of strength eighty; yet their span is but toil and trouble; they are soon gone, and we fly away. Who considers the power of your anger, and your wrath according to the fear of you? So, teach us to number our days that we may get a heart of wisdom" (Ps. 90:2-12).

In our debate, Dr. Brown appealed to 2 Peter 3:8 and claimed Peter was using it to communicate that "God has a different calendar than we do" and therefore NT imminence of "near", "soon", "about to", "quickly", "in a very little while and will not delay" can really mean 2,000 plus years and counting.

There are several points I would like to make on these passages.

Point #1 – Since Dr. Brown admitted that at least some of the OT days of the Lord that were "near" were genuinely near and fulfilled within the lifetimes of their audiences, and Psalm 90:4 is an OT passage, then how is it that "God's calendar of time that isn't ours" didn't change the meaning of "near" in the OT?!? As seen in Ezekiel 7 and 12, God was upset when the false prophets changed the meaning of "near" and "would not delay" to "far off" or to a fulfillment for "many days" beyond their lifetimes. If Dr. Brown's interpretation of 2 Peter 3:8 is correct, then God had no right to be angry and the false prophets could have appealed to Psalm 90:4 and reasoned, "we know Ezekiel is saying the day of the Lord's judgment is 'near' and will 'not be delayed,' BUT,

---

[186] David Green, Ed Hassertt and Michael Sullivan, *House Divided Bridging the Gap in Reformed Eschatology A Preterist Response to When Shall These Things Be? (Ramona, CA: Vision Publishing, Second Edition 2013),* 63-65

remember, 'with the Lord one day is as a thousand years, and a thousand years as one day.' Therefore, really the prophecy could be 'far off,' right?"

If Psalm 90:4 wasn't used in the OT to **change the meaning** of the day of the Lord being "near," it most assuredly wasn't being used by Peter or any NT author that way.

Point #2 – *The context of Psalm 90* is that the generation of unbelievers perished in the desert just as God had determined and promised. They did not outlast God's judgment, for God's word was sure and accurate. The Psalm begins with a reminder going as far back to Adam, who returned to the dust after 930 years. Psalm 90:4 is a contrast of Adam returning to dust, not achieving a thousand years, and God considering man's longest days as nothing or but a "day" in His sight. Even when man may come close to a thousand years—Methuselah lived 969 years (Gen 5:27)—in God's reckoning it is but "a day." As mentioned in Ezekiel 7 and 12, the POINT was not only they were twisting the meaning of "near," but were boasting that they could OUTLAST God's predicted judgment.

The context of the mockers in 2 Peter is similar. In the case of the "mockers," they were mocking Jesus' prediction to come in their generation as if it would not come and they would outlast it. "All things continue" (2 Pet. 3:4) was their response to a definite, imminent prophecy of their demise. But Peter had to point out that they were deliberately forgetting certain aspects of their history, which Psalm 90 covers. When God determines a judgment upon man (Adam returning to dust, the flood, perishing in the wilderness, etc.), it is certain to take place when God says it will, and most assuredly they too would not outlast or dismiss it away. Peter's point is that others, like the mockers within our history, have thought they could outlast or deny God's certain and imminent judgments, but they couldn't. While they appealed to a history lesson of their fathers since the creation of the old covenant age, at the same time they were deliberately leaving out very important things concerning the judgments of their people. So, YES, Jesus is KEEPING His promise and, despite their mocking, they would not outlast His "NEAR" (1 Pet. 4:5-7, 17) judgment coming upon them anymore than others thought they could.

Not only that, but the Rabbis used Ps. 90:15-17 to teach a 40 year, second exodus generation in which Messiah would have a transitionary reign between their old covenant, "this age" and the Messianic "about to come," new covenant age. So, YES, Jesus is KEEPING His promise just as Psalm 90 lays out.

Psalm 90:4 is also brought up in Revelation 20 as well with the Church currently being within the 1,000 year millennial reign. Here were some of my thoughts on this text taken from our book *HD*:

> "Adam falling short of the 1,000-year lifespan by 70 years (Gen. 5:5) may represent his being created a mortal being and perishing in sin outside of God's presence. If this is the case, then it is more than reasonable that the number 1,000 took on the symbolism and representation of Christ's and the church's victory over Death in contrast to Adamic man's vain existence apart from God's salvation (Eccl. 6:6).

> Some Evangelicals and Reformed theologians along with some preterists such as Milton Terry do not understand the long lifespans in the early chapters of Genesis to be literal.[3] They believe that the lifespans were symbolic and contained numerological elements. But even if Adam's lifespan was a literal 930 years, this does not exclude an anti-typical, symbolic 1,000 years in Revelation 20.
>
> When Messiah came as *"the last Adam,"* His reign in and through the church for a symbolic thousand years brought the church not to the dust of the earth separated from God's presence, but to the Tree of Life and into the very presence of God (Rev. 20–22:12). Through faith in and union with Christ as the Last Adam (the Tree of Life and New Creation), Christians have achieved what Adam could not. The church was clothed with *"immortality"*; it attained unto the *"fullness"* of life in AD 70; and it will never die for the *aeons* of the *aeons* (2 Cor. 1:20; 1 Cor. 15:45–53; Rev. 21–22; Jn. 11:26–27)."[187]

Christ and the Church were reigning for a symbolic 1,000 year period (Rev. 20). Old covenant Israel and its "mockers" would not outlast this transitionary or probationary period. They would become a "corpse" picked apart by the Roman vultures/eagles by AD 70, while the Church would continue with Him in the Spirit having eternal life and having dominion over the nations through the everlasting gospel. Selah.

While I would not agree with this commentator on all that he has to say of our text, I would agree that Peter's emphasis is that God was **not** slow or producing a delay to His coming.

The idea that the Lord is not slow is probably an allusion to Hab 2:3: "For the revelation awaits an appointed time; it speaks of the end and will not prove false. Though it linger, wait for it; **it will certainly come and will not delay**." In some Greek translations of the OT, exactly the same word is used for "delay" that 2 Peter uses. Furthermore, one could understand the Greek as saying, "He will not be slow" or "He will not delay." While a similar thought is expressed in Isa 13:22, Sir 35:19 (LXX; 35:22 in the NRSV) is closer to our thought here: "**Indeed, the Lord will not delay, and like a warrior [or "upon them"] will not be patient until he crushes the loins of the unmerciful…**"[188]

Unfortunately, this commentator does not see the significance of my next point (#3) below in connection with these OT references, which he cites in relation to Jesus' and Peter's prediction of a genuine nearness that "will not delay."

Point #3 – The very fact that the mockers (Judaizers – false prophets and teachers) were mocking the reality of Jesus' coming, in light of some of the early church fathers having already died, demonstrates that the coming of the Lord was not a limitless coming but one which was well known to be prophesied to take place within some of

---

[187] Sullivan, ed. David Green, Ibid., *House Douse Divided,* 130

[188] Davids, P. H. (2006). *The letters of 2 Peter and Jude* (p. 278). Grand Rapids, MI: William B. Eerdmans Pub. Co.)

their lifetimes, in their generation and thus "near" to them (Mt. 16:27-28; Mt. 24:27-34; 1 Pet. 4:5-7, 17). The fact that the text implies the false prophets understood NT imminence better than Dr. Brown and other Futurists is a sad commentary indeed.

Point #4 – What would happen if a Bible College or Seminary student asked the instructor in a hermeneutics class, "If I have over 200 clear texts on a given subject and I only have one passage that seems to give a contradictory interpretation of the clear 200, which passage or passages should I go with?"

Everyone knows what the hermeneutics instructor would say (no matter what the denomination). "You go with the 200 clear passages and interpret the one passage in light of the others or in such a way that does not contradict them."

And yet when the Full Preterist has over 200 OT and NT clear texts, which demonstrate the "Day of the LORD" was "near" or "without delay," so many of these same instructors are willing to throw ALL NT imminence concerning the coming of the Lord, judgment and resurrection completely under the bus in their misguided understanding of just one passage (2 Pet. 3:8).

There have been other attempts to get rid of the obvious meaning of NT imminence. Let's briefly address some of them.

The "symbolic", "principle", "ideal" and "eschatological time" view

Simon Kistemaker, in order to walk the creedal party line, decides that the time texts in Revelation should be understood in an "ideal" way or should be somehow "symbolically" interpreted as "…the meaning of eschatological time, expressed not in chronological periods, but in terms of principle."[189]

Response: I hate to sound disrespectful here, but it sounds like someone is smoking weed or crack when I hear bizarre comments like these. Or maybe this is coming from some secular philosophical department somewhere? Or perhaps some liberal neo-orthodox seminary? Unfortunately, none of these are the case. Kistemaker is clearly trying his best to hide behind very vague and so-called "scholarly" or philosophical language. Why? It's because he knows he has no lexical support for making these kinds of comments! I'm sorry, but the truth is that the Futurist and creedal emperor really doesn't have any clothes on here, folks.

This sounds like other kinds of gibberish I hear such as Jesus' Second Coming is "always near" (ex. Anthony A. Hoekema),[190] or "For the NT writers, the nearness of the Parousia is not so much chronological nearness as a "salvation-history nearness."[191]

---

[189] Simon Kistemaker, ed. Keith A. Mathison, *WHEN SHALL THESE THINGS BE? A REFORMED RESPONSE TO HYPER-PRETERISM*, (Phillipsburg, New Jersey: P&R Publishing, 2004), 238.

[190] Anthony A Hoekema, *THE BIBLE AND THE FUTURE*, (Eerdmans Publishing Company, Grand Rapids, MI: 1979), 126

[191] Ibid.

John MacArthur claims the NT authors truly expected Christ's "soon", "will not delay" coming to occur in their lifetimes, but then says that's just what Christ wants all of us to think and expect. Yet MacArthur also affirms that Christ may continue to "delay" His coming another 2,000 years and counting. If language means anything, how on God's green earth can Christ's Second Coming be genuinely "near" and "will not delay" for the inspired writers of the NT, genuinely "near" and "will not delay" for us, and yet at the same time Christ could delay His coming for another 2,000 years?!? MacArthur's friend. R.C. Sproul. correctly called this kind of philosophical mumbo jumbo and exegetical gymnastics as on par with liberal "neo-orthodoxy," and he corrected men like F.F. Bruce for trying to defend similar dribble:

> "When F. F. Bruce speaks of faith making the time be 'at hand,' this sounds all too much like Rudolf Bultmann's famous theology of timelessness, which removes the object of faith from the realm of **real history** and consigns it to a super temporal realm of the **always present hic et nunc [here and now]**."[192]

There is also some irony here for those Futurist, Reformed commentators like Kistemaker, Hoekema, etc. who claim to want to honor God's sovereignty in the redemptive history of men. We hear from them that "God will accomplish what He sets out to do when He says and decrees it to take place" kind of rhetoric. John uses a very strong word in Revelation 1:1 to indicate that the prophecy most assuredly will be fulfilled "shortly" when he says it "**must (Greek *dei*) shortly take place.**" This word means, "necessity **established by the counsel and decree of God**, *especially by that purpose of his which relates to the salvation of men by the intervention of Christ* and which is disclosed in the Old Testament prophecies." The Second Coming or appearing of Christ as our Great High Priest "in a very little while and will not delay" (Heb. 9:26-28—10:37) "relates to the salvation of men," and to teach otherwise is to go against the sovereign decrees and purposes of God! To claim Christ didn't come when He decreed and purposed to is not something any real Calvinist should attempt to teach. Selah.

Not only is a denial of God's sovereignty inseparably connected to a denial of NT imminence, but an indirect attack on the inspiration of Scripture is in view as well. As Gary DeMar writes,

> "Any student of the Bible who does not interpret these time texts to mean anything other than close at hand is in jeopardy of **denying the integrity of the Bible.**"[193]

The inspired writers were "led into all truth…concerning things to come" (the timing and nature of the Second Coming). They were not giving us what they "felt" might happen when they taught Christ was going to come in their lifetimes, generation, soon, etc.

---

[192] R.C. Sproul, *The Last Days According To Jesus* (Grand Rapids, MI: Baker Books, 1998), 108-109

[193] DeMar, *Last Days Madness*, Ibid., (1999 edition), 393, emphasis MJS

The "when Jesus decides to come He will come really fast then" view

"Must **shortly** or **quickly** (Greek *en taxei in the taxos word group*) take place" (Rev. 1:1; see also: 2:16; 3:11; 22:6-7, 12, 20) is a key phrase.

Premillennial Zionist John Walvoord writes of *en tachei*,

> "…indicating a rapidity of execution after the beginning takes place. The idea is not that the event may occur soon, but that **when it does, it will be sudden** (Lk. 18:8; Acts 12:7; 22:18; 25:4; Rms. 16:20)."[194]

Let me summarize this view as teaching "whenever Jesus decides to come, then He will come really quickly." This is like me calling the fire department in an emergency and they tell me, "Don't worry, we will be there "shortly", "quickly" and our arrival will be "near." And yet when they pull up a *week later* after my house has burnt down I say, "I thought you were coming 'quickly.' What happened?!?" And they reply, "Well, what we meant was when we decide to come, then we would drive very quickly at that point." This is how Dispensationalist Thomas Ice has also sought to interpret the *tachos* word family with no success.[195]

Response: None of the translations I have consulted give this imaginative meaning to *en tachei*. Not only this, but Arndt & Gingrich translate *en tachei* (in Lk. 18:8; Acts 12:7; 22:18; 25:4; Rom. 16:20; Walvoord's "proof texts") as "soon, in a short time." And even outside of the Bible (e.g. LXX or Josephus) *taxos* means - yes, you guessed it - "quickly" or "without delay." And even if one were to grant this unsubstantiated meaning to *en tachei*, what of the other Greek words John used to communicate imminence in Revelation such as "near" / "at hand" (Greek *engus*) (Rev. 1:3; 22:10) or "about to be" (Greek *mello*) (Rev. 1:19; 3:10)? Clearly, John is using a wide range of imminent words such as *en tachei, taxos*, and *mello* harmoniously to prophesy that Christ's Second Coming would be fulfilled imminently and not thousands of years later.

The Book of Revelation is filled with a contemporary first century group of Christians experiencing persecution and martyrdom, in which Jesus comforts them by explaining that He will return "soon" and in a "little while" to vindicate them from their first century persecutors and give them "relief" at His appearing from these Jewish persecutors – their "countrymen" the Pharisees, or the "synagogue of Satan" (Rev. 6:10-11; Mt. 23:30-36, Mt. 24; 1Thess. 2:14-16/2Thess. 1:6-7). Jesus was either faithful to return and gave them relief from these first century persecutors or He didn't. It's really that simple.

"Jesus was just saying His coming was a certain event to occur" view

This is what the Greek words actually are in Revelation 22:20 to communicate both genuine imminence and the thought of certainty:

---

[194] John Walvoord, *The Revelation of Jesus Christ*, (Chicago, Moody, 1966), 35

[195] Thomas Ice, Tim LaHaye, Ibid., 103.

"Surely [Greek *nai* – means 'certainly'] I am coming quickly" [Greek *tachu* – means an event will be 'without delay' or take place 'soon'].

Notice the text does not say, "Surely I am coming surely/certainly" (that would be redundant).

If all Jesus was trying to communicate was that His coming was "certain" to happen someday, there were Greek words He could have used instead of the *taxos, engus,* and *mello* word groups!

"Revelation is teaching that the beginning or inauguration of fulfillment was near, not the consummation of fulfillment" view

Perhaps the latest trend, and innovative "scholarly" approach from some Futurists to avoid the obvious, is to claim that the "inauguration" of fulfilled prophecy was genuinely "at hand" when John wrote Revelation, but not the consummation of the prophecy. G.K. Beale writes:

> "The focus of 'quickness' and 'nearness' in vv 1-3 is primarily on inauguration of prophetic fulfillment and its ongoing aspect, not on nearness of consummated fulfillment... Indeed, what follows shows that the beginning of fulfillment and not final fulfillment is the focus."[196]

Response: This is so obviously wrong and it's disturbing that a publisher even paid for these kinds of comments to go into print for the Christian public to read, let alone portray them as "scholarly"! The entire book of "Revelation" or "prophecy [singular] of this book" [singular] was to be fulfilled "shortly" or "soon" (Rev. 1:1; 22:18-20). And everyone knows that the Second Coming and judgment described as taking place "soon" is the "consummative" event, and Pentecost and the giving of the Holy Spirit was the "inauguration" event that took place some 30 years in the past when John wrote!

Summing up OT & NT imminence in light of Psalm 90:4 and 2 Peter 3:8

In examining the "list" of OT Day of the Lord passages that were "near," we found that God was capable of communicating with man in language which he understands "near" and "without delay" to be. There was no exegetical evidence that "near" or "without delay" meant thousands of years, and that this is somehow the way to interpret over 150 direct imminent statements in the NT.

In a couple passages in the OT there were some typological passages or projected imminence passages in which, when the prophecy would begin to be fulfilled in Israel's last days, they would be near. Or when that last days "perverse generation" arrived, then Israel's "end" would be "near."

---

[196] G.K. Beale, *THE NEW INTERNATIONAL GREEK TESTAMENT COMMENTARY NIGT, The Book of Revelation*, (Grand Rapids, MI: William B. Eerdman's Publishing Company, 1999), 182

But once in the NT, since the OT prophesied "last days" and "crooked" or "perverse generation" had arrived, the "nearness" of that day of the Lord had literally come. The harmony between the OT and NT is not the kind of harmony Dr. Brown sees. Brown wants to say that since there are a couple of projected imminence passages in the OT, this must mean that every NT imminence passage must be projected out to thousands of years away. Or because the OT was typological of NT prophecy, the NT also much contain more types of another consummation. No, Jesus and the NT authors communicate that "all that is written" in the Law and Prophets would be fulfilled in their generation. There's the harmony in understanding the couple of projected or typological OT passages. The other harmony comes in the fact that the overwhelming "near" Day of the Lord passages (with apocalyptic de-creation language) were fulfilled within the lifetime and generation of the prophet's audience and this is how we are to understand NT imminence. Brown will not acknowledge even ONE NT imminent coming of the Lord passage in the NT as being fulfilled by AD 70. It's because he sees the Full Preterist train coming, as even one of the authors he endorses sees, when he admits that Partial Preterism will lead to Full Preterism.

While no one disagrees that the OT predicted partial or typological fulfillments, what Brown and men like Hollett are unwilling to see is that the NT writers are developing the imminent eschatological "not yet" anti-types to be fulfilled at the end of the old covenant age in AD 70. This is one of the reasons why I asked Dr. Brown in the cross-examination period to demonstrate from the book of Hebrews or any NT book where Jesus or the author goes from the OT physical typological promises, gives them a spiritual and imminent anti-type fulfillment, and THEN goes back to develop a physical distant fulfillment. He simply claimed the author of Hebrews didn't have to give one example to support his system of OT physical type to the "true" and "better" spiritual anti-type AND then BACK to physical fulfillments. Neither the book of Hebrews nor ANY NT passage supports Brown's carnal Premillennial Kingdom-on-earth position.

God sovereignly decreed or "set a day" on His eschatological "calendar" that was "about to be" (Acts 17:31YLT) fulfilled concerning Jesus' truly imminent Second Coming in judgment by AD 70. He communicated its nearness in language we understand. If we want to honor how this language is used in the OT, honor God's sovereignty and honor the inspiration and infallibility of the Scriptures, we must interpret imminence with its usual literal meaning.

Psalm 90:4 and 2 Peter 3:8 NEVER changed the meaning of what "far off", "many days" or "near" means. Daniel and Revelation contain the same eschatological promises and God communicated consistently in language man can understand concerning the prophetic material of both inspired books. Daniel was told to "seal up" his vision because the time of fulfillment was "far off" or would be fulfilled in "many days" from Daniel. Daniel was told that he would die and not be able to witness the event. Yet John was told the exact opposite: "Do NOT seal up" the vision because the time of fulfillment was "near" and he could live to witness it (cf. Mt. 16:27-28→Jn. 21:21-23).

Daniel	Revelation
• "The vision of the evenings and the mornings that has been told is true, but **seal up** the vision, **for it refers to <u>many days</u> from now**" (Dan. 8:26) • "and came to make you understand what is to happen to your people **in the latter days**. For the vision is for **days yet to come**." (Dan.10:14) • "But you, Daniel, shut up the words and **seal the book, until the time of the end.**" "…go your way till the end. And you **shall rest and shall stand in your allotted place at the end of the days.**" (Dan. 12:4, 13)	• "And he said to me, "**Do not seal up** the words of the prophecy of this book, **<u>for</u> the <u>time</u> <u>is</u> <u>near</u>**" (Rev. 22:10)

Review and Concluding "the Big Three"
(Mt. 10:17-23; Mt. 16:27-28; Mt. 24:3-34)

When we examine the coming of the Son of Man passages in Matthew 10:17-23 and Matthew 16:27-28, we find that they are abbreviated forms or snapshots of what Christ would fully develop in the Olivet Discourse (Matthew 24-25). And in all three cases, Jesus promised that His Second Coming event would be fulfilled in some of the lifetimes and the contemporary generation of the first century church:

Matthew 10:17-23/16:27-28 & Parallels	The Olivet Discourse
1). Delivered up to **councils** and **synagogues** (Mt. 10:17)	1). Delivered up to **local councils** and **synagogues** (Mrk. 13:9)
2). Brought before **governors and kings** to be **witnesses to the Gentiles** (Mt. 10:18)	2). Brought before **governors and kings** to be **witnesses to the Gentiles** (Mrk. 13:9)
3). **Holy Spirit** would speak through them (Mt. 10:19-20)	3). **Holy Spirit** would speak through them (Mrk. 13:11)
4). Family members would **betray and kill each other**, all men would hate the disciples, but he that would stand firm to **"the end"** would be **"saved"** (Mt. 10:22)	4). Family members would **betray and kill each other**, all men would hate the disciples, but he that would stand firm to **"the end"** would be "saved" (Mrk. 13:12-13)
5). The disciples would not have run out of cities of refuge to flee to as they were being persecuted, preaching the gospel **to the cities of Israel, before the Son of Man would come** (Mt. 10:23).	5). The disciples (and later Paul) were to preach the gospel to the **then known "world" and "nations"** at that time **before "the end"** (of the OC age) and coming of **the Son of Man would take place** (Mt. 24:14/Mrk. 13:10).
6). Christ comes **in glory** (Lk. 9:26)	6). Christ comes **in glory** (Mt. 24:30)
7). Christ comes **with angels** (Mt. 16:27)	7). Christ comes **with angels** (Mt. 24:31)
8). Christ comes **in judgment** (Mt. 16:27)	8). Christ comes **in judgment** (Mt. 24:28-31;25:31-34)
9). Christ and the kingdom come **in power** (Mrk. 8:38)	9). Christ and the kingdom come **in power** (Lk. 21:27-32)
10). Some in the **crowd would live** to witness the Second Coming (Mt. 16:28)	10). Some in the **crowd would live to** witness the Second Coming (Lk. 21:16-18)
11). Some in the **crowd would die** before the Second Coming (Mt. 16:28)	11). Some in the **crowd would die** before the Second Coming (Lk. 21:16)
12). Christ was **"about to come"** and would be ashamed of some in His contemporary **"this generation"** (Mt. 16:27YLT/Mrk. 8:38)	12). All of this would occur and be **"near"** and **"at the door"** in His contemporary **"this generation"** (Mt. 24:33-34/Lk. 21:27-32)

The Bible skeptics, who now include Muslims and Talmudic Jews, are dead wrong in thinking that Jesus predicted that He would float down on a literal cloud to bring an end to planet earth and world history in His contemporary generation. He clearly was prophesying the end of the old covenant age and the de-creation of Israel's world or heaven and earth.

Dispensational Zionists who parade themselves as "prophecy experts" do nothing but twist the teachings of our Lord here. The Olivet Discourse has nothing to do with current world events, nor is its content being fulfilled "right before our eyes in the Newspapers," etc. The Church needs to get back to Biblical hermeneutics and exegesis.

Yet not all is lost. When we combine the sounder observations of the Church, we arrive at the Biblical position:

Major Premise: The coming of the Son of Man in the Olivet Discourse is the ONE Second Coming event to be fulfilled at the end of the age or when heaven and earth pass away (Classic Amillennialism).

Minor Premise: But the coming of the Son of Man throughout the Olivet Discourse is the spiritual coming of Christ to be fulfilled in the AD 30 – AD 70 "this generation," that is, in the events of AD 67 – AD 70. It was at this time that Christ brought an "end" to Israel's old covenant "age" or "heaven and earth" and ushered in the new covenant spiritual one (Partial Preterism).

Conclusion: Therefore, the coming of the Son of Man in the Olivet Discourse is the spiritual coming of Christ to be fulfilled in the AD 30 – AD 70 "this generation," that is, in the events of AD 67 – AD 70. It was at this time that Christ brought an "end" to Israel's old covenant "age" or "heaven and earth" and ushered in the new covenant spiritual one ("Reformed and always reforming" - Sovereign Grace Full Preterism).

While some Partial Preterists, such as Gary DeMar and Keith Mathison, have admitted that the coming of Christ in Matthew 10:22-23, Matthew 16:27-28 and Matthew 24-25 (along with every reference to Christ's coming in the book of Revelation) was spiritually fulfilled in AD 70, they depart from common sense and even their own creedal position which states that the coming of Christ in the Olivet Discourse and throughout the book of Revelation is the actual Second Coming event.

Their *system is forced* to teach that Christ had little or nothing to say of His Second Coming and that God would work through Paul later in developing this revelation and doctrine in 1 Thessalonians 4 and 1 Corinthians 15. This doesn't even pass the smell test. Most of Christianity understands that Paul is following Jesus' teaching in the Olivet Discourse, and many admit that he too expected the Second Coming to occur in the lifetimes of his contemporaries:

If A (Matthew 24) is = B (1 Thessalonians 4)		
Christ returns from heaven	24:30	4:16
With voice of Arch Angel	24:31	4:16
With trumpet of God	24:31	4:16
Caught/gathered together with/to Christ	24:31	4:17
"Meet" the Lord in the clouds	24:30 & 25:6	4:17
Exact time unknown	24:36	5:1-2
Christ comes as a thief	24:43	5:2
Unbelievers caught off guard	24:37-39	5:3
Time of birth pangs	24:8	5:3
Believers not deceived	24:43	5:4-5
Believers to be watchful	24:42	5:6
Exhorted to sobriety	24:49	5:7
Son/sunlight shining from east to west / Sons of the Day	24:27, 36, & 38	5:4-8

And if B (1 Thessalonians 4) is = to C (1 Corinthians 15)		
The sleeping to be raised	4:13-14	15:12-18
The living to be caught/changed	4:15-17	15:51-52
Christ's coming (Greek: *Parousia*)	4:15	15:23
At the sound of the trumpet	4:16	15:52
Encouraged to stand firm	4:18	15:58
Same contemporary "we"	4:15-17	15:51-52
Then A (Matthew 24 & Parallels) is = to C (1 Corinthians 15)		
Christ to come (Greek: *Parousia*)	24:27	15:23
His people to be gathered/changed	24:31	15:52
To come with the sound of a trumpet	24:31	15:52
To be "the end" (Greek *telos*, the goal)	24:3, 14	15:24
Kingdom consummation (goal reached)	Luke 21:30-32	15:24
All prophecy fulfilled at this point	Luke 21:22	15:54-55
Victory over the Mosaic Law/Temple	Mt. 24:1	15:55-56
Same contemporary "you" or "we"	Mt. 24:2ff	15:51-52

Two or More Things that are Equal to Another Thing are Also Equal to Each Other		
Matthew 24	**1 Thessalonians 4**	**1 Corinthians 15**
At His coming (24:27-31)	At His Coming (4:16)	At His Coming (15:23)
At the trumpet (24:31)	At the trumpet (4:16)	At the trumpet (15:52)
Dead raised, All Gathered (24:31)	Dead raised (4:16)	Dead raised (15:35-44)
All living gathered (24:31)	Living caught together to Him (4:17)	Status of living changed (15:51)

Once again, we solve the heated division within the orthodox Christian church and continue the work of reformation in the area of eschatology, solving this debate:

Major Premise: The analogy of faith and parallels between Matthew 24-25 and 1 Thessalonians 4-5 and 1 Corinthians 15 teach us that Paul is simply developing and elaborating on the doctrine of our Lord's ONE return at **the** end of the age (Classic Amillennialism and Historic Premillennialism).

Minor Premise: But the coming of Christ in the Olivet Discourse was fulfilled spiritually in Jesus' contemporary generation to bring about the end of the old covenant age in AD 70 (Partial Preterism – mostly Postmillennialists)

Conclusion: Therefore, since Christ's ONE Second Coming event in the Olivet Discourse was spiritually fulfilled at the end of the old covenant age in AD 70, and since the analogy of faith and parallels between the Olivet Discourse and 1 Thessalonians 4-5 / 1 Corinthians 15 teach us that this is the same event, then Christ's ONE Second Coming event was fulfilled spiritually at the end of the old covenant age in AD 70 ("Reformed and always reforming" – Sovereign Grace Full Preterism).

The "historical context" and eschatology of the Dead Sea Scrolls supports NT imminence

Having given the "grammatical context," or the exegetical case, for Full Preterism, we now turn our attention briefly to look at the "historical context" of NT imminence by examining the beliefs of the Qumran Community as found in the Dead Sea Scrolls.

The Qumran Community (most likely the Essenes), looking at Daniel 9:24-27; Habakkuk 2; Ezekiel 38-39 and other OT passages, also believed that they were the 40 years, "last days" generation that would witness the end-time war of Gog and Magog. They likewise believed that this war was imminent and would be waged between Rome (Kittim) and apostate Jerusalem (1QpHab 7:1-2; 1QpHab 9:5-11, 1QpHab 12:5-13; 11QMelch). We will discuss this war in the next chapter.

They also embraced a more spiritual hermeneutic of the Ezekiel 40-48 temple, viewing themselves as God's new Jerusalem and Most Holy Place dwelling (4Q416, 418). They anticipated a new Jerusalem and a new temple where atonement would not come by means of physical burnt offerings of animals, but by a spiritual sacrifice "of lips of justice like a righteous fragrance" (1QS ix 4-5).

I have addressed the significance of 11QMelch where Messiah had to gather his people, perform atonement and judge the wicked along with the Watchers and Satan within the 10th Jubilee which would have begun between AD 17 – AD 28 and needed to end by AD 70.

It is very difficult to ignore there were Jewish beliefs of a spiritual resurrection and a resurrection to take place 40 years after Messiah or after His 40 years transitional reign from the old covenant "this age" to the "age about to come." My exegesis of the Second Coming of the Son of Man and the resurrection event to occur at the end of the old covenant age in AD 70 has a strong "historical context" argument to support it.

The Qumran Community would eventually go to Jerusalem around AD 66 – AD 67 to fight against Rome hoping that Messiah would come and defeat both Rome and apostate Jerusalem while establishing them as the true children of light. However, we can imagine as they were coming to Jerusalem to engage in this physical conflict (having rejected Jesus as Messiah), the Christians heeding Messiah's prophecy, were leaving the city and were delivered as the true sons of the Kingdom and continue today functioning as the New Covenant New Jerusalem/Most Holy Place dwelling of God with our gates open bringing healing to the nations with the gospel (Rev. 21:16—22:17).

Chapter Six:

The Christian Full Preterist Solution: The End of the Old Covenant Age Battle of Armageddon / Gog and Magog Fulfilled AD 67 – AD 70

By far, the connected terms "Armageddon" and the "end of the world" are the two most talked about subjects among those who speculate on Jesus' teaching in the Olivet Discourse and the book of Revelation. Evangelical so-called "prophecy expert" Zionists flood the TV and radio airwaves and litter the Prophecy section of "Christian" bookstores. This section, unfortunately, sells the most books. Apparently, professing and uneducated Christians like carnal carrot-and-stick fiction. Because Dispensational Zionists have mega churches or are presidents of so-called Christian Universities, they are the ones invited on FOX News to pontificate upon Bible prophecy, Islam, Israel, Russia, and current events in the Middle East. From the inception of the Dispensational Zionist movement (which especially gained ground in the 60's and 70's), the subjects of Armageddon and current events go unchallenged and are just expected to go together and be settled fact. Of course, it is about as "settled" as the so-called "science" is on climate change or vaccines.

I think it's safe to say that most Christians and even non-Christians have an idea that the battle of Armageddon or Gog and Magog is predicted to take place somewhere in the book of Revelation. However, if you asked these same individuals where this same end-time or last days battle was predicted in the OT, and which of these OT texts Jesus uses to develop His eschatology, most would have no clue. So let's begin in the OT and see how Jesus interprets these passages on the end-of-the-age war before digging into the book of Revelation.

When did Jesus say "the end" and the "last days" war of Daniel 9, Daniel 12 and Isaiah 2-4 would be fulfilled?

The Coming of the Son of Man / the Time of the End / "the War" of Daniel 7; 9 & 12

There is a majority consensus among scholars that the prophetic book of Daniel contains recapitulation (that is, the same events are described differently) in chapters 7, 9 and 12. Therefore, these chapters will be our focus.

Daniel 7:13-22

In Daniel 7 we learn that Messiah, or the Son of Man, and His Kingdom would come during the time of the fourth world power (the Roman Empire). The Old Greek

Septuagint describes one "like the Son of Man coming upon the clouds" coming "*as* (not up to) the Ancient of Days" and receiving service/worship from the nations (OG LXX Dan. 7:13-14 – John, following the OG LXX in His description of Christ coming upon the clouds both as the Son of Man while at the same time being the eternal Ancient of Days and the "First and Last" in Rev. 1:7-18).

In Daniel 7, Daniel is also told that the Messiah's coming upon the clouds as the Ancient of Days to establish and receive His "Kingdom" would occur after a severe time of persecution for His saints took place (cf. Dan. 7:21-22ff.). We learn in chapter 7 and chapter 2 of Daniel that this kingdom is spiritual and eternal and thus much different than the previous four earthly kingdoms.

Daniel 9:24-27

I have already addressed two important factors of this important prophecy in the previous chapters. First was the time period of the seventy sevens or 490 years according to Jewish first century expectation found in the Dead Sea Scrolls (using the Jewish calendar), being the period from the destruction of the first temple by the Babylonians in 420 BC to the destruction of the second temple by the Romans in AD 70 (490 years). I also demonstrated how the six events of verse 24 were fulfilled by AD 70. I now turn our attention to the war that would culminate in the last half or the last seven:

- *"And after threescore and two weeks shall Messiah be cut off, but not for himself: and the people of the prince that shall come shall destroy the city and the sanctuary; and **the end** thereof shall be with a flood, and unto the end of **the war** desolations are determined." And he shall confirm the covenant with many for one week: and in the midst of the week he shall cause the sacrifice and the oblation to cease, and for the overspreading of **abominations he shall make it desolate**, even until the consummation [the end], and that determined shall be poured upon the desolate" (Dan. 9:26-27).*

The first prince of verse 25, of which the prophetic word of Jeremiah foretold, was Cyrus. Cyrus' actions correspond to the first Jubilee period (7x7 = 49 years) that would set in motion the next series of Jubilee sevens. The second Jubilee period of sevens, or cycle, is referring to the re-building of Jerusalem under Ezra and Nehemiah (62 x 7 = 434 years) leading up to the coming of Messiah or the fulfillment of the last seven. "AFTER" these two prophetic Jubilee periods (49 + 434 = 483 years), another prince or Messiah arrives to accomplish the redemption and judgment of the last prophetic seven years.

Jesus begins His earthly ministry (3 ½ years) announcing that the soteriological and eschatological Jubilee they were expecting out of Daniel 9 and Isaiah 61 had arrived and He was the fulfillment (around AD 27). After His 3 ½ years of earthly ministry, in fulfilling the first half of the last seven, He is "cut off" (crucified). After this there is a second exodus generation of transition (the "already and not yet") between the old covenant "this age" and the in-breaking new covenant "age about to come" that will climax in the fulfillment of the last 3 ½ years between AD 67 – AD 70.

Jesus, who is referenced by the expression "the people of the Prince," would send His armies/people to destroy the city during this period. Remember Jesus said that "the King" (that is Christ Himself) would "send *His armies*" (Romans) to kill those murderers and burn their city (Jerusalem)" (Mt. 22:7). Just as God was sovereign in the OT and came upon the clouds through His armies (the Babylonians or Assyrians, etc. to judge Israel), Messiah/Jesus would sovereignly come upon the clouds through sending His army (the Romans) to judge and desolate her in AD 70.

Daniel 12:1-7

We now turn to Daniel 12 where we learn additional material about the same time period Daniel 7:13-22 and Daniel 9:24-27 has addressed. Daniel 12 is addressing the eschatological "end" of the seventy sevens and connects the "desolation" of the coming war during the last half of Daniel's final seven, that is "…for a time, times, and half a time…" (3 ½ years) with having the effect of "when the power of the holy people would be completely shattered" (Dan. 12:7). This is the end result of "the war" Daniel predicted in Daniel 9:26.

Jesus interprets the timing of the desolation and the war of Daniel 9:26-27 / Daniel 12:1-7

Since I have already given the reader an in-depth exegesis of the Olivet Discourse, I will just remind you of "**all**" of the events that Jesus said would be fulfilled within His contemporary "**this generation**" (AD 30 – AD 70): 1) the signs 2) destruction of the temple 3) end of the old covenant age 4) His coming 5) the tribulation 6) the great commission *7) abomination of desolation / the war [armies surrounding Jerusalem]* 8) resurrection and 9) the arrival of the kingdom (cf. Mt. 24-25/Lk. 21).

Our focus here is on #7, which Jesus says is the fulfillment of the desolation and war of Daniel 9:26-27 and 12:1-7 which was to last 3 ½ years:

- "And after threescore and two weeks shall Messiah be cut off, but not for himself: and the people of the prince that shall come shall destroy the city and the sanctuary; and **the end** thereof shall be with a flood, and unto the end of **the war** desolations are determined." And he shall confirm the covenant with many for one week: and in the midst of the week he shall cause the sacrifice and the oblation to cease, and for the overspreading of **abominations he shall make it desolate**, even until the consummation [the end], and that determined shall be poured upon the desolate" (Dan. 9:26-27).

- "But when **you see <u>Jerusalem surrounded by armies</u>, then know that its <u>desolation</u> has come near**. Then let those who are in Judea flee to the mountains, and let those who are inside the city depart, and let not those who are out in the country enter it, for these are days of vengeance, to fulfill all that is written" (Lk. 21:20-22).

Previously I harmonized this with Matthew 24:15 and summarized our passage to mean, "When you [the disciples and first century Christians] see the abomination of the Gentile Roman armies surrounding and standing in/on the holy place of the land of

Jerusalem, then know its desolation has drawn near. Then let those who are in Judea flee to the mountains, and let those who are inside the city depart…"

Luke's account further describes the end of the Jewish age war between the Romans and the apostate Jews in AD 67 – AD 70 resulting in:

- "They will fall by the edge of the sword and be led captive among all nations, and Jerusalem will be trampled underfoot by the Gentiles, until **the times of the Gentiles** [the 3 ½ years of Daniel 12:7 and Revelation 11:1-2] are fulfilled" (Lk. 21:24).

Jews falling by the edge of the sword and being led captive among all nations is an old covenant curse for Israel found in Deuteronomy 28:64-68 for violating the Mosaic covenant. This creates a problem for most Premillennial Zionists and Christians with other eschatological views since they believe the old covenant ended at the cross or by AD 70. This being the case, how can an old covenant Mosaic Law (which ended thousands of years ago) curse be applied to modern Israel? But since the old covenant (and its curses) was "ready to vanish" (Heb. 8:13) after the cross, but still in effect for the Jews of the first century to experience (the days of vengeance), the war of AD 67 – AD 70 fits perfectly.

Jesus interprets Isaiah 2—4 the "last days" "the war"

Isaiah 2-4 predicts Jerusalem's "last days", "in that day", "Day of the Lord" coming by which Jerusalem's "mighty" would "fall by the sword" and "in the war" (cf. Isa. 2:1 - 3:25). In that day or during this war, men are described as fleeing to the caves in the rocks and holes in the ground. At the time of this war, God would come in "majesty" and "shaking" Jerusalem's "earth/land" or kingdom (2:10-19).

Jesus clearly identifies the time of this last days war for Jerusalem as the events leading up to AD 70 in Luke 23, where on his way to the cross he prophesies against Jerusalem, saying,

- *"…Daughters of Jerusalem, do not weep for me, but weep for yourselves and for your children. For behold, **the days are coming** when they will say, 'Blessed are the barren and the wombs that never bore and the breasts that never nursed!' **Then they will begin to say to the mountains, 'Fall on us,' and to the hills, 'Cover us'**" (Lk. 23:28-30).*

Clearly futurists who admit that this passage was fulfilled in AD 70 fail to look at the context of Isaiah 2-4 which necessitates that the "in that day", "last days", "Day of the Lord" (Isa. 2:9-21) *"war" (Isa. 3:23) is what* causes men and women to flee and to call to the mountains and hills to cover or hide them in the events during the Roman-Jewish War of AD 67 – AD 70!

In Isaiah we also learn that it is through this coming "war" and "Day of the Lord" judgment that God would forgive the remnant among Jerusalem for her sin of bloodguilt: "…when the Lord has washed away the filth of the daughters of Zion and cleansed the bloodguilt from the heart of Jerusalem by a spirit of judgment and a spirit of burning" (Isa. 4:4).

Jesus once again connects this last days "war" with Jerusalem's sin of bloodguilt when the vindication of the martyrs would be fulfilled, i.e. at His coming in judgment in the Pharisees' contemporary "this generation" to make their "house" or temple desolate in AD 70 (cf. Mt. 23:31-39).

Since Dispensational Zionists, such as Thomas Ice, admit that such passages as Luke 21:20-24, Luke 23:28-30, and Matthew 23:31-38 were fulfilled in Jesus' contemporary generation when Rome surrounded and desolated Jerusalem in the events of AD 67 - AD 70, and since Jesus is stating that Daniel's last half of the last seven of Israel's "last days" war would be fulfilled then, then Dispensational Zionism falls on its face yet again!

Let's now turn to the book of Revelation and see if John's eschatology lines up with Jesus on when and why the "time of the end" war was to be fulfilled.

Revelation 11; 16; 19 and 20

Everyone seems to agree that the book of Revelation is John's version of the Olivet Discourse. Therefore, we should expect to have John's eschatology on "THE war" line up with Jesus' eschatology on the end of the old covenant age war. After all, Jesus predicts the war would be "near" within His "this generation," and toward the end of that generation John informs us that the content of his prophecy (including Armageddon and the Gog and Magog war) would be fulfilled "shortly" at the "soon" coming of Christ (Rev. 1:1 - 22:20).

There also seems to be consensus that the book of Daniel and Revelation uses prophetic recapitulation and that John picks up where the prophet Daniel left off. What was to be "sealed up" because the time of fulfillment was "far off" in Daniel's day is "not" to be sealed up in John's, because the time of fulfillment was "at hand" (Rev. 22:10).

Revelation 11 – Measuring of the Temple & Trampling of the City by the Gentiles for 3 ½ yrs.

This "end" or "time of the end" (not end of time) war of Daniel 9:26 and Daniel 12:1-7 is during the three and a half years "when the power of the holy people would be completed shattered" (Daniel 12:7). Likewise, Revelation is when old covenant Jerusalem ("where the Lord was crucified") would be trodden down by the unclean heathen or Gentile nations for a period of "42 months" or 3 ½ years (Rev. 11:1-2, 8).

The protection of the Church in the war described as measuring the Most Holy Place

- *"Then I was given a measuring rod like a staff, and I was told, "Rise and measure the temple [Gk. naos – The Most Holy Place] of God and the altar and those who worship there, but do not measure the court outside the temple; leave that out, for it is given over to* **the nations [the Gentiles Lk. 21:24]**, *and they* *will **trample the holy city for forty-two months [3 ½ years – "TIMES of the Gentiles" Lk. 21:24]** (Rev. 11:1-2).*

The measuring of the Most Holy Place section of the temple[197] is a symbolic act depicting the new covenant Christian worshipers would be protected from God's coming wrath implemented through the trampling of Jerusalem by the Zealot and Roman armies for the 3 ½ year period that was imminent in John's day (AD 67 – AD 70).

Measuring can be a symbol for preservation, protection or building up (e.g. Zech. 2:1). Like John, Ezekiel measures a perfectly cubed (Most Holy Place) temple that is "like a city…where the Lord is" (cf. Ezek. 40-48). As we have discussed in the previous chapter, the Church is that temple where the Lord dwells in the new covenant age (Ezek. 37:27=2 Cor. 6:16; Ezek. 47=John 7:37-39=Rev. 21-22).

The only other place in Revelation where measuring is used, it is used in a positive way to describe the new covenant Jerusalem as a perfect square or as God's Most Holy Place dwelling (Rev. 21:9-16).

Some have argued that *"the holy city"* in Revelation 11:2 cannot be Old Testament Jerusalem because that city was no longer holy after the veil was ripped in two in about AD 30. In this argument, it is implied that the holy covenant that was established with terrible and blazing fire, an earthquake, darkness, gloom, fear, trembling, whirlwind, and the staggering blast of a trumpet (Heb. 12:18–21) came to a final end in God's sight with the tearing of the veil (which was later sewn back together). And, therefore, earthly Jerusalem ceased to be holy at that time.

In contrast to this futurist myth, the author of Hebrews taught that the covenant that began with momentous signs was going to end with momentous signs *in the near future*:

> "And His voice shook the earth then [at Mount Sinai], but now He has promised, saying, "Yet once more I will shake not only the earth, but also the heaven." And this expression, "Yet once more," denotes the removing of those things which can be shaken, as of created things [the old covenant world], in order that those things which cannot be shaken [the kingdom of Christ] may remain. Therefore, since we receive a kingdom which cannot be shaken, let us show gratitude, by which we may offer to God an acceptable service with reverence and awe; for our God is a consuming fire" (Heb. 12:26–29).

The old covenant did not vanish when Christ died on the cross (Heb. 8:13). Therefore, Jerusalem was still holy after Christ died because it was still the covenant city of God, even though it was being "shaken" and was being nullified (2 Cor. 3:7, 11–12) through

---

[197] Jay Adams, *THE TIME IS AT HAND*, (Philadelphia, PA: self-published, 1969), 68-69

the age-changing power of the cross. It was still the holy city of God even though it had become "Babylon", "Sodom," and "Egypt" because of its sins.

To the holy-yet-hardened Jewish nation belonged "*the adoption as sons and the glory and the covenants and the giving of the Law and the temple service and the promises*" (Rom. 3:2; 9:4). Those blessings were all still intact even after the Jews murdered the Lord and persecuted His church (1 Thess. 2:15). The unbelieving Jewish nation was still in the kingdom of God after the death and resurrection of Christ, but its days were numbered. It was soon to be cast out of the kingdom in the Parousia of Christ in the consummation of the ages (Matt. 8:12; 13:41; Gal. 4:21–31).

The tearing of the veil was *a sign* of the coming judgment upon that generation and its temple and world. The biblical record is clear that the old covenant law remained in force for the Jews, both believing and nonbelieving, even after the cross, until "*heaven and earth*" passed away in AD 70 (Heb. 8:13; 2 Cor. 3:7–18; Matt. 5:17–19; Acts 21:20–26; 24:17).

Like the book of Daniel, the book of Revelation is presented in a common prophetic recapitulation construct – again, meaning these are simply different ways of describing the same end-time war or judgment scene. There is only one final war or end-time judgment in Revelation, and it is consistently referred to in John's use of the Greek phrase "to gather them for **the** war" (cf. Rev. 16:14; 19:19; 20:8). The definite article "the" is purposely placed in front of "war" to describe one very specific and important end-time war.

Before leaving Revelation 11, it is important to see the continuity between it and the war or battle of Gog and Magog as described in Revelation 20. In chapter 11 the new covenant Church is being protected and described as the Most Holy Place structure of temple worship. In Revelation 20:7-9; 21:16, the New Jerusalem or "beloved city" is also measured and protected from the persecution and warring "nations" seeking to devour her.

Revelation 16 – "the war" and Armageddon

The texts I want to develop here in Revelation 16 are primarily verses 14-16, 19-20:

- *"They are demonic spirits that perform signs, and they go out to the kings of the whole world, to gather them for **the battle (or the war)** on the great day of God Almighty. "Look, I come like a thief! Blessed is the one who stays awake and remains clothed, so as not to go naked and be shamefully exposed." Then they gathered the kings together to the place that in Hebrew is called **Armageddon**" (Rev. 16:14-16).*

- *"The great city split into three parts, and the cities of the nations collapsed. God remembered **Babylon the Great** and gave her the cup filled with the wine of the fury of his wrath. **Every island fled away and the mountains could not be found**" (Rev. 16:19-20).*

The first point I would like to make and that we should pay careful attention to, is that the context for the gathering of the armies in "Armageddon" and the coming "THE war of the Great Day of God" that ensues in Revelation 16, is for *the purpose* of judging Babylon. Therefore, to understand when this war takes place, we need to identify **who** Babylon is in the prophecy.

Earlier in Revelation 11:8 we are told that Babylon or this "great city" is old covenant Jerusalem – *"where our Lord was crucified."* So "Armageddon" and "the war" here has nothing to do with Babylon or the great city being the Roman Catholic Church, or the lands or nations of modern-day Iran, Iraq, Syria, Muslims, China, the Russians, or even modern Israel. This is a "war" and judgment upon old covenant Jerusalem.

The rest of the prophecy tells us **why** "the war" comes about or why Babylon is to be judged. In chapters 17-18 we learn that it is because old covenant Jerusalem, or Babylon, has played the harlot and has a history of killing all the prophets God sends to her, and that Babylon has gotten drunk off the blood of the apostles, prophets, and martyrs (again, that Jesus promised to send to her in Matthew 23, before He judged that generation and desolated their temple). As a result, God then judges her because she has now filled up the measure of their suffering, and thus the cup of God's wrath is now full and ready to be poured out. The time of avenging the last apostles and prophets Jesus had sent to her, along with all the blood of the martyrs going as far back as Genesis, had come!

The coming "Great Day" of God's judgment and wrath in Revelation 16, in relation to bringing judgment upon Israel's sin of bloodguilt, has also been previously addressed in Revelation 6. In Revelation 6 John is consistent with Jesus' time frame of "the war" and vindication of the martyrs as developed in Isaiah 2-4. John tells us that the vindication for the martyrs would be in a "very little while" after their number would be completed. This corresponds with Jesus' teaching in Matthew 23 where He says the blood of the martyrs would be filled up or completed within their generation.

John, like Jesus in Luke 23, also cites the last days war and coming Day of judgment of Isaiah 2—4 in Revelation 6:15-17. Here people are seeking to hide themselves, in caves and among the rocks of the mountains, from the majesty of the Lord's "Great Day" of judgment coming. And in both Revelation 6 and our Armageddon prophecy here in Revelation 16, parallel de-creation language is used. "Every mountain and island was removed" in chapter 6 is parallel to "every island fled away and the mountains could not be found" in chapter 16. So thus far John is using the last days war of Isaiah 2-4 against old covenant Jerusalem for shedding the blood of the martyrs and announcing that they would be judged imminently in that first century generation just as Jesus used Isaiah 2-4 in Luke 23:28-30 and Matthew 23:31-39.

So then what relationship does the term "Armageddon" have with "the war of the Great Day of God"? Armageddon simply means "Mount Megiddo." And yet there is no "mountain" there because it is a plain, with the closest mountain being Mount Carmel. This term and the geographical locations are referred to because they function as a symbol for famous battles Israel and her enemies had there. As David Chilton and Farrer explain,

> "Megiddo" thus was for St. John a symbol of defeat and desolation, a "Waterloo" signifying the defeat of those who set themselves against God, as Farrer explains: "In sum, Mt. Megiddo stands in his mind for a place where lying prophecy and its dupes go to meet their doom; where kings and their armies are misled to their destruction; where kings and their armies are misled to their destruction; and where all the tribes of the earth mourn, to see Him in power, whom in weakness they had pierced."[198]

Others such as Dr. Michael Heiser make a connection that this war takes place in literal Jerusalem known as "the Mount of Assembly." Here is a sampling of Heiser's points,

> "…the Hebrew phrase behind John's Greek transliteration of our mystery Hebrew term is actually *h-r-m-'-d*. But what does this mean? If the first part (h-r) is the Hebrew word *har* ("mountain"), is there a *har m-'-d* in the Hebrew Old Testament?"[199]

> "The phrase in question exists in the Hebrew Bible a *har mo'ed*. Incredibly, it is found in Isaiah 14:13·…"[200]

> "The result in the case of Armageddon is dramatic. When John draws on this ancient Hebrew phrase, he is indeed pointing to a climactic battle *at Jerusalem*. Why? Because Jerusalem is a mountain—Mount Zion. And if Baal and the gods of the other nations don't like Yahweh claiming to be the Most High and claiming to run the cosmos from the heights of Zaphon/Mount Zion, they can try to do something about it.

> And of course they do. Armageddon is about how the unbelieving nations, empowered by…the prince of darkness—Lord (*ba'al*) of the dead, prince Baal (*zbl ba'al*), Beelzebul—will make one last, desperate effort to defeat Jesus at the place where Yahweh holds council, Mount Zion, *Jerusalem*."[201]

This now harmonizes with Jesus' teaching in Matthew 24; Luke 21 and the book of Revelation--with the end of the [old covenant] age war taking place when the Romans *would surround and tread Jerusalem* (the city that crucified the Lord) beneath their feet in the events of AD 67 – AD 70.

Christ coming as "a thief" in the following verse is another way of describing the coming of "the Great Day of God." And we know from Revelation 3:3, 11 that Christ coming as a thief was His AD 70 "soon" coming. Not only this, but His coming as a

---

[198] David Chilton, *Days of Vengeance*, (Fort Worth, TX: Dominion Press, 1987), 412

[199] Michael S. Heiser, *THE UNSEEN REALM Recovering the Supernatural worldview of the Bible*, (Bellingham, WA: Lexham Press, 2015) 371

[200] Ibid.

[201] Ibid., 373

thief once again connects this event to Christ coming in the generation of AD 30 - AD 70 (cf. Mt. 24:34-43).

In putting this together so far, we learn:

Major Premise: Revelation 16-18 teaches us that the gathering for "the war" in "Megiddo" was for the purpose of bringing judgment upon the great city of Babylon (identified in 11:8 as old covenant Jerusalem – "where the Lord was crucified") for shedding the blood of the martyrs.

Minor Premise: But the war designed to judge old covenant Jerusalem and vindicate the martyrs in Revelation 16-18 is referring to the same "Great Day" of judgment and vindication of the martyrs in Revelation 6 to take place "in a very little while," and is the "last days" war of Isaiah 2-4.

Conclusion: Therefore, both Jesus and John prophesied that "the war" and vindication of the martyrs in Isaiah 2-4 would be fulfilled in the AD 30 - AD 70 "this generation" or "in a very little while," when Jerusalem (or Babylon the great city) would be judged in "THE war" between AD 67 - AD 70.

Revelation 19 - "the war" with the Beast

- *"And I saw the beast, and the kings of the earth/land, and their armies, gathered together to make [THE] war against him that sat on the horse, and against his army" (Rev. 19:19).*

Again, chapters 18-19 are contextually tied to the defeat of the "great city" of "Babylon," which in Revelation 11:8 and Matthew 23 has been identified as Jerusalem where Jesus was crucified, and the persecutor of the OT prophets and NT apostles and prophets Jesus would send to her.

Revelation 19:11-21 is simply another recapitulation of the same end-time battle and judgment we have seen in chapters 11 and 16 - except described differently with different imagery, etc.

Amazingly, the Dispensational Zionist "prophecy experts" claim that the rider of the white horse in Revelation 6:2 is the "antichrist," but there is absolutely no exegetical evidence for this. Here in chapter 19, once again the rider of the white horse is described as Jesus Christ. In chapter 6 Christ comes on the white horse (His Second Coming) conquering – thus vindicating the martyrs "in a very little while" in the "great day of His wrath," pouring out the covenant curses of Deuteronomy 28 upon the land of Israel. We previously saw Jesus appealing to the old covenant curses of Deuteronomy 28 in connection with the end-time war in the Olivet Discourse.

Identifying the beast(s) which fit the "shortly" and "soon" AD 67 – AD 70 context

Since here in Revelation 19 we see that the end-time war involves "the beast," we should probably address how the book of Revelation addresses the beast(s) theme throughout.

A). The beast as Nero and Rome

Beast – Beasts in Daniel represented the four Gentile Kingdoms (Babylon, Medes & Persians, Greece and Rome) that would rule over Israel (Dan. 7:1-7). But the fourth beast took on qualities of the other three, and was more "dreadful and exceedingly strong" than the others. It also is described as taking on some of the attributes of the other beasts (Dan. 7:7) as we see in Revelation 13. This could be simply because Rome was the fourth beast and had consumed and assimilated those other world empires, and she thus takes on those characteristics and power as well.

The beast is described as having 10 horns, seven heads, and rising out of the sea.

The 10 horns – is possibly a reference to Rome whereby she was divided into 10 provinces making up the Empire, which were: Italy, Achaia, Asia, Syria, Egypt, Africa, Spain, Gaul, Britain, and Germany.[202]

The seven heads – is most likely a reference to the seven hills of Rome, which was a symbol of the imperial city. Revelation 17:9-10 informs us that the seven heads are seven mountains on which the harlot (apostate Israel) sits.

Rising out of the sea – is referring to Satan calling on this beast from the sea which often times in Scripture represents the Gentiles, or in this case would be Rome.

Most Partial and Full Preterists see the corporate "beast" in this chapter to be the Roman Empire and her head to be Nero. With Rome and Nero being the beast, the following evidence is given in the book of Revelation:

- Rome was known to be the famous "city on seven hills," and the seven heads is later interpreted as seven mountains (cf. 17:7).

- The beast comes up out of the sea, and the sea in Scripture often times represents Gentile nations and powers, as do fierce animals with horns (13:1-2).

- The seven heads are not just seven mountains, but seven kings (17:9-10), of which five have fallen or have previously died when John is writing (Julius, Augustus, Tiberius, Gaius, and Claudius), the current one "now is" (the sixth being Nero), and when the seventh (Galba) comes, his reign would be brief.

- Rome and Nero persecuted and killed Christians with ferocity – "prevailing" against them for a time, as even Daniel 7 predicted, before they would inherit the kingdom. Nero was known as a "beast" and put Christians on stakes, lit them on fire and rode his chariot naked. He also was crazy and often placed young boys in animal skins and raped them.

- Nero committed "blasphemies" through making coins of himself, depicting himself as the sun god or a new Apollo worthy of worship (13:5-6, 8).

---

[202] F.W. Farrar, *The Early Days of Christianity* (Chicago & New York: Bedford, Clarke & Co., 1882) 532

- Archaeologists have documented the Hebrew spelling (Nrwn Qsr - Nero Caesar) which comes to 666 or six hundred and sixty-six. Alphabets also functioned as a numerical system (n = 50; r = 200; w = 6; n = 50; q = 100; s = 60; r = 200) – which gives us 666.

- If one did not take the mark of the beast (that is, acknowledging that he was the supreme king – "we have no king but Caesar"), Rome made the buying and selling of goods difficult and often times put them to death for not making this declaration.

- Nero was engaged in a war with the Jews for 42 months or 3 ½ years – from November AD 64 – June AD 68 (13:5).

- After Nero died, the Roman Empire seemed to have come to an end with several civil wars erupting, but the Empire recovered and revived (13:3, 7).

B). The beast as purely Jewish view

However, some Preterists have proposed that the beast in Revelation was not Nero and Rome, but the Jewish-led Zealot movement working with the religious Jewish false prophets. The following evidence is provided for this position:

- Israel was known for having seven hills or mountains as well: 1). Mt. Ararat (ark landed here) 2). Mt. Moriah (temple here) 3). Mt. Sinai (law given to Moses) 4). Mt. Nebo/Gerizim (Samaritans worship here) 5). Mt. Carmel (transfiguration) 6). Mt. Tabor (Jesus tempted here) and 7). Mt. Olivet (Jesus arrested here).

- The ten horns refer to 10 Jewish generals who were given authority in AD 66 - AD 67. The seven heads or kings are said to correspond to seven Zealots within the family of Hezekiah.

- The Zealots worked with the Jewish false prophets to try and persuade the people to stay and fight Rome. They persecuted and even killed Jews who didn't see their vision of how the messianic kingdom was allegedly about to come through them.

- This beast has characteristics of other world Gentile powers (cf. also Dan. 7). OC Jerusalem is described elsewhere in Revelation as Gentile powers such as Egypt, Babylon, Sodom and Gomora.

- The NT develops the Jews as being the primarily guilty party in being the "accusers" of Jesus and the Christians with heresy and blasphemy.

- The Jews and Zealots within Jerusalem between AD 66 - AD 70 were described by Josephus as "beasts" that were devouring their own through civil war.

- The Jewish leadership kicked Christians out of the synagogues and they were treated as dead to their families and communities. Jews would not buy from or sell to Christians, and they didn't permit Christians to buy from them or sell their products to them.

Josephus describes the Jews in Jerusalem between AD 67 - AD 70 as a Jewish "beast" devouring their own flesh (the infighting between the priests, Zealots, and Idumeans that would eventually burn down their own city).

Adam Maarschalk argues that the beast here in Revelation 19 is not Roman but Jewish. He connects the beast's fate in Daniel 7 and Revelation 19 thus:

> "...I watched till the beast was slain, and **its body destroyed** and **given to the burning flame**" (Daniel 7:11).
>
> "Then **the beast was captured**, and with him the false prophet who worked signs in his presence, by which he deceived those who received the mark of the beast and those who worshiped his image. **These two were cast alive into the lake of fire** burning with brimstone" (Revelation 19:20).
>
> If the Roman Empire was the beast of Revelation, how was this empire captured, slain, destroyed, burned, and cast into the lake of fire? Rome actually came out of the Jewish-Roman War (AD 66 -73) stronger than ever. History tells us that Rome was stronger in the second century AD than it was in the first century AD.
>
> Someone might say that this applied to Nero, who is said to be the beast in a singular sense. Nero was indeed killed – with his own sword, but he was not captured, and he was not burned. Nor did he go down at the same time as any false prophets who worked with him.
>
> It was Israel that was captured, slain, destroyed, and burned – as we can see in great detail in 'Wars of the Jews' by Josephus."[203]

And of the false prophets working with the Zealots Adam writes,

> "Josephus wrote the following about numerous false prophets who deceived the Jews during the time of the Procurators Felix (52-58 AD) and Festus (59-62 AD):
>
> "These works, that were **done by the robbers**, filled the city with all sorts of impiety. And now **these impostors and deceivers** persuaded the multitude to follow them into the wilderness, **and pretended that they would exhibit manifest wonders and signs, that should be performed by the providence of God.** And many that were prevailed on by them suffered the punishments of their folly; for Felix brought them back, and then punished them. Moreover, there came out of Egypt about this time to Jerusalem one that said he was a prophet, and advised the multitude of the common people to go along with him to the Mount of Olives..."

---

[203] Adam Maarschalk, *Who Was the Beast? (Five Clues) – Long Island Conference Presentation*, https://adammaarschalk.com/2017/04/09/who-was-the-beast-five-clues-long-island-conference-presentation/

In Wars 2.13 – 4:6, Josephus wrote about various false prophets and deceivers who worked to persuade the people to revolt against the Romans and who killed those who refused to revolt:

"There was also another body of wicked men gotten together… **These were such men as deceived and deluded the people under pretense of Divine inspiration, but were for procuring innovations and changes of the government; and these prevailed with the multitude to act like madmen**, and went before them into the wilderness, as pretending that God would there show them the signals of liberty…for **a company of deceivers and robbers got together, and persuaded the Jews to revolt**, and exhorted them to assert their liberty, **inflicting death on those that continued in obedience to the Roman government**, and saying, that such as willingly chose slavery ought to be forced from such their desired inclinations; **for they parted themselves into different bodies, and lay in wait up and down the country, and plundered the houses of the great men, and slew the men themselves, and set the villages on fire; and this till all Judea was filled with the effects of their madness.** And thus, the flame was every day more and more blown up, till it came to a direct war."

In Wars 6.5.1-2 Josephus talked about how, when the temple was burned down, the number of people killed in that blaze was especially high because so many people listened to the words of a false prophet. Josephus also revealed that this false prophet was one of **many** false prophets <u>**who had been hired**</u> by the Zealots to control the people and keep them from fleeing from their control:

"**A false prophet was the occasion of these people's destruction**, who had made a public proclamation in the city that very day, that God commanded them to get upon the temple, and that there they should receive miraculous signs of their deliverance. **Now there was then a great number of false prophets suborned [hired] by the tyrants to impose on the people**, who denounced this to them, that they should wait for deliverance from God; **and this was in order to keep them from deserting**" (Maarschalk, Ibid.).

C). Beast as Satan / Dragon / Ancient Serpent / Seven Headed Beast of Underworld

During the Roman-Jewish War, we can't forget that angelic armies were seen fighting in the sky and clouds as witnessed and verified by Jewish and Roman historians. This supports what the books of Daniel and Revelation teach on the "Watchers", "Angels", "Michael," and "Satan" all being involved in the last days war.

I believe this also corresponds with the historical fact that the multi-headed beast theme within the ancient world view involved the underworld of Satanic or demonic figures who influenced, mirrored and imaged their evil through world kings and empires to do their bidding. They described their gods or heroes as slaying this multi-headed beast. John demonstrates that only the Lamb had power to slay Satan and throw him in the Lake of Fire or, as Paul says, God would "crush" him "shortly" at His "soon" and or "at hand" coming in AD 70 (Rms. 13:11-12; 16:20/Gen. 3:15).

The ancient beast came from the abyss/sea and influenced Nero and the Romans to persecute Christians and then turn and devour Jerusalem. The abyss in the ancient world was understood to be a watery spiritual underworld area right beneath the ocean.

Revelation 13 addresses two beasts – one from the sea (cf. Rev. 13:1) and another on the land (cf. Rev. 13:11).

David Chilton introduced chapter 13 in his Revelation commentary with the ancient two-beast theme of Leviathan (sea beast) and Behemoth (land beast), admitting that the beast theme involves much more than just human rulers and kingdoms:

> "In a visual, dramatic sense, the mighty Roman Empire did seem to arise out of the sea, from the Italian peninsula across the ocean from the Land. More than this, however, the Biblical symbolism of the sea is in view here. The sea is, as we saw in 9:1-3, associated with the Abyss, the abode of the demons, who were imprisoned there..."[204]

G.K. Beale gives a scholarly treatment of how these two beasts and the seven-headed beast theme was understood in the ancient world and within Judaism:

> "The depiction of the two beasts in ch. 13 is based in part on Job 40–41, which is the only OT depiction of two Satanic beasts opposing God. Commentators cite the Job passages but rarely discuss them or develop their relationship with Revelation.[176] These two beasts are echoed throughout Revelation 13, particularly from the LXX. One is a land "beast" (θηρίον, 40:15–24) to be slain by God with a "sword" (40:19 MT; cf. Rev. 13:10, 14). The other is a sea "dragon" (δράκων, Job 40:25) who conducts a "war waged by his mouth" (40:32). "Burning torches" and "a flame" go "out of his mouth" (41:11, 13). "There is nothing on earth like him" (41:25). Both are thus given demonic attributes, and both are described as "made to be mocked by the angels" (40:19; 41:25 LXX).[177]

> The Job text alludes to a primordial defeat of the dragon by God (cf. 40:32 LXX; so also *Midr. Rab.* Exod. 15.22), but also implies a yet future battle (40:19, 20–24 LXX; 41:25 LXX), which is necessitated by the sea beasts' continued attitude of defiance (e.g., 41:33–34 MT). Though the beast was defeated, he continues to exist in a subdued condition (Job 7:12; Amos 9:3; cf. *Apoc. Abr.* 10; 21). On the assumption that the beginning of history must be recapitulated at the end of history, Judaism crystallized the implicit expectation of Job. Rev. 12:1–11 also echoes this Jewish tradition. The tradition held that on the fifth day of creation God created Leviathan to be in the sea and Behemoth to dwell on land (*1 En.* 60:7–10; *4 Ezra* 6:49–52; *2 Bar.* 29:4; *b. Baba Bathra* 74b–75a; *Pesikta de Rab Kahana*, supplement 2.4). These two beasts were symbolic of the powers of evil and were to be destroyed at the final judgment

---

[204] Chilton, Ibid., 326

(so explicitly in *2 Bar.; Midr. Rab.* Lev. 13.3; and *b. Baba Bathra* 74b, and implied in the other three texts just cited above).

This tradition may come into use here in the Apocalypse because people in Asia Minor thought whatever came "from the sea" as foreign and whatever came from the land as native. That is, one of the initial expressions of the first beast was Rome, whose governors repeatedly came by sea to Ephesus. Roman ships literally seemed to be rising out of the sea as they appeared on the horizon off the coast of Asia Minor. The second beast represented native political and economic authorities.

Vv 1–2 are a creative reworking of Dan. 7:1–7. The "beast coming up from the sea" and his "ten horns" are based respectively on Dan. 7:2–3 and Dan. 7:7, 20, 24. Many understand the "seven heads" as a reference to an ancient Near Eastern sea monster myth from before the time of Daniel (Leviathan with seven heads in *CTA* 5.I, 1–3; 3.III, 37–39; cf. also Job 40–41; Pss. 74:13–14; 89:10; Isa. 27:1; 51:9; *Odes Sol.* 22:5)."[205]

In the ancient world (Jew or Gentile) talk of sea beasts or seven-headed beasts or dragons were understood to apply both to underworld evil influences mirrored and imaged through their evil human rulers and kingdom partners who worshipped them.

The great red dragon with seven heads is introduced in Revelation 12 where it seeks to devour the Church or New Israel of God, but she flees to the wilderness and is safe. This is simply a prophetic and apocalyptic description of the same end time war and flight Jesus described for us in Luke 21:20-24, which we looked at previously.

As I laid out in our discussion of Isaiah 11, the gospels are filled with the second exodus theme. Due to space limitations, I will not develop that theme in Revelation. But for the sake of our discussion, let's re-visit Isaiah 51 where God described taking Israel out of Egyptian bondage and parting the sea as not only creating the "heavens" and "earth," but a ***slaying of a sea beast/dragon***: "Was it not you who cut Rahab in pieces, who ***pierced the dragon***?" (Isa. 51:9).

In Hebrew "Rahab" is understood to be a chaotic dragon sea monster. G.K. Beale demonstrates that the Septuagint version of Ezekiel 29:3 reads, "Pharaoh the great dragon,"[206] connecting the evil earthly power to this spiritual underworld being.

In Isaiah 14 and Ezekiel 28, the King of Tyre is understood in terms of being a mere man and yet as Satan or an angelic figure.

In Revelation 9, the siege of Titus for five months is connected to the activity of the abyss and demonic locusts. This is but yet another example of the demonic underworld working through evil rulers. G.K. Beale writes the following on Revelation 9:11:

---

[205] Beale, Ibid., 682-683

[206] Ibid., 633

> "Abandon" is depicted "as the hellish home of Belial, the satanic "asp," in 1QH 3(11). 16, 19, 32. There the "pit" and "abyss" open and fulminate out billows, arrows, and "the spirits of the asp" (3[11]. 16-18; 5[13].27) against hardened hypocrites (3[11].25-27), "leaving [them with] no hope."
>
> These Jewish sources refer to "angels of destruction from the pit, who inflict "most sorrowful chagrin and most bitter misfortune" as allies of the spirits of perversity and darkness."[207]

These Jewish sources Beale appeals to demonstrate that these demonic spirits cause men to believe false doctrine and worship them while the righteous are protected from such. There may be a play on Apollyon and Apollo and how the Romans understood their leaders and false worship (see Daniel Dutra Morais's comments below). It seems to me that God is using Satan and the demonic, working through the Romans, Zealots and Pharisees to judge and destroy Jerusalem and vindicate the early Christians who they had persecuted.

Beale points out that some connect the "destroying angel" in the first exodus (Ex. 12:23) with the descriptions here in Revelation 9:1, 4-5, 11:

> "...the "destroying angel...the angel of death, to whom is given the power to destroy, but has no dominion" over the Israelites (Targ. Pal. Exod. 12; Targ. Pal. And Jer. Exodus 4 use the same titles for the angel who opposed Moses). Jubilees repeatedly identifies this angel as "prince Mastema," another name for Satan and therefore a parallel to the angel of Rev. 9:11 (the "king" of the demons; Jub. 11:5; 17:16; 18:9, 12; 48:2-15). This prince-angel was the one who tried to kill Moses on his return to Egypt and who struck down the Egyptian deluge, so that he became known as "chief of the [evil] spirits" (Jub. 10:7-8; 11:5; 19:28). Not only does "the destroyer" oppose Moses, but he opposes the Israelites after they leave Egypt (Wis. 18:22-25)."[208]

> "...OT and Jewish tradition based on Exodus 12 affirms both that God is the one who struck down the firstborn and that he used an angelic agent to execute his will [Exod. 12:23]. The Satanic source of the plagues is also noted in Wis. 17:14 (where the plague of darkness came from "the bottoms of ...hell"). In Hermas, Vision 4:1, the seer has a vision of "a huge beast, like some sea monster, and from its mouth flaming locusts were pouring out."[209]

Daniel Dutra Morais makes even more of a connection with Titus and the events of AD 70:

> "The name Apollyon is a Greek play on words for "Apollo" (Apollon in Greek) and "Destroyer." Revelation 9:11 reads, "They had as king over them the angel of the Abyss, whose name in Hebrew is Abaddon and in Greek is Apollyon (that is, Destroyer)." Abaddon means "destruction or ruin" which is "apoleia" in Greek. Though Abaddon means "destruction or ruin" it is truly the place of

---

[207] Ibid. 503
[208] Ibid.
[209] Ibid., 502-504

destruction or ruin which in Greek is Hades or bussos or abussos (Abyss). Why does John call the angel of the Abyss the name for "destruction" or "the place of destruction" in Hebrew but then use the Greek word "Apollyon" meaning "destroyer" which is not an exact Greek translation of the Hebrew Abaddon? John appears to call the angel of the Abyss "Apollyon" rather than using more exact Greek translations of Abaddon like "apoleia," Hades, "bussos" or "abussos" because of the similarity between the words "destroyer" (Apollyon) and Apollo (Apollon) in Greek. In other words, this word selection appears to be a word play for "Apollo" (Apollon) and "Destroyer" (Apollyon).

The fact that Apollyon is used to intentionally call to mind the god Apollo is hinted at throughout Revelation 9. The Anchor Bible Dictionary says the following concerning the link between Apollyon and Apollo:

In one manuscript, instead of Apollyon the text reads "Apollo," the Greek god of death and pestilence [or plague like the plague of locusts mentioned in Revelation 9] . . . . Apollyon is no doubt the correct reading. But the name Apollo (Gk Apollon) was often linked in ancient Greek writings with the verb apollymi or apollyo, "destroy." From this time of Grotius, "Apollyon" has often been taken here to be a play on the name Apollo. The LOCUST was an emblem of this god[.]" [Emphasis mine.]

Concerning this perceived link between Apollyon and Apollo, Isbon Beckworth writes, "Some (Boss, Holtzm.-Bauer, al.) find in the name Apollyon an indirect allusion also to the god Apollo, one of whose symbols was the locust and to whom plagues and destruction were in some cases attributed (see Rosher, Lex. d. Griech. N. Rom. Mythol. s.v.)[.] The use of the name Apollyon is meant to call attention to this agent's identification with the Greek God Apollo (hence the plague and locust imagery as well as implicit references to "destroy" in Revelation 9) and his active role as the "destroyer" of Jerusalem. So, who could this be, and why is this figure called the "Destroyer" in Greek so as to imply a link to Apollo?

__The earthly reflection__ of Apollyon is Vespasian's son Titus, the commander of the Legio XV Apollinaris (Fifteenth Apollonian Legion). Initially the commander of the Fifteenth Legion, Titus then went on to succeed his father as general over all the Roman legions during the Jewish War after his father had become Caesar, a title also bestowed on Titus at his father's coronation. As Caesar, Titus was entitled to worship as a god in the imperial cult, and like Apollo, the son of Zeus, could also be labeled the Son of God--a perfect title for the beast.

At the start of the Jewish War, Titus was the general of the Fifteenth Legion. With Apollo as its patron, the Fifteenth Legion was suitably nicknamed Apollinaris, a name meaning "devoted to Apollo." **_The Fifteenth Legion would always carry an emblem of Apollo or one of his holy animals wherever it went. Not surprisingly, the locust was one of Apollo's holy animals. Now it is easy_** *to see why the author of Revelation chose locusts to symbolize the soldiers of the Roman army following the precedence set in Joel. So "devoted to Titus" was his army that at the taking of the Jewish temple, they unanimously declared him emperor of Rome in fulfillment of v. 11 in which Apollyon is said to have been "king over them."*

This play on words for "Apollo"--the god of death and plague--and "Destroyer" in the name Apollyon perfectly describes the man directly responsible for the remaining plagues of Revelation who was the "destroyer" of Jerusalem. And who coincidentally besieged the city FOR EXACTLY 5 MONTHS just as stated in Rev 9:10!" [210]

While at a Berean Bible Church Conference, I had the pleasure of speaking alongside Robert Cruickshank Jr. where he spoke on this subject directly. Here is a helpful quote from his notes addressing Nero being the beast and yet influenced by, and made in the image of, the Satanic beast of the underworld:

In 'THE BACKGROUNDS AND MEANING OF THE IMAGE OF THE BEAST,' Rebekah Yi Liu makes the interesting observation: **"The Bible <u>starts</u> and <u>ends</u> with the making of an image**.

The first mention of making an image is found in Gen 1: the making of human beings in God's image. The language of Revelation 13 alludes to the Genesis story of the creation of human beings. Verbally, the language of Revelation 13 parallels the language of creation in Genesis 1-2. The same nouns occur in both passages, i.e., <u>sea</u> (Gen 1:10, Rev 13:1), <u>land</u> (Gen 1:10, Rev 13:11), <u>beasts</u> (Gen 1: 24, Rev 13:1, 11), <u>image</u> (Gen 1: 26, 27, Rev 13:14)." Drawing on the Septuagint, she notes that "the verbs used for the making of the image are the same" (p. 97).

In Genesis, God **"makes"** man in his own **"image"** (Gen. 1:26) and **"breathes"** life into his nostrils (Gen. 2:7). In Revelation 13, an **"image"** is **"made"** of the Sea Beast, and life is **"breathed"** into it (Rev. 13:14-15). This represents "a reversal of the creation account" (Yi Liu, p. 98).

Verse 15 talks about The False Prophet causing people to worship the image of the Beast. Steven Friesen notes: "Sacrificial activity for the emperors took place in a myriad of contexts. Emperors were worshipped in their own temples, at temples of other gods, in theaters, gymnasiums, in stoas…in judicial settings, in private homes and elsewhere. Imperial cults," says Friesen, "were everywhere" (Satan's Throne, p. 363).

Just as man was made to be *God's image-bearer*, by subduing the earth and bringing order to God's Creation, Nero became the *image-bearer of Leviathan*

---

[210] Daniel Dutra Morais, *Who is Apollyon in Greek Culture*, https://hermeneutics.stackexchange.com/questions/28647/who-is-apollyon-in-greek-culture

(God's age-old enemy) and attempted to bring chaos to God's newly created order – the New covenant Church.[211]

The last of Daniel's four beasts is Rome and it comprises both Roman elements (iron) and that of the apostate Jews and Herodian dynasty (clay) (Dan. 2:40-43).[212] These groups have a love-hate relationship which made the kingdom vulnerable and weak. At first, they both come together in seeking to destroy Christ and the early church, but since clay does not mix or cling with iron, the apostate Jews (clay) rebel against the Romans (iron) and this results in the Roman-Jewish War.

As we move into Revelation, the beast theme is addressing Nero the sixth king, the Roman Empire (the sea beast), the apostate Jews (the land beast) and the Satanic seven-headed beast or dragon from the underworld who is pulling the strings of these other beasts to come against Christ, His saints and to eventually turn on each other in order to tear apart Jerusalem and her temple. Therefore, the judgment of Satan within the beast theme was also fulfilled "shortly" in AD 70 along with the other enemies in the great end of the age war of AD 67 – AD 70.

While the Roman Empire did not end in AD 70, its ability to rule or "shake" God's Kingdom did. The four Gentile world empires that ruled over God's people in Daniel were able to "shake" God's old covenant kingdom (destroy and loot her city and temple). But in AD 70, Rome's power to do so was destroyed and lost because post-AD 70 God's kingdom (city and temple) on earth is set up within the hearts of His people and thus could no longer be shaken, plundered or destroyed as the old had. The riches of this kingdom are found in the righteousness of Christ buried deep within the hearts and souls of His people, never to be taken! It is in this way that the entire statue of Daniel 2 (the four Gentile kingdoms & apostate Jews) comes crashing down when the stone (Christ & His Kingdom) strike it in AD 70.

And while the Roman Beast was not completely destroyed in AD 70, Satan/the Ancient Serpent/the Dragon, whose demonic legions influenced Rome and apostate Judaism, was cast into the Lake of Fire and "crushed" "shortly" in AD 70.

This end-time "the Battle" of Revelation 19 goes on to describe the covenant-cursing divorce and judgment of God's old covenant wife/Jerusalem, while at the same time He consummates His marriage to His new covenant wife/the New Jerusalem (the Church). While the wedding feast takes place for the new covenant Wife/Jerusalem, the old covenant harlot wife/Jerusalem gets fed to the birds - "all the birds gorged themselves on their flesh" (Rev. 19:6-9; 21).

This is in direct harmony with Jesus' teaching concerning the Roman-Jewish War, in that old covenant Judaism would be left a dead body feasted upon by the birds (Mt. 24:28/Lk. 17:37). John is also in lock step with Jesus concerning the eschatological

---

[211] Taken from Robert's notes and lectures at the Berean Bible Church Conference. Special thanks to Robert's work in this area and for sending me his notes.

[212] James B. Jordan, *THE HANDWRITING ON THE WALL - A Commentary on the Book of Daniel* (Powder Springs, GA: American Vision, 2007), 183-184; 380-408.

wedding theme, when at the time of the wedding God was going to send His armies (the Romans) to "kill those [Jewish] murderers" and "burn their city" (Mt. 22:7). Like the unfaithful wife of a priest, Jerusalem is both stoned and burned in the unfolding events of AD 67 – AD 70.

Revelation 20 - the war of Gog and Magog

Men like James Jordan, [213] Gary DeMar[214] and David Lowman believe the battle of Gog and Magog was fulfilled during the time of Esther when Haman gathered the nations of the then known world to come and attack Israel but were defeated by God. Let me seek to summarize the main points of this position:

- "Ezra and Nehemiah both mention the large amounts of silver and gold that the Jews brought back from exile. These are the same items we are told the approaching armies were attacking to plunder.
- The battle with Haman's armies takes place after Israel is returned to the land, during Darius' reign. Ezekiel prophesied until just a few short decades before this time.
- Esther and Ezekiel's enemies from the north both include Persia and Ethiopia.
- In a very short battle [in Esther], the Israelites destroy Haman's army, killing nearly 100,000 despite being greatly outnumbered.
- Both passages state that the Jews were attacked by all of Persia's provinces. DeMar argues well for parallel boundaries between the Persian Empire in Esther's day and Gog/Magog and her allies in Ezekiel's vision.
- In Ezekiel's vision, the Jews were living in unwalled towns. DeMar notes that this was also the case in Esther's day, which makes sense since they were part of the Persian Empire at that time, an empire known for its benevolence and for taking good care of its subjects.
- Haman (the enemy of Esther) is shown to be an "Agagite," and even a "Gogite" in some manuscripts. Also the invaders in Ezekiel's vision would be buried in the Valley of "Hamon-Gog."

Others, such as William Hendriksen, see the first historical and typological reference to the war of Gog and Magog to be during the time of the Seleucids:

> "The expression 'Gog and Magog' is borrowed from the book of Ezekiel, where the term undoubtedly indicates that power of the Seleucids especially as it was revealed in the days of Antiochus Epiphanes, the bitter enemy of the Jews. The center of his kingdom was located in North Syria. Seleucus established his residence there in the city of Antioch on the Orontes. To the east his territory extended beyond the Tigris. To the north the domain over which the Seleucids ruled included Mesheck and Tubal, districts in Asia Minor. Accordingly, Gog

---

[213] James B. Jordan, *The Battle of Gog and Magog*, http://www.biblicalhorizons.com/biblical-horizons/no-2-the-battle-of-gog-and-magog/

[214] Gary DeMarl, (Powder Springs, GA, American Vision Press, 2008).

was the prince of Magog, that is, Syria. Therefore, the oppression of God's people by 'Gog and Magog', refers, in Ezekiel, to the terrible persecution under Antiochus Epiphanes, ruler of Syria."[215]

If this view is correct and the attack of Gog and Magog (Syria under Antiochus Epiphanes) was the last great oppression which Israel endured to close the OT, it stands to reason that John in the book of Revelation would use this as a symbolic or type/anti-type description of the end-time battle to close the old covenant age and to liberate the new covenant Israel of God.

Either way, John is using the symbolism of a past battle of Gog and Magog within Israel's history to depict a future (but "shortly," "at hand," "soon," and "about to be") persecution and battle for John and his contemporaries to experience and relate to.

Also notice that ancient weapons were being used and burned (Ezek. 38:4-5; 39:9), which would fit the warfare, destruction and fire of AD 67 - AD 70 more than it would a description of nuclear or modern-day warfare.

Here we have Satanically-led nations being gathered from the four corners of the earth (or better translated as the *land* of Palestine) to make war and surround the New Jerusalem (the Church). The Greek word here for "earth" is *ge*, which is consistently and accurately translated as "land" in Revelation in Young's Literal Translation. These are not nations gathered from all ends of the globe, but rather are from the world as they knew it (the Roman Empire) or the "land" of Palestine or that of the Jews.

But who are the "nations" involved? Well, the Roman army consisted of all the nations of the then known world that she had conquered, and as we have seen both Nero and Rome were known as a/the "beast" which persecuted and thus waged war against the early Church (the New Jerusalem / the saints God loves).

But the apostate Jews, known to be a part of the beast, also persecuted and waged war against the first century Christians and, as James Stuart Russell points out, they too were understood to be "nations" and "kings":

> "In our Lord's time it was usual to speak of the inhabitants of Palestine as consisting of several nations. Josephus speaks of 'the nation of the Samaritans...'" 'the nation of the Galileans...' etc... Judea was a distinct nation, often with a king of its own; so also, was Samaria; and so, with Idumea, Galilee, Perea...all of which had at different times princes with the title of Ethnarch, a name which signifies the ruler of a nation."[216]

So what we have here is an apocalyptic description of perhaps one or both persecuting powers – the Romans and apostate Jews – seeking to destroy new covenant Jerusalem. Before the Christians fled to Pella, there was in a sense a city (the new covenant

---

[215] William Hendriksen, *More Than Conquerors,* (Grand Rapids, MI, Baker Book House, 7th reprint 1990), 193.

[216] James Russell, *The Parousia,* (Grand Rapids, MI: Baker Book House, third printing, 1990), 105

Jerusalem from above) within a city (residing physically within the walls of the then present old covenant Jerusalem from below).

At some point, the Christians see the sign of Jerusalem being surrounded by armies (Jewish, Roman or both) and flee the city to Pella as the Lord directed them. They were protected by God while the nations who persecuted the Church destroyed each other and were defeated in their effort to destroy the New Jerusalem. In Revelation 21-22, the gates of the New Jerusalem are continually open post-AD 70 in the new covenant age - not only as a symbol for evangelism for the nations to come into her for salvation and healing, but as a symbol that there is no threat of her destruction because God has defeated her enemies and watches over her.

Christian Full Preterism brings together and harmonizes the classic Christian Amillennial view and the Christian Partial Preterist view regarding the time frame of this ONE end-time war in the book of Revelation. Consider the following:

Major Premise: If "THE war" and judgment scenes of Revelation 16-20 are depicting ONE "time of the end" event (through typical prophetic recapitulation – Classic Amillennial View),

Minor Premise: But "THE war" and judgment scenes of Revelation 16-19 were fulfilled in and by AD 70, (Partial Preterist View),

Conclusion: Therefore, "THE war" (which is ONE and the same) and judgment scenes of Revelation 16-20 were fulfilled in and by AD 70 (the Full Preterist View).

The Martyr Vindication Theme

The "soon" Second Coming that took place at the end of the millennium was to vindicate the martyrs here in Revelation 20. Again, this is consistent with what we saw in Revelation 6 and 16-18 along with Jesus' teaching in Matthew 23-24.

Through the imprecatory prayers of the persecuted Church and the cries of the martyrs, they call fire down upon the apostate mountain of old covenant Jerusalem and have it thrown into the sea (Mt. 21:18-22 / Rev. 8:1-8). It was through the preaching of the gospel in the then known world, the filling up the measure of Israel's guilt in their killing of the martyrs, and the imprecatory prayers of the saints that God took the kingdom from Israel and gave it to the Church in her restored, matured, and glorified form.

Concluding Full Preterism and Middle East Eschatology on the Last Days "THE War"

Contrary to the teachings of Muslims, Zionists, and Dispensational Zionists, and the ignorant speculations of Hollywood and the media, the gathering of the armies for "THE war" in the battle of Armageddon and or "The war" of Gog and Magog was an event that was fulfilled in Jesus' contemporary generation and thus "shortly" fulfilled in John's day. When the first century Christians saw the sign of either the Zealot / Idumean armies or the Roman armies surrounding Jerusalem, they left the city and God used these armies to bring desolation and destruction upon the city and temple.

The Church today is not to look to a sign of "wars and rumors of wars" or nuclear developments in the Middle East that allegedly will bring about "THE" final war and "rapture" of the Church. And she most assuredly is not to fund and support them – directly or indirectly!

Chapter Seven:

How was the Resurrection Fulfilled by AD 70?

Jewish Views on the Resurrection

Many Talmudic Zionists, Muslims and Dispensational Zionists simply assume that the only concept of the resurrection of the dead in the OT and during Jesus' day was a biological fleshly one in which an alleged individual's physical/ spiritual body would emerge from the literal grave at the end of time and thus be fitted for the afterlife in the new creation or some paradise on earth. But this is simply not the case.

I like how Lester L. Grabbe points out that, during the Second Temple period, the interpretations of the resurrection in the OT were not all necessarily understood to refer to the physical body. They included the view that the resurrection involved only the souls/spirits of individuals being fit for God's presence either at death, or only their souls were raised at a general judgment of the dead event. He points out that there is no evidence that the physical view was any more dominant than the spiritual view. While lengthy, I think his historical comments will be helpful before we begin an exegesis of the OT and NT resurrection texts and simply assume they are addressing a biological resurrection at the end of time when Jesus or Messiah comes:

> "It is sometimes asserted that the resurrection of the body was the characteristic Jewish belief. This is not borne out by the data. A variety of beliefs seem to be attested about the same time in Israelite history. **One of these was the resurrection of the body, but there is little reason to think that it was earlier or more characteristic of Jewish thinking than the immortality of the soul or resurrection of the spirit**. And it is clear that some Jews still maintained the older belief in no afterlife. The Sadducees (see section 2.7) are one group who thought so; so did Ben Sira. Writing about 190 bce Ben Sira does not seem to think of any life beyond death, as interpreted by the vast majority of scholars. Therefore, it would be quite wrong to refer to any of these beliefs as 'characteristically' Jewish or the Jewish belief on the subject."[217]

---

[217] Lester L. Grabbe, *An Introduction to Second Temple Judaism: History and Religion of the Jews in the Time of Nehemiah, the Maccabees, Hillel, and Jesus,* (T&T Clark Publishing, 2010), see pages 93-96

"The exact form of the resurrection is not always specified, but we should not expect it always to entail resurrection of the body. *Sometimes only the resurrection of the spirit is in mind, as in Jubilees 23:20–22*:

And at that time the Lord will heal his servants, and they shall be exalted and prosper greatly; and they shall drive out their adversaries. And the righteous shall see it and be thankful, and rejoice with joy for ever and ever; and they shall see all the punishments and curses that had been their lot falling on their enemies. And *their bones shall rest in the earth, and their spirits shall have much joy; and they shall know that the Lord is one* who executes judgement, and shows mercy to hundreds, and to tens of thousands, and to all that love him.

Belief in the immortality of the soul is known at least as early as the Book of Watchers (*1 Enoch* 1–36). The souls of the various sorts of people are preserved in hollow places after death (*1 Enoch* 22):

And from there I went to another place, and he showed me in the west a large and high mountain, and a hard rock and four beautiful places, and inside it was deep and wide and very smooth ... Then Raphael, one of the holy angels who was with me, answered me and said to me, These beautiful places are intended for this, that the spirits, the souls of the dead, might be gathered into them; for them they were created, that here they might gather all the souls of the sons of men. And these places they made where they will keep them until the day of their judgement and until their appointed time – and that appointed time will be long – until the great judgement comes upon them.

As the rest of the passage indicates, the souls of the dead are already experiencing reward and punishment in their intermediate state. In this case, the existence of the soul after death seems to be combined with the idea of a final judgement. This may imply a general resurrection, though this is not stated explicitly. In other sections of *1 Enoch,* a resurrection is mentioned (46:6; 51:1; 90:33; 91:10; 92:3–4).

Other sources give no indication of a resurrection at all, only the immortal soul. A good example is Wisdom of Solomon which speaks of the soul (e.g., 3:1–9) but does not mention the resurrection. Whether Wisdom thinks the souls of all are immortal, or only those of the righteous, is debated. Many feel that immortality is not inherent in the soul itself but is a gift given only to the righteous.

The *Testament of Abraham* gives the clearest picture of how the souls are judged after death (Version A 11–14; Version B 9–11). The souls are brought before a throne on which Abel sits as judge. The one who presents the souls for judgement is Enoch, the scribe of righteousness (Version B only). *The judged souls go either through the strait gate which leads to life (for the righteous) or the broad gate to destruction (for the sinners).* Although there is a brief indication of belief in a general resurrection in the *Testament of Abraham* (Version B 7:16), judgement of each individual seems to take place immediately after death, and the emphasis is on this immediate judgement of the soul while the body rests in the grave.

On the other hand, the immortal souls and the resurrection may be combined, as in 2 Baruch 29–30:

> [30:2] And it shall come to pass at that time that ***the treasuries will be opened in which is preserved the number of the souls of the righteous, and they will come out, and the multitude of souls will appear together in one single assembly; and those who are first will rejoice, and those who are last will not be cast down. For each one of them will know that the predetermined end of the times has come. But the souls of the wicked, when they see all this, will be the more discomforted. For they will know that their torment is upon them and that their perdition has arrived.***"[218]

Murray J. Harris after examining the intertestamental period of Judaism agrees:

> "And there is the concept of the immortality of the soul or spirit that is gained at death or at the End [of the Mosaic age], with or without a resurrection of the [physical] body."[219]

In Jewish tradition and exegesis there is also the view that the resurrection takes place 40 years after Messiah,

> "Jewish writings stipulate that forty years after the coming of the Messiah there will be a resurrection of the dead, and all who are lying in dust will rise to new life." (The 13 Principles and the Resurrection of the Dead)

> The Rebbe often quotes the Zohar to the effect that the Resurrection will take place 40 years after the advent of Mashiach. (See Igros Kodesh, Vol. II, p. 75; Sefer HaSichos 5752, Vol. I, p. 274. However, there are also other references in the sichos (e.g., Likkutei Sichos, Vol. XXVII, p. 206; Sefer HaSichos 5733, Shabbos Parshas Balak, footnote 3)."[220]

The fact that the resurrection could be a resurrection of spirits out of Hades in the coming judgment and that it would be fulfilled 40 years after Messiah was cut-off or during His transitionary reign between their old covenant "this age" and the new covenant "age about to come" fits perfectly with the teachings of Jesus and the NT authors. Let's now turn our attention to Christian orthodoxy and see if such a spiritual resurrection in AD 70 can be seen.

---

[218] Ibid.

[219] Murray J. Harris, *FROM GRAVE to GLORY RESURRECTION IN THE NEW TESTAMENT Including a Response to Norman L. Geisler*, (Grand Rapids, MI: Zondervan Publishing House, 1990), 70

[220] (*Historical Jewish Sources*, https://preteristarchives.org/historical-jewish-sources/?fbclid=IwAR2Osz DkXKqp8Z-qv0RFld1hjS6_tDT7hoysllAAjdGQpUOTi03OmHx67Nc

Christian Views of a Spiritual Resurrection in AD 70

Many Christians are unaware that Reformed Partial Preterism teaches that there was a spiritual resurrection of the dead at the coming of Christ in AD 70. This position teaches the exact same concepts I will be developing, in that the OT and NT supports that:

> 1). There was a spiritual, progressive, corporate and covenantal resurrection from the condemnation and death of the old covenant body of Israel being transformed and rising into the imputed righteousness and resurrection life of the new covenant body of Israel between AD 30 - AD 70.

> 2). This spiritual, progressive, corporate and covenantal resurrection is consummated at Christ's coming upon the clouds in the events of AD 67 - AD 70 when God empties the souls from Abraham's Bosom, or Hades, and causes His righteous to inherit God's presence and eternal life.

Unfortunately, the weakness of this position is that both the OT and NT teach that this is the ONE end of the age (old covenant age) consummative resurrection event and not just "a" resurrection.

I will be arguing in this chapter that the above "orthodox" Christian understanding of a spiritual, progressive, covenantal and corporate body resurrection is THE general end of the age resurrection event that was fulfilled imminently by AD 70.

The resurrection of Job 19:25-27?

- *"For I know that my Redeemer lives, and at the last he will stand upon the earth. And after my skin has been thus destroyed, yet in my flesh I shall see God, whom I shall see for myself, and my eyes shall behold, and not another. My heart faints within me" (Job 19:25-27).*

Note how the American Standard Bible translates verse 26 as having the exact opposite meaning as how the physical resurrection proponents would read it: "And after my skin, even this body, is destroyed, then, **without my flesh** shall I see God."

The Anchor Bible reads and understands the Hebrew as "without my flesh" and the NIV concedes that this can be the meaning and adds a note ("from my flesh").

OT and Hebrew scholars Keil and Delitzsch translate the Hebrew in the key verse thus:

> "And after my skin, thus torn to pieces, And ***without my flesh*** shall I behold Eloah..."

And they further elaborate that this text should not be used to support a fleshly resurrection:

"If we have correctly understood עַל־עָפָר, Job 19:25, we cannot in this speech find that the hope of a bodily recovery is expressed."[221]

Barne's Notes on the Bible renders it:

"After I shall awake, **though this body be destroyed, yet out of my flesh shall I see God**."

The Hebrew can actually teach the exact opposite of an expectation of a physical resurrection in that Job is saying "apart from my flesh" or "without my flesh" he would see God. Therefore, this passage could easily be supporting an understanding of a resurrection of the soul in seeing God and, if so, would be consistent with spiritual Jewish views we just looked at.

Some have postulated that Job was one of those raised out of the tombs with Jesus in Matthew 27, and therefore he saw Jesus standing on the earth before He ascended. If so, there is no evidence that Job took a physical body to heaven or ascended with Christ. If such a view was correct (and I don't think it is), then Job's physical resurrection was a "sign" type miracle, and he went into the town testifying of Christ and then would die again, as the purpose of Lazarus' resurrection served.

A more probable interpretation given by Futurists and Preterists alike is that Job is looking for vindication in this life and is not discussing a physical or spiritual resurrection hope in the afterlife. As David Green writes,

"But even if we translate the phrase to read, *"from my flesh"* (i.e., from the vantage point of my flesh), this could be taken to mean that Job expected to see God *within his own lifetime, while still in his flesh*. And, as a matter of fact, *that is exactly what happened.*

After Job's time of tribulation and anguish, his Redeemer at last arose on the dust and answered Job out of the whirlwind (Job 38:1). After God's "archers"/"troops" (i.e., Job's accusers) surrounded and "devoured" Job, and after Job was filled up with the afflictions of his flesh, he was redeemed from his sufferings. He was vindicated as *"a perfect and upright man"* and his enemies were judged (cf. Job 19:29 and 42:79). Thus Job, with his own *eyes*, and *from his flesh*, saw God: *I have heard of You by the hearing of the ear,* ***but now my eye has seen You*** (Job 42:5).

Regarding Job 14:13-17:

O that You would hide me in Sheol, that You would keep me secret, until Your wrath be past, that You would appoint me a set time, and remember me! If a man dies, shall he live again? All the days of my appointed time [literally, "warfare"] *will I wait, till my change come* [or, "until my exchanging or replacement come"]. *You shall call, and I will answer You. You will have a desire to the work of Your hands (*Job 14:13-15).

---

[221] Kiel and Delitzsch, *The Pulpit Commentary*, https://biblehub.com/commentaries/job/19-26.htm

If Job was prophesying concerning the resurrection of the dead in this passage, then we must say that Job was triumphing in the idea that his wretched and miserable condition (his *"warfare"*) would continue for hundreds or even thousands of additional years while in Sheol (Job 14:14), and that only at the end of human history would God's *"wrath"* (Job 14:13) against him pass, and that only then would Job be relieved from his warfare as a battle-wearied soldier is replaced by another (*"changed"*) (cf. Job 10:17; 14:14-15).

Either God remained/remains angry with Job for hundreds or thousands of years after Job's death, or Job was not speaking of a vindication at the resurrection of the dead. As the context leads us to believe, what Job desired was vindication *instead of death*. Instead of resigning himself to dying, stricken of God, Job yearned by faith for vindication and redemption *in his own lifetime*. He hoped that God would not crush him as an enemy, but would instead relent and restore him to Himself (Job 14:14b, 15). As we know, Job's hope was not deferred, as per futurism (Prov. 13:12). Instead, it was fulfilled, and Job was delivered and vindicated in his own lifetime. *"So, the Lord blessed the latter end of Job more than his beginning"* (Job 42:12)."[222]

The resurrection of Daniel 12:2-3

- *"At that time shall arise Michael, the great prince who has charge of your people. And there shall be a **time of trouble**, such as never has been since there was a nation till that time. But at that time your people shall be delivered, everyone whose name shall be found written in the book. 2 And **many of those who sleep in the dust of the earth shall awake, some to everlasting life, and some to shame and everlasting contempt. 3 And those who are wise shall shine like the brightness of the sky above;[a] and those who turn many to righteousness, like the stars forever and ever. 4** But you, Daniel, shut up the words and seal the book, until the time of **the end**. Many shall run to and fro, and knowledge shall increase." (Daniel asks and is told by the angel when all this would be fulfilled in v. 7) **7...**that it would be for a time, times, and half a time, and that <u>**when the shattering of the power of the holy people comes to an end all these things**</u> would be finished" (Dan. 12:1-4, 7).*

Daniel 12:2-3 is by far the most important and clearest OT text on the resurrection. Jesus and the other NT writers appeal to its fulfillment in Matthew 13:39-43, John 5, Acts 24:25, Revelation 20:5-15, and even 1 Corinthians 15.

"All these things" (Dan. 12:7)

Daniel is clearly told in verse 7 that the judgment and resurrection of verses 2-4 would be fulfilled at the same time as the "tribulation" period and during the "time of the end [of the old covenant Mosaic age]." Verse 7 also informs us that this would be a 3 ½ year period of time [the last half of the last seven years of the Daniel 9:24-27 prophecy]

---

[222] Green, Hassertt and Sullivan, *House Divided*, Ibid., 194-195

when God would "shatter the power of the holy people" in the events of AD 67 - AD 70.

Jesus has already connected the "end of the age" resurrection "gathering" and "tribulation" period to be a part of the "all these things" to be fulfilled in Jesus' contemporary "this generation" (Mt. 24:3-34). This "end of the [old covenant] age" gathering is the same event Jesus described in Matthew 13:39-43. Let's get a visual for the parallels and connections:

Since A (Daniel 12) is = to B (Matthew 13):		
Tribulation on national Israel as never before	12:1	13:40-42
Time of the end / end of "this" OC age separation	12:1, 4, 9, 13	13:39-41
Saints rise and shine in the eternal kingdom	12:2-3	13:43
Wicked rise to shame in eternal condemnation	12:2	13:39-42
And if B (Matthew 13) is = to C (Matthew 24-25):		
Pre-kingdom evangelism by Jesus' evangelism	13:37-38	24:14
Tribulation on national Israel as never before	13:40-42	24:21-22
End of "this" age / end of the age separation	13:39-41	24:30-31; 25:31-41
Sons of the day / hour shine with the Son	13:43	24:27, 30-31, 36
Inheritance of and entrance into the kingdom	13:43	25:34/Luke 21:30-32
Then A (Daniel 12) is = to C (Matthew 24-25)		
Tribulation and sanctification / Great Tribulation	12:1, 10	24:21-22
Hour / day / time of the judgment (aka separation)	12:1-2, 4 (OG) LXX	24:36; 25:31-33
Fulfillment at the time of the end / end of the age / the shattering of Israel's world/power or her "heaven and earth" (the temple, etc…)	12:4, 7, 9, 13	24:3, 13-14, 28-29, 34-35
Inheritance of and entrance into the kingdom	12:2-3, 13	25:34/Luke 21:30-32
The sons of the day / hour shine with the Son of life	12:3	24:27, 30-31, 36
Kingdom age evangelism via God's shining ones	12:3	24:14, 25:29
Two or more things that are equal to another thing are also equal to each other		
Kingdom age evangelism	Dan. 12 = Mt. 13 = Mt. 24-25	
Tribulation like never before	Dan. 12 = Mt. 13 = Mt. 24-25	

Time of the end (shattering of Israel's power) / end of the old covenant age (destruction of OC Israel's temple)	Dan. 12 = Mt. 13 = Mt. 24-25
Chosen ones raised and shine to eternal life and wicked raised to eternal condemnation / the righteous raised to shine and tares burn / sheep inherit eternal life / goats to eternal punishment	Dan. 12 = Mt. 13 = Mt. 24-25

Partial Preterist James Jordan now understands the resurrection of Daniel 12:2-3 (and Daniel's personal resurrection [his soul] in verse 13) as being a spiritual and corporate resurrection that took place from Jesus' earthly ministry to AD 70. Jordan even believes that Daniel's soul was raised out of Abraham's bosom according to Revelation 20 in AD 70. Here are some selected quotes from his commentary on Daniel:

- "**The resurrection of [Dan. 12:2]** seems to connect to the evangelistic and teaching ministry spoken of in verse 3; thus, it is some kind of historical resurrection that is spoke of, **a resurrectional event in this world, in our history**."[223]

- "…Daniel 12:2 tells us that in the days of Jesus the **nation will undergo a last spiritual resurrection**, but some will not persevere and their resurrection will only be unto destruction. The Parable of the soils fits here (Mt. 13:3-23): three different kinds of people come to life, but only one of the three different kinds of people come to like, but only one of the three kinds is awakened to persevering, everlasting life.

  During His ministry, **Jesus raised the nation back to life**. He healed the sick, cleansed the unclean, brought dead people back to life, restored the Law, entered the Temple as King, etc. Then, as always, the restored people fell into sin and crucified Him.

  Thus, **a resurrection of Israel is in view**. The wicked are raised, but do not profit from it, and are destroyed. **The saints experience a great distress, and live with God forever and ever**."[224]

- "The death of the Church in the Great Tribulation, **and her resurrection after that event**, were the great proof that Jesus had accomplished the work He came to do. The fact that the Church exists today, nearly 2000 years after her death in the Great Tribulation, is the ongoing vindication of Jesus work."[225]

---

[223] James B. Jordan, *THE HANDWRITING ON THE WALL A Commentary on the Book of Daniel*, (Powder Springs, GA: American Vision, 2007), 618

[224] Ibid., 618-619

[225] Ibid., 620

- "Revelation takes up where Daniel leaves off, and deals mostly with the **Apostolic Age and the death and resurrection of the Church**."[226]
- "What Daniel is promised is that *after his rest in Abraham's bosom, <u>he will stand up with all God's saints</u>* and join Michael on a throne in heaven, as described in Revelation 20, an event that came after the Great Tribulation and in the year AD 70."[227]

After challenging Kenneth Gentry for many years on the timing of the resurrection of Daniel 12, he too has had a recent epiphany recognizing that there had to have been some kind of spiritual resurrection of Daniel 12 fulfilled in AD 70:

- "In Daniel 12:1-2 we find a passage that clearly speaks of the great tribulation in AD 70."[228]
- "…But it also seems to speak of **the resurrection occurring at that time**…"[229]
- "Daniel appears to be presenting Israel as a grave site under God's curse: **Israel as a <u>corporate body</u> is in the "dust"** (Da 12:2; cp. Ge 3:14, 19). In this he follows Ezekiel's pattern in his vision of the dry bones, which represent Israel's "death" in the Babylonian dispersion (Eze 37). In Daniel's prophecy **many will awaken**, as it were, during the great tribulation to suffer the full fury of the divine wrath, while **others will enjoy God's grace in receiving everlasting life**. Luke presents similar imagery in Luke 2:34 in a prophecy about the results of Jesus's birth for Israel: "And Simeon blessed them, and said to Mary His mother, 'Behold, this Child is appointed for the fall and **rise of many in Israel**, and for a sign to be opposed.'"

  Christ Himself points out that some from Israel will believe and be saved, while others will not (e.g., Mt. 10:34-36; 13:11-15), that in the removing of the kingdom from Israel many will be crushed and scattered like dust (Mt. 21:43-45). He even speaks of the saved Jews as **arising from the "shadow of death"** (Mt. 4:16). Though in AD 70 elect Jews will flee Israel and will live (Mt. 24:22), the rest of the nation will be a corpse: "wherever the corpse is, there the vultures will gather" (Mt. 24:28). Indeed, in AD 70 we see in the destruction of the city of Jerusalem (Mt. 22:7) that "many are called, but few are chosen" (Mt. 22:14). Elsewhere he employs the **imagery of "regeneration" to the arising of the new Israel from out of the dead, old covenant Israel in AD 70: "You who have followed Me, in the regeneration when the Son of Man**

---

[226] Ibid. 621

[227] Ibid., 628

[228] Kenneth L. Gentry, JR., *HE SHALL HAVE DOMINION A POSTMILLENNIAL ESCHATOLOGY THIRD EDITION REVISED AND EXPANDED*, (Draper, VA: Apologetics Group Media, 2009), 538

[229] Ibid., 538 emphasis MJS

> **will sit on his glorious throne, you also shall sit upon twelve thrones, judging the twelve tribes of Israel**" (Mt. 19:28)."[230]

- "...it appears that Daniel is drawing from the hope of a future, literal resurrection and applying it **symbolically** to the first century leading up the tribulation in AD 70. That is, he is portraying **God's separating believing Jews out of Israel through the winnowing of Israel in AD 70**."[231]

- "Daniel only picks up on resurrection imagery and, like Ezekiel, applies that to corporate Israel. He is teaching that **in the events of AD 70, the true Israel will arise from old Israel's carcass, as in a resurrection**."[232]

Let's summarize the position of Jordan and Gentry here on what the resurrection of Daniel 12 entails:

1). It is Israel's last spiritual and corporate resurrection.

2). Both Israel and the Church participate in this spiritual, covenantal and corporate resurrection whereby the new covenant Church or new Israel of God is raised out of the corpse of old covenant Israel in AD 70.

3). There was an "already and not yet" type evangelism taking place between Christ's earthly ministry and His coming in AD 70 which brought about the consummative resurrection or "end" of Israel during the events of AD 67 - AD 70.

4). This resurrection resulted in Daniel's soul being raised out of Abraham's bosom to be seated on a throne to reign with Christ and inherit eternal life.

Response – Jordan appeals to the evangelism taking place in the parable of the soils instead of dealing with the evangelism taking place where Jesus actually quotes Daniel 12:2-3, and that is in the parable of the wheat and tares (cf. Mt. 13:39-43). Jesus clearly places this pre-kingdom evangelism and the resurrection of Daniel 12 to be fulfilled at the end of the old covenant age and nowhere else! And as I demonstrated earlier in our discussion of the end of the age in Matthew 24:3 and 13:39-43, a colleague of Jordan and Gentry's is Joel McDurmon, who does admit the end of the age in Matthew 13:39-43 is the old covenant age. This places the resurrection ONLY at the end of the old covenant age and no other time.

It is important to note that Gentry at one time criticized Dispensational Zionism for having two resurrection doctrines (one before and one after the 1,000 year millennial period):

---

[230] Ibid., 538-539 emphasis MJS

[231] Ibid., 539 emphasis MJS

[232] Ibid., 540 emphasis MJS

> "Contrary to dispensationalism and historic premillennialism, there is but **one** resurrection and **one** judgment, which occur **simultaneously** at the end of history: **Daniel 12:2**; Matthew 25:31-32; John 5:28-29…Acts 24:15)."[233]

Gentry NOW says "it appears" there is a double fulfillment of the resurrection of Daniel 12:2-3 (one in AD 70 and another at the end of world history). Yet he argues against other views giving the tribulation period a double fulfillment or any kind of fulfillment beyond the 3 ½ years Daniel mentions, which he correctly sees being fulfilled in the events of AD 67 - AD 70. Daniel is told that "all these things" (the tribulation and resurrection) would be fulfilled together during the "time of the end" [of the old covenant age] or during the 3 ½ years - when Israel's power is completely shattered.

When we harmonize Jordan, Gentry (#1 and #2) and McDurmon on the resurrection of Daniel 12:2-3 and Matthew 13:39-43 we get the biblical position of NT resurrection:

> **Major Premise**: The resurrection of Daniel 12:2-3 is **"one"** general resurrection of the just and unjust to be fulfilled **"at the end of the age"** and forms the resurrection of Jesus' teaching and that of the NT authors [cf. Mt. 13:39-43; John 5; Acts 24:15; 1 Cor. 15; Rev. 20:5-15; etc.] (Gentry #1).

> **Minor Premise (A):** But the resurrection of Daniel 12:2-3 has an "already and not yet" pre-kingdom evangelism connected with it that addresses the inward heart and soul of man or the living (Jordan). This pre-kingdom evangelism is mentioned in Matthew 13:39-43 and 24:14, and was a sign fulfilled before the "end of the old covenant age" in AD 70 (McDurmon).

> **Minor Premise (B)**: But Daniel's soul was raised out of Abraham's bosom in AD 70 at this last spiritual and corporate resurrection in which the new covenant body of Israel was raised out from the old covenant body of Israel in AD 70 (Jordan and Gentry#2).

> **Conclusion**: The **"ONE"** "end of the age" (spiritual, progressive, corporate and covenantal) resurrection of the just and unjust was fulfilled after a pre-kingdom evangelism affecting the hearts of the living, roughly from AD 27 - AD 67. This resulted in the new covenant body of Israel being raised out from the corpse of the old covenant body of Israel, a historic event in AD 70 which also resulted in souls being emptied out of Abraham's bosom to inherit God's presence and eternal life in AD 70 at the end of the old covenant age (the position of the author – "Reformed and always reforming" – Sovereign Grace Full Preterism).

Some get confused over Daniel's phrase "sleep in the dust." This is merely a figure of speech, as David Green points out:

> "The dead were not literally sleeping, nor were they literally in the dust. They were "in dust" only insofar as, in their death, they had not ascended into God's

---

[233] Kenneth Gentry, *The GREATNESS OF THE BREAT COMMISSION*, (Tyler, TX: ICE Publishing, 1990), 142 emphasis MJS

presence in Christ. In terms of the righteousness and life of God, they were earth-bound. From a literal standpoint, they were in Sheol/Hades (the abode of the Adamic dead), and it was from out of Sheol that they were raised to stand before the heavenly throne of God (Dan. 12:1-2)."[234]

Shining like the Sun in the Kingdom

Before leaving the resurrection of Daniel 12:2-3 and Matthew 13:39-43, we should note that Jesus teaches that at the end of the old covenant age "the righteous would shine like the sun in the kingdom" (Mt. 13:43). This connects well with my position of Christ's Second Coming being fulfilled in AD 70 as the great light of the sun shining from east to west in Matthew 24:27 and Luke 17:24. This was a spiritual "within" resurrection for the living and a resurrection for the righteous dead out of Hades or Abraham's bosom in which both groups inherited eternal life.

Before leaving Daniel 12, Gentry and Jordan have understood the resurrection of Daniel 12 to be similar to that of Ezekiel 37 which was a non-biological coming out of the "graves" or covenantal and corporate resurrection. On the subject of coming out of the graves, we turn our attention to how Jesus understands the resurrection of Daniel 12 to be fulfilled in John 5.

The resurrection of John 5:20-29

- *"For whatever the Father does, that the Son does likewise. [20] For the Father loves the Son and shows him all that he himself is doing. And greater works than these will he show him, so that you may marvel. [21] For as the Father raises the dead and gives them life, so also the Son gives life to whom he will. [22] For the Father judges no one, but has given all judgment to the Son, [23] that all may honor the Son, just as they honor the Father. Whoever does not honor the Son does not honor the Father who sent him. [24] Truly, truly, I say to you, whoever hears my word and believes him who sent me has eternal life. He does not come into judgment, but has passed from death to life. [25] "Truly, truly, I say to you, an hour is coming, and is now here, when the dead will hear the voice of the Son of God, and those who hear will live. [26] For as the Father has life in himself, so he has granted the Son also to have life in himself. [27] And he has given him authority to execute judgment, because he is the Son of Man. [28] Do not marvel at this, for an hour is coming when all who are in the tombs will hear his voice [29] and come out, those who have done good to the resurrection of life, and those who have done evil to the resurrection of judgment" (Jn. 5:20-29).*

Commentators have long understood that Daniel 12:2 is the source for Jesus' teaching on the resurrection in John 5:28-29 because the only OT passage which mentions a resurrection for both the righteous and the wicked is Daniel 12:2. This, and the only OT passage addressing "eternal life," is Daniel 12:2. G.K. Beale points out an additional connection, in that Jesus is following the (OG) LXX of Daniel 12:1-2, 4

---

[234] Green, Hassertt, Sullivan, *House Divided Second Edition*, Ibid., 178

when it comes to this coming resurrection "hour" of both believers and unbelievers.[235] Beale points out that Jesus gives the resurrection hour of Daniel 12:1-2 a soteriological and eschatological "already and not yet" period:

> "…notice that Jesus also clearly refers to the same Daniel prophecy in verses 24-25 and applies it to people presently (or imminently) coming to life ("an hour is coming and *now is*").[236]

He provides this helpful chart and adds:

Daniel 12:1-2 (OG)	John 5:24-25, 28-29
12:1: "And at that hour… 12:2: "Many of those who sleep in the width of the earth will arise [*anatesontai*]…some unto eternal life and others to reproach…and to eternal shame."	5:24: "…he who hears My word, and believes Him who sent Me, has eternal life, and does not come into judgment, but has passed out of death into life." 5:25: "…an hour is coming and now is, when the dead will hear the voice of the Son of God, and those who hear will live." 5:28: "…for an hour is coming, in which all who are in the tombs will hear His voice," 5:29: "and will come forth; those who did the good deeds to a resurrection [*anatasin*] of life, those who committed the evil deeds to a resurrection [*anatasin*] of judgment."[237]

> "Jesus understands the Dan. 12 prophecy [and the coming 'hour'] to have begun fulfillment."[238] "Dan. 12:1-2 refers to the hour of tribulation followed by resurrection. In fact, the 'hour' of Dan. 12:1 is further understood as 'the hour of the end' in Dan. 12:4 OG."[239]

But as we have seen in combining the writings of James Jordan, Kenneth Gentry and Joel McDurmon, in Daniel 12:1-3 and Matthew 13:39-43, Jesus has placed the "already and not yet" of the resurrection as having its consummation at the end of the old covenant age in AD 70. This was when Israel and the Church were receiving eternal life and being raised from the death of the fleshly old covenant body of Israel into the spiritual new covenant body of Israel. This last "already and not yet" resurrection for

---

[235] G.K. Beale, *A New Testament Biblical Theology: The Unfolding of The Old Testament In The New* (Grand Rapids, MI: Baker Academic, 2011), 131-132.

[236] Ibid., 131

[237] Ibid., 132

[238] Ibid., 132

[239] Ibid., 132

Israel would result in souls being raised out of Abraham's bosom or Hades into God's presence.

I was able to share Beale's concept of the already and not yet hour of Daniel 12 and John 5 with my co-author, David Green, in our second edition of *House Divided*, along with the chiastic structure connecting "the coming hour and now is" of John 4 with John 5. Green was able to add an even better response to Strimple on this key passage:

> "In order to understand John 5:28 and 29, we must first look three verses above it, in John 5:25, where Jesus said that the hour *"now is"* when *"the dead shall hear the voice of the Son of God, and they that hear shall live."* As most Reformed interpreters agree, Jesus in that verse was referring to the preaching of His death and resurrection. The preaching of that message commenced at Pentecost. *"The dead"* were physically living people who were *spiritually dead in sin*, and *"the voice of the Son of God"* was the gospel. Having heard the gospel, those who were spiritually *"dead"* were spiritually resurrected. They *lived* in that they received eternal life through faith in the gospel (*"the voice of the Son of God"*).
>
> Then, in verses 28 and 29, Jesus expanded His teaching on the resurrection to include those who were not only spiritually dead, but who were also physically dead. He did not call them "dead" (as He had already called the living who were spiritually dead), but He referred to them through another figure of speech as *"all who are in the graves."* They were not literally in their graves or tombs, of course, but were in Hades/Sheol.
>
> What is often missed in this passage is that, like the physically living in verse 25, the physically dead in verse 28 were *also* going to live by means of hearing Christ's *"voice."* As we know from verse 25, that *"voice"* is *the gospel*. The physically dead therefore were going to hear the gospel (cf. 1 Pet. 4:6.) and were, *as a result of hearing the gospel*, going to be resurrected (regenerated, born from out of death and Hades). This means that the physically dead were, like the physically living, *spiritually dead*. And this inescapably means that both the physically living and the physically dead were going to be *spiritually* resurrected by means of the gospel-voice of the Son of God. One resurrection in two main stages: First, the last days saints; then, the Old Testament dead (*"the rest of the dead"* in Revelation 20:5). Note the parallels between John 4:21, 23 and John 5:25, 28:
>
> 1. ..[T]he hour cometh, and now is, when the true worshipers shall worship the Father in spirit and in truth. . . . (Jn. 4:23)
>
> 2. .[T]he hour cometh, when ye shall neither in this mountain, nor yet at Jerusalem, worship the Father. (Jn. 4:21)
>
> 1. . [T]he hour is coming, and now is, when the dead shall hear the voice of the Son of God: and they that hear shall live. (Jn. 5:25)

2. . . . [T]he hour is coming, in the which all that are in the graves shall hear His voice. . . . (Jn. 5:28)

These two sets of prophecies are parallel. They speak of the same timeframes, which were these:

Pentecost (AD 30)

1. The true worshipers would worship the Father in spirit and in truth.

1. The dead would hear the voice of the Son of God, and live.

Fall of Jerusalem (AD 70)

2. God's worshipers would no longer worship Him in Jerusalem.

2. All who were in the graves would hear His voice.

After hearing the gospel, the dead were raised out of their Adamic graves (Hades) in the end of the age. And those among them who believed the gospel received eternal life in the kingdom of God. But those who hated the gospel (those who had done evil) were raised out of Hades only to stand before God and to enter into "eternal punishment" / "the second death" (Matt. 25:46; Jn. 5:28-29; Rev. 20:14)."[240]

Excellent Job by David Green! Let me briefly point out the chiastic structure connecting "the hour that was coming, and now is" of John 4-5 that didn't make it in the second edition:

(A) [T]he hour cometh (the "not yet"), when ye shall neither in this mountain, nor yet at Jerusalem, worship the Father (Jn. 4:21).

  (B) [T]he hour cometh, and now is (the "already"), when the true worshipers shall worship the Father in spirit and in truth. . . (Jn. 4:23).

  (B) [T]he hour is coming, and now is (the "already"), when the dead shall hear the voice of the Son of God: and they that hear shall live (Jn. 5:25).

(A). [T]he hour is coming (the "not yet"), in the which all that are in the graves shall hear His voice. . . (Jn. 5:28).

This is interesting in that Kenneth Gentry considers the "already and not yet" of "the coming hour and now is" of John 4 to refer to AD 27/30 – AD 70 in that the "not yet" of the "hour" was realized in AD 70 when the earthly temple was destroyed; the Church now worships God in spirit and in truth as we commune with Him as God's Mount Zion. In appealing to John 4:21-23 Gentry writes,

---

[240] Green, Hassertt, Sullivan, *House Divided Second Edition*, Ibid., 179-178

"The New Testament anticipates this ***imminent*** change of the old typological temple era into the new final era of spiritual worship."[241]

For Gentry, Jesus' teaching in John 4:21-23

"...**concludes the anticipatory old covenant era (John 4:20-23**; Heb. 1:1; 12:18-29), which "will soon disappear" (Heb. 8:13); it finally and forever closes down the typological sacrificial system, reorienting the worship of God (Heb. 9-10); and it effectively universalizes the Christian faith by freeing it from all Jewish constraints..."[242]

Gentry equates Jesus' phrase, "the hour has come" (the eschatological "not yet") with other AD 70 time texts such as "the time is short", "the day is approaching", "it is the last hour," and "in just a little while."[243]

Therefore, since John is linking John 4-5 together with this chiasm, it should be very apparent that the "already and not yet" of the "hour is coming and now is" of John 5 is also referring to the AD 27/30 – AD 70 transition period. If not, why not? Especially since Gentry has already conceded that the resurrection of Daniel 12 was fulfilled spiritually in AD 70 and that John 5 is the resurrection of Daniel 12! And if not, the burden of proof is upon the Futurist and Gentry to prove that the phrase an "hour is coming and now is" in John 5 is being used of a completely different time period than that of John 4:21-23!

It's not difficult to know when the eschatological "not yet" hour of John 4:21 and John 5:28 would arrive when we allow John to interpret himself:

- "And the world is passing away along with its desires, but whoever does the will of God abides forever. Children, **it is the last hour**, and as you have heard that antichrist is coming, so now many antichrists have come. Therefore, we know that it is the last hour" (1 John 2:17-18).

- "And he said with a loud voice, 'Fear God and give him glory, because the **hour of his judgment has come**...'" (Rev. 14:7).

- "'Put in your sickle, and reap, for the **hour to reap has come**, for the harvest of the earth is fully ripe.' So, he who sat on the cloud swung his sickle across the earth, and the earth was reaped" (Rev. 14:15-16).

And, of course, Partial Preterists such as Gentry understand this eschatological "not yet" "hour" of John in these texts as imminently fulfilled when the old covenant world passed away, when Babylon (Jerusalem) was judged, or when Israel's harvest/resurrection was fulfilled in the events of AD 67 – AD 70.

---

[241] Kenneth Gentry, co-authored book, *FOUR VIEWS ON THE BOOK OF REVELATION*, (Grand Rapids, MI: 1998), 89.

[242] Ibid. 46

[243] Kenneth Gentry, co-authored book, *THREE VIEWS ON THE MILLENNIUM AND BEYOND*, (Grand Rapids MI: Zondervan, 1999), 246 footnote 45.

Major Premise: The "already and not yet" resurrection "hour" of Daniel 12:1-4 (OG) is the resurrection "already and not yet" hour of John 5:25-29. The "not yet" consummation to this hour is further described by John in 1 John 2:17-18 and Revelation 14:7, 15-16.

Minor Premise: But the "not yet" resurrection "hour" of Daniel 12:1-4 (OG) was spiritually fulfilled in the "hour/time of the end" described as the 3 ½ years "when the power of the holy people would be completely shattered" – i.e., in the events of AD 67 - AD 70. As John and his contemporaries approached or were in the AD 67 - AD 70 time frame, he stated clearly that the "last hour" of that harvest judgment and resurrection of Israel had come.

Conclusion: The eschatological "already and not yet" hour/time-of-the-end resurrection of Daniel 12:1-4 (OG) and John 5:25-29 was a progressive, spiritual, covenantal resurrection in which the new covenant body of Israel was being raised out of the death of the old covenant body between AD 27/30 – AD 70. It would include "all" the souls of the wicked and righteous being raised out of Abraham's bosom or Hades to either inherit God's presence/eternal life or eternal punishment.

There needs to be compelling evidence that the "hour is coming, and now is" of John 4:21-23 is a different time period than the "hour is coming, and now is" of John 5:25-28, and Gentry provides none!

There needs to be compelling evidence that the spiritual "already and not yet" resurrection Jordan and Gentry give us for Daniel 12:2-3, which took place between AD 27/30 – AD 70, is not the same "already and not yet" resurrection time frame of John 5:25-29, and we receive none.

Just as Jesus placed the resurrection of Daniel 12:2-3 at the end of the old covenant age in AD 70 (cf. Mt. 13:39-43), He consistently took the "coming hour" judgment and resurrection of Daniel 12:1-4 (OG) in John 4:21-23, 5:25-29 as something imminent and to be fulfilled by AD 70.

The last day resurrection of John 6:37-40

- *"All that the Father gives me will come to me, and whoever comes to me I will never cast out. For I have come down from heaven, not to do my own will but the will of him who sent me. And this is the will of him who sent me, that I should lose nothing of all that he has given me, but **raise it up on the last day**. For this is the will of my Father, that everyone who looks on the Son and believes in him should have eternal life, and **I will raise him up on the last day**" (Jn. 6:37-40).*

The "last day" is simply the last day of Israel's "already and not yet" last days eschaton from AD 30 – AD 70. Those living within that generation who believed, and were thus sovereignly called to do so (vss. 37, 44), would be raised up to inherit resurrection eternal life at the same time the dead would (cf. Jn. 11:25-27). God's "longsuffering" was working out His salvation and granting repentance, not willing that any of His Jewish or Gentile elect ones should perish (2 Pet. 3:9-10). As the gospel was being preached throughout the Roman Empire before "the end" of the old covenant age (Mt.

24:14), the Father had given the Son a Jewish remnant and group of in-grafted Gentiles to believe in Him before the events of AD 67 – AD 70 unfolded.

Since God has always been and always will be omniscient, omnipotent and all sovereign, those coming through the gates of the New Jerusalem and partaking of the living waters are also ordained or chosen to do so (Rev. 22:17). This will always ring true as long as there are sinners and the gospel is preached – "Blessed are those you choose and bring near to live in your courts! We are filled with the good things of your house, of your holy temple" (Ps. 65:4).

As the cross is an in-time historical event accomplished for our salvation and the forgiveness of sins, so too was His second appearing apart from sin to save the members of His body, the Church. The first century elect ones were anticipating being raised into eternal life in AD 70. Positionally through Christ's redemptive work - His death, resurrection and Second Coming - His entire body (past, present and future) has been raised and made perfect in His sight. Those who believed in Christ prior to AD 70 were raised at the last day of the old covenant age and they "never die," just as we today who believe the gospel have been raised and "never die." And to that subject we now turn our attention. But before we do, there is no exegetical evidence that John 5-6 teaches a biological resurrection at the end of world history.

A spiritual resurrection for the dead and living in John 11:25-26

- *"I am the resurrection and the life. Whoever believes in me, though he die [OT worthies like Abraham or Daniel along with those who recently died prior to AD 70], yet shall he live [be raised out of Abraham's bosom or Hades to inherit God's presence and eternal life], and everyone who lives and believes in me shall never die [that is not that they would never see biological death, but rather inherit God's "within" Kingdom and presence of eternal life]. Do you believe this (John 11:25-26)?"*

The death that held both the believing dead [in Abraham's bosom or Hades] and the living prior to AD 70 in its grip, awaiting Christ's redemption through the cross and Second Coming, was the *spiritual death* that came through Adam. Consider the following seven points or arguments that support this premise and exegesis.

1). **Common Hebraic parallelism** in our text makes it clear that both "resurrection" and reception of "life" are equivalent to each other in meaning. Therefore, since the reception of "life" through faith means to "never die" (overcoming the spiritual death that came through Adam the very day he sinned), then the "resurrection" for those who had died in faith should have the same or similar meaning. **That is, both the dead and the living would receive spiritual new covenant or resurrection life and enjoy God's presence forever in His kingdom.**

2). An examination of Jesus' "I am" statements also supports a spiritual fulfillment of the resurrection. Thus far in the gospel of John, all of Jesus' "I am" statements are spiritual:

1. I am the Bread/Water of Life (John 6:35) – **spiritual** Bread & Light

2. I am the Light of the world (John 9:5) – **spiritual** Light
3. I am the Door (John 10:9) – **spiritual** Door
4. I am the Good Shepherd (John 10:11) **spiritual** shepherd
5. **I am the Resurrection (John 11:25)** – is this the only "I am" that is physical?
6. I am the True Vine (John 15:1) – **spiritual** vine
7. I am the Way (John 14:6) – **spiritual** way

Those who believe in Christ as "Bread" or "Water" partake of Him, or find this fulfilled spiritually. The same can be true of being in the "Light" and the "Way," abiding in Him as the "Vine," etc.

3). Thus far in the gospel of John, all references to "life" are spiritual (cf. chapters 1, 3, 4, 5, 6, and 10).

4). In John, the primary purpose of miracles (other than proving that Jesus is a prophet sent by the Father, or that He is the Great "I Am") is to point to a **spiritual truth**. Feeding a great multitude is to point to the fact that Jesus is the bread from heaven who gives spiritual eternal life (Jn. 6:26-35). He heals the blind to prove He can heal those who are spiritually blind [thus those who are spiritually dead] (John 9:39). In Mark's gospel, Jesus heals a crippled man to prove He has the power to forgive sin (Mrk. 2:10-11). So here in John 11 Jesus is going to perform a physical sign miracle of raising Lazarus biologically to prove and point to a deeper meaning that He is "the (spiritual) resurrection and (spiritual) life."

5). We must allow John to interpret John elsewhere. In John's version of the Olivet Discourse (the book of Revelation) we learn the following on when and what the resurrection looks like:

> A). The judgment of the dead and/or the resurrection out of Hades into God's Most Holy Place presence is connected to something that would be fulfilled "shortly" or "soon," and therefore by AD 70 and not the end of world history (Rev. 1:1, 22:20).
>
> B). The judgment of the dead [and thus the resurrection of the dead] was connected to when the "great city" Egypt / Sodom / Babylon (old covenant Jerusalem – "where the Lord was crucified") would be judged in AD 70 (Rev. 11:8-19; see also the harvest/resurrection motif in chapters 7 and 14). Revelation 11 also mentions the 3 ½ year period that is connected with the resurrection of Daniel 12:2-7.
>
> C). Revelation 20-22 mentions NO biological resurrection of corpses, just souls being emptied out of Hades at the "soon" Second Coming, bringing an end to the millennial period (Rev. 20, 22:7, 20).

"In the resurrection whose wife will she be"? (Lk. 20:27-40)

- *There came to him some Sadducees, those who deny that there is a resurrection, and they asked him a question, saying, "Teacher, **Moses wrote** for us that if a man's brother dies, having a wife but no children, the man must take the widow*

> *and **raise up offspring for his brother**. Now there were seven brothers. The first took a wife, and died without children. And the second and the third took her, and likewise all seven left no children and died. Afterward the woman also died. **In the resurrection, therefore, whose wife will the woman be?** For the seven had her as wife." And Jesus said to them, "The sons of **this age** marry and are given in marriage, **but those who are considered worthy to attain to that age and to the resurrection from the dead neither marry nor are given in marriage, for they cannot die anymore, because they are equal to angels and are sons of God, being sons of the resurrection**. But that the dead are raised, even Moses showed, in the passage about the bush, where he calls the Lord the God of Abraham and the God of Isaac and the God of Jacob. Now he is not God of the dead, but of the living, for all live to him." Then some of the scribes answered, "Teacher, you have spoken well." ⁴⁰ For they no longer dared to ask him any question" (Lk. 20:27-40).*

This argument by the Sadducees (who denied life of the soul/spirit after death) worked well against their Pharisee opponents. Why? Because many of the Pharisees believed that the Mosaic OT Torah would be carried into the new creation or Messianic age. Therefore, the Sadducee challenge could be summarized like this:

> "Since you believe in a physical bodily resurrection to fit men and women to live in the new creation and you believe Torah will be practiced at that time, then explain to us whose wife this woman will belong to once all seven brothers are raised and they are all living in the new heavens and new earth together?!? After all, there are women giving birth in the new creation (cf. Isa. 65:23), so are these illegitimate children? Are these births taking place within Torah-ordained marriages? So is this woman, raised in the resurrection with her seven husbands, going to have children by all of her husbands? Whose wife will she be"?

You can almost hear them chuckling because this was forcing the Pharisees into the practice of polyandry (the practice of a woman having more than one husband at once), which unlike polygamy (which was condoned and practiced under the OT law) was not lawful and was considered an abomination of sorts.

While this argument worked for the Pharisees, it did not work for Jesus. Why?

First, Jesus did not teach that the resurrection involved physical bodies capable and ready to sexually produce (as they had in their lives upon earth). Believers in Abraham's Bosom or Hades would be raised out of Hades into God's presence to be like the angels in heaven, spiritual beings not producing offspring in the spiritual or heavenly realm. They would not be placed upon the earth in physical resurrected bodies to be united with their loved ones or prior spouses.

Secondly, Jesus refutes the notion that the OT law (Levirate marriage law) would be applicable in the new creation or new covenant age. The practice of marrying your husband's brother for the purpose of raising up physical seed was inseparably tied to inheritance laws connected to being "in the land" and was typological and "ready to vanish" in AD 70 (Heb. 8:13). In the new covenant age, sons of the resurrection are produced or "raised up" through the gospel and produce an inheritance found "in Christ" (not "in the land").

Jesus effectively silenced BOTH groups. He silenced the Sadducees who denied that Abraham and the rest of the dead were still alive in the afterlife - "He is not the God of the dead (Sadducees view), but of the living" (inferring that Torah supports and He likewise teaches that Abraham, Isaac, and Jacob were still very much alive).

He also refuted or silenced the Pharisees on two points. First, He did so by teaching that the dead would be raised from Hades to be "like the angels" (not having physical bodies), so the issue of "marrying" and producing biological children is a moot point for them. And for the living who inherit the kingdom and continue in the new covenant Messianic age, the Pharisees were also wrong to think that the Mosaic law (and thus the Leverite marriage law) would continue being applicable.

Jesus' teaching silenced and amazed both groups and the crowd listening to this critical debate on how the resurrection would be played out in the Messianic new covenant age.

This, however, does pose a challenging question to the Talmudic Zionist or Premillennial Zionist, and that is, if you employ a literal hermeneutic to Isaiah 65:17-23 and if everything is perfect in the new creation, then why are there sinners and biological death there and are these births taking place as painless deliveries? And if there is no marriage after the resurrection and within the new creation, are these illegitimate births taking place in Isaiah 65?

Concluding Jesus' teaching on the resurrection

At the beginning of this section, we looked at Jewish and Christian views which taught that at the end of the Mosaic old covenant "this age," or during the "general resurrection judgment," there would be a resurrection of souls or spirits (not a biological fleshly corpse resurrection) out of Abraham's Bosom or Hades to inherit everlasting life in God's presence, or inherit everlasting punishment and condemnation.

We also looked at Christian views which teach that there was a progressive Great Commission "already and not yet" period or "coming hour and now is" between AD 27/30 – AD 70 before the old covenant "this age" would end, whereby the new covenant body of Israel was being raised out from the death of the old covenant body of Israel. Not only this, but at the end of this process in AD 70, souls were raised out of Abraham's Bosom or Hades to inherit God's presence and eternal life while ruling with Him.

In examining Jesus' teaching on the resurrection, we find His teaching to be in harmony with these historical spiritual concepts of the resurrection which were believed by Jews before His ministry in the intertestamental period, and were continued to be believed by some during His ministry. This understanding of the resurrection has even continued with us in an orthodox Christian exegesis of Daniel 12:2-3. We simply argue that Daniel 12:1-4 does not teach two, or double, fulfillments of an "already and not yet" eschaton(s) or resurrection(s) for Israel and the Church separated by thousands or millions of years. The exegetical evidence within Daniel 12:1-7 itself and how the NT develops this passage, supports that there is only ONE consummative "end of the age" resurrection event, and it was fulfilled at the end of the old covenant age in the events of AD 67 – AD 70.

Paul on trial and His hope of an "about to be" resurrection of Acts 23:6-9 / 24:13-15 YLT

- *"Then Paul, knowing that some of them were Sadducees and the others Pharisees, called out in the Sanhedrin, "My brothers, I am a Pharisee, descended from Pharisees. I stand on trial because of the hope of the resurrection of the dead." When he said this, a dispute broke out between the Pharisees and the Sadducees, and the assembly was divided. (The Sadducees say that there is no resurrection, and that there are neither angels nor spirits, but the Pharisees believe all these things.). There was a great uproar, and some of the teachers of the law who were Pharisees stood up and argued vigorously. "We find nothing wrong with this man," they said. "What if a spirit or an angel has spoken to him (Acts 23:6-9)."*

- *"You can easily verify that no more than twelve days ago I went up to Jerusalem to worship. My accusers did not find me arguing with anyone at the temple, or stirring up a crowd in the synagogues or anywhere else in the city. ¹³ And they cannot prove to you the charges they are now making against me. However, I admit that I worship the God of our ancestors as a follower of the Way, which they call a sect. I believe everything that is in accordance with the Law and that is written in the Prophets, "...nor are they able to prove against me the things concerning which they now accuse me. 'And I confess this to thee, that, according to the way that they call a sect, so serve I the God of the fathers, believing all things that in the law and the prophets have been written, having **hope** toward God, which they themselves also wait for, that there is **about to be a rising again of the dead, both of righteous and unrighteous**; and in this I do exercise myself, to have a conscience void of offence toward God and men always" (Acts 24:11-15 YLT).*

- *"And now I stand here on trial because of **my hope** in the promise made by God to our fathers, to which **our twelve tribes hope to attain**, as they earnestly worship night and day. And for this hope I am accused by Jews, O king! Why is it thought incredible by any of you that God raises the dead?" "...To this day I have had the help that comes from God, and so **I stand here testifying both to small and great, saying nothing but what the prophets and Moses said would come to pass**: (Acts 26:6-8, 22).*

Paul's trial and accusations of insurrection

Initially the Pharisee sect, upon hearing that Paul was a Pharisee and on trial for his hope of Israel's resurrection, said, "We find nothing wrong with this man." After all, the real problem was those Sadducees who didn't believe in any afterlife or resurrection. But as time went on, they learned something about his resurrection beliefs that caused them to join in with the false accusation that Paul was guilty of insurrection against Rome. Every time Rome heard his case, the Romans were convinced that Paul was on trial for religious and doctrinal issues with his fellow Jews, and was no threat to Rome.

Futurists assume that, because Paul had a Pharisee background, he must have held to an end of time biological resurrection like all of them believed. But as I began this chapter, I pointed out that there were various views of the resurrection among the Jews, and I don't see any definitive proof here that all sects of the Pharisees believed in a fleshly resurrection.

Since there were some Pharisees, or a sect of Pharisees, present who believed in a physical resurrection of the dead that was inseparably connected with a physical resurrection of national Israel, this created a problem. Why? Because for this sect, it was believed that if you were a Jew and you died outside of the land, you either would not participate and ceased to exist, or resurrection entailed one tunneling his way underground all the way back to the land in order to pop up and be resurrected, living a life in the new age under TORAH. *They did not separate their physical resurrection hopes from their carnal physical land and kingdom hopes of ruling over the Gentiles from Jerusalem with Torah and the temple still in place.*

For Paul, the resurrection was grounded in Jesus being the Resurrection (cf. Jn. 11:25) and His presence within him was his hope of glory (cf. Cols. 1:27). These Pharisees definitely disagreed with any resurrection hope that was connected with Jesus, because after all He had rejected their carnal views of a Messianic kingdom on earth (cf. Jn. 6) and they knew there was no separating the two. They despised this aspect of the resurrection which Paul was in the process of attaining to in Philippians 3—in which he had grounds of boasting as a Pharisee under the law, but he considered that life as having "confidence in the flesh" and to be "lost" in order "to gain life and righteousness in Christ" which the law could not give. In fact, Paul considered that the life he led under Torah as the Pharisee of Pharisees was nothing but "dung/crap" (cf. Phil. 3:3-9). So while Paul did believe in a resurrection of souls out from Hades into God's presence, perhaps the main thing they objected to concerning Paul's hope of an imminent resurrection was that it would not include a physical restoration or resurrection of national Israel under Torah with the temple intact, etc.

For these reasons, Paul had to go. As Don Preston observes,

> "The Pharisees charged Paul with "sedition," but the Roman authorities rejected that charge. They did not believe Paul was inciting anti-Roman rebellion. However, Paul was most assuredly teaching a sedition against the Pharisees and their nationalistic kingdom / resurrection hopes!"[244]

---

[244] Don K. Preston, *Paul on Trial, PAUL, THE PHARISEES AND RESURRECTION*, (Ardmore, OK: JaDon, 2020), 123

"After all, at first they believed that both Jesus and Paul were their allies. But they quickly learned differently and put them both on trial for their teachings on the kingdom and the resurrection. They sought to kill both Jesus and Paul for the very thing they were supposed to believe in!"[245]

Jesus	Paul
Jesus taught / offered the kingdom.	Paul taught / offered the kingdom.
Jews initially accepted the offer.	Pharisees initially thought Paul taught the resurrection like they did.
Jesus rejected the offer of kingship.	The Pharisees came to reject Paul's doctrine of resurrection.
When Jesus rejected the Jewish offer, they put Jesus on trial for being seditious, claiming to be king; as His kingship was not the kind they were claiming, as Pilate affirmed.	When the Pharisees came to understand Paul's resurrection doctrine, they put him on trial with the false charge of sedition; the Romans found Paul innocent of political sedition; the real issue was the resurrection.
Jesus: My kingdom is not of this world / The kingdom does not come with observation.	"We do not look on the things that are seen, but unseen / "The Jerusalem that is above, the mother of us all" / We have here no abiding city, but seek one about to come" (2 Cor. 4:16f. / Gal. 4:22f. / Hebrews 13:14).[246]

For those Futurists who boast that they have the same kind of physical resurrection and kingdom hope the Pharisees who condemned Paul had, we must ask them the following: 1) Do you believe the dead soul hovers over the "Luz bones" of a person, and then will 2) tunnel itself all the way to the land of Israel to be raised in the land, only to then 3) enjoy life in the new age under Torah? We prefer to stick with the spiritual kingdom and resurrection hopes and teachings of Jesus and Paul.

Paul's imminent expectation of the resurrection of Daniel 12:2

Paul's imminent expectation of the resurrection can be found in the following literal translations, properly translating the Greek word *mello* in Acts 24:15 as "about to be":

> "…there is **about to be a rising again of the dead, both of righteous and unrighteous**…" (Young's Literal Translation).

> "having a hope in God, which they themselves also await, that there **is about to be a resurrection, both of the just and of the unjust**" (The Berean Literal Bible).

---

[245] Ibid. 125

[246] Ibid. 75

"having hope toward God, which they themselves also wait for, [that] there **is about to be a resurrection of the dead, both of righteous and unrighteous**;" (Literal Standard Version).

"and having a hope directed towards God, which my accusers themselves also entertain, that **before long there will be a resurrection both of the righteous and the unrighteous**" (Weymouth New Testament).

"Having hope to God, which they themselves also admit, **a rising from the dead about to be, both of just and unjust**" (Smith's Literal Translation).

The Interlinear Literal Translation of the Greek New Testament (1897) and *The Lexham English Septuagint (LES) Interlinear* works also translate *mello* here in Acts 24:15 as "about to be."

What was Paul's source for his resurrection hope? Paul was accused of teaching things contrary to the Law and the Prophets. Yet in his own defense he stood there and boldly countered, saying that he testified and preached no other things except that which could be found in the Law and Prophets. This statement coupled with the fact that there is no other OT text which describes a resurrection for the just and unjust places Daniel 12:2 as Paul's "about to be" resurrection expectation.

Paul declared that the resurrection of Daniel 12:2 was the ONE "hope" of Israel. Notice that Paul does not give the resurrection of Daniel 12:2 a double meaning or double fulfillment! He clearly does NOT teach an imminent spiritual resurrection coming to close the old covenant age in AD 70 and then another future physical one for the just and unjust at the end of world history.

Does this not fit the orthodox Christian view and exegesis of Daniel 12:2 such as that of James Jordan and Kenneth Gentry?

Jordan teaches that the resurrection of Daniel 12:2 is referring to "…in the days of Jesus the **nation [Israel]** will undergo…[one] **last [in AD 70] spiritual resurrection**…" that would result in Daniel's soul being raised out of Abraham's Bosom. Paul says Daniel 12:2 is his and Israel's **one** "hope" (singular) of the resurrection and that it was "about to" take place.

And Kenneth Gentry usually appeals to the Young's Literal Translation and other literal translations when wanting *mello* to be translated as "about to be" in the book of Revelation, so according to that standard why doesn't Paul have an imminent expectation of the resurrection here in AD 70 as well? I cited several translations and Greek works that have no problem with *mello* being translated as "about to" take place.

And what about Gentry interpreting the resurrection of Daniel 12:2 as, "He is teaching that in the events of AD 70, the true Israel will arise from old Israel's carcass, as in a resurrection"?!? There is no other Mosaic old covenant Israel beyond AD 70 in Mr. Gentry's theology, as far as I know of. Paul also does not say that there are TWO hope(s) of Israel regarding the resurrection of Daniel 12:2.

Therefore, Paul interpreted the resurrection of Daniel 12:2 as the ONE "hope" of his contemporary twelve tribes of Israel which was "about to be" fulfilled in the coming events of AD 67 – AD 70 to close the old covenant age. Paul's imminent expectation of the spiritual resurrection of Daniel 12:2-3 is in complete harmony with Jesus' teaching of it in Matthew 13:39-43 and John 5:25-28.

- *"For it is we who are the circumcision, we who serve God by his Spirit, who boast in Christ Jesus, and who put no confidence in the flesh— though I myself have reasons for such confidence. If someone else thinks they have reasons to put confidence in the flesh, I have more: circumcised on the eighth day, of the people of Israel, of the tribe of Benjamin, a Hebrew of Hebrews; in regard to the law, a Pharisee; as for zeal, persecuting the church; as for righteousness based on the law, faultless. But whatever were gains to me I now consider loss for the sake of Christ. What is more, I consider everything a loss because of the surpassing worth of knowing Christ Jesus my Lord, for whose sake I have lost all things. I consider them garbage, that I may gain Christ and be found in him, not having a righteousness of my own that comes from the law, but that which is through faith in[a] Christ—the righteousness that comes from God on the basis of faith. I want to know Christ—yes, to know the power of his resurrection and participation in his sufferings, becoming like him in his death, and so, somehow, **attaining to the resurrection from the dead. Not that I have already obtained all this, or have already arrived at my goal, but I press on to take hold of that for which Christ Jesus took hold of me.** Brothers and sisters, I do not consider myself yet to have taken hold of it. But one thing I do: Forgetting what is behind and straining toward what is ahead, I press ontoward the goal to win the prize for which God has called me heavenward in Christ Jesus. All of us, then, who are mature should take such a view of things. And if on some point you think differently, that too God will make clear to you. Only let us live up to what we have already attained. Join together in following my example, brothers and sisters, and just as you have us as a model, keep your eyes on those who live as we do. For, as I have often told you before and now tell you again even with tears, many live as enemies of the cross of Christ. Their destiny is destruction, their god is their stomach, and their glory is in their shame. Their mind is set on earthly things. But our citizenship is in heaven. And we eagerly await a Savior from there, the Lord Jesus Christ, who, by the power that enables him to bring everything under his control, **will transform our lowly bodies so that they will be like his glorious body**"* (Phil. 3:4-21).

- *"The Lord is near"* (Phil. 4:5).

Many miss the context of Paul's discussion on the resurrection of Philippians 3:21. There is an "already not yet," or what I like to call an "already becoming / transforming and not yet," to Paul's teaching on the resurrection here. Paul considered his life under the old covenant Mosaic law to be garbage or dung, and that he had already attained to some degree of being conformed to the resurrection of Christ. Obviously, this is not a biological resurrection. Paul was not half glowing or something like that. The old covenant Law was "garbage" or "dung/crap" and he was being conformed from that "vile/lowly" old covenant body of Adam and Moses to Christ's glorious new covenant body. This "already transforming and not yet" resurrection process would be completed at the "near" Second Coming event (Phil. 4:5).

Paul and the "about to be" glorification and "redemption of the body" (Rms. 8:18-23YLT)

- *"For I reckon that the sufferings of the present time are not worthy to be compared with the **glory <u>about to be</u> revealed in us**; for the earnest looking out of the creation doth expect the revelation of the sons of God; for to vanity was the creation made subject—not of its will, but because of Him who did subject it—in hope, that also the creation itself shall be set free from the servitude of the corruption to the liberty of the glory of the children of God; for we have known that all the creation doth groan together, and doth travail in pain together till now. And not only so, but also we ourselves, having the first-fruit of the Spirit, we also ourselves in ourselves do groan, adoption expecting—**the redemption of our body;...**" (Rms. 8:18-23 YLT)*

As I discussed in our exegesis of the Olivet Discourse, how one interprets the discourse is how one will understand NT eschatology in general. Why? Because, in a nutshell, it is the eschatology of the NT. So I would agree with those like John Murray who understood the "redemption" of Luke 21 to be Paul's redemption hope here in Romans:

> "Now in **Luke 21:28** . . . [t]his word 'redemption' (apolutrosin), when used with reference to the future, has a distinctly eschatological connotation, the final redemption, the consummation of the redemptive process (cf. **Rom 8:23**...). Hence **analogy would again** point to the eschatological complex of events."[247]

Since Gentry adds Matthew 24:28 as a text supporting his view that the resurrection of Daniel 12:2 was a corporate resurrection for Israel in which the new covenant corporate body of Israel was raised from the corporate corpse/body of old covenant Israel in AD 70, I have added it as a possible parallel. One of Ken's favorite theologians, John Lightfoot, also understands the "redemption of the body" to be a corporate body (the Church).

---

[247] John Murray, *COLLECTED WRITINGS OF JOHN MURRAY 2 Systematic Theology* (Pennsylvania, PA: THE BANNER OF TRUTH TRUST, 1977), 390-391

A = The Olivet Discourse & Luke 17	B = Romans 8:17-23YLT
Suffering to come (Mt. 24:9)	**Present sufferings** (Rom. 8:17–18)
Christ comes in **glory** (Mt. 24:30)	Receive and share in Christ's **glory** (Rom. 8:17–18)
Kingdom would be realized **"within"** a person at Christ's return (Lk.17:21–37; 21:27–32)	Glory to be **"in"** believers (Rom. 8:18)
Redemption and salvation – resurrection (Lk. 21:27–28; Mt. 24:13, 30–31/Mt. 13:39-43)	Redemption and salvation (**"at hand" "nearer"**) – resurrection (Rom. 8:23–24; cf. 11:15–27; 13:11–12)
Birth pains of the tribulation (Mt. 24:8)	**Birth pains** together (Rom. 8:22)
"Heaven & earth" of the old covenant **"age"** was to **"pass away"** (Mt. 24:3, 29, 35)	The old covenant **"creation" of Israel** was "eagerly longing" & "groaning" for "adoption" and "liberation" (Rom. 8:19-23)
All fulfilled in the 1st century AD 30 – AD 70 "this generation" (Mt. 24:34)	All **"at hand"** & **"about to be"** (Greek *mello*) fulfilled (Rom. 8:18-23YLT; 13:11-12; 16:20)
Gentry interprets the resurrection of Daniel 12:2 as old covenant Israel being a **corporate body "corpse" (cf. Mt. 24:28) that would be raised into the spiritual New Covenant Body of Israel in AD 70**	Paul believed the glorification and **redemption of the corporate body of Israel/Church was "about to be" fulfilled** (cf. Rms. 8:18-23--11:25-27—13:11-12)

The creation of men groaning – not planet earth

As we saw in our study of the Olivet Discourse, terms like God establishing the heaven and earth and then destroying or causing the heaven and earth to pass away (Jer. 4) can refer to God forming the creation of old covenant Israel (Isa. 51:15-16) and then causing her to pass away in AD 70 (Mt. 5:17-18; 24:35) – while at the same time establishing a new covenant heaven and earth or new covenant people. This is exactly what we have Paul doing here in Romans 8:18-23. The "creation" here is not referring to the physical planet at all. It is referring to the creation of men, most likely the creation of men of Israel groaning under the law seeking Messianic redemption.

Reformed theologian John Lightfoot correctly associated the "earnest expectation of the creature" and the "whole creation groaning" with the mind and heart of man, and interpreted this passage as having nothing to do with the planet earth, not even poetically:

> ". . . [T]his vanity [or futility] is improperly applied to this vanishing, changeable, dying state of the [physical] creation. For vanity, doth not so much denote the vanishing condition of the outward state, as it doth the **inward vanity and emptiness of the mind**. The Romans to whom this apostle writes, knew well enough how many and how great predictions and promises it had pleased God to publish by his prophets, concerning gathering together and

adopting sons to himself among the Gentiles: the manifestation and production of which sons, the whole Gentile world doth now wait for, as it were, with an **out-stretched neck**."[248]

And again,

"The Gentile world shall in time be delivered from the bondage of their sinful corruption, that is, **the bondage of their lusts and vile affections**, (under which it hath lain for so long a time) into a noble liberty, such as the sons of God enjoy. **If it be inquired how the Gentile world groaned and travailed in pain, let them who expound this of the fabric of the material world tell us how that groaneth and travaileth. They must needs own it to be a borrowed and allusive phrase.**"[249]

Lightfoot is on solid ground here citing 2 Peter 1:4, 2 Corinthians 11:3, and 1 Corinthians 15:33. Not only is there lexical evidence to interpret "vanity", "corruption," and "decay" as ethical and moral putrefaction in the heart and mind of man, but contextually the passage has nothing to do with hydrogen or oxygen or squirrels longing for a better day when they won't get hit by cars.

"Redemption of the body" the corporate body of the Church – not individual biological resurrections at the end of time

John Lightfoot not only interpreted the "creation" of Romans 8 to be the creation of men and NOT the physical planet, but he understood the "redemption of the body" to not be a resurrection of physical bodies, but rather the "mystical [corporate] body" of the Church. In his sermon on "Many Mansions," Lightfoot states:

"And of the same body [in context he is referring to the corporate body of Christ just mentioned in Eph. 4:13] is his meaning in that obscure and much-mistaken place (**Rom. viii.23**; "And not only they," i.e. 'the whole creation,' or πασα κτισις, 'every creature,' which means no other thing, than 'the Gentile or heathen world': not only they groan to come into the evangelical liberty of the children of God, but we, also, of the Jewish nation, who have the first-fruits of the Spirit, groan within ourselves, waiting for the redemption, to wit, the **adoption of our body**:" we wait for the redeeming and adopting of the Gentiles, **to make up our mystical body**."[250]

---

[248] John Lightfoot, *Commentary on the New Testament from the Talmud and Hebraica, Volume 4* (Hendrickson publications), 157. Lightfoot, Hammond, and Gill understand the "creation" to be referring to Gentiles. ". . . Crellius (Comm., Para.) explains it as a reference to regenerate Christians and Le Clerc (Supp., NT) refers it particularly to Gentile Christians." See also John Locke, *The Clarendon Edition of the Works of John Locke*. I tend to see it as more of believers within old covenant Israel groaning under the law (Rms. 7) awaiting Messianic deliverance, but there is no reason to exclude righteous Gentiles also longing for the seed of the woman to deliver them from Adamic death and sin which the Mosaic Law only magnified.

[249] Ibid., 158–159, emphases MJS

[250] John Lightfoot, *Sermon on "Many Mansions,"* cf. https://biblicalstudies.org.uk/pdf/lightfoot/vol06.pdf pp. 322-323

Clearly Lightfoot understood the "creation" to mean the creation of men and not the planet earth, and "redemption of the body" to be the "mystical body" of the corporate Jew/Gentile Church and not an individual physical body. He was ahead of his time!

Paul's reference to the "sufferings of this present time" does not have anything to do with losing one's hair, gaining weight, cancer, etc. Paul's mention of the "sufferings" and "the redemption of the body" have nothing to do with those kinds of issues. The context of the "groaning" of the first-century Christians can be found in the previous chapter. The sufferings Paul has in mind here were eschatological, the birth pains that were to precede Christ's return in AD 70 (Mt. 24:8; Rom. 8:22). They had to do with the last days' persecutions and with the saints of the universal church groaning under the tyranny of sin and condemnation of the Law.

For Paul, sin had produced "death," but obviously not physical death. Contrary to Postmillennial and most Futurist assertions, "the body", "death," and "the flesh" in Romans 5–8 have nothing to do with the idea of men biologically dying as a result of Adam's sin. Paul's concern is with corporate-covenantal death, as even some Reformed theologians teach. Tom Holland is a Reformed theologian who sees Paul's "body" of flesh, sin, and death not referring to our physical flesh but to the corporate body of sin in contrast to the corporate body of Christ—the Church.[251] He counters Gundry's individualistic views of soma in Paul's writings. He also argues for "consistency" in Paul's use of corporate terms. "Bondage," according to the immediate context, had to do with groaning under the condemnation of the Law (cf. Rom. 7:2, 7, 15).

For Paul, the glorification, liberation and redemption of this corporate body/creation was "about to" take place (Rms. 8:18ff.YLT)

Still, one might object that the "redemption" associated with the coming of Christ in Luke 21:27-28 has a clear time text ("this generation") associated with it (v. 32), but the "redemption of the body" in Romans 8 does not; therefore, one might conclude that the two passages are not necessarily parallel. Those who argue this way suggest that the redemption in Luke 21 might simply refer to relief from persecution and nothing more. The premise of their objection, however, is false.

There is an imminence text associated with the redemption of the body in Romans 8. Verse 18 reads, "For I reckon that the sufferings of the present time are not worthy to be compared with the glory **about to be** revealed in us" (YLT; cf. NSRV, AV, & WEY: "soon to be manifested").

At least Partial Preterist Postmillennialists, such as Gary DeMar, concede that the "glory" in Romans 8:18YLT was "about to be" fulfilled in AD 70, but pretend to not know what it is:

---

[251] Tom Holland, *Contours In Pauline Theology* (Scotland: Christian Focus Publications, 2004), 85–110.

"*Whatever* **the glory is it was 'about to be revealed...'**"[252]

DeMar also understands the "salvation of all Israel" in Romans 11 to be fulfilled in AD 70. Thus, the "salvation" and "redemption of the body" in Romans 8 and 11 are not dealing with biological or planetary events at the end of time, but rather imminent redemptive events for the mystical Jew/Gentile corporate body/creation change or resurrection that was to imminently take place in AD 70.

Partial Preterists, such as Kenneth Gentry and Keith Mathison, don't address *mello* here in Romans 8:18. But interestingly enough, according to Gentry and Mathison, one of the things that was "**about to** come after" John wrote Revelation 1:19YLT was the arrival of the New Jerusalem and new creation of Revelation 21:1ff. Mathison and Gentry tell us in their other works that the time texts in Revelation point to a near fulfillment of the passing of "the first heaven and earth." They point out that Revelation 21:1 is referring to the passing of the old covenant "creation" in AD 70 and is a fulfillment of Isaiah 65–66. Gentry even says:

> "The absence of the sea (Rev. 21:1) speaks of harmony and peace **within**. In Scripture the **sea often symbolizes discord and sin** (13:1–2; cf. Isa. 8:7–8; 23:10; 57:20; Jer. 6:23; 46:7; Ezek. 9:10). Christianity offers the opposite: peace with God and among humankind (Luke 2:14; Rom. 5:1; Eph. 2:12–18; Phil. 4:7, 9)."[253]

If the removal of the sea represents the **removal of sin and discord within**, then AD 70 was much more than a physical flight to Pella. It was a soteriological event just as the cross was.

Gentry argues that "when used with the aorist infinitive—as in Revelation 1:19, *mello's* predominant usage and preferred meaning is: 'be on the point of, be about to.' The same is true when the word is used with the present infinitive, as in Rev. 3:10. The basic meaning in both

Thayer and Abbott-Smith is: 'to be about to.'"[254] Gentry is correct. The problem, however, is that when the word *mello* refers to the resurrection and judgment of the living and dead in Acts 17:31; 24:15 and 24:25, it is also used with the infinitive. In the case of Acts 24:15, in a recent article on his site, Gentry appeals to *BDAG* to somehow prove that when *mello* is used with the future infinitive, it communicates certainty and shouldn't be translated as "about to" take place. But, of course, as I pointed out in our exegesis of Acts 24:15, there are translations, lexicons and interlinears that do render *mello* there as "about to."

---

[252] Gary DeMar, *Last Days Madness*, Ibid., 225

[253] Kenneth Gentry, co-authored work/debate, *FOUR VIEWS OF THE BOOK OF REVELATION*, (Grand Rapids, MI: Zondervan, 1998), 89

[254] Kenneth Gentry, *Before Jerusalem Fell: Dating the Book of Revelation* (Tyler, TX: Institute for Biblical Economics, 1989), 141-142, MJS

Not only that, but Gentry and Mathison also fail to address in their writings that *mello* in Romans 8:18 is in the aorist infinitive (which they say has the "preferred meaning" of "be on the point of, be about to") and they make no mention that our passage has two other imminent Greek words within the immediate context – *apokaradokia* and *apekdekomai*. *This* serves to further solidify the translation of *mello* as *"about to be."* And lastly, *BDAG* (Gentry's source for trying to place Acts 24:15 at the end of world history) marks *mello* in Romans 8:18 as being translated "about to be revealed." So much for consistency!

Contextually, there is no reason to not understand Paul's expectation of the "about to be" glorification and "redemption of the body" to be when the corporate new covenant body of Israel was raised from the corporate old covenant body of Israel in AD 70. This body/creation was groaning under spiritual Adamic death (magnified by Torah) and was liberated from that death into the life and liberty of Christ's "at hand" salvation/coming in AD 70. And to that we now turn our attention, in Paul's understanding of when Daniel 12:2-3 would be fulfilled.

Like Jesus, Paul understood the "hour" of Daniel 12:1-4 (OG) resurrection in Romans 13:11-12 to be "at hand"

- *"Besides this you know the time, that the **hour** [Dan. 12:1-4 OG] has come for you to **wake from sleep [Dan. 12:2]**. For salvation [or "redemption of the body"] is nearer to us now than when we first believed. The night is far gone; **the day is at hand** [when the righteous would shine like the Sun when Christ came as the Sun of Righteousness - Mt. 13:43/Mt. 24:27/Mal. 4:2]."*

It is not a stretch to see that Daniel's "hour" in Daniel 12:1-2 (OG) of awaking to resurrection is not only Jesus' eschatological "hour" (John 4:21-23--5:25-28) but also Paul's imminent "hour" here in Romans 13:

Daniel 12	Romans 13
12:1 "And at that **hour**…"	13:11: "…you know what **hour** it is…
12:4: "the hour/time of the **end**"	13:11: "how it is **full time**…"
12:2: "Many of those who **sleep** in the width of the earth **will arise**…"	13:11: "The hour has come for you to **wake up from your sleep**…"

Paul, in Romans 8:18-23YLT and 13:11-12, awaited the "about to be" corporate bodily resurrection of the new covenant creation/body, and he was waiting for her members to "awake" out of the "hour" of "sleep" of Daniel 12:1-4, 7-13. Paul not only sees the resurrection of Daniel 12:2 as "about to be" fulfilled in Acts 24:15, but he also sees it imminently fulfilled in these crucial eschatological chapters in Romans as well.

Paul expected some of his contemporaries to be alive and witness the coming of Christ and the resurrection of 1 Corinthians 15

Space does not permit me to give an in-depth exegesis of every verse of 1 Corinthians 15, but I will address much of it. For a detailed exegesis of 1 Corinthians 15, see my co-authored book, *House Divided Bridging the Gap in Reformed Eschatology* and David Green's exegesis.

Before beginning, I think we need to stick with just the basics on what we have learned so far and ask the following questions and make the following points:

    1). No one disputes that the resurrection of 1 Corinthians 15 is the same resurrection as Daniel 12:2-13.

    2). Having established this, we have learned from the immediate context of Daniel 12 that this resurrection would be at the same time as the tribulation and the "time of the end" – that is, "all these things" would be fulfilled together and during a 3 ½ years period of time "when the power of the holy people would be completely shattered" (Dan. 12:7). As we will see below, Paul expected the eschatological "end" and resurrection of Daniel 12 in 1 Corinthians 15 to take place within the lifetime of some of those he wrote to in Corinth.

    3). Most agree that Jesus' teaching on the "tribulation" and "end of the age" in Matthew 24 is the same "tribulation" and "time of the end" found in Daniel 12:1-4. And yet Jesus indicates that the end of the old covenant age and tribulation would be fulfilled during the times of the Gentiles or the 3 ½ years period of AD 67 – AD 70 in His contemporary "this generation" (Mt. 24:3, 21f.; Lk. 21:20-24, 31-32).

So then if Matthew 24/Luke 21 is equivalent to the same time frame and events as Daniel 12:1-7, and Daniel 12 is the same resurrection as 1 Corinthians 15, lets break this down more and get a logical visual.

A (Mt. 24/Lk. 21)

B (Daniel 12:1-7)

C (1 Cor. 15)

If A (Mt. 24/Lk. 21) is = to B (Daniel 12:1-7, 13)	
Tribulation as never before 24:21-22	Tribulation as never before 12:1
Evangelism 24:14	Leading others to righteousness 12:3
End of the [OC] age 24:3, 14	Time of the end 12:4
Resurrection & inheritance of the kingdom 24:31; 13:43; Lk. 21:31-32	Resurrection & or inheritance of the kingdom 12:2-3, 13/Mt. 13:43
Jerusalem surrounded, trodden down/times of the Gentiles (AD 67 – AD 70) Lk. 21:20, 24	Consummation - 3 ½ years when power of the holy people is shattered 12:7
And if B (Daniel 12:1-7, 13) is = to C (1 Cor. 15)	
Resurrection unto eternal life 12:2	Resurrection unto incorruptibility or immortality 15:52-53
time of the end 12:4	time of the end 15:24
When the power [the Mosaic OC Law] of the holy people is completely shattered 12:7	Victory over "the [Mosaic OC] Law" 15:26

At the "end" of the OC age, OT dead would be raised at the same time the NT righteous living would shine in the kingdom 12:2-3, 13	If the dead of the OT are not raised, neither would those who died in Christ be raised & living unforgiven 15:15-18
Then A (Mt. 24/Lk. 21) is = to C (1 Cor. 15)	
Christ to come (Greek: *parousia*) at sound of a trumpet 24:27-31	Christ to come (Greek: *parousia*) at sound of a trumpet 15:23, 52
"The end" (Greek *telos*, the goal) 24:3, 14	"The end" (Greek *telos*, the goal) 15:24
Kingdom (goal reached) Lk. 21:31-32	Kingdom consummation (goal reached) 15:24
All prophecy fulfilled at this point Lk. 21:22	All prophecy fulfilled at this point 15:54-55
Victory over the Mosaic Law/temple 24:1	Victory over the Mosaic Law 15:55-56
Same contemporary "you" or "we" 24:2ff.	Same contemporary "you" or "we" 15:51-52
"All" of the elect (even the dead) gathered (or raised) in the kingdom 24:31; Lk. 21:28-32	"The [OT] dead" raised with the dead "in Christ" 15:15-18

Two or more things that are equal to another thing are also equal to each other		
Matthew 24/Luke 21	**Daniel 12:1-7, 13**	**1 Corinthians 15**
Gather/raise "all" (dead & living) the elect at "end" of OC age 24:3, 31	OT dead raised with NT saints at the end of OC age 12:2-4, 13/Mt. 13:43	OT dead raised with NT dead & living at "the end" of the OC age 15:15-18, 24, 51
All OT prophecy fulfilled when Jerusalem surrounded & times of Gentiles (3 ½ yrs.) fulfilled Lk. 21:22-24 – AD 67 – AD 70	Judgment and resurrection of the dead fulfilled at the end of the OC age, in a 3 ½ year period when Israel's power shattered	Resurrection of Daniel 12:2-3, 13; Hosea 13:14 and Isaiah 25:8 fulfilled at the end of OC age & in the lifetime of Paul's 1st cent. audience 15:51, 54-55

We have also learned up to this point the following:

4). A Christian orthodox position on the resurrection of Daniel 12 involves an "already not yet" progressive, spiritual, corporate and covenantal resurrection taking place between AD 27/30 – AD 70, whereby the new covenant body of Israel was being raised out from the death of the old covenant body of Israel by AD 70. Can a progressive, corporate bodily resurrection be seen in 1 Corinthians 15?

5). As we have just seen, the Apostle Paul has elsewhere taught under the inspiration of the Holy Spirit that the resurrection of Daniel 12:2 was "about to be" fulfilled or was "at hand" (Acts 24:15YLT; Rom. 8:18-23YLT; Rom. 13:11-12). So the burden of proof would be to prove that Paul's "ONE" resurrection hope which he had in Acts and Romans has now turned into two.

Therefore, as we approach the resurrection of 1 Corinthians 15, we want to see if this critical chapter also involves what we have found thus far in Paul's teaching on the resurrection. That is, does 1 Corinthians 15 teach a corporate body resurrection that was in the process of taking place in Paul's day, which he taught under the inspiration of the Holy Spirit would be fulfilled within the lifetime of some of his contemporaries? We believe so.

There are several exegetical observations which demonstrate that Paul's eschatology in 1 Corinthians 15 is not a depiction of a biological casket-type resurrection for all men that will occur at the end of world history:

- The parallels and analogy of faith with Matthew 24 demonstrate a first century generation fulfillment of 1 Corinthians 15.

- Paul's argumentation and use of logic (*modus tollens*) demonstrate that those who denied the resurrection of the dead at Corinth were not denying the resurrection of Christ or the doctrine of resurrection in general, but a resurrection for a particular group (the old covenant dead of Israel).

- Paul's use of the present passive indicative, as already in the process of being fulfilled, demonstrates it is not an end of time biological resurrection.

- Paul's use of familiar corporate body words and phrases within the Corinthian letters and within his other epistles demonstrates that an individual, biological corpse resurrection is wrong.

- Paul's appeal to, and the contexts of, Hosea 13 and Isaiah 25 demonstrate that an end of the world biological resurrection is not in view.

- There would be no victory over "the death" until victory over the Mosaic Torah, "the law," was reached. This does not fit within a futurist framework, but does within the Full Preterist framework, because "the law" (administration of death) was "soon" to vanish at the end of the old covenant age in AD 70 and thus was truly imminent in Paul's day.

The Parallels – Analogy of Faith

Again, let's look at those parallels which demonstrate that Paul's eschatology here in 1 Corinthians 15 is that of Jesus' in Matthew 24/Luke 21:

1. Christ to come (Greek *parousia*) – Matthew 24:27 = 1 Corinthians 15:23

2. His people to be gathered/changed – Matthew 24:31 = 1 Corinthians 15:51-52

3. Comes with the sound of a trumpet – Matthew 24:31 = 1 Corinthians 15:52

4. To be "the end" (Greek *telos* – the goal) – Matthew 24:3, 14 = 1 Corinthians 15:24

5. Kingdom consummation (goal reached) – Luke 21:30-32 = 1 Corinthians 15:24

6. All prophecy fulfilled at this time – Luke 21:22 = 1 Corinthians 15:54-55

7. Victory over the law/temple – Matthew 24:1 = 1 Corinthians 15:55-56
8. Same contemporary "you" or "we" – Matthew 24:2ff. = 1 Corinthians 15: 51-52

The classic Amillennial and Historic Premillennial positions agree with us that the above parallels support the fact that Paul's eschatological one hope, as expressed in 1 Corinthians 15, is the same teaching and resurrection developed by Jesus in the Olivet Discourse.

However, we also agree with Partial Preterists that Matthew 24 was fulfilled in AD 70.

Therefore, I can use the following historical "reformed and always reforming," and Scriptural "the Scripture alone" / "analogy of faith" argument:

> **Major Premise:** The "Parousia," resurrection "gathering," and "trumpet" call at "the end" of the age of Matthew 24 is the same eschatological "Parousia," resurrection "change," and "trumpet" call at "the end" of the age for Paul in 1 Corinthians 15. Paul's eschatology is the eschatology of Jesus (Classic Amillennialism and Historic Premilllenialism)!
>
> **Minor Premise: But** the "Parousia", "gathering," and "trumpet" call at "the end" of the age of Matthew 24 was fulfilled spiritually in Jesus' contemporary generation at the end of the old covenant age in AD 70 (Partial Preterism, mostly Postmillennial).
>
> **Conclusion: Therefore,** the one and the same "Parousia," resurrection "gathering/change," and "trumpet" call at "the end" in 1 Corinthians 15 and Matthew 24 was fulfilled spiritually in Jesus' generation and thus at the end of the old covenant age in AD 70 (Full Preterism).

1 Corinthians 15:1-15 - ONE Gospel Preached

Most futurist commentaries on 1 Corinthians 15 merely assume that the resurrection of the dead deniers at Corinth denied the resurrection of Jesus and the resurrection in general. It is more than difficult to see how Paul could have still referred to them as "saints," etc. if they believed such! Most who take this position believe Paul's appeal to the 500 who witnessed Jesus' resurrection is the beginning of his correction because the group rejected Jesus' resurrection.

This view has many problems, which we will cover shortly, but in reality Paul lays forth the historical resurrection of Christ in the beginning of the resurrection conflict at Corinth NOT because the resurrection deniers at Corinth denied Jesus' resurrection, but because the Gentile Christians were pridefully and ignorantly denying the resurrection of a Jewish sect (the OC dead ones who had died prior to Christ). This denial was similar to what some Gentile believers were saying about Israel and the Church at Rome (see Romans 11). One group or party was denying the resurrection of the other. The schisms of the various groups at Corinth (1 Cor. 1:10 – 3:23) reach their main conflict here in chapter 15, which Paul now desires to set straight. Paul, being the leader of the erring Gentile party who boasted of themselves and Paul as their leader, now humbles himself among the apostles (vss. 7-9) in order to correct this arrogant spirit. He ties his gospel message in as being ONE with the Jewish leaders (vss. 11-12). The resurrection of Jesus and the gospel message was united and agreed upon in the preaching of Christ's resurrection by all the parties! Paul will use this agreement to make his case against them!

Perhaps some of their misunderstandings and arrogance began as early as Acts 18 when they heard Paul say, "Your blood be upon your own heads; I am clean. From now on I will go to the Gentiles." I believe that a misunderstanding of Paul here and perhaps some of his teaching that Gentiles were one body with the Jews, and that a true Jew was one who had been circumcised of the heart, led to a replacement theology and denial of an old covenant Jewish (the dead ones) eschaton / resurrection. After humbling himself and showing his solidarity with the Jewish leaders in preaching the same doctrine, Paul now begins to correct their error.

1 Corinthians 15:12-19 - Paul's Modus Tollens form of Argumentation

To further prove that the deniers of the resurrection of the dead were not denying Christ's resurrection or the resurrection for all in general, we need to take a look at Paul's form of argumentation. The Futurist view makes no contextual sense if you follow Paul's argumentation and the logic he uses. Paul uses a familiar *modus tollens* or "if then" logical argument. That is, "If P, then Q, and therefore not P."

1) "If P"

- "If there is no resurrection of the dead ones…"

2) Then Q"

- If the dead are not rising (and will rise)…**then** not even Christ has been raised.
- If the dead are not rising (and will rise)…**then** our preaching is useless…
- If the dead are not rising (and will rise)…**then** and so is your faith [useless].
- If the dead are not rising (and will rise)…**then** we are found to be false witnesses about God.
- If the dead are not rising (and will rise)…**then** those also who have fallen asleep in Christ are lost.
- If the dead are not rising (and will rise)…**then** your and my baptism (of suffering & martyrdom) on the part of the dead is meaningless.
- If the dead are not rising (and will rise)…**then** the Father is subject to Christ.
- If the dead are not rising (and will rise)…**then** some of you are ignorant of God.
- If the dead are not rising (and will rise)…**then** why are some undergoing a baptism (of suffering & persecution) on behalf of the dead?
- If the dead are not rising (and will rise)…**then** there will be no resurrection for anyone and we all might as well eat, drink and be merry, for tomorrow we die.

3) "Therefore, not P"

- Therefore, your (resurrection of the dead deniers) premise that the resurrection of the (OC) dead will not take place is false (or "therefore, not P").

Paul's argument is also known as *reduction ad absurdum*. This form of argument demonstrates that a statement (the dead will not rise) is false by showing that a false, untenable, undesirable or absurd result follows from its acceptance. Again, Paul is using things he has in common with them and things that they would affirm in order to overthrow and show how absurd their false premise actually was in saying that the dead ones would not rise.

The Resurrection of the Dead Error Identified

Since the Corinthians believed in Christ's resurrection and a resurrection for those who had died "in Christ," then who is left to deny a resurrection for? In short, the error at Corinth was an extreme view (or a hyper-dispensational or pre-mature replacement theology of sorts) that divided up the people of God in extreme ways. They could not reconcile how the dead prior to Christ's arrival could be raised into or with the body of Christ of which they were now a part. In short, they were denying a key ingredient to "the better resurrection" that the writer to the Hebrews outlines:

> "Women received their dead raised to life again: and others were tortured, not accepting deliverance; that they [the OT or old covenant dead] might obtain a better resurrection: And others had trial of cruel mockings and scourgings, yea, moreover of bonds and imprisonment: They were stoned, they were sawn asunder, were tempted, were slain with the sword: they wandered about in sheepskins and goatskins; being destitute, afflicted, tormented; (of whom the world was not worthy:) they wandered in deserts, and in mountains, and in dens and caves of the earth. And these all, having obtained a good report through faith, received not the promise: God having provided some better thing for us, **that they** ("the [OT/OC] dead") **without us** (the NT/NC saints "in Christ") should not be made perfect" (Heb. 11:35-40).

The resurrection of the dead deniers at Corinth saw the "better things" for those who were "in Christ" (dead or alive – their side of the cross), but could not reconcile how the OT or old covenant dead (on the other side of the cross) could participate in a resurrection with those who had died in Christ or how they could be "made perfect" together in the body of Christ. They had the new covenant "better things," and thus the OT or old covenant dead were left without participation in the better resurrection to come; this was their reasoning and error. They did not deny the doctrine of the resurrection in general, *just the all-ness or oneness (with all of God's of people) to the resurrection*.

Extreme views of excluding even the righteous dead were not uncommon, even among the Jews. Some Jews believed that anyone who died outside of the Promised Land would not participate in the resurrection:

> "The Talmud records speculations on the various matters connected with the process of Resurrection. There was a firm belief that the momentous event would take place in the Holy Land. Some Rabbi took the extreme view that only they who were interred there would share in the future life. 'Those who die outside the land of Israel will not live again; as it is said, "I will set delight in the land of the living." (Ezek. 26:20)—those who die in the land of My delight will live again, but they who do not die there will not'..."
> "Even a Cananite maidservant in the land of Israel is assured of inheriting the World to Come'..."[255]

So, in this extreme view, those righteous dead who died outside of being "in the land" would not participate in Israel's corporate resurrection. Similarly, some at Corinth took Paul's teaching – that all prophecy or all the promises of God were fulfilled spiritually "in Christ" (2 Cor. 1:20) – too far in that they concluded the resurrection could only take place for those who believed "in Christ" (their side of the cross), and all others perished outside of being in Him.

Therefore, since the old covenant dead perished and were not present to place their faith in Christ, then they couldn't be a part of the spiritual new covenant body that was in the process of being raised in their day. They lost sight of the great cloud of witnesses who saw Christ's day and were glad and would thus share in the "better resurrection" with them.

According to both of these extreme Jewish or Christian views, men such as Moses had no resurrection hope but perished outside of being either "in the land" or outside of being "in Christ."

We see a similar inability to reconcile the OT promises made to Israel and how they would be fulfilled in the NT body of Christ coming from modern day Dispensational Zionists who think there are opposing theologies between the OT and NT. There are two completely separate bodies of believers or peoples of God needing two separate comings of Christ, programs of salvation, etc. Of particular interest to our discussion here is the comparison of dividing the OT dead from those who died "in Christ." Dispensationalists such as Charles Ryrie and Dr. Lewis Sperry Chafer argue in the following ways:

> "Those who died before Christ's first advent" are not among "the dead in Christ" (Charles Ryrie).[256]

> "The Old Testament saints were not part of the New Creation in Christ," and "the nation of Israel sustains no relation to the resurrection of Christ" (Dr. Lewis Sperry Chafer).[257]

---

[255] Rev. Dr. A. Cohen, *Everyman's TALMUD*, (New York: E.P. DUTTON & CO., INC., 1949), 361-362

[256] quotes taken from: Curtis Crenshaw and Grove Gunn, *Dispensationalism Today, Yesterday, and Tomorrow*, 204

[257] Ibid.

And again, per Chafer, the dead OT saints were not "in the new federal headship of the resurrected Christ..."[258]

This sounds like elements of the resurrection of the dead deniers' doctrine, and confusion was picked up from Dispensational teaching.

In 1937 William Everett Bell argued against Pretribulationalism, providing evidence that at Christ's Second Coming (after the Tribulation period) all the righteous dead were to be raised. The ever-evolving pre-tribulational rapture theory countered with a two-resurrection view – one for those who died "in Christ" at the "rapture" "coming" and one for those who died outside of being "in Christ" (OT dead not "in Christ") seven years later (after the Tribulation) at the Second Coming. The resurrection of the dead deniers also divided God's people up in a way that was contrary to the teachings of Paul, except that for them the best way to avoid the problem (which they created for themselves) was to entirely deny resurrection for the OT dead and only accept a resurrection for those "in Christ."

These examples (one within the Talmud and modern ones) should be sufficient to demonstrate *how* it could be possible for some to miss how the OT dead could or even would participate in the salvation of the ONE NT or new covenant body of Christ.

Romans 11 & 1 Corinthians 15

Perhaps the best parallel to what is taking place among the Gentile deniers of the resurrection of the dead at Corinth can be found in Romans 11. Paul has to explain that the Gentiles did not completely replace old covenant Israel and that there remained a future eschaton and expectation of fulfillment for her. And this future is explained in such a way that without God fulfilling those promises to old covenant Israel, there would be no forgiveness of sin or resurrection life for the Gentiles (cf. Rms. 11:13-27). In Romans the Gentile arrogance against the Jews was illustrated by an olive tree, branches, and the root to demonstrate the solidarity of the Gentiles with Israel's resurrection and covenant promises. As we will see in our next point, Paul uses the illustration of the "first-fruits" harvest to connect the two.

1 Corinthians 15:20-28 – First fruits and Solidarity

Paul is going to now further his argument to connect Christ's resurrection with that of Israel's, by using the first-fruits analogy. How could the Gentiles deny Israel's role in the resurrection when they themselves (along with the believing Jews) were a part of the first fruits awaiting the harvest at Christ's return (James 1:18, Rom. 8, Rev. 14)? Paul's resurrection hope was the "hope of Israel" and the harvest was Israel's harvest of which they were blessed to be a part or grafted into. To deny "the dead" or Israel's future role in the resurrection/harvest was akin to theologically denying Christ's role and their role at the end of the old covenant age / harvest.

---

[258] Ibid.

First-fruits, Imminence & Analogy of Faith

Whenever the first fruits were offered up as a pledge, this was a symbol that not only the harvest was guaranteed, but that it was already ripe and being cut. Paul uses this argument of Christ being the "first-fruits" resurrection to teach that He controls the destiny of Israel's harvest (the dead), which Paul's first century "we" audience would experience at "the end" of the old covenant age.

The imminence of this coming harvest judgment was first developed by John the Baptist. He warned of an "about to" come wrath and punishment (Mt. 3:7GNT). His ax and winnowing fork were already in His hand – indicating that the judgment and end-time harvest would take place in some of their lifetimes (Mt. 3:10-12).

Jesus also taught a spiritual sowing and coming judgment / resurrection harvest which would take place at "the end" of His Jewish audiences' "this age" (which was the old covenant age) in Matthew 13:39-43.

The first fruits and harvest resurrection and judgment of Revelation 7 and 14 was to be fulfilled "shortly" at Christ's "soon" and "at hand" AD 70 Second Coming (Rev. 1:1—22:6-7, 10-12, 20).

Paul's inspired teaching on an imminent harvest resurrection to take place at "the end" (of the old covenant age) is in harmony with the teaching and eschatology of John the Baptist, John the apostle and Jesus.

Major Premise: The harvest judgment and resurrection of Matthew 3:7-12, Matthew 13:39-43, Revelation 7 & 14, and 1 Corinthians 15 is ONE and the same with the end of the age harvest resurrection event (Classic Amillennialism).

Minor Premise: But the harvest judgment and resurrection of Matthew 3:7-12, Matthew 13:39-43, and Revelation 7 & 14 was "about to be" fulfilled spiritually and "short" at the end of the old covenant age in AD 70 (Partial Preterism - mostly Postmillennialist).

Conclusion: The ONE and the same harvest judgment and resurrection of Matthew 3:7-12, Matthew 13:39-43, Revelation 7 & 14, and 1 Corinthians 15 was fulfilled spiritually at the end of the old covenant age in AD 70 (Full Preterism).

First-fruits and the Nature of Jesus' Resurrection Body

In Pauline theology, Christ is described as the "First" (first-fruit or first-born - Col. 1:18) from among the dead ones. Since clearly Jesus was not the first to be raised from biological death, many futurists reason that this must then mean He was the first to be raised with a glorified and immortal body the third day, which they assert was different because it could walk through walls and could never biologically die again. However, there is no exegetical evidence that Jesus' biological body that was raised the third day was substantially different (glorified) than the one He had before He was crucified. Prior to His resurrection, He was able to walk on water, disappear in the midst of a crowd and transport / teleport Himself and a boat full of disciples instantly to the shore (defy physics). So just because Jesus could appear or disappear after His resurrection, this does not prove that His body was different and that somehow at the end of history we too will get a "body" like His (that can defy the laws of physics, etc.).

The truth, however, is that Jesus' body wouldn't be glorified until some 40 days later at His ascension/enthronement and just prior to the giving of the Holy Spirit. Therefore, the resurrection body of Christ that came out of the tomb is not the "same" or "first" immortal and "glorified" body that we allegedly will get at the end of world history. If it was and ours will be just like it, then since Jesus still had His wounds, then will Christians be raised without limbs, deformities, etc.?

Yet Jesus was the "first" to overcome covenantal sin/death or spiritual separation that came from Adam the very day he sinned against God and was banished from His presence. Jesus "became sin for us" – that is, He took the full curse (of separation) for His posterity, was raised and 40 days later glorified and restored into the "glory" and presence of the Father He had before the world began. Exactly how Jesus "became sin" and was separated ("My God why have you forsaken Me") on our account contains concepts that we will not be able to *fully* understand (such as the incarnation and trinity), but it is what Scripture teaches nonetheless. At Christ's Parousia in AD 70, He restored God's presence with the righteous dead (OC & NC) along with the living.

Therefore, the purpose of Jesus being raised from the dead on the third day was to be a sign (like all of His other miracles that pointed to a deeper spiritual truth) that validated He alone had conquered the curse (sin/death/separation) which came through Adam. Jesus never came to conquer biological death for Christians. Jesus repeatedly taught that those who believe on Him (alive or dead – Jn. 8:51; 11:25-26) would "never die." In other words, "never die" is synonymous with "eternal life" (i.e. spiritual life and existence in God's presence).

In Adam or in Christ

Through the corporate body of Adam, "all" come into this world spiritually dead and separated from God (15:21-22), while through Christ and His overcoming of that death "all" of His corporate body or covenant posterity will be restored to God's presence and have their sin completely taken away at His *Parousia*. We will pick up Paul's "in Adam" or "in Christ" doctrine and how he addresses these terms and concepts in verses 44-58 and Romans 5-8.

At His Parousia

Paul's teaching on the *Parousia* (15:23) is not different than what Christ taught of His *Parousia* to take place in the AD 30 – AD 70 "this generation" (Mt. 24:27-34, 37). The NT knows of only ONE hope or eschatological *Parousia* of Christ to bring about ONE eschatological "the end" or "end of the age," and that was His *Parousia* to close "the end" or "end of the [OC] age" in AD 70.

Then Comes the End & the Kingdom

"The end" (15:24) here is consistent with Jesus' teaching on the end of the old covenant "this age" to be fulfilled in the AD 30 – AD 70 "this generation" (Mt. 13:39-43; Mt.

24). It is Daniel's "time of the end" (not the end of time) when the resurrection would occur at Jerusalem's destruction in the three and a half years between AD 67 - AD 70 – i.e. "when the power of the holy people would be completely shattered" (Dan. 12: 1-7).

Before we approach 1 Corinthians 15, Paul has already informed us that "the end" of the world was "shortened" and the end of the age was to take place in the lifetime of the Corinthians (cf. 1 Cor. 7:29, 31; 10:11). The miraculous sign and revelatory gifts would confirm the Church until "the end" or Day of the Lord (1 Cor. 1:4-8).

Paul taught that the new covenant Church age was an "age without end" (Eph. 3:20-21), so why would he here be teaching that he expected its end to take place within the lifetime of the Corinthians? It is the old covenant age that is in view and indeed did pass away within the lifetime of Paul's audience. The new covenant age was "about to" fully come in, and therefore the old covenant age was about to end (Eph. 1:21 WUESTNT).

The "increase" (that is the everlasting gospel) of Jesus' government (that is His kingdom and thus His rule in the new covenant Messianic age) is also described as having "no end" in the OT (Isa. 9:7).

Concerning the timing of the consummation of the kingdom, per Daniel chapter seven, the kingdom would arrive in its fulfilled inherited form just after a time of severe persecution (Dan. 7:21) and at Christ's Second Coming (Dan. 7:13, 18, 22). Jesus informs us when Daniel's prophecy would be fulfilled in Matthew 24. He instructs His disciples that just after a severe persecution takes place, the surrounding of Jerusalem with armies (the abomination that causes desolation), and just prior to His *Parousia* the Kingdom would be inherited in the AD 30 – AD 70 "this generation" (Lk. 21:1-32). How many consummations to the Messianic kingdom do Jesus and Paul teach?

Paul's "end" here is connected to the end or fulfillment of the OT Mosaic "THE Law" which was the strength of sin in 1 Corinthians 15:55-56. This is consistent with Jesus teaching that all that was written in the OT would be fulfilled in His generation (Lk. 21:22-32).

Christ's Pre-Parousia Reign & His Enemies Placed Under His Feet

As David and Solomon's reigns over Israel were 40 years, so too was Jesus' pre-Parousia reign (roughly from AD 30 – AD 70). Through the proclamation and power of the gospel, the power of the Holy Spirit given in the midst of imprisonment and persecutions, and the imprecatory prayers of the saints against their first century Jewish persecutors, Christ's enemies were being placed under His feet and would perish at the end of the old covenant age. This is consistent with the teaching of the author to the Hebrews when He instructs us that the first century Jewish "enemies" to be "made his footstool" were "about to" experience a judgment of fire at Christ's "in a very little while" AD 70 coming that could not be delayed (Heb. 10:13-37YLT).

Last Enemy "The Death" Was in the Process of Being Destroyed - The Present Passive Indicative – The Dead Were Rising

Note that death was in the process of BEING destroyed (*present passive indicative*):

> "As a last enemy, [the] death is be***ing*** abolished, for all things He put in subjection under His feet."[259]

Gordon Fee in his work on 1 Corinthians puzzles over this:

> "The grammar of this sentence is somewhat puzzling… The sentence literally reads, '"The last enemy is be***ing*** destroyed."'"[260]

Others comment on the reality of the present tense here:

> "It is difficult to do justice to the present passive καταργεῖται in trans-lation. As it stands, the Greek states, The last enemy *is being* annihilated, (*namely*) death (v. 26). It is arguable that Paul uses the present to denote the *process* of annihilation *already set in motion* by Christ's (past) death and resurrection."[261]

There is no confusion or difficulty over the last enemy of "the death" be**ing** destroyed during Paul's day when we realize that this death was *spiritual* Adamic death, which was being magnified through Israel's Torah – "the law" or "administration of death" (1 Cor. 15:56-57; 2 Cor. 3). When the definite article "the" is in front of death, it is the spiritual death which came through Adam the very day he sinned that is in view.

However, there is understandable confusion and difficulty for the present tense of the death being destroyed for Futurists who assume that biological death and resurrection is the last enemy to be destroyed throughout 1 Corinthians 15. How was biological death in the process of being destroyed in Paul's day and up to ours for the last 2,000 years?!? Are arms sticking up out of the graveyards today, with biological corpses in the process of rising and overcoming death?!? Obviously, Paul has something else in view and Futurists do not understand him correctly.

Related to the problem for the Futurist of "the death" being in the process of "being destroyed" in Paul's day is Paul's use of the present passive indicative in other places in this chapter.

Although it is rare that a translation or commentator will point this issue out here in 15:26 (as I have cited above), they are all virtually silent when the present tense is being used in the following verses:

"But God is giv*ing* it a body" (v.32).

"…it is be*ing*…" (v. 38).

"…it is be*ing* raised in glory…" (43).

---

[259] Wuest, K. S. (1997). *The New Testament: An expanded translation* (1 Co 15:20–28). Grand Rapids, MI: Eerdmans

[260] Gordon D. Fee, *THE FIRST EPISTLE TO THE CORINTHIANS*, (Grand Rapids, MI: Eerdmans pub., 1987), 756

[261] Thiselton, A. C. (2000). *The First Epistle to the Corinthians: A commentary on the Greek text* (1234). Grand Rapids, Mich.: W.B. Eerdmans, emphasis MJS

"…it is be*ing* raised in power…" (v. 43)

"…It is be*ing* sown a natural body, it is being raised a spiritual body…" (v. 43).

Since most think that the giving of a "body" and it being "sown" a natural body and then being raised in glory and power is allegedly addressing a biologically transformed individual body at Christ's Parousia at the end world history, the present tense seems impossible. But when the corporate body of Christ (the old covenant dead who had the gospel preached to them by Christ, those dead "in Christ" and those alive that constitute that ONE body) is in view, Paul's theology/eschatology begins to make more sense. Christ was still in the process of fulfilling OT Scripture and thus the new covenant corporate body was still being raised from and saved from the Adamic and Mosaic body of death.

Let's not forget that Postmillennialists such as James Jordan and Kenneth Gentry believe the resurrection of Daniel 12:2-3 was a progressive spiritual resurrection between AD 30 – AD 70, with Jordan making it clear that this resulted in Daniel's soul being raised out of the realm of the dead ones into God's presence in AD 70. And on the other hand, we have the Reformed orthodox position telling us that the resurrection of Daniel 12:2-3 and 1 Corinthians 15 is ONE and the SAME resurrection event. Therefore, there is simply no reason to not see the progressive and spiritual resurrection that was taking place between AD 30 – AD 70 in both Daniel 12 and 1 Corinthians 15 as being the same "already and not yet" eschaton that resulted in souls being raised into God's presence at Christ's Parousia in AD 70.

According to Paul, the ONE resurrection hope of Israel had already broken in and there was an "already and not yet" reality to it (Rom. 11:7; Phil. 3).

That God May Be All in All

This is the eschatological goal of the NT – that "all" of God's presence (the Father, Son and Spirit) would be in "all" of God's people (the new covenant body of the Jew and Gentile). The Holy Spirit's presence was with the early Church through the charismata and in forming Christ's image (a spiritual transformation) in the Church. But it was only at the Second Coming of Jesus in AD 70 that the Father and the Son would then make their home within the Church (e.g. John 14:2-3, 23, 29; Lk. 17:20-21ff.; Rom. 8:18YLT; Col. 1:27). At the "end" of Christ's pre-Parousia reign, He would deliver the kingdom up to the Father and its process of being changed (2 Cor. 3) would be complete and consummated into its heavenly form.

The promise of God being "all in all" is the fulfillment of the feast of Tabernacles which we covered in Matthew 24:30-31 and Zechariah 12-14.

1 Corinthians 15:29-34 - Baptism on Behalf of the Dead

There has been much debate on the meaning of those being baptized on behalf of the dead (15:29). However, the context would seem to indicate that this is a baptism of suffering that is in view (vss. 30-32; see also Lk. 12:50/Mt. 20:20-23; Mt. 23:29-36; Heb. 11:39-40). Paul's point and overall argument is that if the old covenant dead would not participate in the resurrection, then those Christians (such as himself) who were undergoing a baptism of suffering, persecution and death/martyrdom on their behalf (the ONE body of Christ that included the old covenant dead) were *suffering and perishing in vain*. If the dead would not rise with those who had fallen asleep "in Christ," then one might as well adopt the fatalistic mindset of "eat and drink, for tomorrow we die," for there would be no resurrection for anyone.

1 Corinthians 15:35-58 - The Body (Greek soma) & Consistency within Pauline Theological Terms & Motifs

Much has been said and debated in recent years in regard to Paul's use of the "body" (Greek *soma*) in his various epistles. Many would insist that when Paul uses "body" in his letters to the various churches, he is mostly referring to an individualistic biological or fleshly body. However, theologians such as Tom Holland are developing a proper cultural context in which Paul is writing with a Hebraic mindset, or within a worldview that is rooted in the OT Scriptures, which sees the body more in a corporate sense and context. Holland does a great job developing this in Romans 5-7 and 1 Corinthians 1-12, but we find him inconsistent and dropping the ball in Romans 8 and 1 Corinthians 15.

Holland also has correctly observed that most of the time Paul uses particular theological phrases and terms in a consistent way in writing to the various churches, so that there is little confusion among them.[262] And while we agree with this, we believe Holland is inconsistent with Paul's consistent use of "the law", "the sin," and "the death" in relationship to being "in Adam" or "in Christ" when addressed in Romans 5-8, and also how he understands these terms and themes in 1 Corinthians 15. In Romans, Paul does not use these terms and the "in Adam" / "in Christ" motif to be discussing biological death and resurrection, but rather corporate modes of existence. We argue that Paul uses these terms and motifs virtually the same way in 1 Corinthians 15, and thus he is not addressing a biological death and resurrection motif.

Paul's Seed Analogy & Being Buried Alive

Since the resurrection of the dead deniers did not deny a corporate bodily resurrection for themselves and those who had died "in Christ" (their side of the cross), then what is Paul's point in using the seed analogy? If Paul was correct in what he was saying thus far in his argumentation, then their objection would be something like, "How or what kind of body could the old covenant dead ones possibly be raised in since they died in the state of death found in Adam prior to Christ's coming (thus they were susceptible to weakness, perishable and merely natural), unattached from us who are "in Christ" where resurrection new covenant eternal life is being realized (cf. 15:35)?"

Paul's statement, "When you sow, you do not plant the body that will be…" summarizes their thinking and error. For them, they were the one *spiritual* body that was BOTH being sown spiritually and would be *raised spiritually*. In other words,

---

[262] Holland, Ibid., see 90 – 107 for this discussion

they thought they sowed the same spiritual body that would be, which couldn't be attached to the old covenant body which they believed perished outside of Christ. Paul uses the seed analogy to demonstrate that they (along with the old covenant dead ones) were not sown a spiritual body, but rather *they had the same sowing/seed origins that the old covenant dead ones were in – i.e. still in a "perishable", "dishonorable", "weak", "natural", "Adamic" body of death*. The corporate body of Christ did not originate their side of the cross out of thin air, but it originated in and came out from within the Adamic old covenant body (along with the old covenant dead ones). The resurrection of the dead deniers needed to see that they were still a part of the old covenant body/seed/world (with the old covenant dead) that had not passed away yet.

If Paul had a resurrection of biological corpses in view, then he didn't know how to teach and use illustrations very well. Futurists believe the passage teaches that in biological death the body dies and then is buried or sown into the earth to be raised at the end of world history into a different form. But for Paul in verse 36, the seed/body was not only in the process of being sown (under the earth), it was still alive and concurrently dying only to be raised into a different form. Futurists are at odds with Paul's teaching and illustration, which would amount to burying corpses while alive, only to undergo a process of dying and then to be raised.

In order to understand Paul's buried alive and concurrently dying doctrine, or how the "body" here in 1 Corinthians 15 is not a fleshly individual body but a corporate body, we must allow Paul to interpret himself elsewhere. We will pick this subject up in Romans 5-8, when addressing the nature of the body in Adam or in Christ, when it surfaces again in verses 44-58.

I believe Don K. Preston's thesis of Paul using Hosea 6 – 13 as an *inclusio* as a possible working outline in 1 Corinthians 15 is an excellent observation.

| *"Hosea: The Outline for Paul's Resurrection Hope* ||
Hosea	1 Corinthians 15
1). "He has torn but he will heal, and after two days He will raise us up."	1). Christ rose on the 3rd day according to the Scriptures - Paul introduces Hosea at the very beginning of his discourse and he closes his discourse by quoting Hosea.
2). Israel the Seed (Jezreel–God sows): Israel sown in the earth (2.23).	2). Except a seed– "That which you sow is not quickened unless it die" (John 12).
3). Israel destroyed/died (1.5– I will cause to cease the house of Israel): continuity / discontinuity – Israel destroyed / Israel restored.	3). You do not sow that which shall be (v. 37). That which you reap is not what you sow; that which is spiritual is not first, but the natural.
4). Israel of old - carnal, sinful.	4). It is sown a natural body (v. 42f).
5). Israel sown in the earth (2.23).	5). As we have borne the image of the earthy.
6). Harvest appointed for Judah when I return My people (6.11).	6). Jesus the first fruits (Jesus of Judah), of those who slept - OT saints, i.e. Israel!! (15.12f).

7). Time of the harvest = resurrection (13.14).	7). Resurrection when Hosea fulfilled (15:54-56).
8). Israel like the first fruit (9:10).	8). Christ the first fruit of Israel (15:20f).
9). They transgressed the covenant (6.7; they died (v. 5; 13.1-2, 10) – death for violating the covenant.	9). The strength of sin is "the law" (15.56) –death for violating the Law.
10). New covenant of peace (2:18; Cf. Ez. 37:12, 25f)—> covenant is covenant of marriage.	10). Sit at my right hand…Heb. 10:14– time of the new covenant (Rom. 11:26f.) – the marriage, thus the covenant —> Rev. 19:6.
11). Israel restored in the last days when "David" rules (3.4-5).	11). End of the ages has arrived (10.11); "then comes the end" (15.20f) - Christ on the throne (15.24f).
12). I will be your God. I will be your king! (Hos. 13:10).	12). 1 Corinthians 15:28 (God shall be all in all).
13). Resurrection = restoration to fellowship.	13). 1 Corinthians 15: resurrection when "the sin," the sting of "the death removed."[263]

The resurrection of the dead deniers needed to be reminded that they were a part of old covenant Israel's seed/body that was promised to be raised in the last days harvest to close her age. Without their union into that seed/body, there would be no resurrection for either group.

Israel had been sown in death and captivity, but she was in the process of being raised, united together, and transformed through the good news of the new covenant. Israel's process of being transformed and being sown and rising from old covenant glory into new covenant glory in 1 Corinthians 15 & 2 Corinthians 3 should be viewed together, just as a spiritual seeing of God's face in a glass or mirror found in 1 Corinthians 13 and 2 Corinthians 3-4 should be interpreted together. We must allow Paul to interpret himself, especially when writing to the same church. It's just basic hermeneutics.

In Adam or in Christ & the Corporate Body Cont.

Let's take a look at the Pauline view of being in the corporate bodies of Adam (as a type) and/or in Christ.

*"But the death did reign from Adam till Moses, even upon those not having sinned in the likeness of Adam's transgression, who is **a type** of him who is "about to" [Smith's Literal Translation correctly translates mello here] come"* (Rom. 5:14).

To further demonstrate that the resurrection for those in Christ is a spiritual resurrection is to notice that in Pauline "in Adam" or "in Christ" theology Adam is a "type" and Christ the anti-type. In the book of Hebrews, the first was the physical type and shadow with the second and better being the *spiritual anti-type*. The point is that the anti-type

---

[263] Don K. Preston, 2005, 2712 Mt. Washington Rd. Ardmore, Ok.

is always spiritual, and that is what we see here in 1 Corinthians 15 of the second being a "spiritual body" that the new covenant Israel/Church is raised up into.

As I pointed out earlier, there are many similarities between Romans 5-8 and 1 Corinthians 15. Therefore, let's spend some time here in Romans to see how Paul develops these themes.

In Romans 5:14, the context is involving an eschatological future ("about to") coming of Christ who is the anti-type of Adam. It will be when the future hope of glory in verses 1-5 is realized (which Rom. 8:18YLT says was "about to be revealed") and when they would be saved from a coming wrath in verse 10.

Most Futurists, such as Postmillennialist Keith Mathison, believe that Romans 5:12 teaches that physical death for man and decay for the planet earth came through Adam's sin and thus at Christ's return He will reverse what Adam had brought upon the planet:

> "As Paul explains, death entered the world because of Adam's sin (Roms. 5:12). God's entire work of redemption from the moment of the Fall onward has been aimed at reversing the effects of sin in man and in creation."[264]

However, the immediate context of verse 12 is dealing with *spiritual* salvation described as "reconciliation" being given to the believer in verse 11. The phrase "...death through sin, and so death spread to all men because all sinned..." is discussing *spiritual death,* not physical death, or people would physically die when they "sin." As I discussed before, in Genesis Adam died spiritually the very day he sinned. Through Adam came the reign of spiritual "death" and "condemnation" in verse 18. This spiritual death and condemnation that came through Adam is countered by Christ because through Him the "free gift" of the gospel is "grace" (v. 15), "justification" (v. 16), and a "reign of life" (v.17), which makes one "righteous" (v. 19). These are *spiritual graces upon the heart of man undoing the reign of spiritual death and condemnation brought through Adam.*

Verses 20-21 are important: "Moreover the law entered that the offense might abound. But where sin abounded, grace abounded much more, so that as sin reigned in death, even so grace might reign through righteousness to eternal life through Jesus Christ our Lord." When the Mosaic law entered the picture, it did not make death any worse, but it did increase and magnify the power and reign of spiritual death and sin in the heart of man. This is most eloquently described by Paul in his struggle of what the law produced when it was brought upon his conscience in chapter 7. Saul, the self-righteous Jew, thought they were "alive" under the law, but when they realized that the law could only magnify their sin and it could not completely take it away, they "died" (7:9). Obviously, Paul did not biologically die the day he realized this. The entire context of Romans is dealing with overcoming the spiritual death passed down through Adam, which was magnified through the giving of Torah. This spiritual death was

---

[264] Keith A. Mathison, co-authored book, *WHEN SHALL THESE THINGS BE? A REFORMED RESPONSE TO HYPER-PRETERISM*, (Phillipsburg, NJ: P&R Publishing, 2004), 196

found in the corporate body of the sin, the death, and the flesh which Paul brings out and develops more in chapter 6.

As previously mentioned, fortunately some Pauline reformed theologians are beginning to see what we have in these Pauline terms. Paul is not addressing an individual resurrection of a physical "fleshly" corpse in Romans 6:

> "The concrete mode of existence of sinful man can sometimes be identified with sin as the 'body of sin' (Rom. 6:6), the 'body of flesh' (Col. 2:11), the 'body of death' (Rom.7:24). Accordingly, the life from Christ by the Holy Spirit can be typified as a 'doing away with the body of sin', 'putting off of the body of the flesh, 'putting to death the earthly members', 'deliverance from the body of this death' Rom. 6:6; Col. 2:11; 3:5; Rom. 7:24) ... *All these expressions are obviously not intended of the body itself, but of the sinful mode of existence of man.*"[265]

Quoting T.F. Torrance,

> "In his death, the many who inhered in him died too, and indeed the whole body of sin, the whole company of sinners into which he incorporated himself to make their guilt and their judgment his own, that through his death he might destroy the body of sin, redeem them from the power of guilt and death, and through his resurrection raise them up as the new Israel"[266]

This corporate view of the "body of sin" is also shared by F.F. Bruce:

> "This 'body of sin' is more than an individual affair. It is rather that old solidarity of sin and death which all share 'in Adam,' but which has been broken by the death of Christ with a view to the creation of the new solidarity of righteousness and life of which believers are made part 'in Christ.'"[267]

Holland feels that T.W. Manson has come the closest to the truth:

> "He questioned the traditional assumption that in the phrase 'body of Sin' the term 'of Sin' is a genitive of quality; he argued that it 'does not yield a very good sense'. He took it to be a possessive genitive, and said, 'It is perhaps better to regard "the body of sin" as the opposite of "the body of Christ". It is the mass of unredeemed humanity in bondage to the evil power. Every conversion means that the body of sin loses a member and the body of Christ gains one'"[268]

---

[265] Tom Holland, *CONTOURS OF PAULINE THEOLOGY A RADICAL NEW SURVEY OF THE INFLUENCE ON PAUL'S BIBLICAL WRITINGS*, (Mentor Imprint, Scotland, UK: 2004), 90, emphasis MJS.

[266] Ibid, 91

[267] Ibid., 91

[268] Ibid., 91

And developing the corporate body motif, commenting on Romans 6:6:

> "Also, in 6:6 Paul refers to 'putting off the old man'. Once again this has traditionally been seen as a reference to the sinful self that dominated the life of the believer in the pre-converted state. However, the same terminology is used in Ephesians 2:15 where Paul says, 'to create in himself one new man out of the two, thus making peace'. He then goes on to say in 4:22-23, 'put off your old self (*anthropos* – man), created to be like God in true righteousness and holiness.' The exhortation is parallel to that in Romans 6:6ff. Thus, the new man, which Paul exhorts the Romans to put on, is corporate, for 'the new man' in Ephesians is the church, and the two who have been united to form this new man are the believing Jews and the believing Gentiles. This corporate understanding is further supported by Colossians 3:9-15… The realm where distinctions are abolished (here there is no Greek or Jew, v. 11) is clearly corporate. This is indicated by two considerations. First, 'here' is clearly the realm where all distinctions are abolished, and this is the new man. Second, the meaning of the one body into which they were called (v. 15) is obviously corporate. These descriptions of corporateness are in the context of the description of the old and new self (vv. 9, 10). The rendering of *anthropos* as *self* by the NIV and *sarx* as *flesh* in the AV has inevitably promoted the individualistic understanding and confused the mind of the English reader. Furthermore, that Paul's exhortation is corporate is shown in that he appeals to them, "as God's chosen people clothe yourselves' (v. 12). Thus, identifying the imagery of the old and new man as being corporate, and appreciating that it is part of the description of the 'body of Sin' in Romans 6:6, along with the other considerations we have presented, establishes a corporate meaning for the term the 'body of Sin'."[269]

What is the Soteriological and Eschatological Goal of Christ's Substitutionary Work?

Before we leave the topic of being in Adam or in Christ, we should probably really define what Christ's substitutionary redemption and mission is and what it isn't.

If one defines Christ's substitutionary work to be that Christ died physically so we don't have to, then Christ's redemption has been an epic failure for some 2,000 plus years and counting. But as we have seen, the WUESTNT correctly translates 1 Corinthians 15:26 as "the death" (that came through Adam – spiritual death and separation) which was already in the process of "beING destroyed" due to Christ's work on the cross and what He would imminently do at His Parousia to bring an "end" to the old covenant age in AD 70. If physical death was "being destroyed" in Paul's day and ours, we should expect physical corpses beginning to rise and walk about like the "Walking Dead" show. Or we should see men living to be 200 – 900 years old.

---

[269] Ibid., 95-96

And if the "wages of sin is biological death," and Christ's substitutionary work on the cross was designed to reverse this process, then again why do we still sin and die physically? Jesus said that if one believed in Him and kept his commandments he would "never die." Again, if this is physical death, then once again Christ's work and your faith prove Christ and Christians are epic failures.

But if Christ's substitutionary and redemptive work on the cross and at His Parousia in AD 70 was designed to overcome the spiritual death that came through Adam, now we can understand the following passages:

- "My God, my God, why have you forsaken me?" (Mt. 27:46).

And why Paul teaches:

- *"Therefore, just as sin entered the world through one man, and death through sin, and in this way death came to all people, because all sinned—To be sure, sin was in the world before the law was given, but sin is not charged against anyone's account where there is no law. Nevertheless, death reigned from the time of Adam to the time of Moses, even over those who did not sin by breaking a command, as did Adam, who is a pattern/type of the one [Greek mello] about to come.* **But the gift is not like the trespass. For if the many died by the trespass of the one man, how much more did God's grace and the gift that came by the grace of the one man, Jesus Christ, overflow to the many! Nor can the gift of God be compared with the result of one man's sin: The judgment followed one sin and brought condemnation, but the gift followed many trespasses and brought justification. For if, by the trespass of the one man, death reigned through that one man, how much more will those who receive God's abundant provision of grace and of the gift of righteousness reign in life through the one man, Jesus Christ! Consequently, just as one trespass resulted in condemnation for all people, so also one righteous act resulted in justification and life for all people. For just as through the disobedience of the one man the many were made sinners, so also through the obedience of the one man the many will be made righteous"** *(Rms. 5:12-21).*

- *"God made him who had no sin to be sin for us, so that in him we might become the righteousness of God"* (2 Cor. 5:21).

- *"Truly, truly, truly, I tell you, if anyone keeps My word, he will never see death" (Jn. 8:51). "...and everyone who lives and believes in Me shall never die. Do you believe this" (Jn. 10:26)?*

Here is a chart that may help:

Adam's ONE Trespass	Christ's ONE Righteous Act
Sin entered the world	Righteousness entered the world
Spiritual death entered the world	Spiritual eternal life entered the world

Spiritual death and separation reigned from Adam to Moses w/ Torah magnifying how sinful sin is and how short we fall.	For those in Christ, spiritual eternal life and righteousness reigns and brings us into God's presence.
Many died spiritually in their covenant head of Adam	Many are made alive in their covenant head of Christ
Spiritual judgment and condemnation came through Adam	Spiritual gift of grace brings justification through Christ
One act of disobedience made those in Adam sinners	One act of obedience made those in Christ righteous before God
Christ became sin for us so that →	…we might become the righteousness of God

It should be clear that spiritual death and life and positional truth is what is being communicated here by Jesus and Paul. If we are in Adam, we are subject to sin's power which results in spiritual separation and death from God's presence. But if we place our faith in Christ and we are granted the gift of His grace, then positionally and spiritually we "never die", we "become the righteousness of God," are "justified before Him," and "righteousness reigns in us."

Christ died to sin or became the curse of Adam's sin/death which separated us from God's presence. This "last enemy" and curse of spiritual death is what was in the process of "being destroyed" in Paul's day. When Adam sinned, he died spiritually. Christ lived a perfect life and committed no sin, so He was a perfect sacrifice capable of satisfying God's righteous and just wrath so that "we might become the righteousness of God." Now through Christ's redemptive work on the cross and Parousia, we live in the new covenant creation or the "world of righteousness" and are perfectly forgiven in His sight. And this gift of faith and of His unconditional grace causes us to be born of God whereby we "do not sin, because His seed/presence remains in us, and we cannot sin because we are born of God" (1 Jn. 3:9). That is, a true child of God cannot commit the specific sin "leading to death" (1 Jn. 5:16-18) which would once again bring us into the spiritual death and headship of Adam. Or as John would reinforce his meaning in Revelation 3:12, those of us who are in the righteousness of the New Jerusalem will never leave the gates and return to the spiritual death and darkness of being in Adam.

The Sovereign Grace Full Preterist has a substitutionary redemption that has been "accomplished and applied," which has produced the 100% goal Christ came to accomplish between AD 30 – AD 70. We are "in Christ", "we are His righteousness," and we will "never die" and be found outside of His marvelous grace! We are made perfect before the Father and behold His face because of what Christ has accomplished on the cross and through His "soon" Second Coming (1 Cor. 13:10-12/Rev. 22:4-7, 10, 20). Selah.

Paul's Consistent Use of Terms

Not only do I agree with Holland in his development of Paul being a Hebrew and thinking in Jewish collective or corporate body terms, but I also agree with him that Paul has a "system of theology" that he draws on when he uses certain words, terms, and phrases throughout his various writings:

> "Also, it seems quite inconceivable that a man of Paul's intellectual caliber should be so haphazard as to be indifferent to these alleged inconsistencies. At Paul's instruction, his letters were being passed around the churches (Col. 4:16). **Was he not concerned with consistency?**"[270]

Paul's themes of being in a corporate body, whether in "Adam" or "Christ," in Romans and 1 Corinthians 15, and being raised in the likeness of Christ or experiencing deliverance from "law" (Adam in the garden) or "THE law" (Israel groaning under the Mosaic law), has nothing to do with a casket resurrection from biological death for believers. This is a soteriological resurrection from the spiritual death inherited from Adam. The order of being planted or buried first and then simultaneously dying only to be changed and resurrected into Christ's image is also the same in Romans and 1 Corinthians 15. We will look at this shortly.

Corruption v Incorruption

Here is how Paul elsewhere uses "corruption":

1). "that the creation itself will be set free from its bondage to **corruption** and obtain the freedom of the glory of the children of God" (Rom. 8:21).

We should quote from John Lightfoot once again who not only saw the "redemption of the body" in Romans 8 to be the corporate body of the Church (which we are arguing is also the case here in 1 Cor. 15), but also identified "vanity" "corruption," etc. to be internal spiritual vices within the heart of man:

> ". . . [T]his vanity [or futility] is improperly applied to this vanishing, changeable, dying state of the [physical] creation. For vanity, doth not so much denote the vanishing condition of the outward state, as it doth the **inward vanity and emptiness of the mind**. The Romans to whom this apostle writes, knew well enough how many and how great predictions and promises it had pleased God to publish by his prophets, concerning gathering together and adopting sons to himself among the Gentiles: the manifestation and production of which sons, the whole Gentile world doth now wait for, as it were, with an **out stretched neck**."[271]

And again,

---

[270] Ibid. 107 emphasis MJS
[271] John Lightfoot, *Ibid., Vol. 4* (Hendrickson publications), 157.

> "The Gentile world shall in time be delivered from the bondage of their sinful corruption, that is, **the bondage of their lusts and vile affections**, (under which it hath lain for so long a time,) into a noble liberty, such as the sons of God enjoy. **If it be inquired how the Gentile world groaned and travailed in pain, let them who expound this of the fabric of the material world tell us how that groaneth and travaileth. They must needs own it to be a borrowed and allusive phrase."**[272]

2). "For the one who sows to his own flesh will from the flesh reap **corruption**, but the one who sows to the Spirit will from the Spirit reap eternal life" (Gal. 6:8).

Sowing to the flesh has to do with giving in to internal temptations of the mind and heart, and reaping "corruption" has to do with inheriting (in this world and the next) the consequences of sin. But if one sows to the Spirit, he reaps "eternal life" in this world and the next. "Corruption" does not have to do with biological flesh.

3). "Let no one disqualify you, insisting on asceticism and worship of angels, going on in detail about visions, puffed up without reason by his sensuous mind, and not holding fast to the Head, from whom the whole body, nourished and knit together through its joints and ligaments, grows with a growth that is from God. If with Christ you died to the elemental spirits of the world, why, as if you were still alive in the world, do you submit to regulations—"Do not handle, Do not taste, Do not touch" (referring to things that are **unto corruption** in the using [or perish as they are used])—according to human precepts and teachings? These have indeed an appearance of wisdom in promoting self-made religion and asceticism and severity to the body, but they are of no value in stopping the indulgence of the flesh" (Col. 2:18-22).

"Corruption" here is referring to the seducing Judaizers seeking to influence Jewish, and/or their proselyte Gentile, Christians into going back under the Mosaic Law to be justified before God. Seeking to be justified by the Mosaic Law as a means of salvation meant being under the "corruption" of these false teachers and this system which would soon perish with its teachers in the events of AD 70. Again, "corruption" is an internal reality of the heart and mind connected to sin and false teaching, not a biological change.

4). "His divine power has granted to us all things that pertain to life and godliness, through the knowledge of him who called us to his own glory and excellence, by which he has granted to us his precious and very great promises, so that through them you may become partakers of the divine nature, having escaped from the **corruption** that is in the world because of sinful desire. For this very reason, make every effort to supplement your faith with virtue, and virtue with knowledge, and knowledge with self-control, and self-control with steadfastness, and steadfastness with godliness, [7] and godliness with brotherly affection, and brotherly affection with love. For if these qualities are yours and are increasing, they keep you from being ineffective or unfruitful in the knowledge of our Lord Jesus Christ. For whoever lacks these qualities

---

[272] Ibid., 158–159, emphases MJS

is so nearsighted that he is blind, having forgotten that he was cleansed from his former sins" (2 Peter 1:3-9).

It was the knowledge and life of the gospel that delivered them from the inner "corruption" that was in the Jewish or heathen world of false religion. Peter is consistent with Pauline theology. Paul taught that through faith they were already being transformed into the image of Christ, which was obviously not a biological process that had already begun (cf. 2 Cor. 3:18). And according to Paul in Colossians 3:9-10, Christians were "putting off the old self" and "putting on the new self" as a process of "being renewed in the knowledge after the image of its creator." Being in the "image of the creator", "being transformed into the image of Christ," or "partaking in the divine nature," for Peter and Paul these were non-biological events and had to do with a change of mind and heart which the gospel had produced and was producing within the hearts of Christians.

5). "For, speaking loud boasts of folly, they entice by sensual passions of the flesh those who are barely escaping from those who live in error. They promise them freedom, but they themselves are **slaves of corruption**. For whatever overcomes a person, to that he is enslaved. For if, after they have escaped the defilements of the world through the knowledge of our Lord and Savior Jesus Christ, they are again entangled in them and overcome, the last state has become worse for them than the first" (2 Peter 2:18-20).

Once again, we have a warning to not go back to false religion which enslaved men's hearts and minds to the vices of sin and "corruption," which the inner "*knowledge* of Christ" had delivered them from. As we have seen, this Greek word for "corruption," as used elsewhere in the NT, does not entail a biological corruption of physical flesh needing a biological resurrection or change, nor is it being used this way by Paul in 1 Corinthians 15.

But what of Paul's use of "Incorruption" or "immortality"?

If "corruption" had to do with internal sin, then "incorruption" would seem to be the opposite. The Adamic or Mosaic world and belief system could only produce, expose and magnify the "corruption" of sin in the heart. The new covenant world and body of the gospel imputed Christ's righteousness, resulting in eternal life or "incorruptibility."

1). "He will render to each one according to his works: to those who by patience in well-doing seek for glory and honor and **immortality**, he will **give eternal life**; but for those who are self-seeking and do not obey the truth, but obey unrighteousness, there will be wrath and fury" (Rms. 2:7-8).

Here "immortality" or "incorruptibility" are equivalent to "eternal life." Earlier, we looked at the "already and not yet" (AD 27-30—AD 70) "hour" (Dan. 12:1-4 OG) of the early church receiving eternal or resurrection life, and it had nothing to do with a biological change that was taking place.

2). "Grace be with all who love our Lord Jesus Christ with **love incorruptible**" (Eph. 6:24).

The new covenant gospel and love of Christ for His Church and her love for Him (and family members) cannot be corrupted or fail (1 Cor. 13:7-8).

3). "…who saved us and called us to a holy calling, not because of our works but because of his own purpose and grace, which he gave us in Christ Jesus before the ages began, and which now has been manifested through the appearing of our Savior Christ Jesus, who **abolished death and brought life and immortality to light through the gospel**, for which I was appointed a preacher and apostle and teacher, which is why I suffer as I do. But I am not ashamed, for I know whom I have believed, and I am convinced that **he is able to guard until that day what has been entrusted to me**" (II Tim. 1:10).

To understand this passage better we need to go to chapter four:

> "I do fully testify, then, before God, and the Lord Jesus Christ, who is **about to** judge living and dead at his manifestation and his reign—preach the word; be earnest in season, out of season, convict, rebuke, exhort, in all long-suffering and teaching, for there shall be a season when the sound teaching they will not suffer, but according to their own desires to themselves they shall heap up teachers—itching in the hearing, and indeed, from the truth the hearing they shall turn away, and to the fables they shall be turned aside. And thou—watch in all things; suffer evil; do the work of one proclaiming good news; of thy ministration make full assurance, **for I am already being poured out, and the time of my release hath arrived; the good strife I have striven, the course I have finished, the faith I have kept**, henceforth there is **laid up for me the crown of the righteousness that the Lord—the Righteous Judge—shall give to me in that day, and not only to me, but also to all those loving his manifestation**" (2 Tim. 4:1-8 YLT, BLB, LSV).

Paul was entrusted with the gospel which brings immortality or eternal life to the soul of man. Paul knew severe persecutions were coming for him before the "about to" approaching "day" of the Lord. His confidence was in knowing that God was going to guard his God-given faith and soul as a precious deposit as that day was "about to" come and his life was going to be poured out (just prior to the events of AD 67 – AD 70).

There is nothing here about Paul having a hope that was connected to an "incorruptible" physical body that he would get at the end of world history. His deposit was his faith and assurance that his soul was about to receive the gift of eternal life or incorruptibility and immortality.

Peter defined this "ready to be revealed" "inheritance" as the "**salvation of the soul**" (1 Pet. 1:4-9).

After reading the above verses to see how Paul and the other New Testament writers use them elsewhere, it can be seen that the term "corruption" has reference to life under the Law of Moses and life "in Adam." Notice that it was possible to be under a state of "corruption" without having to be dead physically. Instead, this term had reference to *life under the dominion of sin.*

Likewise, "incorruption" was used to describe those in the body of Christ. Those enjoying the "incorruption" or "immortality" were those who had been added to the body (Church) of Christ by responding positively to the gospel. Just as the Church had to progress towards perfection, the individual Christians within the Church had "incorruption" while at the same time waiting for it to come on the day when God's wrath would be revealed (Romans 2:7). This idea is called by some as the "already but not yet" of eschatology. Because the "already" was not of a physical nature, it makes sense that the "not yet" would be of the same nature. If you saw the head of a dog coming around a corner, you would expect to see the tail of a dog – not of a cat – following shortly thereafter. The dog doesn't change into something else just because it is fully revealed. In like manner, the nature of the incorruption (the spiritual salvation of the soul) remains the same from initiation to consummation.

Natural v Spiritual

1). "Yet among the mature we do impart wisdom, although it is not a wisdom of **this age** or of the **rulers of this age, who are doomed to pass away**. But we impart a secret and hidden wisdom of God, which God decreed before the ages for our glory. None of the **rulers of this age understood this, for if they had, they would not have crucified the Lord of glory**. But, as it is written, "**What no eye has seen, nor ear heard, nor the heart of man imagined, what God has prepared for those who love him"— these things God has revealed to us through the Spirit**. For the Spirit searches everything, even the depths of God. For who knows a person's thoughts except the spirit of that person, which is in him? So also no one comprehends the thoughts of God except the Spirit of God. Now we have received not the spirit of the world, but **the Spirit who is from God, that we might understand the things freely given us by God**. And we impart this in words not taught by human wisdom but taught by the Spirit, **interpreting spiritual truths to those who are spiritual. The *natural person* does not accept the things of the Spirit of God, for they are folly to him, and he is not able to understand them because they are spiritually discerned. The spiritual person judges all things, but is himself to be judged by no one. "For who has understood the mind of the Lord so as to instruct him?" But we have the mind of Christ"** (1 Cor. 2:6-14).

In the next chapter Paul explains when the "things" were coming that the natural man could not understand:

> "So then, let no one glory in men, for all things are yours, whether Paul, or Apollos, or Cephas, or the world, or life, or death, or things present, **or things about to be** — all are yours," (1 Cor. 3:22 YLT).

The rulers of Paul's "this age" were the civil and religious rulers of the old covenant age that had crucified Christ and were "natural" men, unable to discern the spiritual blessings coming under the new covenant creation. They and their system of power and authority were going to "pass away."

Many exegetes are correct to point out that Paul combines the "things" of Isaiah 64:4 with the coming inheritance of the new creation of Isaiah 65:17 in this OT echo. Paul in verses 10-14 teaches that the natural man could not accept these new covenant or new creation "things" that were being revealed by the Spirit because these were "spiritual truths." The natural man cannot understand the things of the Spirit, the new birth or God's people becoming a spiritual "new creation" (2 Cor. 5:17/Isa. 65). The inheritance of the "things" of the new creation of Isaiah 65 were "about to be" received or inherited by the new covenant body of the Church while the rulers of the old covenant "this age" were going to pass away.

2). "Who is wise and understanding among you? By his good conduct let him show his works in the meekness of wisdom. But if you have bitter jealousy and selfish ambition in your hearts, do not boast and be false to the truth. This is not the wisdom that comes down from above, but is **earthly/natural, unspiritual, demonic**. For where jealousy and selfish ambition exist, there will be disorder and every vile practice. But the wisdom from above is first pure, then peaceable, gentle, open to reason, full of mercy and good fruits, impartial and sincere. And a harvest of righteousness is sown in peace by those who make peace" (James. 3:15).

When was the harvest of judgment and righteousness coming?

> "Be patient, therefore, brothers, until the coming of the Lord. See how the farmer waits for the precious fruit of the earth, being patient about it, until it receives the early and the late rains. You also, be patient. Establish your hearts, for the **coming of the <u>Lord is at hand</u>**. Do not grumble against one another, brothers, so that you may not be judged; behold, **the <u>Judge is standing at the door</u>**" (Jms. 5:7-9)

The rich professing Christians were causing division and persecuting the poor Christians in the Church. Some Christians were even getting caught up into natural/earthly thinking that was demonic and from below, not from new covenant living which was "from above." It was important for true Christians to live out their new covenant faith and thus demonstrate that their faith was genuine and without hypocrisy, because the Judge was "at the door" and "at hand." Those who were natural/earthy were like grass and a flower that would soon be burned up or pass away while others would inherit the crown of life (eternal life) at Christ's imminent coming in AD 70 (James. 1:11-12/5:7-9; 1 Pet. 1:24/4:5-7, 17/2 Pet. 3).

3). "It was also about these that **Enoch**, the seventh from Adam, **prophesied**, saying, **"Behold, the Lord comes with ten thousands of his holy ones, to execute judgment** on all and to convict all the ungodly of all their deeds of ungodliness that they have committed in such an ungodly way, and of all the harsh things that ungodly sinners have spoken against him." These are grumblers, malcontents, following their own sinful desires; they are loud-mouthed boasters, showing favoritism to gain advantage. But you must remember, beloved, the predictions of the apostles of our Lord Jesus Christ. They said to you, "**In the last time** there will be scoffers, following their own ungodly passions." It is these who cause divisions, **worldly/carnal/earthy** people, *devoid of the Spirit*. But you, beloved, building yourselves up in your most holy faith and praying in the Holy Spirit, keep yourselves in the love of God, **waiting for the mercy of our Lord Jesus Christ that leads to eternal life**" (Jude 1:19-21).

Judaizers are here described as "carnal" false teachers seeking to place believers back under the Law. 1 Enoch and other Dead Sea Scroll documents predicted that the end of the age judgment of Satan, the Watchers and the wicked would take place in the first century and by AD 70 just as the teachings of Jesus and the NT developed. Very similar to what we just saw in the book of James, being "carnal" or "worldly" has nothing to do with the physical flesh of man, but being corrupted inwardly with sin and being "devoid of the Spirit."

Earthy v Heavenly

The Greek word for "earthy" is only used by Paul here in 1 Corinthians 15:47, 48, 49. However, we can do a study of "heavenly" in the NT to understand what Paul is referring to.

1). "Jesus answered, "Truly, truly, I say to you, unless one is **born of water even the Spirit, he cannot enter the kingdom of God**. That which is born of the flesh is flesh, and that which is born of the Spirit is spirit. Do not marvel that I said to you, '**You must be born from above (or again)**.' The wind[5] blows where it wishes, and you hear its sound, but you do not know where it comes from or where it goes. So, it is with everyone who is born of the Spirit." Nicodemus said to him, "How can these things be?" Jesus answered him, "Are you the teacher of Israel and yet you do not understand these things? Truly, truly, I say to you, we speak of what we know, and bear witness to what we have seen, but you do not receive our testimony. If I have told you earthly things and you do not believe, how can you believe if I tell you **heavenly things** (Jn. 3:5-12)?"

Citizens of the old covenant kingdom were born by flesh and blood, sons of Abraham. But under the new covenant kingdom, one had to be "born from above" through the Spirit and faith in the Messiah/Jesus – "not of flesh and blood, nor of the will of man, **but of God**" (Jn. 1:11-13).

2). "But God, being rich in mercy, because of the great love with which he loved us, even when we were dead in our trespasses, **made us alive together with Christ**—by grace you have been saved—and raised us up with him and seated us with him **in the heavenly places in Christ Jesus**, so that in the **coming ages** he might show the immeasurable riches of his grace in kindness toward us in Christ Jesus. For by grace you have been saved through faith. And this is not your own doing; it is the gift of God, not a result of works, so that no one may boast. For we are his workmanship, created in Christ Jesus for good works, which God prepared beforehand, that we should walk in them" (Eph. 2:4-10).

According to Paul, when would the coming age arrive or when would the full inheritance into this heavenly realm arrive?

"...not only in this age, but also in the **one about to come**" (Ephs. 1:21 WUESTNT).

For Paul, one could experience spiritual resurrection and be in "heavenly places" while being in a physical body. This spiritual existence would continue for the living in the new covenant "age about to" arrive in AD 70. So to be "heavenly" does not mean to undergo a biological change. Paul in 1 Corinthians 15 is teaching that the Church (comprised of the OT dead and the living) was in the process of being raised a "***Spiritual Body***."

3). "But the Lord stood by me and strengthened me, so that through me the message might be fully proclaimed and all the Gentiles might hear it. So, I was rescued from the lion's mouth. The Lord will rescue me from every evil deed and bring me safely into his ***heavenly kingdom***. To him be the glory forever and ever. Amen" (2 Tim. 4:17-18).

Again, within the immediate context, when did Paul see full access into this "heavenly kingdom" to take place?

"I do fully testify, then, before God, and the Lord Jesus Christ, who is ***about to*** judge living and dead at his ***manifestation and his Kingdom***/Reign..." (2 Tim. 4:1 YLT, BLB, LSV).

While Paul had been delivered by the lions of the Jewish persecution, as we have seen elsewhere in his writings and as time progressed, it was revealed to him that he would die and his life would be poured out (martyred). Even if Paul was alive, he understood that he was raised spiritually and currently in "heavenly places," or if he were to die his soul was "about to" experience the inheritance of the "crown of life" (eternal life) and thus the "manifestation of His Kingdom" at Christ's imminent coming. There's no evidence here that to be raised in a spiritual body means to undergo a biological corpse resurrection.

4). "Therefore, holy brothers, you who share in a **heavenly calling**, consider Jesus, the apostle and high priest of our confession, who was faithful to him who appointed him, just as Moses also was faithful in all God's house. For Jesus has been counted worthy of more glory than Moses—as much more glory as the builder of a house has more honor than the house itself. (For every house is built by someone, but the builder of all things is God.) Now Moses was faithful in all God's house as a servant, to testify to the things that were to be spoken later, ⁶ but Christ is faithful over God's house as a son. And **we are his house**, if indeed we hold fast our confidence and our boasting in our hope" (Heb. 3:1-6).

"Thus it was necessary for the copies of the **heavenly things** to be purified with these rites, but the heavenly things themselves with better sacrifices than these. For Christ has entered, not into holy places made with hands, which are copies of the true things, but into heaven itself, now to appear in the presence of God on our behalf. Nor was it to offer himself repeatedly, as the high priest enters the holy places every year with blood not his own, for then he would have had to suffer repeatedly since the foundation of the world. But as it is, he has appeared once for all at the end of the ages to put away sin by the sacrifice of himself. And just as it is appointed for man to die once, and after that comes judgment, so Christ, having been offered once to bear the sins of many, will appear a second time, not to deal with sin but to save those who are eagerly waiting for him" (Heb. 9:23-28).

"But you **have come to Mount Zion and to the city of the living God, the <u>heavenly Jerusalem</u>**, and to innumerable angels in festal gathering, and to the assembly of the firstborn who are enrolled in heaven, and to God, the judge of all, and **to the spirits of the righteous made perfect, and to Jesus, the mediator of a new covenant**, and to the sprinkled blood that speaks a better word than the blood of Abel" (Heb. 12:22-24).

According to the writer of Hebrews, when would the "heavenly Jerusalem/City" arrive?

"For we have no permanent city here, but we are longing for **the <u>city</u> which is <u>soon</u>** to be ours" (Heb. 13:14 Weymouth New Testament, see also "**<u>one about to come</u>**" – Worrell NT; Worsley NT; Smith's Literal Translation)

Through the "heavenly calling" of the gospel, biologically living Christians were already being raised and experiencing and tasting the heavenly realm and calling (having come to or among angels, Christ and the spirits of just men made perfect). Moses was over a physical old covenant "house," while Jesus was an administrator and trailblazer in perfecting the new covenant spiritual "house," which is the body of Christ. In Hebrews 9-10 the spiritual new covenant body is depicted as the "second" (typified as the Most Holy Place house), and when Christ would come in "a very little while and would not delay" in AD 70, the "first" (the "present age" of the old covenant system, or typified as the Holy Place) would not be standing or have legal standing (Heb. 9:1—10:37). This is when the "heavenly Jerusalem/City" that was "soon" or "about to" come did come. Post AD 70, God has raised and filled His spiritual body or house / New Jerusalem / Most Holy Place with His presence (cf. Rev. 21:16—22:17). There was no biological fleshly change or resurrection for the saints to undergo to experience this "better resurrection" under the new covenant. Nor is Paul teaching that a biological resurrection of flesh is necessary to be raised a spiritual or heavenly body in 1 Corinthians 15.

The weakness of Flesh v. Power

1). "Now when Jesus came into the district of Caesarea Philippi, he asked his disciples, "Who do people say that the Son of Man is?" And they said, "Some say John the Baptist, others say Elijah, and others Jeremiah or one of the prophets." He said to them, "But who do you say that I am?" Simon Peter replied, "You are the Christ, the Son of the living God." And Jesus answered him, "Blessed are you, Simon Bar-Jonah! For **<u>flesh and blood</u>** has not revealed this to you, *but my Father who is in heaven*" (Mt. 16:13-17).

The revelation of who Christ is, or entrance into Christ's kingdom, is not something that the power of "flesh and blood" can achieve; it is only something God who is in heaven can grant.

2). "…who were **born, not of blood** nor of the will of the **flesh** nor of the will of man, **but of God**" (John 1:13).

Again, under the old covenant kingdom, one was and could be born of the blood and flesh of Abraham, but under the new covenant kingdom one had to be "born of God", "born from above," and "born of the Spirit." This was and is nothing the power of natural man ("flesh and blood") can achieve.

3). "For I would have you know, brothers, that the gospel that was preached by me is not man's gospel. For I **did not receive it from any man**, nor was I taught it, but **I received it through a *revelation* of Jesus Christ**. For you have heard of my former life in Judaism, how I persecuted the church of God violently and tried to destroy it. And I was advancing in Judaism beyond many of my own age among my people, so extremely zealous was I for the traditions of my fathers. But when he who had set me apart before I was born, and who **called me by his grace**, **was pleased to reveal his Son to me**, in order that I might preach him among the Gentiles, I did not immediately consult with **flesh/anyone**" (Gal. 1:11-16).

Neither "flesh" nor anyone can ultimately be said to bring one into the kingdom. It is solely the work of God and His grace. The power of any man/flesh cannot achieve or bring one into the kingdom ; it is a revelation and birth only God can grant.

Back to the Corporate Body Motif

David Green helps harmonize Paul's corporate body motifs:

> "To find Paul's meaning, we need only find where in Scripture Paul elaborated on the doctrine of a human "body" that had to be sown/planted/entombed and concurrently put to death, in order that it could be made alive and changed in the resurrection of the dead. This takes us to Romans 6-8, Colossians 2, and Philippians 3.
>
> In these Scriptures, especially in Romans 6, Paul teaches that believers had been bodily "planted," through Spirit-baptism, into death / into the death of Christ, in order that the body that had been planted/buried (the "body of Sin," the "mortal body," the "body of Death," the "body of the sins of the flesh," the "vile body") would be abolished / put to death, and then be made alive and changed/conformed to the image of the Son of God in the kingdom of heaven. Note the order: Burial then death.
>
> This sequence in Romans 6 is exactly, step by step, what Paul teaches concerning the resurrection of the body in 1 Cor. 15:36-37 and its context. Romans 6-8 and 1 Corinthians 15 both speak of concurrent body-burial and body-death, followed by consummated body-death, body-resurrection, and body-change. Futurist assumptions notwithstanding, there is no doubt that 1 Corinthians 15 and Romans 6-8 are speaking of the same burial, death, resurrection, and change—and therefore of the same body.

The Body

What then is "the body" that was being put to death in Romans 6-8 and 1 Corinthians 15? What is the meaning of the word "body" in these contexts? Essentially, or basically, the "body" is the "self" or "person/personality" or "individual," whether that of a singular saint or of the singular church universal (the body of Christ).

According to definition 1b of the word σωμα (body) in Arndt and Gingrich's Greek-English Lexicon of the New Testament, the word "body" in Paul's writings is sometimes "almost synonymous with the whole personality . . . σώματα [bodies] =themselves."

Note how that "body" and "yourselves" are used interchangeably in Romans 6:12-13:

Therefore, do not let sin reign in your mortal body that you should obey its lusts, and do not go on presenting your members [of your mortal body] to sin as instruments of unrighteousness; but present yourselves to God as those alive from the dead, and your members [of your mortal body] as instruments of righteousness to God.

Compare also 1 Corinthians 6:15 and 12:27, where "you" and "your bodies" are synonymous:

. . . your bodies are members of Christ . . . . (1 Cor. 6:15)

. . . you are Christ's body, and individually members of it. (1 Cor. 12:27)

See also Ephesians 5:28, where a man's body-union with his wife is equated with "himself":

So, husbands ought also to love their own wives as their own bodies. He who loves his own wife loves himself.

However, the word "body," when it is used in reference to the eschatological resurrection, means more than merely the "self." Paul is not using the word as a common reference to "the whole person."

It does not refer to man's anthropological wholeness (i.e. material body+soul+spirit=the body). Paul is using the word in a theological eschatological sense to describe God's people as they are defined either by the wholeness/fullness (body) of Adamic Sin and Death or the wholeness/fullness (body) of Christ. The body is either the "person" united with Sin and Death, or the "person" united with Christ, whether individually or corporately.

We can begin to see this in Colossians 3:5 (KJV), where the body parts (members) of the Sin-body are not arms and legs or other physical limbs. The members of the "earthly body" were death-producing "deeds," such as "fornication, uncleanness, inordinate affection, evil concupiscence, and covetousness . . . " (cf. Rom. 8:13). Thus, John Calvin wrote in his commentary on Romans 6:6:

"The body of sin . . . does not mean flesh and bones, but the corrupted mass . . . of sin." Since a body is the sum of its parts, and since the parts of the Sin-body are sins/sinful deeds, it follows that "the body of Sin" is not the physical aspect of man.

Instead, the whole of the sins/deeds of the body equals the body of Sin. Or more accurately, the body of Sin was God's people as they were identified with and defined by the Sin-reviving, Sin-increasing, Death-producing world of the Law.

When Paul said that believers were no longer walking according to "the flesh" (Rom. 8:1, 4, 9), he was saying that believers were putting to death the deeds of the "body" (Rom. 8:10-11, 13). The parts/members of the body equaled the deeds of "the body," which equaled the walk of "the flesh." "Flesh" and "body" in this context, therefore, describe man as he was defined by Sin, not man as he was defined by material body parts.

In Colossians 2:11, Paul said that God had buried believers with Christ, raised them up with Him, and had removed "the body of the flesh." "The body of the flesh" was not the physical body. It was the Adamic man/self/person that had been dead in transgressions and in the spiritual uncircumcision of his "flesh" (Col. 2:13). That "body" (or as Ridderbos puts it, that "sinful mode of existence") had been "removed" in Christ and was soon to be changed into the glorious, resurrected "body" of Christ.

As a comparison of Colossians 2:11 and Colossians 3:9 reveals, "the body" of Sin is virtually synonymous with "the old man":

. . . the putting off of the body of the sins of the flesh . . . . (Col. 2:11)

. . . having put off the old man with his practices (Col. 3:9; cf. Eph. 4:22)

Compare also 1 Corinthians 15:42 with Ephesians 4:22:

[The body] is sown in corruption . . . . (1 Cor. 15:42)

. . . the old man being corrupted . . . . (Eph. 4:22)

Compare also the references to "man" and "body" in Romans 7:24:

Wretched man that I am! Who will set me free from this body of Death?

And in Romans 6:6,

Knowing this, that our old man is crucified with him, that the body of sin might be destroyed, that henceforth we should not serve sin. (Rom. 6:6)

And in 1 Corinthians 15:44, 45:

. . . There is a natural body [the old man], and there is a spiritual body [the new Man]. And so it is written, the first [old] man [the natural body] Adam was made a living soul; the last Adam [the last Man, the spiritual body] a quickening spirit.

Since the natural body is nearly synonymous with the old man, we should expect that the spiritual body is nearly synonymous with "the new man," the Lord Jesus Christ. Compare 1 Corinthians 15:53-54 with Ephesians 4:24; Colossians 3:10 and Romans 13:14:

For this perishable [body] must put on the imperishable [body] . . . . (1 Cor. 15:53-54)

and put on the new man [the spiritual body], which in the likeness of God has been created in righteousness and holiness of the truth. (Eph. 4:24)

and have put on the new man [the spiritual body] who is being renewed to a true knowledge according to the image of the One who created him. (Col. 3:10)

But put on the Lord Jesus Christ [the new man, the spiritual body], and make no provision for the flesh in regard to its lusts. (Rom. 13:14)

As most futurists agree, "the old man" and "the new man" are not expressions that describe man in terms of physicality. "The old man" was man as he was in Adam, alienated from God and dead in Sin. He was "the body of Sin." The new Man is man as he is reconciled to God in Christ, the lifegiving Spiritual Body."[273]

The Eschatological Mystery

Elsewhere in Paul's teaching on God's "mystery," he demonstrates how the OT predicted (and the NT revelatory gifts developed) the Jew / Gentile unity in the body of Christ. Here, Paul is demonstrating how the living will be changed and raised with "all" the dead (including the OT dead) together – into the ONE raised and glorified Body of Christ.

The Trumpet Change and Israel's Feasts

While no one disputes that Paul's trumpet change here is the same trumpet catching away in 1 Thessalonians 4:15-17, Partial Preterists object that it is somehow different than Jesus' trumpet gathering at His *Parousia* in Matthew 24:27-31. Of course, this is pure eisegesis on their part and a failure to harmonize Jesus' eschatology with Paul's, as previously demonstrated. While we agree that the coming of Christ in Matthew 24-25 was fulfilled spiritually in AD 70, we disagree with Partial Preterists such as Gary DeMar and Keith Mathison and their un-creedal and unorthodox position that Matthew 24-25 is not the "actual" Second Coming event, and we disagree with their error that Matthew 24-25 is not the same *Parousia* and resurrection event as described for us in 1 Corinthians 15!

---

[273] Green, Hassertt, Sullivan, Ibid., 206-210

Paul is in harmony with Jesus when he says that not everyone in his contemporary audience would die before experiencing Christ's Second Coming trumpet change/gathering into the kingdom (Mt. 16:27-28; 24:30-34/Lk. 21:27-32).

The living would be "changed" not in their physical *biological substance*, but rather in their *covenantal stance* before God. The Adamic and old covenant body of death was natural, weak, mortal, and subject to being perishable. It needed to be clothed and changed by the heavenly man.

The trumpet call at Christ's *Parousia* here is fulfilling multiple OT concepts. It is the trumpet blown at the wedding in Jewish culture that I have discussed in Matthew 24-25.

Jesus has already been described as the "first fruits," so we also have the trumpet being blown to fulfill the first fruits of the harvest / resurrection motif or *Succot* (the feast of harvest).

The blowing the trumpet here also fulfills the typological ceremonial law or the feast of the new moon festival or the feast of trumpets.[274] These last three feasts that were in the ceremonial law had already broken into Paul's "already and not yet" eschaton in Colossians 2-3 and Hebrews 9-12, and they are present here in 1 Corinthians 15 as well. Again, if the trumpet call and resurrection of 1 Corinthians 15 hasn't been fulfilled and the OT Mosaic "the law" (v. 55-56) hasn't been fulfilled, then the Church remains under "every jot and tittle" of the OT Mosaic Law today (Mt. 5:17-19). One cannot posit the end and fulfillment of all of the ceremonial law to be fulfilled at the cross or Pentecost, because the ceremonial feast days composed the entire structure and function for Israel's calendar year. There were three more to be fulfilled post-Pentecost. According to Paul in Colossians and the writer to the Hebrews, those ceremonial type-and-shadow ceremonial laws and feasts were "about to be" fulfilled at Christ's "in a very little while and will not delay" Second Coming (Cols. 2-3; Heb. 9-10:37).

The Perishable to be Clothed with Imperishable – the Mortal with Immortality & 2 Cor. 3-6

Paul is not describing an individual's biological body as being "perishable" and "mortal," but rather the Adamic and Mosaic corporate body as "perishable" and "mortal" needing to be "clothed." To better understand Paul here, again it is important to let him interpret himself.

In 2 Corinthians 3-6 Paul contrasts the glories of the old covenant and new covenant with two houses/temples. In 2 Corinthians 4 the resurrection is in view (vss. 13-14) and closes by expressing that this hope is not grounded on things which can be seen

---

[274] For a good discussion on the present tense found in 1 Corinthians 15 as well as seeing how this chapter fulfills the last three feast days of Israel, see Don K. Preston, *Paul on Trial, PAUL THE PHARISEES AND RESURRECTION* (JanDon, 1405 4th Ave. N.W. #109, Ardmore, OK. 73401, 2020), 95f.

(that are physical and temporal), but on things that cannot be seen (that are spiritual and eternal) (v. 18). The "earthly tent/house/temple" in 5:1 that would be destroyed is the corporate old covenant temple/house/system, and the spiritual "heavenly dwelling/temple/house" is the corporate new covenant system. Their groaning for this house to be revealed from heaven to clothe them is realized in an AD 70 "soon" and "shortly" time frame in the form of the glorified New Jerusalem (which is the corporate body of the Church) coming down from heaven to earth in Revelation 21-22. The NIV correctly captures the "already and not yet" of the New Jerusalem already being in the process of coming down (cf. Rev. 3:12). This already and not yet process is in harmony with the eschatological Pauline process of putting on Christ, being transformed into the image of Christ, dying and rising, looking at God's face spiritually in a dim glass or mirror, a boy maturing into manhood, and here in 1 Corinthians 15 being sown and rising into a spiritual body.

Paul in 2 Corinthians 6:16 further elaborates that the new covenant temple promised in Ezekiel 37:27 (and thus that of 40-47) is the corporate body of the Church. So the corporate and covenantal context between 2 Corinthians 3 extends to chapter 6:16.

The "groaning" to be further clothed in 2 Corinthians 5:2ff., which correlates to the clothing resurrection of 1 Corinthians 15, is the "groaning" and AD 70 imminent "about to be revealing" of God's glory within the Church, which in context results in the full adoption of sons, the liberation of creation (of God's people) and the "redemption of the body" (Rom. 8:18-23YLT).

As we have seen, Gary DeMar admits that the Greek word *mello* in Romans 8:18YLT should be translated as "about to be" and was fulfilled in AD 70. But to admit this is to admit that the events of 18-23 were also fulfilled in AD 70. Lightfoot correctly observed that the "redemption of the BODY" is the corporate body of Christ as in Ephesians 4:13. Of course we agree that there was a corporate bodily change that was "about to be" fulfilled according to Paul, and that was a transformation from groaning in, and being under, the Adamic/Mosaic body of death to be liberated and raised into the glorious and redeemed body of Christ at Christ's coming in AD 70.

Paul's OT Echo's – Hosea 13 / Isaiah 25

As there is a movement within the Reformed and Evangelical community that seeks to develop Paul's Hebraic corporate body origins, which is beginning to see what Full Preterists have seen for the last 30 years, there is also a movement led by Richard Hayes which emphasizes developing the OT context of an OT reference or echo mentioned in the NT. For example, Hayes writes,

> "Thematic Coherence: How well does the alleged echo fit into the line of argument that Paul is developing? Does the proposed precursor text fit together with the point Paul is making? Can one see in Paul's use of the material a

> coherent 'reading' of the source text? Is his use of the Isaiah texts consonant with his overall argument and/or use made of other texts?"[275]

And,

> "Satisfaction: Does the proposed intertextual reading illuminate the surrounding discourse and make some larger sense of Paul's argument as a whole? '...A proposed intertextual reading fulfills the test of satisfaction when we find ourselves saying, "Oh, so that is what Paul means here in passage x; and furthermore, if that's right, then we can begin to understand what he means in passage y and why he uses these certain words in that place."'"[276]

In other words, one is encouraged to find and develop as many similarities between that OT original context and the context and flow of the NT author in order to understand how he is using it. Therefore, it is important to examine what kind of bodily death and resurrection are taking place in Hosea 13 and in Isaiah's little apocalypse (Isaiah 24-28), to help understand Paul's use of them in 1 Corinthians 15:54-55. This will help us understand the kind of bodily resurrection Paul has in mind.

Isaiah 24-28 – Isaiah's Little Apocalypse

Due to Israel breaking her old covenant Mosaic law (primarily for persecuting and putting to death their poor brethren – the sin of blood guilt), Israel's covenantal world undergoes an apocalyptic de-creation and shaking process and she corporately and spiritually dies in the form of being ruled over by Gentile leaders. Through captivity and bondage, Babylon scattered her outside of her land. When Israel repents and is gathered back into the land, she undergoes a spiritual, corporate and covenantal resurrection as described in Ezekiel 37.

In other words, Israel is a corporate Adam, and just as when Adam broke Edenic covenantal law and died a spiritual covenantal death, resulting in him being scattered from God's presence (the garden/temple), so too when Israel broke covenant she underwent a covenantal spiritual death that resulted in her being scattered from God's presence away from her temple and land.

The time of the eschatological wedding is the time of the resurrection (Isa. 25:6-8) and Jesus identifies the time of the wedding as taking place when the Roman armies would judge and burn Jerusalem, or within the AD 30 – AD 70 "this generation" (Mt. 22:1-14; Mt. 24:27-34—25:1-13).

Paul's other reference to Isaiah is his trumpet change which takes place at Christ's *Parousia*, bringing about the resurrection in 1 Corinthians 15:23, 52. This is the trumpet gathering of Isaiah 27:12-13. And, again, this is the OT echo and foundation to the trumpet gathering and trumpet catching away of Matthew 24:30-31 and 1

---

[275] Richard Hays, *The CONVERSION of the IMAGINATION Paul as Interpreter of Israel's Scripture*, (Grand Rapids, MI: Eerdmans Publishing, 2005), 38

[276] Ibid., 41

Thessalonians 4:16-17 that would take place in the AD 30 – AD 70 "this generation," which Paul taught (under inspiration) and thus expected his first century "we" audience to experience.

Hosea

Hosea's context is clear enough as well. Due to Israel's spiritual adultery with Baal and breaking their old covenant law, God gave Israel a certificate of divorcement. The corporate body of Israel breaking the old covenant law resulted not only in a divorce, but it is also described as Israel dying a covenantal and spiritual death. This death is described as God sowing Israel as a seed into the Gentile lands throughout the Assyrian Empire. Once again, we see the same kind of corporate covenantal death that came through Adam and Israel when they broke covenant and became spiritually dead and scattered/separated from God's presence.

But Israel would once again be betrothed and married to God in her "last days." The "last days" are the last days of the old covenant age which ended in AD 70 and is consistent with the "this generation" coming of Christ that results in the eschatological wedding / marriage that takes place in the OT.

Simply put, there is no biological casket resurrection that takes place at the end of world history found in Hosea or Isaiah, which Paul uses as his source for the resurrection in 1 Corinthians 15. The parallels are a spiritual corporate and covenantal resurrection, not an individual biological resurrection. This is consistent with what we have seen earlier when harmonizing Paul with Paul in Romans 5-8 and 1 Corinthians 15.

Victory Over the Mosaic OC "the Law" = Victory Over "the Sin" and "the Death"

Some commentators not only puzzle over the present tense of "the death" in the process of "being destroyed" in Paul's day, but they also puzzle over his reference to the old covenant Mosaic "the law" thrown in with the timing of victory over "the sin" and "the death." These last two references seem to correlate well with the resurrection, but what does the Mosaic old covenant "the law" have to do with it, especially since most Futurists see the old covenant Mosaic law being done away with at the cross or possibly by AD 70?

However, there is no problem for the Full Preterist who correctly sees the resurrection as "about to" take place in Paul's day, bringing an end to the old covenant's "this age" at Christ's "this generation" *Parousia* (Acts 24:15YLT; Mt. 13:39-43; Mt. 24:27-31, 34). When it came to Paul's teaching on the resurrection before his accusers, he claimed he wasn't teaching anything that couldn't be found in the law and prophets – and Hosea 13 / Isaiah 25 / Daniel 12 are resurrection passages contained in the old covenant "the law" and prophets which Jesus said would be fulfilled in the AD 30 – AD 70 "this generation" (cf. Lk. 21:22, 32). Jesus does not posit the old covenant "heaven and earth" of the law and prophets to be fulfilled at the cross, but rather in His generation (Mt. 5:17-18 / Mt. 24:34-35). This is when it was all fulfilled and when that heaven and earth system "soon vanished" (Heb. 8:13).

Death would be swallowed up, and victory over its sting would only be accomplished when victory over "the law" was attained. This was brought to fruition at Christ's first century generation *Parousia* that closed and fulfilled the promises contained in the Mosaic old covenant age of "the law."

Concluding 1 Corinthians 15

After a careful examination of Paul's *modus tollens* logical form of argumenta-tion, it becomes evident that deniers of the resurrection of the dead were not denying Christ's resurrection or those Christians who had died "in Christ" (the new covenant side of the cross). They could hardly be considered as Christians or saints for denying Christ's resurrection. They were in effect denying resurrection to a specific group – the old covenant dead, whom they assumed they had replaced or were not a part of the new covenant body of Christ as they were.

As we have seen, the parallels between Matthew 24 and 1 Corinthians 15 demonstrate that an AD 30 – AD 70 "this generation" and contemporary first century "we" expectation of the *Parousia* and resurrection was realized and fulfilled in AD 70.

When we allowed Paul to interpret himself (using Romans 5-8), we came to a Scriptural understanding of "the [corporate] body" that was in the process of concurrently dying and rising (present tense) and was "about to be" redeemed. The corporate and covenantal context and transformation of the temple/body of 2 Corinthians 3-6 also helped us understand what kind of body the early church was "clothed" with (and continues to be clothed with) at Christ's *Parousia* in AD 70 and beyond.

The examination of Paul's OT texts (Isa. 25 & Hos. 13) to support His resurrection in 1 Corinthians 15 were found to have nothing to do with a casket resurrection of individual biological corpses. Rather, the cohesiveness and harmony for using those OT texts for Paul was to develop a spiritual, corporate and covenantal resurrection to close the old covenant age in AD 70 at Christ's ONE imminent *Parousia*.

When victory over the Mosaic old covenant "the law" came, then victory and resurrection over "the sin" and "the death" was realized. Victory over the old covenant "the law" was realized when all of its promises were fulfilled and/or its "heaven and earth" soon passed away in AD 70 (Lk. 21:22-32; Mt. 5:17-18; Heb. 8:13; 9:26-28; 10:37).

"Orthodox" Postmillennial Partial Preterism teaches that there was a progressive, spiritual, corporate, covenantal resurrection for Israel and the Church between AD 30 – AD 70 which resulted in souls being raised out from the realm of the dead into God's presence at the *Parousia* of Christ in AD 70 (per Dan. 12:1-7,13 and other texts). As we have seen, THIS IS THE resurrection of 1 Corinthians 15! Selah.

Individual Body and Corporate Body

When we read 1 Corinthians 15 or 2 Corinthians 5, it sounds very much like Paul is describing a spiritual individual body as the ONE corporate body of Christ, the Church. And to a degree, I think that is what he is doing. When one died prior to AD 70, we learn that his soul was gathered back to God who created it (Eccl. 12:7). Because Christ had not come, even righteous men were separated from God in Abraham's bosom or Hades. In this state, they were not shadows or ghosts, but had individual, spiritual bodies that reflected the images they had here on earth. God allowed Samuel's soul to be disturbed and come up to visit Saul in 1 Samuel 28:11-20. Here we see that Samuel's soul/spirit had a body that resembled the body and appearance he had while on earth.

We often speak of our aging relatives on their death beds with language such as, "Grandma is in 'her last days'; get a flight out here quickly!" Or "come quickly and say your goodbyes, because 'grandpa is fading away quickly' or 'passing away quickly.'" We realize that there is a transition and transformation that takes place at biological death where the temporal shell of our body goes back to the earth and our spirit or soul (our essence – personality, memories, volition, etc.) receives a different form and can continue in that form forever. In a similar way, the old covenant man/kingdom was never designed to live on this earth forever. He was temporal and would at some point enter into his "last days" and "soon vanish," but at the same time would experience a change or transformation into another form, a spiritual one fit for eternity. God's kingdom is now a kingdom of heaven "not of this world" and we are blessed to be in it. When we die on this side of Christ's Second Coming in AD 70 and the end of the old covenant age, we are blessed to experience this eternal life separated from the distractions of life here on earth. We will have a spiritual body that is recognizable, and will forever live in His majestic presence.

Before leaving the subject of the resurrection, many Futurists have taken 2 Timothy 2:17-18 out of context in order to try and condemn Full Preterism as "heretical." Therefore, before leaving this subject, we should address this crucial passage.

2 Timothy 2:17–18

- *"...and their talk will spread like gangrene. Among them are Hymenaeus and Philetus, who have swerved from the truth, saying that the resurrection has already happened. They are upsetting the faith of some" (2 Tim. 2:17-18).*

Without 2 Timothy 2:17–18, the Futurist doesn't have a biblical leg to stand on in his *condemnation* of Full Preterists.

Far from being an anti-preterist passage, 2 Timothy 2:17–18 is actually a condemnation of the implications of Futurism. Allow me to explain. First of all, Hymenaeus and Philetus were *Judaizers*. They were of a class of deceivers who taught Jewish "myths" and "genealogies" (1 Tim. 1:4; Titus 1:4), and were self-appointed "**teachers of the Law**" (1 Tim. 1:7). They taught believers to abstain from foods (1 Tim. 4:3), no doubt using the Levitical dietary laws as a basis for their teaching.

It is because Hymenaeus and Philetus were Judaizers that Paul compared them to "*Jannes and Jambres*" (2 Tim. 3:8). According to ancient historians, Jannes and Jambres were Egyptian magicians who challenged Moses' authority in Egypt. Like Jannes and Jambres, Hymenaeus and Philetus were teaching the strange doctrines of "Egypt" (Rev. 11:8), and were challenging Paul's gospel-authority, attempting to deceive Christians into believing that God's new wine (the new covenant land of promise) could be contained within the old "Egyptian" wineskins of the old covenant world.

Likewise, in 2 Timothy 2:19, Paul connects Hymenaeus and Philetus to the rebellion of Korah in Numbers 16:5, 26.[277] Korah had led hundreds of the sons of Israel to challenge Moses' authority. As God had destroyed Korah and his followers in the wilderness, so God was *"about to judge"* (2 Timothy 4:1) and destroy the Judaizers, Hymenaeus and Philetus, and others like them (cf. Heb. 3:16–19).

According to the teaching of Hymenaeus and Philetus, because Jerusalem and the temple still stood (in about AD 67) after the resurrection had allegedly already taken place, it irresistibly followed that *"the sons according to the flesh"* were now the heirs of the eternal kingdom and that Paul's Jew-Gentile gospel of grace was a lie. The blasphemous error of Hymenaeus and Philetus was that the world of the Mosaic covenant would remain forever established after the fulfillment of the Law and the Prophets had taken place and the new heavens and new earth (*"the resurrection"*) had arrived.

This "Hymenaean" heresy is the diametric opposite of Full Preterism. According to Preterism, the old covenant came to an eternal and irrevocable termination in *"the resurrection,"* when all things were fulfilled in AD 70. There is absolutely no theological connection between Preterism and Hymenaeus' blasphemous lie of an everlasting *"ministration of death."*

However, there is a clear connection between the heresy of Hymenaeus and the implications of *Futurism*: If *"the Law and the Prophets"* are not fulfilled today, and *"heaven and earth"* have not passed away, and the jots and tittles of the Law have not passed away, and all things are not yet fulfilled, as futurism says, then *logically and scripturally* the Law of Moses remains "imposed" to this day (Matt. 5:17–19; Heb. 8:13; 9:10). This implication of Futurism is *exactly* what the Judaizers, Hymenaeus and Philetus, taught when they said the resurrection was already past in AD 67.

It is also interesting how Paul's apologetic against Hymenaeus and Philetus is similar to that of those in Thessalonica who were teaching that the Day of the Lord had "already" happened (2 Thess. 2:3). Notice Paul says nothing like our opponents try and reason against us, such as,

> "How in the world could you believe anyone teaching that the Second Coming and resurrection have already been fulfilled in AD 70?!? Just look around. We are still here, so the rapture hasn't taken place, has it? Corpses are still in the graveyards, aren't they? The planet hasn't been burned up and everything isn't perfect yet, is it? So how in the world could you believe the Second Coming and resurrection has already been fulfilled or is a past event?"

---

[277] William Hendriksen; Simon J. Kistemaker: *New Testament Commentary: Exposition of the Pastoral Epistles* (Grand Rapids, MI: Baker Book House, 1953–2001), 268.

Futurists constantly feel that these "just look around; there's no physical manifestations of the kingdom" type "arguments" are their first and best appeals at refuting Full Preterism and yet Paul never used them. Why? Because Paul was a Full Preterist and understood that the Second Coming and resurrection were spiritual and unseen events and that they were "about to be" fulfilled in his future. Paul had no beef with those teaching that these were spiritual events. He just refuted the timing of their teaching (AD 70 and the destruction of the temple were still future to Paul and his audience) and their connections with the heresy of the Judaizers seeking to usurp his authority and the Torah-free gospel he preached.

Chapter Eight:

How was the "Rapture" Fulfilled by AD 70?

Laying the context of 1 Thessalonians 4:15-17

1 Thessalonians 1:10

"…for they themselves report what kind of reception you gave us. They tell how you turned to God from idols to serve the living and true God, and to **wait** for his **Son from heaven**, whom he raised from the dead—Jesus, who **rescues us** from the **coming wrath**" (1 Thess. 1:9-10).

"Wait" with eager expectation

The Thessalonians were to *eagerly wait* for Christ. The definition of "wait" (Greek *anaménō*) has to do with an eager anxiousness coupled with a confident trust to complete a process. In this case it involves confidence in trusting Christ's promise to come and vindicate and rescue the first century Thessalonians.

Dispensational Zionist pastor, John MacArthur, writes of this passage:

> "…the immanency of the deliverance was something Paul **felt** could happen in their lifetimes."[278]

Did Paul **just "feel"** that it could happen or did he write it as an **inspired and authoritative apostle being 'led into all truth," trusting** in the very words of Jesus Himself that He would return at the end of the old covenant age, in their generation, and in some of their lifetimes (Matt. 10:22-23; 16:27-28; 24:27-34)?!?

"From heaven"

The definition of "heaven" here can mean the literal sky and clouds where the birds fly, but in Pauline eschatology the term "from heaven" is primarily dealing with God's heavenly dwelling where His presence is along with the angelic hosts.

To "rescue" the Thessalonians to Himself

The definition of rescue here is "*rhýomai* (from *eryō*, "draw *to oneself*") – properly, draw or (pull) *to oneself*; to rescue ("snatch up"); to draw or rescue a person *to and for the deliverer*. To draw or snatch from danger, rescue, deliver." This is more with the

---

[278] John MacArthur, *The MacArthur Study Bible* (Nashville, TN: Thomas Nelson, 1997), 1843

meaning of drawing to one's self rather than merely rescuing from someone or something.[279]

From the *"coming wrath"*

God laid a trap for the Jews who were persecuting the Thessalonians in that they went to Jerusalem for the feast days in and around AD 66/67 in order to experience His wrath. Christians that did go to Jerusalem to fellowship with the Jerusalem Church in AD 66/67 fled the city and were rescued from this wrath.

Jews who especially sympathized with the Jewish revolt were persecuted throughout Rome during this period – 50,000 died in Egypt alone. Christians were known for being peaceful law-abiding citizens contrary to their Zealot counterparts.

Paul's doctrine on an imminent first century coming of Christ and wrath to be poured out upon their persecuting enemies is in line with *Jesus' teaching in Luke 21:20-23 and Matthew 23. This is also the same "wrath" that was "about to come" upon the Pharisees, according to John the Baptist's eschatology (Mt. 3:7-12 GNT).*

Partial Preterists, such as Gary DeMar, concede that the coming of Christ here in 1 Thessalonians 1:10 was fulfilled in AD 70. But Gary fails to do any exegetical work to harmonize his Preterist interpretation of 1 Thessalonians 1:10 with his futurist creedal view of 1 Thessalonians 4:15-17. In both passages, Christ comes "from heaven" to "snatch" or "catch" away His people to Himself. On what exegetical grounds is the first passage apocalyptic while the latter passage is supposed to be a physical biological transformation?!? Why would the Thessalonians think that these are two different comings of Christ "from heaven" to "snatch" or "catch" His people to Himself?

1 Thessalonians 1:10	1 Thessalonians 4:14-17
1). First century audience – "you", "us"	1). First century audience – "we."
2). Eager expectation – imminence	2). "We who are *still alive…*" – imminent expectation
3). Christ comes "from heaven."	**3). Christ comes "from heaven"**
4). Jesus' resurrection is mentioned as a sign or event guaranteeing that the living would be rescued	4). Jesus' resurrection is mentioned as a sign or event guaranteeing the dead in Christ would be raised and the living would be brought into God's presence
5). "Snatches" from wrath but *to Christ*.	**5). "Catches/snatches away"** *to Christ*

---

[279] (Zodhiates, S. (2000). *The complete word study dictionary: New Testament* (electronic ed.). Chattanooga, TN: AMG Publishers).

1 Thessalonians 2:14-20

> "For you, brethren, became imitators of the churches of God in Christ Jesus that are in Judea, for you also endured the same sufferings at the hands of your own countrymen, even as they did **from the Jews**, who both killed the Lord Jesus and the prophets, and drove us out. They are not pleasing to God, but hostile to all men, forbidding us to speak to the nations that they might be saved, **to fill up their sins always**, but the anger **did come (past tense)** upon them – [even] **to the end**! "…For we wanted to come to you—certainly I, Paul, did, again and again—but Satan stopped us. For who is our hope or joy or crown of exultation? Is it not even you, in the presence of our Lord Jesus **at His coming**? For you are our glory and joy" (1 Thess. 2:14-16, 19-20).

We learn several things about this passage in connection with chapter 1.

The "waiting process" of 1:10 is further clarified in chapter two as waiting for their Jewish persecutors to "fill up the measure of their sins" before Christ comes to execute this wrath.

The YLT and JFB catch something interesting about this wrath, in that it had already begun and is actually in the past tense – "forbidding us to speak to the nations that they might be saved, to fill up their sins always, but the anger **did come (past tense)** upon them – [even] **to the end**! (1 Thess. 2:16).

Speaking about the past tense here, JFB says:

> "[This is] not merely partial wrath, but wrath to its full extent, "even to the finishing stroke" [Edmunds]. The past tense implies that the fullest visitation of wrath was already begun. Already in A.D. 48, a tumult had occurred at the Passover in Jerusalem, when about thirty thousand (according to some) were slain; a foretaste of the whole vengeance which speedily followed (Lu 19:43, 44; 21:24)."[280]

*Was this the event or perceived "Day of the Lord" judgment that the false teachers and prophets were saying had "already" been fulfilled in 2 Thessalonians 2? 1 & 2 Thessalonians were written between AD 50-52. The Judaizers wanted a "Christianity" with the Mosaic Law to continue. So they needed a "Day of the Lord" that did not involve doing away with the temple system.

This "wrath" would be fully realized at **"the end"** [or the wrath that would be poured out at "the time of the end" or end of the old covenant age (cf. Dan. 12:4; Mt. 13:39-43; Mt. 24:3ff.)]. Paul is in perfect harmony with Jesus' teaching:

---

[280] *Jamieson-Fausset-Brown Bible Commentary*, free online, https://biblehub.com/commentaries/1_thessalonians/2-16.htm

Matthew 23-24	1 Thessalonians 1-2
1). Prediction of persecution, suffering & death	1). Present persecution & suffering
2). The Jews killed the prophets, Jesus predicts His death (cf. Lk. 17:25), and that of the deaths of the NT prophets He would send in that generation	2). The Jews killed Jesus & the prophets
3). Jesus pronounces seven "woes" upon the Jews	3). Paul says the Jewish persecutors are not pleasing to God
4). Jews sought to hinder Christ from "gathering" and preaching the gospel to Jerusalem's "children" so that they could be saved	4). Jews sought to hinder Paul from preaching the gospel so that others might be saved
5). The Jews were "filling up the measure of their sin"	**5) Paul says the Jews were "filling up the measure of their sins"**
6). Christ was going to come (Gk. *Parousia* – implied from heaven) to deliver Christians and render wrath and judgment upon that first century Jewish audience and upon their temple – in their "this generation"	6). Christ was going to come (Gk. *Parousia* – from heaven) to deliver Christians and render wrath and judgment upon that first century Jewish audience
7) The coming of Christ in salvation and wrath takes place at "the end (*Greek Telos*) of the age" (of the old covenant age)	**7). The coming of Christ in salvation and wrath upon persecutors takes place at "the end" (*Greek Telos*)**
8) Judgment of living (those Pharisees) and dead (judging Cain for Abel's blood) & gathering of all the elect at the trumpet call – in their "this generation"	**8) Judgment of the living**

1 Thessalonians 3:13

> "May he strengthen your hearts so that you will be **blameless and holy** in the presence of our God and Father when our Lord Jesus comes with all his holy ones" (1 Thess. 3:13).

"Blameless" or "spotless"

The Thessalonians would be *blameless (or "spotless")* and *holy* at Christ's *Parousia*. Paul is using the eschatological marriage terminology here of *blameless / holy – without spot*. Keith Mathison writes of this passage in connection with the resurrection:

> "Paul teaches that all believers will be resurrected at Christ's second coming (1 Cor. 15:23). He teaches that all believers will be presented as a spotless bride at *that* time (Eph. 5:25-27; cf. **1 Thess. 3:13**)."[281]

However, as usual, Partial Preterists have a hard time agreeing what passages about the coming of the Lord were fulfilled in AD 70 and which ones are allegedly going to be fulfilled at the end of world history. For example, unlike Mathison, Gary DeMar admits that 1 Thessalonians 3:10 was fulfilled in AD 70. So, if 1 Thessalonians 3:10 is a wedding Parousia/resurrection text inseparably connected to 1 Corinthians 15:23, and yet 1 Thessalonians 3:10 was fulfilled in AD 70, then the Parousia of 1 Corinthians 15:23 was also fulfilled in AD 70 (A=B).

And as we saw earlier, if men like Mathison believe the coming of Christ and wedding or wedding feast of Matthew 8:10-12; 22:2-7; 25:1-13; Revelation 19-21 was fulfilled in AD 70, how does this coming of Christ and wedding motif get magically pushed thousands of years away into another wedding and coming of Christ? Partial Preterists simply offer no explanation.

Christ comes "with all his holy ones" (angels, people, or both)?

First view – Angels: The argument that Christ is coming with angels as His "holy ones" is in how the LXX of Zech. 14:5 is understood (from which this passage and **Mt. 25:31** are derived). *Angelic beings* is how the term is understood in the OT (ex. Job 5:1; 15:15; Ps. 89:5, 7; Dan. 8:13) and in the texts of the intertestamental period (e.g. 1 Enoch 1:9) depicting God's angels as being present on the last day of judgment.

Although the key word "holy ones" is not used in 2 Thessalonians 1:7, but rather the noun form is used to say that Christ comes with His "powerful angels," the concept is the same.

Second view – Saints/people: In 2 Thessalonians 1:10, Christ comes to be glorified "in" His "holy ones," which are people "who have believed," the passage states.

Third view – "all" here refers to both people & angels: Some commentators suggest that both are in view. This is my view after looking at what the OT says, what the intertestamental period teaches, and finally what the NT teaches on the subject.

Let's once again get the contextual flow of Paul's teaching on the coming of the Lord in the previous chapters leading into 1 Thessalonians 4, which demonstrates that Paul only has one coming of the Lord in view here. And if some Partial Preterists are willing to admit that the coming of Christ in 1 Thessalonians 1-3, and even in chapter 5, was fulfilled in AD 70, there is no exegetical evidence to support the idea that the coming of Christ in 1 Thessalonians 4 is a different coming.

---

[281] Mathison, *Postmillennialism*, Ibid., 177

1 Thessalonians 1:10—3:13	1 Thessalonians 4:14-17
1). First century audience – **"you"**, **"us"**	1). First century audience – **"we"**
2). Eager expectation – **imminence**	2). "We who are **still alive…**" – **imminent expectation**
3). Christ comes **"from heaven"**	3). Christ comes **"from heaven"**
4). **Jesus' resurrection** is mentioned as a sign or event guaranteeing that the living would be rescued	4). **Jesus' resurrection** is mentioned as a sign or event guaranteeing the dead in Christ would be raised and the living would be "caught" away into God's presence
5). To be **"snatched"** away from wrath but *to Christ*	5). To be **"caught"** away *to Christ*
6). Christ comes (Greek ***Parousia***)	6). Christ comes (Greek ***Parousia***).
7). **"The end"** (*Greek Telos)* here is Daniel's "time of the end," or at the "end of the age" when the judgment and resurrection takes place (cf. Dan. 12:1-13; Mt. 13:39-43; Mt. 24:30-31; and 1 Cor. 15:24)	7). No one disputes that the resurrection here is the resurrection to take place at **"the end"** in Daniel 12:1-7 or "the end" (***Greek Telos***) in 1 Corinthians 15:24
8). Christ's coming is described with **wedding terminology;** they were to be **"spotless"** or **"blameless"** and "holy" in coming into the presence of their coming Groom	8). Paul uses a well-known **wedding term** in which a bride would **"meet"** her groom
9). Christ comes **with all His "holy ones"** – that is, angels **and the dead** he raises in chapter 4 which constitute the rest of the bride	9). Christ comes **with those dead saints** that He raised out of Abraham's bosom or Hades to go "meet" them so that they all could be "with the Lord forever

And since so many agree with us that Paul is simply following Jesus' eschatology in Matthew 23-24 or Luke 21, let's get a visual of these parallels:

1 Thessalonians 1:10—3:13	Matthew 23-24/Luke 21
1). First century audience **"you"**, **"us"**	1). First century audience **"you"**
2). Eagerly wait – **imminence**	2). **"This generation" "near" "at the door"**
3). Christ comes (*Greek **Parousia***)	3). Christ comes (*Greek **Parousia***).
4). Christ comes **from heaven.**	4). Christ comes **on clouds**.
5). To **"snatch"** from wrath *to Christ*	5). To **"gather"** *to Christ*
6). Delivers **from wrath**	6). Saves **from wrath**
7). Jews killed prophets and Jesus & currently persecuting Thessalonians	7). Jews killed prophets & will kill NT prophets Jesus sends (e.g. to Thessalonica)
8). **Jews filling up the measure of their sin** of blood guilt	8). **Jews filling up the measure of their sin** of blood guilt
9). Wrath poured out at **"the end"** (***Greek Telos***)	9). Wrath poured out at **"the end"** or "end of the age" (***Greek Telos***)

10). Christ comes **with all His holy ones** (including angels **and the dead per chapter 4**) – which constitute the rest of the bride	10). Christ comes and sends his angels to **gather all the elect (dead and living)**
11). Christ's coming is described with **wedding terminology** – they were to be **"spotless," "blameless"** and **"holy"** in order to come into the presence of their coming Groom	11). Christ's coming is described with **wedding terminology** – "Here's the bridegroom! Come out and **meet** Him."

1 Thessalonians 4:15-17

- *"For this we say to you by the word of the Lord, that we who are alive and remain until the coming of the Lord will by no means precede those who are asleep. For the Lord Himself will descend from heaven with a shout, with the voice of an archangel, and with the trumpet of God. And the dead in Christ will rise first. Then we who are alive and remain shall be caught up together with them in the clouds to meet the Lord in the air. And thus, we shall always be with the Lord" (1 Thess. 4:15-17).*

A day was approaching when Christ would deliver believers from their persecutions and pour out His wrath upon their persecutors (1 Thess. 1:10; cf. 2 Thess. 1:6–7). When that day came, the Lord descended from heaven with a word of command (or "a shout"), with an archangelic voice, and with a trumpet call of God; and the dead in Christ rose. Then the living in Christ and the dead in Christ were simultaneously "caught up" in "clouds" to "a meeting of the Lord in the air."

Since the cloud-covered mountain is not literal, but is heavenly, neither then was the meeting that took place in the heavenly mountain (i.e., in the clouds in the air) literal. Therefore, the shout, voice, trumpet, mountain, cloud, and meeting of 1 Thessalonians 4:16 are all spiritual antitypes of the literal shout, voice, trumpet, mountain, cloud, and meeting of Exodus 19 and 20 (Heb. 12:18–22).

What we have then in 1 Thessalonians 4:15–17 is the "rapturously" metaphorical language of a prophet who is speaking of antitypical, spiritual realities —the transcendent profundities of Christological glory in and among the saints in the consummation of the ages. If this sounds

like an over-spiritualization, it shouldn't. The Lord Jesus Himself was opposed to a literal removal of the church out of the world:

- "I do not ask You to take them out of the world, but to keep them from the evil one" (John 17:15).

The "rapture" passage is no more literal than the prophecy of Ezekiel 37:4–14. In that passage, God caused a valley full of dry bones to come together. He attached tendons to them and put skin on them. Then He caused the bodies to breathe and they stood on their feet as a vast army. The bones represented the house of Israel. They were hopelessly cut off from the land, and were said to be in "graves." As God had done for the dry bones, He was going to do for the house of Israel.

In the same way, in 1 Thessalonians 4:15–17, God raised up His church —the first fruits of the resurrection harvest— which was anxiously longing for the consummation of redemption and atonement. As a mighty warrior, the Lord issued forth his shout of command and sounded the trumpet of God. Then His spiritual army arose by His power. They met Him on His way to His temple to judge the enemies in His kingdom (Mal. 3:1). That is when God afflicted the persecutors of His church, when He gave His people relief and glorified Himself in them (2 Thess. 1:8–10).

Being revealed with Christ in glory (Col. 3:4) and becoming like Him and seeing Him in His Parousia (1 Jn. 3:2) had nothing to do with escaping physical death or with being literally caught up into the literal sky or with being **biologically** changed. It had to do with God's people, living and dead, being "gathered together" to become His eternal tabernacle, His spiritual body, the new man, the heavenly Mount Zion, and the New Jerusalem in the Spirit. "This mystery is great" (Eph. 5:32), and is therefore communicated in the accommodative "sign language" of prophetic metaphor.

Since our Lord came "with His saints" and destroyed the earthly temple in AD 70 (Heb. 9:8), the church of all ages lives and reigns in glory with Him forever (Rom. 6:8; 2 Cor. 13:4; 2 Tim. 2:11–12). Now whether we are alive or asleep, we "live together with Him" (1 Thess. 5:10). This was not the case in the OT, when to die was to be cut off from the people of God. As Paul says in Romans 14:8–9, "…whether we live or die, we are the Lord's. For to this end Christ died and rose and lived again, that He might be Lord both of the dead and of the living."

- *"According to the Lord's own word" (4:15)*

Reformed theologian G.K. Beale agrees with Full Preterism on two issues here. First, he agrees that Paul is using recapitulation between 1 Thessalonians 4-5 (or that both chapters describe the same coming of Christ and eschatological event). Secondly, he agrees with us that Paul is drawing from Jesus' teaching in Matthew 24:

> "…1 Thess. 4:15-17 describes generally the same end-time scenario as 1 Thess. 5:1-11. Specifically, Paul narrates the resurrection at the end of the age and then **recapitulates** in chapter 5 by speaking about the timing of this event and about the judgment on unbelievers, which will also happen at the same time. That both 4:15-18 and 5:1-11 explain the same events **is discernible from observing that both passages actually form one continuous depiction of the same narrative in Matthew 24**,…"[282]

As I have previously demonstrated, Jesus used recapitulation in Matthew 24-25. In Matthew 24:30-31, Jesus' coming is describing the gathering or resurrection of believers. In Matthew 25:31-46, His coming includes a judgment (and thus

---

[282] G.K. Beale, *The IVP New Testament Commentary Series 1–2 Thessalonians* (Downers Grove, IL: Inter Varsity Press, 2003), 136, emphasis added

resurrection) for the unbelieving dead as well. So, it should not surprise us that Paul is using recapitulation here to connect

1 Thessalonians 4-5. In 4:16-17 the emphasis on His coming is the resurrection of believers. In chapter 5 His coming includes the judgment for unbelievers. One has to be blind not to notice what Beale and Full Preterists see:

> "…both passages [1 Thess. 4-5] actually form one continuous depiction of the same narrative in Matthew 24…"[283]

And yet one has to be equally blind not to notice that Jesus' places this coming in His generation, and this is why Paul is teaching that Christ would come in the lifetime of his contemporaries.

Beale goes on to connect 1 Thessalonians 4-5 with Matthew 24:

> "Other significant **parallels** include: the use of the word Parousia for Christ's coming; reference to Christ's advent as "that day" (Mt. 24:36) or "the day of the Lord" (1 Thess. 5:2); and a description of someone coming to "meet" another (eis apantesin autou, virgins coming out to "meet" the bridegroom in Mt. 25:6; eis apantesin tou kyriou, believers "meeting" the Lord in 1 Thess. 4:17; see further Waterman 1975)."[284]

Once again, the eschatological time of the wedding creates problems for Pre-tribulational Zionists or Partial Preterists. How many eschatological weddings are there?

In the *Reformed Study Bible* edited by Partial Preterists R.C. Sproul and Keith Mathison, we learn this of the connections between Matthew 24:30-31 and 1 Thessalonians 4:15-17:

> "But the language of Matt. 24:31 is **parallel** to passages like 13:41; 16:27; and 25:31 [passages which Postmillennialists such as Mathison and DeMar say were fulfilled in AD 70], as well as to passages such as 1 Cor. 15:52 and 1 Thess. 4:14-17. The passage most naturally refers to the Second Coming."

This is more than a bit odd since R.C. Sproul and Keith Mathison believe and teach that the coming of Christ in Matthew 24:27-30 (and Matthew 25:31) was spiritually fulfilled in AD 70 – and yet we learn in their own Study Bible that these passages "most naturally refer to the Second Coming"!

John Murray, appealing to the "analogy of faith" principle of interpretation in examining Matthew 24:30-31, also connects it to the same event as Paul teaches us here:

> "There is ample allusion to the sound of the trumpet and to the ministry of angels elsewhere in the New Testament in connection with Christ's advent (1

---

[283] Ibid.

[284] Ibid, 136–137

Cor. 15:52; 1 Thess. 4:16). **Hence verse 31 can most readily be taken to refer to the gathering of the elect at the resurrection."**[285]

Let's once again get the visual of what Beale, Murray and The Reformation Bible are seeing that we do too:

If A (Matthew 24) is = B (1 Thessalonians 4)		
Christ returns from heaven	24:30	4:16
With voice of arch angel	24:31	4:16
With trumpet of God	24:31	4:16
Caught/gathered together with/to Christ	24:31	4:17
"Meet" the Lord in the clouds	24:30 & 25:6	4:17
Exact time unknown	24:36	5:1-2
Christ comes as a thief	24:43	5:2
Unbelievers caught off guard	24:37-39	5:3
Time of birth pangs	24:8	5:3
Believers not deceived	24:43	5:4-5
Believers to be watchful	24:42	5:6
Exhorted to sobriety	24:49	5:7
Son/sunlight shining from east to west / Sons of the Day	24:27, 36, & 38	5:4-8
And if B (1 Thessalonians 4) is = to C (1 Corinthians 15)		
The sleeping to be raised	4:13-14	15:12-18
The living to be caught/changed	4:15-17	15:51-52
Christ's coming (Greek: *Parousia*)	4:15	15:23
At the sound of the trumpet	4:16	15:52
Encouraged to stand firm	4:18	15:58
Same contemporary "we"	4:15-17	15:51-52
Then A (Matthew 24 & Parallels) is = to C (1 Corinthians 15)		
Christ to come (Greek: *Parousia*)	24:27	15:23
His people to be gathered/changed	24:31	15:52
To come with the sound of a trumpet	24:31	15:52
To be "the end" (Greek *telos*, the goal)	24:3, 14	15:24
Kingdom consummation (goal reached)	Luke 21:30-32	15:24
All prophecy fulfilled at this point	Luke 21:22	15:54-55
Victory over the Mosaic Law/temple	Mt. 24:1	15:55-56
Same contemporary "you" or "we"	Mt. 24:2ff	15:51-52

---

[285] John Murray, Ibid., 391, emphasis MJS

Two or More Things that are Equal to Another Thing are Also Equal to Each Other		
Matthew 24	**1 Thessalonians 4**	**1 Corinthians 15**
At His coming (24:27-31)	At His coming (4:16)	At His coming (15:23)
At the trumpet (24:31)	At the trumpet (4:16)	At the trumpet (15:52)
Dead raised, all gathered (24:31)	Dead raised (4:16)	Dead raised (15:35-44)
All living gathered (24:31)	Living caught together to Him (4:17)	Status of living changed (15:51)

We readily and clearly can see that Paul is following Jesus' teaching in the Olivet Discourse, but we can also see and agree with the Partial Preterist that the coming of Christ and gathering of the elect are spiritual events fulfilled in Jesus' contemporary "this generation."

- *"...WE who are still alive, who are left till the coming of the Lord..." (v. 16)*

If I were to say, "We who live long enough to see the year 2030," there is no reason to think that I would be assuming that I myself would be among the living in 2030. My only assumption would be that some of us today would be alive in 2030. In the same way, Paul's words imply only that he knew that some of his contemporaries would still be alive when Christ returned, as Christ Himself promised would be the case in Matthew 16:27–28; 24:34.

According to Partial Preterists such as Gary DeMar, all of Paul's "we," "you," and "our" statements in 1 and 2 Thessalonians refer to Paul's own first-century audience and address Christ's coming in AD 70—except for the statements in 1 Thessalonians 4 ("the rapture"). These men magically decide that "we" in 1 Thessalonians 4 means something other than what it means everywhere else in 1 and 2 Thessalonians. Suddenly in chapter 4, "we" includes Christians who potentially will not be alive for a million years from today. Now let us move on from arbitrary constructs of Partial Preterism to a biblical look at "the rapture" passage, 1 Thessalonians 4:15–17.

- *"For the Lord himself will come down from heaven..." (v. 16)*

How had God described His "coming down from heaven" to "reveal Himself" (2 Thess. 2:7) and "rescue" (1 Thess. 1:10) His people being persecuted in the past? Notice how David describes God coming down from heaven to rescue him from his enemies:

> "In my distress I called to the LORD; I cried to my God for help. From his temple he heard my voice; my cry came before him, into his ears. **The earth trembled and quaked** (literally?), and **the foundations of the mountains shook** (literally?); they trembled because he was angry. Smoke rose from his nostrils (literally?); **consuming fire came from his mouth** (remember 2 Thess. 1:7 – Jesus is "revealed **from heaven in blazing fire**…"), burning coals blazed out of it. He parted the heavens and came down (literally?); dark clouds were under his feet. He mounted the cherubim and flew; he soared on the wings of

the wind. He made darkness his covering, his canopy around him— the dark rain clouds of the sky. Out of the brightness of his presence clouds advanced (literally?), with hailstones and bolts of lightning. The LORD thundered from heaven; the voice of the Most High resounded (a literal voice?). He shot his arrows and scattered the enemy, with great bolts of lightning he routed them. The valleys of the sea were exposed and the foundations of the earth laid bare (literally?) at your rebuke, LORD, at the blast of breath from your nostrils. **He reached down from on high and <u>took hold of me</u>; he <u>drew me</u> out of deep waters. He <u>rescued</u> me from my powerful enemy, from my foes, who were too strong for me**" (Ps. 18:6-17).

Christ is coming here in 1 Thessalonains 4:16-17 as God had come from heaven and on the clouds in the OT, as we discussed in our exegesis of the Olivet Discourse. If the Church is willing to admit that the coming of Christ in Matthew 24-25 was fulfilled spiritually with Jesus, describing His coming using common apocalyptic language of the prophets, and the Church is willing to admit that Paul's teaching of Christ's coming here in 1 Thessalonians 4-5 is the same event as described by Jesus in Matthew 24-25, THEN it is no stretch to understand that Paul likewise is using common apocalyptic language of the prophets and that 1 Thessalonians 4-5 was also fulfilled in AD 70 just as Matthew 24-25 was.

In fact NT Wright comes very close to admitting that all of the language of 1 Thessalonians 4:16-17 is common apocalyptic language:

> "Unfortunately it [the language of 1 Thess. 4:16] is also a highly contentious passage, being used with **astonishing literalness** in popular fundamentalism and critical scholarship alike to suggest that Paul **envisaged Christians flying around in mid-air on clouds**. The **multiple apocalyptic resonances of the passage on the one hand, and its glorious mixed metaphors on the other, make this interpretation highly unlikely**."[286]

We couldn't agree more with Mr. Wright in that Paul is using common apocalyptic language. Yet it is not figurative language of a physical resurrection at the end of world history, but rather figurative language of a spiritual resurrection by which souls are raised out of Hades into God's presence, and of God's presence "meeting" the living within their hearts while on earth (cf. Lk. 17:20-37). If it is agreed by the Partial Preterist that the language of Jesus in Matthew 24:30-31 is describing Christ's non-literal coming, on non-literal clouds, with a non-literal trumpet sound, and that the "gathering" is an inward resurrection of giving eternal life that the gospel produces (no biological change), while others correctly see Matthew 24:30-31 and 1 Thessalonians 4:15-17 to be the same event, then we suggest the "catching away" for the living is not into physical clouds (as Wright admits), but is God producing the consummative giving of His presence and of eternal life to His saints while here on earth.

---

[286] N.T. Wright, *THE RESURRECTION OF THE SON OF GOD Christian Origins and the Question of God, vol. 3* (Minneapolis, MN: 2003), 215, emphasis MJS

OT Echo to 1 Thessalonians 4:16

Other than the trumpet gathering and resurrection of Isaiah 27:12-13 (which I have addressed already), G.K. Beale and D.A. Carson connect this coming of the Lord "from heaven" with Isaiah 2:10-12's "in that day", "Day of the Lord" judgment:

> "The main clause of 1 Thess. 4:16, "because the Lord himself will come down from heaven," recalls…the prophetic literature of the OT that envisions "the day of the Lord," when God will come to judge the wicked and save the righteous (**Isa. 2:10–12**;…)."[287]

But they also connect 2 Thessalonians 1:7-9 with Isaiah 2, which reads:

> "This (in context – giving the Thessalonians relief from their Jewish persecutors) will happen when the Lord Jesus *is revealed from heaven* in blazing fire with his powerful angels. He will punish those who do not know God and do not obey the gospel of our Lord Jesus. They will be punished with everlasting destruction and shut out (excommunicated [from the heavenly temple] as they had done to the Christians) *from the presence of the Lord and from the glory of his might.*"[288]

On this passage, Beale and Carson write,

> "…eternal destruction from the presence of the Lord and from the glory of his might." This description clearly echoes the triple refrain of **Isa. 2:10, 19, 21**, where on **the day of the Lord** the wicked are commanded to **hide themselves behind rocks and in caves "from the presence of the Lord and from the glory of his might whenever he will rise to terrify the earth.**"[289]

So, since both 1 Thessalonians 4:16 and 2 Thessalonians 1:7-9 fulfill the coming of the Lord "from heaven" in the judgment found in Isaiah 2, let me remind the reader that Jesus appeals to this same OT passage and understands it to be fulfilled by AD 70:

> "And there followed him a great multitude of the people and of women who were mourning and lamenting for him. But turning to them Jesus said, "Daughters of Jerusalem, do not weep for me, but weep for yourselves and for your children. For behold, the days are coming when they will say, 'Blessed are the barren and the wombs that never bore and the breasts that never nursed!' **Then they will begin to say to the mountains, 'Fall on us,' and to the hills, 'Cover us"** (from Isa. 2:19 and Hos. 10:8) (Lk. 23:27-30).

There's a consensus among the commentators that this passage was fulfilled in God's judgment upon Jerusalem in AD 70. We have found plenty of exegetical evidence that Paul too identifies the Lord coming in the judgment of Isaiah 2 to be fulfilled by AD

---

[287] Weima, J. A. D. (2007). 1-2 Thessalonians. In *Commentary on the New Testament use of the Old Testament* (Grand Rapids, MI; Nottingham, UK: Baker Academic; Apollos), 880, emphasis MJS

[288] Ibid., emphasis MJS

[289] Ibid., 885, emphasis MJS

70. As we saw earlier, even John in Revelation 6:15-17 appeals to the coming of the Lord in His wrath in Isaiah 2 to be fulfilled "in a very little while" to avenge the first century martyrs in AD 70 (cf. Rev. 6:11-17).

- *"...with the trumpet call of God and the dead in Christ will rise first." (v. 16)*

There is definitely a chronological order, with the dead rising first and then the gathering, catching away or change for the living taking place second. Even Jesus addresses the dead first in John 11:

> *"I am the resurrection and the life. Whoever believes in me, though he die [OT worthies like Abraham or Daniel, along with those who recently died prior to AD 70], yet shall he live [be raised out of Abraham's bosom or Hades to inherit God's presence and eternal life], and everyone who lives and believes in me shall never die [that is not that they would never see biological death, but rather inherit God's "within" kingdom and presence of eternal life]. Do you believe this (John 11:25-26)?"*

We agree with the scholarship of G.K. Beale who correctly understands the gathering of the elect at the end of the age in Matthew 24:3, 30-31 in his commentary on 1 & 2 Thessalonians as the resurrection event:

> "Paul's particular combination of references from Matthew 24 shows that he interprets the whole of the Matthean text as referring to woes preceding *the* final coming of Christ (and though Matthew does not explicitly mention the idea of **resurrection, he implies it in the phrase "gather his elect" in 24:31, which implies the gathering of all believers, both living and dead**)."[290]

However, this creates a "thorny problem" for Beale when he begins leaning in the direction of a Partial Preterism in a more recent work where he writes:

> "…it is likely better to see [Matt. 24:30]…fulfilled not at the very end of history but rather in AD 70 at the destruction of Jerusalem, in which the Son of Man's coming would be understood as an invisible coming in judgment, using the Roman armies as his agent."[291]

Beale admits, at least indirectly, that holding to both of these views he has defended creates a "thorny problem" for him that deserves "further study" to resolve. I gave him a copy of our second edition of *HD* and told him we did the "further study" and our exegesis of 1 Thessalonians 4:15-17 solves the "thorny problem" that he has created for himself. But Beale's "thorny problem" is simply a microcosm of the problem that the Futurist Church has as a whole.

- *"Gathered up" (Greek Harpazo) (v. 17)*

---

[290] Beale, Ibid., *1-2 Thessalonians*, 138, emphasis MJS
[291] Beale, Ibid., *A New Testament Biblical Theology the Unfolding of the Old Testament in the New*, 369

The NCV translates *harpazo* as "gathered up," thus giving it a theological and parallel connection to the eschatological gathering of Matthew 13:39-43, Matthew 24:30-31 & 2 Thessalonians 2:1. Other translations render it "snatched away" or "will be seized."

Harpazo means to "take one's plunder openly and violently, catch or snatch away." Sometimes it is addressing someone being pulled, snatched away or rescued by someone from an enemy. But is 1 Thessalonians 4:17 discussing an inward spiritual rescuing into Christ's glory cloud presence, or an outward and upward catching away into physical clouds in the sky and a biological change?

Here are some very clear uses of *harpazo being an inward spiritual event*:

1). Matthew 12:29 – Satan was "bound" and Christ was **"carrying away"** (harpazo) his plunder, which were people that were rightfully His who were held captive by Satan and demons. But how was He doing this? It was by casting out demons (*an inward spiritual reality*), and in some cases actually giving faith to these individuals to follow him (*again an inward spiritual reality*).

2). Matthew 11:12 – "the kingdom of heaven has been forcefully advancing (Christ casting out demons openly and publicly taking Satan's plunder), and (in return) the forceful men (believers) **lay hold of it"** (**harpazo** – through faith, vigor, power, and determination in light of present persecution – such as in the case of John). People were violently laying hold of the kingdom through having faith (a spiritual and inward reality).

3). Matthew 13:19 – In the parable of the sower, the wicked one comes and **snatches away (*harpazo*)** what was sown **in his heart** (*again, an inner spiritual reality*).

4). John 10:12 – The wolf (Pharisees, sons of Satan) sought to **snatch** (*harpazo*) and scatter the sheep/ people of Israel. How did the Pharisees seek to "snatch" and "scatter" the Jews from following Jesus? The first phase involved seeking to deceive them in their hearts and minds (an inward snatching) by convincing them that He was not the Christ by perverting the Scriptures and accusing Him of having a demon, etc. The second phase was a physical excommunication or scattering of Christians from their synagogues.

5). John 10:28-29 – Anyone who has faith in Jesus cannot be **"snatched"** (*harpazo*) out of the Father's hand. That is, he cannot be influenced (snatched inwardly) in his or her mind and heart to leave God. Like Peter, "Where else can we go, Lord? You alone have the words to eternal life." The gift of faith is spiritually preserved in the heart and soul of the believer. He cannot be deceived to the point of committing the sin unto death (1 Jn. 3:9). Again, this is an inner spiritual reality of the heart/mind/soul of man.

6). Acts 8:39 – This simply means that the Holy Spirit directed Philip in His heart and mind (inwardly) to go elsewhere and the Eunuch did not see him again. There's nothing in the text to support the idea that Philip was "raptured" into the atmosphere and was then instantly dropped off miles and miles away from where he was.

The eschatological "already" of the inward kingdom gathering and catching away was spiritual, and the eschatological "gathering" and "catching away" in the kingdom at

Christ's return would also be a spiritual event in AD 70. As we noted in our exegesis of Luke 17:20-37/Lk. 21:27-32, Jesus said when that the kingdom would come at His return (to gather all His elect Mt. 24:31), it would be an experience to occur "within" an individual and not something that could be seen with the physical eyes.

The inward realm of redemption or catching away is further evident from a study of the next two words, "clouds" and "air."

- *"...in the clouds..." (v. 17)*

As I have demonstrated thus far in our study of Christ coming on the clouds in the Olivet Discourse and God coming on the clouds in the OT, this is common apocalyptic language and not referring to physical clouds we see in the sky.

- *To "meet" the Lord... (v. 17)*

This Greek word, to **"meet,"** is wedding language and is only used twice in the NT – here and also in the wedding motif that Jesus develops in Matthew 25:1-13 (which Partial Preterists correctly teach was fulfilled spiritually in AD 70).

In Jewish betrothals and weddings, the groomsmen would go ahead of the groom and blow a trumpet at a time the virgin and her bridesmaids were not expecting. Once at the virgin's father's house, it was customary for the groom to consummate his marriage sexually there before taking her to his father's house where they would continue consummating the union for seven days and having the wedding feast.

This Greek word for "meet" was also often used of a king or dignitary coming to make his home in a city which his empire or kingdom had conquered or was about to conquer. On the news of the imminent coming of the king or dignitary, at the sound of a trumpet the members of the city would go out of the city and "meet" him and escort him back to their home/town. The king's presence was established WHERE the people already lived. Again, the imagery does not support a literal "rapture" of people off of planet earth, but rather of God coming to rule and reign in the hearts of His people where they are – living on planet earth.

- *"...in the air" (v. 17)*

But what of this meeting the Lord in **the "air"** (Greek *eros*)? The *Strong's Greek Dictionary* defines it as: "From 'aemi,' to breath unconsciously, to respire. By analogy, to blow. The air, particularly the lower and denser air as distinguished from the higher and rarer air."

So the point is that this is **the air "in" or "within" us**.

The *Dictionary of Biblical Languages with Semantic Domains* lists Eph 2:2, 1 Thess. 4:17, and Rev 16:17 in its definition of *eros* as meaning "the **space inhabited and controlled by [spiritual] powers**."

The Exegetical Dictionary of the New Testament says of the "air" in Ephesians 2:2 – "…Jewish conceptions, according to which, among other things, the **air is the abode of demons**."

Ephesians 2 refers to Satan as the "prince and power of the *AER*." He dwelt in the spiritual realm which extended to the souls of men. The war we see Christ and Satan fighting in the NT is *for the spiritual condition of men – within their hearts and minds*. Paul goes on to say that Satan "now works **in** the children of disobedience." And consistently Jesus defines His kingdom as something that He is setting up "in" and "within" men, and transforming them into His image spiritually.

Prior to AD 70, Satan used his demonic legions to "possess" individuals within the realm of their minds and the spiritual realm of their being. Satan used the old covenant Mosaic law to blind their spiritual eyes, hearts and minds in the realm of the "air" – within their souls, hearts, and minds to produce an arrogant and zealous self-righteousness which apart from Christ could only lead to utter despair (cf. 2 Cor. 3; Gal. 4:17-18; Rom. 7). Christ "bound the strong man" and was raising and delivering Christians from the darkness and death of this spiritual kingdom realm into His own realm (cf. Eph. 2:1-10). Christ snatched away His beloved and spoke peace and joy into the "air" of her heart, soul, and mind when He said, "It is finished" (Rev. 16:17/Heb. 9-10/1 Cor. 15)!

The powers of Satan, demons, the condemnation of the law, and the spiritual death Adam brought upon men were all conquered by Christ at His *Parousia* in AD 70 for those who put their faith in Him.

Had Paul meant to clearly communicate that believers would physically fly off the planet into the sky and atmosphere above, he would have used the Greek word *"ouranos,"* which clearly states this as its meaning.

The picture of the "rapture" is that Christ came down from heaven in / on a cloud to earth where He gathered the living into His presence, "within" us where we function as His Most Holy Place dwelling and throne through which He rules the nations. This is what we also see in Revelation where the New Jerusalem comes down from heaven to earth and God establishes His presence within His Church *here*.

Let me give further evidence not only that there will not be an end-of-world-history physical rapture of Christians off the planet, but likewise there was not a biological rapture or change of the living in AD 70.

1). Paul could have easily rebuked the false teachers and Christians that were tempted to believe the Lord had "already come" (2 Thess. 2:2) by simply saying, "Aren't you still here and the dead still in their graves? Obviously, He has not come!" But since Paul did not hold to the physical rapture view or a literal resurrection attended by Christ's *Parousia*, he did not argue this way. Obviously, Paul understood the Lord's coming to be a spiritual and unseen event as our Lord taught (Lk. 17:20-37/21:27-32), which was consistent with the "Day of the Lord" language of the prophets in the OT.

2). The coming of Christ in 2 Thessalonians 1:9 is the coming of the Lord in **Isaiah 66:5, 15**, where Isaiah describes Christian **survivors** (66:19) who are found alive on planet earth continuing to preach the gospel in the new creation / new covenant age.

3). As we have seen in our exegesis of Mark 8:38-9:1, the Greek is different than Matthew 16:27-28 and actually teaches that those who were alive to witness Christ's coming *would be able to look back (while still alive on earth) on the historical events of Him coming in power and great glory in the destruction of Jerusalem and thus know that He and His kingdom had* **"already come."**

4). After Christ and the Father come and make their home (dwelling - *mone* - John 14:2, 23) **within the believer**, they were told, "I have told you now before it happens, so that *when it does happen* **you will believe**" (14:29). If they were literally raptured, I don't think they would need to be reminded or exhorted to believe that it had been fulfilled! These words make more sense if it was a spiritual fulfillment that could not be seen with the physical eyes, and therefore it would take faith to believe that the Father and the Son had set up their presence within them.

5). Jesus of course directly promised to not remove the Church off of planet earth (John 17:15). Church history tells us that Christians were not raptured, but that they instead fled to Pella (in modern day Jordan). Historically, Pella is one of the first known Christian churches. Church history tells us that the Apostle John was still alive during Domitian's reign in the mid-AD 90's and that Timothy, Titus, and Luke lived beyond AD 70.

There is simply no exegetical evidence of a physical rapture at Christ's coming in AD 70 or some imagined one at the end of world history. The physical rapture view is probably one of the greatest scams perpetrated upon the Church. It makes the sleeping giant of the Evangelical Church numb to getting involved in our culture and politics because they expect things to simply get worse so that they can get "raptured" just before it gets really bad. After all, "you don't polish brass on a sinking ship." We MUST get involved in our politics and be the salt and light of this great country and that of the world!

Chapter Nine:

How did Jesus Come "In Like Manner" in AD 70?

Acts 1:9-11

- *"And when he had said these things, as they were looking on, he was lifted up, and a cloud took him out of their sight. And while they were gazing into heaven as he went, behold, two men stood by them in white robes, and said, "Men of Galilee, why do you stand looking into heaven? This Jesus, who was taken up from you into heaven, will come in the same way as you saw him go into heaven" (Acts 1:9-11)*

Many Futurists insist that Jesus' physical body was seen for some period of time as He ascended into the sky. However, verse nine simply says, *"He was lifted up, and a cloud received Him from their eyes."* Jesus was certainly seen just before He was *"lifted up"* (Acts 1:9). But it is not at all certain that He was directly seen as He ascended into the sky.

In verse 11, the disciples were told that Jesus would come in a similar manner or way to how they had seen Him enter heaven (the sky). The *continuity* (or similarity - "in a similar way") of Him coming as He had entered heaven is found in the fact that He would come *in the heavenly glory-cloud* of His Father (Mt. 16:27). Jesus was not physically seen after He was received into the glory-cloud. It was while He was hidden from sight in that cloud that He was *indirectly* seen entering the sky. A son can "see his father" as his father's plane is taking off from the runway and off into the sky, without directly physically seeing his father's body. In seeing the plane (which contains his father and the other passengers), he can still correctly say, "I can see dad; there he goes." And He was to come in like manner. Therefore, He would not be physically or directly seen when He came *"in like manner,"* in the cloud, to indwell His church at the end of the old covenant age (Luke 17:20–37; John 14:2–3, 23).

The phrase "in like manner" simply means "in a similar way" – *not exactly* the same way (which seems to be how most falsely interpret the passage). Jesus didn't ascend riding on a horse with a sword proceeding from His mouth, did He? Did "every eye" on the planet earth see Him leave? "The *exact same way*" argument offered by hyper-literalists self-implodes upon itself when they apply other Second Coming passages literally to His ascension event and demand an "exact same way" of fulfillment.

Futurists are not correct when they say that Jesus was going to come back in the same way that He "departed." The Scriptures teach that Jesus would come in the same way He had *entered the sky*. He entered the sky hidden from literal eyesight in the cloud of God's glory.

Here is the order of events:

1. As they looked, He was taken up (Acts 1:9).

2. A cloud received Him from their eyes (Acts 1:9).

These first two events could very well have happened simultaneously. Even Partial Preterist, Keith Mathison, admits that the verse could be translated, "He was lifted up; that is, a cloud received Him out of their sight."[292] It is a very real possibility that Jesus was instantly hidden in the cloud at the moment His feet left the earth.

3. Then the disciples saw Him going into the sky. That is, they looked intently into the sky as He was ascending in the cloud (Acts 1:10–11).

In the Old Testament, God was never literally or directly seen coming in His glory when He judged or saved Israel and other nations. Jesus was not literally seen again after He entered the cloud of God's glory. He was *"taken up in glory"* (1 Tim. 3:16) and *He would come in glory as the Ancient of Days* (cf. Dan. 7:13 OG LXX; Rev. 1:7-17).

The Lord God had become flesh. John bore testimony to the fact that looking at and touching Jesus was to look at and touch God Himself (John 1:14; 1 John 1:1). God was physically seen in the flesh, but this was *temporary* for the second person of the Godhead (Heb. 5:7), even as He had been born into and under the old covenant system with its *temporal* types and shadows (Gal. 4:4; Rom. 5–8; 2 Cor. 3; Heb. 8:13). Though Jesus is no longer in the flesh, He forever retains His human nature. He is forever Man, even as the saints in heaven today, who are no longer in their physical bodies, are still human/man by nature. Neither the Son of Man nor those who are in Him, whether in heaven or on earth, are "nonhuman" as some Futurists theorize.

Ironically, the point of the question, *"Why do you stand here looking into the sky,"* was that Jesus was *not* going to return to His physical form. It was futile for the disciples to long for Jesus to return to the earthly form He had taken when He was born of Mary. In His ascension, Jesus had returned to His pre-incarnate glory. The question of the two men was rhetorical, and it meant, "There is no use in standing here longing for Jesus to return to you and to be as He was in the days of His flesh. He will come, but He will come in the manner you saw Him enter heaven—hidden from physical eyes in the cloud of the Father's glory."

We agree with the majority of commentators and cross reference systems which see the in-like-manner coming of Jesus in Acts 1:11 as being parallel with the coming of Jesus on or in the cloud(s) in Matthew 16:27–28, 24:30–31, 26:64–68; Luke 21:27, and Revelation 1:7. But as we have seen, all of these other texts were fulfilled by AD 70. Partial Preterists agree that all of these other passages were fulfilled in AD 70, yet hold onto Acts 1:11 to support their Futurist creeds. They admit that Christ was figuratively

---

[292] Keith A. Mathison, *From Age to Age: The Unfolding of Biblical Eschatology*, (Phillipsburg, NJ: P&R Publishing, 2009), 459

"seen" (perceived, understood) at a figurative "coming" in/on the clouds in AD 70, but they deny that this was the fulfillment of Acts 1:11.

Partial Preterist Milton Terry, in contrast, took a lucid, biblical approach, seeing Matthew 24:30–31, 34; Acts 1:11; and Revelation 1:7 as all being fulfilled in the fall of Jerusalem at the end of the old covenant age:

> "Whatever the real nature of the *Parousia*, as contemplated in this prophetic discourse, our Lord unmistakably associates it with the destruction of the temple and city, which he represents as the signal termination of the pre-Messianic age. The coming on clouds, the darkening of the heavens, the collapse of elements, are, as we have shown above, familiar forms of apocalyptic language, appropriated from the Hebrew prophets.
>
> Acts i, 11, is often cited to show that Christ's coming must needs be spectacular, "*in like manner* as ye beheld him going into the heaven." But (1) in the only other three places where ["in like manner"] occurs, it points to a general concept rather than the particular form of its actuality. Thus, in Acts vii, 28, it is not some particular manner in which Moses killed the Egyptian that is notable, but rather the certain fact of it. In 2 Tim. iii, 8, it is likewise the fact of strenuous opposition rather than the special manner in which Jannes and Jambres withstood Moses. And in Matt. xxiii, 37, and Luke xiii, 34, it is the general thought of protection rather than the visible manner of a mother bird that is intended. Again (2), if Jesus did not come in that generation, and immediately after the great tribulation that attended the fall of Jerusalem, his words in Matt. xvi, 27, 28, xxiv, 29, and parallel passages are in the highest degree misleading. (3) To make the one statement of the angel in Acts i, 11, override all the sayings of Jesus on the same subject and control their meaning is a very one-sided method of biblical interpretation. But all the angel's words necessarily mean is that as Jesus has ascended into heaven so he will come from heaven. And this main thought agrees with the language of Jesus and the prophets."[293]

The immediate context of verse 8 and the Great Commission

Partial Preterists, such as Keith Mathison, have admitted that when the Great Commission of Acts 1:8 is fulfilled, then the coming of Christ in Acts 1:11 will be fulfilled:

> "The **time frame** [of Christ's Second Coming] **is hinted at** in the preceding context. The disciples are given a commission to be Christ's witnesses "in Jerusalem, and in all Judea and Samaria, and even to the remotest part of the earth" (Acts 1:8). **The implication is** that Christ's visible return **will follow the completion of the mission to the remotest part of the earth**."[294]

---

[293] Milton S. Terry, *A Study of the Most Notable Revelations of God and of Christ* (Grand Rapids, MI: Baker Book House, 1988), 246-247

[294] Mathison, Ibid., *Postmillennialism*, 117

We of course agree that when the Great Commission of Acts 1:8 is fulfilled, then the coming of Christ "in like manner" of verse 9 is fulfilled:

Prophecy – Greek *Ge (world/land)*	Fulfillment – Greek *Ge (world/land)*
"But you shall receive power when the Holy Spirit has come upon you; and you shall be witnesses to Me in Jerusalem, and in all Judea and Samaria, and to the end of the earth/land." [Gk. *ge*] (Acts 1:8)	"But I say, have they not heard? Yes indeed: 'Their sound **has gone out** to all the earth/land [Gk. *ge*], and their words to the ends of the world.'" (Rom. 10:18)
One definition of *ge* – "The *then known* lands, regions, territories, countries, etc..."	
1). In Jerusalem	1). Acts 2 – Jews
2). And Samaria	2). Acts 8 – Samaritans
3). In all Judea	3). Acts 10 – God-fearers
4). To the earth/land	4). Acts 19 – the Gentiles

Partial Preterists have no problem quoting Romans 10:18 to demonstrate how the Great Commission of Matthew 24:14 was fulfilled by AD 70 because it uses the same Greek word *oikumene* ("has gone out to the **ends of the world** [*oikumene*]"). Yet Paul in the very same passage, Romans 10:18, also uses the Greek word *ge* ("has gone out into **all the earth** [*ge*]"). Therefore, if Romans 10:18 can be applied to the Great Commission of Matthew 24:14 as being fulfilled in AD 70, it can also be applied to the Great Commission of Acts 1:8 as being fulfilled by AD 70.

Jews from "every nation under heaven" (Acts 2:4-5) were saved and empowered by the Holy Spirit to go fulfill the Great Commission of Acts 1:8 to "the end of the earth/land" of the Roman Empire. As R.C. Sproul points out, the book of Acts describes four Pentecost events based upon Acts 1:8. Since that is the case, the book of Acts maps out the success of the Great Commission of Acts 1:8 — thus showing how the sign of the Great Commission was being fulfilled and giving Paul his imminent expectation of the resurrection (Acts 24:15YLT).

As we have seen over and over again, Partial Preterists are simply wrong to invent two comings of Christ. Because they do this, it necessitates that they delineate and create two Great Commissions – one fulfilled by AD 70 (Mt. 24:14/Rom. 10:18) and another at the end of world history (Acts 1:8). But the Great Commission, Second Coming and arrival of the kingdom, as taught by Jesus in the Olivet Discourse, is the same event Luke lays out for us in Acts 1-2:

The Olivet Discourse	Acts 1-2
1). Only the Father has authority and knows the **day** and **hour** of the kingdom's arrival (Lk. 17:20-37; Lk. 21:27-32; Mt. 24:36).	1). Only the Father has authority and knows the **time** and **dates** of the kingdom's arrival (Acts 1:3-7).
2). The **Holy Spirit (& charismata) would be given** to boldly **fulfill the G.C.** (cf. Mt. 10:17-23; Mark 13:10-13).	2). The **Holy Spirit (charismata) would be given** to boldly **fulfill the G.C.** (Acts 1:4-8).
3). Jesus would come from heaven upon His glory cloud in their "this genera-tion" (cf. Mt. 24:14-34).	3). Jesus would come from heaven upon His glory cloud in their "this perverse and crooked generation" (cf. Acts 1:11; 2:20-40).

The Second Coming and Great Commission, or the restoration of the nations of Genesis 10-11 and Deuteronomy 32:8-9, is also picked up in Acts 2, so let's briefly examine this passage as well.

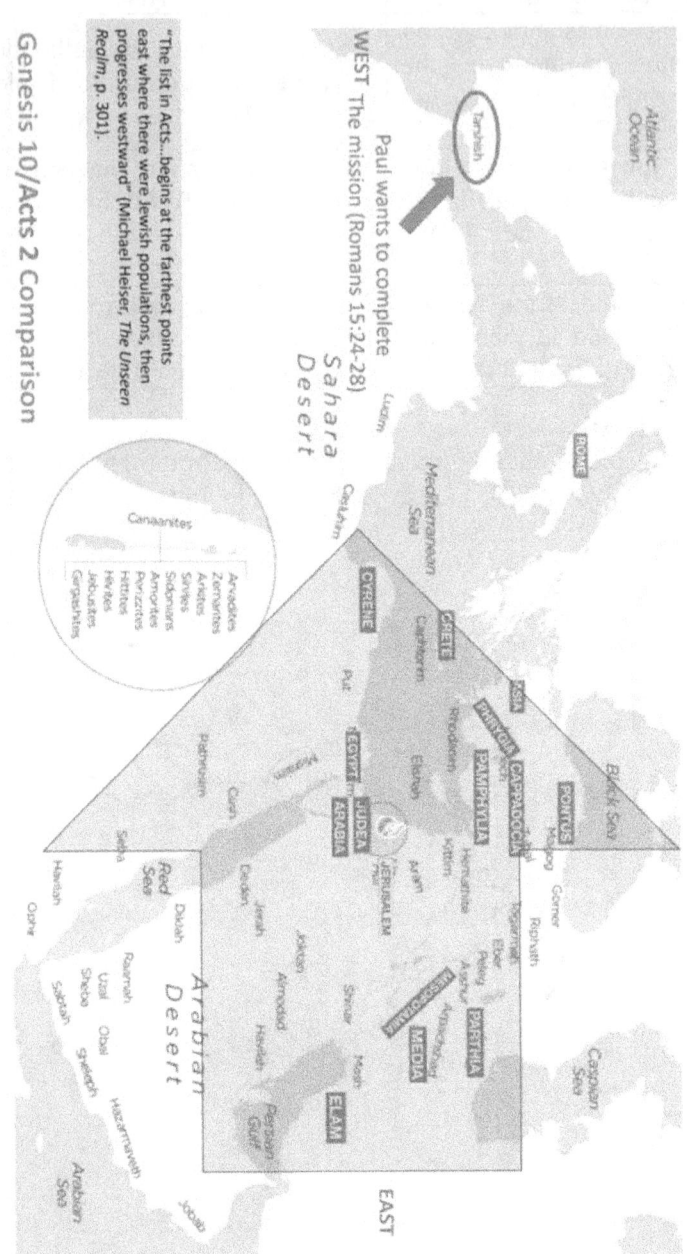

Genesis 10/Acts 2 Comparison

In Acts 2, Luke draws our attention to Peter referencing not just the fulfillment of the outpouring of the Holy Spirit and Second Coming of Jesus in Joel 2, but the restoration and fulfillment of Genesis 11 and Deuteronomy 32 as well.

The Septuagint (LXX) of Acts 2:2-3 references and connects "divided" to Deuteronomy 32:8-9 and "bewildered" to Genesis 11:7.[295] These are deliberate exegetical "echoes" or "hooks" taking us back to these OT passages. In other words, this is the reversing and restoring of God's judgment upon the nations in Genesis 10-11/Deuteronomy 32:8-9 and Him bringing them back together under the uniting and "pure" tongue/language of the gospel of Jesus Christ.

G.K. Beale writes,

> "Why does Luke want readers to see the **link to Genesis 10-11**? Babel's sin of uniting and consequent judgment of confused languages and of people being scattered throughout the earth **is reversed at Pentecost: God causes representatives from the same scattered nations to unite in Jerusalem in order that they might receive the blessing of understanding different languages as if all these languages were one.**"[296]

Josephus on Genesis 11	Peter on Acts 2
They spoke "with other tongues" ["*alloglossous glossais*"] (*Ant.* 1.117; *Ant.* 1.120),	"They began to speak "with other tongues [*heterais glossais*] (Acts 2:4)
God "gave to each his own language" ["*idian hekasto phonen*"] (Ant. 1.118)	"We hear each in our own dialect ["*hekastos- te idia dialekto*"] (Acts 2:6, 8)

Peter Leithart makes a good observation:

> "Pentecost sounds like a repeat of Babel, but, unlike Babel, Pentecostal tongues communicate rather than confuse. Filled with the Spirit, the apostles preach the gospel to everyone in his own language, and the tongues of the Spirit join rather than separate nations. Glossolalia marks the church as an *anti*-Babel.
>
> The apostles announce that all Israel has hoped for has now happened in the cross and exaltation of Jesus. The Spirit's arrival is one of the indicators that Israel's hopes are fulfilled. In contrast to Deuteronomy, the New Testament treats tongues not as an omen of exile but as a sign that exile has ended. Speaking in tongues, the early church isn't being invaded. The church is the invader.
>
> This helps answer our question, To whom was Pentecost a threat? On the one hand, it was a signal to Jews who rejected Jesus as Messiah. Judaism was being "invaded" by a new people who claimed, in Paul's words, to be "true Jews," circumcised in heart rather than flesh (Rom 2).

---

[295] For a detailed explanation of this see: Dr. Michael Heiser, *The Unseen Realm - Recovering the supernatural worldview of the Bible*, (Bellingham, WA: Lexham Press, 2015), 298. The above Genesis 10 / Acts 2 Comparison chart was created by Michael Heiser.

[296] G.K. Beale, *The Temple and the Church's Mission: A Biblical Theology of the Dwelling Place of God,* (Downers Grove, ILL: InterVarsity Press, 2004), 202

On the other hand, tongues were a warning to Rome. Though dominated by Latin in the west and Greek in the east, the empire was polyglot. The sounds of the Pentecostal church told Rome that another multinational empire had invaded and was settling down in Roman territory. No wonder Roman emperors regarded the church as a dangerous rival."[297]

I would agree with Mr. Leithart that tongues were a sign of a uniting force for the nations coming into the fold of God through the Church. BUT tongues also functioned as a sign of judgment and *exile* for old covenant Jerusalem, which would be "cast out" of (exiled from) the kingdom in AD 70 (Mt. 8:10-12; 21:43-45).

Here's a side note on the miraculous and the gift of tongues. The miraculous signs and revelatory gifts of tongues, prophecy and knowledge "ceased" at Christ's "soon", "face to face" coming in AD 70 (1 Cor. 13:8-12/Rev. 22:4-7). Unlike here in Acts 2, where there were known human languages, modern Charismatics engage in learned behavior and speak gibberish.

The theological point of Peter's sermon and the Great Commission is that it is the SEED that will be sent to plant the gospel in the Gentile nations (that were once disinherited by God in Gen. 10-11). These Jews would go back to their synagogues where there were not only Jews but also believing Gentile proselytes and God-fearers. They too would hear the good news of what Messiah had done for them. Form here, God would send the apostle Paul (as another faithful Jonah *from Tarshish*, the end of the ancient world) to make the mission complete and blossom into its fullness, thus bringing the nations back into the fold and kingdom of God. He would do this by going to the Jew first and then the Gentile. No doubt his first stop would be in these synagogues and churches established from Peter's sermon, and then would branch out from there.

Major Premise: The coming of Christ, Great Commission and fulfillment of the kingdom in the Olivet Discourse and Acts 1-2 are the same event (Classic Amillennialism).

Minor Premise: But the coming of Christ, Great Commission and arrival of the kingdom in the Olivet Discourse were fulfilled in Jesus' contemporary "this generation" and at the end of the old covenant age in AD 70 (Partial Preterism).

Conclusion: Therefore, the ONE coming of Christ, Great Commission and fulfillment of the kingdom in the Olivet Discourse and Acts 1-2 was fulfilled in Jesus' and Peter's contemporary "this generation" and thus by AD 70 (Full Preterism – "Reformed and always reforming").

---

[297] Peter Leithart, *THE POLYGLOT POLITICS OF PENTECOST,* https://www.firstthings.com/web-exclusives/2018/05/the-polyglot-politics-of-pentecost

Chapter Ten:

How was the Millennium Fulfilled Between AD 27 – AD 67?

Evangelical Zionists insist that Revelation 20 is teaching a period in which Christ will come and sit on a physical throne from Jerusalem and establish an earthly kingdom for Israel lasting a literal thousand years. Many believe a physical temple will be re-built in which Christ and believers will once again smell the stench of animal sacrifices. Christ comes seven years after the "rapture" of the Church to establish this earthly kingdom which He couldn't pull off at His first coming because Jewish unbelief thwarted His plan, so here in Revelation 20 we have His so-called "plan b" finally come to fruition.

Amillennialists and Postmillennialists disagree and teach that the Church is currently in the millennial period. They believe the thousand year period is a symbolic number as many of the numbers in Revelation are, and that the number 'thousand' is also not taken literally in the OT. Postmillennialists go a step further and say that the thousand years is symbolic of a period that could last millions of years. Of course this is necessary since the world has never seen anything like a "golden age" in which all nations of the world become Christianized or the physical creation undergoes some kind of physical, progressive glorification process.

Psalm 50:10 is often cited, usually by postmillennialists, to teach that "a thousand" symbolizes literally "many thousands or millions." *For every beast of the forest is Mine, and the cattle upon a thousand hills"* (Ps. 50:10).

Postmillennialists reason that God owns the cattle on every hill; therefore "a thousand hills" symbolizes or represents "many thousands or millions of hills." Thus, they reason, we are led by Scripture to interpret the *"thousand years"* in Revelation 20 to mean "many thousands or millions of years."

That reasoning sounds solid at first glance. However, the context of Psalm 50:10 does not lead us to a principle that a symbolic "thousand" always signifies "many thousands." It leads us to the principle that a symbolic "thousand" signifies "fullness." The "thousand" of Psalm 50:10 is interpreted for us two verses later:

"The world is Mine, and the fullness thereof" (Ps. 50:12b).

In Psalm 90:4, a "thousand years" is as "yesterday" and as "a watch in the night." In 2 Peter 3:8, a "thousand years" is as one "day." In those verses, a "thousand" (and "yesterday" and "a watch" and "day") is used to teach us that, to God, a small piece of time is no different than a **fullness** of time (Compare Job 7:7; Ps. 39:5, 90:2, 144:4;

Heb. 13:8; James 4:14.). Thus, in Psalm 105:8, a "thousand" corresponds with "forever": *He has remembered His covenant forever, the word that he commanded to a thousand generations* (Ps. 105:8).

In scriptural usage, a symbolic "thousand" can be likened to "one" (day / yesterday / a watch in the night), or used in reference to millions of hills, or to eternity ("forever"). A "thousand" can be likened unto, or used to represent, a number lesser or greater than a literal thousand. Only its context can determine its literal numerical meaning, but the basic idea that is communicated by the number is "fullness." As G. K. Beale wrote,

> "The primary point of the thousand years is probably **not** a figurative reference to **a long time**..."[298]

How one interprets the thousand years in Revelation 20 depends on one's eschatological framework. The passage does not interpret itself, but must be interpreted by the overall eschatology of Scripture. Within the Preterist interpretive framework, the biblical-eschatological context of Revelation 20 should lead us to interpret the "thousand years" to signify the time of the Christological filling up of all things (Eph. 1:10; 4:10). That time was from the cross of Christ to the Parousia of Christ in AD 70. That was the time during which "the [spiritual] death" which came through Adam and was magnified through "the law" was in process of being destroyed. The literal timeframe of the "thousand years" was roughly forty years.

Reformed theologian G. K. Beale tells us that some Jews considered the length of the intermediate messianic reign to be forty years. He also states that one Jewish tradition made an anti-type connection between Adam's lifespan (almost 1,000 years) and a reign of Messiah for a (possibly symbolic) thousand years or even possibly a literal 70 years to fulfill what Adam failed to achieve, dying at 930 years old.[299] Many Christians have attempted to parallel the thousand years of 2 Peter 3:8 with John's thousand years in Revelation 20:2–6.

Adam falling short of the 1,000-year lifespan by 70 years (Gen. 5:5) may represent his being created a mortal being and perishing in sin outside of God's presence. If this is the case, then it is more than reasonable that the number 1,000 took on the symbolism and representation of Christ's and the Church's victory over death in contrast to Adamic man's vain existence apart from God's salvation (cf. Eccl. 6:6).

Some Evangelicals and Reformed theologians, along with some Preterists such as Milton Terry, do not understand the long lifespans in the early chapters of Genesis to be literal.[300] They believe that the lifespans were symbolic and contained

---

[298] G. K. Beale, *The New International Greek Testament Commentary: The Book of Revelation* (Grand Rapids, Michigan: Eerdmans Publishing Company, 1999), 1018

[299] Ibid., 1018–1019.

[300] Carol A. Hill, *Making Sense of the Numbers of Genesis* (http://www.asa3.org/aSA/PSCF/2003/PSCF12–03Hill.pdf); Milton S. Terry, *Biblical Apocalyptics: A Study of the Most Notable Revelations of God and of Christ* (Grand Rapids, MI: Baker Book House, 1988), 62.

numerological elements. But even if Adam's lifespan was a literal 930 years, this does not exclude an anti-typical, symbolic 1,000 years in Revelation 20.

When Messiah came as *"the last Adam,"* His reign in and through the Church for a symbolic thousand years brought the church not to the dust of the earth separated from God's presence, but to the tree of life and into the very presence of God (Rev. 20–22:12). Through faith in, and union with, Christ as the last Adam (the tree of life and new creation), Christians have achieved what Adam could not. The Church was clothed with *"immortality"*; it attained unto the *"fullness"* of life in AD 70; and it will never die for the aeons of the aeons (2 Cor. 1:20; 1 Cor. 15:45–53; Rev. 21–22; Jn. 11:26–27).

It is odd that Amillennialists and Partial Preterist Postmillennialists understand that the Second Coming of Christ is the event that brings the millennium to its consummation. However, the *only* future coming of Jesus discussed in the book of Revelation is the one that would take place "shortly" or "soon" (Rev. 3:11; 22:6–7, 10–12, 20). Partial Preterists tell us that the coming of Christ in Revelation was fulfilled spiritually and imminently in AD 70, while the Reformed Creeds and Amillennialists tell us that the coming of Christ throughout Revelation is the Second Coming event which ends the millennium. We of course hold both of these orthodox views to be correct.

Please consider the following seven exegetical, orthodox, and historical points which prove that the millennium was roughly a forty years period from AD 27 – AD 67 or AD 30 – AD 70.

1). Imminence

Kenneth Gentry informs us that the book of Revelation is about things which were past, present, and "about to be" fulfilled in John's day (Rev. 1:19, YLT). Therefore, there is no exegetical evidence that Revelation 20 does not fall within these inspired parameters. The millennium was still future when John wrote, and therefore the end of the millennium falls within those things that were "about to be" fulfilled. As Vern Poythress and Simon Kistemaker (also contributors to *The Reformation Study Bible*) have pointed out in their works, if the imminent time texts in Revelation 1:1 and 22:20 are to be taken literally and refer to AD 70, and since they function as brackets or bookends, then the millennium of Revelation 20 would have also been fulfilled by AD 70.

Therefore, both of these views teach that the end of the millennium resurrection and judgment of the dead were fulfilled "shortly" in AD 70. Why would I be considered a "heretic" for agreeing with both?

2). The symbolic nature of the thousand years

As G.K. Beale (the NT editor to *The Reformation Study Bible*) has taught in his commentary on Revelation, the symbol of the thousand years does not have to be taken as describing a long period of time (i.e., thousands or millions of years).

Therefore, the thousand year millennium can be a symbolic depiction of a relatively short period of time – 40 years.

3) Rabbinic typology of a forty year millennial period –historical argument

It has also been acknowledged by Reformed theologians such as Beale that many Rabbis believed that the period of Messiah was to be a transitional stage between "this age/world" and "the age/world to come." These Rabbis (such as R. Adiba) understood this transition period to be 40 years, based upon how long the Israelites were in the wilderness before inheriting the land. This type/anti-type understanding is developed for us in the book of Hebrews (cf. Heb. 3-4; 10:25, 37; 11—13:14, YLT).

And as we have noted from Reformed Partial Preterists such as Joel McDurmon and Gary DeMar, it is within the realm of Reformed orthodoxy to believe that Jesus' and Paul's "this age/world" was the old covenant age, and that "the last days" were the days of transition between the old covenant age and the new covenant age (AD 30 – 70).

But we are also told by Amillennialists that the millennium of Revelation 20 is the period between the NT's "this age" and the "age to come."

We of course agree with all of the above propositions, which when combined, place the millennial period to be a period of roughly 40 years between the old covenant age (which was passing away and ready to vanish) and the new covenant age which was "about to" come in its mature form in AD 70.

4). Recapitulation

Reformed Postmillennial Partial Preterists, such as Kenneth Gentry and James Jordan, are correct to teach that the content of Revelation 1-19 and 21-22 was fulfilled by AD 70, at which time there was a judgment and spiritual resurrection of the dead and arrival of a spiritual new creation or spiritual new heavens and new earth. And Amillennialists, such as Simon Kistemaker and Robert Strimple, are correct to teach that Revelation 20:5–15 *recapitulates* the same judgment and consummation scenes that are depicted in chapters 1–19 and 21–22.

Revelation 1-19 & 20-22 **Partial Preterists correct to teach these things were fulfilled by AD 70**	**Revelation 20 Classic Amillennialists correct to teach these are the same events or judgments in other chapters**
1). Past persecution w/ more persecution to come and vindication of martyr's motif. (Rev. 6 and 12)	1). Past persecution w/ more persecution to come and vindication of martyr's motif
2). Future persecution to last for a "little while" and Satan has "a little while" longer (Rev. 6 and 12)	2). More persecution to come and Satan loosed for "a little while"

3). "Every mountain and island were removed from their places" / "every island fled (Greek *pheugo*), and the mountains were not found" "…for the first heaven and the first earth had passed away" (Rev. 6; 16; 21-22)	3). "The earth and the heaven fled (Greek *pheugo*), and a place was not found for them" (this implies the "new" creation of 21-22 took its place).
4). Judgment of the dead (Rev. 11)	4). Judgment of the dead
5). The last days "the war" of Ezek. 38-39 fulfilled (Rev. 16 and 19)	5). The last days "the war" of Ezek. 38-39 fulfilled
6). Enemies of the Church (beast, harlot, false prophet) thrown in fire (Rev. 17 and 19)	6). Devil thrown in fire (see also "crushed" "shortly" (Rom. 16:20/Gen. 3:15)

Therefore, since Full Preterists hold to both of these reformed and "orthodox" positions in interpreting the book of Revelation, and the end of the millennium resurrection and judgment event was fulfilled in AD 70, why would I be considered a "heretic" for agreeing with both of these "orthodox" and common sense views?

5). Is Revelation 20 an isolated event? The "already and not yet", "this age and the age to come" and the "last days" millennial period

In criticizing the Premillennial view, which often seeks to isolate Revelation 20 from the rest of the New Testament, Amillennialists and many Postmillennialists hold that Revelation 20 falls within the "already and not yet" of the "last days" period in the New Testament, and that this transition period is depicted in the Parable of the Wheat and Tares, or in Matthew 24–25. But as I have shown thus far, it is "orthodox" to believe the "last days" ended with the old covenant age in AD 70, and that the harvest/gathering and coming of Christ in Matthew 13 and 24–25 was fulfilled by AD 70.

Therefore, since the period between "this age and the age to come" is the millennial period, and it was the transition period between the old covenant age and the new covenant age (AD 30 – AD 70), and the "last days" is also the transition and millennial period of Revelation 20 but was also from AD 30 – AD 70, the end of the millennial resurrection and judgment of the dead was fulfilled when the old covenant age passed away and the last days ended in AD 70. Why would I be considered a "heretic" for agreeing with both common sense "orthodox" views?

6). The Second Coming in Matthew 24-25 ends the millennium of Revelation 20

If it is true that a) the coming of Christ in Matthew 24 and 25 is referring to the AD 70 judgment, as Partial Preterists are teaching, and if it is true that b) John's version of Matthew 24-25 is found in the book of Revelation, and if it is true that c) Matthew 24:27 - 25:31ff. is descriptive of the one end-of-the-age Second Coming, judgment, and resurrection event (the creedal position), then d) the Reformed community has some explaining to do, because these "orthodox" doctrines form the "this-generation" forty year millennial view of Full Preterism:

Matthew 24-25	Revelation 20:5-15
1). Resurrection and judgment - Mt. 24:30-31 (cf. Mt. 13:39-43/Dan. 12:2-3); Mt. 25:31-46	1). Resurrection and judgment - Rev. 20:5-15
2). De-creation heaven and earth pass/flee - Mt. 24:29, 35 (cf. Mt. 5:17-18)	2). De-creation heaven and earth pass/ flee - Rev. 20:11 (cf. Rev. 6:14; 16:20; 21:1)
3). Christ on throne to judge - Mt. 25:31	3). God on throne to judge - Rev. 20:11
4). Wicked along with devil eternally punished - Mt. 25:41-46	4). Wicked along with devil eternally punished - Rev. 20:10, 14-15

7). The analogy of faith between Daniel 12:1-13 and Revelation 20

And if it is also true that a) the judgment and resurrection of the dead in Daniel 12:1-4, 13 were fulfilled by AD 70 (per Gentry), and if it is true that b) Daniel 12:1-4, 13 is parallel to Revelation 20:5-15 (classic amillennial view), then c) once again the Reformed community has some explaining to do, in that these orthodox views form the "this-generation" forty-year millennial view of Full Preterism:

Daniel 12:1-2	Revelation 20:5-15
1). Only those whose names are written in the book would be delivered/saved from eternal condemnation (Dan. 12:1-2)	1). Only those whose names are written in the book would be delivered/saved from the lake of fire (Rev. 20:12-15)
2). This is the time for the resur-rection and judgment of the dead (Dan. 12:1-2)	2). This is the time for the resurrection and judgment of the dead (Rev. 20:5-15)

Therefore, the reader should be able to discern that the Full Preterist, AD 27 – AD 67 or AD 30 – AD 70, "this generation" millennial view:

A). is consistent with the teaching of Revelation itself when it comes to imminence and recapitulation…

B). falls within the "orthodox" views of the Reformed church…

C). is in line with the analogy of Scripture and…

D). offers historical support from many Rabbis who promoted a 40 year transitional period between the two ages.

Our view on the millennium is both exegetically sound and orthodox. Finding support for the Full Preterist view of the millennium is not as difficult as many portray it. Selah.

And just as we don't see Revelation 20 discussing the Premillennial Zionist position - Jesus sitting on an earthly throne in Jerusalem with a re-built temple where a priesthood is once again performing animal sacrifices, it also doesn't teach a biological corpse resurrection which all Futurists hold to. The resurrection in Revelation 20 involves the souls of men being released from Hades to inherit God's presence and eternal life or eternal punishment. This fits with Jewish concepts of the resurrection prior to NT times, during Jesus' day and the kind of spiritual resurrection some orthodox Partial Preterists have taught.

Chapter Eleven:

How is the Promise of No More Death, Tears and Pain Fulfilled Today?

All Futurist eschatologies reason that because death, tears, mourning, crying, and pain still exist today, Revelation 21:4 must not be fulfilled.

Response

In Revelation 21:4 (YLT) we read that "***the** death shall not be any more.*" Every Reformed commentator agrees that this verse, along with 1 Corinthians 15:54–55, is describing a future-to-us end of "*the death,*" and that "*the death*" refers to the death that came through Adam in Genesis 2:17. The Douay-Rheims translation renders that verse: "*But of the tree of knowledge of good and evil, thou shalt not eat. For in what day so ever thou shalt eat of it, thou shalt die **the** death.*" The Good News Translation makes it clear when "*the death*" would take place: "*...except the tree that gives knowledge of what is good and what is bad. You must not eat the fruit of that tree; if you do, **you will die the same day**.*"

"*The death*" that came through Adam the very day he sinned was spiritual and not biological. The abolition of biological death was never the purpose of Christ's redemptive work. In 1 Corinthians 15:55–57 (YLT) we read, "*Where, O Death, thy sting? Where, O Hades, thy victory?' And the sting of the death is the sin, and the power of the sin the law; and to God—thanks, to Him who is giving us the victory through our Lord Jesus Christ.*" Whenever Paul uses the definite article "the" in front of "law," he is referring to Israel's old covenant Torah. As 1 Corinthians 15:57 indicates, the Law was not abolished at the cross; but it was "*soon*" to disappear, through the power of the cross, at Christ's *Parousia* in the end of the old covenant age (Heb. 8:13–10:37).

Because "*the death*" is spiritual death (alienation from God) realized through the commandment-breaker Adam and amplified or increased under the Law of Moses (the old covenant), we can see how God gave His elect the victory over "*the death*" at the end of the old covenant age of condemnation. The fact that men die physically is in no way evidence that the "spiritual conflict" of "the death" continues for the Church throughout the new covenant age.

God's people under the old covenant, unlike God's people today, experienced covenantal and spiritual death (cf. Hosea 13:1–14; Isa. 25–27; Ezek. 37). What made physical death dreadful for the saints under the old covenant was that they died with the awareness that their sins had not yet been taken away. In the new covenant creation,

Jesus promises that whether we biologically die in Him or biologically live in Him, we *"never die"* (John 11:25–26). This was not the case before Christ.

Thus, under the old covenant, the residents of Jerusalem wept because they did not have a lasting atonement or eternal redemption. They longed and groaned for the day of Messiah's salvation. Until that day would come, they knew their sins were not put away (Heb. 9:26–28; 10:4, 11). The promise that there would be no more mourning or crying or pain does not refer to any and every kind of mourning, crying, and pain. It refers to mourning, crying, and pain concerning God's people being dead in sin under the condemnation, curse, and slavery of God's law. That sad Adamic state is no more. In the Son, God's people are *"free indeed"* (Jn. 8:36).

As Athanasius wrote in his Festal Letters, iv. 3,

> "For when death reigned, 'sitting down by the rivers of Babylon, we wept,' and mourned, because we felt the bitterness of captivity; but now that death and the kingdom of the devil is abolished, everything is entirely filled with joy and gladness."

Under the old covenant, when David or the nation was exiled from Zion and God's city and temple, there was much inner pain, weeping, and bondage that followed (2 Sam. 15:30; Ps. 137; Isa. 14:3; Isa. 22:4–5; Jer. 9:1; 13:17; Jer. 22:9–10; Lam. 1:16; Joel 2:17). Under the new covenant, the heavenly country and Jerusalem are not subject to being made desolate or shaken by invading armies as was the old (Isa. 62:4; Heb. 12:27–28). The concept of the gates of the New Jerusalem always being open, even at night (Isa. 60:11; Rev. 21:25), is not merely a picture of evangelism; it is also a picture of security for the residents of God's city. The believer, through faith in Christ, is the new covenant creation and it is impossible for him to be exiled from the city (2 Cor. 5:17; Rev. 3:12; 22:12). The new covenant believer is characterized as one whose weeping has ended, because God has forever taken away his sin and united Himself with him (Isa. 60:20; 65:14, 18–19; Jn. 17:21–23).

Christians in the new covenant world do not shed tears in agony and cry out to God to save them from the Adamic death of sin, as Jesus Himself did on our behalf (Heb. 5:7). *"The sting [pain] of the death"* cannot harm us anymore (1 Cor. 15:56) because the power of sin has been removed through Jesus, the Law-Fulfiller who clothes us and indwells us. Now we live and reign with Christ in the new covenant world, wherein dwells the righteousness of God.

It is noteworthy that Partial Preterists avoid any mention of Paul's declaration that Satan would be *"crushed shortly"* (Rom. 16:20) in their discussions of the time texts being fulfilled in AD 70, let alone in the context of Satan being judged at the end of the millennium of Revelation 20. The reason for this is that the majority consensus among all brands of commentators is that the "crushing" of Satan in Romans 16:20 is a direct reference to the *final* "crushing" of Satan as predicted in Genesis 3:15 and Revelation 20. Manifestly, the judgment and wrath that came in AD 70 was not merely "a" "minor" judgment. It was "the" judgment. It was the crushing of Satan.

But Futurists challenge us with the empirical reality that death and Satan could not have met their ultimate demise in AD 70 because, after all, just look around and you will clearly see that people still physically die and there are wars and murders taking place all over the world today. Is this clear evidence that Satan and his demonic hordes are active in our world?

There were certainly times that Satan moved men, such as Judas, to commit sins. But the Bible does not teach us that this was ever *the norm*. James tells us that wars and fights come from within men (James 4:1) instead of from Satan and demons. Satan's primary purpose has come to an end: He can no longer function as *the accuser of the brethren* (Rev. 12:10), because Christ came out of Zion a second time at the end of the old covenant age to put away sin once and for all for His Church (Acts 20:28; Rom. 11:26–27; 13:11–12; Heb. 9:26–28).

Chapter Twelve:

How to Evangelize Muslims, Zionists and Reach Evangelical Zionists

Introduction

This book has confronted the reader with a major paradigm shift. It has eliminated and desolated the Islamic and "Jewish" Zionist argument that Jesus could not be God as He claimed, let alone a prophet, since after all he did not float down on a physical cloud to end world history and set up an earthly kingdom or paradise. I have demonstrated that neither the OT nor Jesus predicted such a new covenant or Messianic kingdom.

According to the book of Daniel and Jesus' teaching, the Messianic kingdom would arrive during the Roman Empire when Messiah would come upon the clouds during a 3 ½ year period of judgment to "shatter the power" of the old covenant people of God. When Christ was revealed from heaven like the sun, He would establish His kingdom "within" His people.

As far as the Evangelical Zionists go, they have radically departed from OT and NT teachings on imminence, apocalyptic language and the nature of the new covenant Messianic kingdom.

We now want to turn our attention on how to reach these various groups with the truths of who Messiah, predicted in the OT and developed in the NT, would be and is. And, when possible, we need to find middle ground by appealing to their own sources of authority.

1). Islam

We looked at the violent theology and eschatology of Islam in chapter one along with all of the false and failed prophecies of Muhammad concerning the Second Coming of Christ. Here we need to investigate what Islam actually teaches concerning our dialog with them and what they teach about the authority of the OT and NT in relation to the Quran.

Are the OT and NT "Scriptures" uncorrupted or corrupted revelations of Allah?

The Quran itself and the early Hadiths teach that god (Allah) gave the Jews the OT Scriptures and Christians the NT Scriptures as a guiding light of infallible, unalterable revelation. The Jews did not corrupt the OT Scriptures, and the Christians did not corrupt the OT Scriptures either, since the NT was the fulfillment and confirmation of the OT. Then Allah allegedly gave Muhammad the guiding light and revelation of the

Quran as a third infallible, unalterable revelation which was built upon the other two revelations. In fact, Allah tells Muslims to go to the "people of the book" (Christians) to confirm these three revelations, and the Quran itself is supposed to be a true consistent, confirmatory revelation with the OT and NT.

It wasn't until very late in Islam's development (1064) that they came up with the doctrine that Allah's revelations to the Jews (the OT) and revelations to the Christians (the NT) have been "corrupted." Why the change? It was because as they did turn to Christians (people of the book) with this challenge and Christians showed them how the Quran was not in any way consistent with the OT or NT, they needed a way out. As the facts and evidence began to mount, something had to be done. So the teaching emerged that Jews and Christians were able to "corrupt" Allah's previous revelations, while somehow he decided to keep the Quran from being corrupted. Therefore, "voila," the problem they created for themselves just magically disappeared.

Here are some passages from the Quran which teach that Allah gave the OT and NT Scriptures as divine revelation that is supposed to be consistent and confirm the revelation given to Muhammad in the Quran:

> Quran 2:113: The Jews say the Christians are misguided, and the Christians say it is the Jews who are misguided. Yet they both read the Scriptures…

> Quran 3:3: He has revealed to you the Book with the Truth, confirming the scriptures which preceded it; for He has already revealed the Torah and the Gospel for the guidance of mankind, and the distinction of right and wrong.

> Quran 3:48 – 50: He [Allah] will instruct him [Jesus] in the Scriptures and in wisdom, in the Torah and in the Gospel and send him forth as an apostle to the Israelites. He will say: "I bring you a sign from your Lord…" "I come to confirm the Torah which preceded me and to make lawful to you some of the things you are forbidden. I bring you a sign from your Lord: therefore, fear God and obey me."

> Quran 5:46-48: After them we sent forth Jesus, the son of Mary, confirming the Torah already revealed, and gave him the Gospel, in which there is guidance and light, corroborating what is revealed before it in the Torah, a guide and admonition to the righteous. Therefore, let those who follow the Gospel judge according to what God has revealed therein. Evil doers are those who do not judge according to God's revelations. And to you we have revealed the Book with the truth. It confirms the Scriptures which came before it and stands as a guardian over them.

> Quran 5:66: If they observe the Torah and the Gospel and what is revealed to them from their Lord, they shall enjoy abundance from above and from beneath.

> Quran 5:68 – 69: Say: "People of the Book, you will attain nothing until you observe the Torah and the Gospel and that which is revealed to you from your Lord"…

> Quran 10:94: If you doubt what We have revealed to you [Muhammad], Ask those who have read the Scriptures before you.

Quran 12:111: There annals point a moral to men of understanding. This is no invented tale but a confirmation of previous Scriptures, an explanation of all things, a guide and a blessing to true believers.

Quran 16:43, 44: The apostles We sent before you were but men whom we inspired with revelations and with Scriptures. Ask the People of the Book, if you know not. To you we have revealed the Admonition, so that you may proclaim to men what was sent down for them, and that they may give thought.

Quran 29:46: Be courteous when you argue with People of the Book except with those among them who do evil. Say: "We believe in that which is revealed to us and which was revealed to you. Our God and your God is one.

Quran 35:31: What We have revealed to you in the Book is the truth confirming previous Scriptures. God knows and observes His servants.

Quran 61:6: And of Jesus the son of Mary, who said to the Israelites: "I am sent forth to you from God to confirm the Torah already revealed…"

Here are passages which clearly teach that Allah's inspired word or revelations (as given in the OT, NT and Quran) **cannot be corrupted by men**:

Quran 6:34: Rejected were the messengers before thee: with patience and constancy they bore their rejection and their wrongs, until Our aid did reach them: **there is none that can alter the words (and decrees) of Allah**. Already hast thou received some account of those messengers.

Quran 6:115: The word of thy Lord doth find its fulfillment in truth and in justice: **None can change His words**: for He is the one who heareth and knoweth all.

Quran 10:64: For them are glad tidings, in the life of the present and in the Hereafter; **no change can there be in the words of Allah**. This is indeed the supreme felicity.

The Hadith on Quran 4:46 and 85:21, 22, "They corrupt the word," means "they alter or change its meaning." Yet no one is able to change even a single word from any book of God. The meaning is that they interpret the word wrongly ["…and he continues to speak about how the Qur'an is preserved"][301]

There are passages in the Quran (2:75-79; 3:78; 4:46-47; 5:12-13, 15; 6:89-92) that MODERN Islamic apologists and groups like ISIS would appeal to in order to support the idea that the Scriptures of the Jews and Christians got "corrupted" and totally changed. However, per the early Hadiths, they simply teach that the Christians or Jews mispronounced, misinterpreted or misrepresented their *meaning* and they needed Muhammad to set them straight on what was "hidden" in them and were not to be

---

[301] Bukhari, *Hadith, vol. 9*, footnote between 642 and 643.

"suppressed" by them. None of these passages in the Quran teach that the actual manuscripts of the Bible have been changed or corrupted!

It wasn't until 1064 that Ibn-Khazem first made the accusation that the OT and NT Scriptures must have been corrupted by the Jews and Christians since these Scriptures are not consistent with the Quran on many doctrinal or historical issues. This "corruption" doctrine of the Christian Bible begun by Ibn-Khazem in 1064 not only contradicts Muhammad, the Quran, and the Haddiths, but also other prominent Islamic teachers such as Ali al-Tabari (855), Amr al-Ghakhiz (869), BUKHARI (870), Al-Mas'udi (956), Abu Ali Husain Bin Sina (1037) and bn-Khaldun (1406).

Some Muslims came up with the theory that Jeremiah 8 teaches that the Jews themselves corrupted the Scriptures - "Behold, the lying pen of the scribes has made it into a lie" (Jeremiah 8:8). But, of course, the context of Jeremiah 8 is discussing God's people turning away from the law and not repenting. The point is that they were so careful to copy it down correctly, but not so careful in following and obeying it! It is exposing their hypocrisy. They were copying the law in vain, because they had no intention at the time of following it. The Hebrew word here, "*sheqer*," has various meanings such as 'untruth, shame, lie or in vain'. The accurate translation, honoring the context, is that the Jews were "writing in vain" the law while not following it. In 1 Samuel 25: 21 the same wording is translated as "it's been useless." They were writing the law "in vain" and it had become useless, because they had no intentions of following it.

There is no mention later of the law having been textually "corrupted," only that they had not obeyed it and would thus be judged by it (cf. Jer. 26:4-6; Dan. 9:1-13).

The irony

It is ironic that ISIS and Islam want to now assert that the Bible has been corrupted when in fact the early Muslim sources admit that there are forgotten and missing chapters and verses of the Quran. Aisha tells us that a sheep ate two chapters, so they were never added and forever lost. Others were memorized by Muslims who died in battle before writing them down, and are thus forever lost. Others were deliberately burned! Some can't even agree on if the modern Quran is even from Allah, and on and on it goes!

Muhammad was illiterate and often exposed that he had very little understanding of the Old and New Testaments, as he tried to mesh the two with paganism through alleged "revelations." Here are some incoherent propositions given by Muhammad, the Quran and Muslims in general on these issues:

> Allah gave the Jews and Christians His revelations and words.
>
> None of Allah's words and revelations can be corrupted because he is all powerful to preserve them.
>
> Jesus allegedly taught Islam from birth, gained a great following, and this prevailing success began from His birth and will last until the "last day."

Jews and Christians are to go to their Scriptures to confirm that Muhammad is a prophet and his revelations are consistent with their Scriptures.

When it is confirmed that Muhammad's teachings and "revelations" contradict the OT and NT, a theory emerges in 1064 that the OT and NT got corrupted. Putting this together we learn:

> Allah is NOT all powerful, because he was not able to preserve his words and revelations given to Jews and Christians.
>
> Allah himself is the one guilty and responsible for the corruption of the NT which teaches the death, resurrection and deity of Jesus (doctrines Muslims hate and will not submit to).
>
> Allah failed to make Jesus' Islamic message and gospel "prevail," because we have no record of any Islamic gospel or Islamic followers for centuries before Muhammad. This is because Allah himself deceived and caused it to not succeed.
>
> The ONLY message or gospel of Jesus that succeeded prior to Muhammad, and the ONLY one that Christians had in their hands to check if Muhammad's revelations were true in Muhammad's day, is the one that taught the death, resurrection, deity of Jesus the Christ and that He would return at the end of the old covenant age (not in Muhammad's generation)!

Another "Islamic Dilemma":

Option #1: If the gospel of Jesus is the authoritative preserved word of God that prevailed up to Muhammad's time, then Muhammad is a false prophet and the Quran is false because the Bible contradicts and exposes it.

And on the other hand…

Option #2: If Christians do not have the authoritative preserved word of God, then the Quran is false because it affirms that the Bible is the authoritative Word of God capable of judging the false teachings and "revelations" of Muhammad in the Quran.

Islam – a non-starter according to "the people of the book" and the Bible itself

As we saw in our study of Daniel 9:24-27/12:7, the office of prophet would "stop" when the Jews were judged and the temple was destroyed in AD 70. Jesus not only places this prophecy to be fulfilled in the events of AD 67 – AD 70, but He also teaches that "all" OT prophecy would be fulfilled at this time (cf. Lk. 21:22-32). Paul and John are consistent with Jesus' teaching when we harmonize 1 Corinthians 13:8-12 with Revelation 22:4-7. The miraculous sign and revelatory gifts of prophecy, tongues and knowledge would "cease" at the "soon" Second Coming of Christ whereby we now spiritually see His face in the new covenant age post AD 70.

The miraculous and confirmatory prophecy of Jerusalem's destruction in AD 70, given by the OT and NT prophets, proves that not only is this revelation miraculous, infallible and trustworthy, but it was also the prophecy and event by which we know the miraculous sign and revelatory gifts "stopped" or "ceased." This in and of itself destroys the claims of Muhammad and the Quran as being divine revelation from the same god of the OT and NT Scriptures.

Was Muhammad the last "seal" or Prophet predicted in Deuteronomy 18 and John 14?

The Quran teaches that Muhammad is the final prophet or "seal" that God has sent:

> "Muhammad is not the father of any of your men, but (he is) the Messenger of Allah, and the Seal of the Prophets: and Allah has full knowledge of all things" (Quran 33:40).

In the Quran (cf. 7:157; 61:6) there is an empty claim that Muhammad was predicted in the Scriptures. After 14 centuries of trying to find him, they finally came up with Deuteronomy 18 and John 14.

ISIS in their literature sought to prove that its caliphate was a sign of the "very soon" Second Coming of Jesus. In its literature they also claimed that Muhammad is the greater prophet predicted by Moses in Deuteronomy 18. Uh, they do realize that if this passage applies to Muhammad, then he should have been stoned for being a false prophet, right?!?

In Deuteronomy 13:1-5; 18:15, 18-20 and other passages, we learn that false prophets were to be stoned or rejected for the following:

1). speaking for God when God had not spoken to them

2). when their "revelations" led God's people away from Him in order to worship other gods

3). if their "revelations" contradicted previous revelations or doctrine found in the Law and Prophets.

4). if they lived an immoral life and committed abominable acts.

Muhammad is guilty of violating ALL of these requirements for being a prophet. Consider the following seven points:

1). Muhammad constantly had doubts that God was speaking through him, giving him alleged "revelations." He thought his revelations were coming from demons and Satan, which depressed him to the point of suicide on several occasions. The reliability of these so called "revelations" rested upon Muhammad's relatives who persuaded him that they were from God – obviously no miraculous confirmation that they came from God or himself!

2). Muhammad, when "prophesying" and receiving "revelations," promoted false gods (praying to three goddesses, resulting in them prostrating themselves down in worship from this "revelation," which were the Satanic Verses that were prompted by Allah himself – Quran 53:19-26; 22:52-53; 17:73-75). Muhammad led people astray from worshipping the true God and Jesus, while at the same time worshipping a false god (Allah).

Some modern Muslims may try and deny that the "Satanic Verses" were ever a part of the Quran, and yet all of their early Muslim sources admit that they were and that this account of Muhammad is true. This puts them in another dilemma:

Option #1: Muhammad did prophesy and support worship involving polytheistic gods, which makes him a false prophet to be stoned according to Deuteronomy 18.

Or

Option #2: All of their most reliable early sources (from which we get the Quran and Hadith) lied or were misinformed, which then means that we can't trust ANYTHING about the Quran and Hadith, because these same sources form them!

3). As already pointed out in this book, Muhammad delivered false prophecies on the arrival of the Antichrist, the last hour, the end of the world, and Second Coming of Jesus to take place at various times: a) in His generation, b) within 100 years of those listening to him, c) Within 500 years (based upon what Muhammad thought the age of the earth was) and d) Islam taking over Constantinople.

4). If Muhammad is a greater prophet than that of Moses, then where are the witnesses to God's revelation and law given to him? Where are the greater signs and wonders that Moses performed? The Quran itself and many Muslims admit that Muhammad performed no miracles.

5). The NT directly affirms that Jesus fulfills Deuteronomy 18, not Muhammad (cf. Acts 3:22-26; 7:37; Jn. 1:45; 5:45-47; 7:4; Heb. 3:2-6). In AD 70, Jesus was revealed from heaven in judgment upon those Jews who did not listen to Him and were "cut off" (Deut. 18:19/Acts 3:23). Jesus produced more miracles than Moses ever did, proving that He was the "last days" prophet Moses predicted would come, establishing a "better" covenant. When God gave Moses revelation, all the people could testify to the miracles before, during, and after this revelation was given, as proof of its divine origin. Likewise, Jesus' miracles were greater than Moses, confirming His message of new covenant salvation found in Him. The Quran affirms that the only "miracle" Muhammad performed was his giving of the Quran (some of which a sheep ate - LOL).

6). Muhammad was a sexual pervert and adulterer. His "revelations" sought to justify having sex with his wives' slave women, taking his adopted son's wife, having sex with a 9-year old girl, dressing up in Aisha's clothing, sucking on men's tongues, etc.

7). Per Muhammad, the Quran and Deuteronomy 18, Muhammad should have been stoned and rejected as a perverted false prophet. Per Muhammad, he should have been "judged" according to the Torah and stoned with that PAGAN Kaaba black stone that Muslims kiss and adore so much.

And what of Islam's appeals that Muhammad was predicted to come in John 14:16-17, 26; 15:26; 16:7?

After proving that there is NO reason to see Muhammad being the prophet of Deuteronomy 18 (except to stone him for being a false prophet), what about the Muslim appeals to finding Muhammad predicted in John 14-16?

1). This text couldn't be more clear that it predicts the coming of the "Holy Spirit" ("Spirit of Truth"), not Muhammad. In examining the literature of ISIS, they claimed that the Greek word *'paraclete'* should be understood as "*Parakleton,*" which would then mean "the praised one," an alleged "direct translation of the name Muhammad, synonymous to the name Ahmad," which means "one defined by praise." Of course, Islam and ISIS cannot produce ANY ancient documents that "*parakleton*" ("the praised one") is in the passage! This is just a minor detail, I guess (LOL).

2). Ironically, John 14-16 affirms the Trinity, which Islam and ISIS deny. The gospel of John also repeatedly confirms that Jesus is God (John 1; 5-6; 10; 14-17). An appeal to the gospel of John destroys the claims of Islam and ISIS.

3). John 14 teaches that the Holy Spirit (the *paraclete*) had already been "with" the disciples and would soon be "in" them. Muhammad came 600 years later and, being a mere man (per Islam), he could not be within the disciples as the Father and Son would be. Again, these are just minor details and problems for Islam here.

4). The Holy Spirit would "remind" and "teach" the apostles about the "things to come" that would be fulfilled in their lifetimes and generation (that is, in AD 70). Since the apostles died long before Muhammad, it's kind of hard to see how he reminded them of anything. The only thing that Muhammad has "reminded" and "taught" Muslims concerning "things to come" is errors and false predictions.

5). This passage teaches that the Second Coming results in the indwelling of the Father, Son and Holy Spirit (Jn. 14:23) – the fulfillment of the spiritual new covenant kingdom promises reached in AD 70 (cf. Lk. 17:20-21/21:27-32).

6). In Islam, ONLY Allah can send Muhammad, and yet in John 14 both the Father and the Son send the "*paraclete*" (Muhammad); thus Jesus is God, per Islam.

7). The Holy Spirit was "with" the disciples by performing miracles in Jesus' name. He continued to be with and in them performing miracles before miracles "ceased" at Christ's very "soon" coming in AD 70 (1 Cor. 13:8-12/Rev. 22:4-7). Again, the Quran teaches that Muhammad had NO POWER and performed NO miracles.

Concluding Islam

Islam and its various groups such as ISIS have killed so many and have deceived millions of their young men to their senseless deaths. The final marching orders of the Quran ends with chapter 9's violent great commission. The NT ends its revelation of Christ having come "soon" in AD 70, and then having the charge for the Church to bring healing to the nations through wielding the sword of the Spirit or preaching the everlasting gospel (Rev. 22:6-20).

Christianity has grown over the years because it confronts and heals man's depravity, while Islam has grown because it has appealed to man's depravity (greed and lust).

ISIS and Islam have sought to prove that the NT is "corrupted" and Jesus was a false prophet because a "very soon" literal Second Coming (attended with a literal earth-ending resurrection) did not take place in His contemporary generation. Therefore, per their own reasoning, we are to reject Muhammad as a prophet because he taught a "very soon" second coming that never materialized. Selah.

The bottom line is that Muhammad was a mentally unstable and illiterate man who simply assumed that the "revelations" he was making up and pawning off actually "confirmed" what the Christians had in their Bibles. It took the Islamic community and religion a very long time to come up with the theory that the Christian Bible got "corrupted" and that this is why the Quran contradicts it. Yet this contradicts the actual teaching of the Quran itself, which informs us that no man can corrupt the words of Allah which are supposed to be his revelations as manifested in the OT, NT and the Quran. If the Bible is from Allah and the Quran says this revelation cannot be corrupted and yet it was, then the Quran is false. If Allah gave the revelation of the Bible and it was not corrupted, then the Quran is once again proven to be false because it contradicts the major doctrines of the Bible on virtually every key doctrine – the deity of Christ, the Trinity, salvation by grace through faith alone, the crucifixion, the resurrection, and the timing and fulfillment of the Second Coming. Therefore, we reject the Quran and Muhammad and humbly implore the Muslim to flee to the Jesus of the OT and NT Scriptures to be saved by His marvelous and free grace.

2). Talmudic Israeli Zionism or Torah Jews

While my focus in this book has been on exposing the violent eschatology of Talmudic or Messianic Israeli Zionism, I do realize there are other Jewish views out there that even reject the modern state of Israel and its Zionism. It is very difficult to find common ground in reaching the Talmudic Zionist when he sees the Talmud as more inspired than the actual Torah or OT Scriptures. But for those Jewish sects that believe the OT is God's infallible revelation to man, we can find common ground and build upon this proposition.

Having said that, my approach here will be in appealing to the OT and what Rabbis have taught about who Messiah would be and when Messiah would come, and see if Christian Full Preterism can help "bridge the gap," so to speak.

The "Jewish" claims against the NT and Christianity

Modern "Jews" portray the NT and Christianity in general as coming up with "a new religion" totally foreign from the OT Scriptures and their Jewish traditions and roots, especially when they examine the NT's portrayal of the virgin birth or Jesus' claims to being eternal and divine, worthy of worship. These doctrines seem to offend them the most. But let's look at their accusations first before correcting them with their own Scriptures and Rabbinical traditions.

1). Modern day "Jewish" apologists claim Messiah was never thought to be a divine being, let alone a savior who could be offered up as a substitutionary offering to forgive the sins of his people:

- "The word "mashiach" does not mean "savior." The notion of an ***innocent, divine*** or semi-divine being who will ***sacrifice himself to save us from the*** *consequences of our own sins is a purely Christian concept that has no basis in Jewish thought."*[302]

2). Modern day "Jewish" apologists also mock the NT and Futurist Christian teaching of the Second Coming of Messiah or Jesus upon the clouds:

- "At first, Christians expected that this "second coming" would come very shortly, and prayed that they would see it in their lifetime. When their prayer was not answered, they began to hope that it would come a thousand years after Jesus' death. This was the millenium or "thousand year kingdom." Finally, after a thousand years passed and Jesus still had not returned, they postponed his "second coming" to an indefinite time.

- We therefore see that the early Christians were forced to radically alter the Jewish concept of the Messiah in order to explain Jesus' failure. This, compounded with the pagan influence in the early church, gave birth to a Messianic concept totally alien to Judaism."[303]

- "...there is **a major historical dilemma** which seems to explain why the doctrine of the second coming was invented. H. M. Waddams, who was the Residentiary Canon of Canterbury Cathedral in 1968, wrote a book [The Struggle for Christian Unity, NY, 1968, p. 10] explaining why it took so many years for the Church to get organized into a formal, organized group. His answer is that even though verses such as Matthew 24:34 may mean that Jesus is referring to a future generation, nonetheless **most of the early Christians** thought that the simple interpretation was correct. It corroborated the impressions that they had of the message of Jesus, and so they **thought that Jesus would return within their own lifetime**. After all, Jesus did say, in Matthew 16:28, "Verily I say unto you, **there be some standing here which shall not taste of death**, till they see the son of man coming in his kingdom." However, after many years went by, and the generation that lived in Jesus' generation had all died, it became rather apparent that Jesus would not reappear in the near future. **The doctrine was therefore changed so that his reappearance was not necessarily going to be in the near future."**[304]

But what if we can show them from the OT Scriptures and through the teachings and traditions of their own Rabbis that there was an expectation for the Messiah to be both a man and a divine being eternal in origin coming to take the form of a man, and that He is worthy of worship?

What if we can prove from their own sources and traditions that the "appointed time" for Messiah to come was around AD 17/19 or AD 26/28?

---

[302] *The Messianic Idea in Judaism*, http://www.jewfaq.org/mashiach.htm

[303] Kaplan, ibid, 32-33. Special thanks to Ed Stevens for that quote.

[304] Samuel Levine, *You Take Jesus, I'll Take God*, (Los Angeles, California USA: Hamoroh Press, 1980), 15-16, bracketed material and emphasis added by Ed Stevens].

What if we can prove from their own sources and traditions that Messiah was to be "cut off" (as a substitutionary offering for the sins of His people) and there would be "forty years" between Him being "cut off" to Him coming upon the clouds in judgment to destroy their temple in AD 70?

What if we can prove from their own sources and traditions that most of them would not "discern" their own "end" in AD 70? What if some taught that if Messiah didn't come before AD 70, then He may never come? Then of course they funneled this failure of Messiah to come by AD 70 into some kind of open theism, in that God changed his mind because they weren't righteous enough for Him to come at "that appointed time" after all. Yet some did claim that Israel has been under a "curse" ever since AD 70.

What if we can prove from their own sources and traditions that Christ coming upon the clouds is common Hebraic apocalyptic language and that Christ predicted an end to the old covenant age/world and not to world history?

What if we can prove from their own sources and traditions that when the Messianic kingdom comes it would be spiritual and within a believer and that the OT never predicts a time when there will be no more earthly wars or a time when God obliterates all evil from the planet? After all, in the new creation of Isaiah 65:17 – 66:24 there are sinners, evangelism, child birth, physical labor and biological death.

Many Jews simply don't understand some of these OT texts, let alone know what some of their own Rabbis have taught concerning them. I think the claims of Christ being the pre-incarnate Word, or God, is the best place to start. I will demonstrate that the doctrine of a divine Messiah and God becoming man was very Jewish during the times of Jesus and even lasting up to around 100 AD until the Jews began making this view heretical.

Messiah ben Joseph and Messiah ben David

But before we get to the relevant texts and Jewish admissions upon which I shall make my case concerning Messiah's divinity and eternal origins, we should point out to the reader that within Judaism there is the concept of two Messiahs – 1). Messiah ben Joseph and 2). Messiah ben David. The Rabbis don't want many Christians to know about Messiah ben Joseph. Why? Because as we have seen, they first begin their propaganda by denying that the Jewish Messiah of the OT and within their traditions will act redemptively to forgive sin, because this sounds too much like the Messiah of the NT. But in the Rabbinic literature Messiah ben Joseph is born in Galilee and dies, being pierced through by mighty enemies at the gate of Jerusalem. His death atones for sin and abolishes the curse of death. And he even appears to undergo a resurrection or transformation.[305]

---

[305] David C. Mitchell, *Messiah be Joseph* (Newton Mearns, Scotland: CAMPBELL PUBLICATIONS, 2016, revised 2021), 1

Messiah ben Joseph is the "Shepherd-Rock," or the "firstborn" sacrificial *shor* ox, that is transformed into the fierce and conquering *rem* ox who will come in Israel's "last days" from the line of Joseph (Gen. 49:24; Deut. 31-33). This white ox will transform the other beasts of the field into white oxen or into his image. And just as Joshua comes from the line of Joseph, so too will Messiah ben Joseph suffer and rise to power like Joseph did. But since Joshua came from the line of Joseph, Messiah ben Joseph will also function as a new Joshua and conquer God's enemies. In Jewish literature, Messiah ben Joseph has a transitionary reign of 40 years before the battle of Gog and Magog,[306] and yet as we have already seen it is also admitted in the Jewish literature (in the Dead Sea Scrolls) that this "last days" war was to be between Rome and apostate Jerusalem between AD 67 – AD 70.

The NT develops Jesus as both the Messiah Yehoshuah as a second Joshua and/or a second Messianic "Son of David." He comes to Israel as the sacrificial "firstborn" who suffers, dies and atones for the sins of His people, transforming them into His image and imputing His righteousness to their account. He is raised / transformed and becomes a mighty conquering King (as Joshua and David were) who has a transitional "this generation" reign of 40 years between the old covenant age which was "passing away" and "ready to vanish" and the maturing new covenant age which was "about to come" in its fulness (AD 30 – AD 70). And just as the first 40 years ends with Joshua conquering Jericho (with the number seven and blowing of trumpets), so Christ judges and "desolates" the temple and the wicked "great city" of old covenant Jerusalem after 40 years at the sound of the seventh trumpet in AD 70 (Rev. 11:1-8). And of course as David reigned for 40 years, placing the enemies of Israel under his feet, Christ was placing His enemies (and those who said they would not have this man reign over Him) under His feet and would have them slain between AD 30 – AD 70.

But once a Christian points out that he is not ignorant of Messiah ben Joseph in the Jewish literature – that is, of his suffering redemptive and atoning role – the propaganda and moving of the goal posts change to something like, "Well, Messiah ben David does not suffer and die for sin." But as we will see, this too is a false statement since Messiah ben David is also mentioned in Jewish literature to be the fulfillment of the suffering servant in Isaiah 53.

We shall now turn our attention to **healing** the **schizophrenic** and **bipolar** *Jewish denial, and yet at the same time admission,* of a suffering, dying and atoning Messiah who is also more than just a man – being divine and having eternal origins – with the consistent and timely arrival and predictions of the Messiah of the NT.

The OT and Jewish views of a human, divine incarnate Messiah

The Jewish apologist against Christianity usually begins a discussion with a Christian by quoting Deuteronomy 6:4, which should be translated as the NJPSV does, grasping the historical and contextual meaning:

---

[306] Mitchell, Ibid., 114-115

"Hear, O Israel! The LORD is our God, the LORD *alone*."

The OT oneness of God within its original context does not discuss the philosophical nature or complexity of God, but rather addresses the context of Israel being commanded to not worship the other gods of the nations, because Israel's God *alone is the one true* God. The Midrash underscores this as well:

> "Hear, O Israel [i.e., Israel/Jacob, our father], the Lord is our God, the LORD *alone*. Just as in your heart there is only ONE (*echad*) so also in our hearts there is only One (*echad*)." To this Jacob replied, "Blessed be his Name, whose glorious kingdom is forever and ever"[307]

In other words, the emphasis is that although Jacob/Israel is worrying about one of his sons being unfaithful, they all reply that they indeed would be faithful to the LORD *alone*. The point is that the LORD *alone* would be the God of Jacob's descendants.

When Jesus addresses this subject in Mark 12:28-30, He establishes that the Father is the only true/one God that is to be worshiped *with one's entire heart* (thus not leaving room for other idols). In John 17:3, Jesus again affirms that His Father is the one and only God. The Messiah's message is to get the people to leave their idols and to serve the one true God.

The complexity of the God-head existed in the OT before we even reach the NT and the Christian view of the Trinity emerges. If the Scriptures said that no one could see God and live (cf. Ex. 33:20), how is it that these same Scriptures taught that people saw Him on the earth (and didn't die) while at the same time He sat enthroned in heaven running the universe? Didn't God come in human form, even *talking and eating* with Abraham, *wrestling* with Jacob and *leading the armies* of Israel? How was God in heaven seated on His throne ruling the universe while at the same time being in the form of a man doing all of these things? The Jews debated and struggled over these issues.

The Aramaic Targums read in the synagogues concerning who the "Word" was

Before examining the Gospel of John and John's description of Jesus as the "Word," let's once again try to get the Jewish cultural and contextual understanding of "the Word" before the Messiah even comes into the world. In the Aramaic Targum (their translation of the Hebrew Scriptures which was read in the synagogues), the "LORD" is substituted with the "Word" or "Word of the LORD" in the following passages: Gen. 1:27, 3:8, 6:6-7, 9:12;,15:6, 20:3, 28:20-21, 31:49; Ex. 14:31, 20:1, 25:22; Lev. 26:9; Num. 10:35-36, 11:23, 14:35; Deut. 1:26, 30; 4:7; 18:19; 31:3; Josh. 1:5; Judges 11:10; Isa. 45:17. In these texts it's the Word that creates. It's the Word that walked in the garden with Adam. The Word is what Abraham believed in and was justified by. It is said they believed in the Word. The Word rose up and returned in saving and justifying

---

[307] *b. Pesahim 56a; Sifre Deuteronomy 31; Genesis Rabbah 98:4*

Israel. The Word was active in decreeing. The Word gave the law. Moses prayed to the Word. The Word is said to sit enthroned in heaven listening to the prayers of Israel. The people rebelled against the Word. The Word led and fought for Israel. The Word passed before the people, etc.

And watch this comparison of Genesis 28:20-21 and the Targum. This is Genesis:

> "If God will be with me and will watch over me on this journey I am taking and will give me food to eat and clothes to wear so that I return safely to my father's house, then the LORD will be with me, **then the LORD will be my God.**"

This is the Targum:

> "If the Word of the LORD will be with me…then the **Word of the LORD will be my God.**"

Clearly, we have seen that belief in the "Word" is what justified Abraham, and here it is **the "Word" that was Jacob's *God*!**

Philo and the "Word

Even the Jew Philo (25 BC – AD 50) understood that the Word (Greek *Logos*) shares the divine identity with God,[308] is "the first-born,"[309] the "man of God,"[310] the "image of God,"[311] and the "second God."[312] While Jesus is the divine Logos and one with the Father, He is also subordinate to the Father. The Father "has given all things into his hand" (Jn. 3:35), "has given Him authority to judge" (Jn. 5:22), and Jesus while being identified as the eternal God understands His role to be from the Father and in submission to His "Father" (Jn. 1:1, 14).

In some contexts, Philo understands the Angel of the Lord to be distinct from YHWH and yet in other contexts the Word is identical (cf. Gen. 16:7-13, 32:24-28; Ex. 23:20, Ex. 23:20; Hos. 12:4-5; Mal. 3:1).[313] Philo sees the Logos as the eldest and chief of the angels. In some places, God is the supreme being and the Logos is next in power being the mediator between God and His creation. Yet in at least three passages Philo describes the Logos as God Himself:

> a.) Commenting on Genesis 22:16, Philo explains that God could only swear by himself (LA 3.207).

> b.) When the scripture uses the Greek term for God, *ho theos*, it refers to the true God, but when it uses the term *theos*, without the article *ho*, it refers not to the God, but to his most ancient Logos (*Somn.* 1.229-230).

---

[308] (Leg. 3, 61, 173; Migr. 6)

[309] (Agr. 12, 51)

[310] (QE II, 62, Marcus, LCL)

[311] (Conf. 28)

[312] (QE II 62, Marcus, LCL)

[313] (Somn. 1.228-239; Cher. 1-3)

c.) Commenting on Genesis 9:6 Philo states that the reference to the creation of man after the image of God is to the second deity, the Divine Logos of the Supreme being and to the father himself, because it is only fitting that the rational soul of man cannot be in relation to the preeminent and transcendent Divinity (QG 2.62)."[314]

I could go on and on and make comparisons and contrasts between Philo and John's gospel, and Philo with the writer to the Hebrews (along with some Pauline Epistles), concerning this same terminology and how each are wrestling with how the divine Logos of the OT LXX breaks into the world of men. It seems that John and the writer to the Hebrews are very familiar with the OT LXX understanding of the *Word / Mediator* motifs and of Philo's use of the *Logos*. They are just explaining HOW this divine being (God) has entered into the world of man as a superior mediator than that of Moses or Philo's impersonal philosophical Logos. God had revealed Himself as the Angel of the Lord and through human theophanies in the OT, but now He has entered in a more personal and redemptive role through the virgin birth and incarnation.

So, once we approach John 1, we can see that John is not coming up with something completely new to Jewish thought and doctrine. He understood what was being read in the synagogues about the Word (*memra*), and writing in Greek He understood what was being taught about the divine *logos* by his Jewish brethren.

As God's plan of redemption is unfolding, there is now more clarity on WHO the "Word" has been all along – Jesus, the eternal Word/Son of God. It is through Him (the Word) that all was made (just as in Jewish thought), except now the Word became a man/flesh and dwelt among us. But even this is not completely foreign because in the OT Scriptures God was seen as a man upon the earth (while at the same time somehow fully Spirit enthroned in heaven ruling and maintaining the universe). The Word/Son of God revealed Himself (theophany) in the form of a man to Abraham, Jacob and Israel prior to his incarnation. But what became of this human body after the Word appeared in it? Since "God is Spirit" (Jn. 4), we know He did not return in His glory with it. This being the case, I affirm that when Jesus ascended in the divine glory cloud and went back into the glory He shared with the Father before the world began, He no longer has had a physical body (Acts 1:9-11; Jn. 17:3-5, 24). We no longer know Him according to the flesh (2 Cor. 5:16). In AD 70 Christ returned in His pre-incarnate form "in His glory" (in His glory cloud) and now has taken up His home (along with the Father and Holy Spirit) *within* the believer – through faith we "believe" this to have taken place (Jn. 14:2-3, 23, 28-29; cf. Lk. 17:20-37, and remember our exegesis of Mark 8:38--9:1).

John 1:14 literally reads that the Word (in the previous context, stated to be God) "lived in a tent" or "pitched his tent" among us just as Jehovah pitched his tent in the forms of the tabernacle and temple in the OT and dwelt in His glory among Israel. Here again, God's presence was both on earth and in heaven at the same time. When God's

---

[314] Marian Hillar, *The Internet Encyclopedia of Philosophy*, https://iep.utm.edu/philo/

presence filled the OT tabernacle, His "glory filled it" (Ex. 40:34-35), and now John says that we have seen His "glory" full of grace and truth. God fills His Son/the Word and through Him all things came about, and in Him is the exact representation of His being (Heb. 1:3).

The promised "seed of the woman" (Genesis 3:15)

This passage was and is understood to be Messianic among those who embrace Judaism. The Targum Yerushaimi states the following of this passage:

> "Nevertheless, there shall be a remedy for the sons of the woman, but for you, serpent, there shall be no remedy. But it shall be that for these [for the sons of the woman] there shall be a remedy for the heel *in the days of the King Messiah*."

If one is functioning within the historical Hebrew worldview, the phrase "seed of the woman" seems out of place in that usually children are referred to as coming from the "seed of the man." The man's sperm is the "seed," and the woman is usually referred to as the fertile soil in which the man's seed is planted to produce offspring. For the modern reader this may sound strange – a Messiah/man who has no human father? But as I previously pointed out, in the Hebrew worldview God took on human form many times in Genesis and the gods came down and walked among women producing hybrids or giants (Gen. 6).

From the beginning, this "seed" is referring to ONE man or Messiah and not two (such as a suffering Messiah ben Joseph and a conquering Messiah ben David).

While not explicitly stated, the death of the Messiah could be implied if the serpent's bite upon His heel is poisonous. If that were the case, a part of the process by which He could overcome and "crush" the Serpent's head would be by rising from the dead. After all, the serpent's bite upon Adam and Eve (so to speak) produced spiritual death that very day and then they were sentenced to physical death to perish in the "dust" outside of the temple/garden some 930 years later. The Messiah would need to reverse the sting or bite of this spiritual death that now separated man from God. Would He take this curse upon Himself in a substitutionary way and experience and somehow take away this sin/death and separation from man?

Therefore, what we have here in seed form is the possibility of two things. First, the Messiah's lineage will come from the woman and thus the possibility of a unique or miraculous conception is in view here. And secondly, Messiah may suffer a lethal bite from the serpent and overcome it somehow. These questions will be answered more fully through the prophets and progressive revelation.

The "Shepherd-Rock" of Genesis 49:24, Messiah ben Joseph

In Genesis 49 we learn that in Israel's "last days" (Gen. 49:1) Messiah or "Shiloh" is not just predicted to come from Judah (Gen. 49:10), but also "from whence/thence" Joseph's line will come the Messiah described as a "Shepherd-Rock" or, as the Septuagint renders, a "Conqueror."

These need not be referring to two Messiahs (Messiah ben Joseph and Messiah ben David), but rather one Messiah being described in different ways.

We now turn to our next passage where it is admitted within Judaism that the "Shepherd-Rock" here in Genesis 49:24 and the "Rock" of Deuteronomy 32 is referring to the Messiah.

The "Rock" of Deuteronomy 32 – both God and Messiah

Old Testament scholar, David C. Mitchell, points out that Jewish interpreters understood the "Rock" of Deuteronomy 32 to be both God and yet Messiah at the same time:

> "Altogether then, the 'Shepherd-Rock' promised to Joseph [Gen. 49:24] is a mighty king. The Septuagint agrees, rendering 'Shepherd-Rock' by one Greek word, *Katischusas*, 'conqueror'. Therefore the coming one promised to Joseph is like the Shiloh world-ruler promised to Judah earlier in the same chapter: he is one whom the nations will obey. And, just as the Shiloh-ruler is to come after Judah's kingdom, a kingdom which has not even appeared at the time of Jacob's prophecy, so the Shepherd-Rock is a divinely-appointed ruler to come after Joseph's time, but one greater and freer than Joseph ever was.
>
> Such an interpretation is not a novelty. Ramban [13th century R. Moshe ben Nahman] says, in his comments on Deuteronomy 32:4, that this Rock from Joseph is the same Rock or Stone as is spoken of in Psalm 118:22.
>
> And he [Moses] said: *Let my teaching fall like rain*. For that which he brought from the heavens, and his speech on the earth, *will fall* upon Israel, and *settle* upon them *like dew* (Deut. 32:2). *For I will proclaim the name of Ha-Shem* in the heavens; *come, declare the greatness of our God* (Deut. 32:3) in the earth. [*The Rock, his work is perfect*, etc. (Deut. 32:4).
>
> And all Israel will say also the rock is Joshua, a sign about this land, for, *From thence a Shepherd-Rock of Israel* (Gen. 49:24). And it was interpreted long ago: *The rock rejected by the builders has become the capstone*; *this is from Ha-Shem*, etc. (Ps. 118:22-23). And that is why Joshua said, *This rock will be a witness between us* (Josh. 24:27). Also, *For behold the rock which I have set before Joshua: upon one rock are seven eyes* (Zech. 3:9). Let the wise understand.
>
> Ramban's comments are triggered by the Rock of Deuteronomy 32:4. This Rock, he says, is not only the ETERNAL, but also Joshua. Writing in his latter years, in the Mamluk-ruled Holy Land, he says it is a sign for 'this land,' and he cites Genesis 49:24, whose Shepherd-Rock he identifies as Joshua. He then proceeds to link the divine Rock of Deuteronomy 32:4 and the Joshua Rock of Genesis 49:24 with the Rock-rejected-by-the-builders of Psalm 118. Now Ramban knew Psalm 118 was written long after Joshua's time. And he knew its rejected Rock had a long history of messianic interpretations [2Q23 and 4Q173 (=4QpPsb) frg. 5, lines 1-6]. So Ramban is not speaking of Joshua ben

> Nun, but of another Joshua Rock yet to come, whom he sees prefigured in the rock set before Joshua ben Jehozadak in Zechariah 3:9. So, when Ramban says that the Joshua Rock is a sign for 'this land,' he foresaw the land of the Israel being reconquered and ruled by another Joshua, one still to come in Ramban's own time, that is, a Joshua messiah, who is the promised Shepherd-Rock."[315]

And again,

> "…he [Ramban] is saying that the Shepherd-Rock promised to Joseph is none other than the Rock of Deuteronomy 32:4, who is the God of Israel himself, the Angel who followed the Israelites through the desert as a thirst-quenching Rock."[316]

Since Deuteronomy 32 is the second-most quoted OT passage in the NT, we should give it some attention here:

1). In Israel's **"last days"**, "evil will befall" them for rejecting God their Rock (31:29, 32:15).

1). Israel was in her **"last days"** with **Christ (as their Rock** – I Cor. 10:4) appearing at the end of the OC age (Acts 2:16-21; Heb. 1:2; 9:26-28).

2). In Israel's "last days" a **"perverse and crooked generation"** would experience the **"end"** and judgment (Deut. 32:5, 20).

2). Jesus, Peter and Paul teach the **"end"** or "end of the [OC] age" as being in their contemporary **"this [perverse & crooked] generation"** (Mt. 23:1-36; 24:3-34; Mark 8:38-9:1; 1 Cor. 10:11GNT; Acts 2:20-**40**).

3). When this terminal generation arrives, God's **"vengeance"** and Israel's "end" would be **"at hand"** (Deut. 32:35).

3). Jesus teaches that the **"days of vengeance"** against "this people" and "land" (His contemporary Jewish nation), along with her "end," would be **"near"** in His contemporary "this generation" when all OT prophecy [e.g. Deut. 32] would be fulfilled (Lk. 21:20-32). Peter declares that the **"end** of all things **is near**" (1 Pet. 4:5-7, 17). Paul identifies his "perverse generation" as the one predicted by Moses which will experience the **"at hand"** Second Coming (Phil. 2:15; 4:5).

4). God's people are **"vindicated"** at this time (Deut. 32:36, 43).

4). In Jesus' contemporary "this generation," He would **vindicate and avenge** all the blood shed as far back as Abel (Mt. 23:30-36). In Revelation **the martyrs are vindicated "in a little while"** (Rev. 6:10-11).

---

[315] Mitchell, *Messiah be Joseph*, Ibid., 16-17

[316] David C. Mitchell, *Jesus The Incarnation of the Word* (Newton Mearns, Scotland: CAMPBELL PUBLICATIONS, 2021), 39

5). Israel is so faithless and wicked that she is identified as **"Sodom"** in her judgment (32:32).

5). Old covenant Jerusalem is so faithless and wicked that she is identified as **"Sodom,"** and her **judgment would "no longer be delayed"** (Rev. 10:6; 11:8).

6). Israel's sin and God's vengeance were **"heaped"** and **"stored up"** for this time of judgment (32:23, 34).

6). Jerusalem had **"filled up the measure"** of her covenantal sin of blood guilt and was judged for it in Jesus' generation (Mt. 23:32-36; 1 Thess. 2:15-16). OC Jerusalem or "Babylon" filled up the cup of her sin (Rev. 17:4).

7). Israel as a covenant people was referred to as **"heaven(s) and earth"** (Deut. 31:30 - 32:1; Isa. 1:1-2; 51:15-16). God would set on **fire the mountains and earth** (32:22).

7). The burning / passing of Israel's "elements" / "heaven(s) and earth" / "mountain" was "near" (1 Pet. 4:5-7/2 Pet. 3; Rev. 8:8/Mt. 21:18-21; Rev. 21-22:10).

8). "I will move them to jealousy with *those which are* not a people. I will provoke them to anger with a foolish nation" (32:21).

8). This would be a "short work," a "nation born in a day" (Rom. 9:25-32; 10:19, 11:11; Isa. 66:8) – when Israel would stumble over Christ and the kingdom would be taken from Israel and given to a "nation" (the Church) bearing the fruits thereof (Mt. 21:43; 1 Peter 2:9).

The Septuagint translation/interpretation of Deuteronomy 32:43 is very interesting. Our most ancient Hebrew manuscript for this particular verse is found in the Dead Sea Scrolls and reads:

> "Rejoice, O heavens together with him; and **bow down to him all you gods [or angels],** for he will avenge the blood of his sons, and will recompense those who hate him, and will atone for the land and his people" (4QDeut^q).

The NT author of Hebrews cites the Septuagint of Deuteronomy 32:43 and sees Jesus as the fulfillment:

> "And when He again brings the **firstborn** [see the **firstborn shor ox** of Deut. 33:13-17] into the world, He says, 'And **let all the angels of God worship Him**'" (Heb. 1:6).

The NT authors identify Jesus as the Messianic "Rock" of Genesis 49 and Deuteronomy 32, who is worthy of worship.

The Messianic "Firstborn" Shor and Rem Ox of Deuteronomy 33:13-17

The Messiah is not just found in Jacob's blessing in Genesis 49, but also in the blessing of Moses found in Deuteronomy 33. From the lines of Joseph would come two oxen which would produce a messianic hero. The first is a "firstborn shor," or a domestic ox exempt from the hard labor of other oxen, but specifically set aside to be a sacrifice for the sin of Israel (Deut. 15:19; Num. 18:17).

The firstborn, domestic, suffering shor ox is transformed into the mighty and wild conquering rem ox. David Mitchel writes:

> "…in Deuteronomy, Joseph's *shor* and rem represent one individual who is to undergo transformation. Even in his lowly state Joseph's *shor* was intrinsically glorious; as it is said, he is Joseph's majesty, or majesty is his. And that is why he is finally endowed with the majestic, fearsome horns of a rem, that is, its kingly corona, its crown of horns. And, being so crowned, it looks like the humble *shor* has become the rem.
>
> …the only option is that the *shor* becomes the rem and is transformed from humiliation to triumph.
>
> And, lest anyone imagine that I have gone completely out on a limb, I call to witness 1 Enoch 90:37-38.

And I saw that a white bull was born, with large horns, and all the beasts of the field and all the birds of the air feared him and made petition to him all the time. And I saw till all their generations were transformed, and they all became white bulls; and the first among them became an aurochs (the aurochs was a great beast and had a great black horn on its head); and the Lord of the sheep rejoiced over them and over all the oxen."

But how does the *shor* become the *rem*? How does one destined to sacrifice become triumphant? Clearly not by evading his fate. Dereliction of duty is not the hero's way. The path to glory must be through the destiny of sacrifice and death. Could this mean some kind of post-mortem resurgence? Perhaps."[317]

The most popular view among the Rabbis, as to who the hero is who wields the horns of Ephraim and Manasseh, is that it was Messiah ben Joseph. Through his sacrifice as the "first born" (death is implied) and victorious transformation (resurrection is implied), He would transform other creatures into His image as a white ox – that is, He would impute His righteousness to them and make them sons of the kingdom.

Psalm 110, Melchizedek and the Messiah

- *Of David, a psalm. YHVH [God] vows to my [David] lord [Messiah/Melchizedek]: Sit at my right hand; till I set your enemies [to be] a stool for your feet. YHVH will send forth your mighty scepter from Zion. Rule amidst your enemies. With you is dominion on the day of your strength. Amidst the shining lights of the holy ones I have begotten you from the womb before the morning star. YHVH has sworn and will not disavow: You are a kohen [Priest] forever, according to my decree, Melchizedek. The Lord at*

---

[317] Mitchell, *Messiah ben Joseph*, Ibid., 23-24

your right hand crushes kings in the day of his wrath. He executes judgment among the nations—fullness of corpses! He crushes the head [or ruler] of the wide earth. From a brook by the road will he drink; so will he lift up [his] head."

- *He [God] says [to Christ] in another place...You are a priest forever according to my/the decree, [O] Melchizedek (Heb. 5:6).*
- *Where the forerunner has entered for us, Jesus, according to my/the decree, [O] Melchizedek, become a high priest forever (Heb. 6:20).*
- *What further need was there for another priest to arise, according to my/the decree, [O] Melchizedek, and not to be named according to the decree of Aaron? (Heb. 7:11)*
- *"For it is declared [of Christ]...You are a priest forever according to my/the decree, [O] Melchizedek (Heb. 7:17)*[318]
- *Your father Abraham rejoiced to see my day [when He came to Abraham as Melchizedek]. He saw and was glad...Truly I say to you, before Abraham was, I am (Jn. 8:56, 58).*

The Psalms in which the Rabbis saw Messiah ben Joseph (and/or combined with Messiah son of David) were 1-2; 22; 60 (here begins an inclusion which ends at 108, which cites some of the same material); 80-81; 86-87; 89; 92; 108; 110. Due to space limitations, we shall focus on Psalm 110, since it is the most quoted OT passage in the NT.

There are some key, and yet basic, important points to make on Jesus' teaching on Psalm 110 in Matthew 22:41-46 and Mark 12:35-37:

> 1). A large part of the Jewish belief that Messiah would be more than a man and have divine eternal origins (prior to Jesus and in His day) was born out of an understanding of the Messiah described in Psalm 110. Daniel 7:13-14, and even non-biblical texts such as *11QMelchizedek; 1 Enoch 46:1; 48:10; 52:4; 4 Ezra 13 [although written post AD 70 around 100],* likewise describe Messiah as both a man and yet much more – having eternal origins, reigning with God in His kingdom, riding upon the clouds of heaven accomplishing atonement for the remnant and exercising judgment for the wicked and fallen Watchers.

> 2). The Pharisees agreed that Psalm 110 was referring to the "Messiah" (Mt. 22:41-42), and no doubt a great many who heard His teaching in the temple agreed as well (Mark 12:35-37). But the question and debate of the day, and the one Jesus enters into here with Psalm 110, is how many understood this passage [and other passages such as the reference to the "Son of Man" in Daniel 7] to teach that Messiah was to be much more than a man – a divine being with eternal origins? What was the theological significance of David calling Messiah his "Lord"?

---

[318] Ibid., 78-79, 84

3). While the crowd in Mark 12 received His exposition of Psalm 110, the Pharisees in Matthew 22 were unable "to answer Him a word." Why? It's because they knew Jesus was teaching that He was the Great "I Am" who existed before Abraham, equal to the Father and the "Son of Man" or Messiah of Daniel 7:13. To admit that Messiah was divine and greater than a mere mortal man would mean that they had to seriously consider Jesus as Messiah and also His claim to be more than a man. This would mean that they needed to submit to His teachings, and at some point renounce their unbiblical traditions and let go of the power they wielded over the people. Their jealousy instead of belief was their downfall.

In Psalm 110:1 there is the promise that the Messiah would be a King, ruling at God's right hand with His enemies functioning as His footstool (Ps. 110:1). In verse 4 there is the promise that Messiah would be more than a King. He would also function as a Priest after the order of Melchizedek. Mitchell correctly translates verse 4 as:

> "You are a *kohen* [priest] forever according to my decree, [O] Melchizedek."[319]

There are not TWO eternal priests, Melchizedek and then one "like" him, Messiah. There is just the Messiah who in the OT took on a human form as the Angel of the Lord, Word or Melchizedek who talked with and blessed Abraham, wrestled with Jacob, was the Rock that traveled with Israel in the wilderness, led Joshua's armies, etc. The Messiah, or Melchizedek of verse 4, is the "Lord" or ruling King of verse 1. In verses 5-7 the Messianic King/Priest rules the nations.

11QMelch also understands the Melchizedek figure to be a divine Messiah with eternal origins who has Kingly and Priestly duties. The author of Hebrews identifies Melchizedek as "without father or mother, without genealogy, without beginning of days or end of life..." (Heb. 7:1-3). Mitchell writes of Melchizedek in Hebrews:

> "Melchizedek is Jesus. Jesus is a priest forever, so is Melchizedek (6:20; 7:3). Both became priests on the basis not of ancestry but of an indestructible life, that is, by virtue of their immortality (7:16). Now, just as in Psalm 110, there cannot be two eternal high priests. So, if Jesus and Melchizedek are both high priests forever, then Jesus and Melchizedek are one and the same person."[320]

But in what way was Melchizedek "made like the Son of God" (Heb. 7:13)? Mitchell answers:

> "This 'likeness' surely refers to Melchizedek's manifestation rather than to his being. After all, Melchizedek, being the Son of God, could not be made to resemble himself in essence any more than he already did. But his manifestation to Avram was made to foreshow his future, incarnate ministry as Jesus. How then did Melchizedek foreshadow the work of Jesus? First, he

---

[319] Mitchell, Jesus the Incarnation of the Word, Ibid., 67-71

[320] Ibid., 75

brought salvation to his friend—to Avram in the battle with the kings. Then he offered bread and wine to refresh the soul of his friend. And, carrying through to Genesis 22, he provided a sacrifice to redeem those under divine sentence of death (Gen. 22:12-14)."[321]

Mitchell gives us the clear "take-home message":

"His enemies finally got the take-home message. He was claiming to be the visible God who was seen in the flesh by Abraham.

It might not have been a matter for stoning if they had believed he was the Messiah. There would surely have been some there who, like Philo or the author of 11QMelch, believed that Melchizedek was the divine Messiah. In theory, the idea was acceptable enough.

But the claimant was intolerable. The one they called illegitimate, demon-possessed Samaritan, who presumed to purge their temple and call them vipers, was claiming to be the divine Messiah, to be Melchizedek who blessed Avraham at the defeat of the kings, to be the Angel-Messenger of YHVH who led Israel out of Egypt and through the desert in the pillar of the cloud and fire, who travelled with them as the thirst-quenching Rock, who appeared to Joshua at Gilgal, to Moses, Samuel, and David in the sanctuary, to be the Logos, the emanation of the divine glory, sent from the right hand of the Ancient of Days to the earth, to illumine, atone, judge, conquer, and inherit.

He was claiming to be Israel's guide since the beginning, he who was born in shame at Bethlehem."

I shall at this point give a brief survey of some of the key places where Psalm 110 is quoted or alluded to in the NT. Psalm 110 references the eschatological "already and not yet," beginning with Christ's ascension in AD 30 and continuing until His truly imminent Second Coming in the events of AD 67 – AD 70 when He placed His enemies under His feet and judged them.

1). Matthew 26:63-64: Here we have a conflation of Daniel 7:13 and Psalm 110:1. Jesus informs the first century apostate High Priest and leaders of Israel who were to crucify Him that they would see [understand or perceive] Him seated at the right hand of the Father and coming upon the clouds to judge them in the events of AD 67 – AD 70.

2). Acts 2:33-36: Peter preaches a sermon on the Day of Pentecost informing Jews gathered from every nation under heaven that they had crucified their Messiah, but He has ascended to the right hand of the Father in fulfillment of Psalm 110. This is the "already."

But Acts 2-3 develops the imminent Second Coming judgment or "not yet" as well. Because they had crucified the Lord of Glory and were living in the terminal "last

---

[321] Ibid., 77

days", "perverse and crooked generation" of Deuteronomy 31-32 and Joel 2, they needed to repent due to the imminent coming "Day of the Lord" (Acts 2:20-21, 40). Chapter 3 is consistent in that if these first century Jews did not heed the words of Jesus as Messiah, He would come from heaven and they would "be destroyed from the people" and thus this would be the judgment of the enemies of Psalm 110 (Acts 3:17-23).

The eschatology in the rest of the book of Acts confirms the imminent, "not yet" judgment of that first century generation in that the judgment of the Jewish world and the resurrection of the just and unjust were "about to be" fulfilled by AD 70 (Acts 17:31 YLT; Acts 24:15 YLT).

3). Hebrews 10:12-37: The author of Hebrews in this one chapter alone tells us that after Christ had become a once and for all sacrifice for sin and was seated at the right hand of God, the "day was approaching" in which He was "about to" judge His first century "enemies" of Psalm 110 with consuming fire at His "in a very little while and will not delay" Second Coming in AD 70 (Heb. 10:12-13, 25, 27 BLB, 37).

4). 1 Peter 3:22—4:5-7, 17: There was a spiritual baptism that was in the process of "saving" (the verb is present tense, active voice) the first century Christians Peter was writing to. It was the spiritual new covenant baptism of faith in which Christians were united to Christ's death, burial, and resurrection (Rom. 6:3-12; Eph. 4:5; 1 Cor. 12:13; Col. 2:11-12). This included an eschatological baptism or testing of "fire" and "suffering" just prior to their "salvation" and "inheritance" that was "ready to be revealed" to them (1 Pet. 1:4-12; 4:12-13; Mt. 20:22-23; Mark 10:38-39).

Psalm 110 is quoted in 1 Peter 3:22, and in the next chapter Peter tells us when the eschatological "not yet" judgment of Psalm 110 would be fulfilled. In 1 Peter 4:5-7, 17 Peter, under inspiration, tells his first century, primarily Jewish, audience that "THE [appointed] time" for "THE judgment" (v. 17) of the "living and dead" was "at hand" (vss. 5-7). *Just as we have seen in Acts 2 and Hebrews 10, whenever the "already" of Christ's ascension of Psalm 110 is cited, it is soon followed by an imminent "not yet" AD 70 consummated judgment of God's enemies.*

In Peter, these enemies subjected to Christ included "angels, authorities and powers" (1 Pet. 3:22). The "judgment" of false teachers and the fallen angels would "not be delayed" (2 Pet. 2:3NLT) and therefore they would be judged in AD 70 when Satan would be "crushed shortly" (Gen. 3:15/Rom. 16:20).

5). 1 Timothy 5:21; 6:13; 2 Timothy 4:1 YLT: Here Paul states that Yeshua Messiah is the Lord who is in the presence of God and the angels, and was "*about to judge* the living and the dead" at "His appearing and His Kingdom" in AD 70.

6). 1 Corinthians 15:24-25: I have already given a rigorous exegesis of 1 Corinthians 15 in this volume and in my co-authored book, *House Divided - Bridging the Gap in Reformed Eschatology*. David Green has as well. The "last enemy" was "the [spiritual] death" that came through Adam, and it was already in the process of "being destroyed" (in the present passive indicative) as Paul wrote (1 Cor. 15:25 WUESTNT).

Not many disagree that it is at Christ's Parousia or Second Coming (1 Cor. 15:23) when the "enemies" of Psalm 110 are judged and the curse of "the last enemy the death" is cast in the lake of fire and removed from God's people. But here in 1 Corinthians 15 Paul expected the Parousia to take place in the lifetime of the Corinthians (1 Cor. 15:51-52), and in Revelation the Second Coming would be fulfilled "shortly" and "soon," being connected with the "three and a half years" coming judgment of AD 67 – AD 70. It was during this period that the last enemy and curse of spiritual death and separation was overcome by Messiah, and those enemies who rejected Him and would not have Him rule over them were brought before His presence and slain by the Roman armies.

7). Revelation 5:13; 7:9-10; 12:10; 22:1, 3: Revelation is filled with allusions to Psalm 110 in references to the Lamb being on a throne, and having authority in His kingdom to judge, etc. Yet John tells us that the events of Revelation would be fulfilled "shortly" and the judgment would take place at the "soon" Second Coming of Christ when Jerusalem ("where the Lord was crucified" – Rev. 11:8) would be judged (Rev. 1:1; 22:6-7, 10-12, 20). This would be a judgment and resurrection of the dead in which souls/spirits were raised and emptied out of Hades to inherit eternal life and God's presence or be cast into the lake of fire with the Devil and angels.

The virgin birth, incarnation and identity of the Son in Isaiah 7:14 & 9: 6-7

- *"Therefore, the Lord himself will give you a sign. Behold, the virgin shall conceive and bear a son, and shall call his name Immanuel" (Isa. 7:14).*

- *"For to us a child is born, to us a son is given; and the government shall be upon his shoulder, and his name shall be called Wonderful Counselor, Mighty God, Everlasting Father, Prince of Peace. Of the increase of his government and of peace there will be no end, on the throne of David and over his kingdom, to establish it and to uphold it with justice and with righteousness from this time forth and forevermore. The zeal of the LORD of hosts will do this" (Isa. 9:6-7).*

OT scholar Michael Brown points out that there is no Hebrew word that specifically and always means "virgin," not *almah* or *bethulah*.[322] But one of the world's leading Semitists, Dr. Cyrus Gordon, who claims to be Jewish and does *not* believe in the virgin birth of Jesus as Messiah, maintains that Isaiah 7:14 may be translated as "virgin."[323] And a famous Rabbi, Rashi, while not holding to a virgin birth in this passage, nevertheless pointed to the view that perhaps this girl was so young that she was *"incapable of giving birth."* So, he is at least proposing some kind of miraculous birth of the "God is with us" son.[324]

The miraculous nature of this virgin birth and the son to be called "God with us" can be more clearly seen and solidified through appealing to how the Greek Septuagint

---

[322] Brown, Vol. 3, Ibid., 20-25

[323] *Almah in Isaiah 7:14*; Gordon, Cyrus H.; JBR 21:106

[324] Brown, Ibid., 30

reads, "Therefore the Lord himself shall give you a sign; Behold, a **virgin [PARTHENOS]** shall conceive, and bear a son, and call his name Immanuel" (Is. 7:14). *Parthenos* is used 15 times in the NT **and it never means anything other than a virgin**. The LXX use of *partheonos* "…would suggest that already before the NT age at least some Jews had come to link the passages in Isaiah 7:14—9:6-7 together and to deduce that there would be an additional, longer-term fulfillment of the birth of a messianic king, portended by a more supernatural conception…"[325]

In addressing Isaiah 9:6-7, Dr. Brown points out that the early Targum and Jewish belief of this passage was understood to be Messianic:

> "The Targum, while explicitly identifying this as a messianic prophecy, renders the verse in Aramaic with an interesting twist, "…and his name will be called from before the One who is wonderful in counsel, **the mighty God who exists forever, Messiah**, because there will be abundant peace upon us in his days."[326]

And there was some consensus that all the names refer to the Son/Messiah and not God (Rabbi Franz Delitzsch, Abraham Ibn Ezra, statements in the Talmudic and Midrashim writings), which would be consistent with the natural ancient coronation ceremony (e.g. by the Egyptians) - applying these four throne names to the new King.[327]

Therefore, we are getting further confirmation of the divine nature of the Immanuel Son of Isaiah 7:14. The virgin birth explains *how* the Messiah would and could be from eternity (the Jewish concept of the "Word") and a "divine human" who was both "Son of Man" and the Ancient of Days coming upon the clouds worthy of worship (cf. OG LXX Dan. 7:13-14). Other views of Daniel 7:13 see Messiah as a younger Ancient of Days or having the concept of the "two powers of heaven." Before looking at other developments of Daniel 7:13 within Judaism, let's look at one more Messianic text associated with Jesus' birth and identifying just who He was prophesied to be.

In Matthew 2 we learn Jesus was prophesied to be born in Bethlehem in fulfillment of Micah 5:2.

- *"But you, O Bethlehem Ephrathah, who are too little to be among the clans of Judah, from you shall come forth for me one who is to be ruler in Israel, whose coming forth is from of old, from ancient days" (Micah 5:2).*

Like Isaiah 7:14/ 9:6-7 and Daniel 7:13-14, Micah 5 was Messianic and predicted a Messianic King "whose goings out are from aforetime, from ancient times [or, 'from days of eternity']. Like Isaiah and Daniel, Micah 5:2 shows that Jesus was not understood to be just a man:

---

[325] G.K. Beale, D.A. Carson, COMMENTARY on the NEW TESTAMENT use of the OLD TESTAMENT, (Baker 2007), 4

[326] Brown, Ibid., 32, emphasis mine

[327] Brown, Ibid., 33-34

"The Targum of the Minor Prophets very explicitly takes this text as Messianic: "And you, O Bethlehem Ephrathah, *you who were too small to be numbered among the thousands of the house* of Judah, from you shall come forth *before me the* **anointed One**, *to exercise dominion* over Israel, *he whose name was mentioned* from of old, from ancient times." (All translations from Targumim of various minor prophets are taken from Cathcart and Gordon 1989. The italicized material reflects changes from the MT here and throughout quotations from the Targumim of all the OT books.) The title "the anointed One" denotes the messianic king...[328]

OT scholar Dr. Michael Heiser discusses in-depth the Jewish view of a second Messianic God figure developed within Judaism long before Jesus arrived, and how the Jews sought to make this view heretical after Jesus (and Christians) began claiming He was the one they were looking for:

"Old Testament Godhead Language

The Old Testament contains elements of (orthodox) Israelite theology and worship that New Testament writers would much later recognize as a Godhead—the view that God comprises more than one personage, each of whom is identified as the presence of Yahweh. Israel derived their understanding of the Godhead from their version of the divine council, or pantheon (i.e., God and His heavenly host), and the binitarian (two persons) language used for Yahweh and other figures that the OT writers identify so closely with Yahweh that they are inseparable, yet distinct.

Israel's Divine Council: An Overview

The closest parallel to Israel's (and therefore the OT's) conception of the assembly of the heavenly host under the authority of Yahweh is the divine council of Ugarit. Practitioners of Ugaritic religion organized the unseen divine world into three (or possibly four) tiers. In the top tier dwelled El and his wife Athirat (Asherah). The second tier was the domain of their royal family ("sons of El"; "princes"). One member of this second tier, Baal, served as the co-regent of El; despite Baal being under El's authority, worshipers gave him the title "most high." The third tier was for "craftsman deities," and (perhaps) the fourth and lowest tier was reserved for the messengers (mal'akhim), essentially servants or staff.

The OT exhibits a three-tiered council (the craftsman tier is absent). In Israelite religion, Yahweh, at the top tier, was the supreme authority over the divine council, which included a second tier of lesser elohim ("gods"), also called the "sons of God" or "sons of the Most High." The third tier comprised the mal'akhim ("angels").

---

[328] Blomberg, C. L. (2007). Matthew In *Commentary on the New Testament use of the Old Testament* (p. 6). Grand Rapids, MI; Nottingham, UK: Baker Academic; Apollos.

Orthodox Yahwism replaced the co-regent slot that Baal occupied with a sort of binitarian Godhead, in which Yahweh occupied both slots. The OT in fact describes Yahweh with titles and abilities that Canaanite literature attributes to both El and Baal. Israelites thus fused El and Baal in their worship of Yahweh—a literary and theological strategy that asserted Yahweh's superiority over the two main divine authority figures in wider Canaanite religion. Within Israelite religion, Yahweh's occupation of both of the two highest tiers resulted conceptually in two Yahwehs—one invisible, the other visible. At times both speak as characters in the same scene, but more frequently, they are virtually interchangeable.

Israel's Binitarian Godhead

The Angel of Yahweh

The relationship between Yahweh and the Angel of Yahweh ("Angel of the LORD") provides the most familiar example of "two Yahwehs." The OT writers at times deliberately make the Angel of Yahweh indistinguishable from Yahweh (e.g., Exod 3:1–14). For instance, according to Exod 23, the Angel has Yahweh's "Name" in him (Exod 23:20–23). This passage gives a glimpse of the Hebrew Bible's "Name theology," in which reference to "the Name" actually refers to Yahweh Himself. Thus, in Exod 23, Yahweh indicates that He is in the Angel. And yet, in other passages, Yahweh and the Angel can be simultaneously—but separately—present (Judg 6). Various OT passages attribute God's deliverance of Israel from Egypt to both the God of Israel and the Angel (e.g., Judg 2:1–3; 1 Sam 8:8; Micah 6:4). In light of Deut 4:37, which states the "presence" of Yahweh was responsible for Israel's deliverance from Egypt, these passages provide a constructive case for binitarianism. The divine presence, of course, is Yahweh Himself, His "essence." Perhaps most tellingly in this theology is the text of Gen 48:15–16, which fuses God and the Angel. Jacob, near death and pronouncing blessing on Joseph's sons, speaks of God's saving action in a way that highlights the fusion of Yahweh and the Angel:

When Israel saw Joseph's sons, he said, "Who are these?" Joseph said to his father, "They are my sons, whom God has given me here." And he said, "Bring them to me, please, that I may bless them." Now the eyes of Israel were dim with age, so that he could not see. So Joseph brought them near him, and he kissed them and embraced them. And Israel said to Joseph, "I never expected to see your face; and behold, God has let me see your offspring also." Then Joseph removed them from his knees, and he bowed himself with his face to the earth. And Joseph took them both, Ephraim in his right hand toward Israel's left hand, and Manasseh in his left hand toward Israel's right hand, and brought them near him. And Israel stretched out his right hand and laid it on the head of Ephraim, who was the younger, and his left hand on the head of Manasseh, crossing his hands (for Manasseh was the firstborn). And he blessed Joseph and said,

"The God [ha-elohim] before whom my fathers Abraham and Isaac walked,

The God [ha-elohim] who has been my shepherd all my life long to this day,

The Angel [ha-mal'akh] who has redeemed me from all evil, May he bless the boys" (Gen 48:8–16).

But this is complicated by the biblical teaching that God is eternal (in that He existed before all things) and that angels are created beings. The explicit parallel of "God" and "Angel," thus, does not imply that God is an angel. Rather, it affirms that this Angel is God. The verb "bless," moreover, is grammatically singular; a plural verb would indicate that Jacob is asking two different persons to bless the boys—the singular thus denotes a tight fusion of the two divine beings—one eternal and one not.

The Angel that embodies Yahweh's presence parallels the role of Baal not only as co-regent but also as the warrior who fights for El. According to Josh 5:13–15, it is the Angel who leads Israel, "sword drawn in his hand," to the promised land as the captain of Yahweh's host. This precise description appears in only two other places in the OT, both in reference to the Angel of Yahweh (Num 22:23; 1 Chr 21:16). Thus, while orthodox worship of Yahweh precluded cosmic rule by two separate and distinct deities (El and Baal in Ugaritic religion, Yahweh plus another distinct deity in Israelite religion), it could tolerate two personages of Yahweh. That the Angel had the Presence (Name) of Yahweh in Him but was a distinct personage meant He was Yahweh's presence, but not Him in His fullness.

The Rider on the Clouds

Another motif in the OT that indicates that there is an Israelite binitarian Godhead is the "Rider on the Clouds." Although this epithet was a well-known title for Baal, the Hebrew Bible consistently uses it and similar designations to refer exclusively to Yahweh (Pss 68:4; 68:33; 104:3; Deut 33:26; Isa 19:1), with one exception: the "son of man" in Dan 7:13. This human figure—though distinct from the Ancient of Days (the enthroned deity described in Dan 7)—bears a title reserved exclusively for Yahweh in the OT.

References to God in the Third Person by Yahweh

In certain OT passages, Yahweh appears to refer to Yahweh, or "God," in the third person: "Then the LORD rained on Sodom and Gomorrah sulfur and fire from the LORD out of heaven" (Gen 19:24) and 'I overthrew some of you, as when God overthrew Sodom and Gomorrah, and you were as a brand plucked out of the burning; yet you did not return to me,' declares the LORD" (Amos 4:11).

The Two Powers in Heaven Doctrine of Judaism

Jewish thinkers in the Second Temple period (circa 516 BC–AD 70)—who were quite familiar with these patterns in the Hebrew text—did not indicate that any of it violated monotheism. Yahweh, quite simply, was alone at the top of the heavenly host, albeit in two forms. In fact, Jewish theologians and writers during this period devoted a great deal of speculation to more precisely identifying the second Yahweh. Their guesses ranged from divinized humans from Israel's history (Adam, Abraham, and Moses were leading candidates) to exalted angels (Gabriel, Michael) to other intermediate figures (e.g., Philo's "the Word"). These guesses were solidified into religious sects, and thus emerged the "two powers in heaven" doctrine of Judaism.

However, the early Christians (who were also Jews), altered the course of these speculations when they identified the second power, or second Yahweh, with Jesus. This identification allowed the first Christian converts—all of them Jews—to simultaneously worship both the God of Israel and Jesus of Nazareth without acknowledging any other god. Affirming Jesus' incarnation as a man went beyond affirming Yahweh embodied in human form—Jesus was crucified as a blasphemer who made Himself equal with God. (The idea that Jesus was the incarnate second Yahweh offended Jews who had formerly accepted the "two powers.") It wasn't until the second century AD that Jewish authorities declared the "two powers" teaching to be heresy.

The Holy Spirit as "Third Yahweh" in the Old Testament

Writers in the OT occasionally make statements about Yahweh that actually reference the Holy Spirit— equating the two. For example, in Isa 63:7, the prophet refers to Yahweh as doing good to His people. But according to Isa 63:9, "the angel of his presence" saved Israel. This is a reference to Yahweh's deliverance of Israel from Egypt. Israel is then recorded as responding by "rebelling" (marah) against and "grieving" (atsab) the Holy Spirit (Isa 63:10). In Psalm 78:40–41, which directly parallels this passage, the same two Hebrew verbs refer directly to God ("they rebelled against him"; "they grieved him"). Consequently, these two passages identify the Holy Spirit with God."[329]

Before we give evidence that Messiah was identified in Daniel 7:13 as the divine cloud rider, we should briefly provide evidence of Messiah being "cut off" and functioning as Israel's "Savior" to forgive sin.

Is/was the Jewish Messiah to be "Savior" or not?

Let's briefly address the modern-day Jewish claim that Messiah was never thought of to be a savior figure in the scriptures,

"The word "mashiach" does not mean "savior." The notion of an innocent, divine or semi-divine being who will sacrifice himself to save us from the

---

[329] Michael S. Heiser, *Old Testament Godhead Language,* Faithlife Study Bible, John D. Barry, Michael R. Grigoni, et al. (Bellingham, WA: Logos Bible Software, 2012), 1-4

consequences of our own sins is a purely Christian concept that has no basis in Jewish thought."[330]

Israel's exodus from Egypt is by far the greatest example of "salvation" or "deliverance" which formed Israel's view that God alone acts as Savior (cf. Ps 106:21; cf. Is 63:8-11; Hos 13:4). This salvation was brought about through the sacrifice of a lamb's blood placed upon the door frames of God's people while the concept of the death of a "firstborn" as an exchange for their salvation and deliverance was born (Exodus 12). This would pave the way for the foundation of Judaism itself – the Temple and sacrificial system necessary to atone for Israel's sins (Leviticus 16).

"Salvation" was connected to the Messiah's (the "King's" or "Anointed One's") work in His coming lowly upon a donkey (Zechariah 9:9 – a passage known to be Messianic in Jewish literature),

*"…if they are meritorious, [he – Messiah will come] with the clouds of heaven [Dan. 7:13]; if not, lowly and **riding upon an ass** [Zech. 9:9]."*[331]

In Zechariah 13:1, we learn that "On that day (the day of Messiah's salvation) a fountain will be opened to the house of David and the inhabitants of Jerusalem, *to cleanse them from sin and impurity*." How would this come about? This was due to the Messianic Shepherd being "struck" and the sheep scattered (Zechariah 13:7-9; cf. also 11:4-14; 12:10; Matthew 26:31, 56). To learn more about the Messiah being "struck" or sacrificed "…to save Israel from the consequences of her sins" (which is being denied by our good "Jewish" friends), we must now turn to Isaiah 53 and examine how some Rabbis understood it.

Let's quote the entire chapter:

"Who has believed our report? And to whom has the arm of the Lord been revealed? For He shall grow up before Him as a tender plant, And as a root out of dry ground. He has no form or comeliness; And when we see Him, *There is* no beauty that we should desire Him. He is despised and rejected by men, A Man of sorrows and acquainted with grief. And we hid, as it were, *our* faces from Him; He was despised, and we did not esteem Him. Surely He has borne our griefs And carried our sorrows; Yet we esteemed Him stricken, Smitten by God, and afflicted. But He *was* wounded for our transgressions, *He was* bruised for our iniquities; The chastisement for our peace *was* upon Him, And by His stripes we are healed. All we like sheep have gone astray; We have turned, everyone, to his own way; And the Lord has laid on Him the iniquity of us all. He was oppressed and He was afflicted, Yet He opened not His mouth; He was led as a lamb to the slaughter, And as a sheep before its shearers is silent, So He opened not His mouth. He was taken from prison and

---

[330] *The Messianic Idea in Judaism*, http://www.jewfaq.org/mashiach.htm

[331] *Babylonian Talmud*, Tractate Sanhedrin Folio 98a

from judgment, And who will declare His generation? For He was cut off from the land of the living; For the transgressions of My people He was stricken. And they made His grave with the wicked—But with the rich at His death, Because He had done no violence, Nor *was any* deceit in His mouth. Yet it pleased the Lord to bruise Him; He has put *Him* to grief. When You make His soul an offering for sin, He shall see *His* seed, He shall prolong *His* days, And the pleasure of the Lord shall prosper in His hand. He shall see the labor of His soul, *and* be satisfied. By His knowledge My righteous Servant shall justify many, For He shall bear their iniquities. Therefore I will divide Him a portion with the great, And He shall divide the spoil with the strong, Because He poured out His soul unto death, And He was numbered with the transgressors, And He bore the sin of many, and made intercession for the transgressors" (Isa. 53:1-12).

Did some of the Rabbis teach this passage was Messianic?

> "**Messiah** …what is his name? The Rabbis say, **'The leprous one'**; those of the house of the Rabbi (Jehuda Hanassi, the author of the Mishna, 135-200) say: 'Cholaja' (The **sickly), for it says, 'Surely he has borne our sicknesses**' etc. (Isa. 53:4)."[332]

And a Targum of Isaiah 53 reads,

> "Behold **my servant Messiah** shall prosper; he shall be high, and increase, and be exceeding strong: as the house of Israel looked to him through many days, because their countenance was darkened among the peoples, and their complexion beyond the sons of men."[333]

The Messiah as a suffering "servant" is also described for us in the previous immediate context (Isaiah 52:13-15, see also Psalm 22). In Isaiah, "Savior" is a consistent title for God communicating His preeminence and His uniqueness over against foreign gods and idols:

> "I, even I, am the Lord, and apart from me there is no savior. I have revealed and saved and proclaimed—I, and not some foreign god among you" (Is. 43:11, 12).

Isaiah further states that God would show himself as Savior in a future blessing and restoration for Israel described in Isaiah 49:26; 60:16. It's simply not accurate that Christians have somehow invented the idea that the Messiah is found in such passages as Isaiah 53 or that Messiah would be a "Savior," saving Israel (and the Gentile believing world) from their sins.

And it is not enough to just say that the "Son" in Isaiah 53 is national Israel and not Messiah. Why? Because within Judaism was also the belief that when Messiah came

---

[332] *Babylonian Talmud (Sanhedrin 98b).*

[333] *Targum Johnathan on Isaiah 53.*

He would recapitulate Israel's redemptive history – primarily to usher in a 40-year second exodus based upon Isaiah 11 and other passages. Jesus is the faithful substitute "Son" and "Vine" who never sinned or failed (unlike the "son" and "vine" of national Israel), and He could be the perfect substitute for man and take His sin justly and fully away.

Let me quote an excellent article by Daniel Mann, a zealous "Jew" who moved to Israel and, after studying Isaiah 53 and what Rabbis taught on it, put his trust in Jesus as His Messiah and Savior:

> **"If anyone was a skeptic about Jews believing in Jesus, I was**. Born to second-generation Jewish American parents in Brooklyn, I experienced much anti-Semitism growing up in the 1950s and '60s. Since my persecutors weren't Jewish, I assumed they were Christian. When I was 14, there was talk that a certain Jewish family in my neighborhood had converted to Christianity. I was filled with disgust. How could Jews do such a thing?
>
> As a young adult, I had a lot of pent-up resentment against Christianity. I enjoyed ridiculing anyone who tried to talk with me about Jesus. But I was spiritually hungry. I moved to Israel, lived on a *kibbutz*, and visited a Hasidic *yeshiva* to ask questions, but I returned to the United States still wondering how to really connect with God – a Jewish God, not a Christian one.
>
> People kept telling me about Jesus. I had a great problem with him. Many Jews had died in his name, and many who hated Jews called themselves Christians. And the idea of someone dying on a cross for me seemed like a bunch of hocus-pocus.
>
> But I kept meeting Christians who seemed genuine in their love and concern for me, and their prayers for me seemed to "work." So finally I prayed, "God, if Jesus is the Savior and Messiah that the Hebrew prophets wrote about, You're going to have to show me."
>
> As I studied the Bible, I began to see how Jesus could have fulfilled many of the prophecies in the Hebrew Scriptures. I also discovered that the New Testament wasn't something arbitrarily tacked onto the Hebrew Bible by people who hated Jews. I was shocked to learn that Jews had written it and that Jesus himself was a Jew.
>
> One of the most convincing passages showing that the Messiah would make the ultimate sacrifice and die for our sins was Isaiah 53.
>
> Present-day rabbis disagree. Rashi (AD 1040-1105) might have been the first to deny that this incredible passage is Messianic. But many Jewish sages, before and after Rashi, saw the Messiah in Isaiah 53.
>
> The highly regarded first-century Rabbi Shimon Ben Yochai stated: "The meaning of the words 'bruised for our iniquities' [Isaiah 53:5] is, that since **the Messiah bears our iniquities**, which produce the effect of his being bruised, it

follows that **whoso will not admit that the Messiah thus suffers for our iniquities, must endure and suffer them for them himself.**"[1]

Rabbi Moshe Alshich, a famous sixteenth-century scholar, asserted: "[Our] Rabbis with one voice, accept and affirm the opinion that **the prophet [Isaiah 53] is speaking of king Messiah.**"[2] In contrast, today's rabbis have rallied around the assertion that the "Suffering Servant" of Isaiah 53 is the nation of Israel and not the Messiah. Let's take a look:

Who has believed our message and to whom has the arm of the Lord been revealed? He grew up before him like a tender shoot, and like a root out of dry ground. He had no beauty or majesty to attract us to him, nothing in his appearance that we should desire him. He was despised and rejected by mankind, a man of suffering, and familiar with pain. Like one from whom people hide their faces he was despised, and we held him in low esteem. (Isaiah 53:1–3)

Throughout Isaiah 53, the masculine singular pronoun "he" is used to designate the suffering servant. This pronoun is very rarely used in regards to Israel. More usually, Israel is referred to as "you," "she/her," and "they/them." But there is no problem at all using "he" in reference to the Messiah.

Surely he took up our pain and bore our suffering, yet we considered him punished by God, stricken by him, and afflicted. But he was pierced for our transgressions, he was crushed for our iniquities; the punishment that brought us peace was on him, and by his wounds we are healed. We all, like sheep, have gone astray, each of us has turned to our own way; and the Lord has laid on him the iniquity of us all. (Isaiah 53:4–6)

Just a quick read through the Prophets will show that Israel could not even bear its own sins, let alone those of others. It was our Jewish people who had "gone astray" and "turned to our own way."

According to the revered twelfth-century Jewish scholar Ramban (Nachmanides), the Redeemer is the Messiah:

Yet he carried our sicknesses, being himself sick and distressed for the transgressions which should have caused sickness and distress in us, and bearing the pains which we ought to have experienced. But we, when we saw him weakened and prostrate, thought that he was stricken, smitten of God. The chastisement of our peace was upon him – for God will correct him; and by his stripes we were healed.[3]

While today's rabbis deny substitutionary atonement – one man dying for the sins of the world – this had not previously been the case. The mystical Zohar records:

The children of the world are members one of another. **When the Holy One desires to give healing to the world, he smites one just man amongst them, and for his sake heals all the rest. Whence do we learn this? From the**

saying, "He was wounded for our transgressions, bruised for our iniquities." (Isaiah 53:5) (Numbers, Pinchus, 218a)

He was oppressed and afflicted, yet he did not open his mouth; he was led like a lamb to the slaughter, and as a sheep before its shearers is silent, so he did not open his mouth. (Isaiah 53:7)

We cannot find any biblical references to affirm that Israel was silent in the face of oppression. But we do find that this is true of Jesus. Before the Sanhedrin, he remained silent. When he finally spoke, it only aided the prosecution:

But Jesus remained silent and gave no answer. Again the high priest asked him, "Are you the Messiah, the Son of the Blessed One?" "I am," said Jesus. "And you will see the Son of Man sitting at the right hand of the Mighty One and coming on the clouds of heaven." The high priest tore his clothes. "Why do we need any more witnesses?" he asked. (Mark 14:61–63)

Jesus astonished Pilate with his silence:

Then Pilate asked him, "Don't you hear the story they are bringing against you?" But Jesus made no reply, not even to a single charge – to the great amazement of the governor. (Matthew 27:13–14)

By oppression and judgment he was taken away. Yet who of his generation protested? For he was cut off from the land of the living; for the transgression of my people he was punished. He was assigned a grave with the wicked, and with the rich in his death, though he had done no violence, nor was any deceit in his mouth. (Isaiah 53:8–9)

Jesus was deprived of justice ("judgment") and was killed. Israel was not "cut off from the land of the living." It is also clearly untrue that Israel "had done no violence, nor was any deceit in his [Israel's] mouth." At times, the prophets charged that our people had morally descended below the Gentiles. The Gospels declare that Jesus' grave was with both the wicked and the rich, as he died with sinners and was buried in a rich man's tomb.

Yet it was the Lord's will to crush him and cause him to suffer, and though the Lord makes his life an offering for sin, he will see his offspring and prolong his days, and the will of the Lord will prosper in his hand. After he has suffered, he will see the light of life and be satisfied; by his knowledge my righteous servant will justify many, and he will bear their iniquities. (Isaiah 53:10–11)

There is no reason to suppose that Israel's death could represent "an offering for sin." Sin offerings had to be without any blemish. But we were covered with them. How could the knowledge of Israel "justify many?" But faith (knowledge) in the Messiah will.

This servant, who dies as a sin offering for the people, will eventually "see the light of life and be satisfied." He will live subsequent to his death – a cryptic reference to the resurrection.

Isaiah says that this servant will bear the iniquities of many. When I first studied this passage as a young man, it began to dawn on me that I personally needed to be forgiven for my wrongdoing, what the Bible calls "iniquities." And this servant – who was looking to me more and more like Jesus – had made that possible."[334]

When this evidence is brought forth, "Jewish" apologists such as Rabbi Tovia Singer claim that the Christian can't produce any Jewish tradition that Messiah ben David fulfills Isaiah 53. But in a radio debate with Dr. Michael Brown, Tovia Singer made such a claim and Michael embarrassed Singer severely. Here are some those quotes provided by Dr. Brown, demonstrating that Messiah ben David is the fulfillment of Isaiah 53:

> "Yet he carried our sicknesses [Isa. 53:4], being himself sick and distressed for the transgressions which should have caused sickness and distress in us, and bearing the pains which we ought to have experienced. But we, when we saw him weakened and prostrate, thought that he was stricken, smitten of God. …The chastisement of our peace was upon him—for God will correct him and by his stripes we were healed—because the stripes by which he is vexed and distressed will heal us: God will pardon us for his righteousness, and we shall be healed both from our own transgressions and from the iniquities of our fathers…
>
> He was oppressed and he was afflicted [v. 7]: for when he first comes, "meek riding upon an ass" [Zech. 9:9], the oppressors and officers of every city will come to him, and afflict him with revilings and insults, reproaching both him and the God in whose name he appears."[335]

Brown goes on to point out that there are others who apply the suffering servant of Isaiah 53 to Messiah ben David, such as Rabbi Moshe Kohen Ibn Crispin (or Ibn Krispen) and Rabbi Mosheh El-Sheikh (or Alshekh).

The coming of the Son of Man in Daniel 7:13 is Jesus the Messiah

In the *Babylonian Talmud*, Tractate Sanhedrin Folio 98a (AD 400-600) we read:

> "…it is written, in its time [will the **Messiah come**], whilst it is also written, I [the Lord] will hasten it! — if they are worthy, I will hasten it: if not, [he will come] at the due time. R. Alexandri said: R. Joshua opposed two verses: it is written, And behold, **one like the son of man came with the clouds of heaven** whilst [elsewhere] it is written, [behold, thy king cometh unto thee …] **lowly, and riding upon an ass!** — if they are meritorious, [he will come] with the clouds of heaven; if not, lowly and riding upon an ass."

---

[334] Daniel Mann, *Isaiah 53: Rabbis, Skeptics, and the Suffering Messiah*, https://www.jewsforjesus.org.au/isaiah-53

[335] Brown, Ibid., Vol. 2, 226-227. This is taken from Nachmanides.

One Rabbi admits both can be fulfilled together,

"It may be suggested that these are not mutually exclusive alternatives. Rather, Messiah will be both powerfully exalted ('on clouds of heaven') and humbly self-effacing ('a poor man riding a donkey')."[336]

Jesus applies both of these OT passages to His redemptive work for Israel through His riding on a donkey – a depiction of His humility and rejection as the suffering servant which begins the atoning and redemptive process – and then Him coming a second time out of the heavenly temple as the High Priest and King coming upon the clouds with salvation and judgment in the events of AD 67 - AD 70.

Jewish Scholar Alan Segal, commenting on R. Akiba and R. Yosi the Galilean disputing over the meaning of the passage, writes:

> "These two rabbis were perplexed by the seeming contradiction in the verses. In one place, more than one throne is indicated by the plural form of the noun. In another place "His (God's) throne was fiery flames" implies only one throne. Does this mean that the 'son of man' in the next verse was enthroned next to God? Rabbi Akiba (110-135 C.E.) affirms the possibility, stating that the other throne was for David. ***Akiba must be identifying the 'son of man' with the Davidic messiah. Nor was R. Akiba alone in the rabbinic movement in identifying the figure in heaven as the messiah. There is some evidence that Judaism contained other traditions linking these verses in Daniel with the messiah.***"[337]

Another Jewish scholar, Jacob Neusner, addresses the 'older' traditions in this way:

> "We focus upon how the system laid out in the Mishnah takes up and disposes of those critical issues of theology worked out through messianic eschatology in other, **earlier versions of Judaism**. These earlier systems resorted to the myth of *the Messiah as savior and redeemer of Israel, a supernatural figure engaged in political-historical tasks as king of the Jews, even a <u>God-man</u> facing the crucial historical questions of Israel's life and resolving them: the Christ as king of the world, of the ages, of death itself.*"[338]

Orthodox Jewish scholar Daniel Boyarin writes on the characteristics of Daniel 7 and the development of Jewish and Christian thought:

> "What are these characteristics?

---

[336] Brown, Ibid., *AJOJ, Vol. 1*, p. 222 re: Schneerson.

[337] Alan Segal, *Part Two. The Early Rabbinic Evidence, Chapter Two. Conflicting Appearances of God*, pp. 47-48. In footnote 21 – 21. b. Hag. 14a Tr. Epstein. Cf. also b. Sanhedrin 38a where other rabbis are said to oppose R. Akiba... (Ibid., 47). And "... R. Hiyya b. Abba answers in Aramaic, rather than in Hebrew, that if a heretic says that there are 'two gods' based on Dan. 7:9f., one is to remind him that God stated that He is the same at the Sea and at Sina..." (Ibid., 42).

[338] *Judaisms and Their Messiahs at the Turn of the Christian Era*, edited by Jacob Neusner, William Scott Green & Ernest S. Frerichs [Cambridge University Press, 1987], 275.

- **He is divine.**
- **He is divine in human form.**
- He may very well be portrayed as a younger-appearing divinity than the Ancient of Days.
- He will be enthroned on high.
- He is given power and dominion, even sovereignty on earth.

All of these are characteristics of Jesus Christ as he will appear in the Gospels, and they appear in this text more than a century and a half [*sic*] before the birth of Jesus. Moreover, they have been further developed within Jewish traditions between the Book of Daniel and the Gospels. At a certain point these traditions became merged in Jewish minds with the expectation of a return of a Davidic king **and the idea of a divine-human Messiah was born**. This figure was then named 'Son of Man,' alluding to his origins in the divine figure named 'one like a Son of Man/a human being' in Daniel. **In other words, a simile, a God who looks like a human being (literally Son of Man) has become the name for that God, who is now called 'Son of Man,' a reference to his human-appearing divinity**…"[339]

And:

"There are many variations of traditions about this figure in the Gospels themselves and in other early Jewish texts. Some Jews had been expecting this Redeemer to be a human exalted to the state of divinity, while others were expecting a divinity to come down to earth and take on human form; some believers in Jesus believed the Christ had been born as an ordinary human and then exalted to divine status, while others believed him to have been a divinity who came down to earth. **Either way, we end up with a doubled godhead and a human-divine combination as the expected Redeemer.***…"[340]

Ancient Jews described the anticipated Messiah with the title "he of the clouds." Boyarin, referring to other scholars such as J.A. Emerton, points out that any good Jew knew that only Yahweh himself rode upon the clouds of heaven in judgment:

"**Clouds–as well as riding on or with clouds–are a common attribute of biblical divine appearances**, called theophanies (Greek for 'God appearances') by scholars. J.A. Emerton had made the point decisively: '**The act of coming with clouds suggests a theophany of Yahweh himself. If Dan. vii. 13 does not refer to a divine being then it is the only exception out of about seventy passages in the Old Testament.**' "…As New Testament scholar Matthew Black puts it bluntly, '**This, in effect, means that Dan. 7**

---

[339] Boyarin, *The Jewish Gospels: The Story of the Jewish Christ* [The New Press, New York, NY 2012], 31-33. These and the following quotes are taken from Sam Shamoun, *Jesus as the Divine Son of God – A Markan Perspective Pt. 2,* http://www.answering-islam.org/authors/shamoun/divine_son_mark2.html.

[340] Ibid., 34; in a footnote, "In these ideas lie the seed that would eventually grow into doctrines of the Trinity and incarnation in all of their later variations, variations that are inflected as well by Greek philosophical thinking; the seeds, however, were sown by Jewish apocalyptic writings."

> knows of two divinities, the Head of Days and the Son of Man.' Those two divinities, in the course of time, would end up being the first two persons of the Trinity."[341]

> "Ancient Jewish readers might well have reasoned, as the Church Father Aphrahat did, **that since the theme of riding on the clouds indicates a divine being in every other instance in the Tanakh (the Jewish name for the Hebrew Bible), we should read this one too as the revelation of God, a second God, as it were. The implication is, of course, that there are two such divine figures in heaven, the old Ancient of Days and the young one like a son of man**."[342]

> "The Messiah-Christ exists as a Jewish idea long before the baby Jesus was born in Nazareth. **That is, the idea of a second God as a viceroy to God the Father is one of the oldest theological ideas in Israel.** Daniel 7 brings into the present a fragment of what is perhaps the most ancient of religious visions of Israel that we can find…"[343]

The presentation of the Son of Man to the Ancient of Days in Daniel 7:13 is perhaps a reference to Christ in His Parousia delivering up the kingdom ("*the saints*") to the Father ("*the Ancient of Days*") in AD 70. *Then cometh the end, when he shall have delivered up the kingdom to God, even the Father; when he shall have put down all rule and all authority and power* (1 Cor. 15:24).

But, again, my preferred interpretation is similar to that of F.F. Bruce. According to the old Greek LXX of Daniel 7:13, the Son of Man came "as the Ancient of Days" on the clouds of heaven, not "to the Ancient of Days."[344] This translation is in harmony with verse 22, which says that it was the Ancient of Days Himself who came in judgment and gave the saints the kingdom. It is also important to point out that John in the book of Revelation alludes to Dan. 7:9, 13 in his description of Christ as being both the Son of Man who comes on the clouds to judge those who had pierced Him (first century Jews) and as the eternal Ancient of Days in Revelation 1:7, 13-17. Again, the context is developing Christ's future "soon" (Rev. 1:1) Second Coming, not His ascension.

Messiah would be worshipped by the nations - and is!

---

[341] Ibid., 39-40.

[342] Ibid., 44.

[343] Ibid.

[344] Some of the early hymns of the seventh, eighth and ninth centuries understood Daniel 7:13 to be Jesus as the Ancient of Days and connected this to His incarnation: "I behold a strange mystery: in place of the sun, **the Sun of Righteousness placed in the Virgin** in an uncircumscribed manner … Today God, He-Who-Is and preexists becomes what he was not; for being God, he becomes a human being without stepping out of his being God. … **The Ancient of Days is born as a child**." (PG 28: 960A-961A = PG 56:389)

Before leaving Daniel 7:13-14, it should be noted that this One likened to the "Son of Man" and "Ancient of Days" coming on the clouds of heaven is **"worshiped"** (vs. 14 NIV – the original Aramaic is *pelach*; some translations render the word to mean divine "service"). In establishing the meaning of a passage or word in a particular text, we need to examine its usage elsewhere in the same book. Everywhere in Daniel, *pelach* is used of divine service or worship. For example, it's used of false gods in Daniel 3:12. In Daniel 3:17-18 we are told that Shadrach, Meshach and Abednego only gave divine service and **worship** to the only living God and would not render divine service and worship to Nebuchadnezzar's false gods. In Daniel 3:28 Nebuchadnezzar gives praise to their God and states that they "*yielded up their bodies rather than serve and **worship** any god except their own God.*" Daniel 6:16, 20 describes Daniel's divine service to the only living God continually, given in hopes that God would deliver Daniel from the den of the lions, which He did. Daniel 7:27 states that when the Ancient of Days would come (cf. vss. 13-14, 22) to give possession of the kingdom to the saints, "all rulers will **worship** and obey him."

A good example of being silent on this issue will be addressed in an article by *Jews for Judaism* covering our next text, Daniel 9:24-27.

Messianic expectations and a Chronomessianic understanding of Daniel 9:24-27

I have already given a brief Christian Full Preterist Chronomessianic exegesis of Daniel 9:24-27, so my only two points here are to demonstrate that:

1). this passage was understood to be Messianic.

2). Messiah had to have come (on the clouds) in Daniel's "expected time" or within the last seven ("week") before the second temple was destroyed in AD 70.

First, our passage was known by Rabbis and Jews to be referring to the Messiah:

- "Our masters taught as follows of the **particular seven-year period at whose end [Messiah] son of David will appear.**"[345]

- "Rav said: All **times set for redemption have passed**, and the matter now depends only on repentance and good deeds (all time calculations had been fulfilled)."[346]

- "R. Samuel bar Nahmani said in the name of R. Jonathan: Blaste be the bones of those who presume to calculate the time of redemption. For they are apt to say, 'Since **redemption has not come at the time expected**, **it will never come**.' Rather, one must wait for it…what then delays its coming? The measure of justice delays it…"[347]

---

[345] *B. San 97a*

[346] *B. San 97b*

[347] *B. San 97b* – "Jews" post AD 70 have come up with clever excuses as to why Messiah didn't come by AD 70. Some claim messiah was alive on earth during this time but because the Jews weren't ready for

This now leads into our second point. *How* and *when* were the Rabbis calculating the "expected time" of Messiah to come in the last seven of Daniel 9:24-27? The Dead Sea Scrolls give us some insight into this question as well as modern Jewish exegesis.

First, we learn from the Dead Sea Scrolls in such sections as 11Q13 (11Melch) that the Messianic deliverer would show up in the 10th Jubilee cycle, or within 490 years of the Daniel 9:24-27 passage (among other texts), and He would accomplish the following: **1). perform the Day of Atonement 2). gather the believers to Himself 3). pour out the days of vengeance upon the wicked and 4). judge Satan and the fallen Watchers** – (directly or indirectly appealing to such passages as Lev. 25; Isa. 27:13; 61:1-11; Dan. 9:24-27; Ps. 7 and Ps. 82).

Margaret Barker is an OT scholar who has done an excellent job of showing how the first century Jews were calculating 10 Jubilee cycles (that is, 10 periods of 49-50 years = 490 years) from the destruction of the first temple around 420 BC to expecting Messiah to arrive in the 10th Jubilee somewhere around AD 17/19.[348] Again, I disagree with her slightly and believe that the 10th Jubilee actually began around AD 26/27 and not AD 17/19. Below are the various ways in which they were calculating Messiah's coming based upon a 49 year or 50 year cycle for the Jubilee, or from the 424 or 422 BC starting date. At best, they could calculate the end to be within 1-2 years, but definitely not know the "day and hour" (Mt. 24:36) of Israel's end. My calculations are the two on the left and Barker's are the two on the right:

---

him God took him to heaven and will have him come back when they are ready. The other is to blame Daniel and claim his calculations were wrong. Both very pathetic. The truth of the matter is that they refused to accept the messianic kingdom of Daniel 2 really would be a spiritual kingdom just as Jesus taught, and thus they would "not discern their end" in AD 70 (cf. Deut. 32).

[348] Margaret Barker, *THE TIME IS FULFILLED JESUS AND THE JUBILEE*, 1999, http://www.margaretbarker.com/Papers/JesusAndTheJubilee.pdf).

Michael Sullivan calculating a Jubilee using the 50 yrs. Jewish tradition of counting & starting at 424 BC	Michael Sullivan calculating a Jubilee using the 50 yrs. Jewish tradition of counting & starting at 422 BC	Margaret Barker calculating a Jubilee using the 49 yrs. Jewish tradition of counting & starting at 424 BC	Margaret Barker calculating a Jubilee using the 49 yrs. Jewish tradition of counting & starting at 422 BC
1st Jubilee 424 BC	1st Jubilee 422 BC	1st Jubilee 424 BC	1st Jubilee 422 BC
2nd Jubilee 374 BC	2nd Jubilee 372 BC	2nd Jubilee 375 BC	2nd Jubilee 373 BC
3rd Jubilee 324 BC	3rd Jubilee 322 BC	3rd Jubilee 326 BC	3rd Jubilee 324 BC
4th Jubilee 274 BC	4th Jubilee 272 BC	4th Jubilee 277 BC	4th Jubilee 275 BC
5th Jubilee 224 BC	5th Jubilee 222 BC	5th Jubilee 228 BC	5th Jubilee 226 BC
6th Jubilee 174 BC	6th Jubilee 172 BC	6th Jubilee 179 BC	6th Jubilee 177 BC
7th Jubilee 124 BC	7th Jubilee 122 BC	7th Jubilee 130 BC	7th Jubilee 128 BC
8th Jubilee 74 BC	8th Jubilee 72 BC	8th Jubilee 81 BC	8th Jubilee 79 BC
9th Jubilee 24 BC	9th Jubilee 22 BC	9th Jubilee 32 BC	9th Jubilee 30 BC
10th Jubilee begins in AD 26 during Jesus' earthly ministry and includes the time of His Second Coming AD 66/67 – AD 70.	10th Jubilee begins in AD 28 during Jesus' earthly ministry and includes the time of His Second Coming AD 66/67 – AD 70.	10th Jubilee begins in AD 17 which is NOT during Jesus' earthly ministry and only extends to the beginning of AD 66.	10th Jubilee begins in AD 19 which is NOT during Jesus' earthly ministry and only extends to the beginning of AD 68.

Even many within modern Judaism take this position:

"422 BC is associated with when the first temple burned **70 Sabbaticals (490 years) before the second temple burned in 70 AD**."[349]

And,

"The 2nd century CE rabbinic work Seder Olam Rabbah, which formed the basis of the era counting of the Hebrew calendar, interpreted the prophecy of seventy weeks in **Daniel 9:24-27** as referring to **a period of 490 years, with a "week" being interpreted as a period of seven years, which would pass between the destruction of the First and Second Temple**."[350]

One *Jews for Judaism* article on this subject, *Daniel 9 – A True Biblical Interpretation*,[351] follows a form of Chronomessianism I agree with for the most part

---

[349] *A Treatise on the Sabbatical Cycle and the Jubilee*, 1866, by Dr. B. Zuchermann, Professor at the Jewish Theological Seminary.

[350] *Missing Years*, Wikipedia.org

[351] *Daniel 9 – A True Biblical Interpretation*, https://jewsforjudaism.org/knowledge/articles/daniel-9-a-true-biblical-interpretation/?fbclid=IwAR1rBmvnmx9_rgQdvxr0IhHHWO2cW6tfDoS33FFYahKQAK70pUwPbHazL0M.

(420 BC – AD 70 = 490 years). [352] I would agree with their criticism of Christian exegetes for not using the Jewish calendar and thus the multiple problems they have of trying to stretch out a fulfillment to AD 70 due to: 1) using the Gentile calendar instead of the Jewish calendar and 2) starting the prophecy with Cyrus or other Gentile kings and dates instead of the prophetic "word" of Jeremiah and thus starting when the first temple was destroyed in roughly 420 BC. In not following this, most Christian exegetes can't get a literal 490 years stretched to AD 70.

But what is missing from the *Jews for Judaism* article is what we covered in our first point – that being, Jews understood this passage to be a prediction of the coming of Messiah and that He needed to show up in the tenth Jubilee and before the destruction of the second temple in AD 70. What JFJ is silent on is first century Judaism's interpretation of such passages as Ezekiel 4:4-5 and Daniel 9:24-27, which see Messiah being cut off within the time frame JFJ has established. Addressing these two OT passages, Lester L. Grabbe writes,

> "There are statements to the effect that a period of **forty years** would elapse between the **death of the teacher** [Messiah] **and the end of the age** [Mosaic OC age]."[353]

JFJ is also silent on the Jewish belief that Messiah would have a transitional reign of **forty years** ("days of Messiah") between the old covenant (OC) "this age" and the Messianic or new covenant (NC) "age about to come." As Dr. Cohen observes,

> "Many Rabbis believed that the period of the Messiah was to be only a transitionary stage between this world [age] and the World to Come [age to come], and opinions differed on the time of its duration. 'How long will the days of Messiah last? R. Akiba said, **forty years, as long as the Israelites were in the wilderness**.'"[354]

In my opinion, no discussion of *11QMelch* is the death blow to the JFJ article. First century Judaism understood Daniel 9:24-27 (and other OT passages) to teach that Messiah had to accomplish atonement, gather His people, and judge Satan and the Watchers within this tenth Jubilee period. The Essenes interpreted Habakkuk 2, the

---

[352] While I agree with JFJ that Daniel 9:24-27 is teaching a literal 490 years from the destruction of the first temple to the second in AD 70, I disagree that the last seven is from AD 63 – AD 70. Daniel's last "seven" (years) of Messiah's redemptive work is divided into two three-and half-year periods: 1) AD 27 – AD 30 (Jesus' earthly ministry, cross, resurrection and ascension) and 2) His Second Appearing in fulfillment of the "Day(s) of Vengeance" between AD 67 – AD 70 to end the OC age and judge Jerusalem by "shattering the power of the holy people" during the last "3 ½ years" Daniel specifically refers to again in Daniel 12 (cf. Isa. 61:2; Dan. 12:7; Lk. 21:20-34).

[353] Lester L. Grabbe, *An Introduction to First Century Judaism: Jewish Religion and History in the Second Temple Period*, (Edinburg: Continuum T&T Clark, 1995), pp. 86-87. Bold emphasis added. Other Jewish Christian scholars, such as Dr. Michael Brown have pointed out that Rashi and others understood Daniel 9:24-27 to be Messianic, *ANSWERING JEWISH OBJECTIONS to JESUS*, Volume Three, (Grand Rapids: MI, Baker Books, 2003, pp. 89-90.

[354] Dr. BOAZ COHEN, *NEW AMERICAN EDITION Everyman's TALMUD*, (New York: E.P. Dutton & CO., 1949), 356.

book of Daniel, and Ezekiel 38-39 to be referring to an end time battle (Gog and Magog) between Rome and apostate Jerusalem in AD 67 – AD 70, and that they were the "final generation."[355] This is consistent with Jesus' eschatology and that of the Jewish NT authors.

It is clearly admitted within Jewish literature that the book of Daniel was the most Messianic of all the prophetic books *and* very clear on the "fixed" time of his coming as found in Daniel 9:24-27. Rabbi Moses Abraham Levi correctly writes,

> "I have examined and searched all the Holy Scriptures and have not found the time for the coming of Messiah clearly fixed, except in the words of Gabriel to the prophet Daniel, which are written in the 9th chapter of the prophecy of Daniel."[356]

The Jewish Messianic view was correct to teach that if Messiah didn't come at the appointed time, then they were in some serious trouble in that he may never come. Others speculated he was alive on earth leading up to the events of AD 70, but because Israel allegedly was not ready for him, God took him to heaven only to bring him back at some time. These excuses are deplorable and fly in the face of good exegesis and logic, but are necessary to keep the system of old covenant Judaism afloat while at the same time attempting to reject Jesus as the only valid candidate for Messiah.

But of course, the truth is that Messiah/Jesus came exactly at the right and appointed time, accomplishing all of His redemptive work between AD 27 – AD 70 (within the last 10th Jubilee or that last 49-50 years period). The problem was, and is today, that they were/are looking for an earthly kingdom which Daniel never prophesied. And in fact, their rejection of their Messiah and His kingdom was predicted in the Song of Moses (Deut. 31-32). In these chapters we learn that in Israel's "last days" there would arrive a "perverse and crooked generation." When it arrived, Israel's "end" would be "near." But most would "not discern what their end" would be! The physical, earthly old covenant kingdom of Judaism and Israel ended in AD 70 when Messiah was predicted to destroy it (coming upon the clouds in judgment in a 3 ½ year period of time [AD 67 – AD 70] to "shatter the power of the holy people Dan. 12:7) and establish His spiritual, everlasting and indestructible new covenant kingdom within the hearts of His New Jerusalem people. Selah.

---

[355] See (*1QpHab 7:1-2; 1QpHab 9:5-11; 12:5-13*).

[356] *Historical Jewish Sources*, https://preteristarchives.org/historical-jewish-sources/?fbclid=IwAR3vY5ANjS-ajVdQBsPTAsqjbFxPM0XrxHMAetCDbgRrgX8sjtz9F5-Lv_M

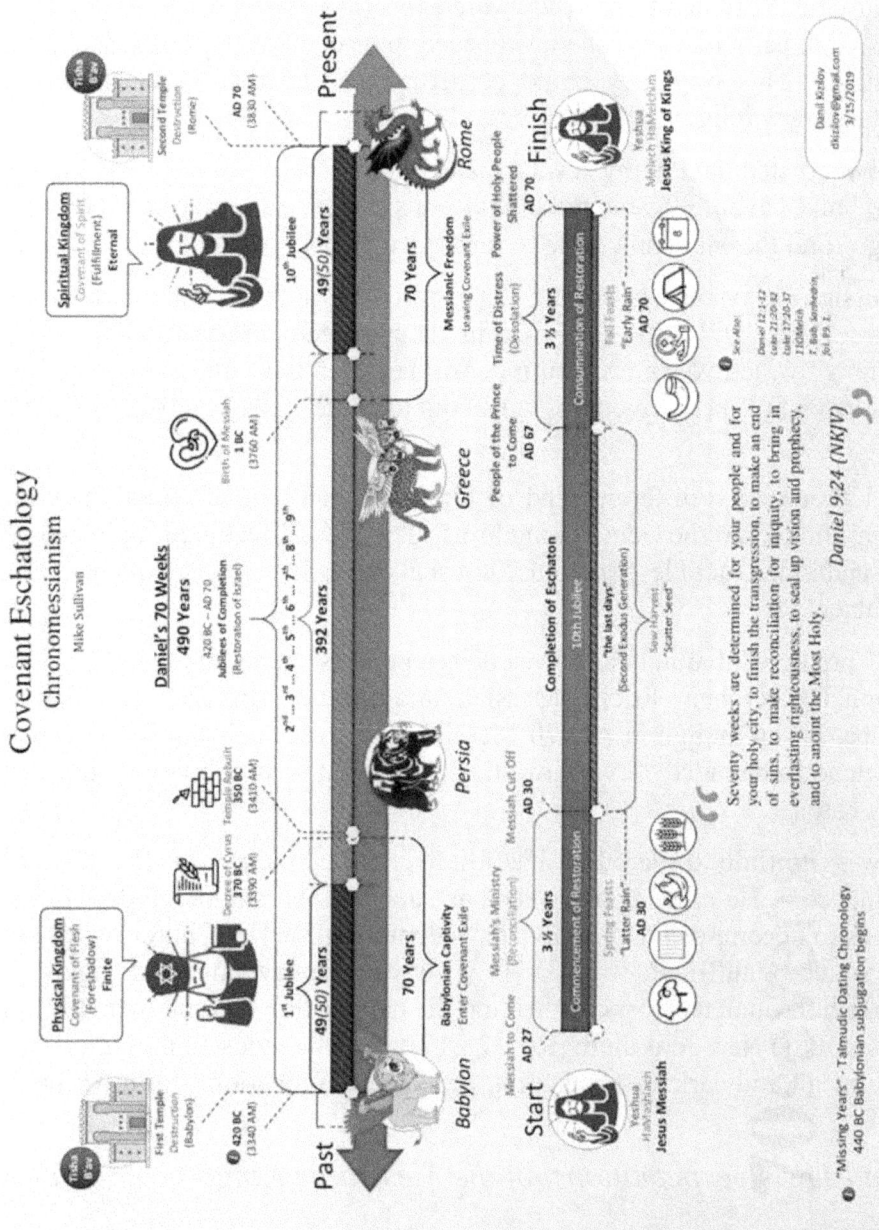

Concluding Israeli Zionism and or Torah Judaism

The OT paved the way for the understanding of how God could both be in a human form and be invisible in heaven ruling the universe at the same time.

The OT predicted, and many Jews expected, a divine God-Man Messiah figure who would be worshipped.

Jews around AD 100 began claiming that views of the Messiah being divine were heretical and could not be believed within Judaism. Why? Because Jesus claimed to be that divine Word and Logos they were expecting. The Christians were winning that battle, so that particular Jewish view needed to be declared heretical and not mentioned if possible. This way they could perpetuate the lie that Jesus and the Christians "invented a new religion which was not Jewish."

The OT predicted, and many Jews expected, that when Messiah arrived, He would be "cut off" and have a 40 year millennial transitionary rule between their old covenant "this age" and the Messianic new covenant "age about to come."

The Messiah (Jesus the Christ) and His inspired NT authors demonstrate how these OT promises were "all" "fulfilled" within their contemporary AD 30 - AD 70 "this generation," which was a transition period between their old covenant "this age" and the maturity of the new covenant "age about to come" (Lk. 21:20-22, 27-32; Mt. 13:39-43).

The OT predicted a different kind of kingdom than that of Israel's previous earthly kingdom and that of the Gentile kingdoms. The Messianic kingdom would be spiritual, eternal and indestructible – and thus "not shaken" as Israel's old covenant kingdom had been subject to.

The OT predicted that in Israel's last days a perverse generation would arrive in which they would reject their "Rock" (Messiah) and thus not "discern" what their near "end" would be. Even though in AD 70 Messiah destroyed their family birth records, they still pretend to be racial "Jews" awaiting a Messiah who will never come, because He already has.

Jesus was rightfully declared by His followers to be their "LORD and God" and thus "worshipped." He remains to be seen as such and worshipped today for keeping His promises to accomplish and apply His redemption for His Church when and how He said it would be fulfilled – by AD 70. Today in the new covenant "age without end," the Church through the gospel is healing the nations and bidding them to come through the gates of the New Jerusalem (Rev. 22:17). This includes an invitation to all modern nations in sin and darkness, including the Rothschild nation begun with blood money in 1948.

OT and Jewish expectations on the Messianic Kingdom and Temple

Introduction

I have briefly covered how so many Jews in the first century were expecting a physical restoration of the kingdom during the days of Messiah and how it was prophesied that they would thus not be able to "discern" their near "end" within Jesus' contemporary "crooked generation" (Deut. 32). This was going to be a "strange work" (Isa. 28:21) for them because they were expecting Messiah to destroy Rome, when in fact Messiah came upon the clouds through the Roman army to judge and destroy them and bring an end to the physical kingdom of Israel!

But we now turn our attention to what the OT teaches concerning the spiritual nature of the coming kingdom and temple promises.

Isaiah 43:18-21 / Isaiah 65:17-8

- *"**Remember not the former things** nor consider the things of old. Behold, **I am doing a new thing; now it springs forth, do you not perceive it?** I will make a way in the wilderness and rivers in the desert. The wild beasts will honor me, the jackals and the ostriches, for I give water in the wilderness, rivers in the desert, to give drink to my chosen people, the people whom I formed for myself that they might declare my praise" (Isa. 43:18-21).*

- *"For behold, I create new heavens and a new earth, and **the former things shall not be remembered or come into mind**. But be glad and rejoice forever in that which I create; for behold, **I create Jerusalem to be a joy, and her people to be a gladness**" (Isa. 65:17-18).*

Within the context of Isaiah 43, we have the coming gathering of the believing remnant Jews and Gentiles into the Messianic kingdom when sin would be forgiven. The exhortation to not covenantally "remember the former things" is a call to discern that God is going to bring the physical old covenant kingdom and expectations to an end. On the flip side, there is an exhortation to "perceive" the spiritual new covenant kingdom that will replace the former one. This Hebrew word for "perceive" can mean to "realize", "know or become known", "reveal," or "hear of." Jesus repeatedly chides the Pharisees in the Gospels that they need to have spiritual eyes to see and ears to hear—in order to spiritually "know" and "understand" His teachings which were in fact contained in the OT (remember Mt. 5:17-18), but concerned "the new [covenant] things" springing up in their midst.

Isaiah 65 prophecies the same time period, except God too would not covenantally "remember" the former things of His old covenant creation and people, because He would cause His new covenant creation and people to replace it/them. In Isaiah 66, this transition when the old covenant creation and people would be judged and mourn, while the new would take their place and be filled with joy, was when the new covenant people would "survive" this Day of the Lord judgment and continue preaching this glory (the gospel of new covenant salvation) to the nations – just as Revelation 22:17 teaches.

Jeremiah 3:15-17

- *"'And I will give you shepherds after my own heart, who will feed you with knowledge and understanding. And when you have multiplied and been fruitful in the land, in those days, declares the LORD, they shall no more say, "The ark of the covenant of the LORD." It shall not come to mind or be remembered or missed; it shall not be made again. At that time Jerusalem shall be called the throne of the LORD, and all nations shall gather to it, to the presence of the LORD in Jerusalem, and they shall no more stubbornly follow their own evil heart" (Jer. 3:15-17).*

There is nothing more symbolic of the power and reality of the physical old covenant kingdom than that of the "ark." Here Israel is told that there is coming a time when the "ark" would not be missed and physically made anymore. Messiah/Jesus the Chief Shepherd would also use other "shepherds" that He would appoint (NT apostles and prophets) to feed the remnant and help them to know and understand that the spiritual nature of the new covenant kingdom Messiah would be established by AD 70. God's presence no longer rests within, or reigns through, the throne/ark of the tabernacle/temple, and thus through the physical kingdom, people and land of fleshly Israel. His kingdom's reign/throne and "presence" is "within the hearts" of His people and thus within the New Jerusalem, whereby we too reign with Him holding rods of iron judging the nations with the gospel. Once converted, the new covenant kingdom and its teachings are written on our hearts and He causes us to obey and follow them.

Haggai 2:6-9

> *"For thus says the LORD of hosts: Yet once more, in a little while, I will shake the heavens and the earth and the sea and the dry land. And I will shake all nations, so that the treasures of all nations shall come in, and I will fill this house with glory, says the LORD of hosts. The silver is mine, and the gold is mine, declares the LORD of hosts. The latter glory of this house shall be greater than the former, says the LORD of hosts. And in this place, I will give peace, declares the LORD of hosts.'" (Hag. 2:6-9).*

This prophecy had a typological fulfillment during the days of Zerubbabel. Within a "little while" (four years or so), God used the Persian King Darius to shake the nations by allowing the Jews to rebuild their temple and to decree that this would ironically be financed by the nations (bringing their gold to them, etc.) who hated them and sought to turn Darius against them (cf. Hag. 1:15; 2:10; Ezra 5-6).

The anti-type is that within "a little while" (four years or so) from when Hebrews 12:26 was written, God shook the nations and the desire of all the nations came, with God's new covenant temple/house being filled with the glory of His righteousness and salvation.

But, of course, the Rabbis had some difficulty with Haggai 2:6-9 because, while it was glorified through the decree and gold brought to it through the decree of Darius and then later through Herod, its physical glory and splender was not greater than that of the first temple built by Solomon. Not only that, but the glory of God's presence filled Solomon's temple and nothing of the sort filled the second (cf. 2 Chron. 5:14; 7:1-3; see also God filling the tabernacle - Ex. 40:34-35). The rabbis also pointed out how there was no ark or Urim and Thummim to go along with God's presence filling the temple. And the promise of "peace" during the time of this temple did not add up with the war and unrest Israel experience from the time it was built until (and during) the period of Rome's dominion over them.

How the glory of the Haggai 2 temple would be greater than that of Solomon's is answered in our next passage which some Rabbis understood to be Messianic.

Malachi 3:1-5

- *"Behold, I send my messenger [John the Baptist in the spirit and power of Elijah – Mal. 4:5], and he will prepare the way before me. And the Lord [God / Messiah] whom you seek will suddenly come to his temple; and the messenger [God / Messiah] of the covenant in whom you delight, behold, he is coming, says the LORD of hosts. But who can endure the day of his coming, and who can stand when he appears? For he is like a refiner's fire and like fullers' soap. He will sit as a refiner and purifier of silver, and he will purify the sons of Levi and refine them like gold and silver, and they will bring offerings in righteousness to the LORD. Then the offering of Judah and Jerusalem will be pleasing to the LORD as in the days of old and as in former years. "Then I will draw near to you for judgment. I will be a swift witness against the sorcerers, against the adulterers, against those who swear falsely, against those who oppress the hired worker in his wages, the widow and the fatherless, against those who thrust aside the sojourner, and do not fear me, says the LORD of hosts" (Mal. 3:1-5).*

John the Baptist is the first messenger, and as we have seen in our study of his eschatology in Matthew 3:2-12 there was "about to come" a "wrath" of fire upon the Pharisees. "THE LORD," and the second messenger, is referring to God / Messiah. Premillennial Zionist Michael Brown writes of rabbis seeing this as Messianic:

> "According to the famous medieval Jewish commentaries of Radak (David Kimchi) and Mesudat David, "the Lord" refers to none other than "King Messiah." However, neither of these commentators took sufficient note of the fact that the Messiah was to come to the Temple that stood in Malachi's day (and note also that it is called "his Temple"—pointing clearly to the divine nature of the "Lord" spoken of here). I ask you, did this happen? If it did, then the Messiah must have come before the Temple was destroyed in 70 C.E.; if not, God's Word failed."[357]

Just as we have seen in our study of Daniel 7:13-14 and Daniel 9:24-27, Messiah had to come not just before the second temple's destruction in AD 70, but He would be very active in its destruction - coming upon the clouds to desolate it! This is what is deliberately missed by Futurist and Premillennial Zionist Dr. Michael Brown. The coming of God/Messiah in the judgment of Malachi 3:1-5 is further described in the next chapter as the "great and awesome day of the Lord" (Mal. 4:5)!

At least Premillennialist John Gill points out what Michael Brown is afraid of, and that is not only was Malachi 4:5 a Messianic text but, according to him, it was fulfilled at Christ's spiritual coming in AD 70:

> "Before the coming of the great and, dreadful day of the Lord; that is, before the coming of Christ the son of David, as the Jews themselves own [cf. T. Bab. Eruvin, fol. 43. 2. & Gloss. in ib.]…[being] the first coming of Christ, reaching to the destruction of Jerusalem: John the Baptist, his forerunner, the Elijah here

---

[357] Brown, *AJOJ, Vol. 1*, Ibid., 77-78

> spoken of, came proclaiming wrath and terror to impenitent sinners; Christ foretold and denounced ruin and destruction to the Jewish nation, city, and temple; and the time of Jerusalem's destruction was a dreadful day indeed, such a time of affliction as had not been from the creation, Matthew 24:21 and the Talmud interprets [cf. T. Bab. Sabbat, fol 118. 1.] this of the sorrows of the Messiah, or which shall be in the days of the Messiah [and Gill points out elsewhere some believing "days of Messiah" would be 40 years, and they were – AD 27 – AD 67 or AD 30 – AD 70 MJS]."[358]

The Church has argued about whether or not Malachi 4:5 is the Second Coming of Christ or His spiritual coming in the judgment through the Roman armies in AD 70. Again, the truth is that both views are true at the same time.

Messiah/Jesus is the Cornerstone of this glorious temple, and in and through the Church (the living stones of His temple) the gospel flows, which brings the riches of His imputed righteousness and peace (presence) to the souls and hearts of those who put their faith in Him. Christ came in the events of AD 67 – AD 70 to burn the old covenant temple and priesthood, and purified and restored it into a spiritual temple and priesthood of new covenant believers.

This spiritual concept of the third or Messianic temple is purely Jewish and in line with what we see the Dead Sea Scrolls teaching. As Tom Holland writes,

> "…texts from the scrolls tell of how the Davidic Messiah would complete his work by establishing a spiritual temple (a building of holiness). It was not a physical building that he was going to construct, it was a spiritual one. It would be made up of the Community Council in conjunction with the 'sons of Heaven.'
>
> …He gave you authority, O ye (4) this was how He **glorified it when you sanctified yourself to him, when He made you a Holy of Holies**…for all [The Children of Salvation (Yesha') and the Mystery of Existence (4Q416, 418)].
>
> In the book of Ezekiel there was the expectation of an eschatological temple; so in Qumran. This expectation was in fact based on Ezekiel's vision in chapters 40-48 [cf. The Words of Michael (4Q529) and The New Jerusalem (4Q554).[359]

Clearly, a spiritual interpretation of the Messianic temple predicted in Haggai 2 and Ezekiel 40-48 was very "Jewish" and contemporary with what Jesus and the writers of the NT were teaching. This temple would be "glorified" through the faith of the believer, and the believing community would function as God's "Holy of Holies" (cf. Ezek. 47/John 7:37-39; Rev. 21:16—22:17).

Not only did the Essenes or the Qumran Community believe they were the spiritual third Messianic temple, but they believed they were the eschatological wife to be

---

[358] Gill, Ibid., free online: https://www.biblehub.com/commentaries/malachi/4-5.htm
[359] Tom Holland, *Contours of Pauline Theology*, Ibid., 22-23

betrothed to God in the wilderness in Israel's last days which would produce salvation for the Gentiles.[360] Didn't John the Baptist identify himself as the "friend of the Groom," calling Israel into the wilderness to repent and get their hearts ready for Jesus – the Messianic Groom, and thus the restoration of Israel?

Concluding outreach methods to modern "Jews"

Thus far we have proven the following to be completely rabbinic Jewish beliefs and traditions which harmonize with the teachings of the OT, NT and thus Christian Full Preterism:

1). According to Rabbinic tradition, the following passages were understood to be referring to Messiah and that He would be a God-man or a divine being having eternal origins - Isaiah 7:14/9:6-7; Micah 5:2; Psalm 110; Deuteronomy 32:4 and Daniel 7:13. When it came to Isaiah 7:14, while some did not recognize this as a purely virgin birth, some did understand it as some kind of a miraculous birth. But the coming "son" is more clearly defined in 9:6-7, which some Jews did see as Messianic with all the titles referring to the Messiah.

2). Jews believed, according to Daniel 9:24-27, that Messiah had to show up at the "appointed time," or at the beginning of the 10th Jubilee (somewhere between AD 17/19 or AD 26/28) and before the second temple was destroyed in AD 70. During this period, He had to gather the people to Himself, perform atonement and judge the wicked, the Watchers and Satan. Not only this, but coupled with Daniel 9:24-27, Daniel 7:13 and Malachi 3:1; 4:5, Messiah would come in judgment to burn and destroy the second temple, coming as the "Sun of Righteousness."

3). But before Messiah would come upon the clouds to burn the second temple within Israel's last and 10th Jubilee period, it was also understood within first century Judaism that passages such as Ezekiel 4:4-5 and Daniel 9:24-27 taught that Messiah would be cut off before a 40-year period which would bring an end to the old covenant age. Likewise, there were rabbis who taught that Messiah would have a transitionary reign of 40 years (a second exodus period or "days of Messiah") between the old covenant Mosaic "this age" and the coming Messianic or new covenant "age to come," which was followed by the resurrection.

The concept of Messiah being "cut off" as a sacrifice for sin is developed by Moses in describing Messiah as the "firstborn ox" (Deut. 33). Jewish literature attributes the suffering servant of Isaiah 53 to be a substitutionary sacrifice and Savior forgiving the sin of Israel. Not only this, but Isaiah 53 was attributed to both Messiah ben Joseph AND Messiah ben David.

4). The teaching of Jesus concerning a spiritual new covenant kingdom is consistent with Daniel's description of the Messianic kingdom and that which is taught in the book of Isaiah. And while in the Dead Sea Scrolls it is defended that there may be two

---

[360] Ibid. 23

Messiahs, a King and then a Priest figure such as Melchizedek, the NT correctly develops Jesus as the fulfillment of both.

5). I have also proven from Deuteronomy 31-32 that most of the Jews would reject their Messiah or "Rock" and not be able to "discern" what their "near end" would be in the "last days", "perverse and crooked generation" between AD 30 – AD 70. Many would pervert who Messiah was, teaching that He would be a military ruler coming to overthrow Rome and set up an earthly kingdom. They did not discern that He was not coming to judge the Romans, but rather that He would judge them through the means of the Roman armies!

Nor has it ever been a Biblical concept that God would save every Israelite, but rather He promised to save only a remnant. Only some would be given eyes to see and discern that not only would the majority reject their Messianic "Rock," but they would likewise not be able to discern His Kingdom to be spiritual in fulfillment of Daniel 2 and 7.

6). The Dead Sea Scrolls also support the position that the end-of-the-age-war of Armageddon, or Gog and Magog, would be fought between the Romans and apostate Jerusalem when the second temple fell in AD 70. God released Satan for the "little while" of AD 67 – AD 70 to "gather the nations" of the Roman and Jewish world to come and try to wipe out the Christians and devour each other and Jerusalem. Jesus was the new Joshua and after 40 years, at the sound of the seventh trumpet, the "great city" of old covenant Jerusalem fell, and the judgment and resurrection of the dead followed (Rev. 11; Rev. 20). This is consistent with the Jewish view that the war of Gog and Magog and the resurrection and judgment of the dead would come after 40 years of Messiah being cut off, or his transitionary reign.

7). As the Dead Sea Scrolls demonstrate, it is completely Jewish to believe that the prophesied glorious temple of Haggai 2, and that of Ezekiel 40-48, consists of believers in Messiah and that God's presence is within them as His Most Holy Place dwelling (Jn. 7:37-39/Rev. 21:16-22 = Ezek. 47; 2 Cor. 6:16 = Ezek. 37:27).

Since the Essenes, or the Qumran Community, believed that they were the spiritual third Messianic temple and eschatological wife to be betrothed to God in the wilderness in Israel's last days, we simply cannot separate the arrival of the Messianic temple and wedding motif from Israel's promises of resurrection, which we now turn to in our last concluding point.

8). In chapter seven I demonstrated that it was completely Jewish to believe that the general resurrection was to take place at the end of the old covenant "this age," which would include souls being raised out of Abraham's Bosom or Hades – either to inherit God's presence and eternal life or eternal condemnation and punishment. It is completely Jewish to not believe in a fleshly corpse resurrection at the end of the new covenant age, but rather to believe in a spiritual resurrection at the end of the old covenant age, following 40 years after Messiah would be cut off. We identify this end of the old covenant resurrection as taking place in the 3 ½ year period of AD 67 – AD 70 just as Daniel 12:2-7 foretold.

Conclusion: Jesus, the NT authors and Christian Full Preterism teach ALL of the above propositions.

Therefore, the charge of the modern "Jew" that Jesus and the writers of the NT "came up with a new religion not consistent with the teachings of Torah and Jewish tradition" has been thrown out and dismissed based upon providing no evidence. Not only this, but the defendant has provided historical and exegetical evidence contrary to the plaintiff's empty assertions.

Not only that, but there is no evidence provided by the plaintiff that he and his people should be considered a race of "God's people" since he cannot prove what Tribe he is from. Not only this, but he and his people have no temple or sacrifices to back the claim that he/they hold to the ancient religion of Judaism. Why? Because the Messiah, predicted within His own Scriptures, burned all of the Jewish genealogical records in the temple when He came upon the clouds through the Roman armies in AD 70. There have been found no OT Scriptures which support the idea that modern Israel is a fulfillment of prophecy. But, to the contrary, there is plenty of evidence that modern Israel was founded upon the wicked blood money of the Khazarian Rothschild Talmudic mafia. Selah.

3). *Evangelical or Premillennial Zionism*

Most modern "WOKE"-type Christians are clueless that the Evangelical, Fundamentalist and Dispensational views they hold to today are relatively new (within the last 150 years or so). Nor do they realize that the Premillennial view of a physical earthly kingdom (be it a thousand years or not) was deemed by the early creeds of the Church as "heresy" and found to be on par with "Jewish dreams and myths" -not reflective of the kingdom taught by Christ and the authors of the NT.

We have seen how the modern Church has turned Biblical prophecy in the OT and especially in the NT completely upside down. They literalize figurative and apocalyptic language in the NT and spiritualize away the clear literal meaning of "this generation", "at hand", "near", "soon", "in a very, very little while", "will not delay", "about to," etc. pointing to the Second Coming and end of the old covenant age to be fulfilled in AD 70. But we must give some of them credit, for they acknowledge that some OT "at hand" cloud comings of God in judgment and even some de-creation events were fulfilled within the contemporary audiences of the prophets and describe the fall of rulers and nations, not the destruction of the planet. Yet when we get to the teachings of Christ and the NT-inspired authors, imminence gets spiritualized away to mean nothing (meaning possibly thousands of years), and to add further to the problem they then literalize apocalyptic language that is designed to be understood figuratively and symbolically to be the end of the old covenant age/world to be referring to the end of world history.

Revival only comes when the Church first submits to the teachings of Scripture and not unbiblical tradition. Once change and revival begins with the Church, then she is able to spread that truth and bring healing to the religions of the world, such as Islam and Zionism / Judaism.

But unfortunately, the Evangelical Zionist movement is plagued with all kinds of false teachings such as Pelagianism, Arminianism and the Charismatic movement (speaking gibberish and making false prophecies in the name of God), etc. This sector of prophesying Christianity brings what many see as a false gospel, is constantly embarrassing the Christian Church with false prophecies, and is known to have a lack of exegetical teaching.

And when it comes to their views on biblical prophecy, the Dispensational Zionist TV mega church, so-called "prophecy experts" have abandoned sound hermeneutics and fallen for sensational newspaper exegesis. And since many within this group also hold to the heretical views of Pentecostalism or the Charismatic movement, it is not uncommon for them to mix their newspaper eschatology with false prophecies of "Jesus is coming soon in our generation" with modern presidents and world leaders either being the Antichrist or being used by God to usher in the alleged end-time war, etc. Proverbs teaches us,

- *"Hope delayed makes the heart sick but when the desire is fulfilled, it is a tree of life" (Prov. 13:12).*

The modern Church has "delayed" the arrival of Christ's Second Coming and His kingdom with this constant "carrot and stick" newspaper eschatology, when Jesus and the authors of the NT said the fulfillment would be "soon" and "would not be delayed." According to Proverbs, this leaves the Church "sick." Christ as the Tree of Life and kingdom has come, and we need not "delay" it! At the heart of this error is not only a misunderstanding of the timing of Christ's *Parousia* and kingdom, but the spiritual nature of His kingdom in general. The Premillennialist makes the same carnal error that Judaism or the Zionist movement make. Both are looking at the OT and expecting the Messiah to establish an earthly kingdom or paradise on earth, in which they will one day rule with Him. No such new covenant kingdom was ever predicted by Daniel and the prophets, let alone by the lips of Messiah / Christ.

Finding common ground with the Evangelical Zionist

While in gross Biblical error, the Evangelical Zionist at least often affirms and wholeheartedly believes that the Bible is the infallible and inspired revelation of God. Therefore, reasoning with them from the Scriptures can be very productive. Many, like myself, have come out of that system to the truth because of our love for the Scripture and the authority it alone has to form sound doctrine ("Sola Scriptura" – "the Scriptures Alone").

Other than the Scriptures themselves, I think the Evangelical Zionist needs to understand that there are other Christian views which have existed for hundreds of years before their views emerged within the last 150 years or so, such as the Protestant Reformed or even Sovereign Grace Churches. And we must look at these views and the historical creeds that came through them. Having said that, we must also be humble enough to admit that the Protestant and Reformed creeds and confessions teach that they may be in error, as previous creeds and confessions have been subject to revision when a better understanding and truth emerged. The Reformation battle cry of

"Reformed and always reforming" did not just stop when we found that the Roman Catholic Church was in gross error on so many doctrines. Nor did it stop with the teachings of one man, Martin Luther. The truth can be found within the two positions of the Reformed Church, which was the subject of my first co-authored book (*HD*):

> 1). **Partial Preterism** – Imminence and fulfillment are accepted. Christ appeared a second time at the end of the old covenant age. There was a spiritual, corporate, covenantal judgment and resurrection of the living and dead which was attended by a passing of the old creation and arrival of the new in AD 70 (Dan. 12:1-4; Matt. 5:17-18; 13:39-43, 24-25; Acts 1:11; Rom. 8:18; 13:11-12; Heb. 8:13; 9:26-28; 10:37; 1 Peter 4:5-7; 2 Peter 3; Rev. 1-22).
>
> 2). **Classic Amillennialism** – The New Testament teaches only one future coming of Christ, general judgment, and resurrection of the living and dead attended by the restoration of creation at the end of the age.

Either the above two propositions form a contradiction, or they have formed the consistent and thus truly orthodox (straight) position of Christian or Sovereign Grace Full Preterism. The latter is the case, which is not only bringing healing and reformation to the Christian Church in the area of eschatology (Bible prophecy), but it is at the same time functioning as a powerful apologetic and evangelistic tool to reach Islam, Zionism and many false cults.

We can only encourage our Evangelical Zionist brothers and sisters to study the Word for themselves using sound principles of hermeneutics / exegesis, and not be lazy and listen to the newspaper exegesis coming from the TV mega church "prophecy experts," then echoed through their local lazy pastors and churches. A reformation of personal study (studying the timing and nature of the coming of Christ and His glorious kingdom) and examining what the Church has collectively taught will lead them in the right direction. Once the sleeping giant of the Evangelical Church takes the beam out of its own eye on these crucial issues, she can then be equipped by the Master to bring healing to Islam, Zionism/Judaism and the various cults. Then and only then can she begin preaching the sovereign and free grace of God's fully established kingdom to them.

Chapter Thirteen:

Pentecostal or Charismatic Zionists Giving Conflicting or Manipulative False Prophecies

The Premillennial Evangelical Zionist movement is filled with Pentecostals and Charismatics who constantly engage in un-Christian behavior all in the name of "worship" and exercising what they think is God's "power" as a part of their "kingdom message." Some of these include: speaking complete gibberish as an alleged "miracle," pushing people on their foreheads, falling on the ground shaking and or "laughing, barking or being drunk in the Spirit." But what is relevant to our discussion is not just their false understanding of modern Israel and pressuring our politicians into war so they can get "raptured," it's also their conflicting and false "prophecies" which they utter in God's name to accomplish their end goal.

This has been of some concern for me in that President Trump's spiritual advisor is Paula White. President Trump has been critical of TV "prosperity preachers," which makes White's appointment puzzling to me. My guess is that President Trump is a new Christian and he has a background of positive thinking, being a successful business man, and he meshed those two together, or that he just hasn't done the proper Bible study to see what a heretic this woman really is.

I personally attended Calvary Chapel of Costa Mesa in southern California for years when I was a young baby Christian, and heard many Charismatic "prophecies" that Jesus was "coming soon" to rapture us. This was based on Chuck Smith teaching this from the pulpit (taking false theology from Hal Lindsey), coupled with bad theology on the prophetic and miraculous gifts. Oftentimes bad eschatology and bad views on the miraculous sign and revelatory gifts go hand in hand.

As if the movement didn't have enough problems on its hands, another recent problem has emerged within these circles concerning Trump's presidency. Some "prophesy" that Trump is the fulfillment of the AntiChrist, or that he is going to deceive Christians and end up putting them in FEMA camps. Others "prophesy" over him concerning how much money he is or is not going to make, or how many terms he will or will not serve, etc. And when they are wrong, they act like it's just no big deal. They claim it's just a small "credibility" or some kind of PR problem that they will be able to fix over time.

Even more concerning are heretics such as Pat Robertson who claim to have made prophecies (guesses) in God's name that Trump would be elected on November 3, 2020 "without question," and then connect them to prophesied "assassination attempts," civil unrest, wars and, yes, you guessed it, the soon end-time events (the so-called end-time war of Ezekiel 38) to be fulfilled in our lifetime.

Obviously, one does not have to be a "prophet" to guess or discern if President Trump would or would not get re-elected. Since President Trump has had multiple attempts on his life in his first term, it doesn't take a "prophecy" to guess those attempts by the deep state would continue. But what is really troubling is that these "prophecies" are tied in with presidents and designed to manipulate them in certain directions. Charismatic Zionists giving U.S. presidents a Cyrus or Messianic complex to defend Israel at all costs in the coming end-time war is the usual suspect, of course. We want our presidents to have solid theology and not be influenced and manipulated to bend to "God's will" – that allegedly being whatever these Charismatic Zionists claim it is or it isn't through their so-called "dreams", "revelations" and "prophetic utterances."

I used to be a Charismatic and recently debated one of the world's renown Zionist Charismatics, Dr. Michael Brown, over 1 Corinthians 13:8-12. I am going to simply give you a few of their arguments, which I used to use myself, and seek to bring some healing and clarity to those ensnared in that movement. These will be brief points. I have an in-depth exegesis on each of these (and more) texts and arguments on my sites: fullpreterism.com and treeoflifeministries.info. Due to space limitations, I will address what I consider to be the top three arguments.

Argument #1: If "that which is perfect" (the Second Coming & arrival of the new creation) has not been fulfilled and we don't see God's face, then the miraculous gifts of prophecy, tongues and knowledge have not "ceased" yet per 1 Corinthians 13:8-12 and Revelation 22:4-7.

The "common ground" we share with this group is that these are parallel passages (they help interpret each other) and the NT does in fact teach that the miraculous sign and revelatory gifts would not cease until the Second Coming and arrival of the new creation were fulfilled. But I have already demonstrated how the Second Coming and new creation were fulfilled "near" in Jesus' contemporary "this generation," and thus "shortly" and "soon" in the book of Revelation (Mt. 16:27-28/Mt. 24:3-34; Rev. 1:1—22:7, 10, 20). There is more we have to say on this crucial text.

Prophecies would cease

The Arndt-Gingrich Lexicon defines *propheteuo* here in 1 Corinthians 13:9 as to "proclaim a divine revelation." And it defines *prophetes* in this way: "prophet as the proclaimer and interpreter of the divine revelation…"[361]

This is in harmony with how OT prophecy and prophets functioned. OT prophets and prophecy were to be 100% accurate, and contained elements of bringing forth divine revelation – God placing His very words into the mouths of the prophets.

---

[361] W.F. Arndt and F.W. Ginrich, *A Greek-English Lexicon of the New Testament* (Chicago: University of Chicago, 1957), 730.

This creates serious problems for Charismatics who claim that, while OT prophets could not be in error, NT prophets and today's prophets may be in error from time to time. Some Charismatic so-called prophets admit that 80% of what they "prophesy" never comes true or is error! They also try to reassure us that they are not like the last days cults who believe their prophets (such as Joseph Smith of the LDS) are bringing forth ongoing divine revelation. Yet in order to try and reassure us of this, they have to begin *re-defining* the meaning of prophecy that their alleged "prophets" are uttering today.

The NT office of prophet and the standard for accuracy is consistent with the OT office and standard of accuracy. As Pastor John MacArthur points out,

> "Biblically speaking, no distinction is made in Scripture between the prophets in either Testament. In fact, the New Testament uses identical terminology to describe both Old and New Testament prophets. In the book of Acts, Old Testament prophets are mentioned in Acts 2:16; 3:24-25; 10:43; 13:27, 40; 15:15; 24:14; 26:22, 27; and 28:23. References to New Testament prophets are interspersed using the same vocabulary without any distinction, comment, or caveat (cf. Acts 2:17-18; 7:37; 11:27-28; 13:1; 15:32; 21:9-11).
>
> Surely, if the New Testament prophetic office were categorically different, as charismatics claim, some distinction would have been made. As Sam Waldron rightly points out, "…To suppose that a difference as important as this would be passed over without explicit comment is unthinkable.""[362]

Charismatics often go to 1 Thessalonians 5:20-22, where Paul exhorts the Thessalonians to "not despise prophetic utterances. But examine everything carefully; hold fast to that which is good; abstain from every form of evil." They reason that if the Thessalonians were to perform "prophetic utterances," that must mean that they should too. And since Paul tells them to "test" what is presented, this must mean the prophecies of Christian prophets can be in error from time to time.

But to "test" the prophecy of a prophet is consistent with OT exhortation as well, and charismatics admit that the standard for an OT prophet was 100% accuracy. Israel needed to test the message of the prophets with previous revelation or the Word because there were false prophets among them. They needed to "test" the prophets and their prophecies (cf. Deut. 13:1-5; 18:20-22; Isa. 8:20; 30:10; Jer. 5:31; 14:14-16; 23:21-22; Ezek. 13:2-9; 22:28; Mic. 3:11). Jesus and the NT writers warned the first century Church that there would be false prophets (Mt. 7:15; 24:11; 2 Tim. 4:3-4; 2 Pet. 2:1-3; 1 Jn. 4:1; Jude 4).

After all, we know there were false prophets even within the Thessalonian church who were Judaizers claiming that Christ had already come prior to AD 70 (2 Thess. 2:2), and therefore the temple and old covenant system was to continue in the new covenant age. Paul warned the Thessalonians that this kind of false prophecy is "evil" and they

---

[362] John MacArthur, *Strange Fire*, (Nashville, TN: Thomas Nelson, 2013), 119-120

should abstain from it. It should have been easy to discern this "prophecy" to be false since Jesus connected His coming with the destruction of the temple and the end of the old covenant age (Mt. 24:3-34). The temple was still standing, and the old covenant system was still active. The prophet and his prophecy were "evil" doctrinally and chronologically.

Contrary to the claims of heretical Charismatics, there is simply no exegetical evidence that NT prophets and prophecy contain "error" to try and justify their track record of failed and false prophecies. President Trump needs to fire Paula White, like, yesterday! Her "counsel" is filled with doctrinal error and will only serve to confuse and weaken his faith, as this false teaching has for many worldwide.

Tongues would cease

The Liddle-Scott Lexicon confirms what we see to be the obvious throughout the book of Acts in that the gift of tongues was a known human language – "a tongue, i.e. the language used by a particular people in distinction from that of other nations: Acts 2:11…"[363]

Paul also informs us in I Cor. 14:5 that when tongues are properly interpreted, they are on the same level as prophecy (proclaiming divine revelation). One who spoke in tongues uttered "mysteries" (1 Cor. 14:2). Of the 28 times "mystery" is used in the NT, it always has the meaning as something that was once hidden but is now revealed. Since tongues were known foreign languages, he who spoke in an untranslated tongue uttered something unknown to man or only known to God. Therefore, the emphasis for Paul was to have it interpreted so that it may edify the body.

It is interesting to note that when the Pentecostal movement first began, they thought they were speaking known human languages as depicted in Acts 2. Therefore, Charles Parham sent them into the mission field only to have them return completely devastated in that no one understood their gibberish. Ever since that time, Pentecostals and Charismatics have sought to **re-define** the Biblical meaning of tongues as they have also done to the meaning of NT prophecy.

Since most Charismatics today do not believe that their tongue speaking is on par with giving divine revelation, as in developing the NT cannon, they have to come up with novel interpretations which prove on one hand that they are not producing cannon-level revelation, while at the same time attempting to justify the non-miraculous nature of their gibberish. Most of the time when they are confronted with the fact that their gibberish is not a known human language like in Acts 2, they say that their gibberish is "tongues of angels" (1 Cor. 13:1).

Commentators such as Adam Clarke are closest to the truth when they bring to light the Jewish historical context and mindset on "the tongues of angels":

---

[363] Free online, https://www.studylight.org/lexicons/greek/gwview.cgi?n=1100.

> "To speak with the tongues of men, among the Jewish interpreters, means, **to speak the languages of the seventy nations**. To the praise of Mordecai, they say that he understood all those languages; and they require that the fathers of the Sanhedrin should be skilled in many languages that they may not be obliged to hear anything by an interpreter. Maim. in Sanh., c. 2.
>
> To speak with the tongues of angels, they thought to be not only an excellent gift, but to be possible; and highly extol Jochanan ben Zaccai because he understood them."[364]

When we begin studying the languages of men and angels, we need to begin in Genesis 11 and how the Jews understood this historical event. They understood that there were 70 angels that came down from heaven with God to confuse man's one language and make it 70 (one angel residing over the 70 nations). They understood the angels to be in charge of teaching these new languages to the 70 nations. Therefore, the angels no doubt had the most knowledge of these languages and therefore spoke them with the utmost of eloquence (something those at Corinth esteemed).

When angels spoke in the OT and NT, it was always in human languages. Because of their intelligence and mastering of men's languages, when they spoke it no doubt was very eloquent (something the Corinthians esteemed in their pride).

It should also be pointed out that the Jewish belief within Paul's day on how angels communicated is different than the Charismatic interpretation. Many Jews believed angels had a language of the heart and mind (didn't use sounds, etc. as they are spirit beings). So to assume that the gibberish of Charismatics today is what is being spoken by angels (literally with literal mouths in heaven) is not the Jewish concept.

So, as we saw with prophecy, once again we have Charismatics needing to *re-define* the meaning of tongues to support their experiences and what they think it is. They imagine, due to their experiences, that tongues should be seen as some kind of private prayer language of pure "angelic" gibberish (not known human languages). This simply cannot be supported using a grammatical, historical hermeneutic.

Parallels between Acts 2 and 1 Corinthians 12-14

John MacArthur does a great job connecting the speaking of tongues in Acts with 1 Corinthians as being known foreign languages:

> "In Acts, Luke uses *laleo* ("to speak") in combination with glossa ("tongues") four different times (Acts 2:4, 11; 10:46; 19:6). In 1 Corinthians 12-14, Paul uses forms of that same combination thirteen times (1 Cor. 12:30; 13:1; 14:2, 4, 5 [2x], 6, 13, 18, 19, 21, 27, 39).
>
> These linguistic parallels carry added significance when we consider that Luke was Paul's traveling companion and close associate, even writing under Paul's apostolic authority. Because he penned the book of Acts around AD 60, roughly

---

[364] Adam Clarke, *Commentary on the Bible*, http://www.sacred-texts.com/bib/cmt/clarke/co1013.htm.

five years after Paul wrote his first epistle to the Corinthians, Luke would have been well aware of their confusion regarding the gift of languages. Certainly, Luke would not have wanted to add to that confusion. Thus, he would not have used the exact same terminology in Acts as Paul did in 1 Corinthians unless what had happened at Pentecost was identical to the authentic gift Paul described in his epistle.

The fact that Paul noted "various kinds of tongues" in 1 Corinthians 12:10 (NASB) does not imply that some are real languages and other are merely gibberish. Rather, the Greek word for kinds is *genos*, from which we derive the word genus. *Genos* refers to a family, group, race, or nation. Linguists often refer to language "families" or "groups," and that is precisely Paul's point: there are various families of languages in the world, and this gift enabled some believers to speak in a variety of them. In Acts 2, Luke emphasized that same idea in verses 9-11, where he explained that the languages that were spoken came from at least sixteen different regions.

Other parallels between Acts and 1 Corinthians 12-14 can be established. In both places, the Source of the gift is the same—the Holy Spirit (Acts 2:4, 18; 10:44-46; 19:6; 1 Cor. 12:1, 7, 11, et al.). In both places, the reception of the gift is not limited to the apostles, but also involved laypeople in the church (cf. Acts 1:15; 10:46; 19:6; 1 Cor. 12:30; 14:18). In both places, the resulting message can be translated and thereby understood, either by those who already know the language (as on the day of Pentecost—Acts 2:9-11) or by someone gifted with the ability to translate (1 Cor. 12:10; 14:5, 13).

In both places, the gift served as a miraculous sign for unbelieving Jews (Acts 2:5, 12, 14, 19; 1 Cor. 14:21-22; cf. Isa. 28:11-12). In both places, the gift of language was closely associated with the gift of prophecy (Acts 2:16-18; 19:6; 1 Cor. 14). And in both places, unbelievers who did not understand what was being spoken responded with mockery and derision (Acts 2:13; 1 Cor. 14:23). ***Given so many parallels, it is exegetically impossible and irresponsible to claim that the phenomenon described in 1 Corinthians was any different from that of Acts 2. Since the gift of tongues consisted of authentic foreign languages on the day of Pentecost, then the same was true for the believers in Corinth.***"[365]

Knowledge would cease

In harmony with the miraculous nature of the gifts of prophecy and tongues, this refers to a specific kind of miraculous gift of knowledge given by God in which one understood the meaning of an OT passage as it related to the new covenant "mystery." For example, James was given this gift when he interpreted Amos 9 as the Gentile inclusion into the one new covenant body/temple (Acts 15:12-17). Even John Wesley

---

[365] John MacArthur, *Strange Fire*, (Nashville, TN: Thomas Nelson, 2013), 140-141 emphasis added MJS

understood that the miraculous gift of knowledge was "…an extraordinary ability to understand and explain the Old Testament types and prophecies."[366]

Daniel prophesied of a time in which "many will go here and there to **increase knowledge**" (Dan. 12:4). This is not referring to airplane/space travel or addressing absolute knowledge of technology or all knowledge in general as many Dispensational Zionist Charismatics have fancifully speculated. It is a knowledge of Messiah and His kingdom that is in view. In context, this is connected with the Great Commission or evangelism of the shining stars (pastors and evangelists) in v. 3 that spread the gospel (the mysteries of the kingdom) between AD 30 – AD 70 and throughout the known Roman world.

Unlike the early transitional Church, we are not seeking knowledge in the OT as to how OT prophecies were being, and would be, fulfilled in the new covenant age – that is, as they pertained to the "mystery" (i.e. the Jew / Gentile union in ONE body). That old covenant body of knowledge was fulfilled in AD 70 and its covenant "soon disappeared" in AD 70 (Heb. 8:13). The new covenant mature man/body stands complete and independent of the old covenant system of types and shadows post-AD 70.

The "gift of knowledge" is not some Charismatic TV "preacher" telling his, or sadly her, 20,000 member church that there is someone out there with cancer and God is going to heal them. Ugh.

"Cease"

Paul uses two Greek words to describe when these miraculous gifts would stop or cease (*katargeo* and *pauo*).

Katargeo simply means to "be done away", "to cease", "to make invalid", "to abrogate", "to annul," or to "be free from a law." Per Paul, the wisdom and rulers of his present old covenant "this age" were in the process of passing away (1 Cor. 2:6). The last enemy, "the death," was in the process of being *annulled* or *destroyed* when "the end" of the old covenant age would take place at Christ's *Parousia* (1 Cor. 15:23-26). God was in the process of giving the Corinthians victory over "the (Mosaic) law" (vss. 55-57). Paul, in his second letter to the Corinthians, continued to teach that the old covenant law of Moses was in the process of "passing away" or being annulled (2 Cor. 3:7, 11, 13, 14).

Pauo means to "cease" or "come to a complete end." Per the writer to the Hebrews, the old covenant law was a shadow of the new covenant things that were "about to" come (Heb. 10:1 – the Greek *mello* is used). **The old covenant law could not have "stopped" (*pauo*) (v. 2) until it had been fulfilled or the new covenant better things which were "about to come" had reached their fullness.** In Hebrews 9 we learn that the old covenant still had a "legal standing" or was still being "imposed" until Christ would appear a second time at the end of Israel's old covenant "last days" age (Heb.

---

[366] Charles Wesley, see Hymn – "Let earth and heaven combine."

9:8-28). The old covenant was "ready to vanish" at Christ's "in a very little while" Second Coming (Heb. 8:13; 10:37).

"But when that which is perfect (Greek telios) comes, the imperfect disappears"

Telios ("that which is perfect") simply means that which has reached its end, matured, has reached its goal, is not complete, wanting in nothing.

According to Paul, those who were *telios*, "mature," in 1 Corinthians 2:6 were not following the ways of their current old covenant "this age," but were following the "wisdom" that comes from the new covenant "things" or way of life. Maturity is the clear meaning here in that Paul gives the example of a child growing into manhood, and when he becomes a man he then puts away the temporal, childish things (cf. 1 Cor. 13:11).

When interpreting a passage, the exegete/interpreter needs to examine the same language being used elsewhere by the author, especially if there was a second letter written to the same church. In this case we have Paul's second letter to the Corinthians to help us understand Paul's teaching of seeing in a glass or mirror the face of God and in what theological context he sees this taking place:

1 Corinthians 13:8-12 "already-maturing-not yet"		2 Corinthians 3:7-14 "already-transforming-not yet"
1. **Love of the new covenant will remain** – unlike the three gifts.		1. **New covenant glory will remain** unlike the Old Covenant glory.
2. Miraculous gifts of prophecy, tongues and knowledge would **pass away.**		2. The old covenant & its glory was **passing away.**
3. **Looking [spiritually]** at God's face through the **mirror** of the old covenant Scriptures as an enigma.		3. **Looking [spiritually]** at the glory [or form] of God through a **mirror** and **being transformed [spiritually]** into the image of Christ from old covenant glory to new covenant glory.
Old Covenant Age (Moses - AD 30)	**Covenantal Transformation (AD 30 – AD 70)**	**New-Covenant Age (AD 70 - Forever)**
Old covenant imposed	Old covenant being nullified	Old covenant/revelatory gifts nullified
Veiled faces	Unveiled face, *as in a mirror, transforming*	Face to face
Slave-child (Gal. 4:1-7)	Adopted child (I Cor. 13:9-12; Gal. 4,4,5)	Man (I Cor. 13:11; Eph. 4:13)
New covenant prophesied	New covenant ratified in Jesus' blood	New covenant remains/ faith, hope, love remain[367]

---

[367] Bottom section of this chart produced by David A. Green.

I would agree with Charismatic D.A. Carson in his *Commentary on the New Testament use of the Old Testament* when he and others correctly connect the seeing of God through a mirror in both 1 Corinthians 13 and 2 Corinthians 3 to be the eschatological "already and not yet" of an unclear seeing of God within "this age" that will be more clearly realized in the "age to come" when Christ returns.

But he has two problems. First, as we have discussed in great detail thus far, the Jews and the NT writers understood "this age" to be the old covenant age of the Law and Prophets, and the "age about to come" as the Messianic or new covenant age (as even Charismatic N.T. Wright admits; the old covenant age is what is in view in Mt. 13:39, 24:3; and Heb. 9:26-28).

Secondly, in 2 Corinthians 3 the "already and not yet" process contextually is addressing the passing of the old covenant age and glory being contrasted with the in-breaking and maturing glory of the new covenant age. This "already and not yet" process was taking place between AD 30 – AD 70 and ended in AD 70 when the old covenant age "soon passed away" at Christ's "in a very little while and would not be delayed" coming (Heb. 8:13—10:37).

According to the Apostle Paul, the "form of the [old covenant] world" was in the process of "passing away" (1 Cor. 7:31). Paul tells us just a couple of verses prior when that would happen: "This is what I mean, brothers. **The appointed time has grown very short** (1 Cor. 7:29ESV). Either the world that was passing away was the old covenant world which did pass away "very shortly" in AD 70, and thus Paul was a prophet and inspired when he wrote this, or Paul had in mind the physical creation and thus Paul is proven to be a false prophet and not inspired.

Major Premise: Both 1 Corinthians 13:8-12 and 2 Corinthians 3:7-14 describe the same eschatological "already and not yet" process.

Minor Premise: But the eschatological "already and not yet" process of 2 Corinthians 3:7-14 covered a time when the in-breaking glory of the new covenant was "increasing" and overlapping with the glory of the old covenant, which was "passing away" between AD 30 – AD 70.

Conclusion: Therefore, the miraculous gifts of prophecy, tongues and knowledge "ceased" or "passed away" when the glory of the old covenant "this age" passed away and the increasing or maturing of the new covenant glory and "age about to come" was matured and brought to its fullness in AD 70.

1 Corinthians 13 / Ephesians 2–4:11-13 Parallels

Having looked at the covenantal context of Paul's "already and not yet" looking-into-a-mirror theme found in 2 Corinthians 3 to help us interpret 1 Corinthians 13, lets now branch out into Paul's other letters to see if they might help us understand Paul's *maturing of the man* as the corporate body theme.

1 Corinthians 12:1-13:<u>10</u> – Greek *Telios* (the mature man)	Ephesians 2:1-4:<u>13</u> Greek *Telios* (the mature man)
Gentiles 12:2; Greeks 12:13	Jew/Gentile discussion 2:11; 3:1; 4:17
"All in all" 12:6, 12	Emphasis on "all" 4:6
Emphasis on oneness and the unity between Jew and Gentile because the same Spirit and miraculous gifts were given to both 12:4-14	Emphasis on oneness and the unity between Jew and Gentile with both benefiting from miraculous gifts given by the one Spirit – Chapters 2-4 * New covenant age "**about to come**" 1:21
Gifts listed: 12:4-11, 27-31; 13:1-3; 14:1-40 – but miraculous gifts listed with "**FIRST apostles, second prophets**…" 12:28	Gifts listed 4:7-11. "Built on the **FOUNDATION** of "**apostles and prophets**" 2:20
Human body illustration 12:12-13, 14ff.	Human body illustration of unity 4:12-16

- *"And He Himself gave some to be apostles, some prophets, some evangelists, and some pastors and teachers, for the equipping of the saints for the work of ministry, for the edifying of <u>**the body of Christ**</u>, till we all come to the <u>unity of THE [New Covenant Christian] faith</u> and of <u>the knowledge</u> of the Son of God, to a <u>perfect (Greek teleios) man</u>, to the <u>measure of the stature</u> of the <u>fullness of Christ</u>;" (Ephs. 4:11-13)*

This maturity process of the "perfect man" (the Church – body of Christ) was the "mystery of Christ" in which both Jews and Gentiles would become fellow citizens and be mutually built up as the **new covenant temple**:

- *"Now, therefore, you are no longer strangers and foreigners, but **fellow citizens** with the saints and **members of the household of God**, having been built on the foundation of the apostles and prophets, <u>**Jesus Christ Himself being the chief cornerstone**</u>, in whom the whole building, being joined together, <u>grows into a HOLY TEMPLE in the Lord</u>, <u>in whom you also are being built together for a dwelling place of God in the Spirit</u>." (Ephs. 2:19-22).*

The arrival of the "that which is perfect" and "the unity of the faith" involved synonymous or synchronous events. Arriving at the "unity of the faith" does not mean when we are all in heaven or that we will believe the same things perfectly. Nor does the existence of many denominations disprove the idea that the unity of the faith arrived in AD 70. In its historical context, the unity of the new covenant Christian faith came in AD 70 when it matured to a place where it no longer had the scaffolding of the unclear, unfulfilled old covenant structure supporting it. Post AD 70, it stands on its own (independent and apart from the old covenant system) and is a *complete and matured temple/man.*

Again, **in context**, this is the Church as the "mystery" being revealed as a maturing boy growing into manhood. This is a maturity of equality of Jew and Gentile, which the old covenant could not bring them into, or to the attaining of the fullness or forgiveness of sin which the old covenant couldn't bring as well. Paul prayed that the Church would grow in their *spiritual* understanding of this *positional knowledge and love* (Eph. 3:14-19).

The list or foundation of the Church described for us in Ephesians 2 and 4, along with 1 Corinthians 12, begins with the apostles and prophets (that is, the unique 12 bringing the inspired revelation of the NT), and many Charismatics correctly affirm that this particular miraculous gift of apostolic office given to the Church has passed away - and so they should. As the OT cannon and revelation is described as the "Law and the Prophets," so the NT is being described as the "apostles and prophets." These are not simply mail carriers with a small "a" kind of apostles, but rather these are the unique, inspired miracle workers with THE capital "A" kind of apostles sent as messengers of Jesus to interpret OT Scripture and form doctrine within the churches as a solid foundation. If it is admitted that the gift of the unique office of the 12 apostles ceased, then the Charismatic must be open to some of the other gifts ceasing around the same time period.

In Ephesians 2-3, we learn that this "building up" until the early Church reached the status of a mature (*telios*) new covenant man or temple is referring to the Jew / Gentile union. Paul says that this process of maturing and growing into the new covenant man and temple was **the "mystery"** not fully revealed in the OT, but was being revealed to him and the other apostles and NT prophets by **divine "revelation."** Jesus promised these unique apostles and prophets that He would send the Spirit to lead **THEM "into all truth concerning things to come" or eschatology** (Jn. 16:13). We can readily see how these two offices of apostles and prophets were unique in their revelatory function and we don't need them anymore, just like we don't need another "cornerstone" to lay the same "foundation." Once the cornerstone and foundation is laid, we don't keep laying it again, and again, and again.

Since there are no more miraculous and revelatory apostles and prophets developing the new covenant "mystery," and since tongues when interpreted functioned as revelatory prophecy (1 Cor. 14:5), the miraculous gift of tongues likewise ceased in AD 70 along with the unique foundational offices of the apostles and prophets.

And, again, there is no debate between the Charismatic and myself when it comes to the miraculous gifts ceasing when the "age to come" arrives. The only problem for the Charismatic is that Paul taught that this eschatological growing into maturity or building up and arriving at the unity of the faith would be achieved

- "not only in this age [the old covenant age], but also in *the one [new covenant age] about to come*" (Eph. 1:21WUESTNT, SLT).

Paul describes the new covenant "age" (Greek *aion*) that was "about to come" as having no end or being "**without end**" (Ephs. 3:20-21). Yet Charismatics believe this is the age in which the miraculous gifts will "end" – the age "without end?!? Paul anticipated that life would go on after the "age about to come" had arrived, or post-AD 70, that is, in the "coming ages" (Eph. 2:7). Here Christ would continue to showcase His grace through His new covenant MATURE body, and those childish and temporal gifts would not be needed.

1 Corinthians 13 / Hebrews 9 Temple imagery & covenant contrast continued

In studying our word "perfect" thus far in Pauline literature, we find it to be connected with the maturing of a boy into manhood theme and temple themes in Ephesians and 2 Corinthians 3:1-6:16. So, let's look at one last eschatological passage in the NT where *telios* is used and see how it too develops the temple motif:

- *"And the lesson which the Holy Spirit teaches is this—that the way into the true Holy place is not yet open so long as the outer tent still remains in existence. And this is a figure—**for the time now present**—answering to which both gifts and sacrifices are offered, unable though they are to give complete freedom from sin to him who ministers. For their efficacy depends only on meats and drinks and various washings, ceremonies pertaining to the body and imposed **until a time of reformation**. But Christ appeared as a High Priest of **the blessings that <u>are soon to come</u>** by means of the greater and more **perfect (Greek telios) Tent** of worship, a tent which has not been built with hands—that is to say does not belong to this material creation" (Heb. 9:8-11WEY).*

Once again, we encounter the "perfect" (Greek *telios*) in the context of contrasting the old covenant with the new. In this particular context in Hebrews, the old covenant represents the Holy Place while the new covenant is represented by the Most Holy Place – in which complete and full access was soon to come. The JFB commentary correctly sees the typology that is being presented:

> "The Old Testament economy is represented by the holy place, the New Testament economy by the Holy of Holies."[368]

Also the theme of seeing God's face is implied since the time when access into the Most Holy Place would be granted is when this perfect face to face experience or unashamed, fully-forgiven, positional reality would be realized.

Some Greek scholars do support that this text is teaching that the old covenant had an "imposed" "legal" "standing" (symbolized by the presence of the Holy Place) until the time of reformation which would "soon" be upon the Hebrew audience. This validates the earlier context of the validity and readiness of the passing of the old covenant law

---

[368] JFB online commentary, ibid.

(Heb. 8:13), and what Jesus taught concerning the legal validity of all the jots and tittles of the law to be in force until all of it had been fulfilled (Mt. 5:17-19).

Again, this is what we see in Revelation 21:15 through chapter 22 in that the New Jerusalem / Bride is the **city described as a perfect cube – The Most Holy Place** coming down – by which God's presence would be with man again. This is when the seventh trumpet is blown and the "mystery" (unity in the new covenant kingdom is fulfilled and access to the ark or Most Holy Place is granted Rev. 10:7; 11:19). This is consummated or realized when the New Jerusalem as the MHP perfect cube (Rev. 21:16 – note there is no rectangular Holy Place connected with it) shortly arrives to earth.

The arrival of the New Jerusalem is also the arrival of the Messianic wedding motif, which we believe may be present in our text when discussing the face to face metaphor or that of knowing.

> *"...then we shall see face to face. Now I know in part; then I shall know fully, even as I am fully known."*

Marriage / Temple Motif

Tom Holland believes bride purchase (with a dowry and not slave purchase) is in view in 1 Corinthians 6:19-20, and Paul again uses bridal and wedding terminology in addressing "the perfect" here in 1 Corinthians 13:

> "That this relationship between the temple and the bride is part of the apostle's thinking is supported by the Hebrew word for bride, *kallah*, meaning 'the complete' or 'perfect one.' This is probably the thinking behind Paul's statement in 1 Corinthians 13:9-12.
>
> This suggestion is also supported by his reference to *knowing*, a term constantly used throughout Scripture of the marriage relationship."[369]

This falls into harmony with the parallels of the face to face sight and the "soon" coming of Christ as the implied Groom coming in Revelation 21-22:7, 20 to consummate His marriage with His bride / New Jerusalem.

And again,

> "This divine marriage is the eschatological goal of the redemption that is in Christ. An echo of it surfaces [again] in 2 Corinthians 5:5 where Paul speaks about the church being prepared for the coming change when she will not be found naked. A further factor that has probably hindered the identification of the wedding theme is the tendency to interpret the passage from an individual perspective. This is not because the grammar demands it, but because tradition has dictated it. As we have seen, the believer is never called the bride of Christ,

---

[369] Tom Holland, *CONTOURS OF PAULINE THEOLOGY A RADICAL NEW SURVEY OF THE INFLUENCES ON PAUL'S BIBLICAL WRITINGS*, (Scotland, UK: Mentor Imprint by Christian Focus Publications, 2004), 120-12.

but the church is. If this is a corporate argument, then the reference to a wedding garment is consistent and makes sense of the flow of the argument. The passage closes with the statement that God would dwell with them (2 Cor. 6:14-18), temple imagery, which is always, as we have seen, closely connected to the theme of the church being the bride of Christ."[370]

I agree with Holland's observations here. Paul is not done with his corporate covenantal contrasts in 2 Corinthians 3, and they extend up to 2 Corinthians 6:16 when Paul identifies the Church as the new covenant tabernacle / temple of Ezekiel 37:27. In 2 Corinthians 5, the "earthly tent" from which they were "groaning" during the transition period is the old covenant house / temple / system, and their desire to be clothed with the building / house from above is the completed / matured new covenant temple / system. And as pointed out earlier, the wedding takes place in Revelation 21-22, whereby the heavenly dwelling comes down from heaven and clothes the church (who is on earth). The New Jerusalem is the "perfect" bride and post-AD 70 we have access to God's intimate "face to face" presence, having fully cast off the veil of the old covenant administration of death.

OT fulfillment – Isaiah 52:8

> "*Thy watchmen shall lift up the voice; with the voice together shall they sing: for **they shall see eye to eye**, when the LORD shall bring again Zion*" (Isa. 52:8).

The Jews understood this passage to be referring to the resurrection. In context, we again have the theme of the arrival of the New Jerusalem and the Church putting on her wedding garments because this is the time of the wedding and resurrection (Isa. 52:1-2; 61:10).

Conclusion - 1 Corinthians 13 / Revelation 21-22

We agree with various views which both recognize that 1 Corinthians 13:10-12 and Revelation 22:4-7 are the same event (Charismatics) and also agree with Partial Preterists that Christ and the spiritual New Jerusalem and new covenant creation arrived at Christ's "soon" coming in AD 70, and therefore we "see His face" spiritually and positionally in the kingdom today. And of course it is not just Charismatics who link these two passages. Oddly some who believe the miraculous gifts have ceased connect them as the same event while somehow trying to maintain that Revelation 21:4-7 is still future. This makes no sense, but at least they are on track as seeing them as the same eschatological event.

Therefore, let me "bridge the gap" within these two orthodox interpretations or parallels of these two passages, and make better sense of them and why we don't see the miraculous sign and revelatory gifts taking place like we see in the gospels and in the book of Acts:

---

[370] Holland, Ibid., 121

Major Premise: Paul's "that which is perfect" of 1 Corinthians 13:8-12 is the "soon" Second Coming of Christ and arrival of the New Jerusalem and new creation of Revelation 22:4-7, 20, which produces the face to face or seeing of God's face (Charismatics and even some non-Charismatics admit this).

Minor Premise: But the "soon" coming of Christ and arrival of the spiritual New Jerusalem and new creation of Revelation 22:4-7, 20 was fulfilled in AD 70. Therefore, positionally and spiritually we continue to see His face clearer today in the new covenant age than in the dark old covenant age (Partial Preterism).

Conclusion: Therefore, "that which is perfect," or the "soon" Second Coming and arrival of the spiritual new covenant New Jerusalem and new creation (which produces a spiritual and positional seeing of God's face today), was fulfilled in AD 70 and is the redemptive and historical event whereby we can know that prophecy, tongues and knowledge "ceased" (Full Preterism).

It is also ironic that Charismatics such as Sam Storms believe the near "this generation" coming of Christ and/or the passing of the heaven and earth in Matthew 5:17-18 and Matthew 24:27-35 is referring to Christ coming in AD 70 and the old covenant creation, but once he gets into the book of Revelation these same "soon" to be fulfilled motifs are somehow pushed to our future. Perhaps Storm's inconsistent hermeneutic is due to him seeing the Full Preterist train coming, which would run down his false Futurism and Charismatic teaching?

Argument #2: If the Church is still in the "last days" and the Great and Dreadful Day of the Lord, or the Second Coming of Acts 2:14-20 has not been fulfilled, then the miraculous gifts of the Church continue for today.

We have already addressed how the evangelism to the "nations" that were gathered throughout the Roman world at Pentecost, and their going back to those nations, fulfilled the Great Commission and the reversing of what took place at the Tower of Babel. So I will not bring that Charismatic argument up here. Let's focus on the language of Acts 2 and Peter identifying the salvation he preached with the coming Great Day of the Lord to take place within their "perverse generation" (Acts 2:20-40).

Common apocalyptic language

A). *"Blood, fire and vapor of smoke"* (Acts 2:19) – This is war language referring to AD 67 – AD 70. As we saw earlier, tongues were for a sign of impending judgment for Israel (1 Cor. 14/Isa. 28).

B). *"Sun turned to darkness & moon to blood"* (Acts 2:20) – This is the language of a lunar eclipse which darkened the sun and turned the moon blood red. Israel, shining like the sun in covenant status with God, would now be extinguished. Her moon or city would become blood red like the moon during an eclipse. After all, they did say, "His blood be on us and on our children," and in AD 67 – AD 70 it was so.

C). *"before the day of the Lord comes"* (Acts 2:20) – As with the judgment and day of the Lord in Malachi 3-4 and Matthew 24:27-30, this passage has historically been referred to as either: 1) The Second Coming closing the "last days" period, or 2) Typical apocalyptic language describing Christ coming in judgment upon Jerusalem with her "last days" old covenant age ending in AD 70. Both are true. This is the Second Coming event which closed the "last days" of the old covenant age in AD 70.

D). *"Everyone who calls upon the name of the Lord shall be saved" "...and [Peter] continued to exhort them, saying, "Save yourselves from this crooked generation."* (Acts 2:21, 40) – That this "Day of the Lord" is referring to AD 70 should be obvious in that Peter's audience is exhorted to be saved from it because it would take place within their contemporary "**this** crooked generation." Peter is referencing Israel's last days, terminal "crooked" or "perverse generation" of Deuteronomy 31; 32:5, 20.

E). *"For the promise is for you and your children and for all who are far off, everyone whom the Lord our God calls to himself"* (Acts 2:38-39). This takes us back to the Great Commission of Acts 1:8 reaching to the end of the earth/land as they knew it (and of them returning back to "all nations under heaven" in 2:5), which was fulfilled just prior to the Lord coming in judgment by AD 70 (Rom. 10:18; 16:25-26; Col. 1:5-6, 23).

Charismatics are fond of quoting this passage and leaving out Peter's exhortation to be saved from *their "crooked generation" in the next verse* (v. 40).

It is ironic that some Charismatics such as "Apostle" C. Peter Wagner are Partial Preterists and argue from Matthew 24 and other texts that the "last days" were from AD 30 – AD 70. Therefore, since the Church is no longer in the "last days," this implodes the Charismatic argument in Acts 2. After all, we should listen to a Charismatic "apostle." Lol.

Many within the Reformed community correctly understand "the last days" in the New Testament to be referring to the end of the old covenant economy in AD 70, and thus we are no longer in them. For instance, Gary DeMar writes,

> "The last days are not way off in the distant future. The end came to an obsolete covenant in the first century. In A.D. 70 the "last days" ended with the dissolution of the temple and the sacrificial system."[371]

David Chilton wrote:

> "The Biblical expression Last Days properly refers to the period from the Advent of Christ until the destruction of Jerusalem in A.D. 70, the "last days" of Israel during the transition from the Old Covenant to the New Covenant (Heb. 1:1–2; 8:13; James 5:1–9; 1 Pet. 2:20; 1 John 2:18)."[372]

---

[371] DeMar, *Last Days Madness*, Ibid., 38.

[372] David Chilton, *The Days of Vengeance*, Ibid., 16, 51.

And John Owen, in his exposition of Hebrews 1:2, wrote,

> "It is the last days of the Judaical church and state, which were then drawing to their period and abolition, that are here and elsewhere called "The last days," or "The latter days," or "The last hour," 2 Peter 3:3; 1 John 2:18; Jude 1:18. . . . This phrase of speech is signally used in the Old Testament to denote the last days of the Judaical church."[373]

R.C. Sproul, in refuting Simon Kistemaker, says that Hebrews 9:26-28 includes both Jesus' first and second comings occurring by the end of the old covenant age in AD 70:

> "**This passage refers to both the first and second appearances of Christ**. The context for his first appearance is 'the end of the ages.' Yet his followers are still waiting for him to appear a second time… If Christ's first coming at 'the end of the ages' has already occurred and if considerable time has elapsed since that coming, then it is impossible to identify 'the end of the ages' with the end of time. **If the second appearing of Christ here refers to his judgment on Jerusalem, it would still fit in the framework of 'the end of the ages' that is not the end of all time**."[374]

The book of Hebrews teaches that they were currently living in, and that Christ came in, the "last days" of an age. Christ coming in the last days of a period of seventy to forty years before the end of the old covenant age was fulfilled makes more sense than Him coming in the "last days" of an age that has now lasted 2000 years and counting, which at this point has now surpassed the duration of the entire Mosaic age.

> **Major Premise**: The miraculous gifts last until the "last days" come to an end (Charismatics).
>
> **Minor Premise**: But the "last days" is the time period from the passing of Israel's old covenant age/world to the maturing of the new covenant age/world, or from AD 30 – AD 70 (Partial Preterists & even some Charismatics).
>
> **Conclusion**: Therefore, the miraculous gifts ended at the end of Israel's "last days" old covenant age in AD 70 (Full Preterist).

Argument #2: Christ would be "with" the Church by performing miracles to accomplish the Great Commission, even to the end of the age (cf. Mt. 28:18-20; Mrk. 16:15-18).

In our exegesis of the Olivet Discourse and in developing Matthew 24:3-14, 34, I showed how the Great Commission (v. 14) was fulfilled within Jesus' generation and by "the end" of the old covenant age in AD 70 (cf. Col. 1:5-6, 23; Rom. 10:18, 16:25-26).

---

[373] John Owen, *The Works of John Owen*, Vol. 19, Ibid., 12–13.
[374] *The Last Days According to Jesus*, Ibid., 106.

Argument #3: Since we are in the eschatological "already and not yet" of the kingdom still being "at hand," we have the same commission as the twelve to "heal the sick, raise the dead, cleanse lepers and cast out demons" (Mt. 10:7-8).

We have already given an exegesis of Matthew 10:17-23 which is connected to Jesus' declaration of the kingdom being "at hand" and the disciples' commission to perform sign miracles in verses 7-8. The kingdom being "at hand" is contextually tied to the coming "day of judgment" (vs. 15) and the Son of Man "coming" when the disciples would be "saved" at "the end" of verses 22-23. All of these events would occur during the "already and not yet" period of AD 30 – AD 70 when the first century Church would be evangelizing Israel and the Gentile world of the Roman Empire. While the disciples were preaching the gospel to Israel and being persecuted, Christ would not exhaust cities of refuge for them to flee to for protection before He came in judgment to "save" them and close the "end" of the old covenant age in AD 70.

We have also examined John the Baptist's eschatology in Matthew 3:2-12 and noted that his declaration of the "kingdom being at hand" was also connected to the "wrath about to come" and the harvest judgment to save the righteous and judge the Pharisees or the unrepentant in AD 70.

Contrary to some of the stories you may hear of what is taking place with missionaries deep within the jungles of Africa (where you can't personally witness), Charismatics are not "healing the sick and lepers" or "raising the dead." Per Paul and the inspiration of the Scripture, Satan was "crushed shortly" (Rom. 16:20/Gen. 3:15) at Christ's coming in AD 70, and Satan and the demonic are not possessing anyone so as to need any casting out of demons or "revivals."

Charismatics such as D.A. Carson agree with us that the coming of Christ in Matthew 10:23 was fulfilled in AD 70, but Carson fails to address what the "end" is, that being the end of the old covenant age, let alone the "at hand kingdom" and "day of judgment" connected to Christ coming in AD 70. He knows that if he identifies the "end" as the "end of the age" here in Matthew 10:23, Matthew would have used the term consistently in Matthew 13:39; Matthew 24:3, 14; and Matthew 28:18-20, and this would destroy his creedal publishing and teaching career as a Futurist and a Charismatic.

The "already and not yet" of the kingdom being "at hand" is connected to the period when the first century disciples would be persecuted in the synagogues and preach the gospel to the towns of Israel just before the Son of Man would come to judge Israel in AD 70. These "at hand" eschatological events connected with the miraculous sign gifts would last until the "end" of the old covenant age would "soon vanish" in AD 70.

Concluding the sign and revelatory miraculous gifts

A miraculous "sign" pointed to something deeper and spiritual. Jesus performed physical miracles to prove that He was God and to point to the deeper and spiritual fulfillment and realities of His kingdom. For example, He would physically heal a man to prove He had the authority to forgive sin (unseen in the spiritual realm), and heal blindness and deafness to prove He had the power and authority to make the spiritually blind and deaf see and hear His teachings about Himself and His spiritual kingdom.

The early church was looking in the dim glass of the OT Scriptures to see how and when they were being fulfilled spiritually in Christ and through the Church. This was like the process of a boy growing to become a mature and independent man, separating himself from his parents. The first century Church was growing and maturing into manhood between AD 30 – AD 70 and would stand mature and independent of the old covenant system when it "soon vanished" in AD 70. Post AD 70, Christ has come and fully forgiven us our sin, and thus positionally we see His face clearly and are fully clothed in Christ's righteousness in the new covenant age. The marriage and feast have taken place; the veil of the old covenant system, and that of death, has been removed in Christ.

The "last days" or "already and not yet" of the "kingdom" being "at hand," was from AD 30 – AD 70. This was also the time when the Great Commission preached to Israel and the Gentile Roman Empire was fulfilled. The charismatic gifts were necessary to confirm the "new" covenant gospel and message which was transforming the physical kingdom into the spiritual. The revelatory gifts were also necessary to develop the NT cannon and show how the OT Scriptures were being fulfilled in Christ and through the Church.

We found no evidence that the miraculous gift of prophecy or the office of prophet changed from the OT and NT – in regard to prophets uttering false and failed prophecies such as the Charismatics do on a regular basis. It is a new interpretation that they have come up with whereby so-called "prophets" and the gift of prophecy may be in error. This re-definition is necessary to justify their vague, un-miraculous "prophecies," or it's given as a backdoor when they fail!

Charismatics have also had to redefine the miraculous nature of "tongues" to not be fluently speaking human languages which they have never studied (as in Acts 2), but to be a "private prayer language" or public gibberish which is purely non-miraculous and learned behavior.

We can only encourage our presidents and politicians to expose these unbiblical manipulative "prophecy experts" as charlatans since they are constantly trying to lead us into an end-time war or into the "endless wars" of the Middle East. They have NO exegetical authority to demonstrate that this end-time war extends beyond AD 67 – AD 70, and they have no "miraculous" gifts or authority to "prophesy" in order to manipulate others to support their "prophecies." Selah.

Chapter Fourteen:

Refutation of Pacifism What Just War Theory in the Middle East is and isn't

- *"If the thief is caught while breaking in and is struck so that he dies, there will be no blood-guiltiness on his account. But if the sun has risen on him, there will be blood-guiltiness on his account. He shall surely make restitution; if he owns nothing, then he shall be sold for his theft."* (Ex. 22:2-3)

As I have demonstrated in this work, seeking to advance a "kingdom of God" theology / eschatology within Islam or Talmudic Zionism through theft and violence [with "Evangelical" or "Christian" support] is not the way Jesus and the NT teach the kingdom of God is to be advanced. But that is not to say there won't be times when we need to defend ourselves, our families and our nation from physical harm and the threat of Communist tyranny or death. What does the Bible teach us about defending ourselves and our country? What does one do when he sees a neighbor being violently raped, robbed and attacked, and they are pleading for you to help them and there is no time to wait for the police? Do you ignore them, or can you get physically involved to help them escape bodily harm or even death from their attacker, even if it means you must kill the attacker? And what if a small and weak country is being unjustly attacked and requests our help? Are we to ignore their cries for help? I think of Islam beheading Christians in small and weak African or Middle East villages, calling out to the US and Christians here for our help. Are we to turn a blind eye and just say, "They are just sheep led to the slaughter" as some pacifists would argue – in their skinny jeans drinking their lattes? Is it inconsistent to be a Christian and a policeman or soldier, as the liberal pacifist argues?

Just and righteous killing in the OT

At various times in the OT, the theocratic kingdom of Israel did advance through the physical sword in taking the Promised Land. God had the Hebrews be enslaved to Egypt for 400 years until the sin of the Amorites had been filled up (Gen. 15:16), and this was for worshipping Baal and sacrificing their children to him, etc. When God had Israel slay HIS enemies in the OT, it was:

1). connected to sacred space under the Mosaic old covenant.

2). just and righteous in that God gave the people of His land time to repent (again from Baal worship and sacrificing children, etc.), and when they didn't it was time for them to be judged (e.g. Numbers 33: 51-53).

3). connected, most of the time, to the office of the prophet whereby the people knew exactly when to go to war. As we previous proved, the office of prophet stopped in AD 70, so if we go to war today it needs to be for self-defense or be a very discernable just war.

Pacifism is present in all kinds of theological and eschatological views and systems, even within Christian Futurism. And, unfortunately, I have seen some Preterists advocating this unbiblical teaching. So I thought we should spend some time looking at what the Bible teaches about justifiable war and address some of the Pacifist "proof-texts."

"Thou shalt do no murder" (Ex. 20:13; Mt. 19:18)

The pacifist usually discards the OT in general, but is fond of quoting this passage in the KJV, which reads, "Thou shalt not kill." The KJV mistranslates the Hebrew (*ratsach*), which is correctly translated as "Thou shalt do no murder." "Killing" indeed ends life, but not all killing is "murder." The OT law distinguishes between [1] various forms of killing and murder done through unjustified greed, malice and wicked intent and [2] justifiable killing like that of manslaughter, self-defense, capital punishment, and in times of just war (Numbers 35: 22-24).

Various individual examples of righteous killing in the OT

Job

In Job 29:5 - 31:33, we learn of Job being a righteous judge, and in Job 29:17 this included "breaking the jaws of the wicked and plucking the spoil out of his teeth." Job didn't get the pacifist memo.

Abraham

When wicked men took Lot and members of Abraham's family, he already had trained 318 men with weapons and pursued them, "smoting" them in a slaughter and recovering his family and property (Gen. 14). Notice that Abraham didn't shrug his shoulders and say, "They must be sheep led to slavery or to the slaughter. I'll just go my own way."

Moses

Moses likewise engages in just vengeance when killing the Egyptian who murdered a Hebrew slave (Ex. 2:11-15). He obviously violated the law of Pharaoh just as his own mother had disobeyed tyrannical civil law when she heard that Pharaoh was going to kill the firstborn among the Hebrew women. She disobeyed and sent baby Moses floating down the Nile. Moses committed an act of insurrection to bring just vengeance upon his Hebrew brother's unjust murder.

Did Moses take the law into his own hands, and, if so, which law? According to Pharaoh's unjust and tyrannical law, Moses was a murderer and a fleeing fugitive from his "justice." But by the Law which God would later give to Moses, he was justified. The NT clearly justifies Moses: "And seeing one of them [Hebrews] suffer wrong, he defended him and *avenged him* that was oppressed, and smote the Egyptian" (Acts 7:24).

David

David, of course, was filled with godly zeal and killed Goliath who threatened and mocked the living God and God's people (1 Sam. 17). David would go on to be filled with the Spirit to kill his "tens of thousands" of God's enemies and enemies of His people (1 Sam. 18:7). David was a "man after God's own heart" who had God Himself "train his hands for war" to "destroy" even his own enemies (1 Sam. 13:14/Acts 13:22; Ps. 144:1; Ps. 18:40).

Yet God at times gave David discernment to not kill unjustly, as in the case of killing Saul, "God's anointed" (1 Sam. 24-28). On the other hand, God condemned David for murdering Uriah, but also granted David the ability to repent over it (2 Sam. 12:13).

Jesus Himself is "the offspring of David" who in the book of Revelation is described not just as a Lamb but also a Lion and Mighty Warrior with His enemies' blood upon Him (Rev. 5:5; 14:20/19:13-15; 22:16). Just as David had God's enemies slain before him during his 40 year reign, Jesus said that those Jews who would not have Him rule over them (from His ascension to His Parousia 40 years later) would be brought before Him and slain in the events of AD 67 – AD 70 (Lk. 19:14, 27).

Ehud

God "raised up a deliverer, Ehud the son of Gera," who in defiance of the ungodly civil authorities (being under the Moabite tyrant, Eglon) assassinated him, which motivated a just rebellion among the people of God who in return killed 10,000 unjust, tyrannical Moabites (Judges 3).

I could go on and discuss judges such as Gideon and Samson, but I think you get the point, so let's move on to the NT where the pacifist believes he is on more solid ground.

The NT: Luke 22:35-38; Matthew 5-7; Matthew 26:52; Romans 12-13 & treatment of soldiers

Luke 22:35-38

- *"And he said to them, "When I sent you out with no moneybag or knapsack or sandals, did you lack anything?" They said, "Nothing." He said to them, "But now let the one who has a moneybag take it, and likewise a knapsack. And **let the one who has no sword sell his cloak and buy one**. For I tell you that this Scripture must be fulfilled in me: 'And he was numbered with the transgressors.' For what is written about me has its fulfillment." And they said, "Look, Lord, here are two swords." And he said to them, "It is enough" (Lk. 22:35-38).*

We could say that Luke 22:36 is Jesus' defense of our Second Amendment. The context of this passage is that the Devil has already filled the heart of Judas to betray Jesus, and they are partaking of what has been called "the last supper." Jesus teaches the disciples that there was coming a time after His death and ascension when they would need to do whatever it took to buy a sword. This was not going to be a peaceful period, as when He sent them out with the 70 and they didn't need to bring a moneybag, etc. Jesus is referring to a period of time when they would be traveling and there might be times when they needed to defend themselves and their families.

The disciples were a bit confused on the timing of this and pointed out how there were two swords right next to Him and that they must be needed for the imminent situation Jesus was addressing. Jesus realized that they were a bit clueless on the timing of when they would need a sword and said, "It is enough." Jesus knew that the imminent historical and redemptive context was that He would be arrested by criminals and it was NOT the time to defend themselves, because it was His predestined mission to be the Lamb slain before the foundation of the earth. This was not the context and time for buying and acquiring a sword, as Jesus previously addressed.

However, Peter did have a sword when the criminal thugs with weapons showed up to arrest Jesus, so let's look at this passage next.

John 18:3-12

- *"So, Judas, having procured a band of soldiers and some officers from the chief priests and the Pharisees, went there with lanterns and torches and weapons. Then Jesus, knowing all that would happen to him, came forward and said to them, "Whom do you seek?" They answered him, "Jesus of Nazareth." Jesus said to them, "I am he." Judas, who betrayed him, was standing with them. When Jesus said to them, "I am he," they drew back and fell to the ground. So, he asked them again, "Whom do you seek?" And they said, "Jesus of Nazareth." Jesus answered, "I told you that I am he. So, if you seek me, let these men go." This was to fulfill the word that he had spoken: "Of those whom you gave me I have lost not one." Then **Simon Peter, having a sword, drew it and struck the high priest's servant and cut off his right ear. (The servant's name was Malchus.) So, Jesus said to Peter, "Put your sword into its sheath; shall I not drink the cup that the Father has given me?"** So, the band of soldiers and their captain and the officers of the Jews arrested Jesus and bound him" (Jn. 18:3-12).*

*"Jesus said to him, "Friend, do what you came to do." Then they came up and laid hands on Jesus and seized him. And behold, **one of those who were with Jesus stretched out his hand and drew his sword and struck the servant of the high priest and cut off his ear. Then Jesus said to him, "Put your sword back into its place. For all who take the sword will perish by the sword**. Do you think that I cannot appeal to my Father, and he will at once send me more than twelve legions of angels? But how then should the Scriptures be fulfilled, that it must be so?" At that hour Jesus said to the crowds, "Have you come out as against a robber, with swords and clubs to capture me? Day after day I sat in the temple teaching, and you did not seize me. But all this has taken place that the Scriptures of the prophets might be fulfilled." Then all the disciples left him and fled" (Mt. 26:50-56).*

Jesus made it clear that He is God (the Great "I am"; "he" is not in the original Greek text) and fully in charge of His arrest in that they all fell down when He answered the thugs. Jesus made it clear that what they were doing was to "fulfill" the Scriptures concerning His coming suffering and crucifixion. Jesus previously told the disciples and Peter that He would go to Jerusalem to suffer and die. Peter "rebuked" Jesus for talking like this and Jesus had to give him a real rebuke for trying to hinder Him from His mission, saying, "Get behind me, Satan" (Mt. 16:21-23). This should have been sufficient exhortation for Peter to not draw the sword out to once again hinder Christ from going to the cross. Everyone falling back when Jesus said "I am" should have also given Peter a clue that he didn't need help from a sword.

The fact is that Peter was carrying a sword, which seems to imply that he and the other disciples carried them for self-defense. Jesus didn't say, "Why do you have that sword?" or "Throw that sword away"! He simply said, "Put your sword *back into its place*," and He put the High Priest's servant's ear back on (you know, just another day of being in control and being God).

We are told by the pacifist that Jesus' words, "He who lives by the sword will die by the sword," mean that Christians are called to be violently mistreated rather than resort to violence or defend themselves. But Jesus had already told the disciples that there would come a time when they really would need a sword and Jesus never told Peter to get rid of his.

So the simple meaning is that since it was God's plan that Jesus be taken, Peter's attack with the sword was not self-defense nor the time in which Jesus said he would need one. To deny or seek to hinder Jesus from being arrested and going to the cross through *offensive assault by the sword* was not the way Christ was going to establish His kingdom (cf. Jn. 18:36). In Peter's mind, I'm sure he thought he was acting in "self-defense" of His Lord and His kingdom, *but in reality at that historical and redemptive moment in time Peter was hindering the kingdom through the sword.*

There is simply no exegetical reason to conclude that the pacifist assumptions laid upon these texts are correct. In fact, Jesus clearly told the disciples that there would come a time to buy or need the sword (for their self-defense, not for His defense that night). We are to assume continuity with the OT Scriptures on this topic of self-defense unless told explicitly not to.

Matthew 5-7

- ***"Do not think that I have come to abolish the Law or the Prophets; I have not come to abolish them but to fulfill them****. For truly, I say to you, until heaven and earth pass away, not an iota, not a dot, will pass from the Law until all is accomplished. Therefore, whoever relaxes one of the least of these commandments and teaches others to do the same will be called least in the kingdom of heaven, but whoever does them and teaches them will be called great in the kingdom of heaven" (Mt. 5:17-19).*

- *"You have heard that it was said, **'You shall love your neighbor and hate your enemy.' But I say to you, Love your enemies** and pray for those who persecute you, so that you may be sons of your Father who is in heaven. For he makes his sun rise on the evil and on the good, and sends rain on the just and on the unjust. For if you love those who love you, what reward do you have? Do not even the tax collectors do the same? And if you greet only your brothers, what more are you doing than others? Do not even the Gentiles do the same? You therefore must be perfect, as your heavenly Father is perfect" (Mt. 5:43-48).*

The pacifist usually seeks to disregard the OT entirely with their interpretation of Jesus' teaching in the Sermon on the Mount. This is odd since most pacifists are Futurists, and so if "heaven and earth" have not passed away (which most believe is the physical creation) then this passage creates a problem for them in that they are to obey "every jot and tittle" of the OT law and prophets until it is all fulfilled or heaven and earth pass away.

And yet there are a growing number of scholars (Futurist and Preterist) who do agree with me that the "heaven and earth" designed to pass away was the old covenant system and temple which passed away in AD 70. Some of them may be pacifists and thus reason, "See, post-AD 70 we are under the new covenant law of love," and the OT is irrelevant on this issue of self-defense and just war – as if this is not consistent with love.

However, our passage simply says that Jesus didn't come to destroy the law but to fulfill it. He fulfilled all aspects of the OT law on our behalf. He fulfilled the sacrificial types and shadows of the ceremonial laws. He also fulfilled the moral law in that He was tempted in all ways and yet was without sin so that He might impute His righteousness to our account. But when all the OT law and prophets were fulfilled by AD 70 (cf. also Lk. 21:22-32), does this mean that even the moral laws in the OT were done away with? No! Those laws are consistent with new covenant living. And self-defense and just war concepts are consistent with OT laws and love, so unless we are explicitly told to NOT do something that was in the OT law, we should seek continuity with it.

The NT does tell us that the old covenant ceremonial laws would "soon vanish," as well as some aspects of the civil laws that were unique to Israel's theocratic old covenant system. Yet moral law was also interwoven into Israel's civil laws. Therefore, I know not to sacrifice animals because the NT tells me that Jesus is a once and for all sacrifice for my sin. I know not to obey a physical Sabbath, because Jesus is my Sabbath rest. I know I don't have to be circumcised and undergo a proselyte baptism in water because God has performed these upon my heart "without" the "hands" of men, and thus I am a citizen of the heavenly kingdom. And I know these were physical "elements" of that old covenant world which perished in AD 70. Therefore, the burden of proof lays upon the pacifist to show us NT texts which **explicitly** break from the moral teachings of the OT when it comes to self-defense, or just war morality when it comes to loving our neighbor and exercising righteousness and justice. The Sermon on the Mount is where they think they can do it, so let's continue.

First, let's develop the proper context of Jesus' teaching on the Sermon on the Mount. Jesus is going to interpret the OT law properly, but he is also going to refute the Pharisee traditions and interpretations about the OT law. When He consistently says, "You have heard it said…but I say to you…," Jesus is referring to the Pharisees and Scribes and their false legalistic use and interpretations of the law, or their liberal interpretations of the OT law that avoided the heart issues connected with the law.

For example, when Jesus says, "You have heard it said, 'you shall love your neighbor and hate your enemy. But I say unto you, Love your enemies and pray for those who persecute you, so that you may be sons of your Father who is in heaven," the phrase *"hate your enemy"* is not found in the OT. The interpretation of the OT law by the Scribes **added to "hate your enemy."** Everything Jesus teaches in this section is consistent with the OT Law itself. As the Reformation Bible correctly adds in its notes on this passage,

> "This was a false conclusion in scribal teaching drawn from the narrow understanding of "neighbor" as simply one's fellow Jew. Jesus shows that the true intent of Lev. 19:18 extends even to one's enemies (Luke 10:29-37). In the same chapter of Leviticus, Israelites are called to love the Gentile sojourner 'as yourself' (Lev. 19:33-34)."

Therefore, Jesus in the Sermon on the Mount is not coming up with something completely new and teaching His followers to disregard the OT law. He is interpreting and building further upon it. Therefore, the pacifist has not met the exegetical burden of proof he is to meet in this crucial section.

A similar passage appealed to by the milquetoast and unbiblical pacifist is:

- "And he said to him, "Why do you ask me about what is good? There is only one who is good. If you would enter life, *keep the commandments*." He said to him, "Which ones?" And Jesus said, "You shall not murder, You shall not commit adultery, You shall not steal, You shall not bear false witness, Honor your father and mother, and, *You shall love your neighbor as yourself*" (Mt. 19:17-19).

Jesus is summarizing #6 - #10 of the Ten Commandments. If you love your neighbor, you won't murder him (#6). If you love your neighbor, you won't sexually violate his covenant he has made with his wife and lust after her or sleep with her (#7). If you love your neighbor, you won't covet or seek to steal his property (#8). If you love your neighbor, you will refrain from lying to him (#9) or coveting his lifestyle and all that he has (#10). It is interesting that the pacifists I have encountered on the Internet are Democrat Socialists, and Socialism is all about coveting and stealing from one's neighbor! I definitely don't want to listen to hypocritical lectures on what it means to love one's neighbor!

The pacifist's idea of "love" is that of the progressive who does not physically discipline his or her child because that is not supposed to be "truly loving," and allegedly comes from some OT barbaric God and is merely abusive in nature. No! Biblical love is consistent with biblical justice both under the OT and new covenant, and the Pacifist has not proven otherwise here to make his or her case. But the Lord loves those he chastises and thus a parent who truly loves his child will likewise administer physical discipline lest the child follow a path in life that will end it or end in hell (Prov. 3:12; 23:13-14). In a similar way, a nation that punishes the criminal doesn't do it out of hate, but rather out of love to protect its citizens and in hopes of reforming the criminal and driving Him to a just and righteous God.

Biblical love and justice in the OT and NT are in perfect harmony in many areas, especially when it comes to self-defense and just war.

Before leaving the gospels, it should be pointed out that in John 7:9-10 and John 8:1-11 Jesus defends the OT death penalty as just and good. Those who curse their parents and mistreat them should be stoned, according to Jesus. And although there may be some textual issues regarding John 8:1-11, the teaching is consistent with the OT. One could not accuse one of a crime they themselves were guilty of. When Jesus says, "He who is without sin cast the first stone," He is being consistent with OT law. If they hadn't slept with this woman themselves or committed sexual sin, Jesus gave them the green light to stone her. But of course, Jesus knew they had slept with her (probably writing their names in the dirt), so they were not qualified to stone her per the OT law.

Romans 12:14-21

- *"Bless those who persecute you; bless and do not curse them. Rejoice with those who rejoice, weep with those who weep. Live in harmony with one another. Do not be haughty, but associate with the lowly. Never be wise in your own sight. Repay no one evil for evil, but give thought to do what is honorable in the sight of all. If possible, so far as it depends on you, live peaceably with all. Beloved, never avenge yourselves, but leave it to the wrath of God, for it is written, "Vengeance is mine, I will repay, says the Lord." To the contrary, "if your enemy is hungry, feed him; if he is thirsty, give him something to drink; for by so doing you will heap burning coals on his head." Do not be overcome by evil, but overcome evil with good" (Rms. 12:14-21).*

Overbearing personal vengeance and being overcome with evil are forbidden, and the teaching on this is consistent between both the OT and NT. There is no evidence here of not being able to defend one's family and country in self-defense.

Romans 13:1-7

- *"Let every person be subject to the governing authorities. For there is no authority except from God, and those that exist have been instituted by God. ² Therefore whoever resists the authorities resists what God has appointed, and those who resist will incur judgment. ³ For rulers are not a terror to good conduct, but to bad. Would you have no fear of the one who is in authority?*

> *Then do what is good, and you will receive his approval, ⁴ for he is God's servant for your good. But if you do wrong, be afraid, for he does not bear the sword in vain. For he is the servant of God, an avenger who carries out God's wrath on the wrongdoer. ⁵ Therefore one must be in subjection, not only to avoid God's wrath but also for the sake of conscience. ⁶ For because of this you also pay taxes, for the authorities are ministers of God, attending to this very thing. ⁷ Pay to all what is owed to them: taxes to whom taxes are owed, revenue to whom revenue is owed, respect to whom respect is owed, honor to whom honor is owed" (Rms. 13:1-7).*

Many pacifists believe that Christians cannot hold public office, be police officers or serve in the military. These are only offices and duties of non-believers to bear the sword and render just punishment, or so we are told.

Yet in the Gospels and in the book of Acts, we see plenty of examples of Christians in government and bearing the sword. In the Gospels, John the Baptist exhorted tax collectors and Roman soldiers who came to him asking what they needed to do, simply saying to not take more than they should (i.e. to line their own pockets), or to be just in their rule and authority and cease from threats and unnecessary violence (Lk. 3:12-14). There was no mention of Christians having to reserve these roles for non-Christians, let alone any evidence that Christian soldiers should lay down their swords! In Acts 10, Cornelius came to Christ carrying the sword as a Roman Centurion. In Acts 13, Sergius Paulus remained the governor after his conversion.

Others twist Romans 13 to teach that only the government has the authority to bear the sword and not the individual citizen. As we have seen, there is zero evidence for this claim. In both the OT and NT, we have seen plenty of examples of individual believers carrying weapons.

Not only this, but our Republic and Constitution ("we the people") gives each individual citizen the right to function as the government, bringing in just political power and to bear the sword, being in perfectly harmony with the teaching of Romans 13. It seems very illogical to me that God wants to work His work of justice and righteousness through unbelievers in government, police and military, but not have Christians being salt and light in those offices to help define what God's righteousness and justice is and to participate in wielding it.

Concluding Pacifism

Nowhere did we find exegetical evidence that Jesus or any author of the Bible taught that Christians cannot possess weapons in order to defend themselves and their families. Nowhere did we see that Christians cannot hold government positions that involve bringing righteous judgment upon, or executing, criminals. In fact, all the exegetical evidence proves that pacifism is an unbiblical and ungodly view of the kingdom. In a time when we need MORE Christians in politics, and in the positions of judge, attorney, police and soldier, these pacifists are claiming that we don't with their false piety and theology!

Besides the Biblical evidence against pacifism is the lack of understanding the differences between our historical situation and that of the early Christian Church. The early Church was a minority within Rome and subject to a totalitarian, tyrannical government. They were not free like us, living under a Republic which was founded upon the principles of securing and defending our life, liberty and pursuit to enjoy our lives.

It was prophesied in the OT and NT that these first century Christians would be martyred by the beasts of Rome and the Jews, and that the Jews would "fill up the measure" of their sin of blood guilt in doing so. No such prophecy exists for Christians post-AD 70. Many Christians will indeed find themselves outnumbered and living under ungodly tyrants (possibly as bad as or worse than Nero and Rome), and it may be the case that there are principles and parallels that can be made for Christians in that setting.

For example, Paul in 1 Corinthians 7 knew that the time was short and the old covenant world was passing away, and because of the "present distress" (prophesied intense persecutions heating up) he advised Christians not to marry, but he said that if they did they were not in sin. This same advice should NOT be given to every Christian throughout the ages. It had a very unique and historical setting. I could use that principle to teach outnumbered Christians in Africa being slaughtered by Islam that it may not be a good time to start a family and that they should read Paul's advice in 1 Corinthians 7. Then I could come home and teach and preach how important it is for Christians here to get married and raise godly families.

We have God-given freedoms and liberties that are found in Scripture and in our Constitution, and the pacifist knows very little about exegeting or interpreting either one properly, especially when they overlap.

Conclusion:

Identifying the enemies and putting together a Christian Bible-centered Republic foreign policy

I realize that Christians may not form the vast majority of the US population, but I do want to put together a chapter identifying the various enemies of our great Republic (foreign and domestic) and at least begin the discussion on how to address them.

At some point we need to have a larger conversation which addresses our Constitution, specifically the Fourteenth Amendment, Section Three in relation to foreign religious and political enemies trying to destroy us from within:

> "No Person shall be a Senator or Representative in Congress, or elector of President and Vice-President, or hold any office, civil or military, under the United States, or under any State, who, having previously taken an oath, as a member of Congress, or as an officer of the United States, or as a member of any State legislature, or as an executive or judicial officer of any State, to support the Constitution of the United States, shall have engaged in insurrection or rebellion against the same, or given aid or comfort to the enemies thereof. But Congress may by a vote of two-thirds of each House, remove such disability."

Let's begin that discussion here and now. It is treasonous to allow into our country those holding to political and religious views that involve desires and goals to destroy us from within. Every citizen and political leader should be held to the standard of defending our Republic from "enemies foreign and domestic":

> "I do solemnly swear (or affirm) that I will support and defend the Constitution of the United States against all enemies, foreign and domestic; that I will bear true faith and allegiance to the same; that I take this obligation freely, without any mental reservation or purpose of evasion; and that I will well and faithfully discharge the duties of the office on which I am about to enter. So help me God."

This section does not affect other oaths required by law. This is not just the law of the land for those placed in office, because the government of the United States and its foundation is formed by "We the People." And this was formed in a Christian belief and worldview whereby our creator has given us these freedoms and rights not just for self-preservation, but so that we can flourish and pursue happiness.

It is this author's conviction that our inability to understand both our Bibles and the Constitution has weakened our great Republic. A revival to understand both properly is necessary for our country to flourish, let alone survive the coming attacks.

Islam

In chapter one, we examined the violent life of Muhammad and the violent religious goals of Islam in general. We looked at the three views of Jihad and, perhaps more cunning and important to understand, the three stages of Jihad. President Trump understood this threat externally more than our closet Muslim President, Obama. President Trump saw ISIS decapitating Christians world-wide and heard their cries for American and Christian intervention. It was nice to have had a president, who understood Biblical just war theory and had Christian compassion, stepping up to defend the defenseless. What would YOU do if you saw a Muslim preparing to decapitate a fellow Christian, you had a gun, and there was no time to call the police to intervene? Would you help and shoot the Muslim or simply watch your brother in Christ be decapitated?

Yet the threat of Islam doesn't just come from a far-away ISIS caliphate or that of Iran. We must also understand how they are using our gracious Constitution and freedoms, along with taking advantage of our entrenched Liberal/Socialist perverted immigration policies to destroy us. We must not allow anyone from other countries to be citizens of ours if they have political or religious ideologies that are contrary to the law of our land (the Constitution) which are designed to destroy us from within ("foreign enemies" who are trying to also become our "domestic" enemies). Islam is such a religion and political system, which we have seen cannot separate "mosque and state." Imposing the life and practices of Muhammad and the violent teachings contained within the Quran itself cannot be separated from the call of Islam to impose Sharia Law upon whatever countries Muslims migrate to in order to infect and influence.

We are called to discern, "discriminate" and vet against such enemies seeking to destroy us from within. There is nothing un-biblical or unconstitutional about what I am proposing.

President Trump was wise to not enrich our Islamic enemies and become slaves when it comes to energy. Becoming energy independent was a wise and foundational step in the right direction.

Recently, China has made alliances with Iran so that they can extend their ungodly world domination ambitions and tentacles into the Middle East.

The slavery of the global Khazarian Zionist one world government and banking system

In chapter two, I gave a brief historical canvasing of the phony "Jews" arising from the Khazarian Empire. We learned that the modern state known as "Israel" was formed and funded by the ungodly Rothschild dynasty and had nothing to do with fulfilling

Biblical prophecy, either in the OT or in the NT (as the unbiblical Evangelical Zionist affirms).

What many may not understand is that our revolt from England did not necessarily arise from the over taxation of tea, but rather our desire to form and regulate our own currency and thus be independent from the tyranny of England. After the French Revolution, the Zionists took over England and their monitory system, thus enslaving them. We had no desire to be under either to enslave us.

While Islam is a great threat, coupled with their new alliance with China, we should not take our eyes off of the much larger enemy to our God-given freedoms and Constitution that arose from the crooks and deception of Zionism. We should never forget when these privately-owned Zionist international banks began to impose, unconstitutionally, the Federal Reserve upon us. As Benjamin Franklin (1706-1790) once correctly wrote,

- "The colonies would gladly have borne the little tax on tea and other matters had it not been that England took away from the colonies their money, which created unemployment and dissatisfaction. *The inability of the colonists to get power to issue their own money permanently out of the hands of George III and the international bankers was the PRIME reason for the Revolutionary War.*"

President Thomas Jefferson (1801-1809)

- "If the American people ever allow private banks to control the issue of their currency, first by inflation, then by deflation, the banks…will deprive the people of all property until their children wake-up homeless on the continent their fathers conquered… The issuing power should be taken from the banks and restored to the people, to whom it properly belongs" (Thomas Jefferson in the debate over the Re-charter of the Bank Bill 1809).

- "I believe that banking institutions are more dangerous to our liberties than standing armies."

- "… The modern theory of the perpetuation of debt has drenched the earth with blood, and crushed its inhabitants under burdens ever accumulating." -Thomas Jefferson

President James Madison (1809-1817)

- "History records that *the money changers have used every form of abuse, intrigue, deceit, and violent means possible to maintain their control over governments by controlling money and its issuance.*"

President Andrew Jackson (1829-1837)

Our first president to seek to "route out" this evil was President Jackson, who said,

- "Controlling our currency, receiving our public moneys, and holding thousands of our citizens in dependence… *would be more formidable and dangerous than a military power of the enemy." "You are a den of vipers, I intend to route you out, and by the eternal God I will route you out*"!

Nicholas Biddle (International Bank enemy of Jackson) responded,

> "[If] This worthy President…thinks he is to have his way with the Bank…He is mistaken." "Nothing but widespread suffering will produce any effect on Congress."

Biddle was responsible for creating a US depression by calling in payment on loans, then restricting loaning, all the while boasting of such. When he did not respond to subpoenas, Biddle was justly arrested for fraud.

Jackson was asked what his greatest accomplishment was, and he said,

- "I killed the [Zionist owned and privately funded] bank."

And he did so temporarily here in the US, but the reality is that this enemy is worldwide and is very determined to infect us, control us and assimilate us like a parasite. They are pervasive throughout history and patient in their planning. The Talmudist Zionist bankers continued their goal to enslave the thriving Christian America during the Civil War.

Abraham Lincoln (1865-1869) wrote:

- "The Government should create, issue, and circulate all the currency and credit needed to satisfy the spending power of the Government and the buying power of consumers. The privilege of creating and issuing money is not only the supreme prerogative of Government, but it is the Government's greatest creative opportunity. By the adoption of these principles…the taxpayers will be saved immense sums of interest. Money will cease to be master and become the servant of humanity."

- "The money power preys upon the nation in times of peace and conspires against it in times of adversity. It is more despotic than monarchy, more insolent than autocracy, more selfish than bureaucracy."

Other world leaders praised Lincoln's efforts to sustain a free and independent monetary system:

- "The death of Lincoln was a disaster for Christendom. There was no man in the United States great enough to wear his boots…I fear that foreign bankers with their craftiness and tortuous tricks will entirely control the exuberant riches of America, and use it systematically to corrupt modern civilization. They will not hesitate to plunge the whole of Christendom into wars and chaos in order that the earth should become their inheritance" (Otto Bismark).

In the zeal of President Jackson, we must "intend to route them out, and by the eternal God" do so with righteous judgment and a swift sword if need be!

Zionist attack of 1871 and US treason committed

I am currently studying this and am by far no authority on the subject of 1871 and what changed in our Constitution. Let me quote some who have seen a radical change:

> "Since the Act of 1871 which established the District of Columbia, we have been living under the UNITED STATES CORPORATION which is owned by certain international bankers and aristocracy of Europe and Britain.
>
> In 1871 the Congress changed the name of the original Constitution by changing ONE WORD — and that was very significant as you will read.
>
> Some people do not understand that ONE WORD or TWO WORDS difference in any 'legal' document DO make the critical difference. But, Congress has known, and does know, this.
>
> 1871, February 21: Congress Passes an Act to Provide a Government for the District of Columbia, also known as the Act of 1871.
>
> With no constitutional authority to do so, Congress creates a separate form of government for the District of Columbia, a ten-mile square parcel of land (see, 'Acts of the Forty-first Congress,' Section 34, Session III, chapters 61 and 62).
>
> The act — passed when the country was weakened and financially depleted in the aftermath of the Civil War — was a strategic move by foreign interests (international bankers) who were intent upon gaining a stranglehold on the coffers and neck of America.
>
> Congress cut a deal with the international bankers (specifically Rothschilds of London) to incur a DEBT to said bankers. Because the bankers were not about to lend money to a floundering nation without serious stipulations, they devised a way to get their foot in the door of the United States.
>
> The Act of 1871 formed a corporation called THE UNITED STATES. The corporation, OWNED by foreign interests, moved in and shoved the original Constitution into a dustbin. With the Act of 1871, the organic Constitution was defaced — in effect vandalized and sabotage — when the title was capitalized and the word "for" was changed to "of" in the title.
>
> THE CONSTITUTION OF THE UNITED STATES OF AMERICA is the constitution of the incorporated UNITED STATES OF AMERICA.
>
> It operates in an economic capacity and has been used to fool the People into thinking it governs the Republic. It does not!
>
> Capitalization is NOT insignificant when one is referring to a legal document. This seemingly "minor" alteration has had a major impact on every subsequent generation of Americans.
>
> What Congress did by passing the Act of 1871 was create an entirely new document, a constitution for the government of the District of Columbia, an INCORPORATED government. This newly altered Constitution was not

intended to benefit the Republic. It benefits only the corporation of the UNITED STATES OF AMERICA and operates entirely outside the original (organic) Constitution.

Instead of having absolute and unalienable rights guaranteed under the organic Constitution, we the people now have "relative" rights or privileges. One example is the Sovereign's right to travel, which has now been transformed (under corporate government policy) into a "privilege" that requires citizens to be licensed.

By passing the Act of 1871, Congress committed TREASON against the People who were Sovereign under the grants and decrees of the Declaration of Independence and the organic Constitution.

The Act of 1871 became the FOUNDATION of all the treason since committed by government officials."[375]

With the Zionists and their US puppets, the Rockefellers and J.P. Morgan aided by President Woodrow Wilson, these entities would crash the economy and establish the unconstitutional Federal Reserve. Years later Wilson would recant his complicity in this horrible affliction he unleashed upon the US:

- "We have come to be one of the *worst ruled, one of the most completely controlled governments in the civilized world – no longer a government of free opinion, no longer a government by…a vote of the majority, but a government by the opinion and duress of a small group of dominant men*. Some of the biggest men in the United States, in the field of commerce and manufacture, are afraid of something. They know that there is a power somewhere so organized, so subtle, so watchful, so interlocked, so complete, so pervasive, that they had better not speak above their breath when they speak in condemnation of it."

Before his death in 1924 he confessed:

- "I have unwittingly *ruined my government*."

Other politicians spoke out:

- "Super-state controlled by international bankers and international industrialists acting together to *enslave the world for their own pleasure*" (Rep. Louis McFadden D-PA).

Some began to see the two forms of government operating in the US because of this wicked Central Banking system:

---

[375] POPEYE, *The Act of 1871: The "United States" Is a Corporation – There are Two Constitutions* http://www.federaljack.com/slavery-by-consent-the-united-states-corporation/?fbclid=IwAR1yHVT 6LcsStnBuV1hKyCbm-huPs_Ssgg3tPdyuojYyVXs2mKgroyFJoy0

- "In the United States today we have in effect **two governments**...*We have the duly constituted Government*...Then we have an **independent, uncontrolled and uncoordinated government in the Federal Reserve System, operating the money powers** which are reserved to Congress by the Constitution" (Rep. Wright Patman, D-TX).

Even *Thomas Edison* criticized this evil institution and accused it of enslaving usury:

- "It is absurd to say that our country can issue $30 million in bonds and not $30 million in currency. Both are promises to pay, but one promise fattens the usurers (the Zionist one world bankers) and the other helps the people."

The treason of Franklin Delano Roosevelt [FDR] (1933-1945)

Tyrants often use or create a crisis to produce fear in the people, in order to manipulate and enslave them to take more freedoms from them. Jacob G. Hornberger explains the theft of the tyrant FDR:

> "...in a major crisis or emergency, people get afraid, so afraid that they are willing to sacrifice their liberty for the pretense of 'safety' or 'security' that government officials are offering them.
>
> Of course, the trade is always sold as being 'temporary.' As soon as the crisis or emergency is over, government officials say, they promise to restore the rights and liberties of the people.
>
> A good example of this phenomenon took place in 1933, when President Franklin Roosevelt issued an executive order commanding every American to deliver his gold coins to the federal government. It would be difficult to find a better example of dictatorship and tyranny than that.
>
> After all, gold coins and silver coins had been the official money of the American people for more than 125 years. That was the official money established by the Constitution, which gave the federal government the power to 'coin' money, not 'print' money. The Constitution had also expressly prohibited the states from making anything but gold tender and silver coins legal tender.
>
> America's gold-coin, silver-coin standard
>
> After the Constitution called the federal government into existence, gold coins and silver coins were issued by the U.S. government. It was the soundest monetary system in history. By forsaking paper money and issuing sound, credible gold coins and silver coins, the U.S. government was precluded from plundering and looting people through inflation and monetary debasement for more than a century. America's gold-coin, silver-coin standard was a major contributing factor of the tremendous increase in economic prosperity and people's standard of living, especially in the late 1800s and early 1900s.

Some college professors today teach their students that the 'gold standard' was a monetary system in which paper money was backed by gold. Nothing could be further from the truth. There was no paper money. The official money of the American people, as established by their Constitution, consisted of coinage — e.g., gold coins and silver coins.

The Constitution permitted the federal government to borrow money. Such loans came in the form of federal bills, notes, and bonds. Sometimes people used these debt instruments to transact business. But everyone knew that they were all promises to pay money — i.e., promises to pay gold and silver — not money themselves.

The Fed and the Great Depression

In 1929, after a decade of extreme monetary manipulation by the Federal Reserve, which had been called into existence in 1913, the stock market suffered an enormous collapse, an event that led to the crisis and emergency known as the Great Depression.

It was that major crisis and economic emergency that Roosevelt seized upon to confiscate the gold-coin holdings of the American people. For some reason, he chose not to also confiscate their silver coins.

Notice something important about FDR's action: The Constitution, which provided for a gold-coin, silver-coin monetary system, can only be amended through the process outlined in the Constitution. Roosevelt did not go through that process. Instead, he simply used the emergency to justify his nullification of the Constitution by executive decree. His action is a perfect example of how crises and emergencies can result in tyranny and oppression.

If an American failed to comply with Roosevelt's order, he was subject to being targeted by federal officials with arrest, prosecution, a felony conviction, and fine and imprisonment. While there were no doubt some Americans who refused to comply and kept their gold hidden, most Americans dutifully complied with FDR's command.

In return, they received Federal Reserve debt instruments. The problem, of course, was that while those debt instruments had previously promised to pay money (i.e., gold or silver), now they were irredeemable. That is, they now effectively promised to pay nothing.

Moreover, shortly after people turned in their gold, Roosevelt intentionally devalued the debt instruments that people were now holding in relationship to gold. In one fell swoop, he had imposed enormous financial losses for the American people.

Why did Americans go along with this revolutionary and illegal transformation of their monetary system and this tyrannical and communist-like nationalization of their gold holdings? One simple reason: The crisis had made them deathly afraid. And when people are overly afraid, they are willing, even eager, to trade away their liberty for the 'safety' and 'security' that public officials are offering them.

The welfare-state

No doubt many Americans convinced themselves that once the crisis or emergency was over, federal officials would restore their gold-coin, silver-coin standard. It never happened. Federal officials were able to use their new paper money standard to finance the ever-burgeoning expenses of the welfare-warfare state way of life that FDR was introducing to America.

Gradually, as a result of the debasement of paper money from ever-increasing inflation of the money supply, silver coins were driven out of circulation. Today, while Americans are once again permitted to own gold (at least for now), the official money of the American people remains paper money, notwithstanding the express terms of the Constitution.

With his gold-confiscation scheme, FDR taught Americans a valuable lesson: Emergencies and crises are the time-honored way that people are induced to sacrifice their rights and liberties at the hands of their own government."[376]

FDR was a Democrat Socialist traitor who himself came from a banking Zionist/Jewish lineage. His grandfather was Isaac Roosevelt, founder of the Bank of New York, and his maternal grandfather was Warren Delano II (also "Jewish"), who made his fortune in the Opium Wars in China.

Unlike Wilson, who regretted his treason, FDR simply admitted that there was an "invisible government" which was enslaving the US:

- "These International bankers and Rockefeller-Standard Oil interests control the majority of newspapers and the columns of these papers to club into submission or drive out of public office officials who refuse to do the bidding of the powerful corrupt cliques *which compose the invisible government*."

He would even give praise (perhaps indirectly) to a former president who had the courage to make a stand against this foe, President Andrew Jackson:

- "The real truth of the matter is, as you and I know, that a financial element in the large centers has **owned the government ever since the days of Andrew Jackson**" (Franklin D. Roosevelt (in a letter to Colonel House, dated November 21, 1933).

Jackson hoped he had killed and routed out the Zionist Central banking system, while FDR helped bring this monster back to life in order to enslave Americans.

---

[376] Jacob G. Hornberger, *FDR's Tyrannical Gold Confiscation,* https://www.fff.org/2020/03/12/fdrs-tyrannical-gold-confiscation/.

The Strategy and foreign US policy in dealing with the Khazarian Globalists

Clearly, our first revolution involved fighting against this Zionist world banking system, with previous presidents seeing that it functioned as an "invisible government" using "deceit and violence," having "more power than a standing army." Some of our presidents sought to fight against it and kill it, while others treasonously allowed it to devour and enslave us. To ignore this enemy and its history, allowing it to enslave our country, is the most destructive thing we can continue to do.

I suggest we "route it out" completely and get back to establishing our own currency and a United States bank. We definitely need to stop giving modern Israel billions (10-15) each year.

While we justify having Israel as an ally to help buffer the West against the advance of Islam, the truth be told, Israel is a much more dangerous threat to us! It is time to let Israel defend herself in the Middle East. If Israel falls, then we can take on the Islamic threat when it comes. Modern Israel is not "God's people" and we are not "in sin" if we don't protect her. This is just unbiblical Evangelical Zionist heresy. There is nothing about modern Israel that shares in a "Judaic and Christian ethic." That country is filled with godless humanism, and its Talmudic religious form is disturbing on many levels.

The Khazarian blackmailing mafia, which funded Jeffrey Epstein in order to gain influence over our government officials, needs to be destroyed within our borders (including George Soros) and exposed and hunted down internationally.

Evangelical Zionism

As long as Evangelical Zionism supports and enables the corrupt Khazarian globalist Zionist system, they too are an enemy hindering the progress of our great Republic.

We can only continue to "red pill" this heretical group with the truth of Scripture. Christian politicians need to do their own study of Scripture and ignore their manipulative, allegedly "Holy Spirit-led prophecies" concerning modern Israel and their attempts to self-fulfill WWIII in order to usher in their so-called "rapture" off the earth. The truth is that the Church will be here a very long time, so she needs to become educated and engaged in the fight with a proper Christian and biblical worldview.

President Trump

I could be wrong, but my sense is that either President Trump was a backslidden Christian for many years or that he has just recently been humbled and is a young Christian. President Trump has stated that it is his desire to leave a legacy and to be known as the most praying President the Whitehouse has ever seen.

But what should we make of President Trump making Jerusalem the capital of Israel and referring to it as "the eternal city"? It appears that Hebrews 13:14 hasn't really settled in yet, among so many other Scriptures. And to make matters worse, his "name it and claim it" female "pastor" is a Charismatic Zionist herself who functions as his official "counsel."

My guess is that this group suffocates and manipulates him as they have other presidents and politicians, and he simply assumes that this is the voice and counsel of the Christian Church. We can only pray that the Lord gives him an intense desire to study Scripture and leads him to better Christian counsel. As I pointed out in chapter three, Ronald Reagan was highly influenced by his mother, who in turn was highly influenced by false teachers and so-called prophets such as Hal Lindsey. One's view of eschatology is very important, especially being the president and seeking to rule our great Republic with Scriptural wisdom and sound praying.

I voted for President Trump twice and I'm proud that I did.

Lincoln once said,

"I believe this government cannot endure, permanently half slave and half free."

This was so true, but neither can it endure, permanently half free and half enslaved to Socialism/Communism. Nor can it endure being enslaved under the Khazarian Zionist one world banking system and give Israel unlimited taxpayer aid! We are either "America first" or we are not. Perhaps it is time for a third Christian Patriot Party to emerge if the Republican Party will not reform its ways and actually begin studying the Scriptures and the Constitution.

Is it time for a third Christian Patriot Party?

I am by no means a historian or a politician, but I have put together 10 common sense Christian patriot points that could serve as a foundation and move the discussion forward.

1). **Monetary System**: Do away with the Federal Reserve. Since the primary reason for the American Revolution was to overthrow England's desire to control our monetary system, we may need to do it again! The original colonies produced their own currency. Presidents Jackson routed out those devils and established silver coins, Lincoln produced greenbacks, and Garfield was sound in his support of a sound US monetary system. Government and elected officials (with term limits) should be responsible to print debt-free money. Amendments should be made to the Constitution to guarantee and protect this right against the wealthy private shadow family/governmental banking system. That system needs to be made illegal. Those seeking to overthrow the Constitutional monetary system will have assets seized (given back to the people) and they will be imprisoned (for theft). No more FAKE & INFLATED MONEY!

2). **Taxation**: Do away with the illegally formed IRS. Create and implement a flat tax to be determined, say 10-20% (flexible on healthcare – see below). If living healthy, the tax can be 10%; if not, it can be up to 20%. Some suggest a "fair tax." These issues need to be rigorously studied and debated.

3). **The Post Office & Freedom of Communication**: The Post Office should be updated and digitalized. They can help create platforms similar to Facebook, YouTube, and Google, guaranteeing free and uncensored speech under the Constitution, which they have a right to. If private Christian citizens won't build these platforms, we have one within the government itself that is designed to facilitate free speech. We need more Christians like Andrew Torba of Gab.com to produce alternative platforms to Facebook and YouTube especially since we have seen how government platforms and agencies can be weaponized against the people. Unfortunately Zionists such Jared Kushner have pressured Andrew Torba and Gab to stifle free speech when it comes to criticizing Zionism as being unbiblical. However, Torba remains faithful to the Scriptures and the First Amendment and did not give in to Kushner's pressure even if that means it won't be the main social media platform Trump will use. We can only encourage President Trump to not listen to Kushner's unbiblical and unconstitutional positions of censorship.

4). **Foreign Policy, Allies & Religious Expression**: There should be no funding to religious extremist countries trying to self-fulfill Armageddon / Gog and Magog, whether Islamic countries or even Israel. Again, the free ride for Israel should be over in that they take billions from us every year! If we aren't supposed to fund Islamic countries that are violent, racist and create conflict, we shouldn't treat Israel any differently.

Modern Israel is NOT OT or NT Israel; the old covenant ended in AD 70. There is no "God's people", "race" of "Jews" that are entitled to any "holy land." That is not only an unbiblical position to take, but also a racist one to hold to. Racism and the victim card will no longer be played on the American people by the so-called "God's people," the Jews.

Freedom of religion does NOT mean supporting ANY religious system that contradicts the Constitution, such as racist or violent Muslims trying to implement Sharia Laws, or Zionists trying to enforce Talmudic Law, which leads to international racism and crimes against humanity.

As I have demonstrated in this volume, the Olivet Discourse and book of Revelation were fulfilled "shortly" in Jesus' contemporary "generation," and therefore the war of Armageddon / Gog & Magog was fulfilled in the events of AD 67 - AD 70. God's kingdom is no longer "in the land" (under the sacred space of old covenant theology), but rather it's "in Christ" and established "within the heart" of a believer (God's people are His sacred space under the new covenant). While neither the new covenant kingdom nor the US *advances* through the sword, we do NOT hold to Pacifism (we believe in self-defense and just war theology).

5). **Economic Energy & Production**: The slogan "America first" should continue to guide production and independence, not just for oil, but also for transportation, food, the medical field, etc.

6). **Healthcare & Medical**: There will be tax incentives for people eating healthily and exercising regularly (physical and blood tests). Our current medical system is great in diagnosing (e.g. CT & MRI) and emergency care, but very poor in treating actual disease. The killing of 300,000 or more a year from the side-effects of unscientific and addictive drugs, along with harmful procedures, will end. A focus on preventative health and real scientific approaches to health will be implemented.

We simply have so many health conditions that are due to our bad diets. We are to be eating 8-10 servings of fruits and vegetables, and hardly anyone does. Instead, we eat way more meat and dairy than we need to, along with processed foods and sugar. Then when our bodies break down, we expect others to pay the bill. This trend needs to stop or this crisis alone will bankrupt our country. If you are going to be free to eat crap, that is your business, but when you break down because of it you don't have a right to reach into my pocket to pay the bill. That's where your freedom ends and mine begins.

Alcohol and Marijuana: Probably both should be legal, especially when taken in moderation and primarily used at home, but illegal when taken in excess. No one should be driving or working under an excessive influence of either. Testing can be enforced for both while driving or at work.

7). **Education**: We need to privatize and use vouchers for K-12, while placing more emphasis on trade schools. Communism and socialism have infected our great country through the educational system, and we have allowed them to re-write our great heritage and history.

If we can free up our economy by getting back to a proper monetary system, we may not be in a situation where two parents are forced to work and live paycheck to paycheck. It's time to actually raise our children and not let their peers at school or ungodly teachers raise them! We need to be much more active in homeschooling or checking in on what our children are learning and who is influencing them.

8). **Abortion, Homosexuality and Transgenderism**: Abortion is simply murder and should be illegal. Homosexual and transgender nonsense should be considered to be biological, psychological and spiritual abnormities or a type of mental disease. We don't treat these individuals as enabling victims, but as those needing serious spiritual and mental health counseling. The Church was warned long ago that once we allow the government to re-define "marriage," etc., these groups would never be satisfied and would continue to infringe upon our rights and inflict harm upon others. And that is exactly what has happened and is continuing to happen.

9). **Immigration & Voting:** No one is allowed to enter the country illegally; violators will be imprisoned and sent back! Voter ID is required in US elections – period. Voter interference will be seen for what it is, not "fraud" but "treason." We either develop a computerized system that is guaranteed to work without interference, or we go back to paper ballots. Every vote that is cast needs a representative from each party present to witness it. Military may also be present to witness and check for treason.

10). **Propaganda, Socialism/Communism**: This should be made illegal immediately! You may not be a citizen of this great land, let alone run for public office, believing in or seeking to promote communism or socialism. We are free as Christians and free as Americans, and you will NOT tread on us any longer!

This is by no means an exhaustive list and I have never really considered myself a political person. But I have watched our country get devoured by socialism/communism, and if we don't turn this direction now our freedoms will be gone within the next 2-6 years.

Concluding with the "missing piece"

Below is a chart listing wealthy families, organizations, political entities, and religious systems that have goals of ruling the world with enslaving or ridding the planet of Christianity. Many Christians believe the CV-19 virus is an end time plague/sign listed in Matthew 24 and that the vaccines are the fulfillment of "666" and the "mark of the beast" in the book of Revelation that communicate the "rapture" is "near" once again. While this work has proven those positions and interpretations to not be exegetically true, the fact remains that history has a way of repeating itself. There will always be evil men wanting to rule the world and oppress Christians to bow to their systems and worldviews. But the Christian need not fear! Because just as Nebuchadnezzar learned -- one cannot stop God and the advancement of His Kingdom in this world:

> At the end of the days I, Nebuchadnezzar, lifted my eyes to heaven, and my reason returned to me, and I blessed the Most High, and praised and honored him who lives forever, for his dominion is an everlasting dominion, and his kingdom is an everlasting dominion, and his kingdom endures from generation to generation; all the inhabitants of the earth are accounted as nothing, and he does according to his will among the host of heaven and among the inhabitants of the earth; and none can stay his hand or say to him, "What have you done?" (Dan. 4:34-35)

God alone raises up and brings down nations and He will sovereignly continue to do so with the Church preaching His "everlasting gospel." She may be prosperous or severely persecuted, but either way She is continually preserved and will thrive and conquer over evil. The Church will be salt and light in this world for a very long time and this must change the way we pray and engage in our culture and politics.

"KNOW YOUR ENEMY"
OPERATION LOCKSTEP / EVENT 201 / TECHNOCRACY / ONE WORLD GOVERNMENT / THE NEW WORLD ORDER / THE WORLD HEALTH ORGANIZATION (WHO) / UNITED NATIONS (UN) / WORLD ECONOMIC FORUM (WEF – AGENDA 2021 & 2030) / BILDERBERG GROUP / TRILATERAL COMMISSION / THE GREAT RESET - "BUILD BACK BETTER" / "CLIMATE CHANGE" - ROTHSCHILD, ROCKEFELLER, RHODES, KISSINGER, SOROS, SCHWAB, GATES, BLOOMBERG, CLINTON, OBAMA, TRUDEAU, BIDEN…
1). Usher in a Socialist/tyrannical One World Government and currency.

2). Depopulate the planet by 80% to make it more manageable and easier to control.
3). Re-allocate the planet's resources and re-distribute wealth.
4). No one will own private land or houses and will eat and drink what they are told.
5). Weaken and destroy the U.S. Constitution or any democracy in the world; weaken and take away 1st and 2nd amendments (unique to the U.S.), and if she falls the rest of the world will also. Eliminate free press and install propaganda and censorship.
6). Open borders to invade Europe and U.S. to further weaken nations.
7). Religion is to worship the earth ("Mother Earth", "Climate Change") or is Satanic. Seeks to purge and depopulate humans from polluting the earth and/or merge humans with machines/transhumanism - humans are evil, especially white Christians.
8). Arrogantly predicts and then ushers in a coronavirus to produce fear and control of nation(s) to usher in their global "reset" to allegedly "build back better."
9). Use coronaviruses to take freedoms away, and usher in endless and harmful vaccines to weaken and control our immune systems. Deadly side effects for millions will crash the medical system over time so they can establish their own. Truthful scientific research exposing them is labeled "debunked science", "anti-science", "fake news," or "conspiracy theory" through the propaganda arm of the media.
10). Use coronavirus and "vaccines" to introduce "vaccine passports" and a "carbon tax" with a goal to track and control populations.
11). Deny and/or ration valid medicines and therapies to the (disobedient) people.
12). *Start WWIII between Israel and Islam – weaken nations financially and militarily.*

ISLAM / QURAN

1). Bring nations to Islam through Sharia Law. Convert to Islam or be be-headed or become a slave to Muslims.
2). Use a nation's gracious immigration laws to lie and deceive infidels, claiming to be a "peaceful religion" while in the minority. When a significant population emerges, wage Jihad and insist on Sharia Law and submission to Islam.
3). Try to self-fulfill a global end-time holy war with the nations of the world.

ISRAELI ZIONISM / TALMUD
1). Non-Jews have no souls and were created to serve the Jews. The Jews will rule the world from Jerusalem. When Messiah comes, each Jew will own 2,800 Gentile slaves in "paradise on earth."
2). Enslave (through interest) non-Jews through privately owned globalist banks, and profit from both sides of wars.
3). Try and usher in Messiah through war and seek to self-fulfill a global end-time holy war with the nations of the world.
CHINA
1). Has over 100,000 spies in the U.S. attending colleges.
2). Buying up our businesses and farmland (along with Bill Gates).
3). Pay off, bribe and/or blackmail (with sex tapes/honey pots) U.S. politicians.
4). Join with Globalists when necessary to weaken America with bioweapons.
5). Collude w/ Socialists in U.S. to install puppet "President" (hack voting machines).

As we wrap up, I hope the reader can see that I have answered all of the questions and challenges given in my preface with exegetical and historical accuracy. And, in doing so, I have provided the Christian Church with an actual "Faithful and True Witness" when it comes to seeing how Christ fulfilled all of His promises.

The "missing piece" to solving the violent Middle East puzzle is to have a correct and biblical view on the timing and nature of Christ's Second Coming, the last days, the end of the old covenant age war of Armageddon / Gog and Magog and the Messianic kingdom. All three of these were fulfilled between AD 67 – AD 70 and prove that Jesus is both Messiah and God as He claimed.

These are essential and foundational truths that need to be embraced and lived out and defended within our communities and the political landscape of our country. Understanding that we are God's sacred space, kingdom of light and New Jerusalem does not translate into an unbiblical and ungodly pacifism. As Christians, we need to be studied and skilled in the Scripture and our Constitution to ensure and defend our God-given liberties. We have many enemies and challenges that lay ahead, but with Christ and His Word to put our trust in, we truly are "more than conquerors in Christ Jesus."

When approaching Islam, Talmudic Zionism (or Torah Judaism) and Evangelical (or Charismatic Premillennialist or Dispensationalist) Zionism, it is not only important to present these biblical truths accurately and with love and humility, but to also use their own sources to refute them and at the same time build our case. I hope the author of this volume has sufficiently accomplished these goals.

My guess is that things may get worse before they get better. It is difficult to see how WWIII is not too far off in the distant future with all three of these religious systems trying to self-fulfill an end time battle, coming of their Messiah (1st or 2nd) and kingdom or carnal paradise on earth. This and a secular one world shadow government and banking system eager to bring it on as well so as to enslave countries into more debt and thus to increase their power even more.

It may take another world war for the Church to figure out what "this generation," "soon," "at hand," "quickly," "about to be," "will no longer be delayed" and "in a very, very little while and will not delay" actually means! This and that the Messianic Kingdom really is "not of this world" and did not come with physical observation, but is "within" the believer. I can only hope and pray that this volume reaches a wide audience at some point and will function as education and a positive informational warfare tool to guide us to a more peaceful Middle East.

Please do feel free to contact me if you have any further questions or if you would like to schedule an interview, speaking engagement or public debate.

Appendix A:

The Roman Catholic Church and Sacred Space and Holy War

Since many unfortunately see the heresy of Catholicism to be among the "three great Abrahamic faiths," I will briefly give a brief history or critique of its attempts to self-fulfill its holy land / holy war eschatology.

To be honest and fair, while the Catholic crusades were a defensive response to the slaughter and theft of Islam from Muhammad's day and throughout the Middle Ages, the Roman Catholic Church with her various popes and monks in times past has sought to motivate her soldiers to fight Muslims - viewing them as the seven-headed beast of Revelation and thus preparing them for the "soon" end-time battle of Daniel 7 and 12, Ezekiel 38, and the book of Revelation:

626 – Avars besieging Constantinople were end-time Gog and Magog.

632 – Muhammad is seen as the "little horn" of Daniel 7.

637 – Muslims capture Jerusalem and the mosque built upon the site of Solomon's temple is seen as a fulfillment of the abomination of desolation" (Dan. 9; 12 and Mt. 24:15).

634-640 – Muslim invasions are seen as "announcing the advent of Antichrist."

691 – The rise of Islam is a sign of the nearness of the end.

700 – Revelations identified the rise of the Islamic Empire as the end-time war of Gog and Magog.

850 – Byzantine Christians saw conquests of Muslims as preparation for "the end."

854-870 – Alvarus of Cordova saw Muhammad crushing the saints, and their execution in Cordova to be the fulfillment of the little horn's persecution of Daniel 7.

Muslims create their own historical propaganda in that, somehow, they were the victims of the Crusades and were actually involved in liberating Christians and living peacefully with them in a pluralistic society under Islamic rule. History tells a different story leading up to 1095 in that Christians in Jerusalem were killed (crucified and beheaded), persecuted and literally marked, their churches burned, etc. (772-937).

This is the BACKGROUND in which Pope Urban II called for the first Crusades in 1095. It was defensive and reactionary in nature to the brutality of Islam over Christians and the theft of their property and lands. The pope's letters and cries for help were to protect pilgrims to Jerusalem who were subject to persecution, and to regain land that was stolen by Muslims.

Many Catholics, such as Robert Spencer, point out that the crusaders were primarily motivated to enter Jerusalem for religious reasons, and if they had to defend themselves they would. He tells us that they did not come for wealth or to oppress Muslims, for they had to sell much to participate in the journey to Jerusalem. However, that is not the entire story. While Spencer is critical of Scott's movie, The Kingdom of Heaven (which portrayed both groups as religious fanatics), the fact remains that some Catholics were motivated by eschatological, "the end is near," and "holy war" religious reasons:

> 1095 – Just prior to the first crusaders sent to Jerusalem, they were seen as ushering in the fulfillment of the book of Revelation whereby they would meet the Antichrist, defeat him, and reign until the end of the world.

> 1191 – Islamic leader Saladin is seen as the sixth head of the dragon (and the "one who now is" - Rev. 17:9) in the book of Revelation, and the seventh was the Antichrist who was already alive in Rome. Yet King Richard the Lionhearted said, "The one who now is [Rev. 17:9] is Saladin, who now oppresses God's Church and holds it captive along with the Lord's sepulcher, the holy city Jerusalem and the land where the Lord walked. But he will soon lose it," because God was going to give him the victory.

> 1213 – 1323 - Beginning with Pope Innocent III, others saw the reign of Muslims and Islamic law in the seven-headed beast of Revelation 13, and that 666 represented the number of years Islam would be powerful until God's crusaders would soon bring it to an end (the beginning and end of the 666 years keeps being adjusted).

> 1249 – The failed crusade of Louis the 9th was a sign that the end was near.

> 1297 – The seven-headed beast of Revelation 13 was the Saracens because, starting with Muhammad, there were seven key Islamic leaders.

> 1329 – 666 represented the years between Christ and Muhammad. The beast of Revelation 13 was the son of Chosroes, the Persian leader who was defeated by Heraclius during the Crusades.[377]

The crusaders were not only motivated to engage in the crusades because this was a "holy war" with a view of an imminent eschatological end approaching, but also because they believed they would be granted redemption and the forgiveness of sins.

---

[377] For the specific documentation for the above dates and the false predictions see: Fracis X. Gumerlock, *The Day and the Hour Christianity's Perennial Fascination with Predicting the End of the World*, (Atlanta, GA: American Vision Pub., 2000), 144-139.

Urban II preached the First Crusade at the Council of Clermont. Many people believed (because this is what the pope told them) that all of their sins would be forgiven if they carried out this momentous task. Like their counter Muslim opponents, they were practically guaranteed a place in heaven by the pope.

Their objectives were to stay the spread of Islam, to retake control of the "Holy Land," and take back their "holy sites," with many of their warriors viewing this crusade as a means of redemption and expiation for sins. Urban II's own letter to the Flemish confirms that he granted "remission of all their sins" to those undertaking the enterprise to liberate the eastern churches (Peters, Edward, ed. (1971), *The First Crusade*, Philadelphia: University of Pennsylvania Press).

Of course, Muhammad and the Quran motivate Muslims for "holy war" by securing them salvation through martyrdom, etc.

Catholic "Christian" European world domination theology can be seen in *The Requerimiento* document, written in 1513 by jurist Juan López de Palacios Rubios of the Council of Castile:

> "On behalf of the King, Don Fernando, and of Doña Juana I, his daughter, Queen of Castille and León, subduers of the barbarous nations, we their servants notify and make known to you, as best we can, that the Lord our God, Living and Eternal, created the Heaven and the Earth, and one man and one woman, of whom you and we, all the men of the world at the time, were and are descendants, and all those who came after and before us. But, on account of the multitude which has sprung from this man and woman in the five thousand years since the world was created, it was necessary that some men should go one way and some another, and that they should be divided into many kingdoms and provinces, for in one alone they could not be sustained.
>
> Of all these nations God our Lord gave charge to one man, called St. Peter, that he should be Lord and Superior of all the men in the world, that all should obey him, and that he should be the head of the whole Human Race, wherever men should live, and under whatever law, sect, or belief they should be; and he gave him the world for his kingdom and jurisdiction.
>
> **And he commanded him to place his seat in Rome, as the spot most fitting to rule the world from**; but also, he permitted him to have his seat in any other part of the world, and to judge and govern all Christians, Moors, Jews, Gentiles, and all other Sects. **This man was called Pope, as if to say, Admirable Great Father and Governor of men. The men who lived in that time obeyed that St. Peter, and took him for Lord, King, and Superior of the universe; so also they have regarded the others who after him have been elected to the pontificate, and so has it been continued even till now, and will continue till the end of the world.**
>
> One of these Pontiffs, who succeeded that St. Peter as Lord of the world, in the dignity and seat which I have before mentioned, made donation of these isles

and Tierra-firme to the aforesaid King and Queen and to their successors, our lords, with all that there are in these territories, as is contained in certain writings which passed upon the subject as aforesaid, which you can see if you wish.

So, their Highnesses are kings and lords of these islands and land of Tierra-firme by virtue of this donation: and some islands, and indeed almost all those to whom this has been notified, have received and served their Highnesses, as lords and kings, in the way that subjects ought to do, with good will, without any resistance, immediately, without delay, when they were informed of the aforesaid facts. And also, they received and obeyed the priests whom their Highnesses sent to preach to them and to teach them our Holy Faith; and all these, of their own free will, without any reward or condition, have become Christians, and are so, and their Highnesses have joyfully and benignantly received them, and also have commanded them to be treated as their subjects and vassals; and you too are held and obliged to do the same. Wherefore, as best we can, we ask and require you that you consider what we have said to you, and that you take the time that shall be necessary to understand and deliberate upon it, and that you acknowledge the Church as the Ruler and Superior of the whole world, and the high priest called Pope, and in his name the King and Queen Doña Juana our lords, in his place, as superiors and lords and kings of these islands and this Tierra-firme by virtue of the said donation, and that you consent and give place that these religious fathers should declare and preach to you the aforesaid.

If you do so, you will do well, and that which you are obliged to do to their Highnesses, and we in their name shall receive you in all love and charity, and shall leave you, your wives, and your children, and your lands, free without servitude, that you may do with them and with yourselves freely that which you like and think best, and they shall not compel you to turn Christians, unless you yourselves, when informed of the truth, should wish to be converted to our Holy Catholic Faith, as almost all the inhabitants of the rest of the islands have done. And, besides this, their Highnesses award you many privileges and exemptions and will grant you many benefits.

But, if you do not do this, and maliciously make delay in it, I certify to you that, with the help of God, we shall powerfully enter into your country, and shall make war against you in all ways and manners that we can, and shall subject you to the yoke and obedience of the Church and of their Highnesses; we shall take you and your wives and your children, and shall make slaves of them, and as such shall sell and dispose of them as their Highnesses may command; and we shall take away your goods, and shall do you all the mischief and damage that we can, as to vassals who do not obey, and refuse to receive their lord, and resist and contradict him; and we protest that the deaths and losses which shall accrue from this are your fault, and not that of their Highnesses, or ours, nor of these cavaliers who come with us. And that we have said this to you and made this Requisition, we request the notary here present to give us his testimony in writing, and we ask the rest who are present that they should be witnesses of this Requisition."

We have one mediator, the God/man/Jesus Christ, who alone can grant and pardon sinners from their sin (cf. 1 Tim. 2:5; Mark 2:1-12). No priest or pope has the authority to do so. Nor do they have Scriptural authority to "rule the world" through violence, theft, and slavery.

The Church is a kingdom of priests (cf. Rev. 1:6) and God rules from His throne in the new covenant / New Jerusalem / temple (i.e. within the hearts of God's people - Lk. 17:20-21ff.; 2 Cor. 6:16/Ezek. 37:27; Jn. 7:37-39/Ezek. 47; Gal. 4:24-27; Rev. 21-22:17). The Roman Catholic Church is wrong on so many levels, and space forbids a detailed treatment. But hopefully seeing how wrong the Catholic Church can be in this area of eschatology (ruling "from Rome" through murder, theft, and slavery), in contrast to how Christ and His kingdom comes to sinners, will cause Catholics to explore many more of her heretical doctrines when it comes to salvation by grace through faith alone.

The Catholic Church no longer seems to just be a heretical works-based cult, but rather a political machine intent on enslaving people's souls and also ruling the monetary systems of countries in a similar way Talmudic Zionism does. So, it also needs to be watched very carefully!

Appendix B:

Two Movie Proposals Designed to be Biblical Information Warfare

A part of this informational warfare that we find ourselves in involves not only a revival of exegetical study and expository preaching from laymen to the pastor, but also interacting on the platforms of our culture. A part of the messaging would include presenting this truth through cinema. Here is my attempt to enter this world with the theology / eschatology defended in this work.

Copyright 2009 Michael J. Sullivan – Thank you in advance for your honesty and integrity.

Introduction / Objective:

Here are two movie proposals or plots that function as "informational warfare" to help solve the problem of Islam, Israeli Zionism and Premillennial Christian Zionism trying to constantly self-fulfill (playing the victim or conquest card) the "in the land", "holy war," and the "end is near AGAIN" battle of Armageddon. The more the Biblical truth gets out there in the US to Evangelical Christians, Jews and Muslims in the Middle East, the more we can heal and get strengthened. The theology that is presented in these proposals has been proven in this volume.

Title: "AD 70 Parousia"

By: Michael J. Sullivan (author, debater, conference speaker, and radio host)
Proposal for: Mel Gibson or whoever sees the vision
Genre: Action / Controversial / Religious

This is a movie that incorporates the success behind such action movies produced by Ridley Scott – *The Kingdom of Heaven* and *The Gladiator* – along with religious controversy drawn from such men as Ron Howard and Tom Hank in *The Divinci Code*. I am no fan of Hank and Howard politically or theologically, but I use them as an example of producing a religious film filled with controversy that takes on a life of its own outside the theater context. If films that are filled with heresy and historical inaccuracies can have an effect on even the Christian churches discussing them in their Sunday School classes, how much more effective would a Christian controversial film be that is filled with exegetical and historical accuracy?

The Historical Setting & Controversial Twist

The religious twist or controversy to this movie, that will make it a financial success and sets it apart from anything that has ever been produced thus far, is that the NT places Jesus' Second Coming during the Roman / Jewish War (between AD 67 – AD 70) and not as an end-of-time event (per the traditional views). While many religious movies have focused on the years AD 26 – AD 33, none have focused on AD 67 – AD 70, let alone to develop this period as the Second Coming and battle of Armageddon or Gog and Magog. We know from church history that Rome surrounded Jerusalem in AD 67 and then briefly retreated. This is when the Christians fled Jerusalem to Pella and were safe (heeding Jesus' prophecy in Luke 21:20-32), while the Jews listened to the false prophets (who Jesus said would come) and were destroyed by the Romans.

Synopsis:

Cornelius (played by _____) is a skilled Roman Centurion warrior who converts to Christianity and begins converting many Roman soldiers to Christ. Word of this reaches Nero (played by _____), who makes Cornelius a gladiator/prisoner. He is forced to engage in combat as punishment for not acknowledging Nero as the one true king or "son of god." Cornelius is separated from his wife and son between AD 63 - AD 66, and is forced to defend himself in the arena against demon-possessed beasts and other valiant gladiators. However, God empowers and sustains Cornelius (placing His Spirit upon him as he did with Samson) through these battles in order to make a statement against Nero and Rome. God miraculously protects him in the arena as a symbol that He will preserve the Church from the Roman beast and Dragon (cf. Rev. 12) seeking to destroy her. As God will ultimately deliver the Christians from the persecutions and wrath of the Jews and Rome in their flight to Pella just before the coming events of AD 67 - AD 70, so too God protects and preserves Cornelius in the arena when he fights for his God, his people and his family (in hopes of being united with them once again).

Cornelius eventually escapes from Roman captivity, only to be captured by John Levi of Gischala (played by _____, who will shortly take over Jerusalem and lead the revolt against Rome). Cornelius eventually breaks free and reaches his family in Jerusalem in AD 66. After the death of Peter at the hands of Nero, God will use Cornelius to lead the Christian Church in Jerusalem to Pella before the Roman - Jewish war (Armageddon Gog and Magog) begins and Titus lays siege to Jerusalem.

Main Characters: Cornelius (_____), Nero (_____), John Levi of Gischala (_____), Vespasian (_____), Titus (_____), Apostle Peter (_____), Josephus (_____).
Budget: $80 – $135 million.
Box office profit: $600 million or more.

Possible obstacle: The budget for a war in Jerusalem will be high. We may look into similar or existing ancient Middle Eastern, Jerusalem-like sets to purchase and build upon instead of building from scratch.

SECOND MOVIE – MODERN APPLICATION
Title: "The Armageddon Conspiracy"
By: Michael J. Sullivan (author, debater, conference speaker & radio host)

Proposal for: Mel Gibson or whoever sees the vision for this project
Genre: Action / Controversial / Religious
Synopsis: There are two stories being played out that will merge together.

Story #1

The main character (Chris Hunt) is an accomplished mixed martial artist, theological scholar and debater.

When Hunt was young, he was homeschooled on the mission field by his parents. His father was a well-known Biblical scholar, but he left that life for the mission field. His father also had a trade being a mixed martial arts instructor on top of preaching to any groups that were willing to hear the gospel. Hunt's father trained him in theology, philosophy and mixed martial arts. Chris will eventually leave his parents on the mission field to attend college in the US and compete professionally in the U.F.C.

However, while Hunt is away his parents experience a violent death at the hands of ISIS, which now leaves Hunt with a sense of loneliness and bitterness toward God and Muslims. Hunt leaves his conservative roots behind and begins teaching theology at a liberal Seminary with a bent toward proving that Jesus is just a good moral teacher with failed prophecy as His legacy. Hunt feels that God had failed him and his parents, and he finds in reading the NT that Jesus Himself seems to have failed the Church, not returning and setting up His Kingdom within His contemporary generation. His arguments are simple, and he presents them to his students year in and year out without any rebuttal: Jesus promised that His Second Coming would take place in the lifetime and generation of His first century disciples (Matt. 10:22-23; Matt. 16:27-28; Matt. 24:34), and since the end of the world did not take place at that time, Jesus' prophecy failed. And since the rest of the NT echoed Jesus' first century time of fulfillment – issuing promises with language like "at hand", "in a very little while", "shortly," and "soon" (e.g. I Pet. 4:5-7; Heb. 10:37; Rev. 1:1, 22:6-7) – it too is a failure and cannot be seen as the "inspired" Word of God as Christians claim it to be.

Hunt regularly mocks his conservative Christian students and tells them that the sooner they realize Jesus was just a man and a failure (like they are and like all people are), the better the rest of their lives are going to be. There's simply no intellectual reason to believe that Jesus is in reality "The Faithful and True Witness" worthy of worship and to be the Lord of one's life, if He couldn't even keep his main promise to the Church. Hunt usually will also give his own brief "testimony" to the class on how God failed him and his parents to ram home his bitter point.

Hunt lays paralyzed in his depression and despair until a new student (Mark) shows up in his Theology class and begins challenging him in a way he has never encountered before. One of his students is a Sovereign Grace Full Preterist and begins showing him how all these predictions pointed to Christ's Second Coming taking place when Jerusalem fell in AD 67 - AD 70, and that the language Jesus uses in Matthew 24 (stars falling, etc.) is apocalyptic language (symbolic/ metaphoric genre) and is not referring to the end of world history and the renewal of planet earth as Hunt erroneously presupposes. Hunt is challenged for the first time that neither Jesus nor the NT writers were ever predicting the end of the world (as commonly taught in most churches), but rather that prophecy involved predictions of Christ's return to bring an end to the old covenant age/world and to establish the new covenant age (which is spiritual).

Hunt's bitterness and pride runs deep and he isn't going to go down easy. He challenges the student to a public debate, knowing that the student has no experience as a public debater like he has. And while this position does make some good points, since Hunt has never heard of it he thinks preparing to refute it will be relatively easy. God begins dealing with Hunt and his faith in his preparation for the debate, but he doesn't totally break down until the closing remarks of the debate as he hears the student's closing remarks, which are not only irrefutable and logically sound but also contain a personal story of hardship that makes Hunt's situation seem trivial.

Hunt is also an accomplished MMA trainer and fighter. Other than trying to lose and dumb himself down in studying the Bible in an effort to find problems and contradictions, Hunt gets a high off of overtraining and trying to be the most accomplished and ruthless fighter the U.F.C. has seen.

After Hunt's conversion, he becomes Mark's friend and Mark begins training with Hunt.

Story #2

Muslim apologist Shabir is from Iran and falsely portrays himself as a peaceful moderate. He comes to the US to debate various Christian theologians, claiming that the Jesus of the NT is a false prophet and that therefore Allah gave Muhammad the Quran as a superior revelation. While this is a legitimate tour by Shabir, no one knows that his inner circle is a terrorist network planning a nuclear attack on US soil, at least no one except two FBI agents who begin noticing some suspicious activity.

Shabir is also an accomplished fighter in the U.F.C. and is using this as an avenue to get into the States.

The merging of the two stories

Shabir challenges Hunt to a debate and to fight in the U.F.C. Tensions are high between the U.S. and Iran, and both countries are pushing both the fight and the debate.

Hunt accepts a debate with Shabir in Los Angeles, California. Chris thinks God has called him to take down Shabir's arguments in a debate, but the mission becomes much more involved as the evening develops. Toward the end of the debate, Shabir and his network take the audience hostage, announcing their plans to detonate their nuclear device. Hunt now has to use his mixed martial arts training and team up with the FBI, along with the audience he has won over in debate, to kill the terrorists and disarm the nuke.

At the same time, extreme Dispensational Zionists such as John Hagee have the president's ear and are trying to convince the president that these are signs of the end times and that the US needs to get ready for Armageddon and do a preemptive strike on Iran while there is time. God is going to use Hunt in a variety of ways to disarm this conflict, and this will also involve educating the president on these issues and the twisted and manipulative theology of Hagee.

Why this movie will be a financial success: Again, this movie involves religious controversies, which does nothing but provide free advertisement and bring in a larger audience. The movie also touches on one of the issues of the day – Islamic eschatology views everything in the news today as a "fulfillment" of their "end-time" prophecies leading to a "holy war" with the West.

Unfortunately, many Dispensational Zionist Christians read their Bibles through the lens of current events (e.g. Hal Lindsey and John Hagee), and they claim that what is taking place today in the Middle East also supports an alleged "imminent end-time holy war" and "rapture" for the Church.

Only through education can these problems come to light, let alone be solved. Making known the fact that these NT "end-time", "holy war" (Armageddon) prophecies were already fulfilled between AD 67 - 70 is a major step in the right direction to healing this conflict.

Characters / Actors: Chris Hunt (_____), Hunt's father, Conner (_____), Mark (_____), FBI agent (_____), and Muslim terrorist (_____).
Budget: $30 – $70 million.
Box office profit: $300 - $500 million or more.

The theology and history behind this movie is 100% solid, as defended in the volume of this work.

Third Movie: I will be developing a third movie where Hunt begins entering politics and becomes a congressman. This will take Hunt on a journey into the depths of the Khazarian mafia and he will learn that this is one of the most cunning and violent enemies he has encountered. The Lord will raise him up both through debate and physical conflict once again to get the US headed in the proper direction in dealing with this Zionist / Globalist enemy of the State.

Also by Michael Sullivan:

Authors-David Green, Edward Hassertt, and Michael Sullivan

This book is a Reformed/Calvinist response to Keith Mathison's multi-authored book When Shall These Things Be, which was a critique and condemnation of (full) preterism. David Green, Edward Hassertt, and Michael Sullivan demonstrate that the advent of preterism in church history is the result of "organic development" from within the historic, Reformed church, and that it represents the uniting of the divided house of Reformed eschatology. As the authors navigate through the confusing maze of the Mathison volume, they overturn the arguments that the authors of that book levied against the truth that Jesus Himself taught in no uncertain terms. This Second Edition includes added material throughout the book, especially chapter four (the response to Mathison's chapter in When Shall These Things Be). It also includes an Appendix in response to critics of the first edition of House Divided.

Armageddon Deception and *House Divided* can also be purchased at www.fullpreterism.com.

www.ingramcontent.com/pod-product-compliance
Lightning Source LLC
Chambersburg PA
CBHW080418230426

43662CB00015B/2138